Managing Change

We work with leading authors to develop the
strongest educational materials in management,
bringing cutting-edge thinking and best learning
practice to a global market.

Under a range of well-known imprints, including
Financial Times/Prentice Hall, we craft high quality print
and electronic publications which help readers to
understand and apply their content, whether studying
or at work.

To find out more about the complete range of our
publishing, please visit us on the World Wide Web at:
www.pearsoned.co.uk

Managing Change

A Strategic Approach to Organisational Dynamics

Fourth Edition

Bernard Burnes

FT Prentice Hall
FINANCIAL TIMES

An imprint of **Pearson Education**
Harlow, England • London • New York • Boston • San Francisco • Toronto • Sydney • Singapore • Hong Kong
Tokyo • Seoul • Taipei • New Delhi • Cape Town • Madrid • Mexico City • Amsterdam • Munich • Paris • Milan

Pearson Education Limited

Edinburgh Gate
Harlow
Essex CM20 2JE
England

and Associated Companies throughout the world

Visit us on the World Wide Web at:
www.pearsoned.co.uk

———————————

First published under the Pitman imprint 1992
Second edition published under the Pitman imprint 1996
Third edition published 2000
Fourth edition published 2004

ISBN 0 273 68336 5

British Library Cataloguing-in-Publication Data
A catalogue record for this book is available from the British Library

10 9 8 7 6 5 4 3 2 1
08 07 06 05 04

Typeset in Sabon 10/12.5 by 30
Printed by Ashford Colour Press Ltd, Gosport

The publisher's policy is to use paper manufactured from sustainable forests.

To Sue, Duncan, Stuart and Hobbes

Contents

For Lecturers:
Available at: www.booksites.net/burnes

- A secure, password-protected site with teaching material
- Complete, downloadable Instructor's Manual
- PowerPoint slides that can be downloaded and used as OHTs

Acknowledgements

The fourth edition of this book, like the previous three, would not have been possible without the generous encouragement and assistance of a large number of people, especially my colleagues and students at UMIST. Space does not permit me to name them all, but I am nevertheless extremely grateful to them, one and all. In addition, Pearson Education deserve many thanks for their encouragement and patience. However, and mostly, I am irredeemably indebted to my wife, Sue. Her painstaking reading and editing of draft after draft of this book have improved it beyond recognition. It is not too much to say that she deserves as much credit as I do for what is good about this book.

Nevertheless, despite all the help and assistance I have received, any faults or shortcomings in the final product are mine and mine alone.

Publisher's Acknowledgements

We are grateful to the Financial Times Limited for permission to reprint the following material:

The sustainable business: continuous search for improvement, © *Financial Times*, 19 August 2002; Realism replaces grand visions, © *Financial Times*, 12 March 2003; How to preserve the soul of management: The increasing sophistication of measurement techniques threatens to reduce executives to robots, © *Financial Times*, 19 September 2002; The master strategist: Michael Porter, © *Financial Times*, 15 August 2003; The great iconoclast: Henry Mintzberg, © *Financial Times*, 5 August 2003; Managers resort to old tools in a crisis, © *Financial Times*, 18 July 2001; Less means more in engineering, © *Financial Times*, 17 October 2002; Weill wields his power at Citigroup: revamp represents ongoing structural changes, © *Financial Times*, 13 June 2002; Microsoft's direct connection to the customer, © *Financial Times*, 31 December 2001; Manage with mother, © *Financial Times*, 2 March 1998.

We are grateful to the following for permission to use copyright material:

Figure 5.1 from Organization Development and Change, 4th edition, by Cummings/Huse. © 1989, reprinted with permission of South-Western, a division of Thomson Learning: *www.thomsonrights.com*. Fax 800 730-2215 Figure 7.1 reprinted with the permission of The Free Press, a Division of Simon & Schuster Adult Publishing Group, from Competitive Advantage: Creating and Sustaining Superior Performance by Michael E. Porter, © 1985, 1998 by Michael E. Porter. All rights reserved. 'Why companies have much to learn from charities' by Keith Leslie, Vaughan Lindsay, Helen Mullings and Neville Salkeld, reprinted by permission of McKinsey & Company. Keith Leslie is a consultant and Helen Mullings is a professional development manager with McKinsey & Company.

In some instances we have been unable to trace the owners of copyright material and we would appreciate any information that would enable us to do so.

Introduction

There is nothing so practical as a good theory. (Kurt Lewin)[1]
All models are wrong, some models are useful. (George Box)[2]

It has become the accepted view that, for society at large, the magnitude, speed, unpredictability and impact of change are greater than ever before. Certainly, over the last 20 years especially, new products, processes and services have appeared at an ever-increasing rate. Local markets have become global markets. Protected or semi-protected markets and industries have been opened up to fierce competition. Public bureaucracies and monopolies have either been transferred to the private sector or have themselves adopted much more market-orientated practices. Most commentators appear to share Hammer and Champy's (1993: 23) view that '... change has become both pervasive and persistent. It *is* normality.'

In the last decade, and perhaps especially since the third edition of this book was published in 2000, organisations appear to have gone though a whirlwind of change. In the 1990s, there was a takeover and merger boom of unprecedented proportions (Burton *et al*, 1996; *The Economist*, 1998). Indeed, on a single day in 1997, Western Europe saw some $130 billion of mergers and acquisitions, whereas the entire total for the previous year was only $250 billion. In America, Warner (1997: 3) commented that:

To find a similar period of economic change and merger frenzy, you might need to go back all the way to the 1890s ... Out of it were born such companies as Standard Oil and American Tobacco, the very prototypes of the vertically integrated modern corporation.

This period leading up to the millennium is usually referred to as the dotcom boom. It is easy to see why this should be so given the rise of the Internet, the publicity given to dotcom companies and, with hindsight, ridiculously-inflated prices paid for any business that had the suffix .com. Moreover, as Warner indicated, the boom touched almost every sector of the global economy, not just Internet-associated businesses. For example, even in the epitome of the 'old economy', the motor industry, merger fever was rife. The coming together of Daimler-Benz and Chrysler in 1998 created the fifth largest vehicle company in the world, with a turnover of $130 billion. In the same year, the takeover of Rolls Royce by Volkswagen was another step in its attempt to transform itself into a global company, whereas Ford continued to gobble up smaller

[1] Lewin (1943/4: 169).
[2] Quoted in Norrie (1993).

companies, such as Volvo, in order to maintain its global position. In the financial sector, the $160 billion merger of Citicorp and Travellers in 1998 was just the largest example of a positive frenzy of merger activity. In the UK, the de-mutualisation of building societies and their takeover by larger financial institutions was another example of the same forces at work. Similarly, in the rest of the European financial services industry, in advance of the Euro, cross-border mergers were especially prevalent. The 'urge to merge' seemed present in all industries; Guinness and GrandMet came together to form Diageo, one of the world's largest food and drink companies, and the on–off merger of Glaxo and SmithKline Beecham, which finally materialised in 2000, showed that the pharmaceutical industry was not immune to the lure of merger.

Though led by the dotcom boom, each merger or acquisition had its own rationale. The underlying motives appear to have been a combination of the forces of globalisation, technological advances, trade liberalisation and changes of governments, especially in Eastern Europe, all of which were reshaping entire industries. However, even faster than the dotcom bubble had risen, it burst with devastating consequences. Ironically, what seemed to signal its demise was the merger between the Internet company AOL and the film, TV and publishing company Time Warner. This deal, hailed as the triumph of the new economy over the old, created a company which was initially valued at $327 billon. Within a week of the announcement of the merger in January 2000, AOL's value fell by $25 billion and continued to fall. By the time the deal was finally closed, the value of the combined company had fallen from $327 billion to $106 billion (Sirower, 2003). The fall of the rest of the dotcom sector was in many cases, especially the WorldCom scandal, even more spectacular, with many companies disappearing altogether. Most commentators now believe that the dotcom boom was really a 'dotcon' boom, with the rise in share prices being driven by froth, lies and illegality (Cassidy, 2002; Cellan-Jones, 2003; Kaplan, 2002). It was the collapse and exposure of companies in the dotcom and other sectors whose value had risen spectacularly only to fall spectacularly that led the American investment guru, Warren Buffet, to make his now famous remark that 'It's only when the tide goes out that you see who has been swimming with their trunks off.'

Organisational change is not just limited to companies involved in mergers and acquisitions. In the UK for example, in the 1990s, survey after survey showed that organisations of all sizes and in all sectors were undertaking a wide variety of change initiatives. These included restructuring, delayering, the introduction of new products and services, outsourcing and, especially, culture change programmes (Coulson-Thomas and Coe, 1991; Ezzamel *et al*, 1994; Industrial Society, 1997; Worrall and Cooper, 1997, 1998).

The point of this brief review is not to chronicle the rise and fall of the dotcom boom, but to show that over even short periods of time, organisations have to cope with very different types of challenges. These range from rapid growth, mergers and acquisitions, and the emergence of new technologies and new competitors, to falling markets, depressed economies, de-mergers and consolidations, and the collapse of some customers, suppliers and competitors. However, it would be wrong to portray these events as affecting all organisations equally. Just as the dotcom companies were most affected by the dotcom boom and bust, just so there were organisations and industries who were relatively unaffected by either the boom or the bust, such as agriculture and mining. Similarly, the public sector tends to be much less affected by the pace and magnitude of economic fluctuations than the private sector. In the UK, for example, whilst the rest of the economy has been relatively stagnant, the public sector has continued to grow significantly (Turner, 2003).

So, although many claim we are living through a period of unprecedented and unpredictable change, not everyone is affected to the same degree. Indeed, as Chapter 1 will show, the history of the past 200 years could well be characterised as successive periods of unprecedented change. In fact, given that it was the ancient Greeks who coined the phrase 'change is the only constant', we should perhaps remember that the history of the human race is one of massive change and dislocation. Each generation seems to yearn for some golden past that has been swept away by progress, and each generation, building on past knowledge, develops new ways of coping with and managing change. Therefore, perhaps we should be less concerned with the overall level of change and instead be asking: how can each organisation best cope with the degree of turbulence it faces?

Though change management would not be considered particularly important if products and markets were stable and organisational change was rare, it would be considered even less of an issue if it were easily managed and success could be guaranteed. Alas, there is substantial evidence that this is not the case. The literature abounds with examples of change projects that have gone wrong, some disastrously so (*see* Brindle, 1998a; Burnes and Weekes, 1989; Bywater, 1997; Cummings and Worley, 1997; Howarth, 1988; Kanter *et al*, 1992; Kelly, 1982a, 1982b; Kotter, 1996; Stace and Dunphy, 1994; Stickland, 1998). Indeed, two of the most respected commentators in the field of organisational change, Beer and Nohria (2000), claim that nearly two-thirds of change efforts fail. Though this seems a staggeringly high failure rate, studies of particular types of change initiatives do appear to come to similar conclusions.

Unlike a company's turnover, an industry's performance or a nation's gross national product, no one gathers statistics on how successful organisations are at managing change. Nevertheless, over the years, particular types of change initiative have attracted sufficient attention for it to be possible to gauge the degree of success achieved in implementing them. There are three types of organisational change which, because of their perceived importance, have received considerable attention: the introduction of new technology in the 1980s; the adoption of Total Quality Management (TQM) over the last 20 years; and, in the last 15 years, the application of Business Process Re-engineering (BPR).

The micro-electronics revolution of the 1980s, which saw the rapid expansion of computers and computer-based processes into most areas of organisational life, was the subject of a great many studies. These found that the failure rate of new technology change projects was anywhere between 40 per cent and 70 per cent (AT Kearney, 1989; Bessant and Haywood, 1985; McKracken, 1986; New, 1989; Smith and Tranfield, 1987; Voss, 1985). Nor do the problems in this area appear to be teething troubles limited to the 1980s. In 1998, the UK government had to admit that its £170 million programme to replace the computer system that holds the National Insurance records of everyone in the country was in such a mess that the system had collapsed, throwing its social security system into turmoil (Brindle, 1998a, 1999).

The move by European organisations to adopt Total Quality Management began in the mid-1980s (Dale and Cooper, 1992). Although TQM appears to be central to the success of Japanese companies, the experience of Western companies has been that it is difficult to introduce and sustain. Indeed, one of the founders of the TQM movement, Philip Crosby (1979), claimed that over 90 per cent of TQM initiatives by American organisations fail. Though a 90 per cent failure rate seems incredibly high, studies of the adoption of TQM by companies in the UK and other European countries show that they have experienced a failure rate of 80 per cent or more (AT Kearney, 1992; Cruise O'Brien and Voss, 1992; Dale, 1999; Economist Intelligence Unit, 1992; Whyte and Witcher, 1992; Witcher, 1993; Zairi *et al*, 1994).

Business Process Re-Engineering was hailed as 'the biggest business innovation of the 1990s' (Mill, 1994: 26). Though less well documented than either new technology or TQM, Wastell *et al* (1994: 37) concluded from the available evidence that 'BPR initiatives have typically achieved much less than they promised'. Other studies of BPR have come to similar conclusions (Coombs and Hull, 1994; Lessem, 1998; Short and Venkatraman, 1992). More specifically, Bryant (1998) cites a reported failure rate for BPR initiatives of 80 per cent, Breslin and McGann (1998) put the failure rate at 60 per cent, whilst Bywater (1997) puts the figure at 70 per cent. Even the founding father of BPR – Michael Hammer – acknowledges that in up to 70 per cent of cases it leaves organisations worse off rather than better off (Hammer and Champy, 1993). Indeed, such was the perceived failure of BPR that, according to Huczynski and Buchanan (2001: 559), by the mid-1990s, many commentators 'were claiming that the approach had been discredited'.

Therefore, even these three types of well-established change initiatives, for which a great deal of information, advice and assistance is available, are no guarantee of success. This is perhaps why managers consistently identify the difficulty of managing change as one of the key obstacles to the increased competitiveness of their organisations (Hanson, 1993; Industrial Society, 1997; Worrall and Cooper, 1997).

To many, this must seem paradoxical. On the one hand, there is now more advice on how to manage change than ever before. On the other hand, the failure rate of change initiatives is astronomical. The two quotations at the beginning of this Introduction hold the key to this paradox. What almost everyone would like is a clear and practical change theory that explains what changes organisations need to make and how they should make them. Unfortunately, what is available is a wide range of confusing and contradictory theories, approaches and recipes. Many of these are well-thought-out and grounded in both theory and practice; others, unfortunately, seem disconnected from either theory or reality. Also, though change theory requires an interdisciplinary perspective, each of the major approaches tends to view organisations from the disciplinary angle of their originators – whether it be psychology, sociology, economics, or whatever – which can result in an incomplete and biased picture. So, regardless of what their proponents may claim, we do not possess at present an approach to change that is theoretically holistic, universally applicable, and which can be practically applied. Nevertheless, we do know that, to paraphrase George Box, whilst all change theories are partial, some theories are useful. This means that for those wishing to understand or implement change, the prime task is not to seek out an all-embracing theory but to understand the strengths and weaknesses of each approach and the situations in which each can best be applied.

There can be few who now doubt the importance to an organisation of the ability to identify where it needs to be in the future, and how to accomplish the changes necessary to get there – although there is a great deal of dispute about how difficult or possible this is. Some might assume that managers do not need to understand organisation theory, strategy theory, change theory or any other theory in order to manage and change their organisations, but this would be to underestimate the extent to which managers and others in organisations are influenced, assisted or potentially misled by theory. Increasingly, managers are exhorted to adopt the teachings of the latest management guru. Nevertheless, as Part 1 will demonstrate, and as Mintzberg and Quinn (1991: xii) observed:

> One can, however, suffer not just from an absence of theories, but also from being dominated by them without realizing it. To paraphrase the words of John Maynard Keynes, most 'practical men' are the slaves of some defunct theorist. Whether we realize it or not, our behavior is guided by the systems of ideas that we have internalized over the years. Much can be learned by bringing these out into the open, examining them more carefully, and comparing them with alternative ways to view the world – including ones based on systematic study (that is, research).

These 'systems of ideas', or organisation theories as they are more commonly called, are crucial to change management in two respects. First, they provide models of how organisations should be structured and managed. Second, they provide guidelines for judging and prescribing the behaviour and effectiveness of individuals and groups in an organisation.

To understand why and how to change organisations, it is first necessary to understand their structures, management and behaviour. As Mintzberg and Quinn indicate, it is clear that in many organisations there is no clear understanding of these theories. It follows that choices with regard to the appropriateness of particular structures and practices, the way they are chosen and implemented, are founded on limited knowledge and perhaps false assumptions. Change cannot hope to be fully successful under these circumstances. On the contrary, a full understanding of these theories is necessary if informed choices are to be made when instigating and implementing change. For this reason, these will be examined critically in relation to each other, and also in comparison with how organisations actually operate, as opposed to how theorists suppose them to. The aim is not to provide a 'hands-on' practical guide to organisational change – though readers should find this book useful in that respect as well. Rather the aim is to provide an understanding of the theories and approaches to change that are on offer, to indicate their usefulness and drawbacks, and to enable the reader to choose for her- or himself which 'models are useful' and when.

The central purpose of this book, then, is to aid this search for understanding both by describing and discussing the key approaches to and theories of organisational change, and by setting these within the broader framework of the development, operation and behaviour of organisations and those who populate them. The intention is to allow those who study and carry out organisational change to make their own judgments about the benefits, applicability and usefulness of the approaches on offer. Therefore, the key themes underpinning the book are as follows:

- There is a need to understand the wider theoretical and historical context within which organisations operate and the pressures and options they face for change.
- Organisational change cannot be separated from organisational strategy, and vice versa.

- Organisations are not rational entities *per se*, though those who manage them strive to present their deliberations and decisions as being based on logic and rationality.
- There is a strong tendency to present the various approaches to change as being limited in number and mutually exclusive. However, in practice, the range of approaches is wide, and they can be and often are used either sequentially or in combination.
- The appropriateness of each of the available approaches is dependent upon the type of change being considered and the constraints under which the organisation operates, although these constraints and objectives can themselves be changed to make them more amenable to an organisation's preferred approach to change or style of management.
- Organisations and managers can and do exercise a wide degree of choice in what they change, when they change and how they change.

The book is organised into four parts.

Part 1: The rise and fall of the rational organisation provides a comprehensive review of organisation theory and behaviour. Chapter 1 deals with the development of organisations from the Industrial Revolution through to the early years of the twentieth century, when the first fully-fledged organisation theory, the Classical approach, appeared. This is followed in Chapter 2 with reviews of the next two organisation theories to appear: the Human Relations approach and Contingency Theory. Chapter 3 examines and compares the three main and most influential contemporary approaches to structuring and managing organisations: the Culture–Excellence and organisational learning approaches, primarily developed in the West, and the Japanese approach. Chapter 4 sets the review of organisational theories in a wider context by reviewing the postmodern, realist and complexity perspectives on organisations. Chapter 5 examines the importance and implications of culture, power and politics. Chapter 5, and Part 1, conclude that, by accident and design, organisation theories attempt to remove choice from organisations by specifying what they need to do in order to be successful. However, the review of culture, power and politics, together with evidence from the earlier chapters, shows that managers do have a wider scope for shaping decisions than much of the organisation literature suggests. This theme of managerial choice is continued in Part 2.

Part 2: Strategy development and change management: past, present and future comprises five chapters, examining the literature on strategic management and change management. Chapters 6 and 7 examine the dominant approaches to strategy, and the main tools and techniques available to organisations for its development and implementation. In particular, these two chapters draw attention to the differences between the Prescriptive and Analytical schools of strategy, and they highlight the importance of the relationship between organisational strategy and organisational change. Chapters 8 and 9 review the two dominant approaches to organisational change: the Planned approach and the Emergent approach. These chapters show that both approaches have their strengths and weaknesses, and that neither separately nor in combination do these approaches cover all change situations. Chapter 10 goes beyond the Planned and Emergent approaches to develop a *Framework for Change* that relates the various change situations organisations face to the range of approaches to managing change on offer. Chapter 10 concludes Part 2 by arguing that, though organisations face significant constraints on their freedom of choice, these constraints can be influenced and changed in order to allow organisations to choose the particular approach to strategy and change that best suits them.

Part 3: Case studies in strategy development and change management comprises three case study chapters. The ten studies they contain are all of real organisations, though in some cases their names and some of the details that would identify them have been changed to protect confidentiality. Nevertheless, the situations described are drawn from real life and show the opportunities, difficulties and constraints faced in developing strategy and implementing change.

Part 4: Managing choice comprises the concluding three chapters of the book. Chapter 14 combines the insights and perspectives from Parts 1 and 2 to analyse the ten case studies presented in Part 3. From this, the chapter identifies key lessons for the theory and practice of organisational change and paves the way for the Choice Management–Change Management model of organisational change presented in Chapter 15. This model, which comprises three interlinked processes – choice, trajectory and change – provides an understanding of how managers and organisations can and do exercise choice and manage change. Given the importance attached to the role of managers in developing strategy and managing change, Chapter 16 reviews what managers do and how they do it. In particular, the role of leadership and management development is examined and related to approaches to change management. The chapter and the book conclude that if, as argued, managers have considerable choice over what to change and how to change it, then this lays a considerable responsibility on their shoulders. How organisations change and develop has enormous consequences, not just for their employees and owners but for society at large. In order to minimise social fragmentation and exclusion, and the destruction of the natural environment, managers need to act in the broader interests of all their stakeholders – employees, shareholders, themselves and the wider community.

The fourth edition

Since the publication of the third edition of this book, I have received many helpful comments and suggestions for improving and developing this book both from my own students and colleagues at UMIST and from readers and users elsewhere. I am very grateful for these and have tried to utilise them in preparing this fourth edition. In particular, this edition reflects the growing influence of the Internet and globalisation on organisations, includes material on realism and complexity theories to counterbalance the postmodernist perspective, the linkage between approaches to change and approaches to management has been made more explicit, five new case studies have been provided, and there is more practical guidance on managing change. Whilst retaining a similar structure and approach to the third edition, this edition has been expanded from 14 to 16 chapters, and all the chapters been updated and revised, some substantially so. The main changes from the third edition are as follows:

- Part 1 has been expanded from four to five chapters. Chapter 4 now concentrates on competing perspectives on organisations, namely the postmodern, realist and complexity perspectives. The new Chapter 5 contains an expanded review of culture, power, politics and choice.

- Part 2 has also been increased four to five chapters. This has enabled the revision and separation of the two chapters on Planned and Emergent change, Chapters 8 and 9, from the new Chapter 10 which develops and presents the Framework for Change, which has itself been revised and expanded.
- Part 3 includes five new case studies: three in Chapter 11, and one each in Chapters 12 and 13.
- Chapter 15 has been lengthened to provide more practical guidance on managing change.
- The last chapter, now Chapter 16, has been expanded to incorporate a discussion of globalisation, and a better linkage between management styles and varieties of organisational change.
- Last but not least, a glossary of terms has been added to the book to explain less familiar words and phrases.

Part One

The rise and fall of the rational organisation

Chapter 1

From trial and error to the science of management

The rise of organisation theory

Learning objectives

After studying this chapter, you should be able to:

■ understand the development of work organisation from the Industrial Revolution until the end of the nineteenth century;

■ appreciate the reasons for the antagonistic relations between labour and employers in the nineteenth century;

■ discuss the different roles played by technology and people in the development of the factory system;

■ describe the main features of the Classical approach;

■ understand why the Classical approach developed as it did in the USA, France and Germany;

■ discuss the differences and similarities between the work of Taylor, Fayol and Weber;

■ list the main advantages and disadvantages of the Classical approach to structuring organisations and designing jobs;

■ describe the key features of the Classical approach to organisational change.

| Exhibit 1.1 | The case of Scientific Management |

Fundamentals of Scientific Management

The principal object of management should be to secure the maximum prosperity for the employer, coupled with the maximum prosperity for each employé.

The words 'maximum prosperity' are used, in their broad sense, to mean not only large dividends for the company or owner, but the development of every branch of the business to its highest state of excellence, so that the prosperity may be permanent.

In the same way maximum prosperity for each employé means not only higher wages than are usually received by men of his class, but, of more importance still, it also means the development of each man to his state of maximum efficiency, so that he may be able to do, generally speaking, the highest grade of work for which his natural abilities fit him, and it further means giving him, when possible, this class of work to do.

It would seem to be so self-evident that maximum prosperity for the employer, coupled with maximum prosperity for the employé, ought to be the two leading objects of management, that even to state this fact should be unnecessary. And yet there is no question that, throughout the industrial world, a large part of the organization of employers, as well as employés, is for war rather than for peace, and that perhaps the majority on either side do not believe that it is possible so to arrange their mutual relations that their interests become identical.

The majority of these men believe that the fundamental interests of employés and employers are necessarily antagonistic. Scientific management, on the contrary, has for its very foundation the firm conviction that the true interests of the two are one and the same; that prosperity for the employer cannot exist through a long term of years unless it is accompanied by prosperity for the employé, and *vice versa*; and that it is possible to give the workman what he most wants – high wages – and the employer what he wants – a low labor cost – for his manufactures.

Source: Frederick Winslow Taylor, *The Principles of Scientific Management*, 1911, p. 1.

Introduction

In Britain and the rest of the industrial world today, it is almost impossible to imagine life without the plethora of organisations that comprise and make possible our everyday life. Yet organisations in their modern form – indeed, in almost any form – were virtually unknown before the Industrial Revolution, 200 years ago. In the intervening period, as Morgan (1986) remarked, we have developed into an 'organizational society'. However, not only have organisations, in their many shapes, sizes and manifestations, come to reach into every facet of our lives, but they have also acquired an equally diverse range of theories, nostrums and semi-sacrosanct beliefs about how they should be structured, managed and changed.

This chapter sets out to explore and discuss the origins of organisations, from the Industrial Revolution to the early years of the twentieth century, when the first detailed and comprehensive organisation theory emerged. As Exhibit 1.1 shows, two of the overarching and complementary characteristics of this period were the conflict between workers and managers, and the search for a systematic, scientific, and above all efficient approach to running organisations. The key themes of this chapter are as follows:

■ Although industrialisation was primarily concerned with the move from a subsistence economy to a money-market economy, the main enabling mechanism for this was the creation of the factory system.

- The pattern and purpose of industrialisation varied from country to country. Whilst in Britain and the USA it was very much driven by individuals seeking profit maximisation, in mainland Europe a different approach can be seen. In Germany in particular, but also in France, industrialisation was largely state-sponsored, and aimed more to further the economic and military objectives of the state than to increase the profit-making capacity of individuals.
- The development of organisation theory was synonymous with the need by managers to legitimate and enhance their authority to initiate change.

The chapter begins by showing how the rapid expansion of national and international commercial activity created the conditions for the British Industrial Revolution, from which emerged the factory system, the precursor of all modern organisations. It is argued that the driving force behind this development was the merchant class. It will also be stressed that two key features of the early factory system were its *ad hoc*, trial-and-error nature, and the antagonistic relationship between owners and employees, or – to use the terminology of the times – masters and servants.

The chapter then goes on to show that British industrial practices, methods and technologies were 'exported' to other European countries and the USA, with similar results in terms of employer–employee relations. As the nineteenth century progressed, and organisations grew in number and size, trial and error increasingly gave way to more considered and consistent approaches to work organisation. This development was especially pronounced in the USA and continental Europe, as industrial leadership moved away from Britain and towards these areas.

What emerged, separately, were three different but complementary attempts by Frederick Taylor in the USA, Henri Fayol in France and Max Weber in Germany to replace the *ad hoc*, rule-of-thumb approach to organisations with a universally applicable blueprint or theory for how they should operate. These three approaches, each focusing on different organisational aspects, coalesced into what later became known as the Classical school of organisation theory. This approach to organisations is characterised by the horizontal and hierarchical division of labour, the minimisation of human skills and discretion, and the attempt to construe organisations as rational-scientific entities. It is argued that one of the key objectives of the Classical school, especially the Scientific Management component, was to legitimise the managerial right to plan and implement change by showing that it was the only group able to analyse the work situation scientifically and rationally, and to devise the most appropriate and efficient methods of operation.

The chapter concludes by arguing that the Classical approach, whilst being a significant advance on what went before, was badly flawed. In particular, its view of human nature and motivation was not only inaccurate, but also alienated workers from and made them resentful of the organisations that employed them. However, the precepts of the Classical school were not solely aimed at constraining workers' ability to make and block change; in addition, by laying down hard and fast rules of what was and was not best practice, they constrained management's freedom of action, thus alienating many managers as well as workers.

With hindsight, the attempt by Taylor, Fayol and Weber each in their own way to formulate a system of reciprocal obligations between managers and workers appears to be less a decisive break with the past and more an attempt to recast feudalism in a more scientific-rational framework. Certainly, in the late nineteenth century, French, German and American managers of European descent did share a recent and common feudal heritage which might make them well-disposed towards a system that substituted a code of joint obligation in place of management–worker conflict. Indeed, in Germany the rise of bureaucracy that Weber described was itself a direct product of the Prussian feudal tradition. However, though many managers undoubtedly did long for and believe in an – albeit mythical – age when workers readily did as they were told, this ignored the fact that most American immigrants left Europe to escape just such a system, whilst French workers took pride in the belief that their Revolution had ended feudal despotism. Only in Germany was it possible to say that the feudal tradition remained strong, though not unopposed.

The rise of commerce and the birth of the factory

The pivotal event that shaped the world into the form we now see around us was the British Industrial Revolution, which began in the late eighteenth century. Before it, most societies were based on small-scale, self-sufficient agricultural production, with the vast majority of the population, some 80–90 per cent, living in the countryside. By the end of the nineteenth century, after the Industrial Revolution had run its course, the reverse became the case, in the leading industrialised countries at least, with most people living in urban centres and depending on industrial and commercial activities for their livelihood (Landes, 1969).

Britain was the pioneer industrial country; it was the model that other European nations and the USA sought to emulate in their attempts to transform traditional agrarian economies into urban societies based on science and technology (Kemp, 1979). The key development of the Industrial Revolution towards this process of societal transformation was the creation of the factory system. It was this that gave the impetus to and created the model for all that was to follow. As Weber (1928: 302) pointed out, the factory's distinguishing characteristic was '... in general ... not the implements of work applied but the concentration of ownership of workplace, means of work, source of power and raw materials in one and the same hand, that of the entrepreneur'. Or, to put it another way, it was the way the entrepreneur 'organised' the elements of production that distinguished it from what went before.

This tells us what changed, but it does not explain why or how in a few score years organisations came to dominate our lives. To answer this, it is necessary to appreciate the great surge of economic activity – especially the international trade in textile products – that arose in the seventeenth and eighteenth centuries. This trade gave an enormous impetus to textile production in Britain, which in turn had a knock-on effect in all other spheres of economic activity (Mathias, 1969).

Before and during the early part of the British Industrial Revolution, textile production was carried out as an agricultural by-occupation based on family units. However, as demand increased in the eighteenth century, some 'men and women [became] specialist spinners or weavers, thinking first of wool, treating work on the land as, at most, a by-occupation' (Ashton, 1948: 23). Allied to this, a new mechanism sprang up to link producer and consumer: the 'putting-out' system, whereby a large merchant would 'put out' work to a number of independent domestic producers.

The advantage to the merchant was threefold: it was cheap – there were few overheads; it was flexible – production could be easily expanded or contracted; and it avoided the difficulties involved in directly employing a workforce. However, as demand continued to increase in the late eighteenth century, this system became more complex and more costly, and eventually it became too cumbersome (Pollard, 1965). The chain of intermediaries linking producer to consumer became increasingly difficult for the large merchant to control. There were many problems with the putting-out mechanism: dishonesty (on both sides) was rife; deliveries were late; and quality often poor. Laws attempting to control producers could do nothing to rectify the fundamental weaknesses in the system. The incompatibility between the large and complex organisation of distribution and the multitude of tiny domestic workshop units, unsupervised and unsupervisable, was bound to set up tensions and drive merchants to seek new ways of production – ways whereby they could establish their own managerial control over the production process (Pollard, 1965).

There was also an incompatibility between different cultures. For the merchant, the expansion of markets was a chance to maximise profits in order to live in the grand style. For the rural domestic producer, involved in long hours of back-breaking work, it created the conditions for increased leisure. As Marglin (1976: 35) commented: '... wages rose and workers insisted on taking out a portion of their gains in the form of greater leisure. However sensible this may have been from their own point of view, it is no way for an enterprising capitalist to get ahead.'

Therefore, it was the merchant who began the move towards the factory system – not because the merchant had an innate desire to run factories or exercise direct control over labour, but in order to take full advantage of expanding market opportunities to reap ever greater rewards.

Nevertheless, there was no headlong rush to create a new economic order overnight. The earliest factories, if that is not too grand a word for them, were small, unpowered weaving or spinning sheds that used existing technology and methods. A few very large factories – such as Wedgwood's Etruria Works in Stoke-on-Trent – were established, but these were the rare exceptions. Indeed, in 1780, the investment in fixed equipment and stock in the textile industry, which was the leading edge of the Industrial Revolution, was only £10 per worker, and the average factory employed no more than 10 or 12 people. By 1830, when the textile industry had grown to employ 100,000 people and the average factory size was 137, the investment in fixed equipment and stock had only increased to £15 per worker, and 50 per cent of the workforce were still home-based (Hobsbawm, 1968; Pollard, 1965; Tillett, 1970). Given this situation, it is hardly surprising that capital investment was quickly recovered and that it was running expenses, mainly wages and raw materials, which formed the bulk of manufacturing costs. It is this, and the original motive for moving to the factory system in the first place (to have greater control over labour), which explains the prevailing attitude of employers towards labour in the nineteenth century.

The relationship between employers and employees

British employers based their attitude towards employees on two basic propositions:

1 Labour is unreliable, lazy and will only work when tightly controlled and closely supervised.

2 The main controllable business cost is labour; therefore the key to increased profits is to make it cheaper, and/or increase its productivity, by getting employees to work harder, or for longer hours, for the same, or less, money.

In this respect, as contemporary writers such as Charles Babbage (1835) and Andrew Ure (1835) observed, workers' skill was seen as at best an inconvenience and at worst a threat, because it could be scarce, costly and allow workers a strong bargaining position.

As might be expected, employers' hostility was reciprocated by labour. Workers exhibited a strong dislike for, and reluctance to become part of, the factory system. As Pollard (1965) noted, this was for three main reasons:

1 It involved a wholesale change of culture and environment and the destruction of small, tightly knit communities in which they lived. Hard though the life of cottage industry was, it had given workers a measure of independence and some control over what they did, when they did it and how.

2 The discipline of the factory was harsh and unremitting with men, women and small children all expected to work long hours, often seven days a week, in appalling conditions.

3 Given the lack of alternative organisational forms on which to establish factory life, employers often modelled them on workhouses or prisons. Indeed, to square the circle, some workhouses and prisons turned themselves into factories and their inmates into little more than slaves. Thus factories acquired the same stigma as was attached to prisons and workhouses.

Therefore, the antagonism that existed between owners and workers was based on a genuine clash of interests – one which has echoed through the industrial world ever since.

If this picture of the factory system in the nineteenth century seems bleak to us, it is nevertheless accurate, as is shown in the work of its proponents such as Charles Babbage and Andrew Ure, social reformers such as Seebohm Rowntree, political activists such as Frederick Engels and contemporary novelists such as Charles Dickens. Nor was this aspect of industrialisation restricted to Britain. Studies of other European countries and the USA have shown similar tensions, sometimes even more violent, between the old and the new methods of working, and between employers and employees (Bruland, 1989; Chapman and Chassagne, 1981; Mantoux, 1964; Pelling, 1960).

In defence of the factory owners, who must take responsibility for what emerged, it should be said that their own experience was limited and there were no textbooks to guide them. That they should 'copy' what models existed reflected both the common view of labour amongst the owning classes, and a lack of alternative organisational forms on which to base the emergent factory system. As other nations industrialised, notably Germany, France and the United States, they too adopted similar organisational forms and espoused similar attitudes towards labour. Partly this was because they were seeking to emulate Britain's success by copying her approach. It was also because these societies, like Great Britain, were riven by hierarchical and horizontal divisions that were inevitably reproduced in the workplace.

■ Industrialisation and the organisation of work

The system of organising work that came to characterise industrial life in Britain and most of continental Europe, and even the USA, by the end of the nineteenth century was based on the hierarchical and horizontal division of labour. Though this represented a significant break with the past in terms of how work had previously been organised, it was not out of step with the social stratification of European society nor with feudal traditions of obedience. The articulation and propagation of the principle of the division of labour owed much to the work of Adam Smith. In his book *The Wealth of Nations*, published in 1776, Smith used the now famous example of pin-making to illustrate what he saw as the advantages of the division of labour. He pointed out that a pin could be made entirely by one person doing everything, or by a number of people each specialising in one aspect of its production. For three reasons, he believed the latter was more efficient:

1 A worker who constantly performs one simple task will quickly acquire greater dexterity than one who performs a variety of tasks.
2 It avoids the loss of time necessitated by one person moving from one task to another.
3 The concentration of attention on one special task leads to the invention of machines that aid the productivity of labour and allow one person to do the work previously performed by many.

Smith's ideas were given flesh and form in Britain by pioneering factory owners such as Josiah Wedgwood, and Matthew Boulton and James Watt. At his Etruria pottery works, Wedgwood developed a production system that split the work process down into separate departments, each with its own specialist supervisor. Work was organised almost on a flow-line basis with the skill involved in each operation reduced to a minimum in order, in Wedgwood's own words, 'to make machines of men as cannot err' (quoted in Tillett, 1970: 37). Matthew Boulton and James Watt developed a similar approach at their Soho Works in Birmingham in the 1770s. They also kept detailed production records, a practice virtually unknown at the time (Roll, 1930). Wedgwood, Boulton, Watt and a few others were the architects of the factory system. By their organisation of work on and off the shopfloor, they created models that later managers would copy and adapt to their own needs and circumstances.

This approach to the organisation and control of work spread outwards from Britain. As Bruland (1989: 165) observed:

> There was a fairly direct international diffusion of these changes from Britain, the originating economy: British workers, in most parts of Europe, played a significant role in spreading the new work systems, in training local workers, and in the adaptation of the work force to the new rhythms of work.

As the nineteenth century progressed, this approach to work organisation became more developed and systematised. Charles Babbage (1835) developed a method of applying the division of labour principle to the detailed analysis of any job. He emphasised the need for and advantage of dividing tasks between and within mental and manual labour. He envisaged three 'classes' employed in the work process: the entrepreneur and his technical specialists who would design machines and plan the form of work organisation; operative engineers and managers who would be responsible for executing such plans and designs, based on only partial knowledge of the processes involved; and the mass of employees, needing only a low level of skill, who would undertake the actual work. Thus, in Babbage's (1835: vii) view:

> ... the master manufacturer, by dividing the work to be executed into different processes, each requiring different degrees of skill or force, can purchase exactly the precise quality of both which is necessary for each process ...

Though coming from separate traditions, Smith's work was also in tune with the Prussian bureaucratic school, and undoubtedly the efficient organisation of German industry in the late nineteenth century owes much to a combination of the two approaches.

The pioneers of these developments in work organisation, whether in Britain, Germany or other European countries, tended to be strict disciplinarians who used their personal authority to impose the new working arrangements on a usually reluctant workforce (Chapman and Chassagne, 1981). Therefore, change tended to be managed by imposition and force rather than negotiation and agreement. Nor is it surprising that it should be so. In the main these were countries which had been, in the recent past, feudal economies dominated by warrior elites. In Germany, this was still the case. Even where, as in France, there had been a decisive break with the past, this seems merely to have reinforced rather than removed patterns of social rigidity and authoritarianism.

In such situations, resistance to or questioning of change was unlikely to be met by understanding or tolerance. Predictably, there was strong resistance, both active and passive, to the introduction of new working patterns and methods (Kriedte *et al*, 1981). Though this resistance could and did take the form of physical violence against factories and equipment, a more frequent manifestation was high labour turnover. One of the largest Manchester cotton spinning firms, McConnell and Kennedy, had an average turnover in the early nineteenth century of 100 per cent per year, a high but not uncommon rate (Fitton and Wadsworth, 1958; Pollard, 1965). A similar situation existed in other European countries. In Germany, for example, employers 'were generally satisfied if they achieved partial success in creating a stable core of skilled workers ... Turnover was the most persistent labour problem confronting employers' (Lee, 1978: 460). This situation clearly gave those workers whose skills were most in demand a significant bargaining position, which allowed them to raise their wages and determine the pace of work. However, it also acted as a spur to employers to seek methods of reducing their reliance on skilled labour (Bruland, 1989). One of the main ways that entrepreneurs responded was through technological developments aimed at replacing or reducing employers' reliance on skilled labour.

A contemporary observer of the nineteenth century industrial scene, Andrew Ure (1836: viii–ix), drew special attention to the role that technology could play in this process:

> By developing machines ... which require only unskilled instead of skilled labour, the cost of labour can be reduced [and] the bargaining position of the worker reduced.

It becomes clear why workers not only opposed the advent of the factory system but also, even when it became established, continued to oppose strongly changes in work practices and the introduction of new equipment. Even in the present day, where change tends to be preceded by consultation and its beneficial effects are stressed, there is still a tendency for those concerned to feel apprehensive of, if not downright resistant towards, change (Smith *et al*, 1982). Therefore, in a harsher and more authoritarian age, where organisational and technological change was seen as a weapon in the battle for control of the workplace, it is not surprising that change management should be achieved by imposition and coercion, and occasion the response that it did.

Nevertheless, despite the increasing opposition of 'organised' labour, the work practices associated with the factory system gradually permeated every aspect of industrial and commercial life, albeit only on a piecemeal basis. Even by the end of the nineteenth century, there was no unified or accepted approach that managers could apply to organisations in their entirety, though in Germany the application of the Prussian bureaucratic model allied to the approach to industrial organisation of Adam Smith was proving influential. Yet the developing factory system could not shake off the legacy of its origins or ignore the continuing battle between labour and management over control, rewards and skill. As the following shows, this was as much the case in continental Europe and the USA as it was in Britain.

Europe

The history of Europe since 1800, at least in economic terms, is essentially the history of industrialisation, of structural change through which industrial sectors grew and non-agricultural sectors came for the first time to dominate economic life. In general, for most of the nineteenth century, continental Europe lagged behind Britain in terms of industrial development. However, just as Britain was something of a patchwork quilt in terms of the pace of development of individual industries and regions, so too was the rest of Europe (Davis, 1989). As Pollard (1981) explained, European industrialisation developed from a few core regions. In Britain, southern Lancashire, the West Riding of Yorkshire, and that part of the West Midlands called the Black Country were the engines of growth. In northern Europe, the area between the Scheldt, the Meuse and the Rhine rivers had a special role to play, whilst to the east, Silesia, Bohemia and Moravia became leading centres of industrial progress. In the south, it was northern Italy and Catalonia that led the way.

Nevertheless, though mainland Europe did have its pockets of progress, industrialisation did not spread from these at the same rate nor in the same manner as it had in Britain. The most outstanding feature of British industrialisation was its self-generating or autonomous nature. Nowhere else could these conditions be exactly reproduced. To use an analogy, once the wheel has been invented, others cannot reinvent it. What they can do is adopt it and adapt it to their needs and circumstances.

Therefore, Britain became a model to be consciously followed. In the same way that Japan became a focus for study, discussion and emulation by Westerners in the 1980s, so Britain was similarly regarded in the early nineteenth century. Regular visits were made by foreign governments and private entrepreneurs to discover and copy British methods and technologies. In some instances, British investors, entrepreneurs and inventors were encouraged by the governments of France, Germany and other European states to help develop their economies – all with the aim of reproducing and overtaking Britain's industrial lead.

For some, especially Germany and France, the process of industrialisation was less a matter of material progress by organisations and individuals pursuing profit maximisation, and more concerned with the maintenance of their position in the world. Just as they sought to challenge Britain's military might, so they sought to emulate her industrial power. They could not and would not let Britain dominate the world without a struggle. Therefore, though the advent of industrial capitalism was in all countries characterised by the rise of a class of industrialists who aggressively sought to maximise their own wealth, the context in which this occurred varied from country to country.

In Britain and the USA, the context favoured individual entrepreneurs pursuing their own self-interest. In Germany, and to a lesser extent France, industrialisation was sponsored by the state and for the state. The prime motive was to build the economic and military might of the state rather than the wealth of the individual. Where these were compatible, the state was happy to maintain a watching brief. However, where free enterprise and competition were seen as counter-productive to the objectives of the state, it intervened to reduce competition either through the creation of cartels and monopolies, or by state ownership/funding, as was the case with much of the European railway system. In Denmark, on the other hand, the operation of the market was constrained not by the state but by the creation of cooperatives, which allowed small-scale farming and business, and the way of life they represented, to survive where in other countries such enterprises were overwhelmed by larger competitors.

Therefore, though other countries used Britain as a model and benchmark, the actual process of industrialisation in each depended upon the unique political, social and economic circumstances that prevailed there. In some cases these gave primacy to profit maximisation, in others the interests of the state held sway, whilst in further cases sectional interests successfully challenged the power of the market. Consequently, influential though the British example was, once the necessary technique, capital and enterprise were introduced abroad and any element of conscious emulation had worn off, the industrialisation assumed a different character (Kemp, 1979). The continental countries did not and could not simply duplicate British experience.

There were, however, some fundamental similarities. All European societies, to a lesser or greater extent, were structured on a hierarchical basis, with those in positions of power strongly influenced in their view of the rest of society by feudal traditions of subservience and obedience. This was as much the case in post-revolutionary France as in Britain, and even more so in Prussia and Russia. It follows that the organisational forms and labour relations that characterised the emerging factory system in Britain found fertile ground elsewhere in Europe (Cipolla, 1973).

Despite this, other countries did not copy Britain unthinkingly or on a wholesale basis. As latecomers, they could, especially with the encouragement of the state, leapfrog some of the stages of industrialisation, which was one of their principal advantages, but they could not close the gap between themselves and Britain overnight. Ashworth (1987) commented that even as late as 1850, apart from Belgium, Europe had little mechanised industry to speak of; however, 50 years later, Germany had overtaken Britain as the leading industrial nation, and other nations were also poised to do so. The reasons for this are many and complex, involving social and political as well as economic factors (Mathias and Davis, 1989). A brief look at industrial development in Germany, France and Scandinavia illustrates this.

Germany

Within the space of a generation in the middle years of the nineteenth century, Germany was transformed from a collection of economically backward states forming a political patchwork in central Europe into a unified empire, driven forward by a rapidly expanding, technologically driven industrial base (Kemp, 1979). Germany's progress was so rapid that, though it industrialised much later, by the end of the nineteenth century it had overtaken Britain as the world's premier industrial nation. This transformation, accompanied as it was by the deliberate resort to military force as an instrument of national policy, and an atmosphere of fierce nationalism, represented an event of major historical significance (Borchardt, 1973).

The two key factors that were primarily responsible for the nature and pace of German industrial development were the geographical and political conditions of the country, and the fact that German industrialisation was state-promoted rather than market-driven.

To look first at geography and politics: not until the late nineteenth century did Germany possess an integrated territory with an economic and administrative centre. Up to the nineteenth century, Germany was a collection of feudal fiefdoms that often warred with each other, rather than a unified nation. In 1789, 'Germany' comprised some 314 independent territories each with their own rulers, internal markets, customs barriers, currencies and trading monopolies. This internal fragmentation, as much as anything else, was probably the key obstacle to industrial progress. This did not change until the Congress of Vienna in 1815, which reduced the number of German states to 39. Each individual state then began to remove internal customs barriers and develop better communications systems, which opened the way for greater economic cooperation with other states.

However, unlike other countries, economic progress was neither driven nor accompanied by a democratisation of society. German society in the nineteenth century remained dominated by a feudal hierarchy. This was characterised by Prussian 'Junkerdom' with its military traditions and ambitions, and its autocratic behaviour. Unlike their counterparts in other countries, the German nobility were not diminished by industrial progress; rather they managed to seize the reins of commercial power to bolster their position. This was due, in many instances, to their retention of regional monopolies over trade, industry and the supply of labour.

This leads on to the second key feature of German industrialisation – the fact that it was state promoted rather than free-market driven. The drive for industrialisation, especially in Prussia, which came to dominate the rest of Germany, was not primarily motivated by economic reasons. Rather, industrialisation was seen as the process of building a strong and powerful state in which the old nobility continued to dominate. Therefore, for Germany, the fact that industrialisation was accompanied by the development of a strong military machine and the continued dominance of the Prussian Junkers was not an unfortunate coincidence, but its major objective.

Industrial progress in Britain exerted a strong influence on Germany. This was partly because it provided a model to emulate, but mainly because Germany saw industrial power and military power as two sides of the same coin. Unless Germany could catch up with and overtake Britain's industrial lead, Germany felt that it would be relegated to the status of a second-class state.

The transformation of Germany into an industrial superpower owed much to the role played by Prussia. From the early nineteenth century onwards, Prussia used its economic and military position as the most powerful German state to subdue the other German states and exclude possible rivals, especially Austria. The prime weapon in the Prussian arsenal was the creation of an all-German customs union (the *Zollverein*). Because of its size, Prussia could determine the rules for the *Zollverein* and, whenever and wherever it was extended, could ensure it was to Prussian advantage.

The customs union, because it opened up trade, also gave a boost to the development of better transportation and communication links, especially railway building (though the latter really took off once the Prussian military came to appreciate its strategic significance for the rapid transit of troops and materials). It seems very clear that, more than the emergence of any one industry, it was the creation of a single market and the boost to consumption that this brought about which was the key factor in Germany's economic progress in the nineteenth century (Kemp, 1979).

By 1834, practically all of Germany was included within the customs union and, though it did not come about until 1871, this provided the essential precondition for political unification. The fact that both political and economic unification were driven by and dominated by Prussia gave German industrialisation its unique character. The new German state that was established in 1871, for all its acceptance of universal suffrage and a national parliament, remained an autocracy ruled by the Hohenzollern dynasty, which still rested on the support of the traditional landed nobility of eastern Germany. It incorporated the bureaucratic and militarist traditions of the old Prussia and remained profoundly conservative.

Indeed, it was the adoption of the Prussian bureaucratic model by both state and industry, combined with close links between both, which gave German industry its unique character. Unlike Britain, where the majority of firms remained relatively small and business operated in an *ad hoc* fashion, with each company pursuing its own interests, in Germany large, bureaucratically structured organisations became the norm. In addition, the state did not hesitate to intervene directly, for example when it nationalised the railways, if it believed the private sector could not or would not serve the national interest.

Given that the state saw German industry as almost an extension of government, it is not surprising that it sought to bolster managerial authority and restrict workers' rights. This also very much reflected the Prussian autocratic tradition of expecting and enforcing obedience from those lower down the social order. Therefore, in most – though not all – enterprises, employers took the view that they had a right to treat their workers however they pleased. A German employer regarded himself as a patriarch, as the master in his own house in pre-industrial terms, with total responsibility for the whole social organism of his enterprise and generally well beyond this. This type of self-esteem made German employers particularly unyielding in any situation of conflict.

One consequence of this was that the industrial and political climate became increasingly radical after the political and economic unification of Germany in 1871, though to no great effect. This period also saw the rapid development of the German economy. In 1870, the leading British enterprises were much bigger than their largest German competitors; by 1900, this position had been reversed. In many cases this was the result of governmental and banking encouragement to move to vertical integration. Also, cartels and monopolies, frowned upon elsewhere, received official endorsement in Germany, which allowed more orderly growth and longer-term investment decisions than might otherwise have been the case.

By the end of the nineteenth century the German economy had outstripped its British counterpart, but had not succeeded in avoiding either the same debilitating conflict between employers and employees, or the rise of political groups and parties which challenged the nature and purpose of capitalism. However, the influence of the Prussian autocratic tradition, the development of a strong bureaucratic approach within both private and public sector organisations, and the close relationship between industry and state, meant that industrial and political resistance was met by a unified and implacable alliance between employers and government. Though prepared to use welfare provisions, sickness benefit, old age pensions, etc., to reduce social tensions, the state was not prepared to cede one iota of industrial or political authority.

France

As in Germany, the process of industrialisation in France was driven by the desire to emulate Britain, rather than by any form of 'spontaneous combustion'. However, despite having the advantage of much earlier state encouragement than Germany, France's industrial revolution was late in starting and did not reach maturity until towards the end of the nineteenth century (Dunham, 1955; Fohlen, 1973). The slow and late development of industry in France appears to have been caused by two key factors: political change and agrarian stagnation, both of which were inextricably linked with the French Revolution of 1789.

In the eighteenth century, little separated France and Britain in industrial terms. With much encouragement from the monarchy, French industry adopted British machines and equipment. British entrepreneurs and inventors were even persuaded to establish factories in France. During the last years before the French Revolution, the King paid great attention to the economy. A twin-track approach to industrial development was instituted. On the one hand, much state aid and encouragement were poured into industry; whilst on the other hand, there was the suppression of every obstacle to individual entrepreneurship, whether they be the privileges of the craft guilds or the ancient rights of the aristocracy.

Though these initiatives gave a significant boost to industrialisation, progress was halted, and even reversed, by the French Revolution in 1789 (Marczewski, 1963). To an extent this is surprising, given that those who dominated the Revolutionary Assemblies were men of property and substance, though drawn from the law and professions rather than the business world. They believed in upholding property rights, abolishing hereditary privilege and vested interests, and providing a favourable climate for entrepreneurship. They also introduced laws that placed employees in an inferior legal position to their employers and which prohibited them from combining for the purpose of bargaining. Nevertheless, the benefits of these to entrepreneurs were outweighed by other consequences of the Revolution. Foremost amongst these was the loss of France's colonial empire, together with its isolation, by the British naval blockade, from key markets such as the United States. The result was not only that France lost crucial imports and exports, but also that it was cut off from the prime source of technical and organisational innovation, Britain.

It was not until the final defeat of Napoleon in 1815 that France was once again able to concentrate on developing its economy rather than fighting wars. As before, the state took a lead in encouraging economic development, notably through the development of roads, canals and, later, railways. It also sought to stimulate the domestic economy by introducing import controls. However, this seems only to have allowed industry to keep outdated methods and equipment and maintain higher prices longer than might have been the case if it had not operated in a protected market. Only after 1850, with the upsurge in economic activity across Europe and the coming to power of Napoleon III, does the French economy really seem to have taken off.

The other main factor which held back industrialisation was the backward state of agriculture. The peasantry were already developing as an important group even before the French Revolution. However, the price they exacted for supporting the Revolution, the ownership of the majority of agricultural land, made them a powerful but reactionary force to which all sections of the property-owning classes had to pay attention. The consequences of this for industrialisation were twofold. First, the agricultural sector, unlike its counterparts Britain and Germany, remained self-sufficient and inefficient for most of the nineteenth century. As such, it was incapable of generating either wealth for investing in industry or demand for manufactured goods produced by industry. Second, by depressing the rate of population growth, it prevented the mass population exodus from the countryside to the towns and thus starved industry of a ready supply of cheap labour. This situation was further exacerbated by the continuing opportunities for home work which, by supplementing agricultural incomes, extended the viability of rural life longer than might otherwise be the case.

Nevertheless, the continued existence of a large rural population, even up to the dawn of the twentieth century, was not just a product of land ownership and the presence of home work. It also owed a great deal to the presence of import barriers which allowed peasants to maintain, in comparison with their British counterparts, inefficient production methods, and reduced the need either to borrow money for new equipment or to sell plots that were too small to be viable.

Import barriers also produced a strong bond of self-interest between peasants and factory owners, both of whom saw free trade as a threat to their way of life. As one observer commented, 'Competition was always possible in France, it simply did not happen to be a preferred form of conduct' (Sheahan, 1969: 25).

For industrialists, the result was similar. The absence of foreign competition, allied to low levels of domestic demand, allowed the typical business to remain family-owned, and also relatively small. Finance for industrial expansion was raised from family members rather than financial institutions, which in turn restricted the size of the banking sector. Indeed, such was the shortage of domestically generated capital and risk-orientated entrepreneurs that the building of railways, so vital to the development of the French economy, could not have taken place without foreign capital and state support (Kemp, 1979).

Therefore, unlike Britain, industrialisation in France was never driven by, or resulted in, individual enterprise or profit maximisation. For the state, the objective was a strong France. For the peasant and small entrepreneur, the objective was to make a reasonable living in the context of the rural and urban cultures they supported and valued.

Scandinavia

Having looked at how the three largest and most advanced European countries – Britain, Germany and France – industrialised, we shall now move on to examine how three of the smaller states – Sweden, Denmark and Norway – responded to the challenge of industrialisation. In 1800, the total population of these three countries was just over four million people: Sweden, 2.35 million; Denmark, 0.93 million; and Norway, 0.88 million. By 1910, it was still less than 11 million: Sweden, 5.5 million; Denmark, 2.8 million; and Norway, 2.4 million. The historical links between these countries were very close, and up to the First World War they operated a monetary union. Although, owing to their seafaring traditions, each had occupied a position of importance on the international stage, by the mid-nineteenth century the standing of all three countries had declined. In fact, Norway and Sweden had become two of the poorest countries in Europe, which was a prime reason for the large-scale emigration from these countries to the USA in the nineteenth century (Milward and Saul, 1973).

Despite growing pockets of industrial production, in the nineteenth century their domestic economies were weak, and all three countries depended heavily on exporting the products of their agricultural, mining and forestry industries to their more industrialised neighbours, especially Britain. That they were able to adapt their export efforts to the changing demands of the international economy bears witness to the entrepreneurial skills of these countries.

However, political, economic and social developments in these three countries in the nineteenth century, particularly in Denmark, laid the foundations for the creation of the 'Nordic model' of industrial relations, which emerged in the 1930s. This arose from the so-called 'historic compromise' between capital and labour, which extended cooperation between employers and social democratic governments over national economic policy into the industrial relations field. At a national level, it was agreed that the efforts of social democratic governments to bring about economic growth would not challenge the capitalist nature of production. Trade unions accepted this approach in exchange for basic trade union rights. This paved the way for an end to lock-outs and other such tactics by employers, and the creation of government-backed approaches to industrial democracy and further extensions of workers' rights (Dolvik and Stokland, 1992; Ferner and Hyman, 1992; Kjellberg, 1992).

These developments happened at different times and at a different pace in each country. Denmark led the way in the late nineteenth century, and Norway and Sweden followed a decade later, though the 'Nordic model' did not really establish itself fully until the 1930s and 1940s. However, the close ties between these three countries meant that political and industrial developments in one affected the other two. Hence the phrase 'Nordic model' was coined to describe similarities between the tripartite approaches adopted by government, employers and trade unions in each country, and the fact that these were distinct from practices elsewhere in Europe (or the rest of the world for that matter). However, for the moment, we are more concerned with the process of industrialisation in the nineteenth century and how this paved the way for these later developments.

For **Sweden,** the nineteenth century brought a rapidly rising population, which was matched by an increasingly productive agricultural sector that not only fully met domestic needs, but also developed a strong export market in grain, especially to Britain. The productivity of agriculture reflected the growing flexibility and commercialisation of this sector, facilitated by a series of gradual and peaceful rural reforms.

The iron trade also occupied an important position in the Swedish economy for much of the nineteenth century. This was due in no small part to its ability to adopt technological innovations, mainly from Britain, and the ability of Swedish ironmasters to seek out new international markets. By the end of the century, this had led to fewer but larger units of production, and the industry began to reflect the structures and methods of the leading European producers.

Despite the growth of agriculture and iron production, the most spectacular element in the growth of the Swedish economy was the boom in timber exports (Jorberg, 1973). Up to the 1830s, Swedish exports were only a fraction of those of Norway. However, the increasing urbanisation of Britain, and growing demand for timber from France and Germany, transformed the pattern of demand and supply. By the 1860s, softwood accounted for 40 per cent of all Sweden's exports, a situation that lasted well into the 1880s.

With over 20 million hectares of productive forest, Sweden possessed the largest such area in Europe, after Russia. The growth in markets was matched by the introduction of new methods and techniques, especially the use of steam engines and fine-bladed saws at the mills. The transfer of land ownership from the state to the private sector, in the early nineteenth century, also aided the development of the timber industry by allowing entrepreneurs to obtain timber rights often at ridiculously low prices, sometimes for no more than a sack of flour. Such a situation attracted many ruthless entrepreneurs whose regard for reforestation and conservation was negligible.

This combination of high demand, cheap wood and ruthless entrepreneurs created the conditions for a very sharp boom in timber exports, at least in the short term. Although after 1875 the state reversed its policy and began to reacquire forests, the timber companies also began to buy farmland, with its attendant forest rights. Gradually, the industry came to be dominated by a few large companies, some of which were foreign-owned. However, this concentration of ownership did make it easier for the state to oblige producers to take a more responsible approach to conservation and reforestation.

Given the dominance of the forestry industry, which relied almost exclusively on waterways for transportation, it is not perhaps surprising that railways came late to Sweden – not until the 1850s. It is also not surprising, given this situation, that it was government push rather than demand pull which gave the impetus to the Swedish railway system. Remarkably, by 1914, Sweden had 2.5 km of railway per 1000 inhabitants, twice that of any other European country. It also had a thriving industry producing rolling stock and engines for both the domestic and export markets (Jorberg, 1973).

Nevertheless, in 1870, industry and handicrafts only employed 15 per cent of the population. There were no industrial centres to rival those of Britain, Germany and France. Even the iron districts were small separate communities. However, after 1870, there was a rapid expansion of the Swedish industrial base, so much so that in the 40 years up to 1914, the Swedish economy grew faster than any other in Europe. Even so, to put this picture into perspective, it should be noted that all the workers involved in Swedish engineering exports in 1912 totalled no more than those to be found in one large German railway works.

For a small country, dependent on its natural resources, Sweden's progress was significant. There were a number of reasons for this. First, changes in the eighteenth century had removed barriers to social mobility and created the conditions for the emergence of entrepreneurs. Second, these entrepreneurs showed an unrivalled ability to exploit Sweden's natural resources and take advantage of developing export markets. An additional factor was the high quality of the Swedish educational system. This provided an educated workforce able to adapt to changing industries, technologies and products. Therefore, though it would be wrong to underestimate the great asset of Sweden's natural resources, neither should one forget the contribution made by human capital. The combination of a less hierarchical society than elsewhere in Europe and a well-educated and skilled workforce clearly paved the way for the advent of the social democratic approach to society which became the hallmark of Sweden in the twentieth century.

On the other hand, it would be misleading to forget that, as elsewhere in Europe, industrialisation was a harsh process. Entrepreneurs could be very rapacious, and much of the technology and many of the methods they employed were imported from the more advanced nations, especially Britain. Consequently, though the Swedish government tended to be more keen to intervene than was the case in Britain, industrialisation was accompanied by the same sort of clashes between capital and labour, and the growing incompatibility between an agricultural economy based on self-sufficiency and a capitalist economy based on money.

By the end of the nineteenth century, Sweden had developed a small industrial base, by comparison with Britain, Germany and France, but one that was flexible and competitive. However, the organisation of labour and the technology deployed tended to be imported from the bigger industrial nations. It imported the poor labour relations that existed elsewhere as well.

Though Sweden's industrial base was modest by international standards, it was in advance of that of Denmark and Norway (Jorberg, 1973). For **Denmark**, as for Sweden, it was changes to agricultural production that gave a large boost to the economy in the nineteenth century.

Traditionally, Denmark had relied on the export of two commodities, grain and cattle (though, in the eighteenth and the first half of the nineteenth centuries, its economy also benefited considerably from its colonial possessions in Asia and the West Indies, particularly in terms of sugar production and the slave trade). Trade in the former grew rapidly in the nineteenth century. However, much of the grain was produced on marginal land, which was no longer economically viable after the collapse of world grain prices in the 1870s. After the early 1880s, imports outstripped exports.

On the other hand, the keeping of livestock and dairy produce showed a remarkable growth throughout the century. By the end of the nineteenth century, Denmark had a thriving export trade in butter and beef. By 1913, Denmark exported 80 per cent of its butter production, mainly to Britain where it had 40 per cent of the market; in that year, only Holland and Argentina exported more live cattle than Denmark. The latter part of the nineteenth century and the early twentieth century also saw a twelvefold rise in the production and export of pork (Milward and Saul, 1973).

One hindrance to the export of pork was the incompatibility between the large scale of the export market and the numerous small producers. However, this was overcome in the 1880s with the establishment of the first cooperative bacon factory. By 1914, 53 per cent of pig breeders were supplying to cooperatives. The idea of cooperatives to buy, process and sell produce had grown up in the dairy industry, and was later taken up by egg producers as well as pig breeders. Similar organisations were also used to purchase bulk feedstuffs and fertilisers. The impetus behind the development of cooperatives was the smaller farmers' fear of being exploited by their larger colleagues, who could afford to purchase the latest technology exclusively for their own use (Jorberg, 1973).

Therefore, unlike most other European countries, Denmark found a method of making small-scale farming production compatible with large-scale international demand. Nor were these cooperatives purely economic and technical organisations. Though this was their primary purpose, they also had a social and political role, and were anti-landowner. The growth of cooperatives along with their attendant 'folk high schools' was crucial, not only in educating farmers, but also in uniting them as an effective political force. Indeed, the party of small farmers, in alliance with the social democrats, headed governments from 1909 to 1910 and from 1913 to 1920. Not only does this show the political influence and socialist leanings of the cooperative movement, but it explains the emergence of the 'Nordic model' in Denmark some 20 years earlier than in the other two Scandinavian countries. The development of cooperatives was also one of the main reasons why there was no reduction in the numbers employed in Danish agriculture in the nineteenth century.

Though in some ways Denmark had a relatively thriving economy, its industrial base was, even relative to its size, on a more modest scale than in Britain, France or Germany. As an example, by 1911, the Danish cotton industry employed only 3,282 people, no more than one big mill in Britain. In total, there were only 108,000 workers employed in factories at this time.

In contrast, there was a tremendous growth in the service sector, not just in transport and communications, but also in financial and trading services. These latter tended to be concentrated in Copenhagen, where by 1910 half the country's population lived. By 1911, service activities accounted for 36 per cent of the occupied population, as averse to 32 per cent in Norway and 19 per cent in Sweden.

One of the remarkable features of Danish industrialisation in the nineteenth century was the degree to which it preserved rather than destroyed the peasant and craft traditions. In agriculture, this was mainly due to the rise of cooperatives for processing and selling produce. In industry, the need to cater mainly for a small and discerning home market, allied to a well-educated workforce, kept alive the craft tradition, and – for most of the nineteenth century – the guild system. Even in 1914, 84 per cent of Danish workers were still in establishments employing five or less people. By contrast, in Sweden in 1912, only 24 per cent of workers were in establishments employing 10 or less people.

Therefore, if Denmark was less industrially advanced than some bigger European countries, it could however claim to have avoided the clash of cultures and the rise of industrial conflict that characterised the industrial revolution elsewhere in Europe.

Just as the process of industrialisation differed considerably between Sweden and Denmark, so was also the case with **Norway**. Like the other two countries, it was dependent on exports, but in Norway these were service-based rather than product-based. Shipping was its chief earner. In 1880, shipping accounted for 45 per cent of all exports.

Its links with Sweden and Denmark tended to be political rather than economic. Up to 1814, it was part of the Kingdom of Denmark, and in that year the King of Sweden also became the King of Norway. However, Denmark sided with France during the Napoleonic Wars and as a consequence of Napoleon's defeat lost the sovereignty of Norway to Sweden. Norway was given its own parliament and constitution, though its political and economic ties with Sweden were considerable until it achieved full independence in 1905.

Of the three Scandinavian countries, Norway was slowest to industrialise and, unlike the other two, this was neither preceded nor accompanied by the modernisation of agriculture. Nor was the stimulus to industrialisation generated internally. Rather, when industry really began to flourish, just before the First World War, it was brought about by an influx of foreign capital wishing to take advantage of Norway's potential for cheap hydroelectricity.

However, up to this point, Norway had made few steps towards becoming an industrial economy. In agriculture, Norway was held back by a combination of poor soils, difficult climate and extremely inefficient internal communications. Indeed, a marked feature of the Norwegian economy was the very poor contact and bad communications between various regions within the country, no doubt a consequence of the mountainous terrain, which meant that it was often easier to import goods from abroad rather than to move them from one part of Norway to another (Jorberg, 1973). This led to a dual economy: the increasingly prosperous urban areas which grew rich on the export of goods and services, and a subsistence agricultural economy in the countryside.

Accordingly, the towns prospered and the countryside stagnated with small peasant farmers tending to be the agricultural norm into the twentieth century. At the end of the nineteenth century, such was the low level of productivity of Norwegian agriculture that butter exports, worth 3.3 million Kr, were dwarfed by imports of grain and animal feedstuffs worth 83 million Kr. Norway had no other food exports of importance, except for fish (Milward and Saul, 1973).

On the other hand, Norway was mercifully free of the social rigidity of many other European countries where the nobility stood at the top of the social pyramid. Instead, uniquely, merchants and gentlemen farmers formed the top layers of society, serfdom was rare, and there was a lack of the social injustice that seemed inevitably to accompany industrialisation in the more advanced countries. This may account for the willingness of employers and trade unions, particularly in the metal industries, to favour cooperation over conflict from the early 1900s (Dolvik and Stokland, 1992; Kjellberg, 1992).

The staple industries of the Norwegian economy in the nineteenth century were fishing, timber and shipping, along with a shipbuilding industry that was a product of all three. In the early years of the century, it also exported iron, but this trade was virtually killed by British and Swedish competition after Danish trade protection was abolished in 1814. The main employers were shipping, where some 33,000 were employed in the merchant marine in 1860, and fishing, both of which had only weak links to the rest of the economy. There was also a small, fragmented, engineering

industry, which in 1850 only comprised 12 factories employing a total of 200 workers. From the 1840s there was a rapid growth in the textile sector. Even so, in 1860
this still only accounted for 3,000 workers out of a total of just under 20,000 industrial workers. The biggest industrial sector was forestry, employing almost one in
three workers (Jorberg, 1973).

Therefore, because of its small population size, the lack of demand from the countryside, and the reliance of the towns on exports for their prosperity, Norway's
industrial expansion was linked very closely to the export trades. When exports
boomed, domestic demand increased; when exports fell, so did domestic demand. In
addition, because its industrial sector was small, Norway found it difficult to generate
capital domestically. As an example, in 1870, half of the mining industry was foreign-
owned. However, with the development of closer economic links with Sweden in
1873, the market for Norwegian industry was expanded considerably.

Developing quite separately from the rest of the economy, the real growth industry
of the nineteenth century was shipping. Shipping emerged during the eighteenth century as a subsidiary of the timber trade, but in the nineteenth century it developed
entirely independently of Norway's own transport needs. Instead, it catered to the
needs of other countries, especially Britain and Denmark and their colonies. It owed
its existence to the country's shipbuilding tradition, the availability of local timber
and the ready supply of cheap labour. From 1850, the industry grew rapidly, growing
fivefold in the years up to 1880, by which time it was the third largest in the world,
greater even than that of France and Germany. However, after 1900, the industry
declined, owing to a fall in freight rates and to the advent of steam-powered vessels.
The industry was very fragmented, which meant that raising capital was difficult.
Though this was not a problem with the small, wooden ships that had been the back-
bone of the industry, it became one with the need for larger, much more expensive,
steam-powered vessels. Also, Norway lacked both the raw materials, iron and steel,
and the skills to build steam ships. Indeed, in the immediate pre-war years, only
20 per cent of the industry's requirements were met from home production. Even so,
in 1914, the Norwegian shipping industry was the fourth largest in the world behind
Britain, the USA and Germany, though there were signs that it was in decline.

The advent of hydroelectric power at the end of the nineteenth century did, however, make a significant difference to Norway's industrial development. Once the
technology had been established, no country in Europe was better placed to exploit it
than Norway, with its plentiful supply of waterfalls. However, to turn this into a reality required both capital and a use for the resultant cheap electricity. Both of these
were to come from abroad. By 1914, hydroelectric power, financed by foreign capital,
was used to produce synthetic fertiliser and aluminium. The attraction for foreign
investors was cheap power. Almost all of the output was sold abroad, much of it
without further processing. These developments had a significant impact in terms of
increasing Norway's foreign earnings. The result was that some 14 per cent of the
industrial labour force was directly employed by foreign firms by 1909, with considerable numbers being indirectly employed. These workers tended to be concentrated
in the more capital-intensive industries and larger workplaces. This led to a law being
passed which limited foreign ownership of Norwegian industry.

In many respects, with the stagnation of timber and shipping, the advent of
modern chemical and metal industries was highly desirable. In another respect,

though, they also showed the weakness of Norwegian industrialisation. Both these industries were heavily dependent on foreign capital; both were capital- as opposed to labour-intensive; and neither developed or needed a local supply or distribution network. Therefore, neither really impacted greatly, at least in the pre-war period, on the wider Norwegian economy. For this reason, in relation to its Scandinavian neighbours, Norway remained a relatively poor country, which certainly accounted for the large waves of emigration it experienced in the nineteenth and early twentieth centuries. In relation to political democracy and educational provision, though, particularly for women, it was in advance of most other European countries before 1914.

Considering these three Scandinavian countries as a whole, the picture of industrialisation by the early twentieth century was very mixed. Sweden was probably the most advanced, with Denmark not far behind but Norway trailing somewhat. However, because of population size, natural resources and history, none had developed an industrial base capable of competing with those of the leading European countries.

As elsewhere in Europe, all three tended to import methods and technologies from the more advanced countries, especially Britain. It would appear that the process of industrialisation, where it was reliant on foreign capital and methods, tended to reproduce the British experience of poor labour relations. However, particularly in Denmark, there were signs that different organisational forms allied to existing social structures and expectations, together with the growth of social democracy, held out the promise of avoiding the vicious employer–employee clashes experienced elsewhere.

Nevertheless, in Europe as a whole, for the most part, those who created and controlled the large business organisations that were becoming the norm still had to rely on their own experience and judgment, but with growing frustration over their inability to control and organise these bodies fully and effectively. There was also a realisation amongst some that, whilst change was inevitable, they lacked an effective and, as far as their employees were concerned, acceptable way of managing it. Therefore, by the end of the nineteenth century, there was a growing awareness of the need to develop an approach to organising work that was more systematic and less harsh and arbitrary than what had gone before. Although this was already, to an extent, taking place in Germany with the rise of bureaucracy, the USA was the country where the most conscious and consistent search was being pursued for a comprehensive theory of how to structure and run organisations.

◼ The USA

In the USA, for a number of reasons, the need for a workable, overall approach to organisational design and control, which legitimised the authority of managers to initiate change, was perhaps more acute than anywhere else. The USA had industrialised far more rapidly and on a larger scale than any other nation. Only in the 1860s, after the Civil War, did the USA begin to industrialise in earnest, but by 1914 it had become the premier industrial nation, with the highest per capita income in the world. In the period 1860 to 1914, employment in manufacturing rose from 1.3 million to 6.6 million, and the population as a whole rose from 31 million to 91 million (Habakkuk and Postan, 1965). The USA at this time was still very much influenced

by Europe, and initially at least adopted similar approaches and methods in organising and running industry. However, the size of the typical American organisation
quickly grew much larger than those in Europe. Whilst the average British and French
business was still the small, family-owned firm, in the USA it was the monopoly,
which dominated an entire industry, or the conglomerate, which had substantial hold-
ings in several industries. As an example, in 1900 Dale Carnegie sold his steel
company for the enormous sum of $419 million to a group of financiers. They
merged it with other steel concerns to create a monopoly steel producer employing
200,000 workers and valued at $1.3 billion. This was at a time when the British steel
industry, which had led the world, comprised 100 blast furnaces owned by 95 separate companies.

As might be imagined, the numbers of Americans employed in factories and offices
grew rapidly – almost tripling between 1880 and 1910 (Levine, 1967; Zinn, 1980).
The rocketing increase in demand for labour could not be met by the indigenous population alone and was fuelled by successive waves of immigration. Whilst solving one
problem – the shortage of labour – this created others. The culture shock of industrial
work, a foreign language, and problems of housing and social integration created
enormous pressures in American society. Alongside this was the arbitrary and ruthless
discipline of the factory system, where workers were treated as so much industrial
cannon fodder. It was a time of rapid social, technological and organisational change:
a time where entrepreneurs did not so much expect to manage change as to impose it,
and those who could not or would not accept this situation were treated harshly.
Consequently, most industries found themselves sitting on a pressure cooker which
could, and frequently did, explode in unexpected and violent ways. If
management–labour relations were poor in most European countries, they were far
worse in the USA (Pelling, 1960).

The American approach to industrial development owed little to government aid or
encouragement, and much to individual entrepreneurship. For this reason American
entrepreneurs had much more in common with the free market approach to industrial
expansion of their British counterparts than to the state-sponsored traditions of
Germany or France. Therefore, the German approach to industrial organisation,
bureaucracy, which might seem appropriate given the size of American companies,
was not attractive. In any case, it tended to operate best in situations where growth
and demand was stable or predictable, which in Germany the government tried to
facilitate. However, American growth patterns were volatile and unpredictable.

Consequently, there was great pressure to find organisational arrangements that
would allow employers to control and organise their employees in a manner that
reduced conflict, was cost-effective, and was applicable to the American environment
and philosophy. It was also becoming recognised that it was not sufficient just to
develop a more systematic approach to the organisation of work; there was also a
need to develop an approach to managing change that would persuade workers to
accept rather than reject or resist the introduction of new methods, techniques and
technologies. Therefore, with the spirit of endeavour, determination and confidence
that seemed so much a part of the American character at this time, managers and
engineers set out to remedy this situation. Though similar developments were taking
place in Europe, they lacked the intensity, commitment and scale of events in the
USA. This is no doubt why one of the earliest and most enduring approaches to

organisation theory emerged in the USA, and why the USA has continued to dominate the development of organisation theory.

Organisation theory: the Classical approach

As can be seen, at the end of the nineteenth century there was a clear need to replace the rule-of-thumb approach to organisational design and management with a more consistent and organisation-wide approach. This was not because of an academic interest in the functioning of organisations, though this was present, but in order to improve their performance, enhance their competitiveness and – an increasing concern at the time – to sustain and legitimate managerial authority. This was certainly the case in the USA, where explosive growth and a workforce suffering from culture shock had created dangerous social pressures that questioned the legitimacy of managerial power, and even the capitalist system itself. This was also true in Europe: although Europe industrialised earlier, it was not only having to come to grips with the increase in size and complexity of business life, but it was also facing considerable, and unexpected, competitive pressure from the United States.

Nevertheless, these difficulties could not quench the innate optimism of the age. It was a time, much more than now, when people dealt in certainties and universal truths. There was a feeling of confidence that any goal, whether it be taming nature or discerning the best way to run business, could be achieved by the twin power of scientific study and practical experience. All over the industrialised world, groups of managers and technical specialists were forming their own learned societies to exchange experiences, to discuss common problems, and to seek out in a scientific and rational fashion the solution to all organisational ills: to discover 'the one best way'.

Out of these endeavours emerged what was later termed the Classical approach to organisational design and management. As the name suggests, it was an approach that drew heavily on what had gone before; taking from writers such as Adam Smith and practitioners such as Josiah Wedgwood and leavening their ideas with contemporary experience, views and experiments. This approach, reflecting the age in which it emerged, portrays organisations as machines, and those in them as mere parts which respond to the correct stimulus and whose actions are based on scientific principles. The emphasis was on achieving efficiency in internal functions; seeing organisations as closed and changeless entities unaffected by the outside world. Though this approach first originated in the early part of this century, its influence on managerial practices and assumptions is still strong today, but its credibility amongst academics has waned (Kelly, 1982a, 1982b; Rose, 1988; Scott, 1987).

The Classical approach, or the Scientific-Rational approach as it is sometimes called, whilst not being homogeneous, is characterised by three common propositions:

- **Organisations are rational entities** – they are collectivities of individuals focused on the achievement of relatively specific goals through their organisation into highly formalised, differentiated and efficient structures.
- **The design of organisations is a science** – through experience, observation and experiment, it has been established that there is one best universal organisational form for all bodies. This is based on the hierarchical and horizontal division of labour and functions, whereby organisations are conceived of as machines which,

once set in motion, inexorably and efficiently will pursue and achieve their pre-selected goals.

■ **People are economic beings** – they are solely motivated by money. This instrumental orientation means that they will try to achieve the maximum reward for the minimum work, and will use whatever bargaining power their skills or knowledge allow to this end. Therefore, jobs must be designed and structured in such a way as to minimise an individual's skill and discretion, and to maximise management control.

The key figures in the development of the Classical approach were Frederick Taylor (1856–1915) and two of his main promoters, the pioneers of motion study, Frank and Lillian Gilbreth (1868–1924 and 1878–1972 respectively) in the USA, Henri Fayol (1841–1925) in France and Max Weber (1864–1920) in Germany. All were writing in the first two decades of the twentieth century, though Weber's work was not generally available in English until the 1940s. Below is an outline of their work.

■ Frederick Taylor's Scientific Management

Frederick Winslow Taylor was born into a prosperous Quaker-Puritan family in Germantown, Pennsylvania in 1856. Although he passed the entrance exam for Harvard Law School, instead of becoming a lawyer as his family wished, in 1874 he took a manual job in an engineering company and became a skilled pattern maker and machinist. In 1878, he joined the Midvale Steel Company as a labourer, but eventually rose to become its Chief Engineer. Having had enough of working for other people, in 1893 he set up his own consultancy (Sheldrake, 1996). Taylor was an accomplished and talented engineer, and became a leading authority on metal cutting and a successful inventor; however, it is for his contribution to work organisation that he is most famous (or infamous).

Taylor was a highly controversial figure during his lifetime and still remains so more than 80 years after his death. This was partly because his theory of management was a direct challenge to both workers and managers. However, a large part of the hostility he generated during his lifetime was due to his own character. Rose (1988: 23) stated that 'Taylor was a notorious neurotic – many would not hesitate to write crank; and there is even a case for upgrading the diagnosis to maniac.' He was certainly a zealot when it came to promoting his own ideas, and would brook no challenge to them, whether from workers or management. Not surprisingly, though he attracted devoted followers, he also engendered fierce dislike.

Through his experience as a shopfloor worker, manager and consultant, Taylor made a major contribution to the development of managerial theory and practice in the twentieth century (Locke, 1982; Rose, 1988). Yet his original attempts to improve productivity (or, as he put it, to stamp out 'soldiering') were less than successful. Not only was his use of sacking, blacklisting and victimisation counter-productive, but also the bitterness that this provoked haunted him for the rest of his life. It was his failure to achieve change by, as Rose (1988: 37) termed it, 'managerial thuggery' that led him to seek an alternative method of change management that the workers, and management, would accept because they could see that it was rational and fair. Thereafter, his prime preoccupation became the pursuit and promotion of a scientific approach to management.

Drawing on his work at the Midvale Steel Company and the Bethlehem Steel Company, Taylor constructed a general ideology of efficiency. It was only in 1911, when a group of his supporters met to discuss how better to promote his work, that the term 'Scientific Management' was first used to describe his approach to work organisation (Sheldrake, 1996). Though initially sceptical, Taylor embraced the term and there can be little doubt that the publication, in the same year, of his *Principles of Scientific Management* laid the foundation stone for the development of organisation and management theory. Taylor's primary focus was on the design and analysis of individual tasks; this process inevitably led to changes in the overall structure of organisations. Such was the impact of his work that it created a blueprint for, and legitimated, the activities of managers and their support staff. In so doing, he helped to create the plethora of functions and departments which characterise many modern organisations.

Before Taylor, the average manager tended to operate in an idiosyncratic and arbitrary manner with little or no specialist support. Taylor saw this as being at the root of much industrial unrest and workers' mistrust of management. Though criticised for his anti-labour postures, Taylor was also highly critical of management behaviour, which may account for this group's initial lack of enthusiasm for his ideas (Scott, 1987). After Taylor, managers were left with a 'scientific' blueprint for analysing work and applying his 'one best way' principle to each job in order to gain 'a fair day's work for a fair day's pay'.

These last two phrases sum up Taylor's basic beliefs:

■ It is possible and desirable to establish, through methodical study and the application of scientific principles, the one best way of carrying out any job. Once established, the way must be implemented totally and made to operate consistently.
■ Human beings are predisposed to seek the maximum reward for the minimum effort, which Taylor referred to as 'soldiering'. To overcome this, managers must lay down in detail what each worker should do, step by step; ensure through close supervision that the instructions are adhered to; and, to give positive motivation, link pay to performance.

Taylor incorporated those beliefs into his precepts for Scientific Management, comprising three core elements: the systematic collection of knowledge about the work process by managers; the removal or reduction of workers' discretion and control over what they do; and the laying down of standard procedures and times for carrying out each job.

The starting point is the gathering of knowledge:

> The managers assume ... the burden of gathering together all the traditional knowledge which in the past has been possessed by the workman and then of classifying, tabulating and reducing this knowledge to rules, laws and formulae ...   (Taylor, 1911a: 15)

This lays the groundwork for the second stage: increased management control. As long as workers possess a monopoly of knowledge about the work process, increased control is impossible. But once the knowledge is also possessed by managers, it becomes possible not only to establish what workers actually do with their time, but also by 'reducing this knowledge to rules, laws and formulae', to decrease the knowledge that workers need to carry out a given task. It also, importantly, paves the way for the division of labour.

The last stage is that 'All possible brain work should be removed from the shop and centred in the planning ... department ...' (Taylor, 1911b: 98–9). The divorce of conception from execution removes control from the worker, who no longer has discretion as to how tasks are carried out.

> Perhaps the most prominent single element in modern scientific management is the task idea. The work of every workman is fully planned out by management ... and each man receives in most cases complete written instructions, describing in detail the task which he is to accomplish, as well as the means to be used in doing the work. ... This task specifies not only what is to be done but how it is to be done and the exact time allowed for doing it.
>
> (Taylor, 1911a: 39)

Allied to this last element was Taylor's approach to worker selection and motivation. Taylor carried out many experiments to identify and reward workers. He believed that organisations should only employ 'first class men' and they would only get the best results if they were paid by results. As he commented on his time as a consultant at the Bethlehem Steel Company (Taylor, 1911a: 18–21):

> The Bethlehem Steel Company had five blast furnaces, the product of which had been handled by a pig-iron gang for many years. This gang consisted, at this time, of about 75 men. ... Our first step was the scientific selection of the ... proper workman to begin with. We therefore carefully watched and studied these 75 men for three or four days ... A careful study was then made of each of these men. We looked up their history as far back as practicable and thorough inquiries were made as to the character, habits, and ambitions of each of them. Finally, we selected [Schmidt] ...] as the most likely man to start with. ... Schmidt started to work, and all day long, and at regular intervals, was told by the man who stood over him with a watch, 'Now pick up a pig and walk. Now sit down and rest. Now walk – now rest,' etc. He worked when he was told to work, and rested when he was told to rest ... And throughout this time he averaged a little more than $1.85 per day, whereas before he had never received over $1.15 per day ... One man after another was picked out and trained to handle pig iron ... receiving 60 per cent more wages than other workmen around them.

The 'task idea' allied to Taylor's approach to selecting and rewarding workers completes the process of gaining control over workers by managers. The workers become 'human machines', told what to do, when to do it and how long to take. But, more than this, it allows new types of work organisation to be developed, and new work processes and equipment introduced; thus workers move from having a monopoly of knowledge and control over their work to a position where the knowledge they have of the work process is minimal, and their control vastly reduced. The result is not only a reduction in the skills required and the wages paid, but also the creation of jobs that are so narrow and tightly specified that the period needed to train someone to do them is greatly reduced. This removes the last bargaining counter of labour: scarcity of skill.

According to Taylor, this transforms not only workers' jobs but also managers' jobs:

> The man at the head of the business under scientific management is governed by rules and laws ... just as the workman is, and the standards which have been developed are equitable.
>
> (Taylor, 1911b: 189)

Taylor stated that the 'scientific' basis and equal applicability of his methods meant they were neutral between labour and management; therefore they legitimated managerial action to analyse and change work methods, because managers are merely applying science to determine the best method of work. As Exhibit 1.1 shows, he claimed that his approach benefited both the worker and the company. The worker was enabled and encouraged to work to his maximum performance and be rewarded with a high rate of pay, whilst the company benefited from a high rate of output:

> It is absolutely necessary, then, when workmen are daily given a task which calls for a high rate of speed on their part, that they should also be insured the necessary high rate of pay whenever they are successful. This involves not only fixing for each man his daily task, but also paying him a large bonus, or premium, each time that he succeeds in doing his task in the given time ... . The remarkable and almost uniformly good results from the *correct* application of the task and the bonus must be seen to be appreciated.   (Taylor, 1911a: 63)

Though seen as something of an anti-trade unionist, which he probably was, as the above implies, he was also strongly critical of management. He believed that many of the problems organisations faced in implementing change were due to the arbitrary and inconsistent approach of managers. In fact, though trade unions were very suspicious of Scientific Management in general and Taylor in particular, managers seemed even more antagonistic. Indeed, after his death, Taylor's acolytes spent much time in the 1920s wooing the American unions with a considerable degree of success; they never achieved the same success with management (Rose, 1988). The main reason for this was that, though managers were anxious to find an approach that would curtail labour resistance to change and improve productivity, they were not prepared to subject themselves to a similar degree of discipline.

As Taylor's biographer, Copley (1923: 146) stated in relation to managerial resistance to Scientific Management at the Bethlehem Steel Company:

> Let us consider what Taylor was contending for. It was essentially this: that the government of the Bethlehem Steel Company cease to be capricious, arbitrary and despotic; that every man in the establishment, high and low, submit himself to law [i.e. that managers should obey the principles of Scientific Management].

Taylor believed passionately in the need to reform managerial authority: to base it on competence rather than the power to hire and fire. However, it is one thing to ask one's subordinates to change their ways and accept new rules and methods; it is another thing entirely for management to acknowledge that they too need to change, and change radically. No wonder that Taylor met managerial as well as worker resistance.

Nevertheless, even though managers resisted the full implementation of Taylorism, the new and rapidly expanding breed of industrial engineers, charged with developing and implementing new methods, techniques and technologies, found in Taylor and his contemporaries' work a blueprint for transforming the workplace and increasing their control and status. One consequence of this, brought about by the use of job cards and other forms of work recording and analysis systems, was a massive increase in the amount of paperwork that needed to be processed. Managers complained about the growth of 'industrial bureaucracy', but the benefits it brought by enabling average times and costs, etc., to be calculated easily outweighed the increase in clerical costs.

Nowhere was this demonstrated more dramatically than at Henry Ford's Highland Park plant – the home of the world's first mass-produced motor car, the Model T Ford. From 1909/10, when 18,664 Model Ts were sold, sales and production doubled year-on-year. However, every increase in production required a commensurate increase in the plant's workforce. In 1911/12, the plant produced 78,440 Model Ts with 6,867 employees. The next year production doubled and the number of employees doubled. Not surprisingly, Ford was desperate for ways of increasing employee productivity. The solution he adopted was to redesign the assembly operation around Scientific Management principles, and then couple this with the introduction of the moving assembly line. This allowed Ford once again to double production, but this time the workforce actually decreased (Lacey, 1986). So the 1910s saw the birth of the twin, and very much related, neologisms that both dominated and revolutionised industrial life for much of the twentieth century – Taylorism and Fordism.

Throughout the 1920s, the adoption of Scientific Management grew in America, though rarely in the full form laid down by Taylor. It was also introduced on a very limited basis into Europe, but met with much scepticism from managers and hostility from workers (Rose, 1988). Only in Russia did there seem any great enthusiasm for it. Indeed, Lenin saw Scientific Management combined with common ownership as the prime basis for Russian industrialisation: 'We must organize in Russia the study and teaching of the Taylor system and systematically try it out and adapt it to our own ends' (Lenin, 1918: 25). Taylor's work also attracted some interest in Japan. However, it was not until after the Second World War, through the auspices of the Marshall Plan for rebuilding Europe's war-torn economies, that Scientific Management was promoted and adopted on any significant scale outside America. Ironically, the contribution of American trade unions, through their role in the Marshall Plan, was crucial in promoting Scientific Management in European enterprises (Carew, 1987).

Taylor claimed that his system was innovative and unique, which indeed it was in terms of the way he synthesised and systematised a host of previously disparate practices and presented them as scientific and neutral (Aitken, 1960; Rose, 1988). Yet in reality, it can be seen that Taylor drew on many of the management practices and negative attitudes towards labour that were prevalent during the nineteenth century. He was also heavily indebted to many contemporaries and associates who helped develop the work study techniques necessary to implement Scientific Management, especially Henry Gantt and Carl Barth, who worked closely with him (Kempner, 1970; Sheldrake, 1996). Perhaps his greatest debt was to Frank and Lillian Gilbreth. As well as being the pioneers of motion study, they were the driving force in establishing the Society for the Promotion of Scientific Management, which was later renamed the Taylor Society, and did much to promote Taylor's work both before and after his death in 1915 (Rose, 1988; Sheldrake, 1996).

■ The Gilbreths and motion study

Much of modern work study (a central element of the Classical approach) owes its origins to the methods and techniques of motion study developed in the first quarter of the twentieth century by Frank and Lillian Gilbreth (*see* Gilbreth and Gilbreth, 1914). Their work on motion study was initiated by Frank Gilbreth, who was a contemporary of Taylor's. In many respects their careers were similar. Taylor, turning his back on Harvard Law School, began his career on the shopfloor and later rose to eminence as a manager and management consultant. Frank Gilbreth, after passing the entrance exam for but declining to enter the Massachusetts Institute of Technology, rose from being a bricklayer to running his own construction and consultancy companies. He was also, along with his wife, a leading campaigner for Scientific Management.

Although the development and promotion of motion study was begun by her husband, there is no doubt that Lillian Moller Gilbreth was an equal partner. Despite contemporary prejudices against women and education, she obtained Bachelor's and Master's degrees in English. She was only denied a doctorate in psychology by the University of California because family commitments prevented her, after her thesis had been approved, from spending the post-thesis year on campus that the regulations required (Sheldrake, 1996; Thickett, 1970).

In justifying their work, Frank Gilbreth stated in his 1909 book on bricklaying that motion study:

> ... will cut down production costs and increase the efficiency and wages of the workman ... To be pre-eminently successful: (a) a mechanic must know his trade; (b) he must be quick motioned; and (c) he must use the fewest possible motions to accomplish the desired results.
>
> (Quoted in Sheldrake, 1996: 28)

The Gilbreths developed a number of procedures for breaking work down into its constituent components. Flow process charts were used which split human motion into five basic elements: operations, transportation, inspection, storage and delay. Arising out of this, they developed a method of minutely analysing tasks which broke handwork into 17 basic elements. Examples of these are as follows:

Grasp Begins when hand or body member touches an object. Consists of gaining control of an object.

Release Begins when hand or body member begins to relax control of object. Consists of letting go of an object.

Plan Begins when hand or body members are idle or making random movements while worker decides on course of action. Consists of determining a course of action. Ends when course of action is determined.

The purpose of this microanalysis was not only to establish what was done, but also to discover if a better method of performing the task in question could be developed. In this respect, they did much original work in establishing the distinction between necessary and unnecessary movements. The latter were to be eliminated immediately and the former further analysed in more detail to see if they could be improved, combined or replaced by special equipment.

If this sounds remarkably similar to Adam Smith's observations on pin-making, mentioned earlier, this is no accident. The Classical approach is descended from Smith through the nineteenth century pioneers of work organisation. Though remarkable in the level of minute detail to which they reduced the motions individuals make when undertaking manual tasks, the Gilbreths were only, as they saw it, taking Smith's maxims to their logical conclusion. If in the process they give the impression of dealing more with machines than people, that too is no accident. Like others who propounded the Classical approach, they viewed organisations and workers very much as machines. The work study methods developed by the Gilbreths and their successors are still widely used today, not just in manufacturing industries, but in all areas of life from hospitals to computer programming (Grant, 1983).

The Gilbreths were also concerned that, having established the best way to carry out a task, this should not be undermined by selecting the wrong person to carry it out or by creating the wrong environment. Therefore, they set about analysing employee selection and establishing environmental criteria with the same determination they had applied to analysing work performance. However, in neither case could they achieve the same microanalysis that characterised their work study technique; what finally emerged were effectively opinions based on their own 'experience', rather than being the product of experiment and observation.

The Gilbreths, like Taylor, were devoted to one objective – to discover the best method of doing any job. The difference was that whereas Taylor was concerned with reducing the time taken to perform a task, the Gilbreths were more concerned with reducing the motions taken to accomplish the task. Though this differing emphasis did lead to some friction with Taylor (Nadworthy, 1957), they were, none the less, among his main promoters and saw their efforts as complementary to, and aimed at enhancing, Scientific Management. The fact that work study is now often labelled 'time and motion' study perhaps shows this. Like Taylor, they saw themselves as creating a neutral system that benefited both labour and management. They felt that any increase in boredom or monotony brought about by their methods would be compensated for by workers' opportunities to earn more money.

While the Gilbreths and Taylor devoted their efforts to improving the productivity of individual workers, there were others who took a wider but complementary perspective.

Henri Fayol and the principles of organisation

Born in 1841 and educated at the *lycée* in Lyon and the National School of Mines in St Etienne, Fayol was promoting his ideas in France at the same time as Taylor was propounding his views on Scientific Management in the USA. He began his working life as a mining engineer in 1860 and, in 1888, was appointed Managing Director of an ailing mining company, which he quickly turned into a much-admired and financially strong enterprise. He retired as Managing Director in 1918, though he stayed on the Board until his death in 1925. In his 'retirement' he founded the Centre d'Etudes Administratives, whose role was to propagate Fayol's ideas through management education. He chaired weekly meetings of prominent industrialists, writers, government officials, philosophers and members of the military. This direct contact with opinion-formers and decision-makers is undoubtedly one of the main reasons why the Centre had such a profound influence on the practice and theory of management in both the public and private sectors in France.

Fayol did not draw his views on organisations solely from his own experience as a manager. His education at one of the *grandes écoles*, and his subsequent career as an executive of a large mining company, placed him among the elite of senior administrators in business, government and the armed forces. Therefore, though he spent his working life in the coal mining industry, his practical knowledge of business was informed by and fits within the intellectual and administrative traditions of French society.

His working life, in the late nineteenth and early twentieth centuries, coincided with a period of rapid industrialisation in France. It was a time when industrial unrest was rife, with frequent strikes by railway workers, miners and civil servants. As was the case in the USA, in this period of rapid growth and change, there was an unwritten consensus that French business and government needed a theory of management, no matter how basic (Cuthbert, 1970). Unlike Taylor and the Gilbreths, however, Fayol's focus was on efficiency at the organisational level rather than the task level: top down rather than bottom up (Fayol, 1949). Though this clearly reflects Fayol's own practical experience, it also shows the combined influence of the French intellectual tradition, with its preference for addressing philosophies rather than practicalities, and the administrative tradition, which sought to identify and lay down general rules and restrictions applicable to all situations.

Given his background, it is not surprising that Fayol was more concerned with general rather than departmental or supervisory management, and with overall organisational control as averse to the details of tasks. This does not, however, place him in opposition to Taylor. Rather the combination of Taylor's work at the task level and Fayol's at the organisational level make their views complementary rather than contradictory. In addition, both emphasised strongly the need for professionally educated managers who would 'follow the rule' rather than acting in an arbitrary or *ad hoc* fashion.

As the following shows, Fayol (like all the Classical school) was concerned with developing a universal approach to management that was applicable to any organisation:

> There is no one doctrine of administration for business and another for affairs of state; administrative doctrine is universal. Principles and general rules which hold good for business hold good for the state too, and the reverse applies.   (Quoted in Cuthbert, 1970: 111)

Therefore, in business, public administration, or indeed any form of organisation, the same universal principles apply. According to Fayol, these are as follows (quoted in Mullins, 1989: 202–3):

1 **Division of work.** The object is to produce more and better work from the same effort, through the advantages of specialisation.
2 **Authority and responsibility.** Wherever authority is exercised, responsibility arises. The application of sanctions is needed to encourage useful actions and to discourage their opposite.
3 **Discipline.** This is essential for the efficient operation of the organisation. Discipline is in essence the outward mark of respect for agreements between the organisation and its members.

4 **Unity of command.** In any action, any employee should receive orders from one superior only; dual command is a perpetual source of conflicts.

5 **Unity of direction.** In order to coordinate and focus effort, there should be one leader and one plan for any group of activities with the same objective.

6 **Subordination of individual or group interests.** The interest of the organisation should take precedence over individual or group interests.

7 **Remuneration of personnel.** Methods of payment should be fair, encourage keenness by rewarding well-directed effort, but not lead to over-payment.

8 **Centralisation.** The degree of centralisation is a question of proportion and will vary in particular organisations.

9 **Scalar chain.** This is the chain of superiors from the ultimate authority to the lowest ranks. Respect for line authority must be reconciled with activities that require urgent action, and with the need to provide for some measure of initiative at all levels of authority.

10 **Order.** This includes material order and social order. The object of material order is avoidance of loss. There should be an appointed place for each thing, and each thing should be in its appointed place. Social order requires good organisation and good selection.

11 **Equity.** There needs to be fairness in dealing with employees throughout all levels of the scalar chain.

12 **Stability of tenure of personnel.** Generally, prosperous organisations have a stable managerial team.

13 **Initiative.** This represents a source of strength for the organisation and should be encouraged and developed.

14 **Esprit de corps.** This should be fostered, as harmony and unity among members of the organisation are a great strength in the organisation.

According to Fayol (1949), it is the prime responsibility of management to enact these principles. Consequently, in order to achieve this, he prescribed the main duties of management as follows:

- **Planning** – examining the future, deciding what needs to be done and developing a plan of action.
- **Organising** – bringing together the resources, human and material, and developing the structure to carry out the activities of the organisation.
- **Command** – ensuring that all employees perform their jobs well and in the best interests of the organisation.
- **Coordination** – verifying that the activities of the organisation work harmoniously together to achieve its goals.
- **Control** – establishing that plans, instructions and commands are correctly carried out.

Fayol was a gifted and highly successful businessman who attributed his success to the application of his principles rather than personal ability. Certainly, he was one of the pioneers of management theory, and many of his principles are still taught and practised today. However, part of the success of his work lay in the fact that he was writing for a receptive audience, and at a time when management practice and ideas were becoming international currency. Just as Taylor's system arose at the time when a need for a management theory had grown amongst the business community in the USA, so Fayol's was aimed at a similar demand in France, where the business community was developing rapidly but in an unplanned way.

Unlike Taylor, though, he attempted neither to denigrate trade unions openly nor to castigate managers. Nor did he share with Taylor a belief that the interests of managers and workers were necessarily the same or ultimately reconcilable. He did, however, believe that much industrial unrest could be eliminated by fairer, more consistent, and firmer management, particularly where this reduced the need for trade unions or their ability to organise. He also believed in the need to educate and train managers. His views were not seen as a direct attack on existing managers; rather, they were in harmony with the approach taken by managers in the larger private enterprises and those operating in government and the armed services. This is not surprising because, by and large, they and Fayol were educated in the *grandes écoles* and shared a common intellectual approach. In addition, Fayol did not generally try to impose his ideas directly on individual organisations. Instead, he preferred to influence managers indirectly through a process of education. In the light of the reaction in America to Taylor's attitude, many would consider this a wise move.

Though there were attempts in France to promote '*Fayolisme*' in opposition to Taylorism, Fayol rejected this, preferring to see them as complementary (Sheldrake, 1996). As Urwick (1949: 9–10) commented in the Introduction to the English version of Fayol's book on *General and Industrial Management*:

> The work of Taylor and Fayol was, of course, essentially complementary. They both realized that the problem of personnel and its management at all levels is the key to industrial success. Both applied scientific method to this problem. That Taylor worked primarily at the operative level, from the bottom of the industrial hierarchy upwards, while Fayol concentrated on the managing director and worked downwards, was merely a reflection of their very different careers.

The USA and France were not the only countries where developments in management practice and thought were being studied and documented. In Germany, at this time, Max Weber was charting the growth and merits of bureaucracy.

Max Weber on bureaucracy

Weber was born in 1864 into a well-to-do Prussian family. He pursued an academic career, obtaining a doctorate in 1889. In 1894, he was appointed Professor of Political Economy at the University of Freiburg, and in 1896 he accepted the Chair in Economics at Heidelberg. Unfortunately, in 1897, he suffered a mental breakdown, which plagued him for many years. He resigned from his university post and spent much of his time travelling in Europe and the USA. He also moved the focus of his academic studies from economics to sociology.

Weber was an ardent German nationalist, and, at the age of 50, he volunteered for military service in the First World War. Until his honourable discharge in 1915, he was responsible for establishing and running nine military hospitals. Despite this, he was a fierce and open critic of the Kaiser, whom he accused of being a dilettante hiding behind the divine right of kings. He believed that Germany's problems at home and abroad could only be solved if the monarchy were replaced with a constitutional democracy. After the war, he became a member of the Commission that drew up the Constitution for the Weimar Republic, and once again took up university teaching, this time in Munich. Unfortunately, when he died in 1920, most of his work was unpublished and his papers were in a state of chaos. It was not until the 1930s that his work began to be organised and published, and it was the 1940s before his work on bureaucracy was published in English (Sheldrake, 1996; Weber, 1948).

There is a considerable affinity between Weber's work on bureaucracy and Fayol's work on the principles of management. Both were concerned with the overall structuring of organisations, and the principles which guide senior managers in this task. Though a contemporary of Fayol and Taylor, it is unlikely that they were aware of his work on bureaucracy, though the reverse is possible (that he may have been aware of their work).

However, unlike Taylor and Fayol, Weber was never a practising manager. His observations on administrative structures and organisational effectiveness arose from his study of the development of Western civilisation. From this, Weber concluded that the rise of civilisation was a story of power and domination. He noted (Weber, 1948) that each social epoch was characterised by a different form of political rule, and that for a ruling elite to sustain its power and dominance, it was essential for them both to gain legitimacy and to develop an administrative apparatus to enforce and support their authority.

Weber (1947: 328) identified what he called 'three pure types of legitimate authority':

1 **Rational-legal** – resting on a belief in the 'legality' of patterns of normative rule, and the right of those elevated to authority under such rules to issue commands.
2 **Traditional** – resting on an established belief in the sanctity of immemorial traditions and the legitimacy of those exercising authority under them.
3 **Charismatic** – resting on devotion to the specific and exceptional sanctity, heroism or exemplary character of an individual person, and of the normative patterns or order revealed or ordained by them.

For Weber, legitimacy is central to almost all systems of authority. He argued that there are five concepts on which rational-legal authority is based. According to Albrow (1970: 43), these are as follows:

1 That a legal code can be established which can claim obedience from members of the organisation.
2 That the law is a system of abstract rules which are applied in particular cases, and that administration looks after the interests of the organisation within the limits of the law.
3 That the man exercising authority also obeys this impersonal law.
4 That only *qua* [in the capacity of] member does the member obey the law.
5 That obedience is due not to the person who holds authority but to the impersonal order that has granted him his position.

Weber argued that, in the context of the rational-legal authority structures which prevailed in Western societies in the early twentieth century, the bureaucratic approach to organisation was the most appropriate and efficient. Under bureaucracy, laws, rules, procedures and predefined routines are dominant and not subject to the vagaries and preferences of individuals. They give form to a clearly defined system of administration – whether it be public administration, such as a government department dealing with pensions and social security payments, or private administration, such as an insurance company – where the execution of routine, pre-programmed procedures is all-important. Weber considered this approach to be both appropriate, because it was the ideal tool for a centralised administration where the legitimacy of those in power was underpinned by the rule of law, and efficient, because the bureaucratic approach mechanises the process of administration in the same way that machines automate the production process in factories.

Weber frequently asserted that the development of bureaucracy eliminates human fallibility:

> Its [bureaucracy's] specific nature, which is welcomed by capitalism, develops the more perfectly the more bureaucracy is 'dehumanised', the more completely it succeeds in eliminating from official business, love, hatred, and all purely personal, irrational and emotional elements which escape calculation. (Weber, 1948: 215–16)

Bureaucracy is characterised by the division of labour, a clear hierarchical authority structure, formal and unbiased selection procedures, employment decisions based on merit, career tracks for employees, detailed rules and regulations, impersonal relationships, and a distinct separation of members' organisational and personal lives. It must, however, be borne in mind that Weber's bureaucratic model (or 'ideal' organisation), though inspired by developments in Germany at the time, was a hypothetical rather than a factual description of how most organisations were structured. It was his view of the characteristics that organisations should exhibit in modern societies based on rationality and law. How Weber saw these organisational characteristics supporting and reproducing rational-legal authority is best seen by contrasting them with the traditional administrative forms based on patronage (*see* Table 1.1) (Weber, 1947 and 1948).

For Weber, therefore, bureaucracy provided a rational-legal form of organisation which distinguished itself from, and eradicated the faults and unfairness of, previous administrative forms by its mechanical adherence to set rules, procedures and patterns of authority. It removed the system of patronage and eliminated human variability, replacing it by the rule of law. In Weber's view, the principles of bureaucracy, especially the legitimation of authority and the subordination of all in the organisation to the same rules and procedures, were universally applicable to all organisations, big or small, public or private, industrial or commercial.

It can be seen that Weber's belief in the standardisation of, and obedience by all to, rules and procedures is the counterpart of the standardisation of production techniques advocated by Taylor and akin to the principles of administrative management prescribed by Fayol. Also, just as the work of Taylor and Fayol can be understood as representing a combination of their backgrounds and the state of the societies in which they lived, so is this the case with Weber. The Prussian bureaucratic tradition dominated both the public, and to a large extent, the private sectors in Germany. It was seen by the ruling elite as the ideal method for ensuring that the objectives of the state and the objectives of individual enterprises were adhered to. It also fitted in with the Prussian militaristic tradition of unquestioning obedience to superiors, which was

Table 1.1 Comparison of Weber's concept of rational-legal authority with traditional authority

Characteristics of rational-legal authority	Characteristics of traditional authority
Areas of jurisdiction are clearly specified: the regular activities required of personnel are allocated in a fixed way as official duties.	The allocation of labour is not defined, but depends on assignments made by the leader, which can be changed at any time.
The organisation of offices follows the principle of hierarchy: each lower office is controlled and supervised by a higher one. However, the scope of authority of superiors over subordinates is circumscribed, and lower offices enjoy a right of appeal.	Authority relations are diffuse, being based on personal loyalty, and are not ordered into clear hierarchies.
An intentionally established system of abstract rules governs official decisions and actions. These rules are relatively stable and exhaustive, and can be learned. Decisions are recorded in permanent files.	General rules of administration either do not exist or are vaguely stated, ill-defined, and subject to change at the whim of the leader. No attempt is made to keep permanent records of transactions.
The 'means of production or administration' (e.g. tools and equipment or rights and privileges) belong to the office, not the office-holder, and may not be appropriated. Personal property is clearly separated from official property, and working space from living quarters.	There is no separation of a ruler's personal household business from the larger 'public' business under their direction.
Officials are personally free, selected on the basis of technical qualifications, appointed to office (not elected), and recompensed by salary.	Officials are often selected from among those who are personally dependent on the leader, e.g. slaves, serfs and relatives. Selection is governed by arbitrary criteria, and remuneration often takes the form of benefices – rights granted to individuals that, for instance, allow them access to the ruler's stores, or give them grants of land from which they can appropriate the fees or taxes. Benefices, like fiefs in feudalistic systems, may become hereditary and sometimes are bought and sold.
Employment by the organisation constitutes a career for officials. An official is a full-time employee and looks forward to a lifelong career in the agency. After a trial period, he or she gains tenure of position and is protected against arbitrary dismissal.	Officials serve at the pleasure of the leader, and so lack clear expectations about the future and security of tenure.

a prevalent view in both public and private organisations. It must be remembered, of course, that the state and private enterprises in Germany were not primarily obsessed with profitability or individual aggrandisement. The key objective was to build Germany as the premier military and industrial power in Europe. Competition at the level of the individual or the individual enterprise was a concept that carried much less force in Germany, and even France, than in the USA or Britain. German industry and government were more concerned with ensuring that all sections of the country pulled in the same direction. Where competition threatened this, it was eliminated by the state, either by direct intervention, such as nationalisation of the railways, or by indirect intervention, through the formation of cartels and monopolies. In carrying out this grand plan for German development, bureaucracy was found to be the ideal tool.

In Germany, the advent of the First World War highlighted the incompatibility between industrial bureaucracies based on the rule of law, and a government run on autocratic lines for militaristic ends. Weber argued that the rule of law applied not only to the operation of organisations but also, and more importantly, to the running of society. If society was not based on the rule of law, if democratically elected governments did not hold power, then the authority of those who ruled must be called into question. This was the basis of Weber's attacks on the Kaiser and the military during the First World War. He believed that, in the modern age, rational-legal authority, based on democratically elected governments and laws governing property rights, was the best and most effective way for society and organisations to be governed. For Weber, the rise of bureaucracy and the rise of liberal democracy went hand in hand.

As can be seen, bureaucracy did not need a Taylor or a Fayol to develop or promote it; it already existed, was accepted by management, and was prospering, in Germany and other advanced countries, especially in the public sector. What Weber did was to give it intellectual respectability by arguing that it was particularly suited to the needs of (what he saw as) the rational, secular and increasingly democratic societies that were becoming the norm in the Western world.

The appeal of bureaucracy, to governments and large organisations at least, can be seen in the way that bureaucracy is an ever-present and pervasive feature of modern life. However, it would be misleading to give the impression that its development in Germany, or elsewhere, was uncontentious. In Germany, in the early years of the twentieth century, it tended to be the purpose and consequences of bureaucracy rather than its principles that were attacked. At an overall political level, the growth of radical parties of the left reflected growing concerns over Germany's military aims and the state's concomitant close links with business, and in particular its perceived preference for aiding capital rather than labour. At the level of the individual enterprise, the growth of militant trade unions, often linked to the parties of the left, reflected the growing frustration of workers who resented the autocratic approach of management and its resistance to collective bargaining.

Conclusions

It is not an inevitable fact of life that modern societies are characterised by organisations, of all shapes and sizes; this is the product of a particular combination of circumstances. The rise of capitalism in Britain and other European countries in the seventeenth and eighteenth centuries created new opportunities and new problems that could not be accommodated under the old order. The result was a move away from self-sufficient, autonomous, individual units to collective units of production controlled by an entrepreneur. It was entrepreneurs who, in pursuit of ever greater profits, created the factory system in Britain which became the basis of modern organisational life. The central features of the factory system were autocratic control, division of labour, and antagonistic relations between management and labour.

Though starting at different times and moving at their own pace, most European countries, followed by the USA, adopted and adapted the British approach to industrial organisation. However, as the nineteenth century progressed, the nature of industrialisation began to vary from country to country, reflecting the unique circumstances and needs of the host society. In Germany, the objectives of the state determined that large-scale public and private bureaucracies became the norm. In France, the state also played a role in shaping industrialisation, but in this case it was to perpetuate small-scale, inefficient business and agricultural operations. In both countries, individual pursuit of profit maximisation was less important than in either Britain or the USA. In Scandinavia, especially Denmark, the emergence of a more collective and less ruthless approach to industrialisation could be discerned.

Nevertheless, in the transition from a subsistence economy to a money economy, one clear image stands out above all else: the antagonism between employers and employees. The factory did not emerge because it was a more efficient means of production *per se*; it emerged because it offered entrepreneurs a more effective means of controlling labour. This meant that the factory was also a battleground, with employers seeking to impose new conditions and technologies, and workers – when they could – attempting to resist change.

As the nineteenth century progressed, managers became increasingly aware of the shortcomings of their *ad hoc* and inconsistent responses to new challenges and opportunities, and the counter-productive nature of resistance to change. The need for a more coherent approach to structuring and running organisations was required: one that legitimated managerial authority, especially to initiate change. This crystallised into the Classical approach.

Though writing in different countries and from different perspectives, the proponents of what later came to be known as the Classical approach all adopted a similar perspective towards what they saw as one of the main issues for modern societies: how to create organisations that efficiently and effectively pursue their objectives. Taylor, supported by the work of the Gilbreths and others, concentrated very much on the operational level, arguing for his 'scientific' method of analysing, designing and managing jobs. However, his insistence on the consistent and unbiased application of scientific principles, and the emphasis he placed on all members of an organisation obeying rules and procedures, were as much a challenge to managerial beliefs and behaviour as they were to the beliefs and behaviour of shopfloor workers. Fayol, in contrast, was concerned less with operational issues and more with the overall administration and control of organisations. Therefore, to an extent, his could be called a top-down approach, whilst Taylor was working from the bottom up. Weber sought to put organisations in a wider historical and societal context, bringing together both the detailed tasks to be carried out in organisations and the general principles governing them.

Though Taylor's approach required a radical change in managerial behaviour and a significant increase in organisational bureaucracy, the objective of his system was to improve the productivity and efficiency with which manual workers carried out the tasks ordained for them by management. Everything else was, as Taylor would have put it, the outcome of pursuing this objective to its logical conclusion. The need to provide managers with rules and systems for running the entire enterprise, and not just that part of it dealing with manual labour, was a means of achieving his objective rather than a prime aim. This is where the work of Fayol and Weber has proved so crucial: together with Taylor's work, it comprises a system for running an entire business in a coherent, standardised and consistent fashion.

Therefore, taken together, their views are, broadly, complementary, and reflect an approach to organisations and people based upon a number of basic assumptions:

- There is a 'one best way' for all organisations to be structured and operate.
- This approach is founded on the rule of law and legitimate managerial authority.
- Organisations are rational entities: collectivities consistently and effectively pursuing rational goals.
- People are motivated to work solely by financial reward.
- Human fallibility and emotions, at all levels in the organisation, should be eliminated because they threaten the consistent application of the rule of law and the efficient pursuit of goals.
- For this reason, the most appropriate form of job design is achieved through the use of the hierarchical and horizontal division of labour to create narrowly focused jobs encased in tight standardised procedures and rules, which remove discretion, dictate what job-holders do and how they do it, and which allow their work to be closely monitored and controlled by their direct superiors.

Seen in the context of the early twentieth century, when there appeared to be a substantial questioning of – and challenge to – managerial authority by workers, the Classical approach had many merits: not least in its attempt to replace arbitrary and capricious management with rules and procedures that apply equally to everyone in the organisation.

Similarly, it is important to see this work in terms of what went before. Weber explicitly drew on history to support his views; the historical debts of Taylor and Fayol, though not openly acknowledged in their work, are clearly there. From Smith, through Wedgwood, Boulton and Watt, Babbage and Ure can be traced key elements of the Classical approach: the division of labour, the distrust of human variability, the need for written rules, procedures and records, and the need for rational and consistent management and objectives. Parallel to these are key themes that run through other aspects of nineteenth century life: the search for the rational, scientific, universal principles that govern the natural world, the belief in the Protestant work ethic, the emergence of Social Darwinism, the greater democratisation of societies, and the gradual reduction of laws favouring one class or group over another.

All these strands coalesced – not always neatly – in the Classical approach, creating (in retrospect) the first real and consistent attempt at a theory, a set of guidelines, for constructing, managing and changing organisations. However, given that it grew out of and was designed to meet particular circumstances, so its appropriateness began to be questioned and criticised as these circumstances changed.

Taylor and his adherents have been criticised both for their lack of scientific rigour and for their one-dimensional view of human motivation (Burnes, 1989; Kelly, 1982a, 1982b). Indeed, as Rose (1988) argued, Taylor portrayed human beings as 'greedy robots': indifferent to fatigue, boredom, loneliness and pain, driven solely by monetary incentive. For Taylor, material incentives are the only effective incentives to work. For this reason, he opposed everything else in the workplace that, in his opinion, undermined managers' attempts to introduce individual incentive systems, whether it be friendships, group loyalty, trade unions, or whatever. Taylor has also been attacked for over-emphasising the merits of the division of labour. The critics' argument is that the creation of jobs which have little intrinsic satisfaction leads to poor morale, low motivation and alienation. Indeed, such are the forces aligned against Scientific Management that it is difficult to find a facet of it that has not been attacked (Littler, 1978; Locke, 1982).

Fayol has been attacked on three fronts: first, that his principles are mere truisms; second, that they are based on questionable premises; and third, that the principles occur in pairs or clusters of contradictory statements (Massie, 1965; Simon, 1957). In addition, Fayol, like Taylor, can be construed as being against trade unions. Certainly, he believed in the pre-eminence of management and its right to make changes how and when it wanted, so long as these were based on his general principles. He also believed, unlike Taylor, that management and labour were fundamentally in conflict. Therefore, his recommendations were partly aimed at eliminating the conditions in which trade unions can flourish, in the interests of his overall aim of establishing the legitimacy of managers to manage.

Weber's arguments for bureaucracy have also received criticism. For instance, Udy (1959) questioned Weber's assertion that bureaucracies are necessarily rational, whilst Parsons (1947) suggested that Weber puts forward contradictory arguments for the basis of authority within bureaucracies. Robbins (1987) pointed out that bureaucracy is most frequently attacked for encouraging goal displacement:

- Rules become ends in themselves rather than means to the ends they were designed to achieve.
- Specialisation and differentiation create sub-units with different goals which then become primary to the sub-unit members. Not only does this lead to conflict between sub-units, but the accomplishment of sub-unit goals becomes more important than achieving the organisation's overall goals.
- Rules and regulations become interpreted as setting minimum standards of performance rather than identifying unacceptable behaviour. Staff can become apathetic and merely perform the bare minimum of work.
- The unthinking and rigid application of standardised rules and procedures can lead to their being applied in inappropriate situations, with dysfunctional consequences.

Robbins (1987) also pointed out that bureaucracy can alienate both employees and customers or clients. For the former, being treated as mere cogs in a machine leads to a sense of powerlessness and irrelevance. For the latter, being presented with a rigid and faceless organisation, which appears to serve its own ends rather than those of its customers or clients, can be frustrating and, when the provision of welfare services is involved, even heartbreaking. Mullins (1993) also pointed out that bureaucracy is often associated with secrecy and attempts to prevent legitimate public access to vital information on the performance of government and large organisations. Weber's work on bureaucracy has also received criticism because of his lack of attention to informal and social processes, in particular the way that individuals and groups can and do struggle to promote their own interests and goals above those of others in the organisation (Crozier, 1964).

It should also be noted that, though broadly complementary, the approaches of Taylor, Fayol and Weber were developed separately and with different objectives in mind. There are, consequently, tensions and inconsistencies between them. Fayol stresses the importance of *esprit de corps* and individual initiative. Taylor and Weber would find the former irrelevant and the latter dangerous. Likewise, the unchanging rigidity of bureaucracy, as portrayed by Weber, leaves little scope for the continuous search for improvement in methods and productivity advocated by Taylor and Fayol. Taylor's advocacy of functional supervision, which in effect meant a worker being responsible to different supervisors for different aspects of his/her job (some four or five supervisors in total), would have been viewed as a threat to discipline and good order by both Weber and Fayol, who were fierce advocates of unity of command – each worker should receive orders from one superior only.

One of the main criticisms of the Classical approach as a whole is that its view of people is negative. Bennis (1959: 263) called the Classical perspective one of 'organisations without people' because it is founded on the belief that people can be reduced to the level of cogs in a machine. It can also be argued that, in any case, it is impossible to remove the element of human variability from the running of organisations and that attempts to do so are counter-productive. Rather than making people work more efficiently in pursuit of organisational goals, it alienates them from their work and makes them resentful of it (Mayo, 1933). This is a point developed by Argyris (1964), who argued that the Classical approach restricts the psychological growth of individuals and causes feelings of failure, frustration and conflict. Instead, he believes that the organisational environment should provide a significant degree of individual responsibility and self-control; commitment to the goals of the organisation; productiveness and work; and an opportunity for individuals to apply their full abilities. These developed as central issues for the proponents of the Human Relations approach, which emerged in the 1930s as a reaction to the 'de humanised' Classical approach. This, together with Contingency Theory – the third approach to organisations to emerge in the twentieth century – will be discussed in the next chapter.

Test your learning

▪ Short answer questions

1 What was Adam Smith's main contribution to the development of work organisation?

2 What was the putting-out system?

3 What was the main impetus for the move to the factory system?

4 What are the key tenets of Scientific Management?

5 According to Fayol, what are the prime functions of a manager?

6 What was Weber's main justification for advocating bureaucracy?

7 What are the implications for organisational change of the Classical approach?

▪ Essay questions

1 To what extent can the move to the factory system be seen as a clash of cultures as averse to a clash of economic systems?

2 Evaluate the case for seeing the work of Taylor, Fayol and Weber as forming a coherent school of thought.

Suggested further reading

1   Wilson, JF (1995) *British Business History, 1720–1994*. Manchester University Press: Manchester.

Despite its title, this book neither confines itself to British history nor examines business in a narrow sense. Amongst other things, John Wilson's book provides an excellent review of the development of management in Britain, Germany, Japan and the USA from the early days of the Industrial Revolution.

2   Pollard, S (1965) *The Genesis of Modern Management*. Pelican: Harmondsworth.

Though published over 30 years ago, Sydney Pollard's book still provides one of the best descriptions of the development of management, and the reaction of labour, in the eighteenth and nineteenth centuries.

3   Rose, M (1988) *Industrial Behaviour*. Penguin: Harmondsworth.

Michael Rose's book provides a well-researched and thorough account of the rise and development of Scientific Management.

4   Sheldrake, J (1996) *Management Theory: From Taylorism to Japanization*. International Thompson Business Press: London.

Michael Sheldrake gives an excellent summary of the lives and contributions of Taylor, Fayol and Weber.

5   Taylor, FW (1911) *The Principles of Scientific Management*. Dover (1998 edition): New York, NY, USA.

This is perhaps the most cited, if least read, of all management books. However, as it numbers only 76 pages and is couched in quite accessible language, it is well worth reading.

Chapter 2

Developments in organisation theory

From certainty to contingency

Learning objectives

After studying this chapter, you should be able to:

- understand the reasons for the emergence of the Human Relations approach;
- identify the key features and key proponents of the Human Relations approach;
- list the advantages and disadvantages of the Human Relations approach;
- describe the differences between the Human Relations approach and the Classical approach to organisational design;
- discuss the reasons for the emergence and popularity of Contingency Theory;
- identify the key features and key proponents of Contingency Theory;
- state the advantages and disadvantages of Contingency Theory;
- appreciate how Contingency Theory seeks to incorporate both the Classical and Human Relations approaches;
- recognise the implications for organisational change of the Human Relations approach and Contingency Theory.

Exhibit 2.1   Organisations as cooperative systems

Functions of organizations

An organization is a system of cooperative human activities the functions of which are (1) the creation, (2) the transformation, and (3) the exchange of utilities. It is able to accomplish these functions by creating a cooperative system, of which the organization is both a nucleus and subsidiary system, which has also as components physical systems, personal systems (individuals and collections of individuals), and social systems (other organizations). Accordingly, from the viewpoint of creation, transformation, and exchange of utilities, the cooperative system embraces four different kinds of economies which may be distinguished as (a) a material economy; (b) a social economy; (c) the individual economies; and (d) the organization economy. ... The individual economy ... consists on one side of the power of the individual ... to do work (physical acts, attention, thought); and on the other side the utilities ascribed by him to (1) material satisfactions, (2) other satisfactions which we shall here call social satisfactions.

The economy of the individual is constantly changing, because of (1) physiological needs, (2) exchanges made with others, (3) the creation of his own utilities, and (4) other changes in his state of mind, that is, his values or appraisal of utilities, physical and social.

Source: Chester Barnard, *The Functions of the Executive*, 1938, pp. 240–2.

Introduction

The emergence of the Classical approach was one of the most significant events in the history of organisation theory and practice. From the 1920s until the 1960s, in the public sector, and in large private sector concerns, bureaucracy was unquestionably seen as the 'one best way'. The other key element of the Classical approach, Scientific Management, was less well received. In the USA, the death of the irascible Taylor did much to overcome the early opposition to Scientific Management, especially among trade union leaders. It was enthusiastically taken up by capitalists in Japan and communists in Russia, though it met with stiff resistance in other European countries. In the 1930s, Scientific Management and a streamlined version, the Bedeaux system, were rejected by both unions and management in a large number of European countries, though after the Second World War, it was heavily promoted as part of the Marshall Plan for the rebuilding of Europe (Carew, 1987; Rose, 1988).

Despite its growing dominance, from the 1930s, the Classical approach began to encounter both intellectual and practical opposition. This is shown clearly in Exhibit 2.1, which makes three assertions about the nature of organisations and individuals which strike at the very heart of the Classical approach:

1 Organisations are not machines but cooperative systems. To operate effectively and efficiently, they require the active cooperation of workers and not just their passive obedience.
2 People are motivated by a range of rewards, including social esteem, not just monetary ones.
3 Motivating factors change over time; what motivates a person one day may be ineffectual the next.

To add insult to injury, many of these assertions, including Exhibit 2.1, came from practising managers rather than 'unworldly' academics.

Therefore, although the Classical school could claim much success, especially in the USA, there was also a rising tide of conflicting evidence. This could have led to the development and strengthening of the Classical approach, and clearly this did happen to an extent (see the work of Ralph Davis, 1928, on rational planning). However, as this chapter will show, what emerged were two new approaches to organisations: the Human Relations approach, which originated in the 1930s and in which Chester Barnard was a key figure, and the Contingency approach, which was developed in the 1960s.

The first half of this chapter describes the Human Relations approach. This approach was a reaction against the mechanistic view of organisations and the pessimistic view of human nature put forward in the Classical approach. It attempted to reintroduce the human element into organisational life, and claim for itself the title of the 'one best way'. In particular, it contended that people have emotional as well as economic needs, and that organisations are cooperative systems that comprise informal structures and norms as well as formal ones. This left managers with something of a dilemma: which 'one best way' should they adopt, the Classical or Human Relations approach.

As the second half of this chapter will show, it was in response to this dilemma that Contingency Theory developed in the 1960s. Contingency Theory began by questioning and rejecting the idea that there is a 'one best way' for *all* organisations. Instead, it argued for a 'one best way' for *each* organisation. It did not, therefore, reject the Classical approach and the Human Relations approach; instead it maintained that the structures and practices of an organisation are dependent (i.e. contingent) on the circumstances it faces. The main contingencies it proposed were environmental uncertainty and dependence, technology and organisation size. After discussing the merits and drawbacks of the Human Relations approach and Contingency Theory, the chapter concludes that neither appears to be the solution to all known organisational ills that their proponents claim. In particular, it is argued that both fail to reflect and explain the complexities of day-to-day organisational life.

The Human Relations approach

Even while the Classical approach was still struggling to establish itself, the seeds of a new approach to organisational design were already being sown. The origins of what later became known as the Human Relations approach can be traced to studies on work fatigue carried out in Britain during the First World War and work in the USA, at the same time, on employee selection, which gave new insights into employee motivation (Burnes, 1989). This work was developed and extended in the 1920s by Myers (1934) in Britain and Mayo (1933) in the USA, providing new perspectives on organisational life. These studies gave substance to a growing suspicion that the Classical view of organisations as being peopled by human robots motivated by money was badly flawed. Indeed, in 1915, the United States Congress took a stand against the use of Taylor's techniques in their establishments – although Scientific Management was becoming more accepted in private industry and was beginning to cross national boundaries, not always successfully (Rose, 1988). Similarly, though the growth of bureaucracy was gathering pace, so too was people's antagonism towards faceless, machine-like organisations where employees and customers alike lost their individuality and became numbers.

In addition, as Davis and Canter (1955) argued, it is necessary to recognise that jobs and work organisation are social inventions put together to suit the specific needs and to reflect the culture, ideology and the governing concept or ethos of the time. Therefore, to understand the emergence of the Human Relations movement, it is necessary to be aware of the changes taking place in Western society prior to and just after the Second World War.

In the 1930s, in many countries, there was the emergence of a more collectivist ethos than had previously been the case. In the USA, this was brought about by the reaction to the Depression of the 1920s and 1930s. The election of FD Roosevelt and the advent of his 'New Deal' introduced a new element of collective provision and concern into a previously highly individualistic nation. It also heralded the advent of 'Big Government' in the USA. In Europe, this collectivist ethos led to greater social concern; collective provision was led by the Scandinavian countries, and reflected the election of social democratic governments and a general mood of cooperation rather than conflict in industry in these countries. Similar developments also became the cornerstone of the rebuilding of Western Germany after the end of the Second World War. The legacy of the collective effort needed to win the war was also evident in the UK with the construction of the Welfare State.

It was in the USA in the 1930s and 1940s that substantial evidence first emerged in print which challenged the Classical view of organisations and allowed the Human Relations approach to stand alongside, if not quite supersede, it. The main precepts of the Human Relations approach were almost diametrically opposed to those of the Classical approach. In particular, it argued the following points:

- **People are emotional rather than economic-rational beings.** Human needs are far more diverse and complex than the one-dimensional image that Taylor and his fellow travellers conceded. People's emotional and social needs can have more influence on their behaviour at work than financial incentives.
- **Organisations are cooperative, social systems rather than mechanical ones.** People seek to meet their emotional needs through the formation of informal but influential workplace social groups.
- **Organisations are composed of informal structures, rules and norms as well as formal practices and procedures.** These informal rules, patterns of behaviour and communication, norms and friendships are created by people to meet their own emotional needs. Because of this, they can have more influence on individual behaviour and performance, and ultimately on overall organisational performance, than the formal structure and control mechanisms laid down by management.

For these reasons, organisations can never be the predictable, well-oiled machines envisaged by the Classical approach. Therefore, in most respects, the Human Relations approach represents a distinct break from the ideas of the Classical school. However, in two important ways, similarities exist. The first is their shared belief in organisations as closed, changeless entities. Once organisations have structured themselves in accordance with the correct precepts, then, regardless of external or even internal developments, no further changes are necessary or desirable. This leads on to the second similarity: proponents of both believed they had discovered the 'one best way'; regardless of the type, nature or size of organisation, their precepts were the correct ones.

With that in mind, we can now begin to examine in detail the case for Human Relations. Despite the work of precursors, no one doubts that the Human Relations approach began in earnest with the famous Hawthorne Experiments.

Elton Mayo (1880–1949) and the Hawthorne Experiments

Elton Mayo was born in Adelaide, Australia in 1880. He had a somewhat chequered career. He failed three times to qualify as a medical doctor, and eventually became a lecturer in logic, psychology and ethics at the University of Queensland in 1911. There he developed a strong interest in the political problems of industrial society, and a life-long commitment to achieving social and industrial harmony. However, he was never very happy at Queensland and, in 1922, he emigrated to America. There, Mayo was fortunate in that his ideas on resolving industrial conflict attracted the attention of the Laura Spelman Rockefeller Memorial Foundation, which funded his entire career at the Harvard Business School. In effect, this meant that Mayo could pursue his own research without let or hindrance from university authorities. This was a major factor in the single-mindedness and success with which he undertook his work.

Elton Mayo is considered by many as the founder and leading light of the Human Relations movement. On his retirement as Professor of Industrial Research at Harvard Business School in 1947, Mayo was one of the most celebrated social scientists of the age. In praise of his achievements, the business magazine *Fortune* wrote of him:

> Scientist and practical clinician, Mayo speaks with a rare authority that has commanded attention in factories as well as Universities. His erudition extends through psychology, sociology, physiology, medicine and economics, and his experience comes from a lifelong first-hand study of industry.   (Quoted in Smith, 1998: 222)

Much of his fame rested on the 'Hawthorne Experiments' carried out at Western Electric's Hawthorne Works in Chicago in the 1920s and 1930s. However, within 10 years of his departure from Harvard, his reputation was in tatters: his expertise as a researcher was seriously questioned, his work was criticised for being too 'managerialist' and, perhaps most importantly, his contribution to the Hawthorne Experiments was considered as no more than a public relations exercise for Western Electric (Rose, 1988; Sheldrake, 1996; Smith, 1998).

The Hawthorne Experiments, as Gillespie (1991: 1) commented:

> ... are still among the most frequently cited and most controversial experiments in the social sciences ... They are acclaimed as a landmark study in both sociology and psychology ... Surveys in the key developments in organization and management theory consistently note the seminal contribution of the experiments to their field.

Yet, for most of the 80 years since the Hawthorne Experiments were initiated, it has been difficult to identify Mayo's exact role (Smith, 1987). That the name of Elton Mayo is inextricably linked with the Hawthorne Experiments is undeniable. That Mayo publicised and was given credit for masterminding these is also undeniable. Until recently, though, key questions have remained unanswered: did Mayo design and implement the experiments himself? What was the role of his colleagues at Harvard? How frequently did he visit the Hawthorne Works? Now, with the availability of family records and other archival material, Smith (1998) claims to have answered Mayo's detractors and to have re-established him both as the key figure in the Hawthorne Experiments and as the dominant figure in the Human Relations movement. Nevertheless, given the vehemence of Mayo's critics (Rose, 1988), one suspects that the debate over the 'Mayo mystique' is not yet over.

Despite the difficulty in separating out the myth from the man, we should not let that undermine the significance of the Hawthorne work or what we know of Mayo and his colleagues' contribution, even if we cannot clearly identify who did what. The Hawthorne programme was originally devised by Western Electric's own industrial engineers in 1924. Western Electric was the manufacturing division of the American Telephone and Telegraph Company. The Hawthorne Works, which at the time employed some 30,000 people, was considered a prime example of the application of the mass production techniques and work organisation methods advocated by Frederick Taylor and Henry Ford. However, this was tempered by the company's personnel and welfare policies which provided pension, sickness and disability benefits, a share purchase plan, medical treatment, extensive recreational facilities and a system of worker representation. This example of 'welfare capitalism' had the twin aims of reducing worker dissatisfaction and resisting trade union influence (Sheldrake, 1996).

The first phase of the Hawthorne Experiments, which lasted on and off until 1927, was the Hawthorne Illumination Tests (HIT), which were designed to examine the effects of various levels of lighting on workers' productivity. The engineers established control and experimental groups: the latter were subject to different levels of illumination as they carried out their work whilst the lighting of the control group was left unchanged. At the outset this looked like a standard Scientific Management experiment in the mould of Taylor and the Gilbreths. What the engineers were expecting was a set of unambiguous results that would allow them to establish the 'one best' level of illumination. This did not happen and, instead, data began to emerge that challenged the very basis of Scientific Management.

The engineers had expected the performance of the experimental group to vary with increases and decreases in illumination and for an optimum level to be established, but as the illumination was varied, so output continued to increase. Indeed, output only decreased in the experimental group when the lighting became so dim that it was difficult to see. More puzzling still, output in the control group, where no changes were made, also increased.

In 1927 the company began the second phase of the Hawthorne Experiments. Building on the HIT work, the company wanted to establish the effects on productivity of increased rest periods, a shorter working day, a reduced working week, free refreshments, changes to payment systems, better and friendlier communication, and a relaxation in the customary discipline usually imposed by first line supervisors. The first group to be involved were six women in the Relay Assembly Test Room (RATR). As Gillespie (1991: 59) noted:

> [Their] privileged status and a modicum of control over work days brought about a strong identification with the test room among the workers ... With the introduction of refreshments during the morning rest period, the women's status soared higher still.

By 1929, productivity in the RATR group had increased by some 30 per cent. In the interim, the company also initiated a further series of experiments in which, from 1928 onwards, Elton Mayo and his colleagues were closely involved. In the years that followed, successive groups of workers were subjected to changes in hours, payment systems, rest periods, etc. The subsequent changes in output, and the reasons put forward for these, undermined many of the assumptions regarding organisations and human behaviour previously perceived as sacrosanct (Mayo, 1933; Roethlisberger and Dickson, 1938).

The experiments were monitored continuously; from this work, Mayo and his colleagues concluded that it was not the changes in working conditions that affected output, but the fact that those workers involved had been singled out for special attention. This acted to increase their morale and make them want to perform better. It was the very fact that they were being studied which produced the increased performance; this later became known as the 'Hawthorne Effect'. This accounted for the improved performance by the original HIT control group, even with no changes to the lighting in their area: they also felt 'special' because they were being studied. These findings led Mayo and his group to move the focus of their work away from the reaction of individual workers to changes in their working conditions. Instead, they began to investigate the role and behaviour of the 'informal' groups that workers themselves established, and the norms and attitudes of these groups.

As a result of this work, Mayo and his colleagues put forward two major propositions that came to form the core of the Human Relations approach. The first related to the importance of informal groups within the formal structure of organisations. The Western Electric studies demonstrated the need to see the work process as a collective, cooperative activity as opposed to an individual, isolated one. The studies showed in particular the important effect that the informal, primary work group has on performance. These groups tend to develop their own norms, values and attitudes that enable them to exert strong social, peer group pressure on individuals within the group to conform to group norms, whether this be in relation to the pace of work or attitudes towards other groups and supervisors. Taylor, years before, had also noted the pressure that groups of workers could exert over their members to make them conform; however, he believed that this was abnormal behaviour which could be remedied by tight managerial control. What the Western Electric studies demonstrated was that far from being abnormal, such behaviour was perfectly normal.

The second proposition put forward by Mayo and his colleagues was that humans have a deep need for recognition, security and belonging. Rather than being purely economic beings, it was argued that the Hawthorne Experiments demonstrated that workers' performance and attitudes could be influenced more by their need for recognition and security, and also by the feeling of belonging engendered by informal groups. This latter point in particular reflected, in Mayo's view, a deep-seated desire by humans as social beings for intimacy, consistency and predictability. Where these social certainties were lacking, workers would deliberately seek to manufacture them by creating their own informal work groups. Therefore, rather than seeking to eradicate or undermine the workings of these informal groups, as Taylor had advocated, the Western Electric studies showed that management needed to gain the collaboration and cooperation of such groups if they were to get the best performance from workers.

It is generally agreed (Mullins, 1989; Rose, 1988) that the Western Electric studies had a dramatic effect on management and organisation theory. The studies ushered in an era where the Economic Man of the Classical approach was supplanted by Social Man. It was no longer possible for managers to ignore the effects of organisational structures and job design on work groups, employee attitudes and management–worker relations. The crucial issue became one of social relationships – Human Relations – in the workplace. In future, the focus of good management practice would shift to the importance of leadership and communication in order to win over employees. As the 1930s and 1940s progressed, other work began to emerge which both substantiated and broadened those findings.

◼ Chester Barnard (1886–1961) and cooperative systems

Chester Barnard was born in Malden, Massachusetts in 1886. On leaving school, he became a piano tuner, but later attended Harvard University where he studied economics. On leaving university, he went to work for the American Telephone and Telegraph Company, in whose subsidiary, Western Electric, the Hawthorne studies were carried out. He was initially employed as a statistician, but quickly rose to hold a number of senior executive positions including, by the age of 41, becoming President of the New Jersey Bell Telephone Company. He also established his credentials as a prolific writer and lecturer with strong links to a number of universities, including Harvard. On retiring in 1948, he became President of the Rockefeller Foundation.

Barnard is best known for his book *The Functions of the Executive* (1938), which has a comparable place in the Human Relations literature to that of Fayol's work in the literature of the Classical school. In this work, Barnard put forward the idea of organisations as cooperative systems. In so doing, this gave him a double claim to fame: not only did he draw attention to the cooperative nature of organisational life, but he was also one of the first to treat organisations as systems rather than machines. He was in frequent touch with Mayo and his colleagues at Harvard, and closely followed their work at Western Electric. Therefore, although *The Functions of the Executive* was a personal and idiosyncratic work, reflecting Barnard's own distinct views and opinions, it was far from being bereft of academic substance. Indeed, his book was the first systematic attempt in English (Weber's work on bureaucracy was still not translated into English at this time) to outline a theory of organisations as a whole. In this respect, Barnard can claim both to have made a substantial contribution to the Human Relations approach and to have laid the ground work for subsequent writers such as Selznick and Simon (Robbins, 1987; Scott, 1987).

Barnard had close links with Harvard Business School and, along with Elton Mayo, Talcott Parsons (who first translated Weber's work into English) and Joseph Schumpeter, was a member of the Harvard Pareto Circle. This group was established to discuss and promote the work of the Italian sociologist Vilfredo Pareto, whose writing placed great emphasis on social systems and social equilibrium (Sheldrake, 1996).

The influence of Pareto's social systems view can be seen in Barnard's depiction of organisations as cooperative systems. An organisation is a cooperative system, he argued, because without the willingness of its members to make contributions to and to pursue its goals, it cannot operate effectively. Like others who espoused the Human Relations approach, he believed cooperation could not be achieved solely by monetary incentives. Instead, he advocated a mixture of monetary and non-monetary inducements. Similarly, cooperation by itself would not be effective unless an organisation also possessed a common purpose: clear and realistic goals and objectives that the organisation's members could understand, relate to and pursue. Establishing this common purpose, in Barnard's opinion, had to be the responsibility of those at the top of the organisation, but achieving it required the cooperation of those at the bottom, and all levels in between. This leads to another of Barnard's assertions: the flow of authority is not from the top down but from the bottom up. He defined authority not as a property of management but as a response by subordinates to superiors. If subordinates did not respond willingly and appropriately, then no authority existed. In this example, as in many others, he both reflected the influence of and supported the findings of the Western Electric studies, which drew attention to the ability of workers through social groupings to facilitate or frustrate the will of management.

In order to avoid a negative response from workers, Barnard advocated systematic and purposeful communication. He saw communication, through both formal and informal structures, as being the key function of the executive. Indeed, he portrayed the organisation as a purposeful, coordinated system of communications linking all participants in a manner that not only encouraged the pursuit of the organisation's common purpose, but also legitimated the premises on which it was based. However, he argued that this does not happen automatically or accidentally; it is the product of effective leadership. This is why Barnard stressed the key role of the executive in leading the organisation by facilitating communication and motivating subordinates to high levels of performance; such developments could only come from the top. He also saw the executive as having a role in shaping and reinforcing the organisation's value systems or, as modern writers would put it, its culture.

Given the emphasis placed by Barnard on the setting and pursuit of clear objectives, and in his approach in general, there is a degree of overlap with the work of the Classical School. However, what significantly distinguishes him from them is his insistence on the non rational, informal, interpersonal, and indeed moral basis of organisational life. His view of effective leadership also distinguishes him from the Classical school. Rather than seeing leadership as dependent on position, Barnard argued that successful leadership arose from the interplay between the individual leader, the followers and the context.

Above all, Barnard rejected the idea of material incentives being the only incentives to make people work purposefully. Indeed, he saw them as being 'weak incentives' that needed to be supported by other psychological and sociological motivators if organisations were to be successful in achieving their common purpose. In thus challenging the effectiveness of material incentives, he was to receive substantial support a few years later from a more academic source.

■ Abraham Maslow's (1908–1970) hierarchy of needs

Abraham Maslow was born in Brooklyn, New York in 1908. He trained as a psychologist at the University of Wisconsin and, apart from a brief period working in the family business, spent his working life in academia. Maslow was one of the first to differentiate between and classify different types of human need. For Taylor and his adherents, there was only one form of need: material/monetary need. Mayo *et al* and

Barnard took a different view; they drew a distinction between material and non-material needs, but made no distinction within these two categories. Maslow (1943) identified five distinct forms of human need which he placed in a hierarchical order. He argued that, beginning at the lowest level, a person had to satisfy substantially the needs at one level before they could move up the hierarchy and concentrate on 'higher order' needs.

In ascending order, the five levels in Maslow's hierarchy of needs are:

- **Physiological needs** – hunger, thirst, sleep, etc.; only when these basic needs have been satisfied do other needs begin to emerge.
- **Safety needs** – the desire for security and protection against danger.
- **Social needs** – the need to belong, to gain love and affection; to be in the company of others, especially friends.
- **Esteem needs** – these reflect a person's desire to be respected – esteemed – for their achievements.
- **Self-actualisation needs** – self-actualisation is the need to achieve one's full potential. According to Maslow, this will vary from person to person and, indeed, may differ over time, as a person reaches a level of potential previously considered unattainable and so goes on to strive for new heights. For these reasons, self-actualisation is a continuously evolving process throughout a person's lifetime.

Maslow (1943: 383) recognised that there were weaknesses in his theory of needs: 'Since, in our society, basically-satisfied people are the exception, we do not know much about self-actualisation, either experimentally or clinically.' He accepted that the strength of the hierarchy might differ with individual circumstances – some people's aspirations may be so deadened by their experiences that they would be satisfied by having enough to eat. He also saw that cultural differences between societies could have an impact on the extent and order of needs. Nevertheless, he did believe that his theory was generally applicable and that where people's higher aspirations were thwarted or unmet, the result was likely to be frustration and de-motivation.

Though not designed specifically for organisational analysis, but rather in the context of life in general, it can be seen why Maslow's work was so readily accepted by proponents of the Human Relations approach. For them, it explained why in some situations Tayloristic incentives were effective, whilst in other situations, such as the Hawthorne Experiments, other factors proved more important.

Applying Maslow's hierarchy of needs to human behaviour in organisations, it can be seen that people will first of all be motivated by the desire to satisfy physiological needs through monetary rewards. Once those have been substantially satisfied, however, workers will seek to satisfy – be motivated by – their safety needs, such as job security and welfare benefits. In a similar fashion, once safety needs are substantially met, these will fade into the background and social needs will come to the fore; people will want to be accepted as part of a group, to share common intents and aspirations with the group, to experience the bonds of friendship and loyalty. Clearly, these social needs played an important role in the Hawthorne Experiments, as did esteem needs. After social and esteem needs are substantially met, finally self-actualisation needs come to the fore. However, as mentioned above, the need for self-actualisation never wanes but tends to act as a continuing spur to further achievements.

Clearly, Maslow's work cannot be transferred fully into the organisational setting, given that the constraints on freedom of action imposed by most jobs do not allow individuals to approach, let alone attain, self-actualisation (Rose, 1988). Even very basic physiological needs are beyond the reach of many millions of people in the world. Nevertheless, in pointing to the negative effects of thwarting an individual's aspirations, and in distinguishing between types of intrinsic (non-material) and extrinsic (material) motivators, and arguing that, at any one time, it is the unmet needs which act as positive motivators, Maslow has had an enormous impact on job design and research (*see* Child, 1984; Smith *et al*, 1982). The influence of Maslow's theory of needs can be seen in the work of other exponents of Human Relations, especially Douglas McGregor.

Douglas McGregor (1906–1964) and Theory X–Theory Y

Douglas McGregor was born in 1906. He received his doctorate in psychology from Harvard, and spent much of his working life at the Massachusetts Institute of Technology where, from 1954 until his death in 1964, he was the first Sloan Fellows Professor. McGregor is one of the most widely cited Human Relations writers. He developed his views from his personal experience and observations as an academic, consultant and university administrator rather than from empirical research.

In his book *The Human Side of Enterprise* (1960), McGregor argued that decisions taken by top managers on the best way to manage people were based on their assumptions about human nature. McGregor maintained that there are basically two commonly-held views of human nature: a negative view – Theory X; and a positive view – Theory Y. He believed that managers' behaviour towards their subordinates was based upon one or other of these views, both of which consist of a certain grouping of assumptions about human behaviour.

Theory X, which he believed dominated the literature and practice of management, consists of the following assumptions:

- The average person dislikes work and will avoid it wherever possible.
- Employees must be coerced, controlled or threatened with punishment if they are to perform as required.
- Most people try to avoid responsibility and will seek formal direction whenever possible.
- Workers place security above other factors relating to employment and will display little ambition.

Theory Y, on the other hand, comprises a group of assumptions that give a much more positive view of human nature:

- Most people can view work as being as natural as rest or play.
- Workers are capable of exercising self-direction and self-control.
- The average person will accept and even seek responsibility if they are committed to the objectives being pursued.
- Ingenuity, imagination, creativity and the ability to make good decisions are widely dispersed throughout the population and are not peculiar to managers.

Theory X and Theory Y are not statements about what people are actually like, but rather the general assumptions that managers, and the rest of us, hold about what people are like. The fact that such views may not have a base in reality is irrelevant if managers act as though they are true. Managers who adhere to Theory X will use a combination of stick and carrot methods to control their subordinates, and will construct organisations that restrict the individual's ability to exercise skill, discretion and control over their work. Those managers who adhere to Theory Y will adopt a more open and flexible style of management. They will create jobs that encourage workers to contribute towards organisational goals and allow them to exercise skill and responsibility, and where the emphasis will be on non-material incentives.

Obviously, Theory X is akin to the Classical view of human nature and organisational design, whereas Theory Y falls more in the Human Relations tradition. Though McGregor favoured Theory Y, he recognised that it could not be fully validated. Instead, he saw Theory Y as a challenge to the orthodoxy of Theory X and, as he put it (McGregor, 1960: 53), as an 'invitation to innovate'. He argued that there was nothing inevitable about which approach to adopt. The choice lies with managers; those who adhere to Theory X will create a situation where workers are only able and willing to pursue material needs (as Maslow observed). Such workers will be neither prepared nor in a position to contribute to the wider aims and objectives of the organisation that employs them. Managers who follow Theory Y precepts are likely to receive an entirely different response from their employees; workers will identify more clearly with the general interests of the organisation, and be more able and more willing to contribute to their achievement.

Though stressing the element of choice, McGregor, along with other Human Relations adherents, believed that changes in the nature of modern societies meant that organisations were moving, and should move, more in the direction of Theory Y.

■ Warren Bennis (1925–) and the death of bureaucracy

By the 1950s and 1960s, the Human Relations approach and the values it espoused were in the ascendancy. One clear sign of this was the widely-held view in the 1960s that bureaucracy was dying and being replaced by more flexible, people-centred organisations that allowed and encouraged personal growth and development. One of the main exponents of this view is Warren Bennis.

Warren Bennis trained as an industrial psychologist and held a number of senior academic appointments, including Professor of Management at the University of Southern California. He is now best known for his work on leadership, and has acted as an adviser to four US presidents. In terms of the Human Relations movement, Bennis (1966) is credited with coining the phrase and making the case for 'the death of bureaucracy'. Bennis argued that every age develops an organisational form appropriate to its time. Bureaucracy was, in his view, appropriate for the first two-thirds of the twentieth century but not beyond that. He believed that bureaucracy emerged because its order, precision and impersonal nature was the correct antidote for the personal subjugation, cruelty, nepotism and capriciousness that passed for management during the Industrial Revolution.

Bureaucracy, he stated, emerged as a creative and wholesome response to the needs and values of the Victorian Age. Up to this point, there is little to distinguish Bennis from Weber; however, he then went on to argue that the Victorian Age, and its needs, were dead and that new conditions were emerging to which bureaucracy was no longer suited. These conditions were:

- **Rapid and unexpected change** – bureaucracy's strength lies in its ability to manage efficiently the routine and predictable; however, its pre-programmed rules and inflexibility make it unsuitable for the rapidly changing modern world.
- **Growth in size** – as organisations become larger, then bureaucratic structures become more complex and unwieldy, and less efficient.
- **Increasing diversity** – rapid growth, quick change and an increase in specialisation create the need for people with diverse and highly specialised skills; these specialists cannot easily or effectively be fitted within the standardised, pyramid structure of bureaucratic organisations.
- **Change in managerial behaviour** – the increasing adoption of the Human Relations approach by managers challenges the simplistic view of human nature put forward by the Classical school, which underpins bureaucracy. If coercion and threats administered in a depersonalised, mechanistic fashion are counter-productive as a way of controlling people in organisations, then the case for bureaucracy is severely diminished.

For Bennis and others such as Daniel Bell (1973), Alvin Toffler (1970) and EF Schumacher (1973), bureaucracy was rightly dying and being replaced by more diverse, flexible structures which could cope with the needs of the modern world.

Job Design: operationalising Human Relations

Though intellectually strong, the Human Relations school remained operationally weak up to the 1950s and 1960s because, unlike the Classical school, it lacked a clear set of operational definitions and guidelines that allowed organisations to understand and implement it in the same way that they could with Scientific Management or bureaucracy. The advent of the Job Design movement in both the USA and Europe rectified this.

In the last 50 years, Job Design, or work humanisation as it has also been called, has become a powerful technique for rolling back the worst excesses of the Classical school, especially in the area of manual work, where Scientific Management and its clones have had such an impact. It was in America in the 1950s that Davis and Canter (1955), influenced by the work of the Human Relations school, questioned the Tayloristic basis of job design and work organisation. They suggested that it would be possible to design jobs that satisfied not only human needs but also organisational ones as well. They argued that increased job satisfaction and increased organisational performance went hand in hand. Since then many other writers, especially in Europe, have contributed to the development of Job Design theory (Davis *et al*, 1955; Guest, 1957; Hackman and Oldham, 1980; Likert, 1961; Trist *et al*, 1963; Warr, 1987).

Job Design is a direct attack on the precepts of the Classical approach. Whereas Taylorist tradition seeks to fit people to rigidly defined and controlled jobs, Job Design theorists argue that jobs can and should be fitted to human needs. The basic tenets of Job Design are relatively straightforward and follow on from the work of the proponents of the Human Relations approach, especially Maslow. It is argued that the Classical approach to jobs, with its emphasis on fragmenting jobs and reducing workers' autonomy and discretion, is counter-productive to both individual fulfilment and organisational performance. This is because boring, monotonous and meaningless jobs lead to poor mental health and feelings of dissatisfaction. In turn, this can result in lack of motivation, absenteeism, labour turnover and even industrial unrest (Arnold *et al*, 1998).

The solution to these problems follows from the analysis. If Tayloristic trends in job design are counter-productive, then they should be reversed and 'variety, task completeness and, above all, autonomy' should be built into jobs (Wall *et al*, 1984: 15). Such a move would promote workers' mental health and job satisfaction, bringing in turn increased motivation and performance. Just as Taylor believed his approach would benefit both workers and management, so too do the proponents of Job Design; the difference is that the benefit to the worker is personal fulfilment rather than increased wages, though in both systems the benefit to management is increased productivity (Friedman, 1961; Hackman and Lawler, 1971; Herzberg *et al*, 1959; Kelly, 1982a, 1982b).

In practice, there are three main variants of Job Design:

- **Job enlargement,** which concentrates on increasing work variety by combining previously fragmented tasks together, or by rotating people between different types of work (Guest, 1957).
- **Job enrichment,** which concentrates on increasing workers' control over what they do by rearranging work so that some of the responsibilities previously borne by supervisors and support staff are given to individuals or, more often, semi-autonomous work groups (Herzberg, 1968).
- **Socio-Technical Systems theory,** which is a variant on Job Design involving a shift of focus from the individual job to the organisation as a whole. Socio-Technical Systems theory sees organisations as being composed of interdependent social and technical systems. The theory argues that there is little point in reorganising the social system in isolation from the technology being used, and that the level of performance achieved is dependent on the degree of fit between the two. This view sees technology as acting as a limitation on the scope for redesigning individual jobs (Davis, 1979; Dunphy and Griffiths, 1998; Trist *et al*, 1963). It follows, therefore, that Job Design must go hand-in-hand with technological change if it is to be successful.

Job Design emerged and attracted so much attention in the 1950s and 1960s for three main reasons:

1 The first flows from the work of Maslow (1943). As workers have become better educated and more affluent, their higher order needs such as self-actualisation have come to the fore. This means that in order to obtain the best performance from workers, jobs have to be designed to meet their psychological as well as their financial needs (Kelly, 1982b).

2 As markets have become more global, more competitive and more volatile, organisations need to be more responsive to the needs of their customers. This requires workers to be more flexible, possess a greater range of skills, and be able to work as part of a team rather than on an individual basis (Aglietta, 1979; Streeck, 1987).

3 Low unemployment in the 1950s, 1960s and 1970s led to high rates of labour turnover and absenteeism and endemic industrial unrest in industries and organisations with poor job design (Pruijt, 1997). This was certainly a major reason for Volvo's adoption of Job Design in the 1970s (*see* Chapter 12).

Since the 1950s, the USA and most European countries have initiated some form of officially sponsored 'Work Humanisation' programme. Not surprisingly, Norway and Sweden, with their traditions of industrial cooperation and democracy, and what was West Germany, with its post-war commitment to industrial consensus and worker rights, led the way in terms of financial and legal backing. Norway initiated the process with its Industrial Democracy Project (1962–1975). Sweden has probably been the most consistent, however, establishing the Work Environment Fund in 1972, with a budget of SEK 500 million per year, and creating the New Factories Programme at the same time. In 1976 it enacted the Co-determination Act, which ensures that trade unions have a right to be consulted on all major changes in working conditions. In 1977, the Swedish government created the Centre For Working Life (later the Institute For Work Life Research) to initiate and promote work humanisation. In the 1980s, it initiated the Swedish Development Programme (1982–1987), the Leadership, Organisation and Co-determination Programme (1985–1990), and the People, Data, Working Life Programme (1987–1992). Germany has seen a similarly consistent approach with the Humanisation of Working Life Programme (1974–1989) and the Work and Technology Programme (1989–). Germany also provided subsidies (around DM 100 million per year) to encourage the adoption of Job Design practices (Pruijt, 1997).

Some of the Job Design initiatives in these countries were inspired by Norwegian researchers such as Einar Thorsrud, who propagated the concept of semi-autonomous work groups. Others derived from the work on the socio-technical systems approach carried out by the Tavistock Institute in London (Auer and Riegler, 1990). In the UK, however, despite the presence of the Tavistock Institute and the establishment of the Work Research Unit in 1974, official backing has been noticeably lukewarm. Indeed, even the modest expenditure devoted to the Work Research Unit was cut back considerably in the 1980s, and the Unit has now been disbanded. Successive UK governments now seem to share the American view that 'Quality of Working Life' programmes are the purview of individual organisations rather than something to be promoted by government.

To a great degree, the popularity of Job Design seems to have fluctuated with employment levels. In the full-employment era of the 1950s and 1960s, governments and employers in the West seemed relatively receptive to it. With the recessions of the 1970s and 1980s, however, interest fell away in most countries. The exceptions were Sweden and Germany, both countries where unemployment remained relatively low in the 1970s and 1980s. Despite this, there can be little doubt that Job Design precepts have permeated Western society on a significant scale, and provide the main operational alternative to the Classical approach; as Pruijt (1997) noted, however, Tayloristic work practices have proved far more persistent than the proponents of Job Design had expected.

■ The Human Relations approach: summary and criticisms

Though many tend to associate the Human Relations movement exclusively with the work of Mayo, the above shows that it is a much more diverse school of thought. Indeed, some have argued that to call it a school owes more to academic convenience than to reality (Rose, 1988). Nevertheless, there are continuing and overlapping themes in the work of the writers cited above which strongly bond them together. The first, and most obvious, is their almost total rejection of the Classical movement's mechanistic-rational approach towards people and organisation structures. As Dunphy and Griffiths (1998: 21) noted:

> In particular, they attacked the notion of employees as interchangeable parts, stressing that individual employees had different motivations; that the specialisation of labour and deskilling had created widespread alienation and demotivation; and that excessive supervision had crushed employee initiative.

The second and more fundamental feature is that whilst approaching the issues involved from different perspectives and emphasising separate aspects, they create an organisational model that possesses both coherence and plausibility.

The Human Relations model stresses three core elements:

- leadership and communication;
- intrinsic job motivation (as well as extrinsic rewards);
- organisation structures and practices which facilitate flexibility and involvement.

These elements are underpinned by two central propositions:

- **Organisations are complex social systems**, with both formal and informal social structures, and are not mechanical contrivances. Therefore, they cannot effectively be controlled by close supervision, rigid rules and purely economic incentives.
- **Human beings have emotional as well as economic needs.** Organisation and job structures need to be designed in such a way as to enable workers to meet both their material and non-material needs. Only in this way will workers perform efficiently and effectively in the best interests of the organisation.

It is not difficult to see why the Human Relations approach proved popular. In a period when many people were becoming increasingly worried about the growth of impersonal bureaucracies, it provided an attractive alternative. It is an approach that stresses that human beings are not mere cogs in a machine but that they have emotional needs: humans want to 'belong', achieve recognition, and develop and fulfil their potential. As mentioned earlier, the Depression of the 1930s and the Second World War and its aftermath created, in the USA and Europe, a greater sense of collectivism and community than had hitherto been the case; another reason why the Human Relations doctrine found such a ready audience. Also, implicitly, it offers an approach to change management that has a surprisingly modern ring to it. The stress on organisations having clear objectives, effective communication systems and proactive leadership, coupled with the need to obtain the willing cooperation of employees, are central to many modern approaches to change management.

Despite its attractiveness and plausibility, a substantial and often vitriolic body of opinion came to be ranged against the Human Relations approach in the 1950s and 1960s (Rose, 1988). Economists rejected the argument that non-material incentives have a potentially stronger motivating influence than material incentives. The emphasis placed by the proponents of Human Relations on people's need for 'togetherness' and 'belonging' was seen by some as a denial of individualism. Others thought that it belittled workers and portrayed them as irrational beings who, given the chance, would cling to management as a baby clings to its mother. It was also attacked from both a management and a trade union viewpoint. Some of the former felt that its supposedly powerful manipulative techniques were either useless or inoperable; whilst representatives of the latter saw Human Relations as a vehicle for manipulating labour, and undermining – or attempting to eliminate – trade unions. Sociologists criticised it for attempting a sociological analysis of organisations without taking into account the larger society within which each organisation exists (Kerr and Fisher, 1957; Landsberger, 1958; Rose, 1988; Whyte, 1960).

Many of the criticisms were clearly directed at the work of Mayo and his colleagues, including inconsistencies between them. Landsberger (1958), for example, was one of the first to point out the difference between Mayo's (1933) interpretations of the Hawthorne Experiments and those of his colleagues, Roethlisberger and Dickson (1938), though Smith (1998) disputes this and many of the other criticisms of Mayo. However, by no means were all the criticisms levelled at Mayo and his colleagues. Maslow's work, a key theoretical cornerstone of the Human Relations approach, was found to lack empirical substance when researchers attempted to validate it, and certainly later theories of motivation seem to adopt a different approach (Arnold et al, 1998; Hall and Nougaim, 1968; Lawler and Suttle, 1972; Sheldrake, 1996). Similarly, Bennis's views were attacked. The Aston Studies in the 1960s (Pugh et al, 1969a, 1969b) showed that bureaucracy was growing rather than declining. Also, Miewald (1970) argued that Bennis did not understand the nature of bureaucracy; in his view, far from being rigid, it could and did adapt to changing and dynamic environments. Kelly (1982b) also attacked the proposition that increased job satisfaction leads to increased performance.

There is one further criticism of the Human Relations approach, one that it shares with the Classical approach: it claims for itself the title of the 'one best way'. Yet, the question was posed, how can any approach claim that there is only one method of structuring and managing organisations, and that it holds good for all organisations and for all time? Indeed, the seed of this criticism can be found in Bennis's (1966) work, where he argued that organisations in the last third of the twentieth century would experience rapid and unexpected change, continue to increase in size – with the problems of complexity which this brings, and become more diverse and specialised. Clearly, whilst not explicitly advocating it, Bennis was making the case for an approach to organisations that recognised not only that they face different situations but also that these are not stable over time. Similarly, Trist et al's (1963) argument regarding the need to fit social systems to technical ones can also be seen as making a case for a situationalist approach to job design. Indeed, the most telling argument against the 'one best way' approach is that presented by Davis and Canter (1955), mentioned earlier. If jobs and work organisation are social inventions designed to meet the needs of societies and organisations at particular points in time, then there can never be a one best way for all organisations and for all times. What is needed, instead, is an approach that links approaches to work design to the particular context to which they are best suited. In the 1960s and 1970s, such an approach emerged.

The Contingency Theory approach

Contingency Theory emerged in the 1960s out of a number of now classic studies of organisation structure and management (*see* Child, 1984; Mullins, 1989; Scott, 1987). Since the 1970s, it has proved – as a theory at least – to be more influential than either the Classical or Human Relations approach. In essence, Contingency Theory is a rejection of the 'one best way' approach previously sought by managers and propounded by academics. In its place is substituted the view that the structure and operation of an organisation is dependent ('contingent') on the situational variables it faces – the main ones being environment, technology and size (Burnes, 1989). It follows from this that no two organisations will face exactly the same contingencies; therefore, as their situations are different, so too should their structures and operations be different. Consequently the 'one best way' for *all* organisations is replaced by the 'one best way' for *each* organisation.

One of the clear distinctions between Contingency Theory and its predecessors was pointed out by Scott (1987: 23):

> The previous definitions tend to view the organisation as a closed system, separate from its environment and comprising a set of stable and easily identified participants. However, organisations are not closed systems, sealed off from their environments but are open to and dependent on flows of personnel and resources from outside.

As Robbins (1987) noted, there is wide agreement that the systems approach offers important insights into the working of an organisation. Systems theory is not new: it has been used in the natural and physical sciences for years. However, its application to business organisation only really emerged in the 1960s. The systems approach views the organisation both as a whole, and as part of a larger environment. The idea is that any part of an organisation's activities affects all other parts. Organisations, rather than being closed (as previous theories assumed), are viewed as open systems operating within a wider environment and having multiple channels of interaction (Mullins, 1993). Therefore, organisations are not in complete control of their own fate; they can be, and often are, affected by the environment in which they operate, and this can and does vary from organisation to organisation.

One of the earliest writers to lay the groundwork for Contingency Theorists was Herbert Simon. Writing in the 1940s (Simon, 1957), he criticised existing approaches as providing managers with nothing more than proverbs or lists of 'good practice' based on scant ideas, many of which contradicted each other. He argued that organisation theory needed to go beyond superficial and over-simplified precepts, and instead study the conditions under which competing principles could be applied.

Nevertheless, it was not until the 1960s that a considered approach emerged, which broke with the Classical and Human Relations movements' attempts to establish a universal approach suitable to all organisations. The former had concentrated on the formal structure and technical requirements of organisations, and had attempted to establish sets of general principles. The latter, the Human Relations movement, focused on the informal aspects of organisations and the psychological and social needs of their employees. As with the Classical approach, this produced lists of good practice and desired objectives, but it lacked precise guidance on how these should be applied.

Contingency Theorists adopted a different perspective, based on the premise that organisations are open systems whose internal operation and effectiveness is dependent upon the particular situational variables they face at any one time, and that these vary from organisation to organisation. This is consistent with evidence that not all organisations – or even all successful ones – have the same structure, and that even within organisations, different structural forms can be observed (Mintzberg, 1979). Though many situational variables, such as the age of the organisation and its history, have been put forward as influential in determining structure, it is generally agreed that the three most important contingencies are:

- **Environmental uncertainty and dependence.** It is argued that the management of any organisation is undertaken in circumstances of uncertainty and dependence, both of which change over time. Uncertainty arises because of our inability ever to understand and control events fully, especially the actions of others, whether outside or inside an organisation. Because of this, forecasting is an inexact and hazardous enterprise. Similarly, the dependence of management upon the goodwill and support of others, whether they be internal or external groupings, makes an organisation vulnerable, and may in some circumstances even threaten its very existence. Levels of uncertainty and dependence will vary, but can never be totally eliminated, and must therefore be taken into account – treated as a contingency – when designing organisational structures and procedures (Burns and Stalker, 1961; Child, 1984; Lawrence and Lorsch, 1967; Pugh, 1984; Robbins, 1987; Thompson, 1967).

- **Technology.** The argument for technology being a key variable follows similar lines to that of environment. Organisations creating and providing different products and services use different technologies. Indeed, even those producing similar products may use differing techniques. Given that these technologies can vary from the large and expensive, such as a car assembly line, to the relatively small and cheap, such as a personal computer, the form of organisation necessary to ensure their efficient operation will also vary. If so, there is a need to treat technology as a contingent variable when structuring organisations. There are distinct variants of the case for technology, however, which reflect the different definitions of technology that theorists and researchers have employed. The two best-developed approaches are found in Woodward's (1965, 1970) studies of 'operations technology' and Perrow's (1967, 1970) analysis of 'materials technology'. The former refer to the equipping and sequencing of activities in an organisation's work flow, whilst the latter refer to the characteristics of the physical and informational materials used. Woodward's work tends to relate more to manufacturing organisations, whereas Perrow's is more generally applicable (Hickson *et al*, 1969; Thompson, 1967; Zwerman, 1970).

- **Size.** Some would argue that this is not just *a* key variable but *the* key variable. The case for size being a significant variable when designing organisations has a long antecedence within organisation theory, being first cited by Weber in the early part of the twentieth century when making the case for bureaucracy (Weber, 1947). The basic case is quite straightforward. It is argued that the structure and practices necessary for the efficient and effective operations of small organisations are not suitable for larger ones. For small organisations, centralised and personalised forms of control are claimed to be appropriate, but as organisations grow in size, more decentralised and impersonal structures and practices become more relevant (Blau, 1970; Mullins, 1989; Pugh *et al*, 1969a, 1989b; Scott, 1987).

The main figures in developing and establishing Contingency Theory were academics in Britain and the USA, among whom the pioneers were Burns and Stalker.

■ Tom Burns and George Macpherson Stalker: the importance of environment

The first major study to establish a relationship between organisations' environment and their structure was carried out by Burns and Stalker (1961) in Britain. They examined 20 firms in a variety of industries in order to assess how their structures responded to the environment in which they operated. Their findings were to have a major impact on organisation theory, and provide concrete evidence for rejecting a universal, 'one best way' approach to organisational structure and practice. They identified five different types of environment, based upon the level of uncertainty that was present, ranging from 'stable' to 'least predictable'. They also identified two basic or ideal forms of structure: 'Mechanistic' and 'Organic'. Their data showed that Mechanistic structures were more effective in stable environments, whilst Organic ones were better suited to less stable, less predictable environments.

The Mechanistic structure, which is akin to the Classical approach, has the following characteristics:

■ the specialisation of tasks;
■ closely defined duties, responsibilities and technical methods;
■ a clear hierarchical structure with insistence on loyalty to the organisation and obedience to superiors.

In contrast, the Organic form, which has some resemblance to the Human Relations approach, is characterised by:

■ much greater flexibility;
■ adjustment and continual redefinition of tasks;
■ a network structure of control, authority and communication;
■ lateral consultation based on information and advice rather than instructions and decisions;
■ commitment to the work group and its tasks;
■ importance and prestige being determined by an individual's contribution to the tasks of their work group rather than their position in the hierarchy.

As can be seen, Burns and Stalker neither reject nor accept what went before. Instead, they argued that both the Classical approach and the Human Relations approach can be appropriate, but that this depends on the nature of the environment in which the organisation is operating. In this respect, they not only built on the past rather than rejecting it, but also restored some responsibility to managers. Instead of being called on to adopt blindly the orthodoxy with regard to structure, managers would in future have to assess their organisation and its needs, and then adopt the structure and practices suitable to its situation (Child, 1984; Mullins, 1989; Scott, 1987).

■ Paul Lawrence and Jay Lorsch: the case for environment continued

Burns and Stalker's findings on the relationship between organisational environment and structure were examined and developed by a number of researchers in Europe and the USA. One of the most significant pieces of work was that carried out by Lawrence and Lorsch (1967) in the USA. Their work went beyond that of Burns and Stalker, in that they were interested not only in the relationship between environment and a company's overall structure, but also how individual departments within companies responded to, and organised themselves to cope with, aspects of the external environment that were of particular significance to them. They undertook a study of six firms in the plastics industry, followed by a further study of two firms in the container industry and two in the consumer foods industry. The structure of each of the firms was analysed in terms of its degree of 'differentiation' and 'integration'.

Differentiation refers to the degree to which managers and staff in their own functional departments see themselves as separate and have distinct practices, procedures and structures from others in the organisation. Integration refers to the level and form of collaboration that is necessary between departments in order to achieve their individual objectives within the environment in which the firm operates. Therefore, differentiation is the degree to which departments are distinct from each other, whilst integration refers to the degree to which they have common structures, procedures, practices and objectives at the operational level. Generally, the greater the interdependence among departments, the more integration is needed to coordinate their efforts in the best interests of the organisation as a whole; this may not always be easy to achieve, however. In a rapidly changing environment, the conditions faced by individual departments may differ greatly, and a high degree of differentiation may be necessary. In such a situation, the need for integration is also likely to be great, but the diversity and volatility of the environment are likely to make this difficult to achieve (Cummings and Huse, 1989).

In their study of the plastics industry, Lawrence and Lorsch (1967) found clear differentiation between key departments such as research, production and sales. Research departments were more concerned with long-term issues and were under pressure to produce new ideas and innovations. These departments, in Burns and Stalker's terminology, tended to adopt an Organic form of structure. Production departments on the other hand were, for obvious reasons, concerned with short-term performance targets relating to output, costs, quality and delivery. Such departments tended to operate in a fairly stable environment and had Mechanistic structures. Sales departments tended to fall in between research and production in terms of environment and structure. They operated in a moderately stable environment and were concerned more with getting production to meet deliveries than with long-term issues.

Whilst highlighting the degree of differentiation between key departments, the study also found that the degree of integration was critical to a firm's overall performance. Indeed, the two most successful firms in their sample were not only amongst the most highly differentiated, but also had the highest degree of integration. These findings were confirmed by their studies of the container and consumer foods industries, which showed that differentiation and integration in successful companies varies with the demands of the environment in which they operate. The more diverse and dynamic the environment, the more the successful organisation will be differentiated and highly integrated. In a more stable environment, the pressure for differentiation is less, but the need for integration remains. Therefore, Lawrence and Lorsch found that the most effective organisations had an appropriate fit between the design and coordination of departments and the amount of environmental uncertainty they faced. The most successful firms, however, were the ones that, whilst operating in an environment that required a high level of differentiation, also managed to achieve a high level of integration.

Clearly, in a situation where departments have dissimilar structures, practices and procedures, achieving integration is not easy or conflict-free. Indeed, in such situations, organisational politics can be rife. Lawrence and Lorsch found that the effective firms avoided such a situation by openly confronting conflict, and by working problems through in the context of the overall needs of the organisation. In addition, in firms that dealt successfully with conflict, the success of those responsible for achieving integration was based mainly on their knowledge and competence rather than their formal position. This was because their colleagues in the different departments respected and responded to their perceived understanding of the issues involved. It follows that to achieve high levels of integration and differentiation, an organisation cannot rely solely on the formal managerial hierarchy. This must be supplemented with liaison positions, task forces and teams, and other integrating mechanisms.

As with Burns and Stalker, Lawrence and Lorsch did not reject the Classical and Human Relations approaches *per se*, but instead saw them as alternative options, depending on the environment in which an organisation operates. In looking at the internal operations of organisations in this way, Lawrence and Lorsch raised the issue of dependence as well as uncertainty. This was a subject that James Thompson tackled in greater depth.

■ James Thompson: environmental uncertainty and dependence

Thompson's (1967) influential work took the environmental perspective forward in three important ways. The first was to argue that although organisations are not rational entities, they strive to be so because it is in the interests of those who design and manage the organisation that its work be carried out as effectively and efficiently as possible. In order to achieve this, organisations attempt to insulate their productive core from the uncertainty of the environment. However, it is not possible to seal off all, or perhaps even any, parts of an organisation, given that it must be open to and interact with its environment if it is to secure resources and sell its products. This leads on to Thompson's second major contribution: different levels of an organisation may exhibit, and need, different structures and operate on a more rational or less rational basis. Thompson's third contribution was to recognise that organisational effectiveness was contingent not only on the level of external environmental uncertainty, but also on the degree of internal dependence present. This echoes Lawrence and Lorsch's argument for integration and differentiation; however, Thompson made this point much more explicitly and related it to different structural forms. He formulated a three-type classification in relation to internal dependence:

■ **Pooled interdependence** – where each part of an organisation operates in a relatively autonomous manner, but by fulfilling their individual purposes they enable the organisation as a whole to function effectively.

- **Sequential interdependence** – where the outputs from one part of an organisation constitute the inputs for other parts of the system.
- **Reciprocal interdependence** – where overall effectiveness requires direct interaction between an organisation's separate parts.

Thompson went on to argue that the type of interdependence could be related to the degree of complexity present: simple organisations rely on pooled interdependence; more complex organisations demonstrate both pooled and sequential interdependence; and in the most complex organisations, all three forms of interdependence may be present. Thompson envisaged that each form of interdependence would require distinct methods for coordinating activities. Pooled interdependence would be characterised by standardisation through the use of rules and procedures. Sequential interdependence would require the use of detailed plans and written agreements, whilst reciprocal interdependence would achieve coordination by means of personal contact and informal agreements between members of those parts of the organisation involved.

Therefore, in a nutshell, Thompson's main arguments are as follows:

- Different sections of an organisation will be characterised by varying levels of complexity, rationality and formalisation, depending on the extent to which managers can shield them from the level of uncertainty present in the environment.
- The higher both the overall level of uncertainty and that faced by each area of an organisation, the greater will be the dependence of one area on another.
- As this interdependence increases, coordination through standardised procedures and planning mechanisms will become less effective and the need for more personal contact and informal interaction will grow.
- The more that coordination is achieved through mutual reciprocity in this manner, the less rational will be the operation of the organisation.

Thompson's work is of seminal importance in the development of organisation theory, not only because of the case he made for linking external uncertainty to internal dependence, but also, as a number of writers have observed (*see* Robbins, 1987; Scott, 1987), because of the attention he drew to the fact that technology can influence organisation structures as well as environmental factors. Thompson's contribution in this respect lay in creating a classification scheme for technology, and arguing that technology determines the selection of the specific structural arrangements for reducing the effect of uncertainty on the various functions of an organisation. The issue of technology and structure had been raised earlier in a major study by Joan Woodward published in 1965.

Joan Woodward: the case for technology

In the 1960s, Joan Woodward carried out a major study of 100 UK manufacturing firms in south-east Essex, in order to establish the validity of the claims made by advocates of the Classical approach that the adoption of a bureaucratic-mechanistic structure was essential for organisational success (Woodward, 1965, 1970). After much work, Woodward concluded that no such correlation existed; what she found, however, was that the more successful companies adopted an organisational form that varied according to their main production technology. By technology, Woodward meant not only the machinery being used, but also the way it was organised, operated and integrated into a distinct production process. From her sample, she identified three distinct types of production technology, ranging from least to most complex:

- **Small batch (or unit) production** – where customers' requirements were for one-off or small-volume specialist products.
- **Large batch (or mass) production** – where standardised products were made in large numbers to meet a forecast demand.
- **Process production** – where production was in a continuous flow, such as an oil refinery.

When the firms were grouped in this manner, a pattern emerged that showed that though they apparently differed considerably in terms of their organisational structure, many of the variations for the more successful firms could be explained by reference to the technology employed. Among firms engaged in small batch production, the most appropriate structure appeared to be one with relatively few hierarchical levels and wide middle management spans of control. Woodward noted that technology became more complex as firms moved from small batch to large batch and finally process production. In turn, structures became taller and more narrowly based, with smaller middle management and larger chief executive spans of control. Within each category of technology, the best-performing companies were those closest to the median in the type of structure adopted. Therefore, Woodward's work clearly established a link between technology, structure and success which ran counter to the notion that there was a 'one best way' for all organisations.

Though qualified by later studies (*see* Child, 1984; Handy, 1986; Smith *et al*, 1982), Woodward's research remains a milestone in the development of Contingency Theory. In particular, she demonstrated the need to take into account technological variables in designing organisations, especially in relation to spans of control. Nevertheless, a major drawback of her work was the difficulty of applying it to non-manufacturing companies. This was remedied by the work of Charles Perrow.

Charles Perrow: the case for technology continued

In the USA, Charles Perrow (1967, 1970) extended Joan Woodward's work on technology and organisation structure by drawing attention to two major dimensions of technology:

- the extent to which the work being carried out is variable or predictable;
- the extent to which the technology can be analysed and categorised.

The first, *variability*, refers to the incidence of exceptional or unpredictable occurrences, and the extent to which these problems are familiar and can be easily dealt with, or are unique and difficult to solve. For example, an oil refinery should experience few non-routine occurrences, whilst an advertising agency will encounter many unpredictable and exceptional occurrences. The second major dimension, *analysis and categorisation*, refers to the extent to which the individual task functions can be broken down and tightly specified, and also whether problems can be solved by recourse to recognised, routine procedures or if non-routine procedures have to be invoked. Bringing these two major dimensions of technology together, Perrow constructed a technology continuum ranging from routine to non-routine. With the latter, there are a large number of exceptional occurrences requiring difficult and varied problem-solving techniques to overcome them. Routine technology, on the other hand, throws up few problems, which can be dealt with by recourse to standard, simple techniques.

Perrow argued that by classifying organisations according to their technology and predictability (routine to non-routine) of work tasks, it is then possible to identify the most effective form of structure in any given situation or for any activity. Perrow's routine–non-routine continuum can be equated with Burns and Stalker's mechanistic and organic dimensions for organisation structures. In routine situations, where few problems arise and those that do are easily dealt with, a mechanistic structure is more effective because of the stable and predictable nature of the situation. In a dynamic and unpredictable situation, however, a more flexible, organic form of structure will be more effective in dealing with the non-routine and difficult problems that occur. By formulating his work in this manner (i.e. by combining technology and predictability) it became possible to apply it to non-manufacturing situations. Therefore, Perrow's work both reinforced and extended Woodward's case for recognising technology as a key situational variable to be taken into account when designing organisations. Nevertheless, whilst Perrow was developing his ideas, a further group of researchers were making the case for yet another 'key' contingency – size.

The Aston Group: the case for size

Though there are many proponents of the case for organisational size being a key contingency (see Child, 1984; Robbins, 1987), perhaps the earliest and most ardent were a group of British researchers based at the University of Aston in Birmingham (who became known as the Aston Group). In the 1960s, they carried out a series of studies to examine and identify the relationship between different forms of organisational structures and their determinants (see Pugh et al, 1969a, 1969b). The Aston Group began in the early 1960s by examining a sample of 87 companies, and, as the work developed, further samples were added to their eventually very impressive database. In analysing their results, the Aston Group found that size was the most powerful predictor of specialisation, use of procedures and reliance on paperwork. In effect, what they found was that the larger the organisation, the more likely it was to adopt (and need) a mechanistic (bureaucratic) structure. The reverse was also found: the smaller the organisation, the more likely it was to adopt (and need) an organic (flexible) structure.

This was clearly a major finding. Not only did it support (at least in terms of larger organisations) Weber's earlier work on bureaucracy, but it also struck a blow against those, such as Bennis, who saw bureaucracy as dysfunctional and dying. The work of the Aston Group, along with that of others such as Blau and Schoenherr (1971), who also argued that size is the most important condition affecting the structure of organisations, gave bureaucracy if not a new lease of life then, at least, a new lease of respectability. Bureaucracy, according to the Aston results, was both efficient and effective, at least for larger organisations; and, given the tendency for the average size of private-sector companies and public bodies to increase throughout the twentieth century, its applicability would grow.

There are two explanations for the relationship between size and bureaucracy, both of which have similar implications for organisational efficiency and effectiveness. The first argues that increased size offers greater opportunities for specialisation – the Adam Smith argument, in effect. This will manifest itself in terms of greater structural differentiation and a high degree of uniformity amongst sub-units. In the first instance, this will make managerial coordination more difficult, especially with the emergence of functional autonomy. To counter this, senior managers will move to impose a system of impersonal controls through the use of formal procedures, standardised reporting and control systems, the written recording of information, etc. The second argument reaches similar conclusions, by pointing out that the difficulty of directing ever larger numbers of staff makes it highly inefficient to continue to use a personalised, centralised style of management. Instead a more decentralised system, using impersonal control mechanisms, has to be adopted. The introduction of such a system inevitably leads to the expansion of the administrative core (the bureaucracy) in organisations (Child, 1984).

As with all the Contingency theorists, those who argued for size as the key situational variable were not attempting to reinvent the 'one best way' approach for *all* organisations. Rather they were rejecting it in favour of an approach that saw organisational performance as dependent upon the appropriateness of the organisation's structure for its size. Therefore, like all the Contingency theorists, the Aston school adopted an approach which stressed that there is a 'one best way' for *each* organisation.

■ Contingency Theory: summary and criticisms

The Contingency approach can be considered much more a cohesive school of thought than either the Classical or Human Relations approaches. It has three unifying themes:

- organisations are open systems;
- structure, and therefore performance, is dependent upon the particular circumstances, situational variables, faced by each organisation;
- there is no 'one best way' for all organisations.

The attractions of Contingency Theory are obvious. First, it was in tune with the times in which it emerged – the 1960s and 1970s. This was a period of rapid economic and technological change, with a tendency towards much larger organisations, and a significant increase in domestic and international competition. In this situation, Contingency Theory offered a plausible explanation of not only why these events were causing problems for organisations, but also how to resolve them (Burnes, 1989). Second, on the surface at least, it was simpler to understand and apply than the Human Relations approach. Finally, whilst rejecting the Classical approach, it was, in the main, a rational approach, based on matching known structural options to identifiable contingencies – size, technology and environment.

The approach to change management offered by Contingency Theory was, it follows, similar to that of the Classical school. In a rational fashion, managers should collect and analyse data on the situational variables the organisation faces and match these to the appropriate structural option. The theory then implies that for employees, faced with a plan for change based on such a 'scientific' approach, the only rational course of action is to accept the validity of the situation and cooperate with managers to achieve the required structural changes. However, it is at this point – the attempt to apply Contingency Theory rationally and mechanically – that problems and drawbacks emerge which give rise to a number of major criticisms of this approach, the main ones being as follows:

■ Difficulty arises in relating structure to performance. A number of writers have pointed out that there is no agreed definition of 'good performance', and it therefore becomes difficult to show that linking structure to situational variables brings the benefits claimed (Hendry, 1979, 1980; Mansfield, 1984; Terry, 1976). Indeed, there are a wide range of factors other than structure which can influence performance, not least of which is luck. Davis and Star (1993) showed that seven of the twelve most profitable firms in the world are pharmaceutical companies, and that three of these are producers of anti-ulcer drugs. They conclude that the profitability of the pharmaceutical sector is attributable less to the nature of these organisations than to governments' over-generosity – clearly a case of an industry that is in the right place at the right time.

■ Despite the length of time that Contingency Theory has been in circulation, there is still no agreed or unchallenged definition of the three key situational variables – environment, technology and size. The literature gives a wide and conflicting range of definitions of these, making it difficult not only to establish a link between them and structure, but also to apply the theory (Dastmalchian, 1984; Mullins, 1989; Pugh and Hickson, 1976; Robbins, 1987; Warner, 1984; Wood, 1979).

■ Whilst, as argued above, a relationship has been established between size and structure, it has proved difficult to show that this relationship has an appreciable impact on performance. Some researchers have suggested that the link between size and structure relates to preferred systems of control, which may have more to do with the political and cultural nature of organisations than any attempt to improve performance (Allaire and Firsirotu, 1984; Child, 1984; Mansfield, 1984; Pugh and Hickson, 1976; Salaman, 1979).

■ In examining the link between structure and contingencies, researchers use the organisation's formal organisational structure for comparison purposes. Yet, as the Hawthorne Experiments showed, the actual operation of an organisation may depend more on the informal structures created by workers than the formal ones laid down by management. This was a point made by Woodward (1965) in her study of technology and structure. She noted that organisation charts failed to show important relationships that, taken together, can have a significant impact on performance (Argyris, 1973; Burawoy, 1979; Selznick, 1948).

■ Structure and associated practices and policies may be strongly influenced by external forces (Mullins, 1993). In the UK, privatised utilities are subject to regulation and face restrictions that have a significant influence on how they are structured and operate. Similarly, in the UK, financial service organisations are required to establish 'Chinese walls' between different parts of their business to avoid market-sensitive information being passed from one area to another.

■ Rather than managers being the virtual prisoners of organisational contingencies when making decisions regarding structure, the reverse may be the case. Managers may have a significant degree of choice and influence over not only structure but also the situational variables. Whether this is called 'strategic choice' (Child, 1972), 'organisational choice' (Trist et al, 1963) or 'design space' (Bessant, 1983), the meaning is the same: those senior managers responsible for such decisions can exercise a high degree of freedom in selecting and influencing the technology to be used, the environment in which they operate and even the size of the organisation. Indeed, one of the architects of the technology-structure hypothesis, Charles Perrow, later claimed that technology is chosen and designed to maintain and reinforce existing structures and power relations within organisations rather than the reverse (Perrow, 1983). Other writers made the case for size and environment being manipulated in similar ways (Abell, 1975; Clegg, 1984; Hendry, 1979; Leifer and Huber, 1977; Lorsch, 1970).

■ It is assumed that organisations pursue clear-cut, well-thought-out, stable and compatible objectives that can be fitted into a Contingency perspective. Researchers and practising managers argue that this is not the case, however – in fact, even two of the proponents of Contingency Theory, Lawrence and Lorsch (1967), highlighted the presence and danger of conflicting objectives. In reality, objectives are often unclear, and organisations may pursue a number of conflicting goals at the same time. Clearly, the objectives of an organisation will impact on its situation and its structure. If these objectives are arbitrary, conflicting or open to managerial whim, it becomes difficult to apply a Contingency approach (Abodaher, 1986; Edwardes, 1983; Hamel and Prahalad, 1989; Mintzberg, 1987; Sloan, 1986).

■ The last criticism is that Contingency Theory is too mechanistic and deterministic, and ignores the complexity of organisational life. As argued by the Human Relations school, organisations are by no means the rational entities many would like to believe (a point also made by Thompson (1967) in his support of Contingency Theory). There is a need to see organisations as social systems, with all the cultural and political issues that this raises. In this view, structure is the product of power struggles between individuals and groups within the organisation, each arguing and fighting for their own perspective and position (Allaire and Firsirotu, 1984; Buchanan, 1984; Hickson and Butler, 1982; Morgan, 1986; Pfeffer, 1981; Robbins, 1987; Salaman, 1979).

Therefore, despite its attractiveness, Contingency Theory, like the Classical and Human Relations approaches, fails to provide a convincing explanation for the way in which organisations do and should operate.

Conclusions

For organisations, if not for academics, the key purpose of any organisation theory or approach is to help them analyse and rectify the weaknesses and problems of their current situation, and to assist them in bringing about the changes necessary to achieve their future objectives. Over the past 100 years, the design and management of organisations has moved from an *ad hoc* process based on – at best – guesswork, to one that is highly complex and informed by a host of practical and theoretical considerations. To the uninitiated, it might appear that this has made running organisations an easier and more certain process; yet a close examination of most organisations will reveal that this is far from being the case. Not only are organisations, in general, larger and more complex than in the past, but also the practical and theoretical reference points on which managers can draw are diverse and give conflicting and confusing signals.

Not surprisingly in such a situation, many managers look for simple, foolproof solutions: often ones that, as Douglas McGregor noted, appeal to their own basic orientation – whether that be Theory X or Theory Y. This is one of the reasons why the Classical approach, with its deep roots in the Industrial Revolution and its straightforward mechanical approach to organisations and their members, has proved so enduring – despite strong evidence of its lack of suitability in many situations. This search for simple, often quick-fix, solutions to the problems of organisational life has been manifested in many ways in the last two decades, not least the emergence of a series of 'panaceas' such as new technology, human resources management, Total Quality Management, culture change, etc. This is not to deny the benefits these can bring but, taken on their own, at best they encourage a fragmented approach, and at worst they create an atmosphere of resignation within organisations as one 'flavour of the month' is succeeded by yet another, and none is given the time necessary to prove itself. Clearly, in such situations, without an overall, long-term plan, the result of these various 'solutions' is to make the situation worse rather than better (Burnes, 1991; Burnes and Weekes, 1989).

Organisations clearly need to reject a short-term piecemeal approach, and instead see themselves in their totality and adopt a consistent and long-term approach. But which approach should they choose? We have seen in this and the previous chapter that well-thought-out and well-supported cases exist for a number of different approaches, but each has its drawbacks and critics. It may well be that each is capable of assisting organisations to analyse and understand the strengths and weaknesses of their present situation. Whether they can provide more effective organisational arrangements for the future is more debatable, however. Similarly, it is not obvious how organisations should actually achieve the process of transformation.

The Human Relations movement offers pertinent advice with regard to having clear objectives, good communication and leadership, but is less forthcoming on how change objectives should be set, and the concomitant changes planned and implemented. Contingency Theory though does give a procedure for setting objectives. It stresses the need to identify and analyse the situational variables an organisation faces in order to choose the most appropriate structure. However, it is also silent on the issues of planning and implementation, other than to imply that rational workers will accept rational propositions for change. In addition, even if organisations do manage to implement the recommendations of the Human Relations or Contingency advocates, it is not clear what degree of benefit they would derive from this, given the criticisms of these approaches.

In short, neither of the approaches discussed in this chapter appears to be the solution to all known organisational ills that their proponents seem to claim. They fail to reflect and explain the complexities of day-to-day organisational life that we all experience. In particular, the issue of organisational culture (Allaire and Firsirotu, 1984) gets short shrift; yet, over the last two decades, its importance as both a promoter of and a barrier to organisational competitiveness has become apparent. Nor do they appear to take account of national differences and preferences, or for that matter pay regard to many of the wider societal factors that now impact on our lives, such as the need to show greater social responsibility, whether it be in the area of 'green' issues or equal opportunities. Yet, it is clear that enormous changes are already taking place in the world, and others may be necessary if some of the worst predictions for the future are to be avoided. The next chapter describes three new perspectives on organisational life that, as the old approaches are perceived as inadequate, have become increasingly influential.

Test your learning

■ Short answer questions

1   What were the main findings of the Hawthorne Experiments?

2   Describe Maslow's hierarchy of needs.

3   Briefly discuss Theory X and Theory Y.

4   State Bennis' reasons for declaring the 'Death of Bureaucracy'.

5   Define the term 'contingency' as used by Burns and Stalker.

6   What are the respective attributes of Mechanistic and Organic structures?

7   How did Perrow define technology?

8   According to the Aston Group, size is the key contingency; state their case for this assertion.

9   For each of the following, briefly state its implications for organisational change: (a) Human Relations and (b) Contingency Theory.

■ Essay questions

1   In what ways can the Human Relations approach be said to be superior to the Classical approach?

2   In what manner can Contingency Theory be said to incorporate both the Classical and Human Relations approaches?

Suggested further reading

1   Rose, M (1988) *Industrial Behaviour*. Penguin: Harmondsworth.
    Michael Rose gives an invaluable account of the development of the Human Relations movement and provides an interesting review of the work of Joan Woodward and the Aston Group.

2   Sheldrake, J (1996) *Management Theory: From Taylorism to Japanization*. International Thompson Business Press: London.
    Michael Sheldrake also provides an excellent review of the lives and work of the key figures in the Human Relations movement.

3   Hendry, C (1979) Contingency Theory in practice, I. *Personnel Review*, 8(4), 39–44.
    Hendry, C (1980) Contingency Theory in practice, II. *Personnel Review*, 9(1), 5–11.
    Wood, S (1979) A reappraisal of the contingency approach to organization. *Journal of Management Studies*, **16**, 334–54.
    Taken together, these three articles provide an excellent review of Contingency Theory.

Chapter 3

In search of new paradigms

Learning objectives

After studying this chapter, you should be able to:

- understand the reasons for the emergence of new organisational paradigms in the 1980s and 1990s;
- describe the principal features of the Culture–Excellence approach;
- list the core advantages and disadvantages of the Culture–Excellence approach;
- describe the central elements of the Japanese approach to management;
- understand the key advantages and disadvantages of the Japanese approach;
- discuss the main features of organisational learning;
- appreciate the chief advantages and disadvantages of organisational learning;
- compare the similarities and differences between Culture–Excellence, organisational learning and Japanese management;
- appreciate the implications for organisational change of these three paradigms.

Exhibit 3.1	Continuous improvement

The sustainable business: continuous search for improvement

Kaizen is a Japanese word usually translated as 'continuous improvement'. It is an important component of Japanese management techniques such as Total Quality Management (TQM), and was central to the acclaimed Toyota Production System, developed under the guidance of engineers such as Ohno Taiichi and Shingo Shigeo in the three decades following the second world war. In the 1980s the concept was imported (some would say re-imported) into the US and other Western countries, where it remains a widely discussed – if seldom fully implemented – philosophy.

Kaizen was probably best expressed by an early head of Toyota, Toyoda Sakichi (1867–1930), who declared that no process could ever be declared perfect and there was always room for improvement. Sakichi was a deep thinker, influenced not only by Buddhist philosophy but also by Self-Help, the manual written by the Victorian entrepreneur, Samuel Smiles, which was hugely popular around the world. Both these influences suggested to Sakichi that while perfection would always remain out of reach, in the process of striving for it, considerable good would result.

Kaizen was introduced as a driving philosophy behind improvements in both product and process, and ultimately it became embraced within the larger concept of TQM. In the former area, the early 1950s saw the introduction of American methods of statistical quality control (SQC), originally developed by Walter Shewhart at Bell Laboratories and introduced into Japan by two legendary figures, Joseph Juran and W Edwards Deming. SQC techniques were also popularised in Japan by the quality guru, Ishikawa Kaoru, and were eagerly adopted by many companies, Toyota among them.

Kaizen, as Sakichi said, is about constantly looking for improvement, not just on the shopfloor but across the company. Here an important defect in Western understanding of the concept emerges. Many Western managers continue to believe that kaizen and, more generally, TQM, are primarily production techniques; they have nothing to do with other areas. But TQM as developed at Toyota was all-embracing, including every department in the company. Ultimately, as Tom Peters and Robert Waterman noted in In Search of Excellence, the quest for continuous improvement should dominate the mindset of managers and workers alike. They need to search for improvement everywhere, and to do so, they must learn as much as they can about their work and the environment in which it is done. So the concept of the 'learning organisation' was born; a decade later, it had been worked out in detail by gurus such as Peter Senge and Arie de Geus. The two concepts, the learning organisation and kaizen, can thus be seen as closely linked.

The learning organisation searches continuously for new knowledge from which value can be created. Kaizen provides value through constant improvements in product and process quality, adding value for the company and its customers. Now more than 50 years old, kaizen is coming back into fashion.

Source: Morgen Witzel, *Financial Times*, 19 August 2002, p. 9.

Introduction

Organisations have come a long way from the days when Henry Ford could famously declare: 'A customer can have a car of any colour he wants, so long as it is black' (Witzel, 2003a: 113). Nowadays, the boot is on the other foot; it is a case of consumers dictating to organisations that they should meet their ever-changing tastes, and woe betide the company that fails to meet them. This is why, as Exhibit 3.1 illustrates, so much attention is now paid to continuous improvement. Indeed, such has been the change in attitudes in the past two decades that many now speak of organisations as having gone through a paradigm shift. If this is so, what do we mean by a paradigm shift and what brought it about? Although he did not invent the word, it was the American philosopher of science Thomas Kuhn (1962) who, in his book *The Structure of Scientific Revolutions*, gave a new importance to the notion of 'paradigms'. He defined a paradigm as a universally-recognised scientific achievement that over a period of time provides model problems and solutions to a community of practitioners. Kuhn was interested in how new ideas and frameworks for carrying out scientific work (i.e. paradigms) supplant old ones in the physical sciences. However, from the late 1960s onwards, a growing body of social scientists adopted the Kuhnian approach to their own disciplines with great enthusiasm. In the intervening period, as Burrell (1997) noted, new, varying, competing and controversial definitions of the term have been put forward. As far as its applicability to organisations is concerned, a paradigm can be defined as a way of looking at and interpreting the world; a framework of basic assumptions, theories and models that are commonly and strongly accepted and shared within a particular field of activity at a particular point in time (Collins, 1998; Mink, 1992; Reed, 1992). However, as situations change and people's perceptions change, existing paradigms lose their relevance and new ones emerge. As Handy (1986: 389) noted:

> When Copernicus suggested that the earth was not at the centre of the universe he was, though he knew it not, a paradigm revolutionary. But it was the minds of men that changed, not the motions of the planets, and the way in which they now viewed that same universe had a profound effect on their beliefs, values and behaviour.

In the previous two chapters we have discussed the paradigms that, in the West at least, have emerged and become common currency in the field of management and organisation theory. Though these paradigms have their adherents as well as critics, increasingly managers have experienced real difficulties in achieving competitive success when applying them in today's turbulent, complex and diverse business world. In consequence, especially over the last two decades, both academics and practitioners have been searching for new recipes for organisational success.

It was in the USA that the search for new paradigms first became apparent. It was the rise of Japanese industrial and economic might that forced American businesses to question what they did and how they did it, as Morgan (1986: 111) observed:

> During the 1960s the confidence and impact of American management and industry seemed supreme. Gradually, but with increasing force, through the 1970s the performance of Japanese automobile, electronic, and other manufacturing industries began to change all this. Japan began to take command of international markets ...

The productivity gap between Japanese and American companies was starkly highlighted in a *Harvard Business Review* article by Johnson and Ouchi (1974). The authors claimed that Japanese workers, assembling the same product using the same technology, were some 15 per cent more productive than their American counterparts.

> For an American audience this was a shocking statement, confirming the worst fears of a decline in the USA's competitive edge over the rest of the world. Since the Second World War American manufacturers had grown accustomed to out-producing and out-performing every

foreign competitor. The era of the Cold War had led Americans to believe that the only danger to their general security sprang from communism and specifically the Soviet Union. The notion that their comprehensively vanquished enemies and strategic clients, the Japanese, might be poised to overhaul them technically and even economically was unpalatable, even unbelievable.

(Sheldrake, 1996: 185)

It was not only the USA that took fright; in the 1970s and 1980s, all over the Western world, businesses and governments too woke up to the Japanese challenge. Even West Germany, which prided itself on producing well-engineered and high-quality products such as BMW and Mercedes cars, found that the Japanese were producing cars such as the Lexus that were not only half the price, but also better-engineered and of far superior quality (Williams *et al*, 1991).

Nor was it just the Japanese challenge that frightened the West. The 1970s also saw the return of unemployment and inflation, both assumed to have been eliminated, and the occurrence of the two 'oil shocks', which highlighted most Western nations' precarious reliance on imported energy. Therefore, old certainties were being challenged and new orthodoxies began to arise. Rather like Copernicus, Japan made the West see the world, and its place in it, from a new perspective.

Organisations have become increasingly aware that in the last 20 years or so, the world has turned on its axis. The days of the mass production of standardised products appear to be over; the key words for the future are variety, flexibility and customisation. As Perez (1983) and Freeman (1988) argued, a new techno-economic rationale is emerging. This new rationale has three main features:

- A shift towards information-intensive rather than energy- or materials-intensive products.
- A change from dedicated mass production systems towards more flexible systems that can accommodate a wider range of products, smaller batches and more frequent design changes – 'economies of scale' are being replaced by 'economies of scope'.
- A move towards the greater integration of processes and systems within companies and between suppliers and customers, which permits a more rapid response to market and customer requirements.

These developments have been given a variety of names. In the 1970s, Daniel Bell (1973) heralded 'The Coming of Post-Industrial Society'. In the 1980s, other writers spoke of the 'post-Fordist' or 'post-Taylorist' era (Whitaker, 1992). Increasingly, in the 1990s, the term 'postmodernism' was used to describe the changes taking place in the world in general and organisations in particular (Hassard, 1993). These terms, particularly the debate around postmodernism and its alternatives, will be discussed in Chapter 4. For now, however, what we need to recognise is that it is not necessarily that the nature of organisations themselves has changed fundamentally, though significant changes in size, technology and complexity have certainly taken place. It is rather that, like those who listened to Copernicus, we are seeing their role in the established order from a different perspective and beginning to see new possibilities and new challenges.

It is the emergence of these new possibilities and challenges that has motivated Western organisations to undertake a fundamental reassessment of their objectives and operations, rather than a mere change in fashion or managerial whim – though this is obviously present as well (Huczynski, 1993; Kennedy, 1994). In effect, what we can see from the beginning of the 1980s is the emergence of a paradigm shift, or, to be more accurate, the search for new, more appropriate paradigms. It seemed as if the changes taking place in the business environment were so enormous and rapid that existing paradigms, whatever their past merits, were breaking down and new ones emerging.

In this chapter, we examine the three proto-paradigms that have come to dominate Western managerial thinking and writing over the last two decades: the Culture–Excellence approach, the Japanese Management approach and the Organisational Learning approach. As Exhibit 3.1 shows, there is a tendency to link them together or treat them as though they are largely the same. As this chapter will show, however, they are distinct approaches to running organisations with different origins and differing implications for management. Culture–Excellence arose as an attempt to counter Japanese competitiveness by drawing on and re-shaping the American and British traditions of individualism and free market liberalism. It emerged in the early 1980s, and its principal exponents (Tom Peters and Robert Waterman, 1982; Rosabeth Moss Kanter, 1989; and Charles Handy, 1989) have attempted both to predict and to promote the ways in which successful (excellent) companies will and should operate in the future.

The Japanese Management paradigm is a very different animal. It has been developed in Japan over the last 50 years, and not only is it being extensively practised there, but, at least until recently, its success was not disputed. Because of the success of the Japanese economy and Japanese companies in the 1960s, 1970s and 1980s, the Japanese approach attracted much interest in the West – a classic case of 'if you can't beat them, join them'. This was especially the case in the UK, where Japanese inward investment (by household names such as Honda, Nissan and Toyota) generated a great deal of debate regarding the impact and merits of 'Japanisation' (Ackroyd *et al*, 1988; Dale and Cooper, 1992; Hannam, 1993; Turnbull, 1986; Whitehill, 1991). This was also the case in the USA, where Japan and Japanese methods were seen, in turn, as either a threat or a lifeline to American industrial pre-eminence (Kanter *et al*, 1992; Pascale and Athos, 1982; Peters, 1993; Schonberger, 1982).

The third approach, organisational learning, came to the fore in the early 1990s. Leading management thinkers, in particular Chris Argyris (1992), have been interested in organisational learning for over 40 years. However, it is only in the last 15 years that the concept has become popularised as an engine for organisational competitiveness through the work of Senge (1990) in the USA and Pedler, Boydell and Burgoyne (1989) in the UK. One of the key benefits claimed for organisational learning is that it is a universal approach which draws on and is consistent with both Western and Japanese organisational traditions (Hedlund and Nonaka, 1993; Probst and Buchel, 1997).

Though the Culture–Excellence and Japanese approaches have some similarities, for example the resemblance between the Japanese passion for quality and the Culture–Excellence school's fervent advocacy of the pursuit of excellence, the two also have significant differences, as will be shown. Whilst the Japanese approach has clearly influenced the Culture–Excellence thinkers, the influence of the latter in Japan has been small. The two may be competing approaches in the West, but certainly not in Japan. Nevertheless, both are dynamic and developing paradigms, with some common elements, and consequently a merging or a blending of the two in the West is not beyond all possibilities. The organisational learning approach, though it draws on both Western and Japanese organisational traditions, is by no means an attempt to fuse or merge the Culture–Excellence and Japanese approaches. Instead, it represents yet another attempt to provide Western countries, particularly the USA, with an approach to managing organisations that will allow them in the twenty-first century to enjoy the sort of dominance they enjoyed for much of the twentieth century.

Nevertheless, it will be argued in the conclusion to this chapter that, although these three proto-paradigms offer new possibilities, they also raise familiar controversies, not least regarding the role and treatment of people. Therefore, as the following discussion of the three approaches will show, whilst attempting to become new paradigms, they still have to answer old questions.

The Culture–Excellence approach

Though predominantly a North American perspective, the Culture–Excellence approach has also found its adherents in Europe. Therefore, the examination of this approach will draw on the work of key writers from both sides of the Atlantic, namely Tom Peters and Robert Waterman, Rosabeth Moss Kanter and Charles Handy. The writers are all practising and internationally-recognised management consultants; Handy and Kanter are distinguished academics as well. Consequently, though their work is attempting to predict and promote the way firms will or should operate in the future, it is firmly based on what they believe the best companies are doing now or planning to do in the future.

These three perspectives formed the spearhead of the movement that simultaneously charted and created the new organisational forms that have begun to appear over the last 20 years. Their work – though both complementary and distinct – is of profound influence in shaping our understanding of what the future holds in the field of management. This work will now be examined in detail, starting with the American perspectives of Peters and Waterman, and Kanter, and concluding with Handy's British perspective.

■ Tom Peters and Robert Waterman's search for excellence

Tom Peters has been, arguably, the most influential management consultant of the last two decades. His books sell in millions, his seminars fill auditoriums, and his newspaper column is syndicated across the world. He is also said to be one of the highest-paid management consultants in the world, reputedly charging some US$25,000 per seminar back in 1987 (Huczynski, 1993). He catapulted to international fame when he co-authored, along with Robert Waterman, *In Search of Excellence: Lessons from America's Best-Run Companies* (Peters and Waterman, 1982), which is the best-selling management book of all time. It is difficult to overestimate the impact this book has had. At a time when Western economies were on the rocks and Japanese companies appeared to be sweeping all before them, *In Search of Excellence* seemed to offer a way, perhaps the only way, for Western companies to regain their competitiveness (Crainer, 1995).

Exhibit 3.2	The 7 S framework

Strategy: plan or course of action for the allocation of scarce resources in order to achieve specified goals.

Structure: the main features of the organisation chart and how the various parts of an organisation are linked.

Systems: the organisation's formalised procedures and processes.

Staff: the composition of the workforce, i.e. engineers, managers, etc.

Style: the behaviour of key managers and also the cultural style of the organisation.

Shared values: the guiding concepts and meanings that infuse the organisation's members.

Skills: the distinctive capabilities possessed by individuals, groups and the organisation as whole.

Source: Peters and Waterman (1982)

The origins of the book lie in a major study of the determinants of organisational excellence, which Peters and Waterman carried out when working for the management consultants McKinsey and Company. They used the now-famous McKinsey 7 S Framework (*see* Exhibit 3.2), which they had developed jointly with Richard Pascale and Anthony Athos, to study 62 of America's most successful companies.

Peters and Waterman concluded that it was the four 'soft' Ss (staff, style, shared values and skills) that held the key to business success. In stressing the 'soft' Ss, they challenged the rational theories of management described in previous chapters. They argue that the rational approach is flawed because it leads to the following:

- **Wrong-headed analysis** – situation or information analysis that is considered too complex and unwieldy to be useful. This is analysis that strives to be precise about the inherently unknowable.
- **Paralysis through analysis** – the application of the rational model to such an extent that action stops and planning runs riot.
- **Irrational rationality** – where rational management techniques identify the 'right' answer irrespective of its applicability to the situation in question.

In the light of these criticisms, Peters and Waterman argue that the analytical tools that characterise the rational approach should only be used as an aid to, rather than a substitute for, human judgment. They believe that it is the freedom given to managers and employees to challenge the orthodox and to experiment with different solutions which distinguishes the excellent companies from the also-rans. In place of the rational approach, Peters and Waterman argue that there are eight key attributes that organisations need to demonstrate if they are to achieve excellence:

1 A bias for action.
2 Close to the customer.
3 Autonomy and entrepreneurship.
4 Productivity through people.
5 Hands-on, value-driven.
6 Stick to the knitting.

7 Simple form, lean staff.

8 Simultaneous loose–tight properties.

These are discussed in more detail below.

1 A bias for action

One of the main identifiable attributes of excellent companies is their bias for action. Even though they may be analytical in approach, they also favour methods that encourage rapid and appropriate response. One of the methods devised for achieving quick action is what Peters and Waterman term 'chunking'. Chunking is an approach whereby a problem that arises in the organisation is first made manageable (i.e. broken into 'chunks') and then tackled by a small group of staff brought together specifically for that purpose. The main reason for the use of such groups, variously called project teams, task forces or quality circles, is to facilitate organisational fluidity and to encourage action. Key characteristics of these groups are as follows:

- They usually comprise no more than ten members.
- They are voluntarily constituted.
- The life of the group is usually between three and six months.
- The reporting level and seniority of the membership is appropriate to the importance of the problem to be dealt with.
- The documentation of the group's proceedings is scant and very informal.
- These groups take on a limited set of objectives, which are usually determined, monitored, evaluated and reviewed by themselves.

Chunking is merely one example of the bias for action that exists in excellent companies and reflects their willingness to innovate and experiment. These companies' philosophy for action is simple: 'Do it, fix it, try it.' Therefore, excellent companies are characterised by small, *ad hoc* teams applied to solving designated problems which have first been reduced to manageable proportions. Achieving smallness is the key, even though the subject or task may be large. Smallness induces manageability and a sense of understanding, and allows a feeling of ownership.

2 Close to the customer

Excellent companies really do get close to the customer, while others merely talk about it. The customer dictates product, quantity, quality and service. The best organisations are alleged to go to extreme lengths to achieve quality, service and reliability. There is no part of the business that is closed to customers. In fact, many of the excellent companies claim to get their best ideas for new products from listening intently and regularly to their customers. The excellent companies are more 'driven by their direct orientation to the customers rather than by technology or by a desire to be the low-cost producer. They seem to focus more on the revenue-generation side of their services' (Peters and Waterman, 1982: 197).

3 Autonomy and entrepreneurship

Perhaps the most important element of excellent companies is their 'ability to be big and yet to act small at the same time. A concomitant essential apparently is that they encourage the entrepreneurial spirit among their people, because they push autonomy markedly far down the line' (Peters and Waterman, 1982: 201). Product champions are allowed to come forward, grow and flourish. Such a champion is not a blue-sky dreamer, or an intellectual giant. The champion might even be an ideal thief. But above all, the champion is the pragmatist; the one who latches on to someone else's idea, and doggedly brings something concrete and tangible out of it.

In fostering such attitudes, the excellent companies have what they label 'championing systems', consisting of the following:

- **The product champion** – a zealot or fanatic who believes in a product.
- **A successful executing champion** – one who has been through the process of championing a product before.
- **The godfather** – typically, an ageing leader who provides the role model for champions.

The essence of this system is to foster, promote and sustain the budding entrepreneur. It is claimed that the three elements of the championing system are essential to its operation and credibility.

Another key part of this system is that, in some companies, product champions tend to be allocated their own 'suboptional divisions'. These are similar to small, independent businesses and comprise independent new venture teams, run by champions with the full and total support of senior management. The suboptional division is independent in that it is responsible for its own accounting, personnel activities, quality assurance and support for its product in the field. To encourage entrepreneurship further, teams, groups and divisions are highly encouraged by the companies' reward structures to compete amongst themselves for new projects.

Autonomy and entrepreneurship are also encouraged by the type of no-holds-barred communications procedures adopted by excellent companies. These exhibit the following characteristics:

- **Communication is informal** – even though there are lots of meetings going on at any one time, most meetings are informal and comprise staff from different disciplines gathering to talk about and solve problems.
- **The communication system is given both physical and material support** – blackboards, flip-charts and small tables that foster informal small group discussions are everywhere. The aim is to encourage people to talk about the organisation: what needs changing; what is going on; and how to improve things around the place. There are also people, variously described as dreamers, heretics, gadflies, mavericks or geniuses, whose sole purpose is to spur the system to innovate. Their job is to institutionalise innovation by initiating and encouraging experimentation. They can also call on staff in other divisions of the organisation to assist them in this process, as well as having financial resources at their disposal.
- **Communication is intensive** – given the freedom, the encouragement and the support (financial, moral and physical) in the organisations, it is no wonder that the level of communication between and amongst workers is not only informal and spontaneous but also intense. This is borne out by the common occurrence of meetings without agendas and minutes. Also, when presentations are made in these meetings, questioning of the proposal is unabashed and discussion is free and open. Those present are expected to be fully involved in such meetings and there are no 'sacred cows' that cannot be questioned.

This intense communication system also acts as a remarkably tight control system, in that people are always checking on each other to see how each is faring. This arises out of a genuine desire to keep abreast of developments in the organisation rather than any untoward motive. One result of this is that teams are more prudent in their financial expenditure on projects. Another is that the sea of inquisitors act as 'idea generators', thereby ensuring that teams are not dependent entirely on their own devices to innovate and solve problems. This usually also ensures that all options are considered before a final decision is made. The concomitant result of this fostering of creativity is that senior management is more tolerant of failure, knowing full well that champions have to make many tries, and consequently suffer some failures, in the process of creating successful innovations.

4 Productivity through people

A cherished principle of the excellent companies is that they treat their workers with respect and dignity; they refer to them as partners. This is because people, rather than systems or machines, are seen as the primary source of quality and productivity gains. Therefore, there is 'tough-minded respect for the individual and the willingness to train him, to set reasonable and clear expectations for him, and to grant him practical autonomy to step out and contribute directly to his job' (Peters and Waterman, 1982: 239). There is a closeness and family feeling in such companies; indeed many of the 'partners' see the organisation as an extended family. The slogans of such companies tend to reflect this view of people: 'respect the individual', 'make people winners', 'let them stand out', 'treat people as adults'.

5 Hands-on, value-driven

Excellent companies are value-driven; they are clear about what they stand for and take the process of value-shaping seriously. There is an implicit belief that everyone in the organisation, from the top to the bottom, should be driven by the values of the organisation; hence the great effort, time and money spent to inspire people by and inculcate them with these values:

> ... these values are almost always stated in qualitative, rather than quantitative, terms. When financial objectives are mentioned, they are almost always ambitious but never precise. Furthermore, financial and strategic objectives are never stated alone. They are always discussed in the context of the other things the company expects to do well. The idea that profit is a natural by-product of doing something well, and not an end in itself, is almost always universal.
> (Peters and Waterman, 1982: 284)

Implanting these values is a primary responsibility of the individual members of the management team. They set the tone by leading from the front. Coherence and homogeneity must, however, first be created among senior management by regular meetings (both formal and informal). The outcome of this is that management speak with one voice. They are passionate in preaching the organisation's values. They unleash excitement, not in their offices, but mainly on the shopfloor where the workers are. Inculcating these values, however, is a laborious process and persistence is vital in achieving the desired goal.

6 Stick to the knitting

Acquisition or internal diversification for its own sake is not one of the characteristics of excellent companies. They must stick to the knitting – do what they know best. But when they do acquire, they do it in an experimental fashion, by first 'dipping a toe in the water'. If the water does not feel good, they get out fast. Acquisitions are always in fields related to their core activities and they never acquire any business that they do not know how to run. As a general rule, they 'move out mainly through internally generated diversification, one manageable step at a time' (Peters and Waterman, 1982: 279).

7 Simple form, lean staff

A guiding principle in excellent companies is to keep things simple and small. Structurally, the most common form is the 'product division'. This form, which is rarely changed, provides the essential touchstone that everybody understands and from which the complexities of day-to-day life can be approached. Since the use of teams, groups and task forces for specific projects is a common stock-in-trade of these companies, most changes in structure are made at the edges, such as by allocating one or two people to an *ad hoc* team. By adopting this approach, the basic structure is left in place, while all other things revolve and change around it. This gives these organisations great flexibility but still enables them to keep their structures simple, divisionalised and autonomous.

Such simple structures only require a small, lean staff at the corporate and middle management levels. This results in there being fewer administrators and more doers: ' ... it is not uncommon to find a corporate staff of fewer than 100 people running a multi-billion-dollar enterprise' (Peters and Waterman, 1982: 15). Therefore, in excellent companies, flat structures, with few layers, and slimmed-down bureaucracies – which together allow flexibility and rapid communication – are the order of the day.

8 Simultaneous loose–tight properties

This is the 'firm and free' principle. On the one hand, it allows the excellent companies to control everything tightly, whilst on the other hand allowing and indeed encouraging individual innovation, autonomy and entrepreneurship. These properties are jointly achieved through the organisation's culture – its shared values and beliefs. By sharing the same values, self-control and self-respect result in each person becoming their own, and everyone else's, supervisor. The individual members of the organisation know they have the freedom, and are encouraged, to experiment and innovate. They also know that their actions will be scrutinised and judged, however, with the utmost attention paid to the impact they have on product quality, targets and, above all, the customer. The focus is on building and expanding the frontiers of the business. The ultimate goal is to be the best company, and in the final analysis, this is the benchmark against which the discipline and flexibility of the individual will be measured.

Therefore, Peters and Waterman maintain that the main attributes of excellent companies are flat, anti-hierarchical structures; innovation and entrepreneurship; small corporate and middle management staffs; reward systems based on contribution rather than position or length of service; brain power rather than muscle power; and strong, flexible cultures.

Peters and Waterman's vision of the organisation of the future, based on their study of leading American companies, has proved extremely influential, not only in the business world but in academia as well. This is not to say (as will be shown later) that they are without their critics; however, there is little doubt that they laid the groundwork, especially in highlighting the important role played by culture, for other leading thinkers whose work draws on and gels with theirs.

Their vision of the future has not stood still. Peters formed his own consultancy, The Tom Peters Group, and has used this as a vehicle for developing and implementing the Culture–Excellence approach. Though not fundamentally changing his view of the need for excellent organisations, in *Thriving on Chaos* (Peters, 1989) he argued that none existed in the USA. In *Liberation Management* (Peters, 1993), he placed more emphasis on the need to break organisations into smaller, more independent, more flexible units. Only by doing this, he argued, would managers be 'liberated', and thus able to achieve their – and their organisation's – full potential. In this book, Peters maintains that the age of the large corporations such as IBM and General Motors is over. He sees such companies as outmoded and uncompetitive dinosaurs, which are doomed to extinction unless they change rapidly and irreversibly. Peters argues that only rapid structural change can create the conditions for entrepreneurial cultures to emerge that both liberate managers and empower workers. Indeed, this book is nothing short of an out-and-out attack on the very existence of corporate America.

The Circle of Innovation: You Can't Shrink Your Way to Greatness (Peters, 1997a) is perhaps his most iconoclastic book. Even the format of the book is different from what has gone before. Indeed, its use of a multitude of different images, font types and font sizes and, in some cases, almost surreal page layouts, makes it more like a pop video than a traditional book. The message could not be clearer: just as this book is innovative in its format, so organisations must be innovative if they are to survive. His attack on present and past organisational practices, stability and any sense of permanence is keener and more vitriolic than ever. Professionalism, rules, balance, propriety, logic and consensus are all outmoded concepts, he argues. Peters (1997a: 76) quotes Dee Hock, founder of the Visa Network, who said: 'The problem is never how to get new, innovative thoughts into your mind, but how to get the old ones out.' For Peters, organisational forgetting is far more important than organisational learning. Future success, he argues, is not related to what an organisation has done in the past, nor what is bringing it success now, but how innovative they will be in identifying new products, services and markets. He makes a strong, almost messianic, plea for organisations to centre themselves on innovation. Peters argues that innovation demands obsession, tension, being provocative, and having no market peers looking over your shoulder. As firms achieve parity in terms of quality and costs, he believes that only a constant commitment to being different, to continuous innovation, will allow companies to differentiate themselves from their competitors. Just as quality was seen as everyone's job in the 1980s, so Peters maintains that innovation must also become everyone's job now. In terms of structure, organisations must adopt a network or even a virtual structure, where small groups and even individuals have the freedom to self-manage themselves, to make connections and break connections as they see fit. Indeed, the subtitle of this book could well be 'Anarchy Rules!'

Whereas in *In Search of Excellence*, he and Robert Waterman put forward their eight attributes of excellence, this book is structured around his 15 points on The Circle of Innovation, which are:

- Distance is dead.
- Destruction is cool.
- You can't live without an eraser.
- We are all Michelangelos.
- Welcome to the white-collar revolution.
- All values come from the professional services.
- The intermediary is doomed.
- The system is the solution.
- Create waves of lust.
- Tommy Hilfiger knows.
- Become a connoisseur of talent.
- It's a woman's world.
- Little things are the only things.
- Love all, serve all.
- We're here to live life out loud.

Trying to follow Peters' train of thought through his various books is like trying to catch mist – just when you think you have got it, it slips through your hands. Indeed, Peters (1997a: xv) takes pride in his inconsistency: '"They" call me inconsistent. I consider that a badge of honor.' Originally he saw the pursuit of 'excellence' as the only way to save corporate America from annihilation by its Japanese competitors (and thus maintaining the USA as the premier industrial nation). Then, in *Liberation Management*, Peters (1993) argued that corporate America needed to be destroyed in order for America to survive. The message from *The Circle of Innovation* is that, with the business world in a permanent state of chaos, the only way for any organisation to survive is by constantly reinventing itself through a ceaseless process of innovation and change.

Nevertheless, though he offers some new tools and techniques, and the tone of his work has become more strident and zealot-like over the years, in essence he is still promoting the concepts first developed in *In Search of Excellence*. The market is not simply the final arbiter of success, but the only arbiter. Meeting the ever-increasing appetite for instant gratification is the only way to survive. Innovation, i.e. autonomy and entrepreneurship, is now the prime attribute of excellence and the only guarantee of success. Peters' (1997a: 493) view of how organisations should be run is, perhaps, best summed up by a quotation he cites from the racing driver Mario Andretti: 'If things seem under control, you're just not going fast enough.'

Rosabeth Moss Kanter's post-entrepreneurial model

Kanter is one of America's leading management thinkers. As well as being a professor at the Harvard Business School and a former editor of the *Harvard Business Review*, she is also a leading and influential management consultant with her own company, Goodmeasure Inc., reputedly charging some $17,000 per hour for her services in 1987 (Huczynski, 1993). Her early work concerned Utopian communities, such as the Shakers, but she then went on to study business organisations. Kanter first came to prominence with her (1977) book, *Men and Women of the Corporation*. This was an intensive examination of corporate America, which she saw as bureaucratic, unimaginative and uninspiring. In her next book, *The Change Masters* (Kanter, 1983), she offered her personal recipe for overcoming what she saw as the malaise and lack of competitiveness of the USA. The book painted corporate America as being in transition; it recognised that the corporatism of the past no longer worked, but was not sure where the future lay. Kanter (1983) argued that it lay in American and not Japanese ideas, and particularly in unleashing individual dynamism through empowerment and greater employee involvement.

Though her earlier books were clearly in tune with Peters and Waterman's work, it is Kanter's (1989) *When Giants Learn To Dance: Mastering the Challenges of Strategy, Management, and Careers in the 1990s* that most complements and develops their work by attempting to define what organisations need to be like in the future if they are to be successful. Kanter called for a revolution in business management to create what she termed post-entrepreneurial organisations. She used this term:

> ... because it takes entrepreneurship a step further, applying entrepreneurial principles to the traditional corporation, creating a marriage between entrepreneurial creativity and corporate discipline, cooperation, and teamwork.   (Kanter, 1989: 9–10)

Kanter maintained that:

> If the new game of business is indeed like Alice-in-Wonderland croquet, then winning it requires faster action, more creative manoeuvring, more flexibility, and closer partnerships with employees and customers than was typical in the traditional corporate bureaucracy. It requires more agile, limber management that pursues opportunity without being bogged down by cumbersome structures or weighty procedures that impede action. Corporate giants, in short, must learn how to dance.   (Kanter, 1989: 20)

She argues that today's corporate elephants need to learn to dance as nimbly and speedily as mice if they are to survive in our increasingly competitive and rapidly-changing world. Companies must constantly be alert and on their guard, and keep abreast of their competitors' intentions. By evaluating the response of modern organisations to the demands placed upon them, Kanter produced her post-entrepreneurial model of how the organisation of the future should operate. She sees post-entrepreneurial organisations as pursuing three main strategies:

1 Restructuring to find synergies.
2 Opening boundaries to form strategic alliances.
3 Creating new ventures from within: encouraging innovation and entrepreneurship.

These are detailed below.

1 Restructuring to find synergies

Synergy occurs where the whole adds up to more than the sum of its constituent parts. In an age where resources are scarce, one of the priorities of organisations is to make every part of the business add value to the whole. The essence of this approach is to identify and concentrate on the core business areas and to remove all obstacles and impediments to their efficient and effective operation. Therefore, all non-core activities are eliminated, and authority is devolved to the appropriate levels of the business: those in the front line. In practice this means selling off a company's non-core activities and ensuring that what remains, especially at the corporate and middle management levels, is lean and efficient. Nevertheless, it is not sufficient merely to have a strategy of reducing the size of the organisational bureaucracy. Companies must also ensure that the essential tasks that these people previously carried out are still undertaken. This can be accomplished in a number of ways, such as the use of computers to carry out monitoring and information-gathering; devolving greater responsibility and power down to individual business units; and contracting out services and tasks previously carried out in-house.

The result is to create flatter, more responsive and less complex organisations that have a greater degree of focus than in the past. Kanter argues that such radical changes need to be well planned, however, and executed with care and in a way that ensures that employee motivation is increased, not eliminated.

2 Opening boundaries to form strategic alliances

With the slimming-down of the organisation and the contracting-out of some of its functions, there arises the need to pool resources with other organisations; to band together to exploit opportunities and to share ideas and information. These alliances take three forms: service alliances, opportunistic alliances and stakeholder alliances. The first, a service alliance, is where two or more organisations form a cross-company consortium to undertake a special project with a limited lifespan. Such alliances are usually considered when the resources of the various partners are insufficient to allow them to undertake the project by themselves. For this reason, and not surprisingly, many such alliances involve research and development (R&D) projects. The collaboration between Ford and General Motors on research into the development of new materials for making cars is an example of this. This approach allows organisations to mobilise resources, often on a large scale, whilst limiting their exposure and protecting their independence. It is the limited purpose of the consortium that makes it possible even for competitors to join together for their mutual benefit.

The second form, an opportunistic alliance, comprises a joint venture whose aim is to take advantage of a particular opportunity that has arisen: ' ... the two principal advantages behind this kind of alliance are competence-enhancing ones: technology transfer or market access or both' (Kanter, 1989: 126). An example of such an alliance was the link-up between the Rover Group and Honda Motors; the former gained access to Japanese know-how, whilst the latter gained greater access to the European market. However, as Kanter (1989: 126) pointed out, such alliances are not always equally beneficial: ' ... once one of the partners has gained experience with the competence of the other, the alliance is vulnerable to dissolution – the opportunity can now be pursued without the partner.'

The third form, a stakeholder alliance, unlike the previous two, is seen as a continuing, almost permanent partnership between an organisation and its key stakeholders, generally considered to be its employees, customers and suppliers. There is a growing awareness among employees, trade unions and management of the need to see each other as partners in the same enterprise rather than rivals. A similar case is made for treating customers and suppliers as partners too. The main reason for the organisation to exist is to serve its customers; therefore, there is a need to keep close to them, not only to be aware of their present concerns and future needs, but also to gain ideas regarding potential joint product development. In the same way, the organisation relies on its suppliers, who will in any case want to get closer to them as their customers. Stakeholder alliances have gained a growing band of adherents in Britain in recent years, especially, though not exclusively, amongst Japanese companies such as Nissan Motors (Partnership Sourcing Ltd, 1991a; Wickens, 1987). As Kanter points out, major innovations in technology and organisational systems require longer-term investments. Companies can only enter into such investments if they are secure in the knowledge that their key stakeholders are themselves committed to the same aims and approach.

The result of these alliances is that structures and positions within organisations will change, sometimes quite dramatically. This is especially the case amongst senior and line managers, but even previously protected groups – such as R&D specialists – will also see their roles and responsibilities change. They will have to work more closely not only with colleagues internally, but also with external groupings.

3 Creating new ventures from within – encouraging innovation and entrepreneurship

Traditional organisations face a difficult balancing act between gaining the full benefits from existing mainstream business, and, at the same time, creating new activities that will become the mainstream business of the future. Kanter argues that there is a feeling in many traditional companies that opportunities are being missed owing to their inability to give staff the flexibility to pursue new ideas and develop new products. The job of creating new products or ventures used to be the sole domain of the strategic planners or the R&D departments. However, in the post-entrepreneurial organisation, this will no longer be the case: innovation will move from these specialised domains to the centre stage. As the case studies in Part 3 will show, some organisations are deliberately forming new, independent units or entirely restructuring themselves to nurture innovation and entrepreneurship. New cultures are being created which encourage and aid innovation, and old barriers and restrictions are being eradicated. As a result of such changes, the innovative potential of employees is being tapped, and a proliferation of new ideas, products and ways of working is emerging.

■ The consequences of the post-entrepreneurial model

There is no doubt that the post-entrepreneurial model carries profound implications for both organisations and their employees. However, Kanter, unlike Peters and Waterman, does not see these new developments as being an unalloyed blessing, especially in the case of employees. In particular, she draws attention to three areas where the changes will have a major impact on employees: reward systems; career paths and job security; and lifestyle.

Reward systems

Employers and employees will increasingly come to look for new and more appropriate ways of rewarding and being rewarded. Indeed, with the advent of performance-related pay, in both the private and public sectors, there is already a gradual change from determining pay on the basis of a person's position and seniority to basing it on their contribution to the organisation. These changes are being driven by four main concerns: cost, equity, productivity and entrepreneurial pressure (*see* Exhibit 3.3).

Exhibit 3.3	Drivers for changes to reward systems

Cost – the concern is that the present system is too expensive for companies that must conserve resources to be competitive.

Equity – organisations are concerned to ensure that employees are fairly rewarded for their efforts.

Productivity – organisations want to adopt reward systems that motivate high performance from employees.

Entrepreneurial pressure – companies are aware that the present system does not always adequately reward entrepreneurs for their efforts.

Source: taken from Kanter (1989)

These concerns are being approached through the application of three different, though not necessarily mutually exclusive, payment methods. The first is profit-sharing, whereby the pay of the employee is pegged to a company's performance. This means that salaries are not fixed but instead are related, by the use of a predetermined formula, to the profit of the organisation over a given period of time, usually the previous financial year. The second method is the use of individual performance bonuses, which are paid on top of basic salary and are related to a predetermined performance target. This method has the advantage of enabling individuals to establish a direct correlation between their personal effort and the bonus payment they receive. Though this method is not new, the sums involved are – sometimes as much as twice basic salary. The last is the venture returns method, which represents perhaps the most radical break with the past. This is a scheme whereby entrepreneurs and inventors within an organisation are given the opportunity to earn returns based on the performance, in the market place, of the particular products or services for which they are responsible. Through this mechanism, the entrepreneur or inventor remains within the corporate fold but is paid on a similar basis to the owner of a small, independent business. The advantage is that they get the personal satisfaction and reward of running their 'own' business, whilst the larger organisation benefits from having highly-motivated and innovative people in charge of part of its operations.

The picture created by new reward systems is not, of course, totally rosy. Where there are winners, there may also be losers; not everyone will have the opportunity or drive to be an entrepreneur, or will be in a position that lends itself to some form of bonus system. Also, many people who currently benefit from reward systems based on seniority and position may find they lose out. Older workers, established in organisations and well down their chosen career path, could be particularly adversely affected by such changes. In addition, such payment systems may be divisive and create conflict. Kanter stresses the need for teamwork, yet a situation where some members of the team are receiving high bonuses is bound to create tensions which undermine cooperation and collaboration. It may be that profit-sharing schemes, which encompass everyone in the organisation, overcome this threat to teamworking, but if everyone receives the same share of the profits irrespective of their individual contribution, the motivating effect is likely to be diminished. The result of these various approaches to pay could be minimal in terms of motivation, or could even be demotivating and indeed drive out the most experienced people in the organisation.

Careers and job security

As organisations have become slimmer and more tasks are contracted out, organisation structures are becoming flatter as entire layers of hierarchy are dispensed with. The resultant effect threatens the demise of traditional forms of career path. Kanter argues that the idea of staying with one organisation and climbing the corporate career ladder is being replaced by hopping from job to job, not necessarily in the same organisation. Therefore, instead of people relying on organisations to give shape to their career, in future the onus will be on individuals to map out and pursue their own chosen route.

This change is also affecting skill development in organisations. It will no longer be sufficient just to be skilled in a particular job or specialism, because these will certainly change over time or even entirely disappear. Increasingly, individuals are finding that the concept of job security is being replaced by 'employability security' – the ability to adapt and enhance one's skills so as to be able to perform well in different types of jobs and organisations. Careers, therefore, are being shaped by professional and entrepreneurial principles: the ability to develop and market one's own skills and ideas, rather than by the sequence of jobs provided by one company. People will join organisations or accept particular jobs not, as in the past, because of job security or career progression, but in order to develop their skills, add to their knowledge and enhance their future employability.

Kanter argues that:

> ... what people are increasingly working to acquire is the capital of their own individual reputation instead of the organisational capital that comes from learning one system well and meeting its idiosyncratic requirements. For many managers, it might be more important, for example, to acquire or demonstrate a talent that a future employer or financial investor might value than to get to know the right people several layers above in the corporation where they currently work.
>
> (Kanter, 1989: 324)

Having painted this picture, it must also be acknowledged that there are contradictions and dilemmas that need to be resolved. What is being created are organisations and cultures that facilitate innovation and entrepreneurship, and change and flexibility. These will be organisations where employability and loyalty are transient concepts and what matters, almost exclusively, is the individual's present performance rather than their past or potential future contribution. The two main dilemmas from the organisational perspective are, therefore, how to reconcile the above with their stated objective of treating employees as long-term partners, and how to motivate employees to work in the organisation's interest rather than their own interest. This is an especially pointed dilemma in the case of the champions and entrepreneurs on whom it is argued the future of organisations depends. This is because it is this group of highly marketable individuals who are most likely to see their careers in terms of many different jobs and organisations.

Workers' lifestyle

There are now many organisations where people have been given greater freedom to innovate and experiment, where there are strong financial rewards for increased performance levels and where people are given greater control over their area of the business. There is little doubt that in such situations people are expected, and indeed wish, to work longer hours and centre what social life they have around their work. Indeed, there is now much evidence that in most developed countries people are working longer hours then they did a decade ago (Kodz *et al*, 2003). To encourage this, many companies now provide key employees with 'concierge' services that do their shopping, find them plumbers, sort out their new car and even find them a new house and arrange the move. The purpose of this is, of course, to allow staff to focus more effectively on their job. Nevertheless, where there are benefits to the organisation, there may also be disbenefits to the individual:

> The workplace as a centre for social life and the workmate as a candidate for marriage mate is, on one level, a convenience for overloaded people who have absorbing work that leaves little time to pursue a personal life outside. It is also an inevitable consequence of the new workforce demographics. But on another level, the idea is profoundly disturbing. What about the large number of people whose personal lives are not contained within the corridors of the corporation? What about the people with family commitments outside the workplace?
>
> (Kanter, 1989: 285)

We already know the adverse cost that such work patterns can have on people's physical and mental health and on their family life. Indeed, there is now a growing tendency among senior managers of both sexes to give up work or move to less well-paid but less demanding jobs (downshifting) in order to spend more time with their families (Carvel, 2002; Frith, 2003). One particularly high-profile example of this in the UK was the decision in 2003 by the Minister of Health, Alan Milburn, to step down in order to spend more time with his children as they grow up. This 'downshifting' phenomenon may be the reason why Kanter believes unmarried or divorced executives are thought to be preferred to their married counterparts by some companies because it is assumed they can focus more on their job given their lack of home life. Therefore, the line between motivation and exploitation may be a narrow one, and crossing it may benefit neither the individual nor the organisation.

Much of Kanter's work supports the view of Peters and Waterman in terms of the need for and direction of organisational change. Certainly, on the issues of innovation and entrepreneurship, culture and flexibility, and structure and jobs, there is much common ground. To an extent we might expect this, given that they are all writing from an American perspective, and basing their views on the experience and plans of leading American companies. Where they differ, however, is that Kanter takes a much more critical view of these developments. In particular, she draws attention to the contradiction that lies at the heart of the post-entrepreneurial model: are people – their skills, motivation and loyalty – central to the success of the organisation of the future, or are they just another commodity to be obtained and dispensed with as circumstances and their performance require?

Like Peters, Kanter has developed her earlier work but in a broader context. In *The Challenge of Organizational Change*, she and her co-authors (Kanter *et al*, 1992) turn their attention to the issue of managing change, and propose 'Ten Commandments for Executing Change' (*see* Exhibit 3.4).

Looking at approaches to change, Kanter *et al* (1992) distinguished between 'Bold Strokes' and 'Long Marches'. The former relate to major strategic decisions or

Exhibit 3.4	Ten Commandements for Executing Change

1. Analyse the organisation and its need for change.
2. Create a shared vision and a common direction.
3. Separate from the past.
4. Create a sense of urgency.
5. Support a strong leader role.
6. Line up political sponsorship.
7. Craft an implementation plan.
8. Develop enabling structures.
9. Communicate, involve people and be honest.
10. Reinforce and institutionalise change.

Source: Kanter *et al* (1992: 382–3)

economic initiatives. These, they argue, can have a clear and rapid impact on an organisation, but they rarely lead to any long-term change in habits or culture. The Long March approach, on the other hand, favours relatively small-scale and operationally-focused initiatives that are slow to implement and whose full benefits are achieved in the long term rather than the short term. However, the Long March approach can impact on culture over time. Bold Strokes are initiatives taken by a few senior managers, sometimes only one; they do not rely on the support of the rest of the organisation for their success. The Long March approach, however, does. Without the involvement and commitment of the majority of the workforce, such initiatives cannot succeed.

Kanter *et al* argue that these can be complementary, rather than alternative, approaches to change, though in practice companies appear to favour one or the other. Nevertheless, companies may need both the Bold Stroke and the Long March if they are to succeed in transforming themselves.

Kanter's, unlike Peters', works go far beyond the confines of the individual business enterprise to look at the workings of society as a whole. She co-authored a book, *Creating the Future*, with Michael Dukakis, the former Governor of Massachusetts (Dukakis and Kanter, 1988) and worked on his failed campaign for the US Presidency. The influence of Dukakis and successive Democrat administrations in Massachusetts can be seen in Kanter's more recent book *World Class: Thriving Locally in the Global Economy* (Kanter, 1997). Here she argues that if local communities and regions are to achieve economic security, they must see themselves as competing bodies in a mercilessly competitive global economy. Kanter paints a picture of the global economy as one where free enterprise reigns supreme and where goods, and many services, can be supplied from anywhere in the world. She points out that in the 1980s and 1990s, both blue- and white-collar American jobs were exported to whichever part of the world offered the lowest labour costs. Though supporting this example of the working of the free-enterprise system as being ultimately to everyone's benefit, Kanter argues that if local communities and regions are to survive and prosper in such a fierce climate, they must learn how to defend themselves. In particular, she argues for an interventionist local state which forms alliances with local private enterprises and manipulates the local economy. By creating a business-friendly taxation system and by the selective use of public expenditure for education and infrastructure projects, it can aim to attract and retain employers, especially large corporations.

In *Innovation: Breakthrough Thinking at 3M, DuPont, GE, Pfizer, and Rubbermaid* (Kanter *et al*, 1997), Kanter returns to the internal world of the organisation and the tried and tested ground of the Culture–Excellence approach. The core arguments of the book are neatly summed up on the dust jacket, which states that inside you will discover:

- Why it is impossible to approach innovation from a business school mentality.
- Why investigations of any cost or size will fail if tied too tightly to current market-place needs.
- Why managers must learn to operate more intuitively.
- Why cross-functional teams are more productive than any other organisational configuration.
- How fostering a competitive internal environment results in a healthy, creative tension and hungry, entrepreneurial employees.

These points are fleshed out by drawing upon the practices of the companies in the book's title and the editors' own, anecdotal, experiences. In a book whose Foreword is written by Tom Peters, it is not perhaps surprising that many of the arguments mirror those of Peters' own book on innovation (Peters, 1997a). Indeed, the key thrust of the book is succinctly summed up in a phrase from Tom Peters' (1997b) Foreword: 'Tomorrow's victories will go to the masters of innovation! Period!' It speaks volumes for the credibility which the Culture–Excellence approach has achieved in the business world that, after nearly two decades, its two leading American proponents are still in agreement about what it takes to achieve success.

In the next (and last) section on Culture–Excellence, we will examine the emergence of new organisational forms from the perspective of a leading British theorist: Charles Handy.

Charles Handy's emerging future organisations

Charles Handy is one of Britain's leading management thinkers. Indeed, in a 1997 European league table of global management gurus, he was placed third; all the others in the top ten were American (Rogers, 1997). Handy was educated at Oxford University and the Sloan School of Management at the Massachusetts Institute of Technology. He has been an oil executive, an economist and a professor at the London Business School. He has also acted as a consultant to a wide range of organisations in business, government, the voluntary sector, education and health.

Handy's first book, *Understanding Organizations*, which was published in 1976, has become a standard text on management courses and is now in its fourth edition (Handy, 1993). However, the book that brought him to public prominence and where he first began to articulate his views about the future direction of organisations was *The Future of Work* (Handy, 1984). As with Kanter and Peters, his work was inspired by the rise of Japan and the apparent decline of the West. In particular, he was concerned with the high level of unemployment in the UK at that time. Handy argued that if organisations were to survive and meaningful jobs were to be created for all those who wished to work, then both organisations and individuals would have to change the way they perceived jobs and careers. It was in his book *The Age of Unreason* (1989) that Handy fully articulated his views on the requirements for organisational success. He argued that profound changes were taking place in organisational life:

> The world of work is changing because the organisations of work are changing their ways. At the same time, however, the organisations are having to adapt to a changing world of work. It's a chicken and egg situation. One thing, at least, is clear: organisations in both private and public sectors face a tougher world – one in which they are judged more harshly than before on their effectiveness and in which there are fewer protective hedges behind which to shelter. (Handy, 1989: 70)

He asserted that British companies were fast moving away from the labour-intensive organisations of yesteryear. In future, new knowledge-based structures, run by a few smart people at their core who will control a host of equally smart computerised machines, will be the order of the day. Already, he noted, leading British organisations were increasingly becoming entities that received their added value from the knowledge and the creativity they put in, rather than from the application of muscle power. He contended that fewer, better-motivated people, helped by clever machines, could create much more added value than large groups of unthinking, demotivated ones ever could.

Like Peters and Kanter, Handy believes that the emerging future organisations will be smaller, more flexible and less hierarchical. Similarly, he also believes that the new organisations will need to treat people as assets to be developed and motivated, rather than just so much industrial cannon fodder. However, he does not assume that the future will be without diversity in relation to the organisational forms that emerge. Unlike Peters and Waterman, and to a lesser extent Kanter, he recognises that companies will continue to face differing circumstances and will need to respond in different manners. Therefore, instead of trying to re-establish a new 'one best way' for all organisations, with all the contradictions that arise from such attempts, Handy identifies three generic types of organisation that he argues will dominate in the future:

1 The Shamrock organisation.
2 The Federal organisation.
3 The Triple I organisation.

These are detailed below.

1 The Shamrock organisation

This form of organisation, like the plant of the same name with three interlocking leaves, is composed of three distinct groups of workers who are treated differently and have different expectations: a small group of specialist 'core' workers; a contractual fringe; and a flexible labour force.

The *core workers* are the first leaf, and the main distinguishing feature of the Shamrock form of organisation. These are a group of specialists, professional workers which form the brain, the hub or what we might call the 'nerve centre' of the organisation. These are people who are seen as being essential to the organisation. It is these few intelligent and articulate personnel in whose hands and heads reside the secrets of the organisation. They are both specialists and generalists, in that they run the organi-sation and control the smart machines and computers that have replaced, to a large extent, much of the labour force. This ' ... all puts pressure on the core, a pressure which could be summed up by the new equation of half the people, paid twice as much, working three times as effectively' (Handy, 1989: 118–19).

For their well-rewarded jobs, they are expected to be extremely loyal to the organi-sation, and to live and breathe their work. It is their responsibility to drive the organisation forward to ever greater success; to be flexible enough to meet the con-stantly-changing challenge of competitors and the equally changing and sophisticated needs of customers. Core workers operate as colleagues and partners in the organisa-tion, as opposed to superiors and subordinates. In a very real sense, it is their company, and as such they expect to be recognised and rewarded for their roles and achievements, rather than the position they occupy on the organisation's ladder. It fol-lows that they are managed differently – by consent: asked and not told what to do.

The *contractual fringe* is the second leaf of the Shamrock. A central feature of Shamrock organisations is their smallness in relation to their productive capacity. This is achieved by two methods: firstly, as mentioned above, by the use of machines to replace people; and secondly, by the contracting-out to individuals and other organisa-tions of services and tasks previously done in-house. This leads to the creation of a contractual fringe, who may or may not work exclusively for the company in question. They are contracted to carry out certain tasks, for which they are paid a fee based on results, rather than a wage based on time taken. The arguments put forward in favour of such arrangements are numerous, but tend to boil down to three main ones:

- **It is cheaper** – companies only pay for what they get.
- **It makes management easier** – why keep the people on the payroll with all the attendant human management problems if it is not necessary?
- **Workload balancing** – when business is slack, it is the contractor who bears the impact of the reduced workload.

The *flexible labour force* is the third and fastest-growing leaf of the Shamrock and comprises a pool of part-time workers available for use by organisations. These are people with relevant skills who are not in need of, or who cannot obtain, full-time employment, but who are prepared to work on a part-time basis.

Increasingly, among this group of flexible workers are women who left their skilled jobs to raise families, but who are willing to return to work on a part-time basis, while still maintaining their child-rearing commitments. Included in this also is the growing army of young or retired executives, who prefer to hop from one job to another, doing bits and pieces of work on a part-time basis. These workers are some-times referred to as temps (temporaries) or casuals. The growth of this group can be measured by the proliferation of employment agencies, catering solely for these groups, which have been established in the United Kingdom since the early 1980s. However, the flexible workforce never

... have the commitment or ambition of the core. Decent pay and decent conditions are what they want, ... They have jobs not careers and cannot be expected to rejoice in the organisation's triumphs any more than they can expect to share in the proceeds, nor will they put themselves out for the love of it; more work, in their culture, deserves and demands more money.

(Handy, 1989: 80–1)

The picture, therefore, of the Shamrock organisation is one where structure and employment practices allow it to be big in terms of output, whilst being small in terms of the number of direct employees. For the latter reason, it is lean with few hierarchical layers and even less bureaucracy. It achieves this by the application of smart machines and a combination of part-time staff and subcontractors, whose work can be turned on and off as circumstances dictate. However, in a departure from past practice, the people involved may be highly skilled and competent. This also has the advantage of requiring much less office and factory accommodation than more traditionally-organised companies. Other than the core staff, the rest are all scattered in different organisations or their own homes, often linked through sophisticated communication systems.

Such organisations, with their flexibility and skills, are well-suited to the provision of high-performance products and services to demanding and rapidly-changing markets. The beauty of it all, as Handy argues, is that they do not have to employ all of the people all of the time or even in the same place to get the work done. According to Handy, small is not only beautiful but also increasingly preferable.

2 The federal organisation

This is the second type of generic organisation that Handy sees as becoming dominant in the future. He defines this type of organisation as a collection or network of individual organisations allied together under a common flag with some shaped identity. Federations arise for two reasons. The first is that, as Shamrock organisations grow bigger, the core workers begin to find the volume of information available to them to make decisions increasingly difficult to handle. Secondly, they constitute a response to the constantly-changing and competitive environment of the business world. Modern organisations need not only to achieve the flexibility that comes from smallness, but also to be able to command the resources and power of big corporations.

As Handy (1989: 110) puts it:

> It [Federalism] allows individuals to work in organisation villages with the advantages of big city facilities. Organisational cities no longer work unless they are broken down into villages. In their big city mode they cannot cope with the variety needed in their products, their processes, and their people. On the other hand, the villages on their own have not the resources nor the imagination to grow. Some villages, of course, will be content to survive, happy in their niche, but global markets need global products and large confederations to make them or do them.

Federalism, therefore, implies the granting of autonomy to Shamrocks. Autonomy requires that Shamrocks are headed by their own separate chief executives, supported by a team of core workers, who take full responsibility for running the company. In such situations the Shamrocks become separate, but related entities, under the umbrella of the Federal Centre. With the devolving of power to the Shamrocks, who still remain in the Federal portfolio, the Federal Centre is left to pursue the business of providing a common platform for the integration of the activities of the Shamrocks. The Federal Centre has the role of generating and collating ideas from the different Shamrocks and making them into concrete, achievable strategic objectives. Therefore, the Federal Centre is concerned mainly with the future; with looking forward, generating ideas, and creating scenarios and options of what the future will look like. All this is done with the ultimate aim of moving the organisation forward and keeping it ahead not only of its rivals, but also of its time.

Another feature of the Federal organisation is what Handy refers to as the 'inverted do'nut'.

> The do'nut is an American doughnut. It is round with a hole in the middle rather than the jam in its British equivalent ... This, however, is an inverted American do'nut, in that it has the hole in the middle filled in and the space on the outside; ... The point of the analogy begins to emerge if you think of your job, or any job. There will be a part of the job which will be clearly defined, and which, if you do not do, you will be seen to have failed. That is the heart, the core, the centre of the do'nut ... [but] ... In any job of any significance the person holding the job is expected not only to do all that is required but in some way to improve on that ... to move into the empty space of the do'nut and begin to fill it up.
>
> (Handy, 1989: 102)

Through this approach, the Federal organisation seeks to maximise the innovative and creative potential of staff members. It does this by specifying the core job, the target and the quality standard expected of a given product or service. Outside of this specified domain, within the do'nut's empty space, however, staff members are given enough room and latitude to challenge and question existing ideas, to experiment and to come up with new methods of doing things, and new products or services. The aim is to encourage enquiry and experimentation that lead to higher standards. It follows from this that the essence of leadership under a Federal system is to provide a shared vision for the organisation; one which allows room for those whose lives will be affected by it – either directly or indirectly – to modify it, ponder over it, expand it, accept it and then make it a reality. Leadership in such situations is about providing opportunities for staff to grow and test their potential to the limit.

3 The Triple I organisation

This is the third of Handy's new organisational forms, although in fact it comprises a set of principles rather than a structural model. From the above, it is clear that both Shamrock and Federal organisation types introduce new dimensions into the world of work. Traditional perspectives are being transformed, and the established criteria for judging organisational effectiveness are being re-evaluated. Issues such as the definition of a productive contribution to work, reward systems, managerial skills and many more are being examined in the light of new management ideas. Indeed, according to Handy, we appear to be on the verge of a revolution in management thought and practice.

An examination of the attributes of the core workers in both Shamrock and Federal organisations gives an indication of what will constitute the new formula for success and effectiveness in tomorrow's companies. The core workers, as seen by Handy, use their *Intelligence* to analyse the available *Information* to generate *Ideas* for new products and services. Thus we find that Handy's first two organisational forms contain the seeds to produce his third form, the Triple I – organisations based on Intelligence, Information and Ideas. Since the three Is constitute the prime intellectual capital of the new organisations, clearly the Triple I principle applies most importantly to the core group of workers who are in a position to possess these attributes.

In future, it is argued, the equation for organisational success will be Triple I = AV, where Triple I = Intelligence, Information and Ideas, and AV = Added Value, either in cash or kind. This will be an organisation 'obsessed with the pursuit of truth, or, in business language, of quality' (Handy, 1989: 113). This will not depend solely on human ability but will be a combination of smart people and smart machines. Therefore, organisations of the future will increasingly have to (a) invest in smart machines to remain competitive and effective; (b) recruit skilled and smart people to control the machines; and (c) ensure that this group of skilled people is rewarded equitably.

For the Triple I organisation to emerge and remain successful, it must keep the skills, knowledge and abilities of its staff up to date. This means that it must become a learning organisation; one that provides a conducive environment for the development of its intellectual capital. Time and effort must be consciously and officially devoted to learning and study, at all levels of the organisation. The core, especially, must spend more time than their equivalents in more traditional companies on thinking and study: meeting with other external professionals and experts, going on study tours and listening more to 'partners' within the organisation, all with the objective of improving the organisation's human capital. The new organisations will be dynamic, interactive societies where information is open to all, freely given and freely received. In the Triple I organisation, everyone will be expected to think and learn as well as to do. Nevertheless, it is the core worker from whom most will be demanded. Such people will be increasingly

> ... expected to have not only the expertise appropriate to his or her particular role, but will also be required to know and understand business, to have the technical skills of analysis and the human skills and the conceptual skills and to keep them up to date.
>
> (Handy, 1989: 124)

This is one of the key features that make the Triple I organisation unique; it is a hotbed of intellectual discourse, where the prevailing culture is one of consent rather than instruction. Staff are unsupervised in the traditional sense, and instead are trusted to do what is right and given room to experiment with new ideas and concepts. Finally, the flexibility of such organisations, and the unpredictability of the environments in which they operate, mean that careers will become more variegated and less permanent.

As can be seen, therefore, Handy's view of the future shape of organisations does not appear dissimilar to that of Kanter, and Peters and Waterman. However, he does depart from their views in at least two crucial respects. Firstly, he explicitly acknowledges that not all organisations will adopt the same form or move at the same pace. His three generic forms indicate that organisations will have to exercise choice and judgment in order to match their particular circumstances to the most suitable form. Also, it is clear that he views this as an evolutionary as well as a revolutionary process: companies cannot immediately become a Triple I type of organisation; they have to develop into one over time. Secondly, he explicitly states what is only hinted at by the other writers, namely that in the new organisations where everyone is to be treated as an equal 'partner', some will be more equal than others, i.e. the core workers will be treated and rewarded in a more preferential manner than the contractual fringe or the flexible labour force.

Handy does not give specific guidance as to how existing organisations can adapt themselves to take on these new forms, although he does indicate that a lack of empowerment and self-belief amongst individuals in organisations presents a major obstacle to change. However, in an earlier work (Handy, 1986), he does state very clearly that fundamental change is a long-term process and that people tend to react emotionally rather than rationally to change.

After the publication of *The Age of Unreason*, Handy appeared to grow increasingly concerned with the unanticipated consequences of his prescriptions for the world of work. This is made clear in the first paragraph of his 1994 book, *The Empty Raincoat*:

> Four years ago, my earlier book, The Age of Unreason, was published. In that book I presented a view of the way work was being reshaped and the effects which the reshaping might have on all our lives. It was, on the whole, an optimistic view. Since then, the world of work has changed very much along the lines which were described in the book. This should be comforting to an author, but I have not found it so. Too many people and institutions have been unsettled by the changes. Capitalism has not proved as flexible as it was supposed to be. Governments have not been all-wise or far-seeing. Life is a struggle for many and a puzzle for most.
>
> What is happening in our mature societies is much more fundamental, confusing and distressing than I had expected.   (Handy, 1994: 1)

In *The Empty Raincoat*, Handy returns to and restates many of the themes of his earlier work, but with two differences. Firstly, he explicitly acknowledges that the types of careers that these new organisational forms will create will have a severely adverse effect on the home life of employees, especially senior managers. They will be called on to be company men and women above all else, including their families.

Secondly, there is an almost evangelical feel to the book. This is especially noticeable in the latter section of the book, where Handy argues that the modern world has taken meaning out of people's lives and that, whilst the pursuit of profit may motivate senior managers:

> Not many in the lower realms of the organisation can get excited by the thought of enriching shareholders. 'Excellence' and 'quality' are the right sort of words, but they have been tarnished by repetition in too many organisations.   (Handy, 1994: 265)

This more pessimistic view of the future is still there in his 1997 book, *The Hungry Spirit* (Handy, 1997: 3):

> Many of us are, I believe, confused by the world we have created for ourselves in the West ... the new fashion for turning everything into a business, even our own lives, doesn't seem to be the answer. A hospital, and my life, is more than just a business.
>
> What good can it possibly do to pile up riches which you cannot conceivably use, and what is the point of the efficiency needed to create those riches if one third of the world's workers are now unemployed or under-employed as the ILO calculates? And where will it end, this passion for growth? ... I am angered by the waste of so many people's lives, dragged down by poverty in the midst of riches. I am concerned by the absence of a more transcendent view of life and the purposes of life, and by the prevalence of the economic myth which colours all we do. Money is the means for life and not the point of it.

In the book, Handy argues that, in the West, people's spiritual needs have been sacrificed to the pursuit of their material needs; and he examines the options, and where the responsibility lies, for putting balance back into people's lives. In particular he is concerned with the distribution of wealth, the role that education can play in giving everyone a good start in life, and how we can look after ourselves whilst having a care for others as well. He even touches on, perhaps, the biggest question of all: 'What, ultimately, is the real purpose of life?' (Handy, 1997: 5). In addressing these issues he ranges widely, looking at markets, organisations and the role of business, government and religion. He believes the answer lies in the pursuit of 'Proper Selfishness'. This is a redefinition of individualism; he sees individuals as moving away from the pursuit of narrow self-interest, and instead realising that it is in their best interests to pursue a fairer society for all. Though he identifies a role for government and business in creating Proper Selfishness, he believes it is individuals themselves who bear the main responsibility for its achievement. In particular, he draws attention to the role of individual entrepreneurs in changing the world:

> Entrepreneurs, whether social or commercial, often discover aspects of themselves in the pursuit of something beyond themselves. Such people are not content to let the status quo be the way forward. They itch to make a difference ... Almost accidentally, corporations have become the nursery for frustrated entrepreneurs. They should turn this to a positive account and do it more deliberately, in the hope that they can retain some of the best for themselves, including women, while seeding the community with the others. The workplace has always been the real school for life. Perhaps it just needs to change its curriculum a little to tune in with the new age of personal initiative.   (Handy, 1997: 262)

Handy calls for a new sense of purpose for individuals, organisations and society. He wants to see a strong ethical approach to business and society, and a recreation of the concept that people exist to help and serve each other as well as themselves. These are sentiments that many of us would probably share but, unfortunately, he fails to show how the unleashing of individual entrepreneurship and the creation of the new organisational forms he advocates will aid this search for meaning. Instead, he asks us to put our faith in the goodness of people and to be optimistic about the future. A recurrent theme in Handy's work, however, has been the many paradoxes thrown up by contemporary society, especially the presence of dire poverty amidst extreme wealth, and the potential of technology for creating meaningful work compared with the increasing tendency for the quality of life to decline. Therefore, it seems strange that the one paradox that Handy appears to ignore is that the forms of organisations that he advocates may well be creating the poor jobs and poverty he deprecates.

■ Culture–Excellence: summary and criticisms

That the Culture–Excellence approach has had a major impact on the thinking of Western businesses, especially in the UK and USA, is beyond question. *In Search of Excellence* has sold over six million copies, making it the best-selling management book of all time. Largely as a result of its success, its authors, especially Tom Peters, have become successful and influential consultants. Rosabeth Moss Kanter and Charles Handy have likewise achieved the pre-eminence in business circles that they had previously only occupied in academia. A look in the business section of any bookshop will show that there are also many more authors who have jumped on the bandwagon. Indeed, barely a day seems to go by without the publication of yet another blockbuster proclaiming that it has discovered the recipe for success. Some of these achieve a degree of prominence in business circles, though many seem to disappear without trace. Nevertheless, the fact that publishers keep publishing them, and that in different ways and shapes they repeat and project the Culture–Excellence message, emphasises the thirst by managers for the message.

Nor is it just a case that managers buy them to leave them on the shelf. Over the last two decades, on both sides of the Atlantic, managers have been attempting to re-shape their companies along the Culture–Excellence lines. In 1997, a survey by the Industrial Society showed that in the UK alone some 94 per cent of respondent organisations either had recently been through or were going through a culture change programme (Industrial Society, 1997).

The reason for its emergence, and for its continuing popularity, was that in a world where old certainties had disappeared, where new and more dangerous competitors seemed to appear every day, it rejected the communal and corporatist approach of the Japanese, and offered instead a recipe for success that was in tune with the free market liberalism, with its stress on individualism, that has dominated much of the West for the last two decades. Nor was it merely a rehash of what had gone before. The Culture–Excellence approach to organisations is significantly different from previous approaches; although we might note that the new forms, especially Handy's Shamrock type, bear an interesting resemblance to the first budding of organisational life during the Industrial Revolution. The entrepreneurial style of management, the stress on a privileged core of skilled workers, and the contracting-out of whole areas of organisational activities are all hallmarks of the early industrial organisations. However, the big differences between then and now relate to the level of sophistication and complexity of the new organisations that are emerging, the degree of integration of both internal functions and external relationships, the grade of intelligence and skill required of all staff, whether they be core or periphery – and, of course, the conditions of employment. For Watson (1986: 66), who coined the term Culture–Excellence school to describe proponents of this approach, there is one further and crucial difference:

[In these new organisations] what brings the activities of the organisational members to focus upon those purposes which lead to effective performance is the existence of a strong and clearly articulated culture.   (Watson, 1986: 66)

It is this which makes it clear that the Culture–Excellence approach that has been developing over the last two decades is remarkably different from most of the theory and practice that has grown up in the last 100 years.

Peters, Kanter and Handy argue that organisations are entering a new age, where familiar themes are taking on different meanings and are being expressed in a new language. Contrasting the old with the new, they argue that what is important in the new is not muscle power, but brain power: the ability to make intelligent use of information to create ideas that add value and sustain competitiveness. The new organisation is flatter in structure, though it might be more accurate to say that structure is decreasing in importance and that its role as a directing and controlling mechanism is being taken over by cultures that stress the need for, and facilitate, flexibility and adaptation (though in passing we should note that Peters (1993) also sees the dismembering of hierarchical structures as an important step in creating these new cultures). The Culture–Excellence approach is sounding the death knell of hierarchical organisations and the concept of promotion through the ranks. Careers and skills are taking on new meanings, as are established ideas of reward.

In future, it is argued, careers are likely to depend on the individual and his/her ability to remain employable. In turn, the skills needed for 'employability' will tend to be generic and broad-based rather than organisation- or function/specialism-specific. Likewise, career paths and promotion will no longer be shaped by the particular employing organisation and its structures and criteria, but will be driven more by individuals creating their own opportunities by taking on new roles and responsibilities, either in one organisation or, more likely, by moving from company to company. As for pay, it seems that this will take the form not so much of a wage related to the particular post occupied, but more that of a fee paid for actual performance.

On human relations, the message being transmitted is that the new forms of organisations will treat their employees in a more responsible and humane fashion than has been the norm. Employees will be seen and treated as 'partners', capable of making a substantial contribution to the growth of the organisation. This approach, it is argued, will manifest itself in a tough-minded respect for the individual, who will receive training, be set reasonable and clear objectives, and be given the autonomy to make his/her own contribution to the work of the organisation. The new organisations will seek to develop open, flexible and pragmatic cultures, which help to maintain a learning environment that promotes creativity and entrepreneurship amongst all employees.

Another feature of the new organisational forms, it is claimed, will be their ability to grant autonomy and encourage flexibility and initiative whilst at the same time keeping tight control of their operations. Like so much else, this is to be achieved through culture rather than structure, and values rather than rules. Everything is to be monitored closely, not by the watching eye of superiors, but by the creation of a homogeneous environment in which all take an equal responsibility for, and legitimate interest in, the work of their colleagues.

Clearly, the new organisation forms that are being promoted offer much that is admirable and worth supporting. Equally clearly, their adherents and promoters raise more questions than they answer. To an extent this is inevitable when dealing with something that is emerging rather than an existing and concrete reality. However, as this concept has been around for nearly two decades, this is no longer the case. Therefore, it would be remiss to ignore or gloss over the questions and dilemmas that seem apparent. Many writers have drawn attention to the shortcomings of the Culture–Excellence approach. Carroll (1983) and Lawler (1985) were both scathing about the methodological shortcomings of the research on which Peters and Waterman's (1982) book was based. Indeed, Peters himself appears to have admitted that he and Waterman 'faked' some of the data in order to obtain their results (Kellaway, 2001). This would seem to give additional support to Wilson's (1992) claim that the book lacks any apparent empirical or theoretical foundations. Though Wilson's criticisms may seem somewhat exaggerated, it is certainly arguable that the

Culture–Excellence approach does have serious weaknesses, especially in three areas that are crucial to the operation of organisations:

1 **People**. There are serious concerns and contradictions regarding the role and behaviour of people in the new organisations. On the one hand, they are proclaimed as the chief asset of the new organisations. On the other hand, there are clearly different grades of employee, from core to periphery, and these different grades will be treated and rewarded in a markedly dissimilar manner; furthermore, none of the different grades can expect any real job security. The new organisations will only value employees as long as they and their areas perform to the highest of standards. Not only does this pit individual against individual, but also one part of the organisation against another. Whilst healthy competition may enhance organisational competitiveness, from what we know of motivation theory (Arnold *et al*, 1998) it is not clear that the Culture–Excellence approach is that healthy. The Culture–Excellence approach also encourages teamwork, yet the pursuit of individual advancement and reward often leads to conflict rather than cooperation (Schein, 1988).

2 **Politics**. Though Western companies traditionally either deny the existence of internal struggles or argue that such behaviour is perverse, it is clear that the struggle for resources, power and survival is as great within organisations as it is between them (Buchanan and Badham, 1999; Pfeffer, 1981; Robbins, 1986). As stated above, the recommendations of the Culture–Excellence school would seem to exacerbate political behaviour by and between individuals and groups, yet in the main they ignore this drawback to their approach, even though it is potentially damaging to both organisational and individual performance.

3 **Culture**. The proponents of Culture–Excellence are advocating a 'one best way' (one best culture) approach for all organisations, irrespective of their size, environment and other circumstances. Also, as Wilson (1992) pointed out, it assumes a simple causal relationship between culture and performance. Nevertheless, for the proponents of the Culture–Excellence school, culture is the great cure-all – the creation of a culture of excellence is seen as answering all questions and solving all problems. This assumes that the creation of new cultures will itself be unproblematic. However, as the Chapter 5 will show, culture and politics appear to be the Achilles' heel of approaches to managing organisations.

It would also be remiss of us if we ignored the differences between the main proponents of Culture–Excellence. Peters is a free market liberal in the classic American mould. He believes that individual and organisational competition untrammelled by government is what makes societies strong. Kanter agrees with most of this, but believes that local communities, working with big business, have a positive role to play in attracting and keeping well-paid jobs for their communities. Handy is also committed to the free market, but has become increasingly concerned with the outcome of his prescriptions. He appears to be turning his back on pure individualism, arguing instead for a less rapacious, more caring capitalism, driven by what he terms 'Proper Selfishness' and more concerned with the collective good than individual wealth creation. Though Peters and Kanter may continue to hold to the Culture–Excellence line, it is difficult to see that the direction which Handy is now taking is consistent with it.

There is one final concern that is wider than the Culture–Excellence approach *per se* or its impact on organisations, but which is reflected in the differences between Peters, Kanter and Handy. The move towards creating segmented workforces of the type described by Handy (1989), and the emphasis on the temporary nature of employment championed by Peters and Waterman (1982) and Kanter (1989), are part of a continuing trend in the West, driven by neo-liberal economic and social policies, towards worsening job security and conditions of service, in order to create a vast pool of under-employed, especially part-time, labour that can be turned on or off as the situation dictates.

In the UK in 1993, for example, some 9.7 million workers (38 per cent of all UK workers) were either part-time, temporary, self-employed, on a government training scheme, or unpaid family workers – an increase of 1.25 million since 1986. Similarly, the proportion of men in employment who were part of the flexible workforce rose from 18 per cent in 1981 to 27.5 per cent in 1993 (Watson, 1994). This tallies with Hutton's (1995) argument that the UK is now more socially divided than at any time since the Industrial Revolution. In particular, he maintains that the UK is a 30/30/40 society – the marginalised, the newly insecure and the advantaged – and that this not only raises the spectre of increased social tensions, but is a positive disadvantage to wealth creation. Hutton's attack on the adverse effects of neo-liberal market policies is supported by others, notably Saul (1997), who points out that the income gap between the highest- and lowest-paid workers in the UK is greater now than at any time since 1880, when records began. Figures published by the UK government (Brindle, 1998b) show that since 1979, whilst the richest 10 per cent of the population have seen their incomes grow by 70 per cent in real terms, the bottom 10 per cent of the population have suffered a cut in real income of 9 per cent. In the same period, poverty in the UK has almost tripled. As White (1999) noted, this increase in poverty has had an especially adverse impact on children. In 1979, 1 in 10 children lived in poverty. In 1996/7, the figure was 1 in 3. The reason for this increase appears to be very clear: 32 per cent of children now live in families without a full-time worker. Nor is this bleak picture restricted to the UK. As Dunphy and Griffiths (1998) point out, in 1980, the Chief Executive Officers of the 300 largest US companies had incomes 29 times that of the average manufacturing worker; ten years later, their incomes were 93 times greater. By 2000, the average CEO salary was 531 times greater (AFL-CIO, 2003). Indeed, the founder of Microsoft, Bill Gates, has a personal fortune that is greater than the combined wealth of the 106 million poorest Americans (Elliott and Brittain, 1998). On a world scale, the estimated wealth of the 11 richest individuals is more than the combined GDP of the 49 least developed countries (Trade, 2003). Much of the economic and labour market liberalisation in the 1980s was justified by 'trickle-down' economics – the view that as the rich got richer, then some of this wealth would trickle down to the rest of society and, therefore, society as a whole would become wealthier. This clearly does not appear to be the case. Not surprisingly, if one looks at the poorest nations in the world, the situation is much worse, with malnutrition, poverty and disease on the increase (Gittings, 1998). In the 1990s, the number of people in sub-Saharan Africa living on less than $1 a day increased from 47 to 49 per cent, and in eastern and central Europe it increased from 7 to 20 per cent (Elliott, 2003). In the USA, Robert Reich, who was Secretary of Labor in the first Clinton administration, and other leading figures have warned of the dangers of a social chasm opening up between an ever-increasing rich elite, holed up in guarded compounds, and a jobless, impoverished majority (Elliott, 1997; Reich, 1997). Indeed, as a sign of this, there are now more private security guards in the USA than there are publicly-employed police (Dunphy and Griffiths, 1998). Contrast this with the case of Japan, discussed next, where, traditionally, at government and organisation level, full employment has taken precedence over profit and underpinned its voracious appetite for economic expansion (Holden and Burgess, 1994).

Despite these concerns and criticisms, Culture–Excellence has become the most influential approach to running organisations in the USA and Europe, as is apparent from the many articles on its merits and case studies of its use that appear regularly in management journals. However, since the 1950s, the Japanese have been developing an alternative approach to structuring and managing organisations that is not only markedly different from the Culture–Excellence one but also has a proven track record of success.

The Japanese approach to management

The last 50 years have seen the rebirth of Japan. Reduced almost to ashes at the end of the Second World War, by the 1980s Japan had built an industrial empire second to none. Even now, despite its economic ills of the last decade, it is still the second largest economy in the world. As Morgan (1986: 111) stated:

> With virtually no natural resources, no energy, and over 110 million people crowded in four small mountainous islands, Japan succeeded in achieving the highest growth rate, lowest level of unemployment and, at least in some of the larger and more successful organizations, one of the best-paid and healthiest working populations in the world.

Though writers suggested many reasons for Japan's success, ranging from culture to economic institutions, time and again, its approach to managing organisations was cited as the key factor (Hunter, 1989; Laage-Hellman, 1997; Sako and Sato, 1997; Schonberger, 1982; Smith and Misumi, 1989; Whitehill, 1991).

Before proceeding to examine what is meant by the Japanese approach to management, it is useful briefly to trace Japan's development as an industrial nation. Up to the middle of the nineteenth century, Japan was an intensely nationalistic society which practised a deliberate policy of isolating itself from the outside world. Therefore, for most of its inhabitants, Japan was the world. It was a feudal country that laid strong emphasis on obligation and deference, and where obedience to authority in general, and to the Emperor in particular, was unquestioned (Sheridan, 1993).

For all its deliberate isolation, Japan was a sophisticated and well-educated country with a high degree of literacy. Education was based on a set of Confucian principles which stressed unquestioning obedience to the family; total loyalty to one's superiors; and reverence for education and self-development. The abiding influence of these can still be seen in Japanese society today, and underpins the strength of Japanese organisations (Smith and Misumi, 1989). However, from the mid-nineteenth century, Japan began to experience internal tensions. The feudal aristocracy experienced escalating financial difficulties whilst the merchant class, considered social inferiors, began to prosper. At the same time, it became clear that the growing military might of other countries posed a potential threat to Japan. In response to these developments, Japan adopted a twin-track policy of economic and military growth, not dissimilar to that being developed in Germany at this time (Hunter, 1989).

Missions were dispatched abroad to study and bring technologies and practices back to Japan. On one such visit in 1911, Yukinori Hoshino, a director of the Kojima Bank, became acquainted with the work of Frederick Taylor and obtained permission to translate his work into Japanese. Following this, Taylor's Scientific Management principles, and allied approaches to work study and production management, were rapidly and enthusiastically adopted by the Japanese (McMillan, 1985). Indeed, such was the impact of Taylor's work that, according to Wren (1994: 205), it ' ... led to a management revolution, replacing the entrepreneur-dominated age'. By the 1920s, Japan had moved from being an agrarian economy to one dominated by industry. Like many Western countries, industrialisation was accompanied by considerable industrial conflict, sometimes violent (Urabe, 1986). However, unlike most Western countries, this was not accompanied by a growing democratisation of society. Instead, democratic tendencies were quashed by a growing coalition between industry and the military that promoted intense nationalism and led, almost inexorably, to Japan's involvement in the Second World War. After Japan's defeat, its shattered society was occupied by the USA, which stripped the Emperor of his traditional powers and established a Western-style democracy (Sheridan, 1993; Whitehill, 1991).

Given the state of the Japanese economy after the Second World War, the success of its reconstruction is nothing short of miraculous. The Korean War in the 1950s proved a stroke of good fortune for Japan, in that the USA used Japan as an important staging post for troops and supplies. This injected billions of American dollars into Japan's economy. However, perhaps much more important was America's contribution to management education in Japan. In the immediate post-war years, Japanese companies acquired a reputation for bitter industrial disputes, shoddy workmanship and poor quality. The main responsibility for tackling these problems lay with American engineers working for the Civilian Communications Section of the Occupation Administration (Sheldrake, 1996). Four men in particular have been credited with turning this situation around and creating the basis of Japan's fearsome reputation for the productivity of its workforce and quality of its products: Charles Protzman, Homer Sarasohn, Joseph Juran and W Edward Deming. Interestingly, the last three of these had all worked at Western Electric's Hawthorne Works and were, therefore, familiar, though not necessarily always in agreement, with the Human Relations approach. All of them were far removed from the narrow concept of the engineer. They took a wide view of how enterprises should be run and in particular of the need for managers to show leadership and gain the commitment of their workforces. Their approach, which covered business policy and organisation as well as production methods and techniques, was enthusiastically received, adopted and disseminated by the senior managers who attended their courses and lectures. As Horsley and Buckley (1990: 51) noted, Deming, especially, met with enormous success:

W E Deming became a legend in Japan. He gave hundreds of lectures ... to eager managers on the vital importance of statistical quality control ... Among his pupils were many who were to become captains of Japanese industry in the 1960s and 1970s, heading firms like Nissan, Sharp and the Nippon Electric Company (NEC). The annual Deming Prize for good management was highly coveted in the 1950s, and is still being awarded today.

Nevertheless, despite the economic and technical assistance of the USA, there is little doubt that the main credit for the country's success can be attributed to the hard work, commitment and intelligence of Japanese managers and workers. Under the umbrella of a supportive economic and political framework, Japanese enterprises overcame their severe industrial relations and quality problems of the 1950s and created the distinctive and hugely successful Japanese approach to developing and managing their businesses that allowed them to take the world by storm in the 1970s and 1980s (Fruin, 1992; Pascale and Athos, 1982; Sako and Sato, 1997; Sheldrake, 1996; Smith and Misumi, 1989).

■ What is the Japanese approach to management?

As one might expect, it is difficult to find an all-embracing definition of the Japanese approach to management that satisfies all commentators or can be found in all Japanese companies. In particular, there are distinct differences between larger and smaller enterprises in Japan, and in the treatment of full-time and part-time, and male and female employees in all enterprises (Cole, 1979; Laage-Hellman, 1997; Sako and Sato, 1997). Indeed, such are these differences that some argue there is either no such thing as a distinctive Japanese approach to management or that, if it does exist, no one has been able to capture it accurately (Dale, 1986; Keys and Miller, 1984; Sullivan, 1983). Nevertheless, the vast majority of observers do seem to agree that it exists and can, broadly, be defined (Abegglen and Stalk, 1984; Ackroyd et al, 1988; Hatvany and Pucik, 1981; Holden and Burgess, 1994; Pascale and Athos, 1982; Smith and Misumi, 1989).

Perhaps the most influential work, and still the best-selling book, on Japanese management was William Ouchi's (1981) *Theory Z: How American Business Can Meet the Japanese Challenge*. Drawing on the theoretical insights of Douglas McGregor and Chris Argyris, Ouchi argued that Japanese success stemmed from the involvement and commitment of the entire workforce. In turn, he argued, this was built upon a set of internally consistent norms, practices and behaviours based on trust and strong personal ties between the individual and the organisation, particularly their immediate work group. Ouchi drew particular attention to practices such as lifetime employment, slow evaluation and promotion and collective decision-making. Many other writers have also tried to capture the essence of Japanese management.

McKenna (1988) believes that the key elements are lifetime employment, the seniority principle with regard to pay and promotion, and enterprise unionism (this will be explained later). Pang and Oliver (1988) agree with McKenna but also draw attention to training and education, company-based welfare schemes, quality circles and manufacturing methods such as Just-in-Time production. Keys and Miller (1984) point to long-term planning, lifetime employment and collective responsibility as being the hallmarks of Japanese management. Laage-Hellman (1997) emphasises the presence of a consensus-seeking decision-making process, incremental planning through the development of a long-term vision and the use of short-term action plans, passive owners who do not usually interfere with managers, strategies that give priority to long-term growth and survival, and the effective use of external resources through partnerships with suppliers and customers. Other commentators have also come up with similar lists.

One of the most quoted of these is by Pascale and Athos (1982) who used the McKinsey 7 S Framework (*see* Exhibit 3.2), which they had developed jointly with Tom Peters and Robert Waterman, to analyse Japanese management. Like Peters and Waterman's Culture–Excellence approach, Pascale and Athos stressed the four 'soft' Ss (staff, style, shared values, and skills). This was not to dismiss the 'hard' Ss (strategy, structure and systems), but to emphasise that the real difference between Japanese companies and their Western counterparts was that the latter tended to concentrate on the 'hard' Ss and ignore the 'soft' Ss. Pascale and Athos argued that, in contrast, Japanese companies had developed the ability to combine and blend the 'soft' and 'hard' Ss to their competitive benefit. Their work differed from other studies of Japanese management at the time by examining the management style of Japanese companies operating in the USA. In a similar vein, Peter Wickens, who was Personnel Director of Nissan Motor Manufacturing (UK) Ltd for over 10 years, also commented on the transfer of Japanese management to the West. In his 1987 book, *The Road To Nissan*, written when he was still at Nissan, he argued that the Japanese approach can be characterised by three factors: teamwork, quality-consciousness and flexibility. Interestingly, after he left Nissan, Wickens (1995) commented that Ouchi and others tended to miss, or underplay, one very important element of Japanese companies – their very strong control culture, especially in relation to shopfloor workers.

The factors identified by the above writers can be separated into two categories: those relating to personnel/industrial relations issues and those relating to business/manufacturing practices.

Personnel issues

The dedication, commitment and ability of Japanese workers is seen as a major factor in the success of Japanese companies. Though much credit for this has been given to the culture of Japanese society, especially its Confucian tradition of obedience and loyalty, similar levels of motivation have been reproduced in Japanese companies operating in the West (Wickens, 1987), which would imply that other factors are also at work. Chief among these is the crucial role played by the personnel policies prevalent in many Japanese enterprises, especially the larger ones. The core of the Japanese approach to personnel comprises a combination of practices and policies designed to align their behaviour with, and bind employees to, the organisation, and promote their long-term development and commitment. The principal practices and policies concerned are listed below.

1 **Lifetime employment.** Many employees are recruited straight from school or university, and expect, and are expected, to spend the rest of their working lives with the same organisation. This 'guarantee', based as it is on an age-old sense of mutual obligation and belonging, creates an intense sense of loyalty to and dependence on the organisation. Indeed, Holden and Burgess (1994) observed that whilst a Japanese worker might survive the loss of his family, the collapse of his employing organisation would be unbearable. Therefore, lifetime employment is a central feature of the Japanese approach and supports so much else, including a willingness to change and the maintenance of a stable organisational culture. However, the fact that organisations prefer to recruit school or university leavers also makes it difficult for individuals to move between companies once they have accepted an

appointment. It follows that if someone is fired, their chances of securing other employment are negligible.

2 **Internal labour markets.** Most positions are filled from inside the company. This is a corollary to lifetime employment which demonstrates to the employee that satisfactory performance will bring promotion, and it eliminates the potential for tension which can be brought about by the recruitment of outsiders.

3 **Seniority-based promotion and reward systems.** Employees are ranked and rewarded primarily, but not exclusively, on their length of service, and independent of the precise nature of the job they perform.

4 **Teamwork and bonding.** Although Japanese employees are made to feel part of the organisation and see it as some sort of extended family, they are first and foremost a member of a particular workgroup or team. The group is not just a collection of individuals; it is constructed and developed in such a way that it comprises a single entity which takes collective responsibility for its performance. Japanese companies use a variety of techniques, both at work and in a social setting, for bonding team members to each other and to the organisation.

5 **Enterprise (single company) unions.** Unlike the West, Japanese companies tend to allow only one union to represent the interests of the workforce. In addition, Japanese unions tend to be single company or enterprise unions. Indeed, from a Western point of view, they are not so much trade unions as company associations. This is illustrated by the practice of senior managers, at some stage in their careers, being expected to serve as union officials.

6 **Training and education.** Extensive and continuous training and education form an integral part of Japanese personnel policies. This emphasis on the continuous development of employees, to enable them to carry out their work better and to prepare them for promotion, represents a significant investment by Japanese companies in their human capital. Much of the training is done on the job and is always geared to the twin aims of improving organisational performance and individual development. Though encouraged by the company, employees are expected to take responsibility for their own self-development.

7 **Company welfarism.** Many Japanese companies provide a wide range of welfare benefits for their employees. These can cover medical treatment, education for children and even housing. Some of the larger companies are almost mini welfare states in themselves.

Many other practices and policies could be added to the list, but these appear to be at the core. They are designed to instill the following in employees:

- loyalty and gratitude to the company and a commitment to its objectives;
- a sense of security;
- a strong commitment to hard work and performance improvement;
- an atmosphere of cooperation and not conflict;
- a belief in self-development and improvement.

These are the cornerstone of Japanese company life; their presence is the reason why Japanese national culture is often cited as being at the heart of Japan's ability to compete in a world market. These operate within organisation structures which, to Western eyes at least, appear complex, highly formalised and very hierarchical

(Whitehill, 1991). However, these personnel issues cannot be seen in isolation from the working practices that Japanese companies use or the objectives they pursue. It is the combination of the two that makes Japanese companies so effective (Wood, 1991). Without overall direction and the appropriate work systems, even the best skilled and motivated workers are ineffective. This is why Japanese business practices and work systems should receive as much attention as personnel issues.

Business practices and work systems

The Japanese ability to satisfy customers, and thereby capture markets, by developing and producing products to a higher specification and at a lower cost than their competitors, is staggering considering the state of their industry in the 1940s and 1950s. Indeed, even as recently as the 1960s, 'Made in Japan' was synonymous with poor quality. What has changed, or rather what has come to fruition, has been the methods they apply to all aspects of business, but especially to manufacturing (Hannam, 1993). The fact that some of these methods have, quite naturally, Japanese names (such as *Hoshin Kanri* – policy deployment; *Genba Kanri* – workshop management; *Kaizen* – continuous improvement; *Kanban* – a paperless form of scheduling) tends, for the Western audience, to cloak and mystify the core principles and systems being used, and also to disguise how much of these have been adopted from the West. Leaving aside the jargon and terminology, Japanese business practices and work systems can be characterised by three interrelated elements: long-term planning, timeliness and quality.

Long-term planning

This will be discussed further in Chapters 6 and 7, but for now, in brief, let us say that the timescale on which Japanese enterprises operate is far longer than many of their Western competitors, and their focus on building a strong market position similarly contrasts with the short-term profit maximisation objectives prevalent in the USA and UK in particular (Hamel and Prahalad, 1989). Needless to say, this is an enormous advantage when considering investment decisions, whether this be for products, processes or people (Smith and Misumi, 1989).

Timeliness

The Japanese are seen as having a crucial competitive edge in their ability to develop products and bring them to market faster than their competitors. Part of the explanation for this relates to teamwork. Whilst many Western companies are still designing and developing products on a sequential basis (whereby one part of the design is completed before another is begun), the Japanese work in teams to undertake these tasks simultaneously. This form of teamwork extends to working jointly with customers and suppliers as well (Laage-Hellman, 1997). Not only does this cut the overall time required, but it also leads to fewer errors and misunderstandings because all the relevant parties are involved (Womack *et al*, 1990). Another major contribution to the timeliness of the Japanese is a series of practices designed to cut manufacturing lead times. The main one is *Just-in-Time* production. Under Just-in-Time, parts are supplied and used only as and when required. This method reduces stock and work-in-progress and thus reduces cost. However, to achieve this (as proponents of lean/agile manufacturing have stressed) requires everything to be 'right first time', otherwise such a system would quickly grind to a halt for lack of usable parts (Kidd and Karwowski, 1994; Lamming, 1993). Therefore, it is necessary to drive waste and inefficiency out of the system, and the key mechanism for achieving this is the Japanese commitment to quality (Dale and Cooper, 1992).

Quality

The Japanese commitment to quality is now legendary. Their approach owes much to the inspiration of three Americans: MacArthur, Deming and Juran (Wilkinson, 1991). General MacArthur, who (on behalf of the USA) virtually ruled Japan in the early post-war years, encouraged Japanese industry to improve production quality as part of the rebuilding of their shattered industrial base. Deming (1982) showed the Japanese that statistical process control (SPC), and other such techniques, are powerful methods of controlling quality. Juran (1988) showed the Japanese that quality was determined by all departments in an organisation, and thus set them on the road to developing Total Quality Management. Though imported, the Japanese developed the original concepts considerably. In particular, they introduced the concept of continuous improvement – *Kaizen*. Despite the widespread acceptance of the need for improved quality in the West, the Japanese appear to be the only nation so far capable of diffusing successfully the ideas and practices throughout their industry (Dale and Cooper, 1992; Hannam, 1993; Schonberger, 1982; Womack *et al*, 1990).

In any investigation of the Japanese approach to long-term planning, timeliness and quality, it is necessary to recognise the role played by employees in decision-making. Most discussions of Japanese management emphasise the occurrence of upward influence, particularly through the *ringi* system. This is a procedure whereby proposals for new policies, procedures or expenditure are circulated throughout the firm for comment. The proposal is circulated in written form, and is then sent to all who might be affected if it were to be implemented, in ascending order of seniority. The proposal is modified in line with comments, and only when all agree is it implemented. This joint approach to decision-making is also operated through production councils and quality circles, and covers the planning and scheduling of production, work allocation, changes to production methods, problem-solving, etc. (Inagami, 1988). This system of involving large numbers of people in decision-making is the reason why the Japanese are notorious for the slowness with which they make decisions, and famous for their ability to get it right first time (Hannam, 1993; Smith and Misumi, 1989). Moreover, the *ringi* system has another equally important benefit, as Morgan (1986: 93) states:

> The ringi is as much a process for exploring and reaffirming values as it is for setting a direction ... In the American view objectives should be hard and fast and clearly stated for all to see. In the Japanese view they emerge from a more fundamental process of exploring and understanding the values through which a firm is or should be operating. A knowledge of these values, the limits that are to guide actions, defines a set of possible actions. An action chosen from this set may not be the very best, but it will satisfy parameters deemed crucial for success.

One factor only mentioned briefly so far is the importance – or not – of culture to the Japanese approach to management. Certainly, early studies laid great stress on the relationship between Japanese culture and business success (Abegglen, 1958). The argument emerged that it was the nature of Japanese society and its impact on individuals and companies that gave Japan its competitive edge. For this reason, it was argued, the West would never be able to replicate Japanese practices and competitiveness successfully. Indeed, one reason why Pascale and Athos (1982) chose to study Japanese companies operating in America was that Pascale doubted whether American companies could learn much from the Japanese in Japan because their cultures were so different (Crainer, 1995). Obviously, as Hofstede (1980, 1990) showed, national cultures do impinge on organisational practices. However, whether or not this means that such practices cannot successfully be adopted in other societies is another question. A number of studies have undermined the argument for considering the Japanese approach to management to be dependent on Japanese culture. It has been shown that many of the distinctive practices of Japanese companies are relatively new and not embedded in Japanese history, that the role of culture is less influential than other factors, and that the Japanese approach can be successfully replicated outside Japan (Ackroyd et al, 1988; Buckley and Mirza, 1985; Cole, 1979; Marsh and Mannari, 1976; Pascale and Athos, 1982; Smith and Misumi, 1989; Urabe, 1986; Wickens, 1987).

The future of the Japanese approach

In discussing the distinctive Japanese approach to management, we must not forget the strong reciprocal links between government and business, especially the importance of Japanese industrial policy in stimulating and guiding the country's economic progress. This is seen most clearly in the close links between business and the Ministry of International Trade and Industry (MITI). As part of its remit to establish Japan as a leading industrial nation, MITI played a crucial role in establishing national programmes in key industries to encourage joint action, to develop the country's science and technological base, amongst companies and public research institutions. The ultimate goal of these programmes has been to create a strong, competitive and world-class industrial base for Japan. These collaborative programmes have not been at the expense of competition between companies; rather they have helped to improve the competitiveness of all the companies both in relation to each other and, importantly, in relation to international rivals (Laage-Hellman, 1997).

Nevertheless, despite the competitiveness of Japanese firms and the active support of the Japanese government, the economy has been in decline for the last decade. After successfully coping with the second oil crisis of 1979 and the effects of a rapidly-appreciating currency in the mid-1980s, Japan enjoyed sustained economic growth until the early 1990s. However, since then the economy has been in protracted recession, though it is now showing some signs of recovery. Unemployment, at over 5.3 per cent in June 2003, was down 1.9 per cent from the historic high of the previous year (Statistics Bureau, 2003). Nevertheless, successive banking and political scandals have undermined the stability of the political and financial system on which Japan's industrial might was built (Barrie, 1999; Shirai, 1997). This has led to a flurry of political and business reforms, and attempts to introduce Western-style deregulation in order to foster competition and cut costs.

Many explanations have been put forward for the decline of the Japanese economy. One of the most persuasive is that whilst Japan developed a world-class manufacturing base, this was undermined by a failure to develop the rest of its economy to similar standards (Pilling, 2003). In particular, the service sector, especially retailing, is only half as productive as its US counterparts. Similarly, the Japanese public sector is seen as being far less efficient than its Western equivalents. The banking sector also did the Japanese economy no favours by making vast loans to property companies to purchase over-priced land and buildings, which became worth only a fraction of what they paid for them when the asset bubble burst in the 1990s. This explanation helps to explain why, despite all its economic problems, even in the worst years of the 1990s, Japan's economy, and its leading industrial companies, generally continued to outperform those of its competitors in the West (Pilling, 2003; Shirai, 1997). Therefore, its economic problems over the last decade do not appear to invalidate the Japanese approach to management as developed in, and applied to, the manufacturing sector. However, low growth, domestic recession, increasing international competition, technological developments that have led to changes in industrial and job structures, and an ageing population have all created pressures to change the Japanese approach to management (Harukiyo and Hook, 1998; Sako and Sato, 1997; Thomas, 2003).

In the larger Japanese companies, these pressures have led to structural changes designed to flatten the hierarchy and create greater flexibility (Koji, 1998). In the motor industry, in particular, there has also been a weakening of the previously strong supply chain links, with second- and third-tier suppliers being exposed to greater levels of competition (Masayoshi, 1998). Looking at the Japanese approach to production systems, here too there have been changes; but these do not seem to have radically changed the main characteristic of the Japanese approach, which has been one of blending mass production with flexibility (Masayuki, 1998).

Perhaps the area where the pressures for change have been the greatest is in personnel practices, especially those relating to lifetime employment, seniority-based promotion and rewards systems, and the treatment of female workers (Sako and Sato, 1997). As far as lifetime employment is concerned, there is some evidence that the economic, industrial and technological changes of the 1980s and 1990s have had an effect on this (Barrie, 1999). For white-collar workers, especially the older and higher-paid ones, there is evidence that continuous employment within one enterprise is giving way to continuous employment within a group of enterprises (Inagami, 1995; Sako, 1997). In the past, if a worker's job was eliminated, they would be given another one in the same workplace. Increasingly, the tendency is now to transfer redundant workers to another job within the same group or affiliated group of companies but not necessarily the same workplace. In some cases, this can be hundreds of miles away, and can also involve a reduction in pay (Watts, 1998). However, for blue-collar male workers, where the distinctions between East and West were always the most marked, job security seems to have improved, if anything. This is because of the falling birth rate, which has also led to an increase in the retirement age from 55 to 60 or even 65 (Seike, 1997). Research has also shown that whilst the use of part-time (mainly women) and contract labour may be increasing, job security in this area is also increasing (Wakisata, 1997). Therefore, overall, it appears that stability of employment may actually be increasing. In terms of lifetime employment, though there have been some changes to the system, most Japanese managers, as well as workers, do seem to believe it is desirable and feasible to maintain it, especially as it is seen as essential to manager–worker cooperation (Ohmi, 1997; Sako, 1997; Sugeno and Suwa, 1997). As the Finance Director of a large Japanese corporation commented:

> To secure our employees living life in good shape is one of the corporation's duties ... We cannot believe in cutting employees to sustain profitability. It is a kind of failed management philosophy.
> (Quoted in Barrie, 1999: 13)

In the area of the seniority principle, there does seem to be a greater willingness to make changes. There is growing pressure from both employers and unions to consider other criteria, such as ability, as well as seniority when determining pay and promotion (Sugeno and Suwa, 1997). In a 1995 survey, two-thirds of responding managers saw the introduction of ability-based reward and promotion systems as a priority in order to create greater flexibility, although very few managers seemed prepared to abandon the seniority principle totally (Kawakita, 1997; Sako, 1997). Also, it must be remembered that though seniority plays an important part in promotion and reward, ability has always been taken into account as well. Therefore, what seems to be being proposed is fine-tuning of the system rather than its dismantling.

Significant changes do, however, seem to be taking place with regard to female workers. As in the West, there has been a significant increase in the proportion of women in the workforce in Japan in the last 40 years. In 1960, there were 18.1 million working women (40.8 per cent of the adult female population); by 1992, this had grown to 26.2 million (75.4 per cent of the adult female population) (Wakisata, 1997). This growth was accompanied by legal changes to promote equal opportunities and practical assistance with child care arrangements. Like men, women have also benefited from greater security of employment. The average length of service of women workers increased from 4.5 years in 1970 to 7.4 years in 1992; the respective figures for men are 8.8 and 12.5 years. In addition, there seems to be a gradual reduction in the very significant gap between male and female rates of pay: in 1970, women earned on average some 50 per cent of male wage levels; by 1992, this had increased to around 60 per cent. However, for female university graduates in their 20s, the figure was over 90 per cent (Wakisata, 1997).

Therefore, there have been and remain significant pressures on the Japanese economy, which have led to changes in how companies are structured and run, especially their human resource practices, and in their relations with customers and suppliers (Thomas, 2003). However, these do not seem designed to undermine or alter significantly the core of the Japanese approach to management (Harukiyo and Hook, 1998). The strong ties that bind workers and Japanese enterprises together and which lie at the heart of the Japanese approach to management have not weakened (Sako and Sato, 1997). As Shirai (1997: xv) commented, ' ... it appears from all the indicators that the foundations of stable labour–management relations in Japan remain unshaken and intact.'

▪ The Japanese approach: summary and criticisms

It can be seen, therefore, that there are distinctive practices and policies which have a coherence and can be described as 'the Japanese approach to management'. However, it is not simply the merits of the individual practices that have given the Japanese their competitive edge. Rather it is that they are devised and adopted in such a way that they are integrated and mutually supportive of each other; in particular, Japanese companies have a unique way of combining hard and soft practices (Laage-Hellman, 1997; Ouchi, 1981; Pascale and Athos, 1982; Sako and Sato, 1997). This is not to say that this approach is universal in Japan or that all elements are present in those companies who do practise it. However, there is sufficient evidence available to justify stating that it is the dominant approach in Japan at the moment, and has been since at least the 1960s.

This does not imply that it will not change. Indeed, given that most of these practices have been evolving over the last 50 years, it would be surprising if they did not continue to evolve (Smith and Misumi, 1989; Thomas, 2003; Whitehill, 1991). Already, as described above, there is strong evidence to show that changes are taking place. Even in large companies, such as Toyota and Honda, policies of lifetime employment and the reluctance to recruit staff mid-career are being modified, owing to the need to recruit skills that are in short supply, and because of economic and social pressures. These include especially the pressures for equal opportunities for men and women, the implications of an ageing population, and the need to recruit foreigners (Dawkins, 1993, 1994; Thomas, 1993; Wakisata, 1997).

Nevertheless, although the dynamic and innovative nature of Japanese organisations and their passionate devotion to competitiveness are likely to lead to changes in the way organisations are run, it is unlikely that these changes will undermine the core construct of mutual obligation between organisation and employee that lies at the heart of the Japanese system (Ohmi, 1997; Sako, 1997; Sugeno and Suwa, 1997). It also seems more than likely that the changes which are taking place and will take place in the future will enhance, rather than detract from, Japan's economic strength.

The Japanese approach has delivered impressive economic results, but there are those who would question the social cost involved. Japanese workers work longer hours than their Western counterparts, and in addition are expected to participate in many work-related social events (Clark, 1979). There is also considerable evidence to show that Japanese workers are less satisfied with their lot than their Western counterparts, especially in relation to working hours and pay (Kamata, 1982; Lincoln and Kalleberg, 1985; Luthans *et al*, 1985; Naoi and Schooler, 1985; Odaka, 1975).

In many respects this is not surprising. From a Western standpoint at least, Japanese companies appear to operate very oppressive and authoritarian regimes that, through the combination of personnel practices and work systems discussed above, together with peer group pressure, leave workers little option but to conform and perform to very high standards (Kamata, 1982; Smith and Misumi, 1989). This accounts, in part at least, for the common observation that the Japanese are a nation of workaholics. However, there are other serious criticisms of the Japanese approach:

▪ Most companies operate a two-tier labour market, whereby a significant minority of the workforce have good conditions and lifetime employment, at the expense of less well-paid and less secure jobs for the majority, especially women. However, there is now some evidence that this is changing, especially for women (Wakisata, 1997).

- Even those with lifetime employment are little more than slaves to the corporation because they cannot move to other jobs (Morgan, 1986).
- The merits of teamwork are only gained thanks to the unremitting peer group pressure on individuals continually to improve their performance (Kamata, 1982).
- The lack of independent trade unions leaves workers defenceless in the face of managerial pressure to work ever harder (Kazunori, 1998; Yutaka, 1998).

Whatever the merits or demerits of the Japanese approach, there is little doubt that it has had an enormous impact on organisational performance; consequently, many attempts have been made to introduce 'Japanisation' into Western companies (Ackroyd *et al*, 1988; Hannam, 1993; Pang and Oliver, 1988; Pascale and Athos, 1982; Schonberger, 1982; Thomas, 2003; Turnbull, 1986). Despite some reservations about how well the system might travel, Japanese companies have shown that they can transfer their approach to the West. Nissan's Sunderland car assembly plant in the UK was judged by the Economist Intelligence Unit to be the most productive in Europe for the second year running in 1998, whilst in the same year its Smyrna, Tennessee plant was cited as the most productive in North America by the Harbour Report.

On the other hand, transferring the Japanese approach to indigenous Western companies appears to have been more problematic. Even the UK car components industry, which, owing to the presence of Nissan, Honda and Toyota, has received more support and encouragement than probably any industry outside Japan, seems to have failed to adopt the Japanese approach successfully (Hines, 1994; Lamming, 1994). This may be a major reason why many companies in the West, whilst not rejecting the lessons of Japanese management *per se*, are now turning to other approaches to increase their competitiveness, especially organisational learning.

Organisational learning

Though Culture–Excellence and the Japanese approach continue to exert a powerful influence over Western companies, in the 1990s a third approach to organisational success came forward to challenge them: organisational learning. Despite its new-found popularity in the 1990s, organisational learning was not a new concept. The highly-respected American academic Chris Argyris has been writing about organisational learning for over 40 years (Argyris, 1992). However, there can be no doubt that interest in the concept of organisational learning, or the learning organisation as it is sometimes called, grew considerably in the 1990s. As Crossan and Guatto (1996) noted, there were as many academic papers published on the topic in 1993 as in the whole of the 1980s. Many of these articles are dotted with emotive statements such as ' ... the rate at which individuals and organizations learn may become the only sustainable competitive advantage ...' (Stata, 1989: 4). Though statements like this have the power to attract the attention of business leaders, there are really two factors which appear to have moved organisational learning from being a subject for serious academic study to a hot boardroom topic: the pace of change, and the rise of corporate Japan.

There is considerable support for the view that the pace of change is accelerating as never before, and that organisations have to chart their way through an increasingly complex environment. Organisations are having to cope with the pressures of globalisation, changes in technology, the rise of e-commerce, situations where customers and suppliers can be both competitors and allies, and a change in emphasis from quantity to quality and from products to services. To cope with this growing complexity, organisations are recognising the need to acquire and utilise increasing amounts of knowledge if they are to make the changes necessary to remain competitive (Chawla and Renesch, 1995). As Pautzke (1989) stated:

> Careful cultivation of the capacity to learn in the broadest sense, i.e. the capacity both to acquire knowledge and to develop practical abilities, seems to offer a realistic way of tackling the pressing problems of our time.   (Quoted in Probst and Buchel, 1997: 5)

The second, and perhaps main, factor that has generated such interest in organisational learning is the rise of corporate Japan. In attempting to explain and/or combat Japanese penetration of Western markets, many commentators argued that one of the main strengths of Japanese companies is the speed with which they gather information on markets and competitors, and disseminate and act upon this information internally (Nonaka, 1988; Pascale and Athos, 1982). However, Japanese companies' ability to learn, adapt and develop also extended to their commitment to continuous improvement, in processes as well as products, both internally and jointly with customers and suppliers (Laage-Hellman, 1997; Sako and Sato, 1997). The result, as described earlier in this chapter, is their fearsome reputation for producing the right product, in the right time and at the right price. Underpinning this is an ability to translate a commitment to individual learning into organisational learning (Hedlund and Nonaka, 1993; Nonaka, 1988; Ouchi, 1981; Whitehill, 1991). This idea, that the promotion of collective learning is crucial to organisational success, has not only led to the upsurge in interest in organisational learning, but it also provides a bridge between Western and Eastern approaches to managing organisations. For these reasons, Probst and Buchel (1997: 1) argue that 'Organizational learning offers an alternative paradigm by which systems can change, thus permitting us to redefine the economy and society.'

■ What is organisational learning?

The term 'organisational learning' is often used interchangeably with the term 'learning organisation'. The difference, according to Tsang (1997: 74–5), is that:

> Organizational learning is a concept used to describe certain types of activity that take place in an organization while the learning organization refers to a particular type of organization in and of itself. Nevertheless, there is a simple relationship between the two – a learning organization is one which is good at organisational learning.

In effect, the difference appears to be between 'becoming' and 'being'. Organisational learning describes attempts by organisations to become learning organisations by promoting learning in a conscious, systematic and synergistic fashion that involves everyone in the organisation. A learning organisation is the highest state of organisational learning, in which an organisation has achieved the ability to transform itself continuously through the development and involvement of all its members (Argyris and Schon, 1978; Burgoyne et al, 1994; Chawla and Renesch, 1995; West, 1994).

A further, and perhaps more significant, distinction between the two terms relates to those who use them. Argyris (1999: 1) asserts:

> We divide the literature that pays attention to organizational learning into two main categories: the practice-oriented, prescriptive literature of 'the learning organization,' promulgated mainly by consultants and practitioners, and the predominately skeptical scholarly literature of 'organizational learning', produced by academics.

In fact the term 'learning organisation' is used much less now than in the 1980s and 1990s. This appears to be because very few organisations, if any, appear to have achieved learning organisation status (Easterby-Smith, 1997; Probst and Buchel, 1997; Tsang, 1997). For this reason, organisational learning now appears to be the term of choice for both the sceptical and prescriptive camps.

Having said that, one of the problems in coming to grips with organisational learning is that its advocates appear to offer a multitude of definitions or models of what it is; for example:

> Organizational learning is the process by which the organization's knowledge and value base changes, leading to improved problem-solving ability and capacity for action.
> (Probst and Buchel, 1997: 15)
>
> A learning organization is an organization skilled at creating, acquiring and transferring knowledge, and at modifying behavior to reflect new knowledge and insights.
> (Garvin, 1993: 80)
>
> Organizational learning means the process of improving actions through better knowledge and understanding. (Fiol and Lyles, 1985: 803)
>
> An entity learns if, through its processing of information, the range of its potential behaviors is changed. (Huber, 1991: 89)
>
> Organizational learning occurs through shared insight, knowledge and mental models and builds on past knowledge and experience, that is, on memory. (Stata, 1989: 64)

These are only a sample of the definitions that have been advanced. Indeed, it is probably not an over-exaggeration to say that there are nearly as many definitions of organisational learning as there are writers on the topic (Tsang, 1997).

Easterby-Smith (1997) attempts to explain this confusion of definitions by identifying the different disciplinary backgrounds of those writing on organisational learning. He argues that most writers come from one of six disciplines: psychology, management science, sociology, organisation theory, production management and cultural anthropology. Wang and Ahmed (2003) note that it is not just the different disciplinary backgrounds of the proponents of organisational learning that leads to confusion. They identify five different focuses on the concept, and argue that researchers tend to centre their attention on only one of these. The 'five focuses on the concept [are]: focus on the collectivity of individual learning; focus on the process or system; focus on culture or metaphor; focus on knowledge management; and focus on continuous improvement ...' (Wang and Ahmed, 2003: 9).

Like Argyris (1999), Easterby-Smith (1997) also draws attention to the difference between the long-established contributors to the field, the academic sceptics, who have been attempting to analyse, describe and understand learning processes within organisations, without necessarily wishing to change them (e.g. Argyris, 1992; Bateson, 1972), and the relatively newer entrants, the practitioners and consultants, who are attempting to prescribe what an organisation should do to maximise learning (e.g. Pedler *et al*, 1989; Senge, 1990). This is a point also made by Tsang (1997), who notes that, up to the 1980s, it was the analytical writers who dominated the field, but in the 1990s, with the upsurge in interest in organisational learning, it was the prescriptive writers who came to the fore. Though the variety of disciplinary backgrounds and perspectives of those writing about organisational learning helps to explain the plethora of definitions, it does not help to resolve them. For this reason, as Probst and Buchel (1997) state, there is as yet no comprehensive theory of organisational learning. Nevertheless, there is one area where there is growing clarity and agreement: 'In today's environments ... learning is directed increasingly at transformational change ...' (Cummings and Worley (2001: 520). It is the potential of organisational learning to enable organisations to reinvent themselves in order to compete in the changing and increasingly uncertain and competitive environment that is making it such an attractive proposition for many managers.

Although many writers have contributed to the concept of the organisational learning, those who have done most to popularise the concept in the UK are Pedler, Boydell and Burgoyne (1989). However, perhaps the most influential writer of the 1990s was Peter Senge in the US, whose book *The Fifth Discipline* (1990) caught the imagination of corporate America. Its success motivated a whole host of consultants and academics to follow suit and produce books and articles extolling the virtues of the learning organisation, and the steps necessary to become one (Tsang, 1997). Part of the success of his book lies in the fact that it combines the individualism of the Culture–Excellence approach with the knowledge-generating ability of the Japanese approach. Senge argues that there are five interrelated disciplines that organisations need to foster amongst individuals and groups in order to promote learning and success:

1 **Personal mastery** – individual growth and learning.
2 **Mental models** – deeply-ingrained assumptions that affect the way individuals think about people, situations and organisations.
3 **Shared visions** – the development of a common view of the organisation's future.
4 **Team learning** – the shift from individual learning to collective learning.
5 **Systems thinking** – the 'Fifth Discipline' that links the others together and which, he argues, is missing in most organisations:

> The art of systems thinking lies in being able to recognise increasingly (dynamically) complex and subtle structures ... amid the wealth of details, pressures and cross-currents that attend all real management settings. In fact, the essence of mastering systems thinking as a management discipline lies in seeing patterns where others see only events and forces to react to.
>
> (Senge, 1990: 73)

In contrast to Senge, who stresses the attributes an organisation needs to possess in order to learn, others stress the learning styles of individuals and organisations. Perhaps the most influential in this area are Argyris and Schon (1978) who, building on the work of Bateson (1972), proposed a three-level evolutionary model of learning:

- **Level I – single-loop learning.** This is adaptive learning, which involves detecting and rectifying errors or exceptions within the scope of the organisation's existing practices, policies and norms of behaviour in order to ensure its objectives are met. Typical examples of this would be the monitoring of quality standards or adherence to sales targets in order to detect and correct variance. However, this would not feed back into the questioning of, or amendment to, the organisation's original objectives.
- **Level II – double-loop learning.** This concerns going beyond correcting variance in standards and targets and, instead, involves challenging the appropriateness of the organisation's basic norms, values, policies and operating procedures that create these standards and targets in the first place. This is reconstructive learning, which involves reconstructing basic aspects of an organisation's operations. Typically, this might involve questioning whether some functions should be outsourced rather than continuing to be performed in-house or whether the organisation should adopt a flatter, more open structure to remain aligned with its environment. Out of such changes, new practices, policies and norms of behaviour are generated.
- **Level III – triple-loop learning.** This involves questioning the rationale for the organisation and, in the light of this, radically transforming it. A typical example of this might be a traditional manufacturing organisation attempting to reinvent itself as a service company with all the implications for culture, structure and practices that such a move would require.

Burgoyne (1995) suggests that the importance of learning at Level III lies as much in its ability to allow an organisation to create and transform its environments as it does in allowing it to transform itself. He also considers that this is reflected in the ability of the organisation to stabilise the context in which it operates and/or its relationship with it. It is at this level that the concept of the learning organisation can fully emerge.

Cummings and Worley (2001) argue that there are a number of learning interventions designed to help an organisation's members move from adaptive, Level I, learning to transformative, Level III, learning. These comprise three phases, but Cummings and Worley (2001: 522–4) warn that:

Although the phases are described linearly below, in practice they form a recurrent cycle of overlapping learning activities.

1 *Discover theories in use and their consequences.* This first step involves uncovering members' mental models or theories in use and the consequences that follow from behaving and organizing according to them. ...
2 *Invent and produce more effective theories in use.* Based on what is discovered in the first phase of this change process, members invent and produce theories in use that lead to more effective actions and that are more closely aligned with [Level II and Level III] learning. ...
3 *Continually monitor and improve the learning process.* This final phase involves ... – learning how to learn. Here learning is directed at the learning process itself and at how well [Level II and Level III] learning characteristics are reflected in it. This includes assessing OL strategies and the organizational structures and processes that contribute to them.

Cummings and Worley also identify five organisational characteristics that promote organisational learning, as follows:

- **Structure** – this needs to be flat and teamwork-based in order to promote networking both internally and externally.
- **Information systems** – these need to be geared toward the rapid acquisition, processing and sharing of information.
- **Human resource practices** – these need to include appraisal and reward systems which promote the acquisition and sharing of new skills and knowledge.
- **Organisational culture** – this needs to be based on values and norms which promote openness, creativity and experimentation in order to support successful learning.
- **Leadership** – managers throughout the organisation must lead, promote and be involved in organisational learning.

Therefore, as can be seen, Cummings and Worley identify both the phases that organisations need to go through to move from adaptive to transformational learning, and the characteristics which promote organisational learning. Probst and Buchel (1997: 16), on the other hand, take a very different view, claiming that 'Organizational learning is unique to an institution.' That is to say that each organisation can and should find its own way to become a learning organisation. They argue that there are at least four different generic approaches:

- **Learning by developing a strategy** – shaping the organisation's future through a participative and practical learning exercise.
- **Learning by developing a structure** – developing structural forms, such as matrix and network structures, that promote learning.
- **Learning by developing a culture** – the creation of shared values, norms and attitudes that promote collective success over individual attainment.
- **Learning by developing human resources** – developing staff through participative and group-orientated learning.

Despite the diversity and contradictions evident among those promoting the concept of organisational learning, one thing is clear: they all see the main purpose of learning as facilitating organisational change. As with the Culture–Excellence and the Japanese approaches, its popularity owes much to its posited beneficial link to organisation performance. However, unlike them, it is the only organisation theory whose main purpose is to enable organisations to cope with and promote change. As Probst and Buchel (1997: xi) comment:

> ... learning is attracting increasing attention both in academic circles and business practice. One of the main reasons for this is the increasing pressure of change on companies ... The rate of change accelerates steadily, and companies must find their bearings in an increasingly complex environment. The ability to learn is thus of paramount importance. Companies which do not successfully implement organizational changes, and which fail to cultivate their potential to develop, may soon find themselves amongst the losers.

As can be seen, there are considerable arguments in favour of the learning approach; yet, there are also arguments against it.

■ Organisational learning: summary and criticisms

Though there has been a considerable interest in the concept of organisational learning over the past decade, this does not seem to have created the clarity one might have wished for. It is, therefore, difficult to summarise a concept that has been defined in so many different ways and from so many different perspectives. However, there are perhaps five aspects of organisational learning that most writers would agree upon:

- An organisation's survival depends on its ability to learn at the same pace as or faster than changes in its environment.
- Learning must become a collective and not just an individual process.
- There must be a fundamental shift towards systems (or triple-loop) thinking by an organisation's members.
- By adopting organisational learning, an organisation not only acquires the ability to adapt quickly and appropriately to changing circumstances, but it can also transform itself if necessary.
- As well as the ability to transform itself, an organisation can adapt to, influence and even transform its environment.

Presented in this way, it is easy to appreciate the attractiveness of organisational learning. As Huczynski and Buchanan (2001: 135) assert, however, the positive views of organisational learning need to be balanced with the negative ones (*see* Table 3.1).

Table 3.1 **Learning organisation positives and negatives**

Learning organisation positives	Learning organisation negatives
A rich, multi-dimensional concept affecting many aspects of organisational behaviour	A complex and difficult set of practices, difficult to implement systematically
An innovative approach to learning, to knowledge management and to investing in intellectual capital	An attempt to use dated concepts from change management and learning theory, repackaged as a management consulting project
A new set of challenging concepts focusing attention on the acquisition and development of individual and corporate knowledge	A new vocabulary for encouraging employee compliance with management directives in the guise of 'self development'
An innovative approach to organisation, management and employee development	An innovative approach for strengthening management control
Innovative use of technology to manage organisational knowledge through databases and the Internet or intranets	A technology-dependent approach that ignores how people actually develop and use knowledge in organisations

Source: from Huczynski and Buchanan (2001: 135)

Huczynski and Buchanan are not the only ones to draw attention to the more problematic aspects of organisational learning. The major criticisms of organisational learning can be grouped under six major headings:

1 As is apparent from the above review, there is no agreed definition of organisational learning (Burnes *et al*, 2003; Easterby-Smith, 1997; Probst and Buchel, 1997; Tsang, 1997; Wang and Ahmed, 2003). Even Tom Peters (1993: 385), who might be expected to be attracted to the concept, stated that: 'Most talk about "learning organisations" is maddeningly abstract or vague – and perpetually falls short on the specifics.'

2 Despite the volume of publications on the subject, there is a scarcity of rigorous empirical research in the area. As Tsang (1997) pointed out, one of the main reasons for this is that many of those writing on organisational learning are practitioners and consultants seeking to prescribe and sell rather than describe or analyse. He argues that, as well as promoting the concept, they are also trying to promote themselves and the organisations they work for. A similar point was also made by Easterby-Smith (1997: 1107):

> Much of the existing research into learning organizations is based on case studies of organizations that are said to be successful, and these sometimes seem to rely more on public relations than on any rigorous and grounded studies.

If this is the situation, then much of the research on organisational learning, and the recommendations and conclusions that flow from it, have to be treated with a degree of scepticism.

3 As Thompson (1995) pointed out, 'The term organizational learning is actually a misnomer. In fact an organization itself doesn't learn – people learn.' It follows that, in most organisations, the achievement of a high level of organisational learning will necessitate a fundamental shift in how individuals learn. This is not just a case of collecting and sharing information in new ways but, crucially, of thinking in new ways (Argyris and Schon, 1978). This requires individuals to undergo difficult and sometimes painful changes involving unlearning old ways of thinking and the redrawing of their cognitive maps – the way they perceive and make sense of the world around them. Many writers have commented on the serious obstacles to achieving such changes (Argyris, 1990; Hedberg, 1981; Probst and Buchel, 1997; Wang and Ahmed, 2003). However, above and beyond these difficulties lies a further issue. In engineering such changes in an individual's thought processes, it is not just their perception of the organisation that is being changed, but their perception of the world outside work and how they relate to it and to others around them. What are being tampered with are deep-rooted personality traits and constructs that are fundamental to an individual's psychological make-up. In such cases, one has to question not only the extent to which such attempts can ever be successful, but also whether it is even ethically justifiable to try.

4 Probst and Buchel (1997) maintain that organisational learning requires the generation of diversity of opinion and, at the same time, the creation of consensus. They argue that these contradictory tasks can be reconciled and achieved through the development of a collective view of reality. Their view assumes that it is in everyone's interest to participate in organisational learning and the ensuing changes. Although some writers, especially Argyris (1990) and Easterby-Smith *et al* (2000) recognise that there are major barriers to organisational learning, the assumption is that these can be overcome. However, as Chapter 1 demonstrated, much of our

organisational experience since the Industrial Revolution has shown that managers view knowledge and control as almost synonymous. To this end, managers have systematically attempted to reduce workers' knowledge and increase their own (Rose, 1988). As will be discussed further in Chapter 5, organisations are riven by political battles, and the possession and selective use of knowledge is a potent weapon in such situations (Pfeffer, 1981). Beyond that, however, many traditional managers are unlikely to welcome the creation of organisations which encourage openness, and allow subordinates to seek out their own knowledge and question the expertise and authority of their superiors. As Garratt (1999: 205) put it:

> A few, often senior, people can see the concept as highly challenging and unnerving. They are concerned that existing organisational power balances may be upset by too much 'transparency' ...

Given what we know about resistance to change, given what we know about power and politics in organisations, it is surprising, as Blackler and McDonald (2000) and Coopey and Burgoyne (2000) note, that so little attention has been paid to these issues by those investigating and promoting organisational learning.

5   Though Japanese companies are often held up as exemplars of organisational learning, most theory and practical advice in this area has been developed in the West, especially the US. The proponents of organisational learning argue that the recipes they have developed are applicable to all organisations and cultures; nevertheless, many writers have drawn attention to the problem of transferring theories and practices developed in one culture to another (Deresky, 2000; Hedlund and Nonaka, 1993; Hofstede, 1993; Rosenzweig, 1994; Thomas, 2003; Trompenaars, 1993). For example, openness and the encouragement of public debate and criticism are seen as an essential part of organisational learning (Chawla and Renesch, 1995). Although US managers might not find this too difficult to accept, it is doubtful whether, for example, Japanese or Chinese managers, with their tradition of preserving face, would find it so easy (Deresky, 2000). Face involves both maintaining one's own dignity and decorum and, at the same time, not undermining or attacking the dignity and decorum of others. Therefore, Japanese and Chinese managers, and managers from other non-Western countries, might find it very difficult openly to challenge and criticise the behaviour and ideas of others or for others to do this to them (Ho, 1976; Jones et al, 2000; Tsang, 1997). Similarly, as was noted in the previous chapter, proponents of Contingency Theory argued against universal approaches to organisational effectiveness and in favour of a context-based approach (Burns and Stalker, 1961; Woodward, 1965; Child, 1984). In particular, they maintain that theories and practices developed with one sort of organisation/situation in mind may be much less effective in a different set of circumstances (Burnes, 1991).

6   Burnes et al (2003) point out that the case for the general adoption of organisational learning is based on the assumption that all organisations operate in a fast-moving and unpredictable environment. In such a situation, the ability to learn and adapt must be possessed by all members of an organisation and not just a few at the top. Burnes et al argue that this may be the case for companies in the IT sector, but other sectors may experience a much lower level of environmental disturbance. Also, they

maintain, even in fast-moving sectors such as IT, there are companies, such as Microsoft, whose dominant position allows them a degree of predictability and stability (Coupland, 1995; Wallace and Erickson, 1992). In addition, Burnes *et al* pose the question: if an organisation can develop the ability to transform its environment, what is to stop it creating an environment where organisational learning is unnecessary? After all, given the many obstacles and barriers to developing and maintaining organisational learning, this would appear an attractive proposition.

In conclusion, we can perhaps agree with Probst and Buchel (1997: xi) who warn that:

> We should be wary of dismissing it [organisational learning] as the latest fad, since the topic of learning is attracting increasing attention both in academic circles and in business practice.

However, we can perhaps also agree with Mintzberg *et al*'s (1998b: 228) double-edged compliment that:

> ... [organisational learning] is all the rage right now, and mostly for good reasons. But it is no panacea for anything. People have to learn, but they also have to get on with doing the regular work efficiently. (Horses wear blinders for good reasons). There can be a time to learn and a time to exploit previous learning ... So learning is wonderful, but there can be too much of a wonderful thing!

Conclusions

This chapter has examined the three main approaches to managing and structuring organisations that have dominated Western thinking and practice over the last two decades. The proponents of all three approaches claim that theirs is a new paradigm that contrasts sharply and favourably with the organisational theories discussed in Chapters 1 and 2. This does not mean there are not some similarities with what has gone before. For example, the Japanese use the industrial engineering concepts developed by Taylor and his contemporaries to study and design jobs. However, the context in which they are deployed (the lack of payment by results, the use of teamwork and worker involvement, and above all else, guaranteed jobs) is markedly different. In a similar way, the Culture–Excellence approach can be seen to bear some similarities with the Human Relations movement, especially in its emphasis on leadership and communication. However, the emphasis on culture, individual achievement and all-round excellence make it a distinct approach. The same can be said of organisational learning, which builds on, but develops in a wider context, past practices for encouraging individual and group learning.

There are also points of contact between the three approaches themselves. Organisational learning consciously draws on the methods used by the Japanese to gather and use information speedily. In addition, it stresses, as with Culture–Excellence, the importance of individuals in promoting innovation. However, it also clashes with the other two approaches. Advocates of organisational learning stress that it can enable companies to shape and create their environment, whilst supporters of Culture–Excellence stress that organisations have no choice but to adapt to their environment. It is at odds with the Japanese approach in terms of change. The Japanese favour directed continuous incremental change, whereas the organisational learning approach encourages continuous but often undirected adaptation and also transformational change.

There are also points of contact between the Japanese approach and the Culture–Excellence approach (the emphasis on excellence, the importance of culture); but, again, there are marked differences. Lifetime employment and loyalty to the organisation contrast strongly with the stress on the temporary nature of jobs proposed by the proponents of Culture–Excellence. As an example, contrast the threat to thousands of jobs posed by the merger of the Halifax and Leeds building societies in the UK (in order to form the UK's fourth largest bank) with the case of the merger of the Mitsubishi Bank and the Bank of Tokyo in Japan (to form the world's largest bank), where it was stated that maintaining all jobs was a matter of honour (Hughes, 1995; Rafferty, 1995). Likewise, payment by seniority and payment by performance are significant points of departure (though there is an increasing, but still small-scale, use of performance pay in Japan). It is noticeable as well that neither the Culture–Excellence nor the organisational learning approaches really concern themselves with the sort of hard, manufacturing/quality practices so common in Japan.

Finally, the Culture–Excellence school seem obsessed with downsizing and arguing for smallness. The Japanese, on the other hand, are committed to growth. As Ferguson (1988: 57) remarked, in the 1970s and 1980s the USA was not outperformed by small, nimble organisations, but by 'high industrial complexes embedded in stable, strategically-co-ordinated alliances often supported by protectionist governments ... '.

On balance, though there are similarities, these three approaches conflict with, rather than complement, each other. The Japanese approach, with its combination of tried and tested, hard and soft techniques, provides a coherent and comprehensive approach to organisations which stresses both innovation and stability. The Culture–Excellence approach tends to emphasise soft techniques, innovation, dynamism and unpredictability, and, particularly, draws attention to the role of culture. Organisational learning, as an attempt to provide a coherent paradigm for organisational competitiveness, is the newest and least concrete of the three. At one level it has affinities with the other two approaches, but its emphasis on learning as the principal source of competitiveness also distinguishes it from them. This does not mean that if Western organisations become more adept at adopting Total Quality Management and other such techniques, and if Japanese companies broaden their use of external labour markets and adopt more flexible structures, the three may not coalesce, especially given the common emphasis on learning. At the moment, however, they remain competitors rather than collaborators.

Needless to say, none of the three approaches is without its drawbacks or criticisms. In particular, there are five concerns that should be highlighted, relating to 'one best way', people, politics, culture and change management.

One best way

The first three chapters of this book have been concerned with approaches to managing and structuring organisations. The one clear message that has emerged so far is to beware of any theory or proposition which claims that it is the 'one best way' for all situations and all organisations. Yet all three of the approaches we have discussed in this chapter appear to advocate just that.

People

The Culture–Excellence and the Japanese approaches also leave much to be desired with regard to people. Both approaches rely on a workforce split into a privileged core and a relatively unprivileged periphery. Under both approaches there is a strong emphasis on commitment to the organisation taking precedence over all else, even family life. Therefore, long hours and short holidays are the norm under both systems. The Japanese approach appears to offer more job security, at least for the privileged core. However, the price of this is that competition for jobs in the better organisations begins, quite literally, at birth. To get a job with the best companies, applicants have to have been to the best universities; to enter those, they have to have been at the best schools; and to enter the best schools, they have to have been at the best nurseries (Bratton, 1992; Fruin, 1992). The lack of clarity of the organisational learning concept makes it difficult to be certain what the implications of it are for people. However, it does project an intensity of work and commitment that aligns it with the Culture–Excellence approach. Also, its emphasis on restructuring individuals' cognitive processes in order to overcome their resistance to learning is, potentially at least, very worrying. Therefore, taking all three approaches together, one cannot escape the conclusion that the social cost of achieving excellence, in either West or East, is high.

Politics

The issue of organisational power and politics has received extensive attention over the last 20 years (Buchanan and Badham, 1999; Kotter, 1982; Minett, 1992; Pfeffer, 1981, 1992; Willcocks, 1994) and will be explored in Chapter 5. Given that organisations are social entities and not machines, power struggles and political infighting are inevitable. They may not always be prominent, but tend to come to the fore in situations where resources are scarce or organisations are in transition (Morgan, 1986). It is perhaps here that Peters and Waterman, with their notion of total openness and trust to the extent of employees effectively allowing others to monitor their work, could most easily be accused of being out of touch with reality. There is a tendency in the West to treat politics and conflict as illegitimate; but, as Pascale (1993) and Thompkins (1990) argued, conflict is part and parcel of the creative process, and political skills may be a key competence for managers if they are to be successful leaders and persuaders. To ignore the presence of conflict or underestimate its tenacity is usually a recipe for disaster (Kanter et al, 1992; McLennan, 1989; Pfeffer, 1992; Robbins, 1986).

However, in the Japanese, organisational learning and Culture–Excellence approaches, little is said on the subject of organisational politics and conflict. As far as the Culture–Excellence and organisational learning perspectives are concerned, there appears to be an assumption that employees working in smaller business units, having greater autonomy and more satisfying jobs, will work with each other, pursuing a common purpose. As Chapter 5 will show, this is perhaps an unrealistic expectation. It may well be that in Japanese organisations, with their consensual and open approach to decision-making, strong commitment to organisational goals, high peer group pressure and, for some at least, lifetime employment, conflict is either minimised or channelled into creative directions; though Ishizuna (1990), Kamata (1982) and Sakai (1992) have shown that this is not always the case. However, in the West, with companies reshaping their businesses, where job security is being eroded, where an individual's current performance outweighs all other considerations, and where only the fittest and fleetest of foot can expect to survive, it is foolish to deny or underestimate the importance of power and politics or to believe that culture can act as a cure-all.

Culture

This brings us to the next concern to which these three approaches give rise. Proponents of all three approaches treat culture in a rather simplistic fashion. For the Culture–Excellence school, all problems are resolved through the creation of strong, flexible, pragmatic cultures which promote the values of trust, cooperation and team-work. A similar point can also be made with regard to the creation of a learning culture. In neither approach is there any real discussion or acknowledgement of the difficulties in defining or changing culture, despite much evidence to the contrary (Allaire and Firsirotu, 1984; Schein, 1985; Wilson, 1992). Nor do those who seek to promote the Japanese approach treat the subject of culture any more thoroughly. Either it is portrayed as an immutable feature of Japanese companies which prevents the West from adopting the Japanese approach or, more frequently these days, the Japanese approach is seen as somehow independent of culture (Sheldrake, 1996; Smith and Misumi, 1989). Very few writers acknowledge that Japanese companies, like their Western counterparts, can find themselves with apparently inappropriate cultures that they wish to change (Ishizuna, 1990). Therefore, all three approaches clearly leave themselves open to the accusation that they gloss over the difficulty of changing culture. The role of organisational culture will be examined in Chapter 5.

Change management

There is one last issue that should be touched on: the management of change. Organisation theories are also theories of change. Most organisation theories claim to show organisations how to identify where they are and where they should be. They also, either explicitly or implicitly, address the issue of change management.

For the Classical school, change management is relatively easy: it tells organisations what they should be and, because managers and workers are rational beings, they should accept any concomitant changes because it's the logical thing to do! A similar approach is adopted by the Contingency Theorists. The Human Relations movement, on the other hand, sees change as more problematic. Organisations are social systems, change is not a rational process, emotions come into play as well. Therefore, persuasion and leadership play a key role in changing organisations.

The Culture–Excellence approach has little to say about how change should be achieved, despite acknowledging the radical transformation it is advocating. Peters (1993) advocated a 'Big Bang' approach to change: 'change radically and do it quickly' seems to be his advice. Handy (1986), on the other hand, seemed to adopt a more gradualist approach to change – big changes over long periods. Kanter *et al* (1992) advocated a combination of both; they argue that major changes, especially in behaviour, can only be achieved over time. However, they also believe that dramatic gestures are also necessary to improve performance in the short term. Therefore, their approach to change is a combination of 'Bold Strokes and Long Marches'. Taken as a whole, the message from the Culture–Excellence school is somewhat mixed and the process and details are lacking, notwithstanding Kanter *et al*'s (1992) book on change.

Though organisational learning is explicitly directed at enabling organisations to change, its proponents are vague and inconsistent in specifying how one leads to the other, and particularly how the ultimate goal, of becoming a learning organisation, can be achieved (Probst and Buchel, 1997). Nor is it clear how the plethora of change initiatives generated by learning will lead to effective, coordinated and complementary overall change (Easterby-Smith, 1997; Tsang, 1997).

The Japanese approach, however, is more specific. They advocate creating a vision of the future and moving towards it in incremental steps (*Kaizen*) at all levels of the organisation. The Japanese are extremely able at this process, which has given them a reputation as a nation that makes ambitious long-term plans which are slowly, relentlessly and successfully achieved. However, it is debatable whether this approach could work in many Western countries. In the USA and UK in particular, competitive pressures appear to require radical change over a short timescale, and at the same time there appears to be a built-in aversion to long-term thinking, especially amongst the financial institutions who play a pivotal role in the life of most firms.

Therefore, though the organisational learning, Japanese and Culture–Excellence approaches have their strong points, they also have their drawbacks, at least as far as Western companies are concerned. For this reason, none have achieved the same intellectual dominance enjoyed by past paradigms, though the Culture–Excellence approach has come to exert a powerful influence on managerial attitudes and behaviour over the past two decades. However, this lack of a dominant paradigm is not necessarily a cause for despair. Developing paradigms by their very nature will contain dilemmas and contradictions that can only be resolved with experience and the passage of time. This is not a case for ignoring them; rather the reverse. The future is not, hopefully, immutable. Managers are not powerless, they do have some freedom of choice and action, and the possibility does exist to influence the future shape of work by promoting the good and avoiding the bad.

Parts 2, 3 and 4 of this book will further consider managerial choice and the degree to which organisations are free to shape their own future. Before moving on to this, however, the final two chapters in Part 1 will round off the review of organisation theory by examining, in Chapter 4, the case for and alternatives to the postmodern perspective on organisations and, in Chapter 5, the role of culture, power and politics in constraining and enabling organisational choice.

Test your learning

■ Short answer questions

1 What is a paradigm?

2 Why did *In Search of Excellence* become an instant best-seller when it was first published?

3 List the main tenets of the Culture–Excellence approach.

4 What is a Shamrock organisation?

5 What are the main personnel and business issues that make up Japanese management?

6   What are seen as the main benefits of the Japanese approach?

7   Define organisational learning.

8   State the key arguments in favour of organisational learning.

9   For each of the following, briefly state its implications for organisational change: (a) Culture–Excellence, (b) the Japanese approach and (c) organisational learning.

Essay questions

1   What are the main similarities and differences between the Culture–Excellence approach and Japanese management?

2   What are the core tenets of organisational learning and what difficulties might an organisation encounter in introducing it?

Suggested further reading

1   Peters, TJ and Waterman, RH (1982) *In Search of Excellence: Lessons from America's Best-Run Companies*. Harper and Row: London.
    In order to capture the essence of Culture–Excellence, there is no better book to read than the one that began it all.
2   Wilson, DC (1992) *A Strategy of Change*. Routledge: London.
    David Wilson's book provides a pithy and critical analysis of the shortcomings of the Culture–Excellence approach.
3   Sheldrake, J (1996) *Management Theory: From Taylorism to Japanization*. International Thompson Business Press: London.
    Michael Sheldrake provides a brief but good review of the work of Charles Handy and also of the rise of Japanese management.
4   A more comprehensive and up-to-date review of Japanese management can be found in Sako, M and Sato, H (eds) (1997) *Japanese Labour and Management in Transition*. Routledge: London.
5   Probst, G and Buchel, B (1997) *Organizational Learning*. Prentice Hall: London.
    For a brief, comprehensive and comprehensible look at organisational learning, this book is excellent.

Chapter 4

Critical perspectives on organisation theory

Postmodernism, realism and complexity

Learning objectives

After studying this chapter, you should be able to:

- discuss the contribution of postmodernism to organisational theory;
- list the strengths and shortcomings of postmodernism with regard to the design and management of organisations;
- understand the main tenets of the realist perspective;
- discuss the strengths and weaknesses of the realist perspective for organisations;
- describe the influence of complexity theories on our understanding of organisations;
- state the main advantages and disadvantages of the complexity approach to organisations;
- appreciate the limitations of rational approaches to organisations;
- comprehend how postmodernism, realism and complexity widen the scope for organisational choice.

Exhibit 4.1   Realism replaces grand visions

Realism replaces grand visions

Major innovations have had their day in the telecoms sector – at least for the time being. Mobile operators have been forced to become more realistic. This will be apparent at CeBIT, where changes will be small and mainly restricted to the refining of existing services.

'We want to make the benefits of new applications clear,' says Rudolf Groger, head of O Germany, the country's smallest mobile operator. 'Content and customer advantage will be to the fore.' Technology – especially UMTS, the long-awaited third-generation mobile technology being deployed in Europe – will be in the background.

The collapse in the telecom industry's fortunes after the peak year of 2000 pitched it into a deep crisis. Now, cost-saving is the top priority and investment budgets have been slashed.

In Germany alone, companies have paid out around Euros 50bn for their UMTS licences – but the technology, which was supposed to produce big and rapid profits, has not yet overcome its teething troubles. UMTS launches have been postponed until the middle or end of this year and sales expectations have been revised sharply downwards.

Nevertheless, T-Mobile, Vodafone, E-Plus and O are pinning their hopes on new data services, such as the sending of photos by mobile phone. The small pictures, of which 3m were sent by camera telephone in Germany last year, have caught the attention of mobile operators. So-called multimedia messaging services (MMS) are aimed at persuading customers to use their phones more and thus boost turnover.

By 2007, mobile phone users are expected to be spending about Euros 66bn worldwide on data services, and operators must develop strategies now to capture a share of this market, says Ovum, the IT consultancy. Operators have quickly rethought their strategies to emphasise the importance of applications over technology; with MMS, they are keen to offer customers far more ways of spending money than simply sending photos.

In recent years, the mobile industry lost sight of end-users. 'They showed their imaginative ideas but no one could do anything with them,' says Nikolaus Mohr, a consultant at Accenture. At CeBIT, they will make sure this time that their offerings are money-making rather than just visionary.

'Operators thought they could sell customers technologies like UMTS or Wap,' says Nigel Deighton, an analyst at Gartner, the IT consultancy. 'They didn't show people how they could benefit from them.' Now, they are concentrating on practical products. Whereas they used to plan years ahead, the focus is now on customer solutions which can be introduced in the next six to 12 months.

Not surprisingly, the need to cut debts has led to hugely increased pressure for short-term revenues. 'Companies now want to make money rather than constantly launch new innovations,' says Marcus Sander, an analyst with Sal. Oppenheim, the German private bank. 'They have come down to earth. The level of expectations for UMTS has been reduced. Everything is taking longer than the operators thought. The big revenues from UMTS are far in the future'. Even at the beginning of last year, companies were reluctant to believe this.

Source: Kristina Spiller, *Financial Times*, 12 March 2003, p. 2.

Introduction

It is now commonly believed that our world is changing significantly and that we are entering a new era (Berkeley Thomas, 2003; Cooper and Jackson, 1997; Deresky, 2000; Giddens, 2002; Handy, 1997; Hardaker and Graham, 2002; Hatch, 1997; Kanter *et al*, 1997; Peters, 1997a). Whether we refer to this development as 'the Information Age', 'the Age of the Internet', 'the Age of Innovation', 'the Age of Unreason', 'Post Industrial Society', 'the Postmodern Age' or 'Globalisation', the message is the same: what worked in the past will not work in the future, and organisations, like society at large, will have to change in unprecedented and unanticipated ways if they are to survive. However, despite all this talk of a brave new world, in the wake of the dotcom collapse, more and more companies are searching for some form of twenty-first century realism and rejecting the grand visions of the 1990s, as Spiller's article, Exhibit 4.1, illustrates. But, of course, there are many who will argue that their 1990s visions were realistic and that today's reality is too pedestrian and lacking in ambition. This chapter will examine three critical perspectives on organisation theory with a view to understanding how they view 'reality' and the implications of their differing views for organisations.

The previous three chapters have described the development of organisations and organisation theory from the Industrial Revolution through to the present day, in order to show the various approaches to and options for designing and running organisations so as to meet the challenges they face. What has emerged is a somewhat confusing picture of theories which claim, each in their own way, to be the answer to all organisational ills, yet which are all open to potentially damning criticisms. All the theories we have examined claim to give practical and coherent advice to managers on how to structure and run their organisations. Yet it is in their limited applicability to the range and complexity of situations found in everyday organisational life that these theories are most open to criticism:

■ The tendency to assume a unitary frame of reference, in which the interests of workers and managers, blue-collar and white-collar staff, and people of different genders, ethnicity and religions either coincide or can be easily reconciled, is a clear shortcoming in all these theories.

■ The belief of the Classical school and the Human Relations movement that contextual factors – the external environment, size, technology, etc. – are either irrelevant or easily accommodated is another obvious flaw.

■ The assumption by both the Contingency theorists and the proponents of Culture–Excellence that managers are powerless to change the situational variables they face, and have no choice but to accept the prevailing recipe for success, is not borne out in reality.

■ There is a growing scepticism regarding the ability of rational, objective science to provide an explanation for the many and fundamental changes taking place in organisations and the wider society.

■ One of the most serious drawbacks is that only the Culture–Excellence school, and to a lesser extent the organisational learning and Japanese approaches, give any importance to the role of organisational culture – and even then it is treated in a simplistic fashion.

■ None of the theories give serious consideration to the role of power and politics in influencing decision-making in organisations. Not only does this go against a great deal of research that has been produced over the last 20 years, but it also runs counter to most people's own experience of organisational life.

■ Lastly, these theories explicitly or implicitly reject the notion of choice. Their basic argument is that organisations need to follow 'their' recipe for success or they will fail. Yet, if we look at the population of organisations, we can see a vast variety of approaches to their design and management. Some, for periods of time at least, may seem more successful than others, but most organisations appear capable of surviving whether they adopt the current recipe in full, in part or totally reject it.

This, and the following chapter, which is devoted to an examination of culture, power and politics, will address these issues, especially the final three points. This chapter examines three important and critical perspectives on organisations: postmodernism; realism, and complexity. It begins with the examination of postmodernism. This is a loosely-defined philosophical movement which, though originally based in the arts, has become increasingly influential in the social sciences over the last 20 years. It is a way of looking at the world that rejects rationality. Instead, it concentrates on the ways in which human beings attempt to shape reality and invent their world. This is followed by a review of the realist perspective on organisations. Like postmodernism, realism is a philosophical doctrine that was first applied to the arts but has in recent years been taken up by organisation theorists. Also like postmodernists, realists believe that reality is socially-constructed. But, unlike the postmodernists, realists reject the notion of multiple realities. The essence of realism is that there is only one reality and it exists even if we have not yet discovered it. They see both the natural and social worlds as consisting of complex structures which exist even if we are not aware of them or how they influence our behaviour. For realists, events and patterns of events are generated or caused by mechanisms and powers that exist independently of the events they generate. Therefore, realists do not deny the ability of human beings to shape their world, but they see this ability as being limited by an ensemble of real and concrete structures, practices and conventions in society. Contrary to the former two perspectives, the third critical perspective on organisations considered in this chapter, complexity, arose from the natural sciences before being taken up by social scientists. Complexity theories are concerned with how order is created in dynamic non-linear systems. In particular, those applying this approach to organisations maintain that successful organisations need to operate at the 'edge of chaos' and can only maintain this position by the presence of appropriate order-generating rules.

The chapter concludes by arguing that, whilst these three approaches differ significantly, what they have in common is that they open up the prospect that organisations have choices in what they do and how they do it. Rather than being the prisoners of organisational theories or contingencies, managers (potentially) have considerable, though by no means unconstrained, freedom of choice over the structure, policies and practices of their organisations, and even over the environment in which they operate. This then leads on, in Chapter 5, to an examination of the role of culture, power and politics in the identification, shaping and pursuit of choices.

The postmodern perspective

■ From modernism to postmodernism?

As was described in Chapter 3, a sea-change has taken place over the last 20 years in terms of how we view organisations. The Culture–Excellence model, the Japanese approach and organisational learning all have links with the past but they also represent a break with what has gone before. Running alongside these developments and to a large extent giving them a theoretical respectability, albeit mainly an unacknowledged one, is the view that we have moved from the modern to the postmodern world.

For Alvesson and Deetz (1996: 191–2), it was the changing nature of work and competition in the 1980s that forced organisation theorists to question existing and entrenched assumptions about the world:

> The increased size of organizations, rapid implementation of communication/information technologies, globalisation, changing nature of work, reduction of the working class, less salient class conflicts, professionalization of the workforce, stagnant economies, widespread ecological problems and turbulent markets are all part of the contemporary context demanding a research response.

Initially, in the 1980s, much of the debate about the changing nature of the modern world revolved around the posited move from 'Fordist' to 'post-Fordist' or 'neo-Fordist' forms of work organisation. This debate, over the move from mass production to flexible specialisation, initially centred on the work of Piore and Sabel (1984). Their argument was that the age of Taylorism and Fordism, the age of mass production, was dead. Mass production was concerned with the production of standardised goods for stable mass markets using a form of work organisation that was characterised by the intense division of labour, the separation of conception from execution and the substitution of unskilled for skilled labour (Tomaney, 1990). It was argued, however, that the market conditions that allowed Fordism to thrive have passed. The emergence of segmented and highly volatile markets, brought about by changes in consumer tastes and technological innovation, require organisations to be highly flexible in order to succeed in these post-Fordist conditions (Laudon and Starbuck, 1997).

According to Piore and Sable (1984), in the present day only decentralised, worker-run firms have the flexibility, skills and commitment to cope with sudden shifts in consumer demands, volatile input prices and rapid changes in technology. They drew on the operation of loose alliances of small firms in Italy to substantiate their case. Though an attractive proposition to some, there does not appear to have been any great movement to create the decentralised worker cooperatives envisaged by Piore and Sable, as Williams et al (1987) showed. Instead, other writers began to argue in favour of the emergence of neo-Taylorist or neo-Fordist organisational forms (Smith, 1994; Whitaker, 1992). Rather than the age of industrial bureaucracy coming to an end, it was argued that it was going through a two-pronged programme of change. On the one hand, computerised automation was linking together machines and processes and thus eliminating labour. On the other hand, where this was not possible, managers were shifting production to low-wage regions of the world (Froebel et al, 1980).

As Smith (1994) argues, the problem with this perspective is that though it fits, for example, General Motors, it does not fit Toyota, which has proved by far the more successful company. Sayer (1989) complains that the post-Fordist literature is confused, riddled with speculation and is selective in its use of evidence. Piore and Sable (1984) in particular have come in for much criticism, especially in relation to what some see as their over-optimistic view of the developing nature of work (Amin and Robins, 1990). Therefore, though their supporters can point to examples of flexible specialisation and post- and neo-Fordism, the explanations they gave for these and the implications they drew from them seem both partial and particularistic (Whitaker, 1992). Indeed, given the breadth and magnitude of the new organisational developments and forms discussed in Chapter 3, terms such as flexible specialisation, post-Fordism and neo-Fordism seem to have only a limited ability to explain the many changes taking place in organisational life. Nevertheless, what this debate did was to create a receptivity amongst a wider audience for the work of the postmodernists, who provided a more substantial and complex explanation for the changes taking place in the world around us.

Depending on whom one reads, postmodernism is either a relatively new concept or it has been around at least since the 1930s (Appignanesi and Garratt, 1995; Featherstone, 1988a). Certainly, the term became fashionable among young writers, artists and critics in New York in the 1960s. In the 1970s and 1980s, the term became more widely used in architecture, music and the visual and performing arts (Hassard, 1993). However, its adoption by organisation theorists stems from the work of the poststructuralist movement in French philosophy, which emerged in the 1960s. The interest in meaning and interpretation by symbolic-interpretive organisation theorists, drawing on linguistic, semiotic and literary theory, also served to increase interest in postmodernism (Hatch, 1997). In the 1970s and 1980s, it became most closely associated with the work of Jean Baudrillard (1983), Jacques Derrida (1978), Michel Foucault (1977) and Jean-François Lyotard (1984).

Researchers in organisation and management studies came relatively late to postmodernism. It was only in the late 1980s, with, for example, the work of Smircich and Calás (1987) and Cooper and Burrell (1988) that postmodernism started to impact on organisation theory. The interest in postmodernism by many social scientists and organisation theorists stemmed from their growing belief that existing, modernist, theories, such as the Contingency approach, could no longer account for the changes taking place in the world of work and society in general. In particular, there was an increasing scepticism concerning the ability of rational, objective science to provide absolute and unitary knowledge of the world. In its place, postmodernists argue for a relativist position that emphasises multiple realities, fragmentation and subjectivity (Linstead, 1993).

Postmodernism, as the term implies, is something that carries on from, succeeds or takes its frame of reference from modernism. Therefore, it is necessary to understand how the proponents of postmodernism define modernism in order to appreciate their arguments. Modernism is a term used to describe the values, rationale and institutions that have dominated Western societies since the Age of Enlightenment in the eighteenth century. This was the period in which European thought, led by France and Great Britain, is seen as making a decisive break with the superstition, ignorance and tradition of the Middle Ages. In its place emerged a strong belief in progress, economic and scientific rationality, a search for the fundamental rules and laws that govern both the natural world and human nature, and a commitment to a secular, rationalist and progressive individualism (Gergen, 1992; Hassard, 1993). As Hobsbawm (1979: 34) noted, 'Liberty, equality and (it followed) the fraternity of all men were its slogans.' Linstead (1993: 99) commented that the Enlightenment:

... produced a commitment to the unfolding of progress through history, the incremental growth of knowledge through science and the resulting inevitable subordination of nature to culture and the control of man.

Also, as Gergen (1992: 211) stated, modernist 'presumptions remain vital throughout contemporary culture, and have left an indelible mark on theories of organization from early in the [twentieth] century to the present.' Modernists, therefore, assume that the world, both social and natural, and its structuring principles, are accessible through the correct (scientific) methods of observation and analysis. In relation to organisational life, the term modernism is used to describe the form of organisation that has dominated both the public and private sectors over the past 100 years (Biberman and Whitty, 1997). In the previous chapters, we have termed this the Classical or bureaucratic model, though others use terms such as Taylorist, Fordist or machine-era paradigm (Fox, 1994; Smith, 1994; Tomaney, 1990). It is an organisational form which, its proponents argue, is based on rationality, logic and the pursuit of scientific rules and principles. Such organisations are characterised by mechanistic and hierarchical structures based on the extreme division of labour, and control systems that suppress people's emotions and minimise their scope for independent action.

Exhibit 4.2	Some features of postmodernism

Fragmentation: the breaking up of established structures into fragments.

De-differentiation: the blurring or dissolution of established boundaries.

Hyper-reality: confusion and mixing of the real with artificial/virtual realities.

Chronology: interest in the past and its imitation alongside/instead of the future.

Pastiche: the playful mixing of styles of decoration, dress, expression, etc.

Anti-foundationalism: rejection of all basics, absolutes, fundamentals, universals, etc.

Pluralism: all of the above happening simultaneously!

Source: Berkeley Thomas (2003: 214)

As can be seen from Exhibit 4.2, postmodernism offers a very different view of the world from that of the modernists. Postmodernism opposes or denies the validity of the Enlightenment's emphasis on reason, logic and rationality as the foundation of scientific method and the basis for the establishment of truth. Postmodernism challenges the claim of science to establish authoritative or absolute knowledge. Instead, it argues that scientific knowledge is a social construction by the scientific community, and that new scientific paradigms are brought about by changes in the community of scientists rather than scientific discoveries *per se* (Hassard, 1990).

Therefore, for postmodernists, knowledge is relative, not absolute. Postmodernism is, as Watson (1997: 383) states:

A way of looking at the world which rejects attempts to build systematic explanations of history and human activity and which, instead, concentrates on the ways in which human beings 'invent' their worlds, especially through language and cultural innovations.

One of the crucial distinctions between modernists and postmodernists is how they view the nature of language:

> For the modernist, language was simply a tool for the logical representation of the real ... Within the postmodernist view, language ... gains its meaning and significance through its placement within social interchange. Words fail to make sense (they remain nonsense) until there is at least one other person to give assent to their meaningfulness.
>
> (Gergen, 1992: 213–14)

Therefore, if language is a social construct, one cannot take the statements, rules and practices of particular groups and organisations at face value. Instead, taking their cue from Derrida (1978), postmodernists often begin their analysis of a situation or event by 'deconstructing' the language used. Deconstruction is an approach that seeks to reveal and overturn the assumptions underlying an argument, proposition or theory. Overturning assumptions opens up space for previously unconsidered alternatives. In the postmodernist approach, alternatives are left open to multiple interpretations, and the acceptance of multiple, fragmented realities is seen to displace the idea of one unitary transcendent reality (Hatch, 1997). Like many others, the postmodernists recognise that the various stakeholders in an organisation each have different perceptions of what the organisation should do and whose views and interests should be paramount. Where they differ, however, is that they do not believe that there is a correct view or that one view has a right to be paramount. Instead, postmodern management and organisation theory, beginning with a process of deconstruction, ' ... seeks to reconstruct organizations by restoring a sense of harmony and balance in our species, our institutions, and our theories' (Gephart *et al*, 1996: 364).

This leads on to another prevailing theme within postmodernism: self-reflexivity – a critical suspicion of one's own suppositions. If reality and language are social constructs, then, so the postmodernist argument goes, to avoid the modernist error of believing they have discovered a fundamental truth or reality, postmodernists must constantly question and be suspicious of their own assumptions, statements and actions (Lawson, 1985).

Moving on to the links between postmodernism and organisation theory, the concept of self-reflexivity has similarities to Argyris and Schon's (1978) notion of double- and triple-loop learning, which promotes the questioning and challenging of existing organisational assumptions (*see* Chapter 3). Other aspects of Argyris' work also show postmodernist leanings, particularly his questioning of the inner contradictions of research methods (Argyris, 1980). We can also see postmodernist tendencies in Morgan's (1986) *Images of Organizations*, in which he treats existing organisation theories as literary metaphors.

Moving into the heartland of organisation theory, Linstead (1993) argues that under postmodernism, hierarchies of merit, legitimacy and authority give way to networks, partnerships and organisational structures of a shifting, fluid and social nature. These are driven by external forces, such as markets or competition, and are *ad hoc*, short-term, fragmentary and localised. According to Daft (1998), necessity will force postmodern organisations to develop more flexible and decentralised organisation structures with fuzzy boundaries both internally and externally. In such organisations, he believes, leaders will become facilitators who will communicate through informal, oral and symbolic channels, control will be exercised through self-regulation, planning and decision-making will be inclusive and egalitarian principles will hold sway. In a similar vein, Clegg (1990) suggests clear distinctions between modernist and postmodernist organisational forms (*see* Table 4.1).

Table 4.1 Comparison of modernist and postmodernist organisational forms

	Modernist organisations	Postmodernist organisations
Structure	Rigid bureaucracies	Flexible networks
Consumption	Mass markets	Niche markets
Technology	Technological determinism	Technological choice
Jobs	Differentiated, demarcated and deskilled	Highly de-differentiated, de-demarcated and multi-skilled
Employment relations	Centralised and standardised	Complex and fragmentary

Clegg acknowledges that postmodern forms of organisation are somewhat ill-defined. Nevertheless, he argues that they are associated with developments such as flexible specialisation and post-Fordism, and that examples of postmodern organisations can be found in Japan, Sweden, East Asia and Italy. However, he does point out that whilst they can be associated with progressive developments, such as the extension of industrial democracy in Sweden, they can also be linked to more repressive and elitist developments, such as the segmented labour force policies adopted by Handy's Shamrock organisation (*see* Chapter 3). In the Shamrock organisation, there are three classes of employees – *core workers*, the *contractual fringe*, and the *flexible labour force*. Each of these three segments of the organisation's workforce has very different conditions of employment and is treated and valued very differently. Therefore, for Clegg, and an increasing number of organisation theorists, postmodernism has arrived, it is having a major impact on the nature and functioning of organisations, and it will continue to do so.

There are two areas of organisational life to which the postmodernists have paid particular attention: culture and power. The postmodern approach to organisational culture rejects both the integrationist perspective, which sees culture as being shared by all members of an organisation, and the differentiation perspective, which sees organisational unity as being broken by coherent and stable subcultures. Instead, it takes a fragmentation perspective, believing that organisational cultures are inconsistent, ambiguous, multiplicitous and in a constant state of flux (Martin, 1992; Meyerson and Martin, 1987). Hatch (1997: 231) observes of the postmodern perspective on culture that:

> In this view, alliances or coalitions can never stabilize into subcultures and certainly not into unified cultures because discourse and its focal issues are always changing – hence the image of fragmentation.

Therefore, for postmodernists, organisational culture is important, and indeed is clearly linked to their interest in symbols and language. However, postmodernists are sceptical of attempts to manipulate and change culture, as Hatch (1997: 235) points out:

> When you attempt to change organizational culture, while it is true that something will change, generally the changes are unpredictable and sometimes undesirable (e.g., increases in employee cynicism towards cultural change programs) ... Do not think of trying to manage culture. Other people's meanings and interpretations are highly unmanageable.

Where power is concerned, postmodernists take a very different view from most other writers on organisations. They are less concerned with the power that individuals or groups possess, acquire or deploy. Rather they believe that power resides in the combination of linguistic distinctions, ways of reasoning and material practices which make up the body of taken-for-granted knowledge that exists in society and organisations (Alvesson and Deetz, 1996). Perhaps the most influential postmodernist writer on power has been the French philosopher, Michel Foucault (1983). Foucault argues for a strong link between knowledge and power. He believes that knowledge, when it becomes socially legitimised and institutionalised, exerts control over what we think and do. However, there is a power struggle between different bodies of knowledge each fighting for legitimacy and supremacy. For Foucault, though these bodies of knowledge are seeking to represent reality, at the same time they socially create it. He argues that power moulds everyone, both those who use it and those who are used by it. He maintains that power and knowledge depend on each other, so that an extension of a group's power is dependent upon and accompanied by an extension of its knowledge, and *vice versa* (Appignanesi and Garratt, 1995). Gergen (1992: 221) takes a similar perspective, arguing that:

> ... power is inherently a matter of social interdependence, and it is achieved through the social coordination of actions around specified definitions.

The postmodernist perspective on power has important implications for how a particular view of reality comes to the fore and is maintained in an organisation. Rather than being the product of an objective and rational process, it is the product of power and politics in an organisation. In some organisations, there does not appear to be a settled and generally agreed view of reality; rather what we see are competing interpretations put forward by competing groups and individuals. In other organisations, however, a definite view does appear to be held and does appear to be maintained. This is achieved when a coalition of groups and forces is able to wield power and use political processes to achieve a dominant position over others in the organisation. When this occurs, it is their view of reality which takes shape and comes to be accepted. Therefore, not only is power deployed to legitimate their view of the world, but, in turn, its legitimacy bolsters their power.

■ The implications for organisations

What we can see from this review of postmodernism is the influence that both modernism and postmodernism have had on organisational theory and practice in the twentieth century. Clearly, the Classical approach, and especially Weber's contribution, with its emphasis on rationality and scientific knowledge, is very much within the tradition of modernism. Indeed, one can also say that much of the Human Relations literature, with its use of scientific methods to identify the 'one best way', and certainly the literature on Contingency Theory would appear to fall squarely into the modernist camp. On the other hand, the Culture–Excellence approach seems much more comfortable with the rhetoric of postmodernism. Not only does it share a similar view of the current state of the world, i.e. chaotic and unpredictable, but it also shares some of the language. For example, Charles Handy (1989) entitled one of his books *The Age of Unreason*, whilst Rosabeth Moss Kanter (1989) writes of 'post-entrepreneurial' organisations. Though Tom Peters does not necessarily use the language of the postmodernists, the essence of his message, and often the way it is delivered, sits comfortably with postmodernism. The same can be said of organisational learning, with its emphasis on knowledge acquisition, rapid change and, most importantly, the ability of organisations to create their own realities (Hatch, 1997). The Japanese approach, with its inclusion of hard and soft elements, on the other hand, seems to contain happily elements of modernism and postmodernism. Indeed, it may be that one of the main criticisms of modernism and postmodernism is that both come from a Western, especially European, intellectual and cultural tradition and, consequently, do not lie easily with other, particularly Eastern and Islamic, intellectual and cultural traditions (Appignanesi and Garratt, 1995). Nevertheless, at least in the West, postmodernism does appear to be having a powerful impact on both theory and practice in organisations.

In summary, despite the somewhat impenetrable and contradictory nature of the literature, the core of postmodernism concerns the nature of reason and reality. For postmodernists, reason and logic have proved illusory and reality is a social construct. In organisational terms, an organisation, or rather those individuals and groups who dominate it, create their own reality – their own view or views of the world. Whether they see themselves as successful or not, whether they view the world as chaotic, whether they believe they can shape their own future, is to a large part determined not by any objective data or what is happening in their environment as such, but by their own ability to shape their own reality. The extent to which they can impose their view of reality on others both inside and outside will, to a large degree, determine whether they and the organisation are seen as successful or not.

Seen in this light, postmodernism has three important implications for the organisation theories and practices discussed in the previous three chapters. The first implication concerns the nature of organisational culture. As we saw in Chapter 3, the Culture–Excellence school has been highly influential in bringing the issue of organisation culture to the forefront of management thought and practice over the last two decades. In essence, what they argue is that, in order to achieve excellence, managers need to create a strong, unified and appropriate culture for their organisation. A core component of this approach is to manipulate and use language and symbols to create a new organisational reality. Though acknowledging the importance of culture, and sharing a concern with symbols and language, postmodernists, however, view the results of attempts to manipulate and change culture as generally unpredictable and sometimes undesirable. This is because the outcomes depend upon the multiplicity of meanings and interpretations that others in the organisation put on such attempts, which are inherently unmanageable (Hatch, 1997). The second implication concerns the issue of how a particular view of reality comes to the fore and is maintained in an organisation. The answer for postmodernists concerns the role of power and politics. In some organisations, there does not appear to be a settled and generally agreed view of reality; rather what we see are competing interpretations put forward by competing groups and individuals. In other organisations, however, a definite view does appear to be held and does appear to be maintained. This is achieved when a coalition of groups and forces is able to wield power and use political processes to achieve a dominant position over others in the organisation. When this occurs, it is their view of reality that takes shape and comes to be accepted. The final implication relates to organisational choice. As we saw in the three previous chapters, most organisational theorists and practitioners believe that there is a 'one best way' to run organisations. The postmodernist debate, however, has raised significant questions about whether these 'one best ways' represent some form of objective knowledge, or whether they are socially-constructed realities which pertain to particular times, countries, industries and organisations. If organisational reality is socially constructed, then, in theory at least, it is open to organisations to construct whatever reality they wish. From this perspective, organisations have a wide degree of choice about what they do, how they do it and where they do it. Nevertheless, despite the attractions of postmodernism, and despite its strong impact on organisational theory over the past two decades, there are some serious reservations about its validity and usefulness.

Postmodernism – some reservations

Perhaps the main reservation and drawback of postmodernism is, as Alvesson and Deetz (1996) point out, the difficulty in defining the concept. In the social sciences, the term has acquired a wide and often conflicting set of definitions, including a social mood, a historical period filled with major social and organisational changes, and a set of philosophical approaches to organisational and other studies (Featherstone, 1988b; Hassard and Parker, 1993). Hatch (1997: 43) believes postmodernism has been defined in so many different ways that:

> It is impossible to choose a core theory, or a typical set of ideas, to exemplify postmodernism – the incredible variety of ideas labelled postmodern defies summarization, and the postmodern value for diversity contradicts the very idea of unifying these different understandings into a single, all-encompassing explanation.

As Appignanesi and Garratt (1995: 4) observe:

> The confusion is advertised by the 'post' prefix to 'modern'. Postmodernism identifies itself by something it isn't. It isn't modern anymore. But in what sense exactly is it post ...
>
> – as a result of modernism?
> – the aftermath of modernism?
> – the afterbirth of modernism?
> – the development of modernism?
> – the denial of modernism?
> – the rejection of modernism?
>
> Postmodern has been used in a mix-and-match of all these meanings.

The confusion and variety of postmodernism is best summed up by the following list of terms used by postmodern theorists, compiled by Featherstone (1988a: 197):

modern	postmodern
modernity	postmodernity
modernité	postmodernité
modernisation	postmodernisation
modernism	postmodernism

Not only, as Featherstone shows, do postmodernists attribute different meanings to each of the above terms, but also they do not share common agreement about what the individual terms mean either. Indeed, Burrell (1988: 222) remarked of one of the key influences on the postmodernist debate, Michel Foucault, that:

> ... it is important to note that Foucault's iconoclasm takes him into positions which are not readily defensible and his refusal to retain one position for longer than the period between his last book and the next is certainly problematic.

As well as the difficulty in defining postmodernism, there are also powerful voices who defend modernism and attack postmodernism as a form of intellectual nihilism or of neo-conservatism (Aronovitz, 1989; Callinicos, 1989). Hassard (1993: 119) states that:

> The most influential critic of postmodernism, however, is Jürgen Habermas ... [he] argues that theories of postmodernism represent critiques of modernity which have their ideological roots in irrationalist and counter-Enlightenment perspectives ... Habermas suggests that as many French writers [especially Derrida, Foucault and Lyotard] take their lead from the counter-Enlightenment statements of Nietzsche and Heidegger, this can be interpreted as a disturbing link with fascist thinking ... Habermas wishes to defend robustly 'a principle of modernism', which he suggests is an unfinished project that holds great, unfulfilled emancipatory potential.

Lyon (2000) argues that the critics of postmodernism fall into the following three camps:

1 Those who claim there has never been a fully modernist era and claim there cannot, consequently, be a 'post' modernist one.
2 Those who maintain that the current developments in society are merely an extension of what has gone before rather than any significant break with the past.
3 Those who accept that the world is entering a new age, but see globalisation (*see* Chapter 16) and not postmodernism as its defining characteristic.

Therefore, a number of serious reservations have been expressed regarding the validity of postmodernism. These include its lack of consistency and clarity, that its proponents misread the current state of the world, that it may be correct but it is not important, and its posited alignment on the far right of the political spectrum. Its proponents accept that the postmodernist message is not always clear and consistent but, in the main, they would reject most of the other criticisms, especially that it is an ideology of the right. On the other hand, there can be little doubt that the postmodernist message has provided some justification and encouragement for the neo-liberal policies, such as privatisation and deregulation, adopted by most Western governments in the last 20 years. Nevertheless, regardless of the merits or not of postmodernism, there are two other non-modernist perspectives on organisations which are also having a significant impact on organisation theory: realism and complexity.

The realist perspective

What is realism?

As the above showed, there appear to be two dominant philosophical perspectives on the social world: the modernist, or positivist, perspective which believes in objective reality, logic and reason, and the postmodernist perspective, which see multiple and competing realities which are socially constructed. In the field of organisations, over the past 20 to 30 years, it is the postmodernist perspective which has come to the fore. However, Ackroyd and Fleetwood (2000a) argue that there is an alternative to both. They point out that there is much substantive research on organisations that is based on neither modernism (positivism) nor postmodernism. This work is based on a long-established seam of social science which strongly maintains that, in order to understand and explain events, it is necessary to take into account both social structures, such as organisations, routines, rules and power, and the meaning that individuals and groups apply to these. Underpinning this work are well-developed philosophical doctrines that are neither modernist nor postmodernist. One of the most important of these is realism, which offers support for a non-modernist and non-postmodernist approach to organisations and management (Ackroyd and Fleetwood, 2000b). The essence of realism, as Easton (2000: 207) notes ' ... is that there is a reality "out there" waiting to be discovered.'

Since the 1970s, realism has been applied to the social sciences by a number of writers (Bhaskar, 1979, 1986; Collier, 1994; Harré, 1972; Outhwaite, 1987; Sayer, 2000). However, though few have explicitly applied it to management, it does appear to underpin much work in the field of institutional and regulation theory, and there is now a growing interest in its application to the wider issues of management and organisations (Ackroyd and Fleetwood, 2000b). As with postmodernism, the term realism has influenced many areas such as the arts, literature, philosophy and the social sciences, and the term tends to be used differently in each of these areas. However, the core belief of realists is that many entities exist independently of us and our investigation of them. Therefore, unlike postmodernists, realists assert that social entities, such as markets, class relations, gender relations, ethnic groupings, social rules, etc., exist, are real and can be discovered, though this does not mean that discovering them will be easy. As Easton (2000: 207) succinctly puts it, 'We see through a glass darkly but there is something there to see.'

Realism and organisations

Tsoukas (2000) states that realist philosophers see both the natural and social worlds as consisting of complex structures that exist independently of our knowledge of them. For realists, events and patterns of events are generated (are caused to be brought about) by causal mechanisms and causal powers that operate independently of the events they generate. Realists seek to identify the generative structures, i.e. the causal mechanisms that bring about events, and to identify their capabilities, i.e. their causal powers (Harré and Madden, 1975; Harré and Secord, 1972). However, though these causal mechanisms possess certain capabilities, causal powers, the actual outcome of their operation will be dependent, i.e. contingent, on circumstances. For example, the Japanese approach to management has the potential to engender team-working and organisational commitment, but whether it will or not depends on a whole host of situational variables, such as the nature of the society in which the organisation operates and the expectations of the employees concerned. Organisations also contain competing and contradictory organising principles, such as class, gender and ethnicity, and they are composed of different groups with their own distinct priorities and agendas that can undermine the dominant causal mechanisms (Reed, 2000). Nevertheless, despite the potential of these competing forces and groups to create disorder, in many cases the interaction between them occurs in such a way that it produces organisational integration, a degree of continuity and stability, and sufficient change to maintain the organisation's viability (Ackroyd, 2000).

In terms of organisations and management, a central issue is the extent to which organisations and their practices are produced by human beings but still exist externally to them and shape their behaviour. Realists are very clear on this point. They argue that whilst the social world, including organisations, is a product of human action, it is not necessarily a product of human design but exists independently of human beings (Connelly, 2000; Easton, 2000). Realists also argue that social phenomena can exist without those involved having any knowledge of them. For example, markets only exist in and through human activity, yet there is no necessity that those people involved should be conscious of the part they play in sustaining them.

Therefore, realists acknowledge the socially-constructed nature of the world but, unlike postmodernists, do not see the world as being merely a social construction (Ackroyd and Fleetwood, 2000b). This can be seen in terms of the structure and operation of organisations. Realists argue that a structure is a set of simultaneously enabling and constraining rules and resources which shape the interactions of those who work in or have to deal with the organisation. That is to say, a structure can be considered as a causal mechanism which has the potential and capability to act in certain ways, i.e. it has causal powers (Giddens, 1984; Manicas, 1980; Tsoukas, 2000). Consequently, as Tsoukas (1992) observes, just because a person may have friendly relations with a bank manager does not by itself mean that the person will be able to obtain a loan – the key issues are the lending rules of the bank and the creditworthiness of the borrower. Organisations may give groups and individuals certain powers but they also prescribe how and when these powers are to be deployed (Whittington, 1989). This does not imply that those concerned know how the rules are generated, the obvious and less obvious ways in which compliance is ensured, or their role in maintaining and developing these rules. Therefore, to continue the banking example, the bank manager knows the lending rules but not necessarily why they are as they are. Also, though he or she is aware of the penalties for non-compliance, they are less likely to be aware of the subtle pressures exerted by cultural norms to behave in certain ways. Yet the lending decision is not a mechanical process. The manager does have the ability to exert judgment and a degree of discretion in what they do.

Likewise, the potential borrower can present their case in a more or a less convincing fashion. This is why the causal powers possessed by a causal mechanism are seen as capabilities and not determinants. Whilst causal powers limit what can be done, and whilst they have the potential to bring about (cause) certain actions to occur, whether they do occur or not is dependent on a range of other factors as well, not least human action or inaction. As a result, when studying management and organisations, realists stress the need to give due weight to both people and structure, and the complex interplay between them. They argue that human action is shaped by the simultaneous constraining and enabling nature of an organisation's structure, which tends to favour certain types of outcome, but that any actual outcome is contingent on the prevailing circumstances (Tsoukas, 1989; Whittington, 1994). In addition, as Kumar (1995) notes, not only do these constraining and enabling forces lie outside the control of those concerned, but those concerned are often unaware of them.

Realists seek to understand and explain events by focusing on the mechanisms, structures, powers and relations that bring them about. In seeking an explanation in this way, realists begin by postulating the existence of a possible mechanism and proceed by collecting evidence for or against its existence and evidence of possible alternative mechanisms (Outhwaite, 1987; Reed, 2000). In revealing the mechanisms which bring about events, realists also seek to engender debates about alternative ways of structuring the social world and alternative forms of relationships, be they concerned with class, gender or power.

The use of realism in the field of management and organisations is most closely associated with the work of Bhaskar. His argument, Bhaskar (1989: 36), is that nothing happens out of nothing:

> ... people do not create society. For it always pre-exists them and is a necessary condition for their activity. Rather society must be regarded as an ensemble of structures, practices and conventions which individuals reproduce and/or transform, but which would not exist unless they did so. Society does not exist independently of human activity ... But it is not the product of it ...

Bhaskar (1986) makes a clear distinction between human action and social structure. He argues that common propositions which are applied to people assume such a distinction: 'He cashed a cheque' assumes a banking system, 'He pleaded guilty' assumes a legal system (Bhaskar, 1979; Connelly, 2000). The two are mutually influential and interdependent but can be analysed separately, and are fundamentally different in that social structures pre-exist and are sustained and changed through human action, but human action is constrained and enabled by social structures. Realists do not deny that there are multiple perspectives or competing claims about the nature of the social world. They also share with postmodernists a recognition of the role of culture, power and politics in shaping organisational choices. However, they reject the possibility that there are multiple realities. Therefore, unlike the postmodernists, they claim that truth exists and what exists can be found, though the finding may be very difficult (Easton, 2000). As Stacey (2003: 7) comments:

> ... realists do not see any inherent limitation on human ability to comprehend reality in its entirety. For them, it is only a matter of time before research progressively uncovers more and more of reality.

Realism is a riposte to both modernism and postmodernism. It attacks the former for placing too much reliance on science, rationality and logic, whilst criticising that latter for rejecting reality in favour of multiple and competing realities. Though it would be unfair to characterise realism as being a half-way house between modernism and postmodernism, it does tend to open itself up to criticism from both camps. The modernists object to the social construction side of the realists' reality, whilst the postmodernists object to the realists' claim that there is only one reality and it can be discovered. However, the battle as to which perspective on the world will carry most weight with organisation theorists is not just between postmodernists and realists; over the last decade, a third perspective, complexity, has entered the fray, which, unlike modernism and postmodernism, owes its origins not to philosophy but to the natural sciences.

The complexity perspective

What is complexity?

Over the last decade, an increasing number of academics and practitioners have come to view organisations through the lens of complexity theories, and this is beginning to have a profound impact on views of how organisations should be structured and changed (Arndt and Bigelow, 2000; Bechtold, 1997; Black, 2000; Fitzgerald, 2002a; Lewis, 1994; MacIntosh and MacLean, 2001; Morgan, 1997; Stacey, 2003; Tetenbaum, 1998; Wheatley, 1992). Complexity serves as an umbrella term for a number of theories, ideas and research programmes that are derived from many different disciplines in the natural sciences (Rescher, 1996; Stacey, 2003; Styhre, 2002). To emphasise the diversity of viewpoints amongst complexity researchers, we will follow Black's (2000) lead and use the term complexity theories rather than theory.

Complexity theories are concerned with the emergence of order in dynamic non-linear systems operating at the edge of chaos, such as weather systems, which are constantly changing and where the laws of cause and effect appear not to apply (Beeson and Davis, 2000; Haigh, 2002; Wheatley, 1992). Order in such systems manifests itself in a largely unpredictable fashion, in which patterns of behaviour emerge in irregular but similar forms through a process of self-organisation, which is governed by a small number of simple order-generating rules (Black, 2000; MacIntosh and MacLean, 2001; Tetenbaum, 1998). Many writers have argued that organisations are also complex systems that, to survive, need to operate at the edge of chaos and have to respond continuously to changes in their environments through just such a process of spontaneous self-organising change (Hayles, 2000; Lewis, 1994; Macbeth, 2002; MacIntosh and MacLean, 1999, 2001; Stacey, 2003; Stickland, 1998).

Complexity theories stem from attempts by meteorologists, biologists, chemists, physicists and other natural scientists to build mathematical models of systems in nature (Gleick, 1988; Lorenz, 1993; Styhre, 2002). In the process, a number of different but related theories have emerged, the key ones being chaos theory (Bechtold, 1997; Haigh, 2002; Lorenz, 1979, 1993), dissipative structures theory (Prigogine and Stengers, 1984; Prigogine, 1997), and the theory of complex adaptive systems (Goodwin, 1994; Stacey et al, 2002). The main difference between these three theories, according to Stacey (2003), is that chaos and dissipative structures theories seek to construct mathematical models of systems at the macro level (i.e. whole systems and populations), whilst complex adaptive systems theory attempts to model the same phenomena at the micro level by using an agent-based approach. Instead of formulating rules for the whole population, it seeks to formulate rules of interaction for the individual entities making up a system or population. However, all three see natural systems as both non-linear and self-organising. There are three central concepts that lie at the heart of complexity theories – the nature of chaos and order; the 'edge of chaos'; and order-generating rules.

Chaos and order

Chaos is often portrayed as pure randomness, but from the complexity viewpoint, it can be seen as a different form of order (Arndt and Bigelow, 2000; Fitzgerald, 2002b; Frederick; 1998). Fitzgerald (2002a) states that chaos and order are twin attributes of dynamic, non-linear (complex) systems, and, within chaos, a hidden order may be concealed beneath what looks completely random. For complexity theorists, chaos describes a complex, unpredictable, and orderly disorder in which patterns of behaviour unfold in irregular but similar forms; snowflakes are all different but all have six sides (Tetenbaum, 1998). Stacey (2003) identifies three types of order–disorder: stable equilibrium; explosive instability; and bounded instability. However, only under the last of these, bounded instability, are complex systems seen as having the ability to transform themselves in order to survive. If systems become too stable, they ossify and die. If they become too unstable, as with cancer, they may get out of control and destroy themselves (Frederick, 1998).

Edge of chaos

Under conditions of 'bounded instability', systems are constantly poised on the brink between order and chaos. Elsewhere, Stacey (Stacey *et al*, 2002) refers to this as a 'far-from-equilibrium' state, whilst Hock (1999) uses the term 'chaordic'. However, the term most commonly used to describe this condition is the 'edge of chaos':

> … complex systems have large numbers of independent yet interacting actors. Rather than ever reaching a stable equilibrium, the most adaptive of these complex systems (e.g., intertidal zones) keep changing continuously by remaining at the poetically termed 'edge of chaos' that exists between order and disorder. By staying in this intermediate zone, these systems never quite settle into a stable equilibrium but never quite fall apart. Rather, these systems, which stay constantly poised between order and disorder, exhibit the most prolific, complex and continuous change …   (Brown and Eisenhardt, 1997: 29)

It is argued that creativity and growth are at their optimal when a complex system operates at the edge of chaos (Frederick, 1998; Jenner, 1998; Kauffman, 1993; Lewis, 1994). It is the presence, or not, of appropriate order-generating rules, which permit self-organisation to take place, that allow some systems to remain at the edge of chaos, whilst others fall over the edge.

Order-generating rules

In complex systems, the emergence of order is seen as being based on the operation of simple order-generating rules which permit limited chaos whilst providing relative order (Frederick, 1998; Lewis, 1994; MacIntosh and MacLean, 2001; Reynolds, 1987; Stacey *et al*, 2002; Wheatley, 1992). As Gell-Mann (1994: 100) puts it:

> In an astonishing variety of contexts, apparently complex structures or behaviours emerge from systems characterized by very simple rules. These systems are said to be self-organized and their properties are said to be emergent. The grandest example is the universe itself, the full complexity of which emerges from simple rules plus chance.

Therefore, the concept of order-generating rules explains how complex, non-linear, self-organising systems manage to maintain themselves at the edge of chaos even under changing environmental conditions. Complex systems have a further trick up their sleeve. Under certain conditions they can even generate new, more appropriate order-generating rules when the old ones can no longer cope with the changes in the system's environment (Bechtold, 1997; MacIntosh and MacLean, 1999; Wheatley, 1992).

■ The implications for organisations

A growing number of academics and practitioners maintain that organisations are complex, non-linear systems, the behaviour of whose members is characterised by spontaneous self-organising underpinned by a set of simple order-generating rules (Arndt and Bigelow, 2000; Bechtold, 1997; Black, 2000; Fitzgerald, 2002a; Lewis, 1994; MacIntosh and MacLean, 2001; Morgan, 1997; Stacey, 2003; Tetenbaum, 1998; Wheatley, 1992).

Frederick (1998) argues that companies who relentlessly pursue a path of continuous innovation succeed because they operate at the edge of chaos, and, indeed, because they inject so much novelty and change into their normal operations, they constantly risk falling over the edge. Brown and Eisenhardt (1997) draw a similar conclusion from their research into innovation in the computer industry. They maintain that continuous innovation is necessary for survival and that this is brought about by a process that resembles self-organisation in nature.

Perhaps the most well-known example of a self-organising organisation is Visa. Visa has grown by 10,000 per cent since 1970, comprises 20,000 financial institutions, operates in 200 countries and has over half a billion customers (Hock, 1999). However, as Tetenbaum (1998: 26) notes:

> ... you don't know where it's located, how it's operated, or who owns it. That's because Visa is decentralised, non-hierarchical, evolving, self-organizing and self-regulating. ... it is a chaordic system conceived as an organization solely on the basis of purpose and principle. Its structure evolved from them.

If organisations are complex systems, management and change take on a new dimension. Beeson and Davis (2000) make the point that whilst it might be fruitful to see organisations as non-linear systems, to do so will require a fundamental shift in the role of management. Like many others (e.g. Boje, 2000; Stacey *et al*, 2002; Sullivan, 1998;

Tetenbaum, 1998; Wheatley, 1992), they point out that self-organising principles explicitly reject cause and effect, top-down, command-and-control styles of management. Brodbeck (2002) suggests that the belief by managers that order and control are essential to achieve their objectives needs to be redressed. Morgan (1997) maintains that complexity will require managers to rethink the nature of hierarchy and control, learn the art of managing and changing contexts, promote self-organising processes, and learn how to use small changes to create large effects. For Tetenbaum (1998), the move to self-organisation will require managers to destabilise their organisations and develop the skill of managing order and disorder at the same time. Managers will need to encourage experimentation and divergent views, even allow rule-breaking, and recognise that '... people need the freedom to own their own power, think innovatively, and operate in new patterns' (Bechtold, 1997: 198). For Jenner (1998: 402), the key to achieving this is a flexible, de-centralised structure.

Brown and Eisenhardt (1997: 29) refer to such flexible structures as 'semistructures', which they maintain ' ... are sufficiently rigid so that change can be organized, but not so rigid that it cannot occur.' They claim that organisations can only survive in highly competitive environments by continuously innovating and improvising, which, they argue, relies on intensive, real-time communication within a structure of a few, very specific rules. Beeson and Davis (2000) echo this point and argue that, in such situations, change becomes an everyday event undertaken by all in the organisation. Brown and Eisenhardt (1997: 28) also claim that in the firms they studied:

> The rate and scale of innovation ... was such that the term 'incremental' seemed, in retrospect, stretched. Yet it was not radical innovation [but] ... a third kind of process that is neither incremental nor radical and that does not fit the punctuated equilibrium model ...

Similarly, Brodbeck (2002) draws attention to studies that cast doubt on the effectiveness of large-scale change programmes (*see* Clarke, 1999; Harung *et al*, 1999). For Styhre (2002), the problem is that such programmes assume that it is possible to predict the outcomes of change and attempt to plan, control and manage it in a rational, top-down, linear fashion.

These writers are depicting organisations operating at the edge of chaos and, therefore, needing to respond continuously to changes in their environments through a process of spontaneous self-organising change in order to survive. However, as in the natural world, this process is driven by order-generating rules that themselves can be subject to transformation in certain situations (Lewis, 1994; MacIntosh and MacLean, 1999, 2001; Stacey, 2003). When this takes place in nature, it is an automatic process; in organisations, this is rarely likely to be the case. As Stacey (2003) argues, people are not unthinking molecules; they can and do exercise free will, they can and do pursue their own objectives, they can and do utilise power and political manoeuvring to gain their own ends, and they can and do interpret events in widely-differing ways. Therefore, self-organisation may not occur even when appropriate order-generating rules are present, nor, if such rules cease to be appropriate, can it be assumed that they will automatically be transformed. Instead both will depend on the nature of the organisation (Griffin, 2002).

MacIntosh and MacLean (2001) provide evidence of the existence and importance of order-generating rules, based on a case study of a long-established manufacturing company that had been in decline for over 30 years. This decline appeared to be caused by a combination of inappropriate order-generating rules (such as 'don't innovate unless it leads to cost reduction') and a rigid structure that stifled innovation. Once this was recognised, the company evolved more appropriate order-generating rules (such as 'better, faster, cheaper') and implemented a new structure that gave greater freedom for self-organisation to its constituent parts.

In order for organisations to promote change through self-organisation, a number of writers have argued that organisations need to operate on democratic principles, i.e. their members will have to have the freedom to self-organise. For example, Bechtold (1997) argues that organisations seeking to adopt a complexity approach need a balanced distribution of power, strong customer focus, a strategy of continuous learning and an orientation towards community service. A further strand in this argument is provided by Kiel (1994), who argues that because small actions can have large and unpredictable consequences, individual human activity assumes great importance. Jenner (1998) claims that for self-organisation to work, authority must be delegated to those who have access to the broadest channels of information that relate to the issue concerned. Nevertheless, Stacey (2003: 278) sounds a note of caution:

> This seems to assume that self-organisation is some new form of behaviour rather than a different way of understanding how people have always behaved. The question is whether such self-organising behaviour produces patterns that block or enable change.

In considering complexity theories and organisational change, one of the key questions is to ask: 'What's new?' (Frederick, 1998). If we look at what appears to be being said about management, structure, behaviour and change, much of it seems very familiar. Writers from Peters and Waterman (1982) onwards have been arguing that managers need to abandon top-down, command-and-control styles, that organisational structures need to be flatter and more flexible, and that greater employee involvement is essential for success (Handy, 1989; Kanter, 1989, 1997; Kanter *et al*, 1997; Kotter, 1996; Peters, 1989, 1993, 1997). However, as the implications listed in Exhibit 4.3 show, there are three areas where those seeking to apply complexity theories to organisations appear to depart from, or significantly extend, the received wisdom of the last 20 years.

Exhibit 4.3   Applying complexity theories to organisations

Implication 1 There will be a need for much greater democracy and power equalisation in all aspects of organisational life, instead of just narrow employee participation in change (Bechtold, 1997; Jenner, 1998; Kiel, 1994).

Implication 2 Small-scale incremental change and large-scale radical-transformational change will need to be rejected in favour of 'a third kind' which lies between these two, and which is continuous and based on self-organisation at the team/group level (Brodbeck, 2002; Brown and Eisenhardt, 1997).

Implication 3 In achieving effective change, order-generating rules have the potential to overcome the limitations of rational, linear, top-down, strategy-driven approaches to change (MacIntosh and MacLean, 1999, 2001; Stacey, 2003; Styhre, 2002).

The basis for *Implication 1* is that unless employees have the freedom to act as they see fit, self-organisation will be blocked and organisations will not be able to achieve continuous and beneficial innovation. The rationale for *Implication 2* is that neither small-scale incremental change nor radical transformational change work: instead, innovative activity can only be successfully generated through the 'third kind' of change, such as new product and process development brought about by self-organising teams. *Implication 3* is based on the argument that because organisations are complex systems, which are radically unpredictable and where even small changes can have massive and unanticipated effects, top-down change cannot deliver the continuous innovation that organisations need in order to survive and prosper. Instead, it is argued that organisations can only achieve continuous innovation if they position themselves at the edge of chaos. This position can only be achieved and maintained through self-organisation, which in turn depends on the possession of appropriate order-generating rules. However, should these rules cease to be appropriate for the organisation's environment, the process of self-organisation allows new, more appropriate rules to be generated. Therefore, in a chicken and egg fashion, order-generating rules create the conditions for self-organisation, and self-organisation creates the conditions that enable order-generating rules to be transformed (Bechtold, 1997; Hoogerwerf and Poorthuis, 2002; Tetenbaum, 1998).

■ Complexity – some reservations

Like postmodernism and realism, complexity has much to commend it. It offers an explanation of the apparent complexity and chaos of modern life and, potentially at least, a way of managing this complexity and chaos. Also, for managers, it is an approach based on 'hard' science and not 'airy fairy' philosophy. Nevertheless, writers have raised three significant reservations about the application of complexity theories to organisations. Firstly, the complexity approach requires a significant shift towards greater organisational democracy and power equalisation. This appears to go far beyond the more limited, and often failed, attempts to redistribute power through empowerment, flatter organisational structures and quality improvement programmes which have been called for over the last 20 years (Eccles, 1993; Foegen, 1999; Lawler *et al*, 1998; Lee, 1999; Pfeffer, 1996; Stohl and Cheney, 2001; Wetlaufer, 1999; Whyte and Witcher, 1992; Witcher, 1993; Zairi *et al*, 1994). Therefore, convincing organisations that they are complex systems is likely to prove far easier than for organisations to achieve the profound internal realignments necessary to implement this concept (Beeson and Davis, 2000; Stacey, 2003).

Secondly, in applying complexity theories to organisations, it is important to bear in mind that, even in the natural sciences, there are variants of these and disputes about their implications (Black, 2002; Stacey *et al*, 2002; Stacey, 2003). As Arndt and Bigelow (2000: 36) observe, they have '... caused consternation as well as delight'. Therefore, one needs to be extremely careful not to treat complexity theories as though they are established, unitary, unquestioned and uncontroversial (Stickland, 1998).

Lastly, in applying complexity theories to organisations, there appears to be a lack of clarity or explicitness regarding how writers are treating them (Arndt and Bigelow, 2000; Brodbeck, 2002; Hayles, 2000; Morgan, 1997; Stacey *et al*, 2002; Stacey, 2003). For example, some see them as a metaphorical device which provides a means of gaining new insights into organisations, whilst others see them as a way of mathematically modelling how and why organisations operate as they do (Stickland, 1998). If the former, then it could be argued that the complexity perspective is just another of the multiple realities so beloved of the postmodernists. If the latter, then its proponents will have to show how mathematical modelling techniques can be applied to complex and dynamic human processes in organisations, though there is no indication that anyone has yet attempted to do so (Stacey, 2003).

Conclusions

In Chapters 1–3, we reviewed the main theories and approaches to structuring and running organisations. These three chapters showed that, over the past 100 years, organisation theory had moved a long way from the mechanical certainties of the Classical school as exemplified by the work of Frederick Taylor. We no longer perceive organisations as simple machines, nor of people as cogs, or 'greedy robots', in those machines. We now recognise the convoluted nature of organisations and their environments, and the even more convoluted nature of human beings. Contemporary approaches to running organisations have attempted to move away from the mechanical certainties of Frederick Taylor and co. by developing theories that focus on, or incorporate, the human–social dimension of organisational life. Consequently, for the Culture–Excellence school, the key issue has been organisational culture; for the Japanese, the key issue has been to blend together the 'hard' and 'soft' elements of organisational life; whereas for the learning school, the main topic has been to understand how humans learn, and how this can be translated from individual learning to collective, organisational learning. Though there are some common elements between all three approaches, there are also major differences. Nevertheless, this has not stopped proponents of all three from seeking to promote their approach as the 'one best way'.

What this chapter has shown is the need to set and understand approaches to running and designing organisations into a wider theoretical frame. None of the three perspectives on organisations reviewed in this chapter were developed specifically with organisations in mind; indeed, their originators might have been somewhat surprised to see this development. Two of them, postmodernism and realism, are based on well-developed philosophical doctrines, and the other, complexity, comes from a great deal of research carried out in a wide variety of disciplines in the natural sciences. All three are inspired by the desire to understand the world around us in its widest context, whether this be art, history, science or why it always seems to rain in Manchester. All three have significant implications for structuring and managing organisations.

Postmodernism, with its denial of an absolute reality and promotion of competing, and socially-constructed, multiple realities, offers enormous scope for the emergence of alternative strategies and choices, but it also stresses the importance of culture, power and politics in how the strategies are selected and legitimised, and how choices are made. The realists reject the concept of multiple realities in favour of just one. They do not deny the socially-constructed nature of their reality, though they claim that it is no less real for all that. Nor do they deny that this social construction offers organisations a great deal more scope for choice and manoeuvre than conventional approaches appear to acknowledge. The difference between these two perspectives is that while the postmodernists believe that anything is possible, the realists see organisations' room for manoeuvre and choice as limited by complex structures in both the natural and social worlds which exist even if we are not aware of them.

Moving on to the complexity perspective, this sees organisations as complex, self-organising systems that, in order to maximise their innovative capacities, need to operate at the edge of chaos. In order to remain in this position, rather than falling off the edge, they need to develop and maintain appropriate order-generating rules. In order to develop and maintain appropriate order-generating rules, organisations are required to become far more democratic than they are now and allow '... people the freedom to own their own power, think innovatively, and operate in new patterns' (Bechtold, 1997: 198). In effect, choice moves from the few to the many. Though it does appear to be the case that organisations can survive for long periods of time without appropriate rules, complexity theorists maintain that this will reduce the organisation's innovative capacity and threaten its long-term survival.

As can be seen, all of these three critical perspectives have important but different implications for organisational life, and each has fundamental differences with the other two. Nevertheless, there is one very important implication which all three perspectives share; this is that organisations do have a wide range of options and choices open to them as to how they are structured and operate. This is the case even if one concedes that some postmodernist realities are more dominant than others, that 'real' social entities, such as markets, class relations, gender relations, social rules, etc., limit choice, or that eventually organisations need to adopt or develop appropriate order-generating rules. If choice is far wider than most organisation theories acknowledge, this poses questions as to how to identify options, and who will make the decisions as to which ones to choose? In Chapter 3, we drew attention to the importance of culture in shaping organisations and the actions of those in them. Chapter 3 also drew attention to the lack of interest paid to power and politics in running organisations and making decisions. In this chapter, especially in considering postmodernism, we have also drawn attention to the role of culture, power and politics in shaping decisions in organisations. In the next chapter, we will return to these issues and show how they impact on the choices made by those who run organisations.

Test your learning

■ Short answer questions

1 What is flexible specialisation?

2 Give three definitions of postmodernism.

3 Using Clegg's (1990) distinction between modernist and postmodernist organisation forms, identify the significant differences between job design under a modernist regime and that under a postmodernist regime.

4 What is realism?

5   What do realists mean by the terms 'causal mechanism' and 'causal powers'?

6   What do complexity theorists mean by the 'edge of chaos'?

7   What are the implications of the complexity perspective for organisational democracy?

8   For each of the following, briefly state their implications for organisational change: (a) postmodernism, (b) realism and (c) complexity theories.

Essay questions

1   What are the implications for organisations of differences between postmodernists and realists in terms of how they view reality?

2   What are 'simple order-generating rules', and how might an organisation identify and modify these?

Suggested further reading

1   Hatch, MJ (1997) *Organization Theory: Modern, Symbolic and Postmodern Perspectives.* Oxford University Press: Oxford.
    Stacey, R D (2003) *Strategic Management and Organisational Dynamics: The Challenge of Complexity.* FT/Prentice Hall: Harlow.
    Taken together, these two books provide a good overview of the postmodernist slant on organisations.
2   Ackroyd, S and Fleetwood, S (eds) (2000) *Realist Perspectives on Management and Organisations.* Routledge: London.
    This edited collection of essays provide an excellent introduction to realism and how it can be applied to organisations.
3   Black, JA (2000) Fermenting change: exploring complexity and chaos. *Journal of Organizational Change Management* (Special Edition), **13**(6).
    Fitzgerald, LA (2002) Chaos: applications in organizational change. *Journal of Organizational Change Management* (Special Edition), **15**(4).
    These two special editions of the *Journal of Organizational Change Management* offer a thought-provoking and informative overview of complexity theories.

Chapter 5

Culture, power, politics and choice

Learning objectives

After studying this chapter, you should be able to:

- understand the main tenets of organisational culture;
- discuss the strengths and weaknesses of the cultural approach to organisations;
- describe the role of power and politics in organisations;
- state the main advantages and disadvantages of the power-politics perspective on organisations;
- understand the scope, methods and limitations for the exercise of choice in terms of organisational design and change.

Exhibit 5.1   The end of choice?

How to preserve the soul of management: the increasing sophistication of measurement techniques threatens to reduce executives to robots

... This week, lulled by the soft-sounding title, I opened a book called Quest for Balance, the Human Element in Performance Management Systems. Inside were pages of boxes, tables, diagrams and acronyms constructed around case studies. It is the kind of book publishers like to describe as a business tool: an instruction manual for those attempting to implement Robert Kaplan's and David Norton's Balanced Scorecard (BSC). The idea is to identify crucial areas of the business – customer satisfaction, for example – that are described as critical success factors (CSFs) and measure them. In the case of customer satisfaction, you could canvass customers, count repeat purchases or work out the time it takes to deal with complaints. These measures are described as key performance indicators (KPIs).

It appears that these systems can produce measurable improvements in organisational productivity. I am sure they do. It makes a lot of sense to concentrate on the features of a business that create value. But what of the people engaged in carrying out the measurements and the people expected to respond? If systemisation removes the discretionary powers of managers, we may begin to ask why we should have managers at all.

When systems and controls are able to measure such critical areas of performance there is no reason why front line employees should not manage themselves and adjust their work habits accordingly. Surely anything that creates more efficient and effective organisations should be a cause

for celebration. But I fear the long-term consequences of this kind of organisation.

Isn't performance management simply a way to control the work of managers? How will people respond to such controls? If you stifle individual initiative, character, discrimination and style, you remove qualities critical to job satisfaction, leaving a mechanical process. How many managers will turn their backs on such systems in the belief that there has to be a better way of living your work?

Pursuit of efficiency improvements has always underpinned the development of management and the organisation of work. Adam Smith was intrigued by the division of labour in a pin factory. One workman, he noticed, would find it hard to make one pin a day but a group of 10 workmen, dividing the task into separate and distinct jobs, could between them make 48,000 pins in a day. Later Frederick Taylor, the founder of work study, believed that his scientific management had discovered the 'one best way' of working.

So manufacturing was reduced to its bare bones, in which a repeated action such as the clockwise turn of a screw became a job in itself. Craftsmanship, artisanship, individuality – even humanity – were abandoned in the search for ever more efficient production. Re-engineering and performance management continue this tradition. All these improvements are finding 'better ways' of doing things for the organisation. But what about personal fulfilment, the stuff that feeds our soul and spirit?

Source: Richard Donkin, *Financial Times*, 19 September 2002, p. 12.

Introduction

The first three chapters of this book described the main and most influential approaches to running organisations that have emerged in the last 100 years. If they can be said to have one common feature, it is that each of them claim to have discovered the 'one best way' to run organisations. The result of this ought to be the type of development described in Exhibit 5.1, the reduction or elimination of managerial choice and discretion. If there is a sure-fire way of running organisations, the main job of senior managers is to see that it is implemented and that no one, especially themselves, deviates from it. If there is a sure-fire recipe for success, then we should see the elimination, or at the very least the downgrading, of senior managerial posts because almost anyone should be capable of implementing the recipe. However, there are three counter-arguments to those who see 'managerial recipes' replacing 'managerial resourcefulness'. The first is that, if this is the case, why have executive salaries increased so dramatically on both sides of the Atlantic in the last decade (AFL-CIO, 2003; Finch and Treanor, 2003)? The second is that, if such sure-fire recipes existed, why is there such a wide disparity in organisational success and why do so few, if any, companies manage to achieve long-term prosperity? The third counter-argument was provided by the discussion of postmodernism, realism and complexity in the previous chapter. This is that rather than being the prisoners of circumstances, rather than being hemmed in by successful recipes, rather than rational beings unquestioningly following rational recipes, managers have a surprisingly wide degree of choice and discretions. Even if one rejects the 'boundless' view of choice advocated by the postmodernists in favour of the 'bounded' view of the realists and complexity theorists, managers are still far from the 'executive robots' perceived by Donkin in Exhibit 5.1. However, if the recipes for success are not straitjackets, if managers are not rational beings, if they do have scope for choice, on what do they base their choices? In this chapter, it will be argued that the answer lies in the areas of culture, power and politics.

The chapter begins with a review of organisational culture. It is shown that many organisations lack a cohesive culture that bonds them together in a common purpose. However, contrary to the arguments of the Culture–Excellence school, even where strong cultures exist, they may not always be appropriate; they may also be undermined owing to the absence of clear or uncontested organisational goals. The review of culture concludes that, firstly, although organisational culture may have important implications for organisational performance, there is little agreement about the nature of culture, whether it can be changed or the benefits to be gained from attempting to do so. Secondly, instead of culture being seen as an all-important and malleable determinant of performance, organisational life in many cases is dominated by political power battles which may be more influential than culture in shaping key decisions. Consequently, the review of culture leads on to an examination of the nature and role of power and politics in organisations. This view of organisations maintains that they are essentially political entities whose decisions, actions and major developments are influenced and determined by shifting coalitions of individuals attempting to protect or enhance their own interests.

In summing up the implications of chapters 4 and 5 for organisations, it is argued that, rather than being the prisoners of organisational theories or contingencies, managers (potentially) have considerable, though by no means unconstrained, freedom of choice over the structure, policies and practices of their organisations, and even over the environment in which they operate. In exercising choice, managers are influenced by organisational theories and constraints, but they are also influenced by their concern to ensure that the outcome of decisions favours, or at least does not damage, their personal interests. The conclusion to this chapter – and indeed of Part 1 of the book – is that, whether illegitimate or useful, political behaviour is an ever-present part of organisational life, and that such behaviour is particularly prevalent when major change initiatives are being considered or implemented.

The cultural perspective

■ What is organisational culture?

As can be seen from the discussion in Chapter 3 of the Culture–Excellence school, and, to a lesser extent, organisational learning and Japanese management, many writers point out that managers and employees do not perform their duties in a value-free vacuum. Their work and the way it is done are governed, directed and tempered by an organisation's culture – the particular set of values, beliefs, customs and systems that are unique to that organisation. Though Peters and Waterman's (1982) view that organisational culture is the prime determinant of organisational performance has been highly influential, other writers stress different, but no less important, aspects of culture. Keuning (1998: 46), for example, argues that the two most important functions of culture are: 'To provide relatively fixed patterns for handling and solving problems ... [and to] ... reduce uncertainty for members of the organization when confronted with new situations.' Nevertheless, as Wilson (1992) noted, so influential has Peters and Waterman's view become that culture has come to be seen as the great 'cure-all' for the majority of organisational ills.

The current fascination of business with organisational culture began in the 1980s with the work of writers such as Allen and Kraft (1982), Deal and Kennedy (1982), and above all Peters and Waterman (1982). Academics, however, had drawn attention to its importance much earlier; as Allaire and Firsirotu (1984) and Albrow (1997) have shown, there was already a substantial academic literature on organisational culture well before the work of Peters and Waterman (*see* Eldridge and Crombie, 1974; Turner, 1971). Blake and Mouton (1969), for example, were arguing that there was a link between culture and excellence in the late 1960s. For all this, organisational culture remains a highly contentious topic whose implications are far-reaching.

Turner (1986) traced the 'culture craze' of the 1980s to the decline of standards in manufacturing quality in the USA, and the challenge to its economic supremacy by Japan. He commented that the concept of culture holds out a new way of understanding organisations, and has been offered by many writers as an explanation for the spectacular success of Japanese companies in the 1970s and 1980s. Bowles (1989), amongst others, observed that there is an absence of a cohesive culture in advanced economies in the West, and that the potential for creating systems of beliefs and myths within organisations provides the opportunity for promoting both social and organisational cohesion. The case for culture was best summed up by Deal and Kennedy (1982), who argued that culture, rather than structure, strategy or politics, is the prime mover in organisations.

Silverman (1970) contended that organisations are societies in miniature and can therefore be expected to show evidence of their own cultural characteristics. However, culture does not spring up automatically and fully-formed from the whims of management. Allaire and Firsirotu (1984) considered it to be the product of a number of different influences: the ambient society's values and characteristics, the organisation's history and past leadership, and factors such as industry and technology. Other writers have constructed similar lists but, as Brown (1995) noted, there does seem to be some dispute over what factors shape organisational culture and those which are an integral part of it. Drennan (1992), for example, lists company expectations as a factor that shapes culture, but these might just as easily be seen as a reflection of an organisation's values which, as Cummings and Huse (1989) point out, are a key component of an organisation's culture. However, the difficulty in distinguishing between the factors that shape culture and those that comprise culture is a reflection, as Cummings and Huse (1989: 421) also point out, of the 'confusion about what the term culture really means when applied to organizations'. Brown (1995: 6–7) estimated that there are literally hundreds of definitions of culture: samples of these are shown in Exhibit 5.2.

Exhibit 5.2   Definitions of culture

The culture of the factory is its customary and traditional way of thinking and doing things, which is shared to a greater or lesser degree by all its members and which new members must learn, and at least partially accept, in order to be accepted into service in the firm.   (Jacques, 1952: 251)

Culture ... is a pattern of beliefs and expectations shared by the organization's members. These beliefs and expectations produce norms and powerfully shape the behaviour of individuals and groups in the organization.   (Schwartz and Davis, 1981: 33)

A quality of perceived organizational specialness – that it possesses some unusual quality that distinguishes it from others in the field.   (Gold, 1982: 571–2)

By culture I mean the shared beliefs top managers in a company have about how they should manage themselves and other employees, and how they should conduct business(es).   (Lorsch, 1986: 95)

Culture represents an interdependent set of values and ways of behaving that are common in a community and that tend to perpetuate themselves, sometimes over long periods of time.
(Kotter and Hesketh, 1992: 141)

Culture is 'how things are done around here'.   (Drennan, 1992: 3)

Whilst there is a similarity between the definitions shown in Exhibit 5.2, there are also some distinct differences: is culture something an organisation is or something it possesses? Does it mainly apply to senior managers or does it embrace everyone in the organisation? Is it a weak or a powerful force? Perhaps the most widely accepted definition is that offered by Eldridge and Crombie (1974: 78), who stated that culture refers:

... to the unique configuration of norms, values, beliefs, ways of behaving and so on, that characterise the manner in which groups and individuals combine to get things done.

Culture defines how those in the organisation should behave in a given set of circumstances. It affects all, from the most senior manager to the humblest clerk. Their actions are judged by themselves and others in relation to expected modes of behaviour. Culture legitimises certain forms of action and proscribes other forms. This view is supported by Turner (1971), who observed that cultural systems contain elements of 'ought' which prescribe forms of behaviour or allow behaviour to be judged acceptable or not. Other writers have suggested a wide variety of different aspects of culture as being important in shaping behaviour. Martin *et al* (1983) pointed to the role of organisational stories in shaping the actions and expectations of employees. They identified seven basic types of story prevalent in organisations which provide answers to seven fundamental questions of behaviour (*see* Exhibit 5.3).

Exhibit 5.3	Fundamental questions of behaviour in organisations

1. Can employees break the rules?
2. Is the big boss human?
3. Can the little person rise to the top?
4. Will I get fired?
5. Will the organisation help me if I have to move?
6. How will the boss react to mistakes?
7. How will the organisation deal with obstacles?

Alongside stories, much attention has been paid to the role of ceremonies, rites and rituals in reinforcing behaviour. As Trice and Beyer (1984) found, these include the following:

■ **Rites of passage** – designed to facilitate and signal a change in status and role through events such as training and induction programmes.
■ **Rites of questioning** – to allow the status quo to be challenged through the use of, for example, outside consultants.
■ **Rites of renewal** – to enable the status quo to be updated and renewed through participative initiatives including strategy development, vision building and job redesign programmes.

Another common theme in the literature is the role of 'heroes'. Peters and Waterman (1982) stressed the importance of corporate heroes in shaping the fortunes of their 'excellent' companies. Deal and Kennedy (1982) likewise saw the corporate hero as the great motivator, the person everyone looks up to, admires and relies on. Indeed, there is a tendency, not just in the USA, to attribute much of business success to the actions and personality of individuals, such as Pierre du Pont, Henry Heinz, Henry Ford, Alfred Sloan, Toyoda Kiichiro, Matsushita Konosuke, Edward Cadbury and Sir John Harvey-Jones. Current corporate heroes include Richard Branson at Virgin, Bill Gates at Microsoft, Chris Gent at Vodafone, Steve Jobs at Apple, Luc Vandevelde at Marks and Spencer and Jack Welch at General Electric.

Brown (1995) compiled a long list of 38 key elements of culture that have been identified by writers in the field, which include organisational climate, metaphors, attitudes, history and basic assumptions. Identifying these separate elements of culture helps us to flesh out and better understand how organisational culture manifests itself and impacts on individual and group behaviour. Nevertheless, as Brown shows, producing lists of elements or focusing on the role of particular elements tends to present a confusing and partial picture of culture. It becomes difficult to determine which are the more and which are the less important elements and, in terms of changing culture, which elements can be easily altered and which are more immutable.

To overcome this lack of clarity, there have been a number of attempts to identify and categorise the constituent elements of culture. Hofstede (1990) developed a fourlayered hierarchical model of culture which ranged from *values* at the deepest level through *rituals*, *heroes* and, at the surface level, *symbols*. In a similar way, Schein (1985) suggested a three-level model, with *basic assumptions* being at the deepest level, *beliefs*, *values* and *attitudes* at the intermediate level, and *artifacts* at the surface level. Based on an analysis of the different definitions of culture, Cummings and Huse (1989) produced a composite model of culture, comprising four major elements existing at different levels of awareness (*see* Figure 5.1).

Cummings and Huse (1989: 421) define these four major elements of culture as follows:

1. *Basic assumptions*. At the deepest level of cultural awareness are unconscious, taken-for-granted assumptions about how organisational problems should be solved ... They represent nonconfrontable and nondebatable assumptions about relating to the environment, as well as about the nature of human nature, human activity and human relationships. [...]
2. *Values*. The next higher level of awareness includes values about what *ought* to be in organizations. Values tell members what is important in the organization and what they need to pay attention to. [...]
3. *Norms*. Just below the surface of cultural awareness are norms guiding how members should behave in particular situations. These represent unwritten rules of behavior. [...]
4. *Artifacts*. At the highest level of cultural awareness are the artifacts and creations that are visible manifestations of the other levels of cultural elements. These include observable behaviors of members, as well as the structures, systems, procedures, rules, and physical aspects of the organization.

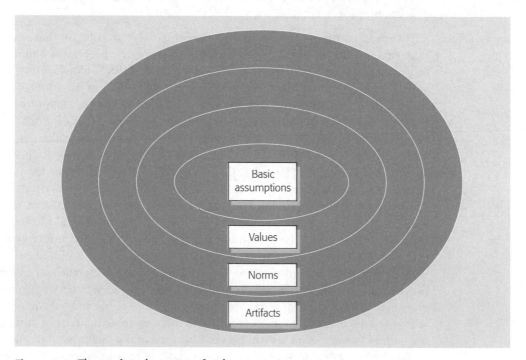

Figure 5.1 **The major elements of culture**
Source: from Cummings and Huse (1989)

However, while the various hierarchical models of culture elements are useful, we should always remember that, as Brown (1995: 8–9) notes, ' ... actual organisational cultures are not as neat and tidy as the models seem to imply'. Where there are cultures, there are also usually subcultures; where there is agreement about cultures, there can also be disagreements and counter-cultures; and there can also be significant differences between espoused culture and culture-in-practice.

This lack of neatness and tidiness has not prevented numerous attempts to define organisational culture, nor attempts to categorise the various types of culture. Deal and Kennedy (1982) identified four basic types of culture:

- The *Tough Guy, Macho culture*, characterised by individualism and risk-taking, e.g. a police force.
- The *Work-Hard/Play-Hard culture*, characterised by low risks and quick feedback on performance, e.g. McDonald's.
- The *Bet-Your-Company culture*, characterised by high risks and very long feedback time, e.g. aircraft companies.
- The *Process culture*, characterised by low risks and slow feedback, e.g. insurance companies.

Quinn and McGrath (1985) developed their own four types of culture:

- The *Market*, characterised by rational decision-making and goal-orientated employees, e.g. GEC under Arnold Weinstock.
- The *Adhocracy*, characterised by risk-orientated and charismatic leaders and value-driven organisations, e.g. Apple and Microsoft in their early days.
- The *Clan*, characterised by participation, consensus and concern for others, e.g. voluntary organisations.
- The *Hierarchy*, characterised by hierarchical, rule-based authority that values stability and risk avoidance, e.g. government bureaucracies.

Perhaps the best-known typology of culture, and the one which has been around the longest, is that developed by Handy (1979) from Harrison's (1972) work on 'organization ideologies'. Handy (1986: 188) observed that 'There seem to be four main types of culture ... *power*, *role*, *task* and *person*'. As shown in Exhibit 5.4, he relates each of these to a particular form of organisational structure.

Exhibit 5.4	Handy's four types of culture

A *power culture*, Handy states, is frequently found in small entrepreneurial organisations such as some property, trading and finance companies. Such a culture is associated with a web structure with one or more powerful figures at the centre, wielding control.

A *role culture* is appropriate to bureaucracies, and organisations with mechanistic, rigid structures and narrow jobs. Such cultures stress the importance of procedures and rules, hierarchical position and authority, security and predictability. In essence, role cultures create situations in which those in the organisation stick rigidly to their job description (role), and any unforeseen events are referred to the next layer up in the hierarchy.

A *task culture*, on the other hand, is job- or project-orientated; the onus is on getting the job in hand (the task) done rather than prescribing how it should be done. Such types of culture

Exhibit 5.4 *continued*

are appropriate to organically-structured organisations where flexibility and teamworking are encouraged. Task cultures create situations in which speed of reaction, integration and creativity are more important than adherence to particular rules or procedures, and where position and authority are less important than the individual contribution to the task in hand.

A *person culture* is, he argues, rare. The individual and his or her wishes are the central focus of this form of culture. It is associated with a minimalistic structure, the purpose of which is to assist those individuals who choose to work together. Therefore, a person culture can be characterised as a cluster or galaxy of individual stars.

Source: Handy (1986)

Handy (1986) believes that role and task cultures tend to predominate in Western organisations. Relating these two types of culture to Burns and Stalker's (1961) structural continuum, with mechanistic structures at one end and organic at the other, we can see that Handy is in effect seeking to construct a parallel and related cultural continuum, with role cultures at the mechanistic end and task cultures at the organic end (*see* Figure 5.2).

This categorisation certainly accommodates the five Western approaches to organisation theory discussed in the previous chapters. However, it is difficult to accommodate Japanese organisations within this framework, as their cultures contain elements of each extreme. As was described in Chapter 3, Japanese companies have very tightly-structured jobs, especially at the lower levels; they are very hierarchical and deferential, whilst at the same time achieving high levels of motivation, initiative and creativity in problem-solving. They tend to be heavily group/team-orientated, with such teams having a great deal of autonomy.

This difficulty of where to place Japan highlights one of the main criticisms of the various attempts to categorise culture, which is that they appear to give insufficient weight to the influence of national cultures on the types of organisational culture that predominate in particular countries. Increasingly over the last decade, and to an extent before, strong reservations have been expressed about the ethnocentric nature of organisational theory; the main reservation concerns the generalisability and applicability of management theories developed in the West, predominately the USA, to

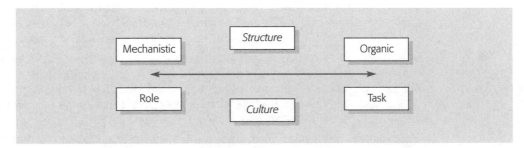

Figure 5.2 **A structure–culture continuum**

the very different cultures and societies of Asia, the middle East and Africa (Deresky, 2000; Ho, 1976; Rosenzweig, 1994; Sullivan and Nonaka, 1986; Thomas, 2003; Trompenaars, 1993). Given that the various typologies of organisational culture all come from a Western, and predominantly North American, perspective, this is an especially serious criticism.

One of the most comprehensive and influential studies of the differences between national cultures was carried out by Hofstede (1980, 1990). He suggested that national cultures can be clustered along the lines of their similarities across a range of cultural variables, as follows:

- the prevailing sense of individualism or collectivity in each country;
- the power distance accepted in each country (the degree of centralisation, auto-cratic leadership and number of levels in the hierarchy);
- the degree to which uncertainty is tolerated or avoided.

Based on these cultural variables, as Exhibit 5.5 shows, Hofstede classified industrialised countries into four broad clusters. However, his findings have to be treated with some caution as his sample was drawn from just one multi-national company, IBM.

Exhibit 5.5   Hofstede's national clusters

1. Scandinavia (primarily Denmark, Sweden and Norway): these cultures are based upon values of collectivity, consensus and decentralisation.
2. West Germany (prior to unification), Switzerland and Austria: these are grouped together largely as valuing efficiency – the well-oiled machine – and seeking to reduce uncertainty.
3. Great Britain, Canada, the USA, New Zealand, Australia and the Netherlands: these lie somewhere between 1 and 2 but cluster on the value they place on strong individuals and achievers in society.
4. Japan, France, Belgium, Spain and Italy: these are clustered on bureaucratic tendencies – the pyramid structure   favouring a large power distance.

Wilson (1992: 90) observed that 'The similarity of the factors in [Hofstede's] national culture study to Handy's (1986) four organizational forms is striking.' However, whilst one can see that Scandinavia can be classed as exhibiting task culture characteristics, and the group containing West Germany can be seen as exhibiting role culture characteristics, the other two groupings (Great Britain *et al* and Japan *et al*) are more difficult to place. Rather than placing Great Britain and the USA in one category, according to where they are positioned on Hofstede's dimensions, it might be more accurate to follow Handy's own lead and say that both task and role cultures are prevalent. This still leaves us with where to place Japan *et al*. From the point of view of Hofstede's dimensions, Japan appears to exhibit characteristics of Handy's role culture. However, as pointed out above, this is only part of the story of Japanese organisational life.

The impact of different national cultures on the management of organisations will be returned to in Chapter 16 when discussing globalisation. However, for now, it is important to recognise that Handy's categorisation of types of culture is very useful, in that it takes us beyond vague generalisations and gives us a picture of differing cultures. Nonetheless, like the other work discussed, it serves to highlight both the difficulty of defining cultures clearly, and also the profound implications of the cultural approach to organisations. These implications fall under four main headings.

Firsly, Deal and Kennedy (1982) argued that behaviour, instead of reacting directly to intrinsic and extrinsic motivators, is shaped by shared values, beliefs and assumptions about the way an organisation should operate, how rewards should be distributed, the conduct of meetings, and even how people should dress.

Secondly, if organisations do have their own identities, personalities or cultures, are there particular types of cultural attributes that are peculiar to top-performing organisations? As discussed in Chapter 3, the Culture–Excellence school reply to this question with a resounding *yes*!

Thirdly, Sathe (1983) argued that culture guides the actions of an organisation's members without the need for detailed instructions or long meetings to discuss how to approach particular issues or problems; it also reduces the level of ambiguity and misunderstanding between functions and departments. In effect, it provides a common context and a common purpose for those in the organisation. However, this is only the case when an organisation possesses a strong culture, and where the members of the organisation have internalised it to the extent that they no longer question the legitimacy or appropriateness of the organisation's values and beliefs.

Fourthly, one of the most important implications is that, as Barratt (1990: 23) claimed, 'values, beliefs and attitudes are learnt, can be managed and changed and are potentially manipulable by management'. O'Reilly (1989) is one of those who clearly believes this is the case. He argued that it is possible to change or manage a culture by choosing the attitudes and behaviours that are required, identifying the norms or expectations that promote or impede them, and then taking action to create the desired effect.

This last implication is particularly contentious, with many writers supporting this view but others arguing strongly against it.

Changing organisational culture: the arguments in favour

That cultures do change is not in question. No organisation's culture is static: as the external and internal factors that influence culture change, so culture will change. But given that culture is locked into the beliefs, values and norms of each individual in the organisation, and because these are difficult constructs to alter, this type of organic cultural change will be slow, unless perhaps there is some major shock to the organisation (Boddy and Buchanan, 2002; Brown, 1995; Burnes, 1991; Keuning, 1998; Schein, 1985). This in itself may not be problematic for organisations, provided that other factors change in an equally slow fashion. However, the argument put forward by the proponents of Culture–Excellence is that a successful culture is one based on values and assumptions appropriate to the environment in which it operates. In addition, like Handy (1986), Allaire and Firsirotu (1984) argued that, to operate effectively and efficiently, an organisation's culture needs to match or be appropriate to its structure. Looking at Figure 5.2, we can see that organisations with mechanistic structures are likely to operate effectively and efficiently if they have role cultures. However, given that an organisation's environment can change rapidly, as can its structure, situations will arise where an organisation's culture may be out of step with changes that are taking place in the environment, structure and practices of the organisation. In such a case, a company that moves quickly to replace a mechanistic structure with a more organic structure to cope with increasing uncertainty in its environment, might find that the change does not improve its effectiveness and efficiency because it had been unable to change from a role to a task culture with equal speed. As Handy (1986: 188) commented:

> Experience suggests that a strong culture makes a strong organisation, but does it matter what sort of culture is involved? Yes, it does. Not all cultures suit all purposes or people. Cultures are founded and built over the years by the dominant groups in an organisation. What suits them and the organisation at one stage is not necessarily appropriate for ever − strong though that culture may be.

Flynn (1993) described how, with the introduction of a more market-orientated philosophy, such a situation arose across organisations in the public sector in the UK. Many similar cases can be found in the private sector (*see* Boddy, 2002; Brown, 1995; Cummings and Worley, 2001; Dobson, 1988; Industrial Society, 1997). In such situations, rather than facilitating the efficient operation of the organisation, its culture may obstruct it.

Therefore, for a variety of reasons, organisations may decide that their existing culture is inappropriate or even detrimental to their competitive needs. In such a situation, many organisations decide to change their culture. A survey of the UK's 1,000 largest public and private sector organisations, carried out in 1988 by Dobson (1988), revealed that more than 250 of them had been involved in culture change programmes in the preceding five years. A similar survey by the Industrial Society in 1997, covering over 4,000 organisations, found that over 90 per cent of respondents were either going through or had recently gone through a culture change programme (Industrial Society, 1997). The survey found that culture change was promoted through a variety of methods including strategic planning, training, organisation redesign to promote teamwork, and changes to appraisal systems. Based on his 1988 survey, Dobson states that the organisations involved sought to change culture by shaping the beliefs, values and attitudes of employees.

Derived from the actions taken by these companies, Dobson identified a four-step approach to culture change:

Step 1 − change recruitment, selection and redundancy policies to alter the composition of the workforce so that promotion and employment prospects are dependent on those concerned possessing or displaying the beliefs and values the organisation wishes to promote.

Step 2 − reorganise the workforce to ensure that those employees and managers displaying the required traits occupy positions of influence.

Step 3 − effectively communicate the new values. This is done using a variety of methods such as one-to-one interviews, briefing groups, quality circles, house journals, etc. However, the example of senior managers exhibiting the new beliefs and values is seen as particularly important.

Step 4 − change systems, procedures and personnel policies, especially those concerned with rewards and appraisal.

Drawing on the work of wide range of researchers, Cummings and Worley (2001) offered their own six 'practical' steps for achieving cultural change (*see* Exhibit 5.6). Though wider in scope in that their approach sets change in a strategic context, the actual mechanics are very similar to those adopted by the organisations Dobson studied.

Exhibit 5.6	Guidelines for changing culture

1. **Formulate a clear strategic vision**. Effective cultural change should start from a clear vision of the firm's new strategy and of the shared values and behaviour needed to make it work. This vision provides the purpose and direction for cultural change.

2. **Display top-management commitment**. Cultural change must be managed from the top of the organisation. Senior managers and administrators need to be strongly committed to the new values and the need to create constant pressure for change.

3. **Model culture change at the highest level**. Senior executives must communicate the new culture through their own actions. Their behaviours need to symbolise the kind of values and behaviours being sought.

4. **Modify the organisation to support organisational changes**. Cultural change must be accompanied by supporting modifications in organisational structure, human resource systems, information and control systems, and management style. These organisational features can help to orientate people's behaviours to the new culture.

5. **Select and socialise newcomers and terminate deviants**. One of the most effective methods for changing culture is to change organisational membership. People can be selected in terms of their fit with the new culture, and provided with an induction clearly indicating desired attitudes and behaviour. Existing staff who cannot adapt to the new ways may have their employment terminated, for example, through early retirement schemes. This is especially important in key leadership positions, where people's actions can significantly promote or hinder new values and behaviours.

6. **Develop ethical and legal sensitivity**. Most cultural change programmes attempt to promote values that emphasise employee integrity, control, equitable treatment and job security. However, if one of the key steps in pursuing culture change is to replace existing staff with new recruits, not only can this send out the wrong message to newcomers and the remaining staff but, depending how staff are selected for replacement, it could also contravene employment laws. Therefore, organisations need to be especially aware of these potential ethical and legal pitfalls.

Source: adapted from Cummings and Worley (2001: 509–11)

Many other writers advocating culture change adopt a similar approach. Some of these, including Peters and Waterman (1982) with their eight steps to excellence, take a very prescriptive line. Others, though, appear to underestimate greatly the difficulty involved in changing culture. An example of this is an article in *Management Today* (Egan, 1994) which took just four pages to show how organisations could quickly, and with apparent ease, identify and change their cultures. Regardless of how its supporters interpret or apply it, however, this type of generic approach to culture has been criticised as being too simplistic, and putting forward recommendations which are far too general to be of use to individual organisations (Brown, 1995; Gordon, 1985; Hassard and Sharifi, 1989; Nord, 1985; Uttal, 1983).

There are other writers who, whilst sharing the belief that culture can be changed, take a more considered view. Brown (1995) warns that organisations must be sure that the problems they wish to address through cultural change are actually caused by the existing culture. He warns that there is a tendency to assume that culture is the root cause of organisational problems, when in fact they might arise from inappropriate organisational structure. He also points out that senior managers may use the issue of culture to redirect blame for poor performance away from themselves and onto the rest of the organisation. In addition, Brown warns against taking an overly simplistic view of culture by believing that organisations have a single unitary culture, or by assuming that all employees can be made to share a single purpose or vision. This was also a point made by Hatch (1997) on behalf of the postmodernists. One of the most influential writers on the subject of culture, Schein (1985), takes a similarly cautious view. He warns that before any attempt is made to change an organisation's culture, it is first necessary to understand the nature of its existing culture and how this is sustained. According to Schein, this can be achieved by analysing the values that govern behaviour, and uncovering the underlying and often unconscious assumptions that determine how those in the organisation think, feel and react. Difficult though he acknowledges this to be, he argues that it can be achieved by:

- analysing the process of recruitment and induction for new employees;
- analysing responses to critical incidents in the organisation's history, as these are often translated into unwritten, but nevertheless very strong, rules of behaviour;
- analysing the beliefs, values and assumptions of those who are seen as the guardians and promoters of the organisation's culture;
- discussing the findings from the above with staff in the organisation, and paying especial attention to anomalies or puzzling features which have been observed.

Schein's approach, therefore, is to treat the development of culture as an adaptive and tangible learning process. His approach emphasises the way in which an organisation communicates its culture to new recruits. It illustrates how assumptions are translated into values and how values influence behaviour. Schein seeks to understand the mechanisms used to propagate culture, and how new values and behaviours are learned. Once these mechanisms are revealed, he argues, they can then form the basis of a strategy to change the organisation's culture.

In a synthesis of the literature on organisational culture, Hassard and Sharifi (1989) proposed a similar approach to that advocated by Schein. In particular, they stress two crucial aspects of culture change:

> Before a major [cultural] change campaign is commenced, senior managers must understand the implications of the new system for their own behaviour: and senior management must be involved in all the main stages preceding change.
> In change programmes, special attention must be given to the company's 'opinion leaders'.
> (Hassard and Sharifi, 1989: 11)

Schwartz and Davis (1981), on the other hand, adopted a different stance with regard to culture. They suggest that, when an organisation is considering any form of change, it should compare the strategic significance (the importance to the organisation's future) of the change with the cultural resistance that attempts to make the particular change will encounter. They term this the 'cultural risk' approach. They offer a step-by-step method for identifying the degree of cultural risk involved in any particular change project. From this, they argue, it is then possible for an organisation to decide with a degree of certainty whether to ignore the culture, manage round it, attempt to change the culture to fit the strategy, or change the strategy to fit the culture. Although Schwartz and Davis' method relies heavily on managerial judgement, they maintain that it constitutes a methodical approach to identifying, at an early stage, the potential impact of strategic change on an organisation's culture, and vice versa.

It should, of course, be pointed out that though Schein's approach and Schwartz and Davis' approach are different, this does not mean they are in conflict or are not compatible. Indeed, both could be considered as different aspects of the same task: deciding whether culture needs to be changed, and, if it does, in what way.

No one should dispute the difficulty of changing an organisation's culture. The work of Schein (1985), Schwartz and Davis (1981), Cummings and Huse (1989) and Dobson (1988) provides organisations with the guidelines and methods for evaluating the need for and undertaking cultural change. Schein's work shows how an organisation's existing culture, and the way it is reinforced, can be revealed. Schwartz and Davis' work shows how the need for cultural change can be evaluated and the necessary changes identified. Finally, the work of Cummings and Huse (1989) and Dobson (1988) shows how cultural change can be implemented.

■ Changing organisational culture: some reservations

One of those who sounds a cautious note regarding the feasibility or advisability of culture change is Edgar Schein. Though he believes that culture can be changed, he also argues that there is a negative side to creating (or attempting to create) a strong and cohesive organisational culture (Schein, 1984, 1985). Such shared values, particularly where they have been seen to be consistently successful in the past, make organisations resistant to certain types of change or strategic options, regardless of their merit.

Schein, in conversation with Luthans (Luthans, 1989), was also critical of the idea that culture change can be achieved by a top-down, management-led approach. Schein (1989) appears to advocate a contingency or context-specific view of culture. Taking an organisational life-cycle approach, he argues that an organisation may need a strong culture in its formative years to hold it together whilst it grows. However, it may reach a stage where it is increasingly differentiated geographically, by function and by division. At this stage, managing culture becomes more a question of knitting together the warring factions and subcultures. In such a case, a strong culture may outlive its usefulness.

Salaman (1979) also pointed out that whilst there may be a strong or dominant culture in an organisation, there will also be subcultures, as in society at large. These may be peculiar to the organisation or may cut across organisations. Examples of the latter are groups such as doctors and lawyers who have their own professional cultures which extend beyond the organisations who employ them. Davis (1985) examined the culture of white- and blue-collar lower-level employees. He found that not only do these groups have their own distinctive cultures, but these can often be in conflict with the dominant (managerial) culture of their organisation. Therefore, subcultures exist in a complex and potentially conflicting relationship with the dominant culture. If that dominant culture is seen by some groups to have lost its appropriateness (and thus legitimacy), then potential conflicts can become actual conflicts. The reverse can also be the case; cultural values and methods of operation which one group adopts may be seen as being out of step with 'the way we've always done things'. This in turn can lead to an undermining of the authority of managers and specialists – endangering the efficient operation of the organisation (Morieux and Sutherland, 1988).

Uttal (1983) is another who expressed caution with regard to the difficulties and advisability of culture change. In particular, he observed that even where it is successful, the process can take anywhere from 6 to 15 years. Meyer and Zucker (1989) went further, arguing that whilst managing cultural change may result in short-term economic benefits, in the longer term it may result in stagnation and demise. Another difficulty in achieving culture change is that, as Brown (1995: 153) notes:

> ... most employees in an organisation have a high emotional stake in the current culture. People who have been steeped in the traditions and values of the organisation and whose philosophy of life may well be caught up in the organisation's cultural assumptions will experience considerable uncertainty, anxiety and pain in the process of change ... Even if there are personal gains to be made from altering the habits of a lifetime these are likely to be seen as potential or theoretical only, as against the certainty of the losses.

Therefore, any attempt to change an organisation's culture is inevitably going to be met with resistance. Sometimes this will be open and organised; often it will be covert and instinctive with people trying to hold on to old ways and protect the old order. Unlike many other forms of change, the main resistance may well come from middle and, especially, senior managers who see their status, power and personal beliefs challenged. This is a point made by Cummings and Worley (2001), who observed that culture change programmes often result in or require the removal of managers from key leadership positions.

As can be seen, there are many writers who draw attention to the difficulties inherent in attempting culture change; however, there are also writers who believe that culture cannot be changed or managed at all. Meek (1988: 469–70) commented that:

> Culture as a whole cannot be manipulated, turned on or off, although it needs to be recognised that some [organisations] are in a better position than others to intentionally influence aspects of it ... culture should be regarded as something an organisation 'is', not something it 'has': it is not an independent variable nor can it be created, discovered or destroyed by the whims of management.

In a similar vein, Filby and Willmott (1988) also questioned the notion that management has the capacity to control culture. They point out that this ignores the ways in which an individual's values and beliefs are conditioned by experience outside the workplace – through exposure to the media, through social activities, as well as through previous occupational activities. Postmodernists, as mentioned in the previous chapter, take a similar view. Hatch (1997: 235) probably speaks for many of them when she gives this advice:

> Do not think of trying to manage culture. Other people's meanings and interpretations are highly unmanageable. Think instead of trying to culturally manage your organization, that is, manage your organization with cultural awareness of the multiplicity of meanings that will be made of you and your efforts.

A further reservation expressed by a number of writers relates to the ethical issues raised by attempts to change culture. Van Maanen and Kunda (1989) argued that behind the interest in culture is an attempt by managers to control what employees feel as well as what they say or do. Their argument is that culture is a mechanism for disciplining emotion – a method of guiding the way people are expected to feel. Seen in this light, attempts to change culture can be conceived of as Taylorism of the mind. Frederick Taylor sought to control behaviour by laying down and enforcing strict rules about how work should be carried out. Van Maanen and Kunda in effect argue that culture change programmes attempt to achieve the same end through a form of mind control. Willmott (1995) expresses similar concerns. He believes that the over-riding aim of culture change is to win the 'hearts and minds' of employees by achieving control over the 'employee's soul'. Watson (1997: 278) concludes that:

> Employers and managers engaging in these ways with issues of employees' self-identities and the values through which they judge the rights and wrongs of their daily lives must be a matter of serious concern. To attempt to mould cultures – given that culture in its broad sense provides the roots of human morality, social identity and existential security – is indeed to enter 'deep and dangerous waters'.

Changing organisational culture: conflicts and choices

As in so much else to do with organisations, there is no agreement amongst those who study culture as to its nature, purpose or malleability. Certainly, few writers doubt its importance, but beyond that there is little agreement. The result, to quote Brown (1995: 5), is that we are presented with 'an embarrassment of definitional riches'. The Culture–Excellence proponents argue that there is only one form of culture that matters in today's environment – strong and flexible – and that organisations should adopt it quickly or face the consequences. The proponents of the Japanese approach to management and the Organisational Learning camp adopt a similar, though less strident, view. Schein (1984, 1985, 1989) agreed that culture is important and that in certain cases a strong culture is desirable. However, in other situations, shared values and strong cultures may have a negative effect by stifling diversity and preventing alternative strategies arising. He also doubts that managers acting in isolation from the rest of an organisation have the ability themselves to change the existing culture or impose a new one. Salaman (1979) also drew attention to the presence and role of subcultures, particularly their potential for creating conflict. Meek (1988) took the view that culture is not amenable to conscious managerial change programmes at all. The postmodernists adopt a similar view. Though they consider organisational culture to be important, they are sceptical of attempts to manipulate and change culture, believing that the outcomes of such attempts are unpredictable and can alienate rather than motivate employees – remember Hatch's (1997: 235) warning not even to 'think of trying to manage culture'.

Despite the lack of consensus amongst writers, there are two main conclusions we can draw from the above review of the culture literature. Firstly, in the absence of unambiguous guidelines on organisational culture, managers must make their own choices based on their own circumstances and perceived options as to whether to attempt to change their organisation's culture.

Secondly, in the absence of strong or appropriate cultures that bind their members together in a common purpose and legitimate and guide decision-making, managers may find it difficult either to agree amongst themselves or to gain agreement from others in the organisation. As Robbins (1987) argued, in such a situation, there is a tendency for conflict and power battles to take place.

Therefore, in understanding how organisations operate and the strengths and weaknesses of the theories we have been discussing in the previous chapters, it is necessary to examine the power–politics perspective on organisations.

The power–politics perspective

Political behaviour in organisations

The cultural perspective on organisational life reinforces the argument developed in previous chapters that organisations are not rational entities where everyone subscribes to, and helps to achieve, the organisation's overarching goals. The power–politics perspective puts forward a similar view, arguing that organisations often act irrationally, that their goals and objectives emerge through a process of negotiation and influence, and that they are composed of competing and shifting coalitions of groups and individuals (Brown, 1995; Buchanan and Badham, 1999; Mintzberg *et al*, 1998; Robbins, 1986, 1987). This perspective began to emerge strongly in the late 1970s and early 1980s, and is especially associated with Jeffrey Pfeffer's (1981) book *Power in Organizations*. Before then, as Gandz and Murray (1980) discovered when they reviewed the literature on organisational politics, there was very little general interest in the topic, and very few publications on it.

Nevertheless, of the early work in the field, Lindblom's (1959) work on the 'science of muddling through' and Cyert and March's (1963) book, *A Behavioral Theory of the Firm*, can be said to have really laid the basis for the later explosion of interest in power and politics in organisations. Writing from the viewpoint of public sector organisations, Lindblom argued that political constraints on policy make a rationalist approach to decision-making impossible. Cyert and March extensively developed Lindblom's work, showing that private sector firms were no less political entities than public sector organisations. The intention behind their work was to provide a better understanding of decision-making by supplementing existing theories, which tended to focus on market factors, with an examination of the internal operation of the firm. Cyert and March characterise firms as competing and shifting coalitions of multiple and conflicting interests, whose demands and objectives are constantly, but imperfectly, reconciled and where rationality is limited or bounded by uncertainty over what is wanted and how to achieve it. Under such circumstances, managers 'satisfice': rather than searching for the best solution, they select one that is satisfactory and sufficient (Simon, 1957).

Cyert and March's work on the political dimension of decision-making and the nature of organisational life now forms part of the received wisdom on organisational behaviour (Mallory, 1997). This is not to refute or marginalise the role of organisational culture. As Handy (1993) observed, the extent to which agreement exists about the tasks an organisation undertakes, how it undertakes them, and the extent to which members of the organisation are committed to achieving them, will be affected by the strength and the perceived legitimacy or suitability of the organisation's culture. Willcocks (1994: 31) took the view that diverse interests are part of organisational culture. They include, he argues, 'for example, the goals, values and expectations of the organizational participants and have been described as cognitive maps or personal agendas'. The importance of the power–politics perspective is that it shows that, even where a strong culture may be present, the cohesiveness, willingness and stability of an organisation's members is unlikely to be uniform either across an organisation or over time. Rather the degree of cooperation and commitment they exhibit will vary with the degree to which they perceive the goals they are pursuing as broadly consistent with their own interests (Mullins, 1993; Rollinson, 2002). Therefore, as Pfeffer (1978: 11–12) commented:

> It is difficult to think of situations in which goals are so congruent, or the facts so clear-cut that judgment and compromise are not involved. What is rational from one point of view is irrational from another. Organizations are political systems, coalitions of interests, and rationality is defined only with respect to unitary and consistent ordering of preferences.

It might be comforting to believe that individuals and groups within organisations are supportive of each other, that they work in a harmonious and cooperative fashion. Such a non-political perspective portrays employees as always behaving in a manner consistent with the interests of the organisation. In contrast, as Robbins (1986: 283) remarked, 'a political view can explain much of, what may seem to be, irrational behaviour in organizations. It can help to explain, for instance, why employees withhold information, restrict output, attempt to "build empires" ... '.

Handy (1986) also observed the tendency for individuals and groups to pursue courses of action that promote their interests, regardless of the organisation's formal goals and objectives. He notes that where individuals perceive that the actual or proposed goals of the organisation or the tasks they are asked to perform are out of step with their own interests, they will seek where possible to bring the two into line. In some cases, individuals and groups may be persuaded to change their perceptions; in others, they may seek to change or influence the goals or tasks. It is this phenomenon of individuals and groups, throughout an organisation, pursuing differing interests, and battling with each other to shape decisions in their favour, that has led many commentators to characterise organisations as political systems (Buchanan and Badham, 1999; Dawson, 2003; Mintzberg et al, 1998; Morgan, 1986; Pettigrew, 1985, 1987; Pfeffer, 1981, 1992).

Zaleznik (1970) stated that where there are scarce resources (which is the case in most organisations), the psychology of scarcity and comparison take over. In such situations, possession of resources becomes the focus for comparisons, the basis for self-esteem and, ultimately, the source of power. Such situations will see the emergence not only of dominant coalitions but also, Zaleznik argues, of unconscious collusion based on defensive reaction. Therefore, whilst some individuals will perceive their actions as 'political' or self-interested, others may act in the same manner, but believe they are pursuing the best interests of the organisation.

Drory and Romm (1988) argued that those in managerial positions are less likely than those in non-managerial positions to define (or recognise) their actions as political. This may be explained by the findings from a survey of 428 managers carried out by Gandz and Murray (1980). They found that managers are more involved in political behaviour, and therefore tend to see it as a typical part of organisational life. If this is the case, it could be argued that the more individuals and groups are involved in political behaviour, the more it becomes the norm, and they become blind to its political nature and see it merely as standard practice. Those less involved in such behaviour, on the other hand, recognise its political nature because it stands out from their normal practices. It is also the case that those lower down the organisation, whilst affected by resource allocation decisions, are less likely, on a regular basis, to be in a position to influence such decisions. For managers, however, arguing for additional resources or allocating existing resources is the normal currency of everyday life. This is reflected in Gandz and Murray's survey, where 89 per cent of respondents thought that successful executives had to be good politicians. Despite this, over 50 per cent of respondents also thought that organisations would be happier places if they were free of politics, and a similar number thought that political behaviour was detrimental to efficiency. As Kanter (1979) and Pfeffer (1992) note, this ambivalent attitude, i.e. believing that political behaviour is necessary but deploring its use, is rife in organisations.

As mentioned in Chapter 4, postmodernists take a very different view of power and politics to that of most other writers on organisations. They are not greatly concerned with the way individuals and groups acquire and hold on to power as such. Instead, they focus on the relationship between power and knowledge, and on the way that power is used to promote particular views of reality and to legitimate particular forms of knowledge in organisations.

Power and politics: towards a definition

Though it is relatively easy to provide simple definitions of power (the possession of position and/or resources) and politics (the deployment of influence/leverage), it is more difficult to distinguish between the two, as was shown by Drory and Romm (1988). They argue that the two concepts are often used interchangeably and that the difference between the two has never been fully settled. Indeed, a brief examination of each shows the difficulty, and perhaps danger, in separating them. First, however, it is also necessary to understand the difference between power and authority.

Robbins (1987: 186) drew an important distinction between them:

> ... we defined authority as the right to act, or command others to act, toward the attainment of organizational goals. Its unique characteristic, we said, was that this right had legitimacy based on the authority figure's position in the organization. Authority goes with the job. ... When we use the term power we mean an individual's capacity to influence decisions. ... the ability to influence based on an individual's legitimate position can affect decisions, but one does not require authority to have such influence.

In support of his view, Robbins quotes the example of high-ranking executives' secretaries, who may have a great deal of power, by virtue of their ability to influence the flow of information and people to their bosses, but have very little actual authority. Pfeffer (1992), whilst agreeing with this view, points out that power can stem from three sources: control over information; formal authority to act; and control over resources. However, he believes this latter source of power is particularly important. We must, Pfeffer (1992: 83) argues, recognise the truth of the 'New Golden Rule: the person with the gold makes the rules.'

On the other hand, Robbins (1987: 194) defines organisational politics as the:

> ... efforts of organizational members to mobilize support for or against policies, rules, goals, or other decisions in which the outcome will have some effect on them. Politics, therefore, is essentially the exercise of power.

Robbins' argument, then, is that power is the capacity to influence decisions whilst politics is the actual process of exerting this influence. This view, that politics is merely the enactment of power, is held by many writers. Gibson *et al* (1988: 44), for example, stated that organisational politics comprises 'those activities used at all levels to acquire, develop or use power and other resources to obtain individual choices when there is uncertainty or disagreement about choices'. This view is also central to Pfeffer's (1981: 7) widely-accepted definition, that organisational politics:

> ... involves those activities taken within organizations to acquire, develop and use power and other resources to obtain one's preferred outcome in a situation where there is uncertainty or descensus about choices.

Pfeffer, like many writers, refers to organisational politics as games. In his major work *Power in Organizations* (Pfeffer, 1981), he took the view that decisions in organisations are the result of games among players with different perceptions and interests. This was a theme developed by Mintzberg (1983) in his comprehensive review of power and politics in organisations. He lists 13 political games that are common in organisations, the key ones being games to resist authority, games to counter resistance, games to build power bases, games to defeat rivals, and games to change the organisation.

Like all games, political ones have particular tactics associated with them. Exhibit 5.7 lists the seven most common ploys used by managers when seeking to influence superiors, equals and subordinates.

Exhibit 5.7	Political ploys

- **Reason** – facts and information are used selectively to mount seemingly logical or rational arguments.
- **Friendliness** – the use of flattery, creation of goodwill, etc., prior to making a request.
- **Coalition** – joining forces with others so as to increase one's own influence.
- **Bargaining** – exchanging benefits and favours in order to achieve a particular outcome.
- **Assertiveness** – being forceful in making requests and demanding compliance.
- **Higher authority** – gaining the support of superiors for a particular course of action.
- **Sanctions** – using the promise of rewards or the threat of punishment to force compliance.

Source: from Kipnis *et al* (1980, 1984), Schilit and Locke (1982)

Robbins (1986) observed that the most popular tactic or ploy is the selective use of reason, regardless of whether the influence was directed upwards or downwards. Although cloaked in reason, arguments and data are deployed in such a way that the outcome favoured by those using the tactic is presented in a more favourable light than the alternatives. Therefore, though reason may be deployed, it is not done so in an unbiased or neutral fashion; it is used as a screen to disguise the real objective of the exercise. In deciding which tactic to use, Kipnis *et al* (1984) identified four contingency variables that affect the manager's choice: the manager's relative power; the manager's objectives in seeking to influence others; the manager's expectations of the target person's/group's willingness to comply; and the organisation's culture.

Having gained a clearer picture of power and politics, we can now move on to examine one of the central issues that arises from this: the distinction between the legitimate and illegitimate use of power and politics.

Power, politics and legitimacy

Thompkins (1990) firmly believed that the use of politics is a direct contravention of or challenge to the legitimate rules of an organisation. Many, however, see organisational politics as existing in a grey area between prescribed and illegal behaviour (Drory and Romm, 1988). Porter *et al* (1983) differentiated between three types of organisational behaviours: prescribed, discretionary and illegal. They believe that political behaviour falls within the discretionary rather than the illegal category. The most common view is that the use of politics in organisations can best be described as non-sanctioned or informal or discretionary behaviour, rather than behaviour that is clearly prohibited or illegal (Farrell and Petersen, 1983; Mayes and Allen, 1977). This definition of politics helps to distinguish between the formal and legitimate use of officially-sanctioned power by authorised personnel, and power that is exercised either in an illegitimate manner by authorised personnel or used by non-authorised personnel for their own ends.

Most organisations and many writers see political behaviour as dysfunctional (Drory and Romm, 1988). Batten and Swab (1965), Pettigrew (1973) and Porter (1976) believed that political behaviour goes against and undermines formal organisational goals and interests. Thompkins (1990), though, argued that political manoeuvring in organisations is due to a failure by senior managers to set and implement coherent and consistent goals and policies in the first place. This results in uncertainties, which in turn lead to conflict between groups and individuals. In such a situation, Thompkins (1990: 24) argues:

> Management is then left without top level guidance to run company operations. They will, then, by their own nature of survival, over a period of time, make decisions that will perpetuate their own safety and security. This is the beginning of political power, where legitimate discipline begins to decline and illegitimate discipline begins to strangle the organisation. In short, the tail begins to wag the dog. 'Politics' in this form is created by the neglect of top executive management.

Pfeffer (1981) took a different view of organisational politics. Rather than political behaviour arising from a lack of clear-cut goals and policies, he suggests that the construction of organisational goals is itself a political process. Nevertheless, this does not always mean that political behaviour is detrimental to organisational effectiveness. Mintzberg (1983) maintains that, when used in moderation, political games can have a healthy effect by keeping the organisation on its toes. Mayes and Allen (1977) took a similar view. Pascale (1993) went further, putting forward the view that conflict and contention are necessary to save an organisation from complacency and decline. The argument that the use of politics and power are central to the effective running of organisations has been most strongly put by Pfeffer (1992: 337–8) in his book *Managing with Power*, in which he argues that:

> Computers don't get built, cities don't get rebuilt, and diseases don't get fought unless advocates for change learn how to develop and use power effectively. ... In corporations, public agencies, universities, and government, the problem is how to get things done, how to move forward, how to solve the many problems facing organizations of all sizes and all types. Developing and exercising power requires both will and skill. It is the will which often seems to be missing.

For Pfeffer, will and skill are exercised through the pursuit of a focused and consistent personal agenda which is implemented through a seven-step programme (*see* Exhibit 5.8). However, Mintzberg (1983) sounds a note of warning. He argues that if too many people pursue their own personal agenda, or if the use of power and politics becomes too aggressive and pervasive, it can turn the whole organisation into a political cauldron and divert it from its main task.

Exhibit 5.8   The use of power and politics

1. Decide what your goals are, what you are trying to accomplish.
2. Diagnose patterns of dependence and interdependence; what individuals are influential and important in your achieving your goal?
3. What are their points of view likely to be? How will they feel about what you are trying to do?
4. What are their power bases? Which of them is more influential in the decision?
5. What are your bases of power and influence? What bases of influence can you develop to gain more control over the situation?
6. Which of the various strategies and tactics for exercising power seem most appropriate and are likely to be effective, given the situation you confront?
7. Based on the above, choose a course of action to get something done.

Source: from Pfeffer (1992: 29)

To an extent, the degree to which the balance between positive and negative benefits is tipped one way or the other in an organisation is dependent on the type of power deployed and how it is used. Etzioni (1975) identified three distinct types of power used in organisations:

■ **Coercive power** – the threat of negative consequences (including physical sanctions or force) should compliance not be forthcoming.

- **Remunerative power** – the promise of material rewards as inducements to cooperate.
- **Normative power** – the allocation and manipulation of symbolic rewards, such as status symbols, as inducements to obey.

Robbins (1986) developed this further by identifying not only types of power but also the sources of power. To Etzioni's three types of power, he adds a fourth:

- **Knowledge power** – the control of information.

> We can say that when an individual in a group or organization controls unique information, and when that information is needed to make a decision, the individual has knowledge-based power. (Robbins, 1986: 273)

Robbins suggests that these four types of power stem from four separate sources: a person's position in the organisation; personal characteristics; expertise; and the opportunity to influence or control the flow of information.

All four types of power can be and are deployed in organisations. The degree to which they will be effective is likely to depend upon the source from which they spring. Coercive power is usually the prerogative of those in senior positions, whilst even quite junior members of an organisation may, in particular circumstances, control or possess information that enables them to exert knowledge power. The interesting point to note is that the use of knowledge power – the selective and biased use of information (often deployed under the guise of reason) – is shown to be effective in gaining willing compliance and cooperation from those at whom it is directed. According to Huczynski and Buchanan (2001), however, the favourite influencing strategies are:

- For influencing up (managers) – the use of reason.
- For influencing across (co-workers) – the use of friendliness.
- For influencing down (subordinates) – the use of reason.

This appears to fit in well with the view of many observers that the use of remunerative and coercive power, i.e. the opposite of reason and friendliness, is often counter-productive because those on the receiving end of such power tend to view it negatively and resent it (Bachman *et al*, 1968; Ivancevich, 1970; Robbins, 1986; Student, 1968).

This is perhaps why the most detrimental outcomes from the deployment of power arise when people feel they are being coerced into a particular course of action that goes against their beliefs or self-interest (Rollinson, 2002). Therefore, irrespective of the source or type of power, it is perhaps the willingness to use it in situations where there will be clear winners and losers, and where the covert activities of warring coalitions turn into open warfare, that leads to the more dysfunctional and damaging consequences. Such battles, where groups and individuals fight to influence key decisions and in so doing bolster their own position, especially where the stakes are high, can end with senior figures either leaving or being forced out of the organisation.

This was the case with BMW, where the battle over the future of Rover's Longbridge plant in the UK led to both Bernd Pischetsrieder, BMW's Chairman, and his long-time boardroom rival, Wolfgang Reitzle, BMW's Marketing Director, being forced to resign (Gow, 1999a; Gow and Traynor, 1999). A similar situation occurred with Pehr Gyllenhammar, the man who ran Volvo for more than two decades. His

1993 attempt to merge Volvo with Renault, the French state-controlled car company, was opposed by a coalition of shareholders and managers, who felt that it was not so much a merger of equals as a takeover by Renault. Both shareholders and managers felt that in such a situation their interests would be damaged, and a very public power struggle ensued, with both sides claiming to act in Volvo's best interests (Done, 1994). Both these cases could be classed as battles between individuals fighting to maintain their own power. However, the reality was that in both cases major issues concerning the future viability of these organisations were at stake. The irony in Volvo's case was that six years after rejecting a merger with Renault because it was seen as disadvantageous to the company's interests, the company sold its car division to Ford Motors, whose work practices were seen as the antithesis of all that Volvo held dear. The battle for control of the advertising agency Saatchi & Saatchi, which resulted in the founders leaving, also shows how a power struggle can leave an organisation damaged (Barrie, 1995; Donovan, 1995). Another very public example of a power clash was the on–off merger of SmithKline Beecham and Glaxo. In 1998, the two companies announced that they planned to merge and form the largest pharmaceutical company in the world, worth an estimated US$165 billion. However, the merger was quickly called off owing to a rumoured clash between SmithKline's Chief Executive, Jan Leschley, and Glaxo's Chairman, Sir Richard Sykes, over who would run the merged company (although given that it later emerged that Mr Leschley's pay, perks and shares package was worth over £90 million, one can understand why he would be reluctant to step down in favour of Sir Richard Sykes (Buckingham and Finch, 1999)). It was only when Leschley and Sykes both announced their retirements that the merger proceeded. In some cases, such clashes can become endemic and linger on even after the initial cause has long gone. Lonrho is a case in point. After the successful battle to oust Tiny Rowland from the company he founded and for so long dominated, Lonrho was split up and sold off. Yet the political battles for control still rumbled on even amongst its demerged parts (Laird, 1998).

Clearly, as the above examples show, the deployment of coercive power can be very damaging; however, other forms of power can also have adverse effects, though perhaps in a more insidious fashion. Thus the use of remunerative power by senior managers in the UK is a good example. In the 1990s, executive salaries ran far ahead of inflation, the pay of salaried staff and company profits (Business Notebook, 2003). This caused much controversy, especially in the now privatised, but once public, utilities such as gas, electricity and water. In these organisations, executives, the so-called 'fat cats', used their power to give themselves extremely generous remuneration packages; whilst at the same time, they cut jobs and wages for many staff elsewhere in their organisations (Smithers, 1995). In general, though, this practice was condoned by both shareholders and governments because the UK economy and UK companies were doing well and those controlling them could argue that they were being rewarded for success. However, the criticisms of fat-cat salaries became more strident and widespread after the economy started to falter. Government, shareholders and trade unions began to sing with one critical voice that those leading companies were being rewarded for failure. Given that amongst FTSE-100 companies the pay of directors rose 84 per cent in the three years to 2003 but the stock market value of these companies fell by 50 per cent, one can understand the outcry (Finch and Treanor, 2003). However, this disgruntlement became even more strident when it was realised that some companies were giving big payoffs to executives who appeared to have failed in their jobs, such as Gerald Corbett, who walked away from Railtrack with a payoff of £3.7m (Treanor and Finch, 2003). The issue is not so much whether the way executives distribute rewards in their organisations is fair or not, but the corrosive effect such a blatant use of power has on employee morale, shareholder support and customer loyalty.

These very public manifestations of power battles in organisations represent merely the tip of the iceberg. They illustrate the tendency for such battles to be fought under the banner of 'the best interests of the organisation'. Political in-fighting, the seeking of allies, the influencing of decisions, and the protection or promotion of one's own or one's group's interests are nearly always justified by recourse to the best interests of the organisation (just as the parties involved in any armed struggle always seem to justify it on the grounds that they have justice on their side). It is not that the participants necessarily believe their own propaganda, though often they do; it is that, without it, they would find it very difficult to justify, to themselves and their allies, the use of blatantly illegitimate tactics such as challenging, undermining or explicitly ignoring their organisation's official goals and policies.

Therefore, in opposing or promoting a particular decision or development, those indulging in even a low level of political behaviour rarely openly declare their own personal interest in the outcome. As Pfeffer (1981) maintained, a major characteristic accompanying political behaviour is the attempt to conceal its true motive. This can be seen from Buchanan and Badham's (1999: 27–9) list of power tactics shown in Exhibit 5.9. Concealing motives is essential because, as Allen *et al* (1979), Drory and Romm (1988) and Frost and Hayes (1979) observed, those involved believe that such tactics would be judged unacceptable or illegitimate by others in the organisation and as such resisted. Accordingly, a false but acceptable motive is presented instead.

Exhibit 5.9	Power tactics

- **Image building** – action that enhances a person's standing, such as backing the 'right' causes.
- **Selective information** – withhold unfavourable information from superiors.
- **Scapegoating** – blame someone else.
- **Formal alliances** – form or join a coalition of the strong.
- **Networking** – make friends with those in power.
- **Compromise** – be prepared to give in on unimportant issues in order to win on the important ones.
- **Rule manipulation** – interpret rules selectively to favour friends and thwart opponents.
- **Other tactics** – if all else fails, use dirty tricks such as coercion, undermining the expertise of others, playing one group off against another, and get others to 'fire the bullet'.

Source: Buchanan and Badham (1999: 27–9)

The picture of power and politics that emerges from Exhibit 5.9 tends to be a negative one, portraying individuals and groups as using power and politics purely to pursue their own selfish interests. However, others take a more positive view. Morgan (1986) offered a model of interests, conflicts and power, accepting that diversity of interests can create conflict. In such circumstances, power and influence are, he suggests, the major means of resolving conflict. Buchanan and Boddy (1992) argue that the use of power and politics is a necessary component in the toolkit of those responsible for managing change in organisations. Seen in this light, political behaviour can have a positive effect on improving the working of organisations by enabling them to manage change more effectively. Pfeffer (1992), in a similar vein, maintains that the use of power is an important social process that is often required to get things done in interdependent systems. In fact, he maintains that a failure to deploy power and politics is harmful:

> By pretending that power and influence don't exist, or at least shouldn't exist, we contribute to what I and others (such as John Gardner) see as the major problem facing many corporations today, particularly in the United States – the almost trained or produced incapacity of anyone except the highest-level managers to take action and get things accomplished.
>
> (Pfeffer (1992: 10)

Perhaps Gardner (1990: 57) sums up the issues involved in the power–politics debate most succinctly when, in relation to those who possess and deploy power, he argues that, 'The significant questions are: What means do they use to gain it? How do they exercise it? To what ends do they exercise it?'

We can see from the above why writers have found it difficult to separate power from politics. Whilst it is possible to examine the potential for power without also examining how power is or might be exercised, for students of organisational life this is rather a sterile endeavour. For the purpose of understanding what makes organisations tick, how decisions are arrived at, why resources are allocated in a particular way and why certain changes are initiated and others not, we have to comprehend both the possession and exercise of power, whether it be by official or political means.

Though Robbins rightly draws a distinction between formal authority and the possession/deployment of power, we should not fall into the trap of assuming that there is not a close relationship between the two. An examination of the ability to exert influence (power) over key decisions and the possession of position (authority) shows that these tend to lie within dominant coalitions rather than being spread evenly across organisations (see Buchanan and Badham, 1999; Pfeffer, 1978, 1981, 1992; Robbins, 1987). The dominant coalition is the one that has the power to affect structure. The reason why this is so important is that the choice of structure will automatically favour some groups and disadvantage others. A person or group's position in the structure will determine such factors as their influence on planning, their choice of technology, the criteria by which they will be evaluated, allocation of rewards, control of information, proximity to senior managers, and their ability to exercise influence on a whole range of decisions (Morgan, 1986; Perrow, 1983; Pfeffer, 1981, 1992; Robbins, 1987). Though the postmodernists would not disagree with this analysis per se, as mentioned earlier, their view of power in organisations is a much broader one. For them, power is the mechanism by which groups in organisations create and reinforce their view of reality. In turn, postmodernists maintain, it is this shaping and construction of reality that, in the main, allows dominant groups in organisations to impose their will on others rather than the use of sanctions and other control mechanisms (Reed and Hughes, 1992).

Managing and changing organisations: bringing back choice

In the previous chapter we examined the postmodernist, realist and complexity perspectives on organisations. The postmodernists argue that reason and logic have had their day, and that organisations are social organisms in which individuals and groups construct their own views of reality based on their own perceptions of the world and their place in it. Realists, whilst accepting the social construction hypothesis, argue that reality does exist and that it imposes limits, though sometimes very broad ones, to what individuals and organisations can do. The proponents of complexity, for their part, see organisations as complex, self-organising systems where, in order to maintain appropriate order-generating rules, choice and decision-making must move from the few to the many. What Chapter 4 showed, with its review of these three perspectives, was that organisations have a great deal more choice and freedom in what they can do and how they can do it than the organisation theories discussed in Chapters 1–3 allowed.

In this chapter we have sought to develop this argument further by looking at how choices are made in organisations and on what basis. The chapter began by examining the literature on organisational culture, which revealed that, despite its popularity as a promoter of organisational excellence, culture is difficult to define, change and manipulate. Strong cultures may have a positive effect on organisations, in that they can bond disparate groups together in a common purpose; and weak cultures may have a negative impact, in that individuals and groups can pursue separate and conflicting objectives. In some situations, however, especially where there is major environmental disruption, the reverse may also be true, with strong cultures being a straitjacket on innovation and weak ones allowing new ideas and new leaders to come to the fore. In such situations, where the organisation's dominant coalition is split, or is so ossified it cannot entertain change, power and politics come to the fore. As Pfeffer (1992: 337) put it:

> Computers don't get built, cities don't get rebuilt, and diseases don't get fought unless advocates for change learn how to develop and use power effectively.

As the examination of the literature on power and politics showed, in cases where a clash of interests and a clash of perspectives is present, where the status quo is being challenged, major decisions about the future direction, structure and operation of an organisation are likely to be dominated by issues of power and politics (Buchanan and Badham, 1999).

Murray (1989: 285), reporting on a major study of the introduction and use of information technology, commented that:

> ... the use of new technology is subject to processes of organizational decision-making and implementation characterized by often conflicting managerial objectives, rationalities and strategies developed through the mobilization of organizational power.

Therefore, as far as Buchanan and Badham (1999), Dawson (1994), Morgan (1986), Pfeffer (1992), Robbins (1987) and many others are concerned, the process of organisational change is inherently a political one.

Though the postmodern, realist, complexity, cultural and power–politics perspectives on organisational life are very different, there are also strong overlaps. In particular, the management of meaning and the creation of legitimacy through the construction and manipulation of symbols is an area of common ground. This can be seen in Pettigrew's (1987) work on organisational change. He maintains that the process of change is shaped by the interests and commitments of individuals and groups, the forces of bureaucratic momentum, significant changes in the environment, and the manipulation of the structural context around decisions. In particular, Pettigrew (1987: 659) argues:

> The acts and processes associated with politics as the management of meaning represent conceptually the overlap between a concern with the political and cultural analyses of organizations. A central concept linking political and cultural analyses essential to the understanding of continuity and change is legitimacy. The management of meaning refers to a process of symbol construction and value use designed to create legitimacy for one's ideas, actions and demands, and to delegitimate the demands of one's opponents ... [Therefore] structures, cultures and strategies are not just being treated here as neutral, functional constructs connectable to some system need such as efficiency or adaptability; those constructs are viewed as capable of serving to protect the interests of the dominant groups. ... The content of strategic change is thus ultimately a product of a legitimation process shaped by political/cultural considerations, though often expressed in rational/analytical terms.

This view that the choice and use of structure, and other key decisions, is the outcome of a political process rather than the application of rational analysis and decision-making has significant implications for organisation theory. Whilst it does not necessarily invalidate the appropriateness or otherwise of particular approaches, it does mean that managerial aspirations and interests are seen as more important than might otherwise be the case. It also means that, rather than being the prisoners of organisation theory (as some might suppose or hope), managers do have significant scope for the exercise of choice with regard to structure and other organisational characteristics.

In his review of the influence of power and politics in organisations, Robbins (1987) noted that no more than 50 to 60 per cent of variability in structure can be explained by strategy, size, technology and environment. He then went on to argue that a substantial portion of the residual variance can be explained by those in positions of power choosing a structure that will, as far as possible, maintain and enhance their control. He points out that proponents of other determinants of structure, such as size, technology, etc., assume that organisations are rational entities: 'However, for rationality to prevail an organisation must have either a single goal or agreement over the multiple goals. Neither case exists in most organisations' (Robbins, 1987: 200). Consequently, he argues that structural decisions are not rational. Such decisions arise from a power struggle between special-interest groups or coalitions, each arguing for a structural arrangement that best suits them. Robbins (1987: 200) believes that whilst strategy, size, technology and environment define the minimum level of effectiveness and set the parameters within which self-serving decision choices will be made, 'both technology and environment are chosen. Thus, those in power will select technologies and environments that will facilitate their maintenance of control.' As both the realists and complexity advocates argue, however, the extent to which those in power can please themselves has limits. Markets do exist, economies can fall as well as rise and, as the dotcom collapse showed, new technologies do not always deliver on their promise. The power–politics perspective, therefore, does not totally undermine the case against the rational view of management.

There is, though, a strong and significant body of literature and evidence that challenges the view of management as rational and neutral implementers of decisions determined by objective data. In particular, the detailed case studies of organisational decision-making and change at ICI and Cadbury Ltd carried out, respectively, by Pettigrew (1985, 1987) and Child and Smith (1987) lend a great deal of weight to the view that management in general, and the management of change in particular, is inherently a political process. Murray (1989) made the telling point that, given the insecurity of many managers' positions, particularly during periods of major upheaval and change, it is not surprising that managers and other groups attempt to influence decisions in order to protect, enhance or shore up their position in the organisation.

Nevertheless, one needs to be wary of ascribing the purpose of all organisational decisions and actions to self-interest. Politics plays a part but, to view Robbin's (1987) finding from another perspective, so too do strategy, size, technology and environment. As the realists would argue, these can act as a constraint on the freedom of action of groups and individuals, as can the need to be seen to act in the organisation's best interests, in line with agreed goals and in a rational manner. Therefore, though the political perspective has become very influential in the last 20 years, it does not explain all actions and all decisions in organisations. We need to see power and politics as an important influence on organisations but not the only influence. Indeed, we need to remember the original objective of Cyert and March's (1963) work on organisational politics. They sought to show that external factors were not the only factors that affected decision-making in organisations. This is not, of course, the same as saying that external factors do not matter. As Child and Smith (1987) show with their firm-in-sector perspective (*see* Chapter 6), the external environment does matter. In a whole host of concrete and symbolic ways, it constrains and impinges on organisational decision-making and behaviour. It may well be, as Robbins (1987) commented, that strategy, size, technology and environment only define the minimum level of effectiveness and set the parameters within which decisions are taken, but this is still a very important constraint on managers. It is also an important rejoinder to those management theorists who have become, as Hendry (1996: 621) notes, ' ... overfocused on the political aspects of the change [decision-making] process'.

In summary, therefore, power and politics are amongst the most important factors influencing decision-making in organisations. Indeed, by linking the arguments of Robbins, Pettigrew and Murray regarding managerial choice of structure to the discussion on culture, two very interesting points arise. Firstly, it was argued by Allaire and Firsirotu (1984), and others, that culture and structure need to be mutually supportive if an organisation is to operate efficiently and effectively. If, as the power-politics perspective argues, structure is in part at least the outcome of self-interested choice by the dominant coalition, the degree of congruence between the two may be due more to accident than design. Secondly, it was also argued earlier that organisational culture is the product of long-term social learning in which dominant coalitions play a key role.

This clearly opens up scope for choices over both structure and culture. However, the development of culture and approaches to changing it are long-term processes. Dominant coalitions, on the other hand, change their composition and priorities over time, sometimes over quite short periods of time. Therefore, although it can be argued that the possibility exists for managers to choose both the structure and culture that best suit their own self-interests, this is only likely to result in a balanced and effective structure–culture nexus if the dominant coalition holds sway and is consistent in its aims over long periods of time.

As many observers have noted, whilst these conditions may exist in some Western companies (e.g. News International under Rupert Murdoch, General Electric under Jack Welch, Vodafone under Chris Gent), these are the exception. In any case, as the departure of Arnold Weinstock from GEC showed (*see* Chapter 11), such situations often rely on dominant individuals to hold coalitions together; when they go, the dominant coalition falls apart and a new one emerges with a radically different vision for the organisation (Brummer and Cowe, 1998; Brummer, 1999). Sometimes the departure of such individuals can even bring an organisation perilously close to collapse, as was the case with GEC when Weinstock stepped down, Apple Computers when Steve Jobs was fired in 1985, and with Tiny Rowland's forced departure from Lonrho in 1995 (Laird, 1998; Morgan, 1986). Indeed, in some companies, so forceful and coercive is the personality of a dominant individual that their will cannot be questioned, and fundamental problems are only discovered once they depart, as was the case with Robert Maxwell and Mirror Group Newspapers (Bower, 1996).

The Japanese experience seems at first glance to follow a similar pattern of dominant coalitions relying on one key person for their legitimacy and direction. In their case, however, when such a person departs, the dominant coalition appears to maintain the unity of purpose (Fruin, 1992; Pascale and Athos, 1982; Whitehill, 1991). Yet even the Japanese are not immune from problems when changing leaders. For example, Nissan's appointment of a new chief executive in 1985 was followed by an attempt to change its culture in order to overcome what were seen as major mistakes by the previous incumbent (Ishizuna, 1990). This and other changes failed and, in the end, Nissan was, in effect, taken over by the state-owned French car-maker Renault.

To sum up, therefore, what we can see is that managers have a degree, arguably a wide degree, of choice or influence over major organisational variables such as structure, technology, environment and perhaps even culture. Despite the arguments of the postmodernists, however, their freedom of action is constrained by a whole host of factors such as market conditions, technological development, organisational goals, policies and performance, their own and other people's self-interests, and the need to portray their actions as being rational and in the best interests of their organisation. In addition, in a reciprocal way, some of the factors over which they have a degree of choice, such as structure and culture, can also limit managers' freedom of manoeuvre. These constraints will vary from organisation to organisation at any one time and, within and between organisations, over time but will never be fully absent. Strong though these constraints may be, however, choice will never be totally absent.

Conclusions

In reviewing the main approaches to and perspectives on organisation theory, Part 1 of this book has shown that, by succeeding stages, these have moved from the mechanical-rational outlook of the Classical school to the, arguably, culture-based perspectives of the Culture–Excellence, Japanese and Organisation Learning approaches, passing through the social perspective of the Human Relations school and the rational perspective of the Contingency theorists. They all argue for a 'one best way' approach (though the Contingency theorists believed in this for 'each' rather than 'all' organisations). Because of this approach they all, in effect, seek to remove choice from managers: do as we tell you, or else! Indeed, it was one of the main claims of the Classical school that it removed discretion not only from workers, but also from managers. As Frederick Taylor (1911b: 189) stated:

> The man at the head of the business under scientific management is governed by rules and laws ... just as the workman is, and the standards which have been developed are equitable.

The role of managers, from these perspectives, is to apply rationally the dictates of the particular theory promoted. To do otherwise would be sub-optimal and irrational.

By building on the discussions of postmodernism, realism and complexity in Chapter 4, this chapter has sought to move managerial choice back to centre stage. By exploring organisational culture, it was shown that the degree to which culture influences behaviour is dependent upon the presence of clear and consistent organisational goals. If these are not present, which appears to be the case in many companies, conflict and disagreement emerge regardless of the nature of the culture. Similarly, if the environment changes to the extent that existing ways of working are no longer appropriate, once again, conflict and disagreement may emerge. In such situations, it is the political perspective on organisational life that offers the better opportunity for understanding how and why decisions are taken, particular courses of action are embarked upon, and why some changes to the management and structure of the organisation are pursued and others discarded.

The examination of organisational politics and power added further weight to the criticisms of the approaches to organisation theory considered in previous chapters, particularly concerning the scope for rational decision-making and choice. To an extent, the key issue was raised when discussing Contingency Theory, namely the question as to whether managers are the prisoners of the situational variables they face, or whether they can influence or change these. Certainly some critics of Contingency Theory argue that managers can, partly at least, influence or choose the contingencies they face. This casts doubts not only on the deterministic nature of Contingency Theory, but also on all organisational theories, because – either openly or implicitly – they are all founded on the notion that organisations face certain immutable conditions that they cannot influence and to which they must therefore adapt.

This does not necessarily mean that the various theories and their attendant structures and practices we have discussed so far in this book are invalid, unhelpful or inapplicable. It does, however, mean that it may be possible, within limits, for organisations, or rather those who control organisations, to decide upon the structure and behaviours they want to promote, and then shape the conditions and contingencies to suit these, rather than *vice versa*. Indeed, as far as the public sector in the UK is concerned, this appears to be exactly what governments have done. From 1979 to 1997, successive Conservative governments took the view that they wanted managers in the public sector to be cost-focused and entrepreneurial, and shaped the conditions in which the public sector operates (i.e. its environment) in order to promote those attributes (Ferlie *et al*, 1996; Flynn, 1993). Following its election in 1997, the 'New Labour' government similarly manipulated the public sector environment to influence managerial behaviour. This can be seen in terms of significant alterations to the NHS Internal Market, the replacement of Compulsory Competitive Tendering with the notion of 'Best Value' in local government, and the reversal of the previous government's policy of contracting out central government activities through the creation of semi-autonomous agencies and the Next Steps initiative (Salauroo and Burnes, 1998).

If – contrary to the dictates of most management theories – organisations are *not* the prisoners of situational variables, as most organisation theories maintain, if those who manage them do have a degree of leeway in what they do, one then has to ask what factors do influence the actions of decision-makers. The review of the power-politics literature showed organisations as shifting coalitions of groups and individuals seeking to promote policies and decisions that enhanced or maintained their position in the organisation. From the literature, a persuasive argument is mounted for seeing politics and power – usually promoted under the cloak of rationality, reasonableness and the organisation's best interests – as a central, though not exclusive, determinant of the way organisations operate.

In particular, though political behaviour appears to be an ever-present feature of organisational life, politics comes to the fore when major issues of structural change or resource allocation are concerned. Such decisions have crucial importance for achieving and maintaining power or position, or even – when the chips are down – for keeping one's job when all around are losing theirs.

Therefore, it is surprising that much of organisation theory, which after all is primarily concerned with major decisions concerning structure and resource allocation, seems to dismiss or gloss over power and politics. Nevertheless, what is clear from this chapter is that managers, despite the constraints they face, have a far wider scope for shaping decisions than most organisation theories acknowledge, and that the scope for choice and the deployment of political influence is likely to be most pronounced when change, particularly major change, is on the managerial agenda.

Having examined the merits and drawbacks of the main organisation theories, and in particular having raised the issue of the way in which major decisions are decided upon and implemented, we can now turn our attention in the following chapters to an in-depth examination of change management.

Test your learning

■ Short answer questions

1 What are Cummings and Huse's four elements of culture?

2 Briefly describe Handy's four types of culture.

3 List three implications of Hofstede's work on national cultures for Western approaches to organisation theory.

4 What does the term 'satisfice' mean?

5 Give three benefits of Robbins' addition of *knowledge power* to Etzioni's three types of power.

6 Define organisational power.

7 Define organisational politics.

8 For each of the following, briefly state their implications for organisational change: (a) organisational culture and (b) power and politics.

■ Essay questions

1 Discuss the following statement: organisational culture is the prime determinant of organisational performance.

2 Explain the concept of dominant coalitions, and discuss how these can prevent organisations dividing into warring factions with individuals and groups pursuing their own personal agendas.

Suggested further reading

1 Brown, A (1995) *Organisational Culture*. Pitman: London.
   Andrew Brown's book gives a useful introduction to the uses and abuses of organisational culture.
2 Pfeffer, J (1992) *Managing with Power: Politics and Influence in Organizations*. Harvard Business School Press: Boston, MA, USA.
   This is an entertaining and very useful guide to the power–politics perspective on organisations.

Part Two

Strategy development and change management: past, present and future

Chapter 6

Approaches to strategy
Managerial choice and constraints

Learning objectives

After studying this chapter, you should be able to:

- discuss the origins, development and popularity of organisation strategy;
- describe the main features of the Prescriptive stream of strategy;
- list the strengths and weaknesses of the Prescriptive stream;
- discuss the key elements of the Analytical stream of strategy;
- state the major advantages and shortcomings of the Analytical stream;
- understand the key differences between the Prescriptive and the Analytical streams of strategy;
- describe the constraints faced by organisations and whether these can be manipulated or overcome;
- appreciate the relationship between strategy and change.

Exhibit 6.1   Michael Porter

The master strategist: Michael Porter

Michael Porter became famous in the 1990s as a consultant on competitiveness to business and governments. In the 1980s, however, he wrote several popular and respected books on business strategy, introducing basic tools of strategic thinking such as the 'five forces' model and the value chain.

It is for this work on strategy that he is likely to be remembered, and his ideas have had a wide impact. In 1999, Fortune called him the single most important strategist working today, and possibly of all time.

Prof Porter was born in Ann Arbor, Michigan, in 1947. He studied at Princeton and Harvard and joined the faculty at Harvard in 1973. He has also become a highly respected consultant, working with companies such as DuPont and Shell, and the US, Canadian, New Zealand and Swedish governments.

Prof Porter views strategy from the standpoint of economics, and his ideas on how strategy should be implemented are based on an understanding of competition and other economic forces. Strategy is not devised in isolation; a company's options will always be limited by what is going on around it.

His famous 'five forces' model shows the constraining impact that competition and environment have on strategy.

The five forces identified by Prof Porter are: the threat of new entrants and the appearance of new competitors; the degree of rivalry among existing competitors in the market; the bargaining power of buyers; the bargaining power of suppliers; and the threat of substitute products or services that could shrink the market.

The strength of each of these forces varies from industry to industry, but taken together they determine long-term profitability. They help to shape the prices companies can charge, the costs they must pay for resources and the level of investment that will be needed to compete.

From the external environment, he turns to the company itself. Companies make products and deliver them to consumers, but they can also add value to the basic product in a variety of ways and through different functions.

Value can be added directly, for example by giving a product new technology features, or indirectly, through measures that allow the company to become more efficient. Prof Porter argues that every product follows a critical path through the company, from its inception to its delivery as a finished article. At every stage along this path there are opportunities to add value. This path he calls the 'value chain'.

The value chain is crucial, he says, because it demonstrates that the company is more than just the sum of its parts and activities: all activities are connected, and what is done at one stage affects work at other stages.

The company needs to examine its value chain and decide where it can add value most effectively to meet competitive pressures in the industry.

These concepts can be applied to entire sectors and national economies as well as individual companies, and Prof Porter went on to develop his theories of national competitiveness in great detail.

Source: Morgen Witzel, *Financial Times*, 15 August 2003, p. 11.

Exhibit 6.2   Henry Mintzberg

The great iconoclast: Henry Mintzberg

Henry Mintzberg had been called 'the great management iconoclast' for his willingness to attack previously sacred concepts in business and management. But his commonsense approach to management problems have won him a broad following, particularly among students and working managers. He is best known for his work on busi-

ness strategy, where he exposed the gap between academic concepts of strategy and reality.

Born in Montreal in 1939, Mintzberg studied engineering and worked for Canadian National Railways before obtaining a doctorate from the Massachusetts Institute of Technology in 1968. He joined the faculty of management at McGill

Exhibit 6.2 *continued*

University, Canada, where he has remained. Mintzberg was interested in defining what managers really do and how they carry out their tasks. He discovered a vast body of what he termed 'managerial folklore': research studies that considered managers rational beings who made decisions based on careful analysis of all available information.

Experience told Mintzberg that managerial work was not like that. Not only was it less structured and ordered than assumed but its true nature was also hard to define. His observations of managers in action confirmed this. He found that decisions were made quickly, often on the move, usually based more on intuition and experience than on considered analysis. Action was more important than reflection. Half the daily management tasks he observed took less than 10 minutes each and only 10 per cent took more than an hour.

The portrait of the manager and his task that emerges from Mintzberg's work is a sympathetic one. Managers are constantly 'firefighting', dealing with problems under pressure. Rather than the best possible solution, they seek the best solution that can be implemented given the resources available. And, says Mintzberg, because each organisation has

its own culture and needs, managers' responses to problems will vary. There may be no one 'right' way to manage a business.

These affect strategy. Academic conceptions of strategy regarded it as the province of top management, who consider and make strategic decisions with detachment. Again, Mintzberg disagrees. In the real world, strategy-making is ad hoc and instinctive, not structured and planned. The concept of 'strategic planning' becomes an oxymoron.

Mintzberg sees this approach to strategy as a virtue. 'Emergent strategy', as he calls it, is strategy that evolves according to need, constantly adjusted and adapted. He also speaks of 'crafting strategy', a process by which managers develop strategy according to the needs of their organisation and environment. Here, strategy creation and implementation are interdependent. He compares the art of strategy making to pottery and managers to potters sitting at a wheel moulding the clay and letting the shape of the object evolve in their hands.

Successful management is about knowing the business – in all its aspects and not just in specialist areas – and an ability to manage through discontinuity.

Source: Morgen Witzel, *Financial Times*, 5 August 2003, p.11.

Introduction

In Part 1 of this book, we discussed the options open to organisations in terms of their structures, cultures and practices. By examining the development of organisational theory in the 200 years since the Industrial Revolution, we saw that, in the beginning, management was almost exclusively concerned with strict labour discipline and long working hours. The methods used to pursue these were *ad hoc*, erratic, short-term and usually harsh and unfair. As the period progressed, more structured and consistent approaches came to the fore. Up to the 1960s, it was the Classical and Human Relations approaches that dominated organisational thinking. With the advent of these two approaches, the emphasis moved more to the effectiveness and efficiency of the entire organisation, rather than focusing purely on discipline and hours of work.

Both these approaches tended to dwell on internal arrangements and to assume that organisation structures and practices were in some way insulated from the outside world. The development of Contingency Theory in the 1960s, with its underlying Open Systems perspective, changed all this. The nature of the environment (both internal and external) in which organisations operate emerged as a central factor in how they should structure themselves. This theme has been continued with the development of new paradigms in the 1980s and 1990s, and the importance of situational variables, especially environmental turbulence, which organisations face is seen by many as an unchallengeable fact (Kanter *et al*, 1997; Peters, 1997a).

However, as argued in Part 1, the degree to which organisations are the prisoners of these situational variables (as averse to being able to exercise influence and choice) is certainly open to debate. Similarly, as shown in Chapters 4 and 5, the credibility of the rational approach to decision-making has been considerably undermined in the last two decades. The increasing appreciation of the complexity of organisational life has been paralleled by a growing recognition that organisations cannot cope successfully with the modern world and all its changing aspects purely on an *ad hoc* and piecemeal basis. Whether decision-makers operate on the basis of rationality or are influenced by personal considerations or organisational cultures, the received wisdom is that for organisations to succeed there must be a consistency and coherence to the decisions taken – which is another way of saying that they must have a strategy (Johnson and Scholes, 1993). Unfortunately, it is easier to say that an organisation needs a strategy than it is to say what that strategy should be or how it should be derived. Perhaps the two most influential writers on strategy over the past 25 years have been Michael Porter and Henry Mintzberg, yet, as Exhibits 6.1 and 6.2 show, their portrayal and understanding of strategy is significantly different.

In this chapter, we shall examine the development and shortcomings of the main approaches to strategy that have been put forward in the last 50 years. It will be shown that, since the end of the Second World War, organisations have begun to take a strategic perspective on their activities. They have increasingly sought to take a long-term overview in order to plan for and cope with the vagaries of the future. In many respects, the development of strategic management has tended to mirror the development of organisational theory. In the 1940s and 1950s, the strategy literature only considered one aspect of an organisation's activities – the external environment. It tended to seek rational, mathematical approaches to planning. With the passing of time, more intuitive and less rational approaches to strategic management have been developed which claim to incorporate the totality of organisational life.

The chapter concludes by arguing that, rather than managers being the prisoners of mathematical models and rational approaches to strategy development, they have considerable freedom of action and a wide range of options to choose from. They are not totally free agents, however; their freedom of action is seen as being constrained or shaped by the unique set of organisational, environmental and societal factors faced by their particular organisation. Fortunately, these constraints are not immutable. As argued in Part 1, it is possible for managers to manipulate the situational variables they face with regard to structure. Similarly, managers can exert some influence over strategic constraints and, potentially at least, can select the approach to strategy that best suits their preferences.

Understanding strategy: origins, definitions and approaches

■ The origins of strategy

It is commonly believed that our concept of strategy has been passed down to us from the ancient Greeks. Bracker (1980: 219) argued that the word strategy comes from the Greek *stratego*, meaning 'to plan the destruction of one's enemies through the effective use of resources'. However, they developed the concept purely in relation to the successful pursuit of victory in war. The concept remained a military one until the nineteenth century, when it began to be applied to the business world, though most writers believe the actual process by which this took place is untraceable (Bracker, 1980; Chandler, 1962). Chandler (1962) put forward the view that the emergence of strategy in civilian organisational life resulted from an awareness of the opportunities and needs – created by changing population, income and technology – to employ existing or expanding resources more profitably.

Hoskin (1990) largely agreed with Chandler's view of the development of modern business strategy since the Industrial Revolution. However, he does take issue with both Chandler and Bracker on two crucial points. Firstly, he argues that the modern concept of organisational strategy bears little resemblance to military strategy, at least as it existed up to the First World War. Secondly, he challenges the view that the origins of business strategy are untraceable. When investigating the emergence of modern strategy he did find a link with the military world, though it was not quite the link that Bracker and Chandler proposed. Like Chandler, Hoskin argues that one of the most significant developments in business management in the nineteenth century occurred in the running of the US railways. Unlike Chandler, however, Hoskin gives the credit for initiating business strategy to one of the Pennsylvania Railway's executives, Herman Haupt. He states that Haupt:

> ... changes the rules of business discourse: the image in which he reconstructs business, on the Pennsylvania Railroad, is that of the proactive, future-oriented organization, which is managed by the numbers ... How does he do so? By importing the practices of writing, examination and grading ... On the Pennsylvania Railroad we find for the first time the full interactive play of grammatocentrism [writing and recording] and calculability [mathematical analysis of the recorded data].
> (Hoskin, 1990: 20)

This approach created the bedrock on which strategic management grew in the United States, especially after the Second World War. It also ensured that strategic management became a quantitatively-orientated discipline, whose focus was on the use of numerical analysis to forecast market trends in order to plan for the future. Hoskin also points out that Haupt was a graduate of the US military academy at West Point, which pioneered the techniques of 'writing, examination and grading' in the military world. From there its graduates, particularly Haupt, took them out into the business world – hence the link between military and civilian management techniques.

Thus it is possible to see why strategic management developed in the way it did – as a quantitative, mathematical approach. We can also see that there are links between the military and business world, but that they are not as some have claimed.

Management strategy has not developed from the approach to military campaigns of the ancient Greeks; instead it has adopted and made its own the techniques of record-keeping and analysis that were developed at West Point in order to measure the performance, and suitability for military life, of the US army's future officer class.

The contribution of the American armed forces to this quantitative approach to strategy did not end with West Point or in the nineteenth century. In 1945, with the end of the Second World War, America experienced an extraordinary trading boom. McKiernan (1992) commented that this forced many American companies to rethink their business planning systems. In order to justify and implement the capacity expansion necessary to cope with the boom, companies began to abandon short-term, one-year, budgeting cycles in favour of more long-range planning techniques. The development of this strategic approach to planning and investment was given a significant impetus when some of the people involved in the USAAF's wartime strategic planning activities returned to civilian life – most notable amongst whom was Robert McNamara, who became Chairman of the Ford Motor Company, Secretary of State under John F Kennedy and President of the World Bank (Moore, 1992). Their main vehicle for influencing business was the Harvard Business School's approach to business policy teaching, which steadily moved the focus of management away from a preoccupation with internal organisational issues (as proposed by the Classical and Human Relations schools) towards an external orientation. This was best exemplified by the development of two important concepts: marketing, with its emphasis on analysing demand and tailoring products to meet it; and systems theory, with its emphasis not only on the interconnectedness of different parts of an organisation, but also the links between internal and external forces.

In the intervening years, first in the USA and later across the Western world, these techniques and approaches have become more widely disseminated and used (Bracker, 1980). Much credit for this must go to three key figures, Kenneth R Andrews, Alfred D Chandler and H Igor Ansoff, for their work in developing and fleshing out the concept of strategic management, and especially for demonstrating the importance of product–market mix. Nevertheless, in highlighting the importance of the outside world, and thus breaking managers' Classical school-inspired fixation with internal structures and practices, they can be criticised for not making the link between the two. So managers moved from believing that internal arrangements alone would bring success to believing that an external, market focus was the key.

◼ The rise and fall of long-range planning

In order to cope with the new and rapidly-changing technological, economic and organisational developments that followed the end of the Second World War, American organisations, which were at the forefront of these developments, began to adopt long-range planning techniques. This necessitated first defining the organisation's objectives, then establishing plans in order to achieve those objectives, and finally, allocating resources, through capital budgeting, in line with the plans. A key aim of this process was to reduce the gap that often occurred between the level of demand that a firm expected, and planned for, and the level of demand that actually occurred (Fox, 1975). Therefore, long-range planning was a mechanism for plotting trends and planning the actions required to achieve the identified growth targets, all of which were heavily biased towards financial targets and budgetary controls. However, this process proved incapable of accurately forecasting future demand and the problem of the gap between the level of expected demand and actual demand remained.

Long-range planning failed for a variety of internal and external reasons (McKiernan, 1992). Internally, many planning systems involved little more than an extrapolation of past sales trends. Little attention was paid to wider external economic, technological or social changes, or even changes in the behaviour of competitor firms. Externally, in the 1960s, the relatively comfortable conditions of high market growth gave way to lower levels of growth, which led to increased competition as companies tried to increase, or at least maintain, their market share to compensate for lower growth. One outcome of this was that strategic planners had to adapt to a world where growth was not steady; it could slow down, increase or be interrupted in an unpredictable and violent manner. Also, unforeseen opportunities and threats could and did emerge. Furthermore, it became evident that closing the gap between the plan and what actually occurred was not necessarily the most critical aspect of strategy formulation. Indeed, since the early 1970s, volatile markets, over-capacity and resource constraints have taken over as dominant management considerations.

Long-range planning techniques could not cope with such environmental turbulence which, to say the least, limits forecasting accuracy. In addition, the nature of American business had begun to change. Slower growth and increased competition led to a situation where large single-business firms, which in the past might have dominated a single industry, were being replaced by multinational conglomerates operating in a wide range of increasingly competitive industries and markets. Therefore, rather than managing a single, unified enterprise, corporate managers found themselves managing a diverse portfolio of businesses. In response to the failure of long-range planning and the emergence of conglomerates, in the late 1960s, the concept of strategic management began to emerge.

Unlike long-range planning, strategic management focuses on the environmental assumptions that underlie market trends and incorporates the possibility that changes in trends can and do take place, and is not based on the assumption that adequate growth can be assured (Elliot and Lawrence, 1985; Mintzberg and Quinn, 1991). In addition, strategic management focuses more closely on winning market share from competitors, rather than assuming that organisations can rely solely on the expansion of markets for their own growth (Hax and Majluf, 1996). This concept sought to take a broader and more sophisticated view of an organisation's environment and, initially at least, was closely associated with a number of portfolio planning techniques which also emerged in the late 1960s (Hax and Majluf, 1996; McKiernan, 1992). As will be described in Chapter 7, these were developed to assist managers in running large, diversified enterprises operating in complex environments. Much of this work was sponsored and used by large American corporations, such as General Electric, in order to identify the market position and potential of their strategic business units (SBUs) and to decide on whether to develop, sell or close them down. This 'positioning' approach to strategic management, the latest variant of which is Porter's (1980, 1985) 'competitive forces model', dominated the practice of strategic management from the 1960s onwards, and to a large extent still does (Galagan, 1997; Rigby and Gillies, 2000). It has also led many companies to adopt a harsh, and to an extent unthinking, approach to business success, which is epitomised by the words of Jack

Welch when he was CEO of General Electric: 'We will run only businesses that are number one or two in their markets' (quoted in Kay, 1993: 339). Therefore, if businesses are not, or do not have the potential to become, leaders in their field, they are sold off or closed down (Koch, 1995).

As Kay (1993), and many others, point out, this approach to strategic management portrays strategy as a rational process whereby managers gather hard, quantitative data on their companies, and from this information come to rational decisions regarding their future. However, from the late 1970s onwards, the rational perspective on strategy has come under increasing attack, not least by the leading management thinker of his generation, Henry Mintzberg (1976, 1978, 1983, 1987, 1994). The main criticisms of the rational approach to strategy are threefold: that hard data are no more reliable, and in some cases less so, than qualitative data; that organisations and managers are not rational entities and do not apply a rational approach to decision-making; and that an organisation's strategy is as likely to emerge from unplanned actions and their unintended consequences over a period of time as it is from any deliberate process of planning and implementation (Child and Smith, 1987; Hatch, 1997; Mintzberg *et al*, 1998a; Pettigrew *et al*, 1992; Stacey, 2003; Whittington, 1993).

Defining strategy

As the above shows, like many other concepts in the field of management, there are many approaches to strategy but none are universally accepted (Stacey, 2003). Indeed, even one of the pioneers of business strategy, Igor Ansoff (1987), warned that strategy is an elusive and somewhat abstract concept. This must be expected when dealing with an area that is constantly developing. Nor should this inhibit the search for a definition, or definitions, because in doing so we can see how the debate on strategy is developing and where the main areas of dispute lie.

Rather than leading to clarity, the eclipse of long-range planning merely heralded the arrival of a range of different perspectives on strategy. As early as the 1960s, two schools of thought vied with each other: the Planning school and the Design school (Mintzberg *et al*, 1998a). The Planning school was based on formal procedures, formal training, formal analysis and a large dose of quantification. Its underlying assumption was that a strategy could be put together and work in the same way as a machine. It led to the creation of strategic planning departments in large organisations, reporting directly to the chief executive; that person's role – though notionally to be the architect of strategy – was to approve the planners' plan. The chief proponent of the Planning school was Igor Ansoff. Ansoff was a Russian–American engineer, mathematician, military strategist and operations researcher whose *Corporate Strategy* was published in 1965 to great acclaim (Koch, 1995). In this book he assumes that the purpose of a firm is profit maximisation, and he portrays strategic management as being primarily concerned with the external, rather than internal, concerns of the firm, especially the matching of products to markets (the product–market mix). The book provides managers with a plethora of checklists and charts to enable them to derive objectives, assess synergy between different parts of an organisation, appraise its competence profile and decide how, where and in which way to expand. Nevertheless, as Koch (1995) remarked, from today's viewpoint, the book, and indeed the precepts of the Planning school as a whole, have not aged well.

The Design school, though sharing some common features with the Planning school, adopted a different, less formal and machine-like approach. It proposed a model of strategy that emphasises the need to achieve a fit between the internal capabilities of an organisation and the external possibilities it faces. Flowing from this, the Design school places primary emphasis on the appraisal of an organisation's external and internal situations. To facilitate this, Kenneth R Andrews developed the now-famous SWOT technique – the assessment of the internal Strengths and Weaknesses of the organisation in the light of the Opportunities and Threats posed by the environment in which it operates (Andrews, 1980). One of the main architects of the Design school was Alfred Chandler. Chandler was one of the most eminent and influential American economic historians of his generation. His main contribution to the Design school is encapsulated in his 1962 book, *Strategy and Structure*, which was based on a major study of US corporations between 1850 and 1920. In the book, Chandler defined strategy as the determination of the basic long-term goals and objectives of an enterprise, and the adoption of courses of action and the allocation of resources necessary for carrying out these goals. The book also suggested three important precepts for running organisations which challenged the conventional wisdom of the time: firstly, that an organisation's structure should flow from its strategy rather than being determined by some universal 'one best way'; secondly, that the 'visible hand of management' was more important than Adam Smith's 'invisible hand of the market' in meeting customer needs; and thirdly, that large organisations need to decentralise and divisionalise in order to remain competitive. Chandler's work proved very influential in shaping the strategy debate over the next three decades.

Nevertheless, like Ansoff, Chandler has attracted his fair share of criticism, especially with regard to his view that structure should follow strategy. Tom Peters (1993: 148), for example, remarked that, 'I understand Chandler's reasoning, but I think he got it exactly wrong. For it is the structure of the organization that determines, over time, the choices that it makes about market attacks' (i.e. its strategy).

The crucial difference between Ansoff and Chandle, and between the Planning and Design approaches, is that the former regards strategy as almost exclusively concerned with the relationships between the firm and its environment, whilst Chandler takes a broader view. His definition includes internal as well as external factors. In particular, he sees issues such as organisational structures, production processes and technology as being essentially strategic. The point he makes is that the external and internal cannot be separated, as the Open Systems theorists would be the first to point out (*see* Scott, 1987). The external affects the internal, and vice versa. Therefore, strategic management must encompass the totality of the organisational domain and must not be restricted to one aspect, such as determining the product–market mix (Andrews, 1980).

This brings us a little nearer a definition but still leaves us with a hazy concept. Henry Mintzberg argued that it is necessary to recognise explicitly that there are multiple definitions of strategy and that we need to use these to manoeuvre through this difficult field. According to Mintzberg *et al* (1998b), there are five main and interrelated definitions of strategy: *plan*, *ploy*, *pattern*, *position* and *perspective* (*see* Exhibit 6.3).

In a manner that has a postmodernist feel to it, Mintzberg *et al* (1998b) do not argue that one definition should be preferred to the others. In some senses they can be considered as alternatives or complementary approaches to strategy. Also, they are useful in adding important elements to the discussion of strategy. They draw our

Exhibit 6.3	Mintzberg's five definitions of strategy

- **Strategy as a plan**. According to this view, strategy is some form of consciously-intended course of action which is created ahead of events. This can be either a general strategy or a specific one. If specific, it may also constitute a ploy.

- **Strategy as a ploy**. This is where strategy is a manoeuvre to outwit an opponent. An example of this is when a firm threatens to lower its prices substantially to deter new entrants into its market. It is the threat to lower prices that is the consciously-intended course of action, and not any actual plan to do so.

- **Strategy as a pattern**. This is where we observe, after the event, that an organisation has acted in a consistent manner over time; i.e. whether consciously or not, the organisation exhibits a consistent pattern of behaviour. We can say from this that an organisation has pursued a particular strategy. This may not be the strategy it intended to pursue, however, but it is the one that has emerged from the action of the organisation. Therefore, though the organisation's realised strategy could be the product of a conscious and deliberate plan, this is often not the case.

- **Strategy as a position**. From this perspective, strategy is about positioning the organisation in order to achieve or maintain a sustainable competitive advantage. Mintzberg *et al* argue that most organisations try to avoid head-on competition. What they seek to achieve is a position where their competitors cannot or will not challenge them. In this sense, strategy is also seen as a game: groups of players circling each other, each trying to gain the high ground.

- **Strategy as perspective**. This definition sees strategy as a somewhat abstract concept that exists primarily in people's minds. For members of an organisation, the actual details of its strategy, as such, are irrelevant. What is important is that everyone in the organisation shares a common view of its purpose and direction which, whether people are aware of it or not, informs and guides decision-making and actions. Consequently, without the need for detailed plans, the organisation, through a shared understanding, pursues a consistent strategy/purpose.

Source: Mintzberg *et al* (1998b)

attention to the distinction between conscious and unconscious strategy, and between emergent and planned strategy. They also highlight the role of the organisation's collective mind in developing and implementing strategy.

In a similar way to Mintzberg *et al*, Johnson (1987) also distinguishes between different views of the strategic management process. As Exhibit 6.4 shows, he argues that there are three basic views that reflect more general distinctions in the social sciences.

Exhibit 6.4	Johnson's three basic views of strategy

- **The rationalistic view** – which sees strategy as the outcome of a series of preplanned actions designed to achieve the stated goals of an organisation in an optimal fashion.

- **The adaptive or incremental view** – which sees strategy evolving through an accumulation of relatively small changes over time.

- **The interpretative view** – which sees strategy as the product of individual and collective attempts to make sense of, i.e. interpret, past events.

Source: Johnson (1987)

One way of considering these various definitions or views of strategy, following on from Morgan (1986), is as metaphors. Morgan (1986) identified eight influential metaphors that are applied to organisations (*see* Exhibit 6.5).

Exhibit 6.5	Morgan's organisational metaphors

- Organisations as machines
- Organisations as organisms
- Organisations as brains
- Organisations as cultures
- Organisations as political systems
- Organisations as psychic prisons
- Organisations as flux and transformations
- Organisations as instruments of domination

Source: Morgan (1986)

Morgan (1986: 12–13) comments that:

> ... our theories and explanations of organizational life are based on metaphors that lead us to see and understand organizations in distinctive yet partial ways. ... By using different metaphors to understand the complex and paradoxical character of organizational life, we are able to manage and design organizations in ways that we may not have thought possible before.

In a similar way to Morgan's use of metaphors, the postmodernist viewpoint, as discussed in Chapter 4, would see the varying definitions of strategy as competing realities which managers attempt to impose on their organisations. Realists would acknowledge that these are different perspectives that do influence organisational strategy, but would also argue that there is a 'real world out there' which has to be addressed if strategies are to be successfully realised. Complexity theorists would take a similar view, acknowledging that different perspectives do exist and are influential but claiming that the social world, like the natural world, is governed by order-generating rules which organisations ignore at their peril. Therefore, whilst most would see Mintzberg *et al*'s and Johnson's definitions of strategy as metaphors or alternative perspectives, some would also argue that they represent competing realities, whilst others would argue that there is only one reality (though this can and does change with circumstances and time).

Nevertheless, the explicit recognition that there are multiple definitions of strategy can help us to make sense of the confusion of terms which litter the literature and which different writers use in different ways. Many writers seem to treat corporate planning, long-range planning, strategic planning and formal planning as synonymous. However, not all would agree. Naylor (1979), for example, defined strategic planning as long-range planning with a time horizon of three to five years. Litschert and Nicholson (1974) disagreed: they state that strategic and long-term planning are not synonymous. They argue that strategic planning is a process which involves making a sequence of interrelated decisions aimed at achieving a desirable future environment for an organisation. Andrews (1998: 51), similarly, defined strategy as a:

> ... pattern of decisions in a company that determines and reveals its objectives, purposes, or goals, produces the principal policies and plans for achieving those goals, and defines the range of business the company is to pursue, the kind of economic and human organisation it is, or intends to be, and the nature of the economic and non-economic contribution it intends to make to its shareholders, employees, customers and communities.

What we can see from the above is that, knowingly or not, writers are using different definitions of strategy and thus interpreting particular terms or phrases in the light of their own implicit or explicit definition. Nevertheless, in the use of these various terms, a certain consensus of opinion does emerge with regard to the basic features of strategic management and strategic decisions. Most of the writers would agree with Johnson and Scholes (1993), who described strategy as:

- concerning the full scope of an organisation's activities;
- the process of matching the organisation's activities to its environment;
- the process of matching its activities to its resource capability;
- having major resource implications;
- affecting operational decisions;
- being affected by the values and beliefs of those who have power in an organisation;
- affecting the long-term direction of an organisation.

Approaches to strategy: the Prescriptive versus the Analytical stream

In defining strategy, especially bearing in mind Mintzberg *et al*'s (1998b) and Johnson's (1987) various definitions, there are two further issues which need to be considered:

1 Is strategy a process or the outcome of a process?
2 Is strategy an economic/rational phenomenon or is it an organisational/social phenomenon?

Taking these two questions together, it can be seen that there are two parallel, competing and, to an extent, interacting streams of ideas. The first, the Prescriptive stream, sees strategy as a controlled, intentional, prescriptive process, based on a rational model of decision-making, which produces complete deliberate strategies (Ansoff, 1965; Argenti, 1974; Steiner, 1969). The second, the Analytical stream, which is more interested in understanding how organisations actually formulate strategy rather than prescribing how they should formulate it, argues that it is the outcome of the complex social and political processes involved in organisational decision-making (Hamel and Prahalad, 1989; Miles and Snow, 1978; Mintzberg, 1987; Pettigrew, 1980; Quinn, 1980a).

The Prescriptive stream grew out of the long-range planning initiatives of the 1940s and 1950s, and is aimed primarily at the practitioners of strategy. Through the work of the Planning and Design schools, this stream dominated the practice of strategy in the 1960s and 1970s. They not only saw strategy as an economic-rational process, but also considered its options and usefulness as primarily restricted to issues relating to market share and profit maximisation (Ansoff, 1965; Porter, 1980). However, with growing disillusionment amongst academics and practitioners over the ability of this approach to deliver competitiveness, a new variant of this approach came to the fore in the 1980s: the Positioning school. This school is most closely identified with Michael Porter (1980, 1985) whose *competitive forces framework* reinvigorated the Prescriptive approach and allowed it to maintain its dominance on the practice of strategy in the 1980s and 1990s (Teece *et al*, 1997). The main difference between the Positioning school and the earlier Planning and Design ones was that:

> Both the planning and design schools put no limits on the strategies that were possible in any given situation. The positioning school, in contrast, argued that only a few key strategies – as positions in the economic market place – are desirable in any given industry: ones that can be defended against existing and future competitors. Ease of defense means that firms which occupy these positions enjoy higher profits ... By thereby dispensing with one key premise of the design school – that strategies have to be unique, tailor-made for each organization – the positioning school was able to create and hone a set of analytical tools dedicated to matching the right strategy to the conditions at hand ...
>
> (Mintzberg *et al*, 1998a: 83)

The work of Porter and the Positioning school will be discussed in more detail in Chapter 7. However, for now, the key points to note are that the three schools that comprise the Prescriptive stream have dominated the practice of strategy within organisations since the 1960s. The reason for this is threefold. Firstly, its proponents set out deliberately to address the needs of industry and commerce by providing them with a blueprint for strategy formulation and implementation. Secondly, the Prescriptive stream interacted closely with a number of leading consultants, notably the Boston Consultancy Group, and business schools, notably Harvard, to promote their work and tailor it to the needs of organisations. By reinforcing and promoting each other, this triple alliance of researchers, consultants and educators created an iron orthodoxy that organisations, especially large ones, felt they ignored at their peril. Finally, because all three groups in this triple alliance were in effect engaged in a business activity, selling strategy as a product, they were able to invest in promoting and developing their product in a way that others were not. As the following examination of the Analytical stream of strategy will show, though, this did not mean that other important perspectives on strategy were not developed or did not achieve acceptance by a wide audience. It did, however, mean that these alternative perspectives have never had the same impact on practice within organisations as those promoted by the Prescriptive stream.

The Analytical stream, which began to appear in the 1970s and represents a more sceptical and more academically-orientated face of strategic management, views strategy not as a process, but as an outcome of a process. Its proponents' emphasis is not on the construction of detailed plans, which in any case they believe to be a misdirected approach, but on the organisational and social aspects of strategy formation. Their argument is that the capabilities of an organisation, in terms of its structure, systems, technology and management style, restrict the range of strategic options the organisation can pursue. Consequently, in a very real sense, it is the day-to-day stream of decisions regarding the development of its capabilities that determines an organisation's strategic direction, rather than the reverse (Mintzberg, 1994).

One of the oft-cited examples for this view is that of Japanese management. Pascale and Athos (1982) and Hamel and Prahalad (1989) argued that Japanese business success is not based on well-thought-out strategies *per se*, but on strategic intent – the commitment of Japanese managers to create and pursue a vision of their desired future. The vision is then used to bind an organisation together and give it a common purpose to which all can contribute. A key part of this common purpose is the identification and development of the core competences and capabilities necessary for the achievement of the organisation's vision.

This theme has been taken up by other Western writers on strategy. Kay (1993) used the term 'distinctive capabilities' rather than 'core competences', but is clearly describing the same thing. He argues that a firm's distinctive capabilities fall under four headings: reputation, architecture (i.e. internal and external structures and linkages), innovation and strategic assets. Kay believes that an organisation's competitiveness is dependent not upon any strategic plan as such, but upon the uniqueness and strength of its capabilities. It is these that allow an organisation to take advantage of opportunities and avoid threats, whether foreseeable or not. In a similar way, Stalk *et al* (1992) used the term 'core capability' in referring to an organisation's practices and business routines; and Grant (1991a) proposed a framework for analysing a firm's competitive advantage in terms of its resources and capabilities.

To an extent, the case made by Kay, Stalk *et al* and Grant is complementary to Mintzberg's (1987) concept of emergent strategy. Based on the many Western companies he had studied, Mintzberg argued that successful companies do not start out with detailed strategic plans. Instead, their strategies emerge over time from the pattern of decisions they take on key aspects of their activities. Mintzberg *et al* (1998a: 189–90) draw a distinction between planned or deliberate strategies and emergent ones:

> Deliberate strategy focuses on control – making sure that managerial intentions are realized in action – while emergent strategy emphasizes learning – coming to understand through the taking of actions what those intentions should be in the first place. ... The concept of emergent strategy ... opens the door to strategic learning, because it acknowledges the organization's capacity to experiment. A single action can be taken, feedback can be received, and the process can continue until the organization converges on the pattern that becomes its strategy.

Clearly, there are similarities between the Japanese strategic intent/competence approach, Mintzberg's and that of Kay and co. However, the Japanese consciously work out their shared vision and consciously pursue it. The Emergent approach, at least in its pure form, lacks the concept of 'vision' and doubts the presence of conscious intent. Mintzberg (1994: 25), though, does recognise that in practice some organisations pursue:

> ... umbrella strategies: the broad outlines are deliberate while the details are allowed to emerge within them. Thus emergent strategies are not bad and deliberate ones good; effective strategies mix these characteristics in ways that reflect the conditions at hand, notably the ability to predict as well as the need to react to unexpected events.

Kay (1993) took a similar view. Whilst doubting the efficacy of corporate vision *per se*, he does stress that the development of capabilities is, or at least can be, a conscious and planned process.

As mentioned in Chapter 4, complexity theories have had an increasing influence on organisation theorists over the last decade. However, their influence on the strategy literature has been limited by the fact that complexity theorists do not appear to share a common view of complexity and organisational strategy. For Stacey (2003: 319–20):

> Strategy comes to be understood as the evolving patterns of an organisation's identity. ... Strategy as the identity of an organisation is continuously constructed and enacted in the interaction of organisational practice.

For MacIntosh and MacLean (2001), strategy also has an emergent dimension to it but, for them, a key feature of strategy is to identify and maintain the appropriateness of the organisation's order-generating rules. It is the presence of appropriate order-generating rules that allow a consistent, and beneficial, pattern of action to emerge which forms the organisation's strategy. Bechtold (1997) and Brown and Eisenhardt (1997) stress that the purpose of order-generating rules is to keep an organisation operating at the edge of chaos. For them, the purpose of strategy is to create an organisation where self-organisation can take place. It is the ability to self-organise that they see as being crucial to maintaining/developing appropriate order-generating rules and thus bringing about beneficial change.

As with complexity theories, population ecology is borrowed from the physical sciences. It is a Darwinist-type approach that focuses on how organisations adapt and evolve in order to survive within the general population of organisations to which they belong (Carroll, 1988; Morgan, 1990). Watson (1997: 273) comments that:

> One way of considering the relationship of organisations to other organisations in the environment is to regard them as involved in a process of natural selection: a fight for survival within the ecological system of which they are part. ... They go through both planned and unplanned 'variations' in their form, and, largely through processes of competition, the environment 'selects' the form which best suits the organisation. Organisations then 'retain' the form which best suits their particular 'niche' or 'domain' ...

Population ecologists do not, therefore, challenge the importance of the fit or correspondence between an organisation and its environment. They do, though, question the extent to which achieving this is a conscious and planned process. In particular, as Pettigrew *et al* (1992: 25) maintain: 'Ecologists are unimpressed by the possibility that managers can turn their organizations round, and instead stress organizational inertia.' This argument echoes Hannan and Freeman's (1977: 957) assertion that:

> ... for wide classes of organizations there are very strong inertial pressures on structure arising from both internal arrangements (for example, internal politics) and from the environment (for example, public legitimation of organizational activity). To claim otherwise is to ignore the most obvious feature of organizational life.

Population ecologists argue that an organisation's survival, the extent to which it achieves a fit with its environment, depends on a combination of the organisation's own (planned and unplanned) actions, the activities of other organisations in its field and a strong element of luck (i.e. being in the right place, with the right combination of characteristics and at the right time).

The stress on luck or serendipity is also present in the work of writers such as Williamson (1991) and Weick (1979). Weick, in particular, views the world as an essentially ambiguous place in which it is unrealistic, and indeed impossible, to make detailed plans. This is clearly a strong challenge to those who emphasise the need for, and ability of, organisations to pursue environmental match or correspondence. However, Child's (1972) concept of equifinality takes this challenge even further. Equifinality, as (Sorge, 1997: 13) notes:

> ... quite simply means that different sorts of internal arrangements are perfectly compatible with identical contextual or environmental states. The principle goes against the idea of a quasi-ideal 'match' which is inherent in the principle of correspondence. Whereas correspondence [i.e. Contingency] theory suggests that rigid and bureaucratic structures are not a good match for volatile and shifting product markets, equifinality theorists claim that it may very well turn out to be a good match but only if the level and diversity of the workforce is large and organization culture produces motivated and flexible actors.

As Mintzberg et al (1998a) note in relation to equifinality, managers need to recognise that achieving a successful outcome is more important than imposing the method of achieving it.

Pettigrew (1985, 1987) and Child and Smith (1987), through their respective studies of ICI and Cadbury, also offered important insights and perspectives on approaches to strategic management and environmental fit. Pettigrew argues that there is a need for a change theory that sees organisations and how they operate in their entirety, one that recognises the importance and influence of the wider environment and appreciates the dynamic and political nature of strategy development and change. He is critical of theories which assume that organisations are rational entities pursuing agreed goals that reflect their best interests. Instead, he argues that organisations have to be understood in the context of the constraints and possibilities offered by the environment in which they operate and in relation to the self-interests of the individuals and groups that comprise them.

Pettigrew, therefore, sees organisations primarily as political systems in which groups and individuals, under the guise of rationality, seek to mobilise support for, and legitimate the pursuit of, strategies and actions that promote or sustain their personal or sectional interests. Particular groups or individuals may achieve a position of dominance, but that dominance is always subject to prevailing intra-organisational and environmental conditions. Therefore, Pettigrew rejects the view that strategy is a rational process of deliberate calculation and analysis. Instead he believes that organisational strategy – though often cloaked in rational and analytical terms – is in reality the outcome of a combination of internal political struggles, between groups and individuals seeking to influence policy in their favour, and external environmental pressures and constraints (this argument was examined in more detail in Chapter 5).

Child and Smith's (1987) firm-in-sector perspective has some similarities with Pettigrew's work; however, they take a more realist perspective, arguing for a stronger determining link between the individual firm and the sector in which it operates, and a lesser role for organisational politics. As shown in Exhibit 6.6, they suggest three areas of firm–sector linkage that shape and constrain the strategies organisations pursue.

Exhibit 6.6   Child and Smith's firm-in-sector perspective

1. **The 'objective conditions' for success**. Though each firm within the sector may pursue a different strategy, these will all tend to focus on or be determined by similar success factors such as customer satisfaction, quality, profitability, etc.

2. **The prevailing managerial consensus**. Within and across a sector, regardless of the organisation in which they work, managers are likely to develop a common and (implicitly at least) agreed view of how firms should operate, the key factors in their industry and the basis on which they compete with one another.

3. **The collaborative networks operating in the sector**. These may be with customers, suppliers, outside experts or even competitors.

Source: Child and Smith (1987)

Child and Smith's (1987) view draws on economic theories of the firm and suggests that the sector, particularly when strongly competitive, determines the path a firm must take for its future success. Though not denying a role for organisational politics, they claim that, unless the strategic decisions a firm takes are consistent with the conditions prevailing in its sector, success may be jeopardised. Therefore, though falling in the Analytical stream, Child and Smith appear to exhibit a greater faith in a rational and linear progression from market sector analysis to strategy formulation and implementation than Pettigrew and many other writers.

The Analytical stream also has a number of other variants, most notably those who see the role and personality of leaders as being the key determinants of successful strategy (Bennis and Namus, 1985). Leadership will be touched on later in this chapter, and covered more extensively in Chapter 16; nevertheless, merely mentioning here it serves to emphasise the somewhat disparate nature of the Analytical stream of strategy. Proponents of this stream are united by a number of factors such as their attempt to understand rather than prescribe strategy; their orientation, mainly, to an academic rather than a business audience; and their view of organisations as complex social entities operating within dangerous, dynamic and unpredictable environments. On the other hand, the proponents of the elements which make up the Analytical stream are divided by their emphasis on different aspects of strategy, such as politics, the industry sector, the general environment, organisational and national cultures, leadership, etc. They are also divided by their explicit or implicit adherence to postmodernist, realist or complexity perspectives. So, although it is true to say that proponents of the Japanese-inspired strategic intent/competence argument came to the fore in the 1990s, it is also true to say that they are challenged by the proponents of the other elements in this stream who still exert a powerful influence on the debate over strategy. It follows that their differences with each other are as important as their differences with proponents of the Prescriptive stream of strategy.

Understanding strategy: choices and constraints

Whilst the above identifies key themes in the debate over organisational strategy, it still presents a somewhat confusing picture. Clearly there is a distinction between those who adhere to the Prescriptive stream of strategy, which arose from the long-range planning approach of the 1940s and 1950s, and the Analytical stream as represented by, amongst others, the strategic intent/competences approach of the 1980s and 1990s. What is not clear, however, is the degree to which a common understanding and perspective exists amongst those collected under the Analytical umbrella. Certainly, a number of writers have tried to argue that a common perspective does exist. Brown and Jopling (1994) believed that the main distinction lies between the writers of the 1950s and 1960s who, they argue, saw strategy as basically concerned with fitting the organisation to its environment, and the writers of the 1980s and 1990s who, they argue, see strategy as focusing on internal issues, mainly to do with the development of core competences. They base their case on a contingency perspective. The earlier approach, they argue, was suitable to organisations operating in relatively stable and predictable environments, who had a limited product range, and where competition was restricted. With the advent of greater competition and more unstable environments, this approach was no longer viable, and firms had to look internally at how they could organise themselves to cope with the new situation. To an extent, this is an attractive analysis. However, though it is true that the earlier writers on strategy – such as Ansoff and company – did concentrate on product–market mix issues, it is also true that later they came to appreciate the link between the outside and the inside (Moore, 1992). Also, whilst Mintzberg and others have concentrated on internal capabilities, the Japanese approach has been to see the internal and external as two sides of the same coin, which is why they emphasise the importance of the strategic outward-looking vision driving the development of internal capabilities.

Nevertheless, such a simple distinction, based on one dimension of organisational life, cannot resolve the complex differences between and within the Prescriptive and Analytical streams. As Mintzberg *et al* (1998a) noted, the strategy field is more eclectic and more populous, in terms of different approaches, than ever before. In such a situation, attempts to fit writers into two camps, whether they be early and late, external and internal, are bound to fail. The multiple-definition view of strategy argued by Mintzberg *et al* (1998b), and particularly their proposition that the various definitions of strategy are both competing and complementary, offers another perspective. Strategy can be considered as either a process or an outcome. It can also be considered as either a rational approach or a political/social phenomenon. The various approaches to strategy do not reflect some underlying truth; rather they are different approaches that organisations can choose (consciously or not) to adopt, depending on their circumstances, objectives and management.

If this is the case, it may be that instead of looking for a theory of or approach to strategy that unifies and encompasses all the others, we should turn the argument on its head and ask, as we did with organisational theory, whether there is a 'one best way' for strategy?

In approaching this question, it is valuable to return to Child's (1972) concept of equifinality. As stated earlier, by Sorge (1997: 13), equifinality 'quite simply means that different sorts of internal arrangements are perfectly compatible with identical contextual or environmental states'. To paraphrase this definition, and to stretch the concept a little further than Child might have intended, it could be argued that different approaches to strategy formulation may be perfectly compatible with positive outcomes. This may especially be the case if one takes account of the growing opinion, as expressed in this and the previous chapters, that though organisations are constrained by their circumstances, they do possess the ability to manipulate and influence these circumstances to their own benefit. If this is the case, then, as Mintzberg *et al* (1998a: 365) maintain, 'the question is not whether there exists strategic choice, but how much'. To approach this question, we need to attempt to classify the various approaches to strategy in order to establish the degree to which they incorporate or exclude choice.

Though the above review of approaches to strategy cannot claim to be all-embracing, it does cover the key protagonists in the area. Whilst it separates the main approaches into two streams, however, it does not provide a classification or taxonomy of the various approaches. Whittington (1993) attempted to make sense of the many definitions and categories of strategy by identifying four generic approaches to strategy: the Classical, Evolutionary, Processual and Systemic (*see* Exhibit 6.7).

Exhibit 6.7   Whittington's generic approaches to strategy

- **The Classical approach**. This is the oldest and most influential approach to strategy. It portrays strategy as a rational process, based on analysis and quantification, and aimed at achieving the maximum level of profit for an organisation. It argues that, through rigorous analysis and planning, senior managers can predict future market trends and shape the organisation to take advantage of these.

- **The Evolutionary approach**. As the name implies, this uses the analogy of biological evolution to describe strategy development. It believes that organisations are at the mercy of the unpredictable and hostile vagaries of the market. Those organisations that survive and prosper do so not because of their ability to plan and predict, which is impossible, but because they have been lucky enough to hit on a winning formula. From this perspective, successful strategies cannot be planned, but emerge from the decisions managers take to align and realign their organisations to the changing environmental conditions.

- **The Processual approach**. This perspective concentrates on the nature of organisational and market processes. It views organisations and their members as shifting coalitions of individuals and groups with different interests, imperfect knowledge and short attention spans. Markets are similarly capricious and imperfect but, because of this, do not require organisations to achieve a perfect fit with their environment in order to prosper and survive. Strategy under these conditions is portrayed as a pragmatic process of trial and error, aimed at achieving a compromise between the needs of the market and the objectives of the warring factions within the organisation.

- **The Systemic approach**. This approach sees strategy as linked to dominant features of the local social system within which it takes place. The core argument of this perspective is that strategy can be a deliberate process, and planning and predictability are possible, but only if the conditions within the host society are favourable. Therefore, to an extent, this is a contingency approach to strategy which can accommodate situations where firms do not seek to maximise profit or bow to market pressures. If the conditions within the

Exhibit 6.7 *continued*

host society are supportive, markets can be manipulated, financial considerations can become a secondary issue, and stability and predictability can be achieved. Also, under such conditions, the objectives managers seek to pursue may be related more to their social background, degree of patriotism or even professional pride, than to profit maximisation. Therefore, from the Systemic perspective, the strategy an organisation adopts and the interests managers pursue reflect the nature of the particular social system within which it operates.

Source: Whittington (1993)

Whittington's categorisation of generic approaches to strategy is extremely useful in making sense of the plethora of approaches on offer. As one would expect, it is not perfect; some writers, such as Mintzberg, could fall under more than one heading, whilst others, like Child and Smith, are difficult to locate. Nevertheless, the Classical approach, with its modernist leanings, would clearly incorporate the work of the Planning, Design and Positioning school and the early Western writers on strategy. The Evolutionary approach has links with both the work of the complexity theorists and population ecologists; Mintzberg's (1994) work on emergent strategy might also fall under this heading. The Processual approach could also cover Mintzberg's work, certainly includes Pettigrew's (1985, 1987) work on organisational politics and sits reasonably comfortably with the postmodernists. The Systemic perspective, which has a realist tinge to it, clearly owes much to the Japanese approach to strategy as described by Hamel and Prahalad (1989).

Whittington (1993) also categorises these four approaches to strategy in terms of how they view outcomes and processes. He argues that the Classical and Evolutionary approaches see profit maximisation as the natural outcome of strategy. The Systemic and Processual approaches, on the other hand, believe other outcomes are both possible and acceptable, such as stability, environmental responsibility or maintenance of an organisation's dominant coalition. With regard to processes, the groupings change. Here the Classical and Systemic both agree that strategy can be a deliberate process. The Evolutionists and Processualists, though, see strategy as emerging from processes governed by chance and confusion.

Whittington's four categories of strategy can be summarised as follows:

- Classicists see strategy as a rational process of long-term planning aimed at maximising profit.
- Evolutionists also believe that the purpose of strategy is profit maximisation, but regard the future as too volatile and unpredictable to allow effective planning. Instead, they advise organisations to focus on maximising chances of survival today.
- The Processualists are equally sceptical of long-range planning, and see strategy as an emergent process of learning and adaptation.
- The Systemic perspective argues that the nature and aims of strategy are dependent upon the particular social context in which the organisation operates.

To an extent, the four approaches to strategy have some similarity to the Western approaches to organisation theory discussed in Part 1. The Classical, Evolutionary and Processual approaches are clearly 'one best way' or 'only possible way' approaches, whereas the Systemic approach offers a Contingency perspective on strategy. They also share some common ground with organisation theory on the issue of rationality. The Classical and Systemic approaches argue that strategy is or can be rational and intentional in its development and objectives. The Processualists believe that it is rational in neither aspect; the Evolutionists take a similar view of process, but appear to adopt a rational perspective on outcomes, in that profit maximisation is seen as the only outcome that guarantees survival.

In their view of the scope for managerial choice and judgment, three of these four approaches to strategy do appear to be more permissive than organisation theory. Clearly, the Classical strategy theorists leave little scope for either: their instruction seems to be to follow the textbook in terms of outcomes and processes or else. However, both the Evolutionists and the Processualists emphasise the need for managers to be fleet of foot and percipient in making key decisions responding to opportunities or threats; although the Evolutionists (rather like Napoleon in his view of generals) appear to believe that, at the end of the day, a lucky manager may be more desirable than an able one. For advocates of the Systemic approach, choice and judgment are important, but tend to be constrained by the limits and objectives of the society in which they are located.

It would appear, therefore, that managerial choice, preference and judgment, for all but the Classicists, do have a role to play in determining not just an organisation's strategy, but also the particular approach to strategy it adopts. In our examination of the strategy literature, however, it is clear that choice is constrained and can only be exercised within limits (from some perspectives, very narrow limits indeed). As Figure 6.1 shows, these limits or constraints, which are suggested by or inferred from the literature, can be classified under four headings.

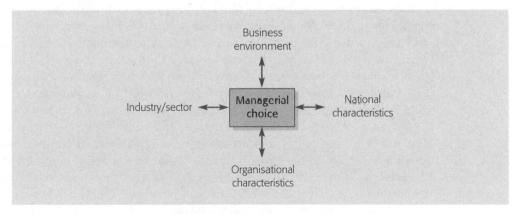

Figure 6.1 Constraints on managerial choice

National objectives, practices and cultures

The case for country-specific constraints very much follows the argument of the Systemic perspective on strategy. This view sees the operation of organisations as strongly influenced by the social system in which they operate. In some cases, such as in Japan and Germany, patriotism, national pride and a collectivist ethos have created a business environment that supports the pursuit of long-term national objectives. This is reflected in the behaviour of individual firms and financial institutions that favour stable growth over the medium to long term, rather than short-term profit maximisation. In Britain and the USA, on the other hand, the climate is far more supportive of individual endeavour and short-term profit maximisation rather than the national interest *per se*.

The difference between these two approaches is neatly summed up in the old saying that 'What's good for General Motors is good for America'. The Japanese would, of course, transpose this to read 'What is good for Japan is good for Toyota'. This view also draws support from Hofstede's (1980, 1990) work on national cultures discussed in Chapter 5. The implication, therefore, is that organisations ignore national norms at their peril: the pursuit of short-term profit maximisation in Japan and Germany is likely to be as difficult, and perhaps as counter-productive, as the pursuit of a long-term strategy of growing market share, which ignores short-term profitability, would be in the UK or the USA. Nevertheless, these constraints are open to manipulation and avoidance. The move by many British companies – Dyson, GKN, etc. – to manufacture outside the UK and/or to form international alliances is an example of this, as is the Japanese trend to establish manufacturing plants in the USA and Europe in order to avoid high production costs on the one hand and import quotas on the other. Another example is the lobbying of governments and national and international bodies for changes in laws and regulations that particular organisations or industries see as operating against their interests.

Industry and sector practices and norms

This follows from Child and Smith's (1987) firm-in-sector perspective. As discussed earlier, they believe that the objective conditions operating in a sector, managers' understanding of the dynamics of the sector, and the nature and degree of inter-firm collaboration all combine to determine the path a firm must take for its future success. This is especially the case where the sector is highly competitive. In effect, Child and Smith's argument is that firms must stick to the rules of engagement in their sector or perish. However, they do concede that, where competition is less intense, then managers have a greater degree of freedom with regard to the selection of strategy. Indeed, the low level of competition may explain how Japanese companies were able to change the rules of engagement to their advantage in many industries in the 1960s and 1970s (Hamel and Prahalad, 1989); although it is also the case that Japanese companies pay less attention to today's sectoral constraints than to re-shaping the rules of the game to create competitive conditions more favourable to themselves (Turner, 1990). Another method of overcoming sectoral constraints and conditions is, as illustrated by Allaire and Firsirotu (1989), by diversifying into new products and different sectors.

Business environment

For nearly all the approaches to strategy that we have discussed, their proponents assume, explicitly or implicitly, that they are operating in a particular type of environment. The Classical approach to strategy is clearly predicated on the existence of a relatively stable and predictable environment. If this exists, then predicting the future and planning accordingly is a much less hazardous exercise than would otherwise be the case. The Systemic view also seems to assume a degree of environmental stability. As the history of Japan and Germany show, however, stability needs to be actively promoted by government–industry cooperation rather than relying on the invisible, and often volatile, hand of the market. For Processualists, and even more so for Evolutionists, the environment is a hostile, unpredictable and uncertain place. Planning is almost impossible, and success comes either from continuously adapting to changes in the environment, or from being in the right place at the right time.

For three of these perspectives, the environment is a given, even if they disagree about exactly what is given. However, for those advocating a Systemic approach, the environment is not a given: it can be changed. As this chapter and Part 1 have argued, there is now a considerable body of evidence from a number of different perspectives to this effect (Hatch, 1997; Morgan, 1986). Shapiro (1989) utilises the tools of game theory to show how firms influence the behaviour and actions of their competitors, and in so doing change the environment in which they operate. In a similar way, Teece *et al* (1997) argue that investments in production capacity, R&D and advertising can all be used to alter an organisation's environment favourably. Weick (1979) takes a different perspective. He argues that the world is so complex and ambiguous that an organisation cannot possibly 'know' its environment. Instead, organisations have to 'enact' their environment; that is to say, they have to develop and act upon their own interpretation of their environment. This is very similar to the learning organisation and postmodernist perspectives, as discussed in Chapters 3 and 4, that organisations have the ability to 'invent' their own reality. The implication from these different perspectives is that though many companies may have to adjust their strategic approach to environmental conditions, some companies may be able to do the reverse. The UK National Health Service is a good example of this. As Burnes and Salauroo (1995) noted, the NHS operated prior to 1990 as a typical government bureaucracy. The government allocated resources and gave policy direction, whilst the NHS centrally planned how resources would be allocated and policies operationalised (i.e. the Classical approach to strategy). This meant that there was considerable stability and predictability in its environment. However, the government of the day wanted the NHS to operate in a more cost-conscious and entrepreneurial mode. To facilitate and encourage this, it changed the way funds were provided and distributed. Rather than funds being given as of right to service providers (e.g. hospitals), they were reallocated to service purchasers (e.g. local doctors) who could decide what to buy and from whom. This creation of a market for the provision of medical services destabilised the environment and made planning and prediction very hazardous exercises (thus making an Evolutionary or Processual approach to strategy more relevant). However, with a change of government in 1997, the pendulum began to swing back. Whilst wishing to retain some of the perceived benefits of a market system, the new government announced that it would modify the purchaser–provider system to create greater stability (Salauroo and Burnes, 1998).

Normally, attempts at manipulating the environment aim to reduce uncertainty, or at least cope with rather than increase, it. Allaire and Firsirotu (1989) identified three ways of coping with uncertainty. The first of these is through predicting and planning (the Classical approach). The second is to restructure for flexibility (the Contingency approach). The third, however, is to manipulate or control the environment. Allaire and Firsirotu cite the examples of Boeing and IBM, who created and subsequently dominated their environments. Another major approach they identify is the use of cooperative strategies – collusion, market-sharing and other methods of reducing competition. An example of this in the UK was the agreement by the main companies in the milk industry to 'carve up the country so they stop competing with each other' for doorstep sales (Cowe, 1995: 40). Perhaps the most famous recent example is Microsoft's attempt to dominate the market for Internet products by providing its web browser 'free' to everyone who bought its Windows operating system. Therefore, as can be seen, there is certainly sufficient evidence to show that it is possible to change, control or manipulate the environment in which an organisation operates, and thus either necessitate or make possible a particular approach to strategy.

Organisation characteristics

Obviously, there are many organisation characteristics that act to constrain or facilitate managerial choice. However, there do appear to be four that have particular importance: structure, culture, politics and managerial style. Apart from the latter, these have been reviewed extensively in Chapters 3 and 4 and can be discussed relatively briefly. An organisation's structure and culture have clear implications for managerial choice in the area of strategy. Organisations with organic structures and task cultures are likely to be resistant to or incapable of operating a Classical form of strategy. Similarly, organisations with mechanistic structures and role cultures are likely to have a somewhat hostile attitude towards Processual or Evolutionary approaches to strategy. Moving on to the issue of organisational politics: where decisions are heavily influenced by individual and/or group self-interest, as averse to organisational objectives, it is unlikely that a Classical or Systemic approach to strategy would be successful. A Processual or Evolutionary approach, though, would have clear applicability.

There remains the subject of managerial or leadership style. There has been considerable interest in recent years in applying Burns' (1978) pioneering work on political leadership to leadership in organisations (Burnes and James, 1995; Beatty and Lee, 1992; and Gibbons, 1992). Burns identified two basic organisational states: *convergent* – a stable state; and *divergent* – where predictability and stability are absent. For each of these states, he argued, there is an appropriate managerial style. Convergent states require managers with a *transactional style* – ones who are good at optimising the performance of the organisation within the confines of existing policy. Divergent states, however, require managers with a *transformational style* – ones who challenge the status quo and create new visions. It follows from this that transactional managers will prefer approaches to strategy that stress continuity and predictability (i.e. the Classical or, in some circumstances, Systemic approach), whilst transformational managers will be more comfortable with a Processual or Evolutionary type of approach. Managerial style will be further discussed in Chapter 16.

As was the case with the other three forms of constraint, organisational characteristics can be amended. The debate on structure and culture has been well covered already, but the level of political behaviour is also open to change. As Pfeffer (1981, 1992) showed, though political behaviour is never absent from organisations, there are situations where it is likely to be more prevalent. In particular, political behaviour is likely to be most evident where major structural changes are taking place that affect the power distribution in organisations. By recognising that this is the case, by taking steps to reduce ambiguity and by trying to increase the transparency and openness of the decision-making process, the ability of individuals to pursue their own interests can be reduced. This is demonstrated by the Japanese *ringi* system, which promotes extensive and open debate over decisions in order to ensure that they fit in with the company's objectives rather than those of sectional interests. As far as changing managerial styles is concerned, although there is evidence that these are shaped and changed by the organisations in which managers work, there is also considerable evidence that senior managers tend to change organisations to fit their style (Morgan, 1986).

■ Choices and constraints: summary

It should be borne in mind that the particular mix of these four forms of constraint will vary from organisation to organisation, even where these operate in the same country and industry. Also, it needs to be recognised that these constraints are as likely to conflict with each other as they are to complement each other: for example, car companies operating in the UK may find that the culture of the UK's financial institutions favours short-term profit maximisation, whilst the car industry appears to require long-term investment in building market share. This may be one reason why the UK motor industry is now mostly foreign-owned. In addition, it should be noted that whilst managers are not obliged to take account of the constraints they face, they may well pay a price for this in terms of the performance of their organisation. Successful firms are likely to be ones whose managers are aware of, and can balance, the various constraints they face. This obviously raises the issue of managerial ability and competence, an issue we shall explore in some depth in Chapter 16.

Therefore, the key point to recognise from the above review is that the type of strategic approach adopted is a matter of managerial choice, but that choice is constrained by a variety of organisational, environmental, sectoral and national factors, as are the outcomes which flow from it. As was argued in Part 1, organisations and managers may be able to influence or change the constraints they face. Therefore, by recognising, as Figure 6.1 shows, that there are real constraints on managerial choice, one is acknowledging that both the realist and complexity perspectives on organisations have much to offer. However, by recognising that some constraints can be consciously manipulated or influenced and changed, one is also acknowledging that the postmodernist's arguments should not be lightly dismissed.

Nevertheless, both the case for managerial choice and the argument for manipulating constraints need to be taken with a pinch of salt. The fact of the matter is that in the West, as noted by many writers, the Classical approach to strategy, latterly through the work of the Positioning school, is still dominant (Joyce and Woods, 2001; Rigby and Gillies, 2000; Teece *et al*, 1997; Whittington, 1993). Also, as noted in Chapter 5, there is a tendency for decision-makers to 'satisfice'. That is to say, rather than undertaking an extensive examination of the issues involved and searching for all the possible solutions, decision-makers tend to accept the first satisfactory solution to a problem (Butler, 1997). This equates to Argyris and Schon's (1978) concept of single-loop learning (*see* Chapter 3). It is also similar to Cohen *et al*'s (1972) comment that decisions are often not taken but happen. They suggest that decisions occur when four independent streams meet: problems, solutions, participants and choice opportunities – the so-called Garbage Can model of decision-making. They argue that when a problem becomes severe it demands attention. Solutions, on the other hand, are answers looking for a problem. Participants are the people in the organisation possessing problems and/or solutions, while choice opportunities are occasions when organisations are required to make a decision. When these four elements come together, decisions occur. Seen in this way, decision-making is not conscious, rational or systematic; on the contrary, decisions are haphazard, accidental and unplanned. From a slightly different perspective, Nelson and Winter (1982) argue that in many cases decision-making is an unconscious and automatic process, based on a repertoire that individuals develop over time of responses to particular situations. This is similar to Ashforth and Fried's (1988) observation that there is a tendency in some organisations for behaviour to become almost mindless – employees and managers, as a result of organisational socialisation and experience, respond automatically to events in a programmed way. Consequently, though the potential for choice exists, the reality is that many managers appear not to exercise it, preferring instead to stick to tried-and-tested, routine, orthodox, textbook approaches – regardless of their suitability.

Yet, it is important to note that, in the academic world, the weight of the argument appears to be shifting from seeing strategy as a rational, mathematical process, to seeing it as the outcome of the ability of an organisation's management to utilise its strengths and competencies in the competitive pursuit of success. There are some writers, however, who believe the reverse is true of the business world, and that more and more firms are opting for rational decision-making approaches to strategy based on value-maximising financial techniques and quantitative analysis of market positions (Grant, 1991b; Teece *et al*, 1997). Whatever the truth or otherwise of this view, the main strategies favoured by organisations – as the following chapter will show – are still, though no longer exclusively, market- and quantitatively-orientated, and certainly give greater credence to rational decision-making than to more qualitative approaches.

Conclusions

Strategic planning or management has moved in and out of fashion over the years and is once again firmly back in fashion (Galagan, 1997; Joyce and Woods, 2001; Rigby and Gillies, 2000). It has developed considerably since it began to be widely used in America in the 1950s and 1960s. No longer is strategy purely about the external world, no longer is it solely seen as a rational, quantitative process. Neither is it any longer seen as a process that is geared towards predicting the future, but instead it seeks to shape or create the future (Joyce and Woods, 2001). Indeed, writers and practitioners from different backgrounds and countries, such as Hamel and Prahalad (1994), Mintzberg *et al* (1998b), Ohmae (1986) and Stacey (2003), have argued that it is not a process at all, but the outcome of a process: an outcome that is shaped not by mathematical models but by human creativity.

The move towards this new, more emergent, perspective on strategy has been brought about by the mounting criticisms against the Classical or Prescriptive approach to strategy. The main criticisms are that it is mechanistic, inflexible, and reliant on quantitative tools and techniques of dubious validity. The result is that organisations who attempt to construct strategies using the Classical approach fall foul of what Peters and Waterman (1982) described as 'Paralysis Through Analysis' and 'Irrational Rationality'. In effect, organisations contort themselves in a vain attempt to make the real world fit the constraints and limitations of their mathematical models, rather than vice versa.

The alternative view, and one that is gaining adherents, is that organisations should move away from exclusive reliance on mathematical models. Instead, human creativity should be brought into play. Senior managers should create a vision of the organisation's future – establish its strategic intent. This should then be pursued relentlessly by the organisation. In the process of doing so, the strategy emerges from the decisions that are taken with regard to resource allocation, organisation structure and the other key areas of operation. From different perspectives, a number of writers have come to the same conclusion. For successful companies, strategy does not appear to be a preconceived and detailed set of steps for achieving a coherent package of concrete goals within a given timescale. Neither does it seem to be a rational process that is amenable to mathematical modelling. Rather, it is the outcome of a process of decision-making and resource allocation that is embarked upon in pursuit of a vision (though even here there is disagreement about how conscious this process is). Such an approach is inherently irrational, inherently unplannable – it cannot be modelled or quantified, though it can and must be pursued with rigour and determination. Needless to say, just as the rational approach to strategy sat easily with a modernist perspective, so the irrational approach sits better with the postmodernist view of the world.

In this chapter, we have suggested a third approach, one which sides with neither the quantitative nor qualitative schools of thought. Instead, it has been argued that the approach to strategy that organisations adopt is or can be the outcome of managerial choice and preference. However, choice in this respect, as in most others, is constrained. The key constraints identified were societal, sectoral, environmental and organisational. Whilst on the face of it this appears to impose severe limitations on the degree of freedom managers have with regard to the choice of strategy, it was also argued that managers can influence or manipulate the constraints they face in order to create their own preferred organisational reality. Therefore, though being very much in the realist and complexity camps, it does not totally reject the postmodernist view either.

This follows on from Part 1, where it was claimed that managers are not the passive creatures portrayed by much of organisation theory. Instead of having to adapt their organisations to the circumstances in which they find themselves, they can attempt to amend or even reinvent the circumstances. So, managers in organisations faced by a dynamic and unpredictable environment could seek to change markets and/or products, influence the behaviour of competitors, or change customers' perceptions, in order to reduce uncertainty and increase predictability. By so doing, an organisation could still function efficiently at the more mechanistic end of the mechanistic–organic spectrum, if that was the type of structure preferred by its managers.

This argument would seem equally applicable to the constraints managers face when choosing an approach to strategy. Some managers might prefer an Evolutionary or Processual approach to strategy, either because it suits their own temperament or because they believe that a hostile and turbulent environment suits them better than their competitors (the move by Rupert Murdoch's newspapers in the UK in the 1990s to start a price-cutting war was an example of this). On the other hand, constraints might be manipulated or changed for ideological reasons, such as the attempt by most Western governments to privatise or introduce market forces into the public sector. The point is that the possibility does exist for managers to choose not only the approach to strategy but also, to an extent at least, the constraints they face.

To choose an approach to strategy is one thing; to apply it is an entirely different matter. As Mintzberg *et al* (1998a and b) observe, whether one takes the view that strategy drives change or that it emerges from the changes an organisation makes, the two are inseparable. Therefore, just as this chapter has reviewed the main arguments with regard to strategy, so the remaining chapters in Part 2 will review the strengths and weaknesses of the main approaches to applying strategy and implementing change.

Test your learning

■ Short answer questions

1 What does Hoskin (1990) see as being the origins of modern business strategy?
2 Define long-range planning.
3 What technique did the Design school develop for assessing an organisation's potential?
4 How do Johnson and Scholes (1993) define strategy?
5 What is the Prescriptive school of strategy?
6 What is the Analytical school of strategy?
7 What is emergent strategy?
8 What is an umbrella strategy?
9 What are the main constraints on organisational choice?
10 Describe the relationship between organisational strategy and organisational change.

■ Essay questions

1 How do Whittington's four generic approaches to strategy relate to the Prescriptive and Analytical schools of strategy?
2 Discuss the following statement: strategy development and implementation can never be a rational process.

Suggested further reading

1 Mintzberg, H, Ahlstrand, B and Lampel, J (1998) *Strategy Safari*. Prentice Hall: Hemel Hempstead.
   Almost anything with Henry Mintzberg's name on it is worth reading and this book is no exception. It provides a succinct and pertinent review of the main perspectives on strategy.

2 Whittington, R (2001) *What is Strategy and Does it Matter?* (2nd edition). Thomson Learning: London.
   In this short and eminently readable book, Richard Whittington challenges much of the orthodox thinking on strategy.

Chapter 7

Applying strategy

Models, levels and tools

Learning objectives

After studying this chapter, you should be able to:

- describe the three basic approaches to strategy that organisations can adopt;
- discuss the three levels of strategic decision-making in organisations;
- list the main strategic planning tools;
- state the strengths and weaknesses of quantitative tools;
- list the advantages and disadvantages of qualitative tools;
- understand why quantitative tools have tended to be preferred to more qualitative ones;
- appreciate the growing interest in vision-building techniques;
- identify the implications for organisational change of both quantitative and qualitative tools and techniques.

| Exhibit 7.1 | Strategy development tools |

Managers resort to old tools in a crisis

Many executives around the world have abandoned 'new economy' management tools such as corporate venturing in favour of tried-and-tested methods to navigate the economic downturn, according to a survey by Bain & Co, the strategy consultancy. Bain's annual 'management tools' survey, involving senior executives from 451 companies in 22 countries, found dissatisfaction was highest with formerly trendy tools that had been seen as offering a path to rapid growth. Forty-two per cent of users last year abandoned corporate venturing – the creation of new businesses using venture capital methods. Thirty-nine per cent dropped 'market disruption analysis', used to identify where to launch businesses in competition with outside start-ups. Customer relationship management, using the internet to identify and retain

valuable clients, was abandoned by 18 per cent of users. The figures compared with an average 11 per cent defection rate from the 25 management tools considered by the survey. Only a third or fewer respondents adopted these new economy tools during the year. Managers reported finding the tools difficult to implement. With corporate venturing, they said their companies had trouble mastering the required venture capital disciplines, including making a quick exit from failing ventures. The most commonly used tools last year were strategic planning, mission and vision statements ... although 77 per cent of respondents said most tools promised more than they delivered.

Source: Alison Maitland, *Financial Times*, 18 July 2001, p. 10.

Introduction

This chapter begins where the previous one ended. Chapter 6 reviewed the main perspectives on strategy. In seeking to understand and define strategy formulation, it identified two streams of thought, the Prescriptive and the Analytical. As the name implies, the Prescriptive stream comprises approaches that seek to 'prescribe' how organisations should undertake strategy but, in so doing, tends to ignore or downplay the irrational and highly convoluted nature of organisational life. The Analytical stream, on the other hand, rather than telling organisations how they should build strategy, seeks to analyse – to understand and describe – the complexity and range of forces that affect how organisations actually do build strategy. This divergence is reflected in their respective views of strategy. The Prescriptive stream, which was the first on the scene and is very much practitioner-orientated, sees strategy formulation as an economic-rational process based on mathematical models. The Analytical stream, which began to appear in the 1970s, represents the more reflexive and more academically-orientated face of strategy. It views strategy not as a process, but as an outcome of a process. Its proponents' emphasis is not on the construction of detailed plans, which in any case they believe to be an unworkable approach, but on the organisational, social and political aspects of strategy formulation.

The two streams represent markedly different perspectives on strategy formulation, and whilst the Analytical stream has tended to win the academic arguments over the last 20 years, the Prescriptive one has had considerably more impact and influence on the practice of strategy. Nevertheless, as the survey by Bain & Co (Exhibit 7.1) shows, though management tools come and go, the use of mission and vision statements has now joined the more quantitatively-orientated strategic planning tools favoured by the majority of companies, though most managers appear to have a healthy scepticism about what can be achieved by either quantitative or qualitative tools.

This chapter begins by examining the three basic types or models of strategy that organisations can adopt: the Competitive Forces model; the Resource-Based model; and the Strategic Conflict model. The chapter then moves on to look at the three levels of strategic decision-making in organisations: corporate, business and functional. This is followed by a review of the main strategic planning tools.

The chapter ends by arguing that one of the principal reasons for the dominance of prescriptive approaches to strategy has been the alliance between leading consultancies and business schools in America to develop, market and update these. In so doing, the Prescriptive school has established itself as the orthodox, safe and practical approach to strategy formulation. Nevertheless, with the take-up of more analytically-based types of strategy, this is beginning to change. As Chapter 6 maintained, the model or type of strategy an organisation should adopt, and the associated planning tools that accompany it, are dependent upon the constraints the organisation faces. However, organisations do not have to fit themselves and their strategies to these constraints. Rather, they have a choice; they can seek to influence or mould the constraints they face in order to make them more amenable to the type or model of strategy they wish to pursue. Therefore, the approach to strategy an organisation adopts may have less to do with the merits of the different models on offer and more to do with the type of organisation it is and the orientation of its managers.

Types of strategies

As the previous chapter demonstrated, there is a wide, and often confusing, variety of approaches to strategy development that organisations can adopt. It follows that the same comment can be made with regard to the types of strategy that organisations do actually adopt in order to achieve competitive advantage over their rivals (Johnson and Scholes, 2002; Joyce and Woods, 2001). However, Teece *et al* (1997) argue that, in the main, there are only three basic types or models of strategy that organisations do adopt in practice, which are as follows.

■ The Competitive Forces model

This stems from the Positioning school and, since its inception in the 1980s, has become the dominant approach to strategy. The central tenet of this approach is the need to align the organisation with its environment, the key aspect of which is the industry or industries in which it competes. Proponents of this view believe that industry structure strongly influences the competitive rules of the game as well as the range of strategies open to the organisation. This model is most closely associated with the work of Michael Porter (1980, 1985) and his 'five forces' framework (*see* Figure 7.1).

Porter argues that it is these five industry-level competitive forces, the bargaining power of buyers and sellers, the threat of potential substitute products and new entrants, and rivalry among existing competitors, that determine the inherent profit potential of an industry. Consequently, he argues, these are the main factors which an

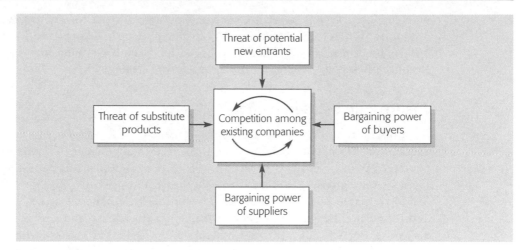

Figure 7.1 Porter's five competitive forces

organisation needs to take into account when developing its strategy. For Porter (1985: 47), strategy is concerned with '... positioning a business to maximise the value of the capabilities that distinguish it from its competitors.' Porter (1980) maintains that there are only three basic generic strategies a firm can adopt in order to outperform competitors: *cost leadership*, *product differentiation* and *specialisation by focus* (these are discussed in more detail below). Porter believes that a firm's ability to increase its profits is dependent on its ability to influence the competitive forces in the industry or to change its market position in relation to competitors and suppliers. This approach obviously has links to Contingency Theory (*see* Chapter 2), given that it is based on a systematic empirical search for relationships between external conditions and internal strategies. In addition, because of its focus on the importance of sector and industry factors, it has an affinity with Child and Smith's (1987) firm-in-sector perspective discussed in Chapter 6.

There is little doubt that the Positioning school in general, and Porter's work in particular, has had a huge influence on the practice of strategy within organisations (Hussey and Jenster, 1999; Johnson and Scholes, 2002). However, as one would expect, it has also attracted considerable criticism. Miller (1992) criticised it as too narrow and inflexible, and thus likely to leave organisations vulnerable if social, technological or economic developments lead, as can happen, to rapid changes in the market place. Mintzberg *et al* (1998a) noted that the Positioning school's assumption of rationality ignores the political nature of organisations; that it is biased towards big business, where market power is greatest, and therefore has little to say to small and medium-sized enterprises; and that its dependence on analysis and calculation impedes both learning and creativity. For Fleisher and Bensoussan (2003), the key weaknesses of Porter's approach are its lack of explicit recognition of the importance of socio-political factors, its lack of a longitudinal focus and that it underestimates the importance of core competences. A further and telling criticism is that the big competitive battles of the last 30 years, especially between Japanese and American firms, tend not to have been won by those who have identified and defended their market position, but by those, such as Toyota and Cannon, who have used their unique resources to change the rules of the game itself (Hamel and Prahalad, 1989, 1994). For these reasons, the last decade has seen a growing interest in both the Resource-Based and Strategic Conflict models of strategy.

The Resource-Based model

In terms of achieving competitive advantage, the Resource-Based view sees above-average profitability as coming from the effective deployment of superior or unique resources that allow firms to have lower costs or better products, rather than from tactical manoeuvring or product market positioning (Fahy, 2000). Such resources include tangible assets, such as plant and equipment; intangible assets, such as patents and brands; and capabilities, such as the skills, knowledge and aptitudes of individuals and groups (Amit and Schoemaker, 1993; Hall, 1993; Wernerfelt, 1995). The resource-based perspective grew from the work of economists who, in seeking to identify the factors which gave rise to imperfect competition and super-normal profits, drew attention to differences between firms in terms of technical know-how, patents, trademarks, brand awareness and managerial ability (Chamberlin, 1933; Learned *et al*, 1965; Penrose, 1959). Consequently, proponents of the Resource-Based view see firms as being heterogeneous in respect of their resources, i.e. no two firms possess exactly the same combination of these. However, this view really came to the fore in the 1980s and 1990s as an explanation for the rise of corporate Japan. It was out of research into the competitiveness of Japanese firms that Prahalad and Hamel (1990) produced their article, *The Core Competence of the Corporation*. In it, they argue that real competitive advantage comes from the ability to build at lower cost and more speedily than competitors those core competences that spawn unanticipated products. They also argue that senior managers should spend a significant proportion of their time developing a corporation-wide architecture for establishing objectives for competence-building. The influential study of the car industry by Womack *et al* (1990), *The Machine That Changed The World*, came to a similar view of Japanese competitiveness. Support for this perspective has also come from a number of studies of Western firms. Cool and Schendel (1988) showed that there are systematic and significant performance differences among firms in the same industry sectors. Rumelt (1991) showed that intra-industry profit differentials are greater than inter-industry differentials. Kay's (1993) work on strategy also comes to the conclusion that an organisation's success comes from developing distinctive capabilities.

Hax and Majluf (1996: 10) state that:

> The essence of the resource-based model ... [is] that competitive advantage is created when resources and capabilities that are owned exclusively by the firm are applied to developing unique competencies. Moreover, the resulting advantage can be sustained due to the lack of substitution and imitation capabilities by the firm's competitors.

The influence of the resource-based view has grown considerably over the last decade (Fahy, 2000). It is now the received wisdom that organisations should, in Peters and Waterman's (1982) phrase, 'stick to the knitting' and discard activities that are not part of their core business and which do not build on their core competences (Hax and Majluf, 1996). Nevertheless, there are criticisms which have been raised against this view of strategy, including the lack of empirical support, complex and ambiguous definitions of resources and that it is merely a rehash of the SWOT analysis (Fleisher and Bensoussan, 2003). In addition, because resources cannot easily or quickly be acquired or developed, in the short run, firms are stuck with the ones they possess. Therefore, depending on the circumstances, and how they change, these firm-specific assets can be either a boon or a curse. Perhaps the main criticism of this approach comes from population ecologists who argue that, because these competences take so long to develop and environments change so quickly, any beneficial match between an organisation's competences and its environment is more likely to be accidental or fortuitous rather than the result of deliberate or foresightful actions by managers (Hannan and Freeman, 1988). This is perhaps why there has also been a growing interest in the Strategic Conflict model, that draws attention to the dynamic nature of organisational strategy.

The Strategic Conflict model

This model harks back to the military metaphor, and portrays competition as war between rival firms. In particular, there is a tendency to draw on the work of military strategists such as von Clausewitz (von Clausewitz *et al*, 2001) and Sun Tzu (Michaelson, 2001) and attempt to apply their military aphorisms to modern business organisations (Mintzberg *et al*, 1998a). Sayings such as, 'No battle plan ever survived the first encounter with the enemy' are used to illustrate not just the dynamic nature of strategy but also the need to respond to competitors who do not always behave as anticipated. In its current manifestation, it came to prominence with the publication of Carl Shapiro's (1989) article, *The Theory of Business Strategy*. Central to this approach is the view that a firm can achieve increased profits by influencing the actions and behaviour of its rivals and thus, in effect, manipulate the market environment. This can be done in a number of ways, such as by investment in capacity (Dixit, 1980), R&D (Gilbert and Newberry, 1982) and advertising (Schmalensee, 1983). However, such moves will have little impact if they can be easily undone; therefore, to be effective, they require irreversible commitment.

Also, it is argued, these various manoeuvres are crucially dependent on what one firm thinks another firm will do in a particular situation. Therefore, the model incorporates the role of strategic signalling as an important mechanism for influencing or intimidating rivals. This includes such practices as predatory pricing (Kreps and Wilson, 1982) and limit pricing (Milgrom and Roberts, 1982). In addition, more recently, the model has come to embrace issues relating to the role of commitment and reputation (Ghemawat, 1991) and the simultaneous use of competition and cooperation (Brandenburger and Nalebuff, 1996).

Therefore, from the strategic conflict perspective, an organisation's ability to increase its profits is dependent on its ability to outwit, out-bluff and out-manoeuvre its rivals. This approach also draws on game theory to understand the nature of competitive interaction between rival firms. Game theory has allowed established intuitive arguments concerning various types of business tactics and strategy (e.g. predatory pricing) to be explained and formalised. In terms of the Prescriptive and Analytical streams of strategy, although Porter (1980) acknowledges the benefits of strategic manoeuvring, it does not fit in with his or the rest of the Positioning school's work. Instead, its emphasis on quick-wittedness, gut instinct and the more emotional elements of decision-making means it sits better with the Analytical stream.

Given that conflict-based strategies do not take account of the wide range of external and internal factors which also contribute to an organisation's competitiveness, its usefulness may well be limited. As Teece *et al* (1997) noted, strategic conflict is likely to be more appropriate in situations where there is an even balance between rivals in an industry (e.g. Coca-Cola and Pepsi) rather than in situations where one organisation has a substantial competitive advantage over its rivals (e.g. Microsoft). In these latter situations, it is perhaps the Resource-Based model of strategy that is of most interest.

These three types or models of strategy are all currently fashionable, though Porter and the Positioning school are the more dominant. They are, however, very different in their emphasis and timescales. The Strategic Conflict model is very much about out-manoeuvring the opposition, and tends to have a short-term focus, although a number of its tactics do have longer-term implications. The Competitive Forces model is concerned with identifying and occupying a defensible market position, and thereby achieving higher profits than others in the industry. This tends to have a medium-term focus. The Resource-Based model has a much longer-term focus than either of the other two. Its proponents believe that organisations need to build strategic competences that, almost through a process of serendipity, will allow it to meet future and unanticipated market needs.

Levels of strategy

It is easier to see how the three types of strategy above are applied in practice by examining the three levels of strategic decision-making in organisations: corporate, business and functional (*see* Exhibit 7.2).

Exhibit 7.2   Levels of strategic decision-making

- **The corporate level**. Strategy at this level concerns the direction, composition and co-ordination of the various businesses and activities that comprise a large and diversified organisation, such as Rupert Murdoch's News International or Richard Branson's Virgin empire.
- **The business level**. Strategy at this level relates to the operation and direction of each of the individual businesses within a group of companies, such as Nissan's car assembly plant at Sunderland.
- **The functional level**. Strategy at this level concerns individual business functions and processes such as finance, marketing, manufacturing, technology and human resources.

Each of these three levels has its own distinct strategic concerns and each can draw on a different battery of strategic tools, techniques and approaches to aid them. Nevertheless, it is important to remember that they are interrelated. Traditionally, it has been assumed that the corporate level sets the direction for each of its constituent businesses and, in turn, these set the direction for their various functions. Though this is true for some organisations, it is now recognised that these three levels interact in an iterative and dynamic fashion (Johnson and Scholes, 2002; Lynch, 1997). Therefore, as Mintzberg (1994) argues, just as business level and functional level strategy can be seen as being imposed or driven by corporate level decisions, so corporate level strategy can be seen as emerging from, or being shaped by, functional level and business level decisions and actions. Consequently, it follows that although there are strategies at the corporate level that have their counterparts at the business and the functional levels, it would be wrong to assume that this is always a product of a top-down rather than a bottom-up process.

Moving on to look at these three levels in more detail: at the corporate level, strategy is said to deal with the 'game plan' for managing diversified enterprises whose activities cut across a number of different areas of business (Fleisher and Bensoussan, 2003). It concerns itself with the questions listed in Exhibit 7.3.

Exhibit 7.3	Corporate strategy questions

- What is the mission of the organisation?
- What are its unique attributes?
- How should the business portfolio be managed?
- Which existing businesses should be disposed of and which new ones acquired?
- What priority and role should be given to each of the businesses in the current portfolio?

The central strategic concerns at the individual business level are:

- How should the firm position itself to compete in distinct, identifiable and strategically relevant markets?
- Which types of products should it offer to which groups of customers?
- How should the firm structure and manage the internal aspects of the business in support of its chosen competitive approach?

Functional level strategy concerns itself with the following issues:

- How can the strategies formulated at the corporate and business levels be translated into concrete operational terms in such a way that the individual organisational functions and processes (marketing, R&D, manufacturing, personnel, finance, etc.) can pursue and achieve them?
- How should the individual functions and processes of the business organise themselves in order not only to achieve their own aims, but also to ensure that they integrate with the rest of the business to create synergy?

Given the different concerns of these three levels, it is easy to appreciate the need to integrate the strategies and structures at these three levels. Otherwise, for example, the corporate level may pursue a strategy of diversification whilst the individual businesses are busy concentrating their efforts on fewer products and markets. However, it is also easy to appreciate why in practice it is so difficult for large diversified organisations to identify and pursue a consistent strategy through all areas of their activities (Joyce and Woods, 2001; Lynch, 1997). As argued in the last chapter, strategy formulation and implementation is not a mechanical process that begins at the corporate level and moves in a linear and logical fashion through to the functional level. Strategy formulation is inherently iterative, and aims to optimise the operation of the organisation in its entirety rather than maximising the product of any one particular part. These issues, and the main differences in scope and focus of the individual levels, can clearly be seen by a brief examination of the types of strategy that are pursued at the corporate, business and functional levels.

Corporate level strategy

Broadly speaking, there are six basic forms of strategy that organisations pursue at this level:

- **Stability strategy** (also known as maintenance strategy). As its name implies, strategies under this heading are designed to keep organisations quiet and stable. They are most frequently found in successful organisations, operating in medium-attractiveness industries, which are faced with unpredictable circumstances outside the range of their normal business experience. Because of their markets and products, such organisations believe they have no need to make sudden changes and have the time and position to allow events to unfold before making any response (Wheelen and Hunger, 1989). A typical example would be an established mortgage lender whose business would both necessitate and allow it to take a longer-term perspective.
- **Growth strategy**. This is possibly the most common form of all corporate strategies, and involves either concentrating on dominating one industry (e.g. Vodafone) or growing by diversification across a number of industries (e.g. Virgin). As a number of writers have suggested (*see* Argenti, 1974; Byars, 1984), its basic attraction is twofold. Firstly, it is claimed that there is a strong and proportional correlation between increased turnover and increased profit. Secondly, the performance of senior managers tends to be measured in terms of the annual increase in turnover and profit. There are those, however, who point out that increases in turnover are not necessarily matched by increases in profits and that, given the need to invest to achieve growth in turnover, growth may actually weaken a company's financial health (Byars, 1984; Drucker, 1974).
- **Portfolio extension**. This is another variant of the growth strategy, but is achieved through mergers, joint ventures or acquisitions, rather than through internally-generated organic growth. The first two of these, mergers and joint ventures, allow growth or development to take place, without the organisations involved having to invest the level of resources that would be necessary if they were operating in isolation. The latter, acquisition, is usually resource-intensive but brings immediate gains in the form of an established and, hopefully, profitable business (Byars, 1984; Little, 1984; Leontiades, 1986).
- **Retrenchment strategy**. This strategy is usually only embarked upon when an organisation is in trouble or, because of adverse market conditions, sees trouble ahead. It usually involves a process of downsizing, i.e. cutting back on numbers employed and activities undertaken. In some situations this may lead to selling off the entire enterprise. The general aim, however, is to cut back in order to match expenditure to projected income, and refocus the organisation so as to be able once again to attain prosperity in the future (Bowman and Asch, 1985; Thompson and Strickland, 1983).

■ **Harvesting strategy.** This involves reducing investment in a business or area of activity in order to reduce costs, improve cashflow and capitalise on whatever residual competences or areas of advantage still remain. This approach can be implemented at different rates depending on the urgency of the situation. Slow harvesting means to reduce financial support at such a slow rate that it almost appears to be a maintenance strategy; at the other extreme, fast harvesting can result in budgets being cut at such a rate that it seems almost indistinguishable from liquidation (Harrigan, 1980; Kotler, 1978; Porter, 1980).

■ **Combination strategy.** The above strategies are not mutually exclusive, and can be linked together in whatever combination seems appropriate given the circumstances of the organisation in question. Combination strategies, however, are clearly more appropriate, or at least more necessary, in large multi-divisional organisations where the circumstances faced by the different activities are likely to vary. Therefore, in such situations, organisations may experience a constant flurry of change, where some parts are being run down and/or disposed of whilst new units are being acquired and other areas of the business rapidly expanded (Glueck, 1978; Pearson, 1977).

The above list is not exhaustive, nor can it be, given that each organisation is free to develop its own strategic variant in relation to its own circumstances. As argued in Chapter 6, it is the circumstances of the particular organisation in question that should dictate the type of strategy adopted by its managers, rather than any attempt to copy what has been successful elsewhere. Though Porter's Competitive Forces model can be applicable to all these forms of strategy, the Strategic Conflict and Resource-Based models appear to be applicable more to situations where growth is being pursued or where companies have a strong market position. Nevertheless, it needs to be remembered that it is the precepts and assumptions of Porter and the Positioning school which still dominates the practice of strategy. A further point to note is that all except the first, maintenance strategy, imply fundamental restructuring of the internal operations of the organisation. In such situations, there are likely to be winners and losers, and managers may be more concerned with preserving their jobs and power than choosing the best strategy for the organisation (Mintzberg, 1994).

Nevertheless, in both America and Europe, over the last 20 years, the tide has been turning against corporate strategy, or rather against the large corporate centres responsible for developing corporate strategy and which wielded so much power in the 1970s and 1980s. The case against them is summed up by Koch (1995: 78) who maintains that:

> Anything other than a minimal [corporate] Centre can only be justified if the Centre adds more value than it costs and subtracts from the business. ... Yet it should be clear that ... independent of their cost, most corporate Centres destroy more value than they add.

This negative view of corporate strategy has, perhaps, been most vociferously championed by Peters and Waterman (1982), but has also received strong support from academic researchers (Goold *et al*, 1994). The result of this is that there has been an increasing tendency to devolve responsibility for strategy from the corporate to the business level.

Business level strategy

Whilst corporate level strategies are mainly concerned with managing diversified enterprises whose activities span a number of different areas, business level strategies relate to the different ways that an individual business unit can compete in its chosen market(s). However, it must be remembered that business level strategies are chosen and deployed within the framework of an overall corporate strategy and not in isolation from it, though the degree of freedom allowed to individual business units in this respect will vary from organisation to organisation (Johnson and Scholes, 2002). To this end, the strategic concerns of managers at the business level tend to be, as Hax and Majluf (1996: 46) note:

> ... the mission of the business, the attractiveness of the industry in which the business belongs, and the competitive position of the business unit within the industry. These are the inputs that determine the strategic agenda of a business and lead to the formulation and implementation of its strategy.

Just as at the corporate level, the available business level strategies are many and varied. Rather than attempt to describe them all, we shall examine the main variants by addressing Porter's (1980, 1985) work in this area.

Porter (1985: 11) argues that there are only two 'basic types of competitive advantage a firm can possess: low cost or differentiation'. He adds to these the 'scope' of the business (i.e. the range of its markets) to create 'three generic strategies for achieving above average performance'. As mentioned earlier, these are cost leadership, product differentiation and specialisation by focus.

Cost leadership

The aim of this strategy is to achieve overall lower costs than one's competitors, without reducing comparable product quality. To do this requires a high volume of sales in order to allow organisations to structure themselves in such a way that they can achieve economies of scale. This strategy, to quote Porter (1980: 15), requires the:

> ... aggressive construction of efficient scale facilities, vigorous pursuit of cost reductions from experience, tight cost and overhead control, avoidance of marginal customer accounts, and cost minimisation in areas like R&D, services, sales force and so on.

Product differentiation

This strategy attempts to achieve industry-wide recognition of different and superior products and services compared to those of other suppliers. This recognition can be accomplished through the design of special brand images, technology features, customer service or higher quality, all of which have implications for the structure and operation of companies. Achieving differentiation is likely to result in insulation against competitive rivalry due to securing customer loyalty. The resultant competitive advantage also leads to increased returns, sometimes through making customers less sensitive to high product price.

Specialisation by focus

In this case the strategy is concerned with selecting (focusing upon) only certain markets, products or geographical areas in which to compete. Porter argues that by focusing in this way, it becomes feasible for a firm to dominate its chosen area(s). The method of achieving domination could either be through cost advantage or product differentiation. According to Porter (1980: 15), however, such niche markets must have certain characteristics which separate them out from the market in general:

> ... the target segment must either have buyers with unusual needs or else the production and delivery system that best serves the target must differ from that of the other industry segments.

If the niche market grows, or is incorporated, into a larger market, then market dominance is unlikely to be retained. In such circumstances, the previously dominant organisation will find itself having to compete for market share with others. In effect, the rules of the game will have changed and a different strategy is required – either attempting to gain cost leadership across the entire market, or adopting a product differentiation policy that neutralises other competitors' cost advantage.

Porter's assertion concerning these three strategies is that they are distinct and cannot be mixed. That is to say, it is not possible to pursue successfully a cost leadership strategy and a product differentiation strategy at the same time because each requires different organisational arrangements to be successful. Also, if a firm does not achieve cost leadership, product differentiation or specialisation in its products, services or market, it is bound to produce low profitability and have below average performance. Porter (1980: 41) refers to these sorts of firms as 'stuck in the middle' because they lack:

> ... the market share, capital investment, and resolve to play the low cost game, the industry-wide differentiation necessary to obviate the need for a low cost position, or the focus to create differentiation or low cost in a more limited sphere.

Nevertheless, influential though Porter's work is, there are many who disagree with him on this point (Mintzberg *et al*, 1998a). Hlavacka *et al* (2001), in a study of public and private hospitals in the Slovak Republic, found that those which pursued a 'stuck in the middle' strategy had the best performance. An earlier study by Dess and Davis (1984) also questioned Porter's view. They found evidence to show that businesses with both a low cost and a high differentiation position can be very successful.

Miller (1992) challenged Porter's assertion that firms should pursue only one strategy. He points out that such strategic specialisation can lead to inflexibility and narrow an organisation's vision. In addition, Gilbert and Strebel (1992) point to the success of 'outpacing' strategies. This is where firms enter a market as low-cost producers and then, once established, differentiate to capture a larger slice of the market. This was the approach, i.e. moving from one successful form of strategy to another, used by Japanese companies to capture Western markets in the 1970s and 1980s (Johnson and Scholes, 2002). In so doing, Japanese firms used a Strategic Conflict approach, but this was underpinned by their commitment to building and developing their core competences. Therefore, though Porter's work has tended to dominate the practice of strategic management in Western firms, both the Resource-Based and

Strategic Conflict models have shown their worth. Nevertheless, regardless of which business level approach to strategy organisations have followed, prompted by the success of Japanese companies, there has been a growing interest in the importance of functional level strategy (Hax and Majluf, 1996; Schonberger, 1982).

■ Functional level strategies

The main functional level strategies concern marketing, finance, R&D, technology, human resources, manufacturing/operations and purchasing. Of the three levels of strategic decision-making, the functional level has probably been the most neglected by Western organisations. This is for three reasons. Firstly, the concentration at both the corporate and business levels on the external world, i.e. the market, led to a lack of interest in the internal operation of organisations. The assumption was that the internal world was malleable, and could and should adjust to the priorities set by corporate and business strategists (Schonberger, 1982). Secondly, key elements of functional level strategy, especially concerning finance, marketing, R&D and technology, were in effect determined and constrained by corporate strategists. Indeed, in many organisations, even the human resource strategy was determined at the corporate level. Finally, even though the 1980s saw a renewed interest in functional level strategy, this tended to be one-sided, stressing soft, personnel-type issues. As discussed in Chapter 3, in seeking to understand and emulate Japanese success, Western researchers created the 7 S Framework: strategy, structure, systems, staff, style, shared values, and skills (Peters and Waterman, 1982; Pascale and Athos, 1982). Though acknowledging that the Japanese were strong in and integrated all the seven Ss, the tendency in the West was to stress the so-called soft Ss: staff, style, shared values and skills. This not only continued to neglect areas such as manufacturing/operations and purchasing, but also, in so doing, failed to produce the sort of integrated corporate, business and functional level strategies that were seen as lying at the core of Japanese competitiveness. Once again, this highlights the difficulty that Western strategy practitioners, consultants and theorists have with creating an approach to strategy that goes beyond focusing on particular aspects and takes an all-encompassing view (Mintzberg *et al*, 1998a).

In examining the corporate, business and functional levels, it can be seen that there are only a limited number of forms of strategy that organisations tend to adopt and which flow from the Competitive Forces, Strategic Conflict and Resource-Based models of strategy discussed earlier. However, the appropriateness of any of these for a particular organisation is, as maintained in Chapter 6, related to the nature of the societal, sector, environmental and organisational constraints it faces. These include the stage of product–market evolution, the competitive position the firm has, the competitive position it seeks, the business strategies being used by rival firms, the internal resources and distinctive competences at a firm's disposal, the prevailing market threats and opportunities, the type and vigour of competition, customer needs, and the conditions that financial institutions place on capital availability, to mention only the more obvious ones (Hax and Majluf, 1996; Johnson and Scholes, 1993; Koch, 1995; Thompson and Strickland, 1983). In addition, it must be acknowledged that generic strategies will always give rise to a host of variants and, therefore, at any one time the choice of the most suitable strategy will be a highly complex task. Indeed, this is what one would expect. If choosing and implementing strategy was easy, then all firms would be successful. But, given that success is usually measured in relative terms, by definition not everyone can be successful; therefore, strategy formulation will and must remain fraught with danger and complexity.

A major point to note, though, is that almost without exception, whatever form of strategy is adopted, it will require the organisation to achieve a fit between its external environment and internal structures, culture and practices. Contrary to the views of earlier writers on strategy (such as Ansoff, 1965), if organisations are driven by their external environment, internal arrangements may, and probably do, need to change, often radically, in order to achieve the desired market-place objectives. This once again emphasises the importance of functional level strategy and shows why it should not be treated as a lesser issue. Nevertheless, it should also be borne in mind, as argued in previous chapters, that the possibility does exist for organisations to shape the external environment to fit in with their internal arrangements. The fact that many do not, may say more about the type of organisation they are than the constraints they face.

Types of organisation

Miles and Snow (1978) developed an important variant of the argument on types of strategy. Rather than attempting to classify the types or levels of strategy that organisations can adopt, they classify the organisations themselves as strategic types, based on the rate at which an organisation changes its products or markets. Miles and Snow identified four strategic types (*see* Exhibit 7.4).

Exhibit 7.4   Classification of strategic types

- **Defenders**. These seek internal stability and efficiency by producing only a limited set of products, directed at a narrow but relatively stable segment of the overall market, which they defend aggressively. Such organisations are characterised by tight control, extensive division of labour and a high degree of formalisation and centralisation.

- **Prospectors**. These are almost the opposite of defenders. They aim for internal flexibility in order to develop and exploit new products and markets. To operate effectively in a dynamic environment they have a loose structure, low division of labour and formalisation, and a high degree of decentralisation.

- **Analysers**. These types of organisation seek to capitalise on the best of both the preceding types. They aim to minimise risk and maximise profit. They move into new markets only after viability has been proved by prospectors. Their internal arrangements are characterised by moderately centralised control; with tight control over current activities but looser controls over new undertakings.

- **Reactors**. This is a residual strategy. These types of organisation exhibit inconsistent and unstable patterns caused by pursuing one of the other three strategies erratically. In general, reactors respond inappropriately, perform poorly, and lack the confidence to commit themselves fully to a specific strategy for the future.

Source: Miles and Snow (1978)

Though Miles and Snow's classification has received empirical support from some researchers (e.g. Shortell and Zajac, 1990), others have questioned its applicability across industries (e.g. Hambrick, 1983). Notwithstanding this, as Waldersee and Sheather (1996) point out, there are some similarities between Miles and Snow's work and Porter's work. They argue that successful firms pursue one of two basic types of strategy – innovative or stability.

Organisations pursuing innovative strategies, which embrace both Porter's product differentiators and Miles and Snow's prospectors, seek to achieve success through reducing price competition by offering products and services that are considered unique in terms of their design, brand image and features. On the other hand, organisations pursuing stability strategies, which embrace Porter's cost leaders and Miles and Snow's defenders, seek to achieve success by locating and maintaining secured niches in stable product areas where they can produce higher-quality or lower-price products than their competitors.

Covin (1991) agrees with the proposition that successful organisations pursue one of two forms of strategy, though he labels them entrepreneurial and conservative. The former falls within Waldersee and Sheather's innovative category, whilst the latter falls within their stability category. Covin argues that the strategy an organisation adopts reflects its basic nature (i.e. its culture). Therefore, for Covin, the selection and pursuit of strategy is driven by managerial style and organisational culture. However, Waldersee and Sheather dispute this. Their work sought to examine the relationship between strategy and managerial style, and whether one drove the other. Their conclusion, which was tentative, was that different types of strategy may predispose managers to act in different ways (i.e. managerial style follows strategy type) rather than managers' styles predisposing them to a particular type of strategy. Yet, recalling Chapter 6's discussion of strategy and the constraints on managerial choice, it could be argued that these writers are taking too narrow and deterministic a view. It might well be that, depending on the constraints faced by managers and their perceptions of these, in some situations strategy does require managers to adopt a particular style of working, whilst in other situations managerial style does influence the nature of the strategy adopted. This discussion of the relationship between managerial style and organisational context will be returned to in the concluding chapter of this book.

Before moving on to examine the strategic tools that organisations have at their disposal, it is important to remember that the concept of strategy (whether at the functional, business or corporate level) is contentious. There are many influential writers who do not believe in strategy as a conscious and planned process (e.g. Mintzberg, 1994; Pettigrew, 1985; and Stacey, 2003). This does not invalidate corporate, business or functional strategies *per se*, but it does mean that they occupy a problematic and contested terrain.

Strategic planning tools

This section briefly reviews the main tools that organisations use to select and construct their strategies. By and large, these tools tend to have either a quantitative or a qualitative bias. In the past, and to a major extent even now, it was the quantitative tools (mathematical models) that tended to dominate. This is largely a reflection of the types of strategy organisations adopt, and a (not unrelated) preference for quantification, especially in the financial arena, in the USA, where many of the leading tools of and approaches to strategy originated (Grant, 1991b; Hax and Majluf, 1996; Moore, 1992). It should be noted, though, that other leading industrial nations, especially Germany and Japan, place less reliance on financial and other quantitative measures in determining strategy (Carr *et al*, 1991; Whittington, 1993). For example, the Japanese electronics giant, NEC, never uses discounted cash flow; and though Toyota does calculate cash flows, it does not take account of them for decision-making purposes (Williams *et al*, 1991). Nevertheless, even in the USA and the UK where financial considerations appear paramount, there has been a movement away from the sole reliance on quantitative techniques, and a growing interest in softer, qualitative tools such as scenario/vision-building (Fleisher and Bensoussan, 2003; Joyce and Woods, 2001; Rigby, 2001). In part, this interest in more qualitative techniques is a result of the perceived failure, especially in the face of Japanese competition, of more quantitative approaches favoured by proponents of the Positioning school to deliver a genuine and sustainable competitive advantage. This interest in qualitative techniques has also received a boost from the growing interest in the Strategic Conflict and Resource-Based approaches to strategy. In addition, it forms part of, and has been given impetus by, the move away from quantification and towards the use of more qualitative techniques in organisation theory in general.

As one would expect, there are an enormous range and number of tools and techniques available to the strategist. However, perhaps the ones that have attracted most attention are, in chronological order:

1 the PIMS (Profit Impact on Marketing Strategy) model;
2 the Growth-Share Matrix;
3 the Scenario construction approach.

The first two focus on corporate and business level strategies and are biased towards large organisations that have an established and significant presence in the markets they serve. The third, though, has no such restrictions or biases and can be applied to a wide range of situations.

PIMS

The PIMS (Profit Impact on Marketing Strategy) programme was launched in 1972 and derived from research by Sidney Schoeffler. This was put into practice by General Electric, who wanted to analyse their operations with the aim of identifying those factors determining business success (Schoeffler, 1980). In 1975, Schoeffler founded the Strategic Planning Institute (SPI), which is linked to Harvard Business School, to provide a permanent base for the PIMS work. Since then, PIMS has grown to become the largest privately owned database in the world, comprising over 200 major corporations and some 2,600 individual business units (McNamee, 1985; Moore, 1992).

The rationale underlying the PIMS model is that certain characteristics of a business and its markets determine profitability. Consequently, understanding these characteristics and acting upon them will aid a company to become more profitable. The model is based upon the belief that there are three major factors which determine a business unit's performance: its strategy, its competitive position, and the market/industry characteristics of the field in which it competes (Moore, 1992). Underpinning the model are two key assumptions. The first is that all business situations are basically alike and obey the same laws of the market place (Schoeffler, 1980). The second is that the future will resemble the past, i.e. if certain linkages between strategy and performance resulted in profitability in the past, they will do so again in the future (Buzzell and Gale, 1987).

PIMS operates as a form of club. It collects information from its member companies relating to such factors as market share, profitability, product quality and investment. This information is fed into the PIMS database and is then used to provide individual members with answers to questions such as:

- What profit rate is 'normal' for a given business?
- What strategic changes are likely to improve performance?
- What are the likely effects on profitability, cash flow, etc., of adopting a particular strategy?

There has been much discussion as to the success of the PIMS. Certainly, some of its users, as well as academic observers, regard it as having only a limited use (Ford, 1981; Mitroff and Mason, 1981). The main criticisms levelled against PIMS are as follows:

- It is flawed because it uses historic data, without consideration for future changes. The argument is that, as organisations operate in a dynamic environment, to use the past to predict the future can be a dangerous exercise. Indeed, PIMS seems to be useful only in a stable environment, where companies stick to doing what they know best. It is even questioned whether PIMS can be regarded as a tool for policy in a strategic sense, since it can be argued that the 'variables' it so relies on, such as market share, are performance variables, not strategic ones (Abell, 1977).
- It is highly analytical, but very limited in solving problems. In addition, because PIMS has to use a very large database for its analysis, it is argued that this creates a major problem for managers in terms of absorbing all the data generated. In turn, since the statistical errors in its output are rarely openly discussed, there is a tendency for managers not to question its findings because 'the computer is always right' (Andrews, 1980).
- Its most famous, and contentious, assertion that profitability is closely linked to market share, and that an improvement in market share can be associated with a proportionate increase in return on investment, is of dubious validity. As Smith (1985) maintains, it could equally be argued that both are due to common factors, such as low costs and good management. It is also said to be responsible for inculcating in managers and consultants a belief that low market share businesses are bad and must either increase their market share or withdraw from the industry in question, regardless of profitability (McKiernan, 1992).
- Most of the factors that govern the forecasts of the model are beyond the control of individual companies. Therefore, since PIMS relies heavily on this data, whatever conclusions it reaches about the fate of a company are final. It is neither comforting nor particularly useful to be told that you cannot do anything to turn a negative forecast around, because the factors responsible are out of your hands (Anderson and Paine, 1978).

- It assumes that a rather large set of quantitative variables, primarily of a financial nature, are sufficient to capture the state of a business and from this determine a realistic strategy (Naylor, 1981). Also, as Mintzberg *et al* (1998a: 99) comment, ' ... finding a correlation between variables ... is one thing; assuming a causation, and turning that into an imperative, is quite another.'
- It is based on the premise that business problems are orderly or well-structured. PIMS thus assumes that the determination or classification of the level of the organisation or business unit, the customer group, the competition, the market and the product line to which the analysis applies are all either well-known or well-specified. It is, therefore, not equipped to handle imprecise, let alone conflicting, definitions of business problems (Koch, 1995; Naylor, 1981).

In summary, the main criticisms of PIMS are that it is too mechanistic, overly complex, based on unreliable data, and cannot cope adequately with dynamic and unpredictable environments. Yet, despite the criticisms levelled against it, many researchers still believe that PIMS is a useful tool (Chang, 1997; Johnson and Scholes, 2002; Thompson, 1996). The PIMS method has also been praised for the insight it has given into the true nature of the relationships between strategic variables such as profit and market share. Obviously, managers deal with these variables and their relationships on a daily basis, but attempts at conceptualising these relationships had been lacking until the advent of the PIMS research programme (Anderson and Paine, 1978; Ford, 1981; Mitroff and Mason, 1981).

This is not, however, to minimise the shortcomings of the PIMS model. It is biased towards, and contains data almost exclusively provided by, large and well-established corporations who already occupy significant positions in their markets. Therefore, as Mintzberg *et al* (1998a: 99) observe, its emphasis is on 'being there' or 'staying there' rather than 'getting there'. It follows that its prescriptions may have little relevance for new, small or innovative businesses seeking to enter new markets.

The Growth-Share Matrix

This was the brainchild of the Boston Consulting Group (BCG) in the USA and is arguably the most famous strategic tool ever developed (Koch, 1995). BCG was formed in 1963 by Bruce Henderson, and it is generally considered to be the pioneer of business strategy analysis. The Growth-Share Matrix, or 'Boston Box' as it is colloquially referred to, arose from two concepts developed by BCG: the experience curve and the sustainable growth formula (McKiernan, 1992).

The experience curve, which Henderson claims to have discovered in the 1960s, suggests that 'as the cumulative production of a product doubles, the cost of producing it seems to decrease by a constant percentage (usually 10 to 30 per cent)' (Mintzberg *et al*, 1998a: 97). From this, BCG concluded that if costs fall in relation to production volume (i.e. experience), then cost must also be a function of market share. Therefore, the company with the largest market share should also have the greatest competitive advantage and, it follows, the highest profit margin.

The sustainable growth formula, which was developed by BCG in the early 1970s, is based on the relationship between growth, investment and returns. It maintains that companies with the highest rate of returns on investments can, theoretically, grow the fastest (McKiernan, 1992).

It was bringing together these two concepts (that the company with the highest returns can grow the fastest and that the company with the highest market share should have the highest profit margin) that created the basis for the Growth-Share Matrix. The matrix is based on the assumption that all except the smallest and simplest organisations are composed of more than one business. The collection of businesses within an organisation is termed its business portfolio. Using pictorial analogies (*see* Figure 7.2), it posits that businesses in an organisation's portfolio can be classified into stars, cash-cows, dogs and problem children (Smith, 1985).

- **Stars** are business units, industries or products with high growth and high market share. Because of this, stars are assumed to use and generate large amounts of cash. It is argued that as they, generally, represent the best profit and investment opportunities, then the best strategy for stars, usually, is to make the necessary investments to maintain or improve their competitive position.
- **Cash-cows** are defined as former stars whose rate of market growth is in decline. They were once market leaders, during the early days when the market was rapidly growing, and have maintained that position as the growth tapered off. They are regarded as businesses with low growth but high market share. Because they are entrenched in the market, they have lower costs and make higher profits than their competitors. These businesses are cash-rich; therefore the appropriate strategy for such businesses is to 'milk' them in order to develop the rest of the organisation's portfolio.
- **Dogs** are businesses that have low market share and which operate in markets with low growth potential. Low market share normally implies poor profit, and because the market growth is low, investment to increase market share is frequently prohibitive. Also, in such situations, the cash required to maintain a competitive position

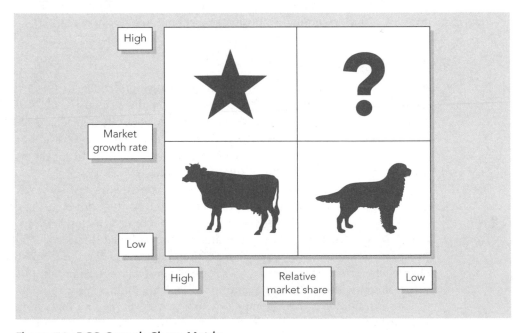

Figure 7.2 BCG Growth-Share Matrix

often exceeds the cash generated. Thus, dogs often become cash traps. It follows from this that, generally, the best strategy is for dogs to be sold off.

- **Problem children** or **question marks**, as they are sometimes labelled, are regarded as having a high growth rate and low market share. They have high cash requirements to keep them on course, but their profitability is low because of their low market share. They are so named because, most of the time, the appropriate strategy to adopt is not clear. With their high growth rate, it might be possible to turn them into stars, by further investment. On the other hand, because of the uncertainty that surrounds this type of business, the best strategy might be to sell them off altogether.

The originators of the Growth-Share Matrix see it as a dynamic tool for assessing and planning market and business developments. For example, the matrix predicts that as growth in their industries slows down, the original stars will move into the position of cash-cows, as long as they keep maintaining their high market share; otherwise they will become dogs. It also claims to predict how cash-cows and dogs will develop as their markets change. Therefore, the Growth-Share Matrix can be used to forecast the development of a business portfolio over a period of time. There are two basic assumptions underlying the matrix: firstly, that those industries, products or businesses that have a high growth rate can be differentiated from those that have a low growth rate; and secondly, that those that have a high competitive position/market share can be differentiated from those that have a low competitive position/market share. Based on these assumptions, the matrix classifies business units or activities according to the growth rate of the industry of which they are part and by their market share (Koch, 1995; McKiernan, 1992; Moore, 1992).

The matrix was widely and rapidly adopted by American corporations in the 1970s. This was for two reasons: firstly, the matrix's simplicity and ease of construction; and secondly, because most large corporations were busy splitting their organisation into strategic business units focusing on particular industries and products. The corporate centres were looking for a simple means of categorising and directing the activities of these units, and the matrix was seen by them as an ideal tool for this purpose. McKiernan (1992), however, argues that its advantages go far beyond merely its simplicity and ease of construction. He maintains that it aids strategic planning, balancing cash flow between businesses, investment decisions, and competitive benchmarking.

Nevertheless, as many commentators note, over the years, the Growth-Share Matrix has attracted its fair share of criticisms as well as praise (Koch, 1995; McKiernan, 1992; Mintzberg *et al*, 1998a). One of the obvious objections to the matrix is the labels it employs for the classification of businesses. Andrews (1980) described these labels as a 'vulgar and destructive vocabulary'. There are, however, other more substantial criticisms concerning the assumptions underlying, and the operation of, the 'Boston Box' (Johnson and Scholes, 2002). The main one is that the uniqueness of an organisation and its problems may not be adequately captured by this or any other tight classification scheme (Hax and Majluf, 1996). This is reflected in the views of Mitroff and Mason (1981), who argue that the critical assumptions underlying the matrix are tautologous and simplistic, e.g. the classification scheme applies to all businesses, because all businesses can be classified as one of the four basic types, or the classification scheme is relevant to all businesses, meaning that all businesses should be able to be classified as one of the four types.

Researchers have also drawn attention to the difficulty in defining and measuring the major variables, such as growth, market share and profitability, on which the matrix relies (Hax and Majluf, 1982; Hax and Nicholson, 1983; Johnson and Scholes, 2002). Hax and Nicholson (1983) also question whether market share really is the major factor determining profitability, and whether industry growth is really the only variable that fully explains growth opportunities? These reservations are echoed by Smith (1985). A further concern is that the matrix assumes that a good portfolio analysis should identify the competitive strengths and the industry attractiveness of each business unit. Alternatives to the Growth-Share Matrix, however, reject this assertion. Instead they start by assuming that these two dimensions cannot be revealed by a single measurement, but require a wider set of critical factors for reliable positioning of the business units (Hax and Majluf, 1982; Hofer and Schendel, 1978). Another reservation, expressed by Fawn and Cox (1985), is the difficulty of defining what constitutes a single business.

One of the most telling criticisms is that many of the companies who have used the matrix found, to their alarm, that all their component businesses were classed as dogs even though these businesses were actually profitable!

Perhaps the key and most common criticism relates to the way the matrix, and other similar tools, have been used. As Hax and Majluf (1996: 313) observe:

> ... matrices tend to trivialise strategic thinking by converting it into simplistic and mechanistic exercises, whose final message is dubious at best. Also the matrix methodology has tended to take strategic analysis and, subsequently, strategic thinking away from managers and into the realms of planning departments.

In the face of such criticisms, a number of modifications were made to the original Growth-Share Matrix. General Electric, for example, in association with management consultants McKinsey, developed the nine-box GE Business Screen Matrix, instead of the original four-way classification (Hax and Nicholson, 1983). A similar system called the Directional Policy Matrix (DPM) was also developed by Shell Chemicals in the UK (Hussey, 1978). Many other organisations, in their turn, developed or employed similar schemes to meet their organisational needs (Koch, 1995; McKiernan, 1992; Patel and Younger, 1978). Nevertheless, portfolio models all seem to attract similar criticisms to those levelled at the Growth-Share Matrix (Fleisher and Bensoussan, 2003; Mintzberg et al, 1998a; Turner, 1990).

Regardless of the merits of these criticisms, even its proponents would not dispute that, like PIMS, the Growth-Share Matrix is primarily suited to well-structured planning problems in which the basic definition of a business unit, product or competition is not an issue (Bowman and Asch, 1985). Unfortunately, because of the uncertain and rapidly-changing nature of business today, such situations are becoming less and less common. This, to an extent, may account for the increase in the popularity of the next approach.

The scenario/vision-building approach

As a way of overcoming some of the criticisms of the above quantitative approaches, scenario-building techniques emerged in the 1970s. The use of scenarios is based on the assumption that, in a rapidly-changing and uncertain world, if you cannot predict the future, then by considering a range of possible futures, an organisation's strategic horizons can be broadened, managers can be opened up to new ideas and, perhaps, the right future can even be identified (Ringland, 1998). Scenarios allow organisations to exercise strategic choice in terms of whether to try shaping the future, adapting to the future or keeping their options open by investing in a range of products, technologies and markets (Courtney *et al*, 1997). Johnson and Scholes (2002: 107) define a scenario as:

> ... a detailed and plausible view of how the business environment of an organisation might develop in the future based on groupings of key environmental influences and drivers of change about which there is a high level of uncertainty.

The rationale for the scenario approach is that it allows an organisation to carry out an intensive examination of its own unique and complex circumstances and needs, rather than attempting to fit itself to standard strategic planning tools such as PIMS and the Growth-Share Matrix (Linneman and Klein, 1979).

Kahn and Weiner (1978) define a scenario as a hypothetical sequence of events constructed for the purpose of focusing attention on causal processes and decision points. For them, the purpose of scenarios is to display, in as dramatic and persuasive a fashion as possible, a number of possibilities for the future. To Norse (1979), scenarios are a means of improving our understanding of the long-term global, regional or national consequences of existing or potential trends or policies and their interaction. Essentially, therefore, building scenarios can be regarded as making different pictures of an uncertain future (business or otherwise) through the construction of case studies, either quantitatively or qualitatively (McNulty, 1977). The quantitative variant of scenario-building, sometimes called the hard method, uses mathematics, models and computers to make pictures of the future, through the production of a vast array of numbers and figures. The main approach, however, is the qualitative, or soft, method, which is essentially intuitive and descriptive; it is based on the resources of the human mind and derived from the methods of psychology and sociology (Joyce and Woods, 2001; Ringland, 1998).

The two main scenario-building approaches that have become well-established are the *Delphi method* and the *Cross Impact method*. However, in recent years, a third approach has become increasingly influential: *vision-building*. Though this bears some relation to other scenario-building techniques, it comes from a different tradition. The scenario approach and especially vision-building have some similarities with the postmodernist view that organisations exist in and represent multiple realities which compete with each other for supremacy (Joyce and Woods, 2001). From the postmodernist perspective, organisations have the ability to create their own reality and, therefore, both scenario- and vision-building can be viewed as processes that assist organisations, or the dominant group within an organisation, to select or construct the reality that most suits their needs. However, scenario- and vision-building are also compatible with the Realist and Complexity approaches described in Chapter 4. For realists, scenarios could provide a way of separating real constraints from the plethora of different perspectives that surround them; whereas for adherents of complexity, they can be used to locate the 'edge of chaos' and the order-generating rules necessary to maintain an organisation in this position.

One of the main functions of scenario-type approaches is that they enable organisations to question the very foundations of their existence, to examine the usefulness of their values and norms. Instead of asking how they can improve what they are doing, they begin to ask: Why are we doing this at all? What alternatives are there? This questioning of basic assumptions is something that is alien to the quantitative tools discussed above, especially given that most managers do not understand the assumptions built into such models in the first place. Indeed, quantitative models appear to remove the necessity for managers to think by providing them with 'answers' rather than information on which to base their own decisions (Hax and Majluf, 1996). The three main qualitative approaches, on the other hand, are designed specifically to make managers think radically about their organisation, its purpose and its future.

The Delphi method

This uses a panel of experts, who are interrogated about a number of future issues within their area of expertise. In the classic application, the interrogation is conducted under conditions whereby each respondent is unknown to the others, in order to avoid effects of authority and the development of a consensual bandwagon. After the initial round of interrogations, the results are reported to the panel and another round of interrogations is conducted. Several rounds may be carried out in this manner.

Results produced from these interrogations may be amenable to statistical treatment with a view to yielding numbers, dates and ranges from them. At the end of the process, depending on whether a quantitative or qualitative approach is taken, either a detailed numerical forecast of the future is obtained, or a more descriptive and richer picture. In both cases, the central tendencies of majority opinion and the range of minority disagreements will also be included (McNulty, 1977; Zentner, 1982).

The Cross Impact method

This is a variation to the Delphi method. It uses essentially the same interrogation method as the Delphi, i.e. a panel of experts; the difference, however, lies in what they are asked to do. The Delphi requires the experts to identify a number of future issues that they think will affect the organisation or business within their area of expertise. The Cross Impact method, on the other hand, asks its panel of experts to assign subjective probabilities and time priorities to a list of potential future events and developments supplied by the organisation. The emphasis is on identifying reinforcing or inhibiting events and trends, to uncover relationships and to indicate the importance of specific events. The accruing data from this exercise are used to create yield curves of the probabilities for each event as a function of time (Lanford, 1972).

Vision-building

As regular surveys by Bain & Co have shown, over the last decade vision-building has established itself as one of the key management tools (Rigby, 2001). Whilst it certainly bears a resemblance to the other scenario-building techniques, it is influenced more by Japanese management practices than by those in the West (Collins and Porras, 1991; Hamel and Prahalad, 1989). Though it is one of the most popular management tools, it is perhaps also one of the least understood and idiosyncratic (Cummings and Worley, 2001; Stacey, 1992). This is perhaps because it is a much less structured approach than the other two scenario-building techniques, and relies more on a company's own management. According to research by Collins and Porras (1997), compelling visions have two components: (a) a core ideology which describes the organisation's core values and purpose; and (b) a strong and bold vision of the organisation's future which identifies specific goals and changes. The major elements of vision-building are as follows:

- the conception by a company's senior management team of an 'ideal' future state for their organisation;
- the identification of the organisation's mission, its rationale for existence;
- a clear statement of desired outcomes and the desired conditions and competences needed to achieve these.

Vision-building is an iterative process that is designed to move from the general (the vision) to the specific (desired outcomes and conditions), and back again. By going round the loop in this manner, according to Cummings and Huse (1989), an ambitious yet attainable future can be constructed and pursued. This owes much to the Japanese, who pioneered the concept of strategic intent on which vision-building is based. The work of Hamel and Prahalad (1989) is of particular importance in this respect. They argued that the strategic approach of Japanese companies is markedly different to that of their Western counterparts. Rather than attempting to lay down a detailed plan in advance, Japanese companies operate within a long-term framework of strategic intent. They create a vision of their desired future – their 'intent' – which they then pursue in a relentless but flexible manner. Hamel and Prahalad quote examples of leading Japanese companies who, in the 1960s, when they were insignificant in world terms, set out to dominate their markets. Honda's strategic intent was to be the 'Second Ford', Komatsu's to 'Encircle Caterpillar' and Canon's to 'Beat Xerox'. These companies then mobilised their resources towards achieving their individual strategic intent. In this, the prime resource they deployed was the commitment, ingenuity and flexibility of their workforces.

Like all approaches to strategic planning, these scenario/vision-building approaches have many criticisms (Cummings and Worley, 2001; Fleisher and Bensoussan, 2003; Joyce and Woods, 2002; Keshavan and Rakesh, 1979; Porter, 1985; Wack, 1985; Whittington, 1993), the main ones being:

- They are prone to subjectivity and bias. The fact that any five management specialists can interpret the same situation in totally different ways is an oft-quoted example of this type of criticism.
- They can encourage retrospection. People's ideas of the future are informed by their knowledge and experience of the past. Since experience is not always the best teacher, scenarios and visions may be based on false assumptions.
- Participants can be strongly influenced in their preference of scenario by their own sectional and personal interests.
- The process cannot be carried out by novices and can, therefore, be time-consuming and expensive in terms of senior management time and outside experts.

- There is much debate about how many scenarios to construct and how they should be used.
- The more radical the vision or scenario, the more difficult it will be to get managers and others to commit to them.
- Visions often require strong visionary leaders, which are in short supply.

Despite these criticisms, the use of scenarios and visions now forms an important part of the managerial tool box (Collins and Porras, 1997; Cummings and Worley, 2001; Leemhuis, 1990; Malaska *et al*, 1984; Smith, 1985).

Therefore, to summarise, there are a wide range of strategic planning tools and techniques available to organisations. In reviewing the main quantitative and qualitative ones, it can be seen that none are without their weaknesses. However, in tandem with the increased use of less prescriptive and more qualitative models of strategy, more qualitative tools and techniques are increasing in popularity.

Conclusions

Just as the aim of Chapter 6 was to examine the main approaches to understanding strategy, the aim of this chapter has been to examine the main approaches to applying strategy. The chapter began by describing the three main models of strategy which organisations have tended to utilise over the last 20 years: the Competitive Forces model; the Resource-Based model; and the Strategic Conflict model. This was followed by an examination of the different organisational levels at which strategy is applied and the main forms of strategic planning tools on offer.

What the examination of these areas has shown is that, in the West at least, it is the approaches, tools and techniques of the Prescriptive stream of strategy that organisations have tended to favour. The continuing prominence of the Positioning school, through the work of Michael Porter, clearly demonstrates the enduring influence of the Prescriptive stream. This of course should not be surprising. After all, the livelihood of those who comprise the Prescriptive stream, whether they be consultants, consultancies, business schools or academics, is dependent to a large extent upon creating a market for its strategic planning products. It is also, probably, the case that when leading consultancies, business schools and large corporations are all arguing for a particular approach, there is enormous pressure on managers elsewhere to follow. To paraphrase the old slogan that 'no one ever got fired for buying IBM', one could also say, 'no one ever got fired for calling in the Boston Consultancy Group or Michael Porter'.

Yet, as this chapter has also shown, the Resource-Based model and the Strategic Conflict model have been growing in importance in the last 15 years. Both tend to be located in and draw support from the Analytical stream of strategy. The Strategic Conflict model has its roots in the perspective of strategy as a battle between warring organisations. As explained, however, its renewed prominence has come both from practical concerns about the applicability of the Competitive Forces model, and from new theoretical insights from areas such as game theory. The Resource-Based approach, on the other hand, owes much to those, such as Prahalad and Hamel (1990), who have sought to understand and explain the Japanese approach to strategy. In both cases it can be seen that strategy is conceived of as an emergent rather than a planned process. Therefore, though the Prescriptive stream of strategy is still extremely influential in determining how managers develop and implement strategies, the influence of the Analytical stream is also growing.

To return, however, to the argument developed in Chapter 6, it would be wrong to fall into the trap of seeing the Analytical stream as being the 'right' way to apply strategy and the Prescriptive as the 'wrong' way, or vice versa. Instead, it may be that approaches from both the Prescriptive and Analytical streams have much to offer organisations, depending on their circumstances or constraints. For organisations with a dominant position in a relatively stable market, an approach from the Prescriptive stream, such as the Competitive Forces model, may be suitable. Likewise for organisations seeking to enter new markets or grow their business over a long time-frame, an approach from the Analytical stream, such as the Resource-Based model, has much to commend it. Similarly, in evenly-balanced competitive situations, the Strategic Conflict model may be more appropriate. This is not, though, to propose a Contingency model of strategy. Rather, as was argued in Chapter 6, what is being suggested is that organisations have a choice; they can seek to influence or mould the constraints they face in order to make them more amenable to the type or model of strategy they wish to pursue. Therefore, as indicated earlier in this chapter when looking at the work of Miles and Snow (1978), the approach to strategy an organisation adopts may have less to do with the merits of the different models on offer and more to do with the type of organisation it is and the orientation of its managers.

Nevertheless, choosing the type or model of strategy to pursue is one thing; implementing it is an entirely different matter. This is especially so if one recognises that the Prescriptive and Analytical streams of strategy have distinctly different, indeed almost opposite, perspectives on implementation. For the former, implementation flows from the organisation's strategic plan. For the latter, the strategy emerges from and is given shape by the actions and decisions organisations make on a day-to-day basis to change and adapt themselves to their circumstances. But no matter which model of strategy one subscribes to, it is only when organisations implement changes that strategies come alive. This highlights the crucial importance of organisational change. Consequently, just as this chapter and the previous one have reviewed the main arguments with regard to strategy, so the next two chapters will review the strengths, weaknesses and implications of the main approaches to change management.

Test your learning

■ Short answer questions

1 What is the Competitive Forces model of strategy?

2 Define the Strategic Conflict model of strategy.

3 Briefly discuss the case for the Resource-Based model of strategy.

4 What are the three levels of strategic decision-making in organisations?

5 Give Miles and Snow's four strategic types of organisations.

6   Describe the Growth-Share Matrix.

7   What is scenario construction?

8   Briefly discuss the implications for organisational change of the following: (a) the PIMS model and (b) vision-building.

■ Essay questions

1   Contrast and compare the strengths and weaknesses of quantitative and qualitative strategic planning tools.

2   To what extent can vision-building be seen as a realist approach?

Suggested further reading

There are a vast number of books on strategy but, unfortunately, no one book covers all the main tools and techniques. However, the following three books, whilst leaning towards the Prescriptive approach, do cover the main strategic planning methods, techniques and processes.

1   Fleisher, CS and Bensoussan, BE (2003) *Strategic and Competitive Analysis: Methods and Techniques for Analysing Business Competition*. Prentice Hall: Upper Saddle River, NJ, USA.
2   Hax, CA and Majluf, NS (1996) *The Strategy Concept and Process* (2nd edition). Prentice Hall: Upper Saddle River, NJ, USA.
3   Joyce, P and Woods, A (2001) *Strategic Management: A Fresh Approach to Developing Skills, Knowledge and Creativity*. Kogan Page: London.

Chapter 8

Approaches to change management

Learning objectives

After studying this chapter, you should be able to:

- describe the main theoretical foundations of change management;
- discuss the contribution of Kurt Lewin to managing change;
- state the core elements of Lewin's Planned approach to change;
- show how Planned change has evolved under the Organization Development movement;
- understand the key differences between Lewin's view of Planned change and that promoted by Organization Development;
- appreciate the benefits of the Planned approach to change;
- list the main criticisms of Planned change;
- describe the incremental, punctuated-equilibrium and continuous transformation models of change.

Exhibit 8.1   The importance of theory

Less means more in engineering

The problem facing diesel engine specialist Royston Marine was clear: it had to increase its production by seven times, immediately, to meet a sudden order from a valued customer, the British Army, for the refurbishment of scores of engines.

The solution, thought Royston managing director Tom Wilkinson, was equally clear – introduce round-the-clock working, with every engineer working on as many engines at once as possible.

He knew, however, that skill shortages and the need to fulfil other orders limited his room for manoeuvre. 'The guys couldn't work 700 per cent harder, they would be carried out on stretchers,' he says. So he was modest – or anxious – enough to seek a fresh perspective from William Callin of the Agility Project, a consultancy based at Durham University's School of Engineering.

In a three-hour discussion in Royston's boardroom in Newcastle upon Tyne, Mr Callin bluntly told Mr Wilkinson that his plan for fulfilling the order was wrong. He made him a bold offer: 'Give me the production line tomorrow for 24 hours and I'll show you what to do.'

Given the challenge facing him, and Mr Callin's record as an automotive engineer, Mr Wilkinson agreed. By lunchtime the next day, Mr Callin had proved to Royston's management that, in manufacturing at any rate, less really can mean more.

Instead of having lots of engines at each stage of the process – stripping, assessing, cleaning, rebuilding, painting and testing – Mr Callin suggested having only one engine at each stage, a 'one-piece flow' approach.

This contradicted Mr Wilkinson's instincts but he could see the virtue in a method of working that was not '10 per cent doing the assembly and 90 per cent looking for the nut'. His employees also warmed to the grand prix pit-stop approach, where a team of workers focus on a single task. 'We could tell straightaway it was going to work,' says diesel fitter Vaughn Blake. 'The parts were all there, so it was much quicker.'

Having previously refurbished one engine a week for the army, Royston was suddenly able to finish more than one a day – without a nightshift and while fulfilling other orders.

Mr Wilkinson is full of praise for Mr Callin and his manager, Karl McCracken, who worked with him to help the company.

For Mr Wilkinson it was the pair's practical, rather than academic, credentials that mattered: 'There were no tutorials, no delay. What we would have done without them, I don't know.' In fact, there is plenty of management theory underpinning Mr Callin's miracle.

Embedding 'living lean' practices, Mr Callin says, means people must adopt new methods with sufficient belief to stick to them when they hit problems. 'When it is going badly, that's exactly when you want it,' Mr Callin says. 'It is showing you your problems.'

Lean manufacturing principles are far from new: the 'elimination of waste' theory underpinning Mr Callin's Royston work was developed by Toyota 50 years ago. The Agility Project engineers appreciate that radical change is never easy.

'You are getting into the way people believe the world is,' says Mr McCracken. 'That takes a long time.' And with so many acute pressures on manufacturing managers, it is hardly surprising, says Mr Callin, that many are nervous of changing methods.

But, he suggests, some managers' hostility to what they see as 'theory' is misplaced. What is batch production, he asks, but the practical implementation of an old theory?

'Everything,' he argues, 'is theory.'

Source: Chris Tighe, *Financial Times*, 17 October 2002, p. 15.

Introduction

This chapter follows on from the discussion of approaches to strategy in the two previous chapters. Chapters 6 and 7 were essentially concerned with approaches to determining and charting an organisation's strategic direction. Underpinning both chapters was the division between the Prescriptive stream of strategy, whose members seek to tell organisations how they should formulate strategy, and the Analytical stream of strategy, whose members seek to understand what organisations actually do to formulate strategy. The former tend to see strategy as a formal, rational and pre-planned process. The latter tend to see strategy as a more messy, less rational, emergent process. Therefore, for the Prescriptive stream, organisational change flows from, and is concerned with implementing, an organisation's predetermined strategy. For the Analytical stream, organisational change is not an outcome of strategy but the process by which it is created and given form. For both streams, change management is vitally important, whether it be for strategy implementation or development.

Consequently, this and the next two chapters will focus on the approaches to planning and implementing the changes required to achieve, or shape, strategic objectives. As the example in Exhibit 8.1 shows, even relatively small change projects require people to discard long-held beliefs; they also need to be robust enough to prevent regression when times get tough. For these reasons, they need to be based on sound and appropriate theory. The chapter begins by describing the theoretical foundations of change management. In particular, it is shown that the three main schools of thought that underpin approaches to change management can be distinguished by their respective concentration on individual, group and organisation-wide issues. This leads on to an examination of the Planned approach, which was developed by Kurt Lewin in the 1940s. This approach dominated both the theory and practice of change management from then until the 1980s, when it met with increasing levels of criticism, especially from those questioning its suitability for organisations operating in dynamic and unpredictable environments. This is followed by a description of the Incremental, Punctuated equilibrium and continuous transformation models of change. The chapter concludes by arguing that, though some of the criticism may be unjustified, the Planned approach does appear to be more suited to incremental change rather than larger-scale and more radical change initiatives.

Theoretical foundations

Change management is not a distinct discipline with rigid and clearly-defined boundaries. Rather, the theory and practice of change management draws on a number of social science disciplines and traditions. Though this is one of its strengths, it does make the task of tracing its origins and defining its core concepts more difficult than might otherwise be the case.

The task is complicated further by the simple fact that the social sciences themselves are interwoven. As an example, theories of management education and learning, which help us to understand the behaviour of those who manage change, cannot be fully discussed without reference to theories of child and adult psychology. Neither can these be discussed without touching on theories of knowledge (epistemology), which is itself a veritable philosophical minefield.

The challenge, then, is to range wide enough to capture the theoretical foundations of change management, without straying so far into its related disciplines that clarity and understanding suffer. In order to achieve this delicate balance, the examination will be limited to the three schools of thought that form the central planks on which change management theory stands:

- the Individual Perspective school;
- the Group Dynamics school;
- the Open Systems school.

The Individual Perspective school

The supporters of this school are split into two camps: the Behaviourists and the Gestalt-Field psychologists. The former view behaviour as resulting from an individual's interaction with their environment. Gestalt-Field psychologists, on the other hand, believe that this is only a partial explanation. Instead, they argue that an individual's behaviour is the product of environment and reason.

In Behaviourist theory, all behaviour is learned; the individual is the passive recipient of external and objective data. Among the earliest to work in the field of conditioning of behaviour was Pavlov (1927). In an experiment that has now passed into folklore, he discovered that a dog could be 'taught' to salivate at the ringing of a bell, by conditioning the dog to associate the sound of the bell with food. Arising from this, one of the basic principles of the Behaviourists is that human actions are conditioned by their expected consequences. Behaviour that is rewarded tends to be repeated, and behaviour that is ignored tends not to be. Therefore, in order to change behaviour, it is necessary to change the conditions that cause it (Skinner, 1974).

In practice, behaviour modification involves the manipulation of reinforcing stimuli so as to reward desired activity. The aim is to reward immediately all instances of the wanted behaviour, but to ignore all instances of the unwanted behaviour (because even negative recognition can act as a reinforcer). This is based on the principle of extinction; a behaviour will stop eventually if it is not rewarded (Lovell, 1980). Not surprisingly, given the period when it emerged, the Behaviourist approach mirrors in many respects that of the Classical school, portraying humans as cogs in a machine, who respond solely to external stimuli.

For Gestalt-Field theorists, learning is a process of gaining or changing insights, outlooks, expectations or thought patterns. In explaining an individual's behaviour, this group takes into account not only a person's actions and the responses these elicit, but also the interpretation the individual places on these. As French and Bell (1984: 140) explain:

> Gestalt therapy is based on the belief that persons function as whole, total organisms. And each person possesses positive and negative characteristics that must be 'owned up to' and permitted expression. People get into trouble when they get fragmented, when they do not accept their total selves ... Basically, one must come to terms with oneself, ... must stop blocking off awareness, authenticity, and the like by dysfunctional behaviours.

Therefore, from the Gestalt-Field perspective, behaviour is not just a product of external stimuli; rather it arises from how the individual uses reason to interpret these stimuli. Consequently, the Gestalt-Field proponents seek to help individual members of an organisation change their understanding of themselves and the situation in question, which in turn, they believe, will lead to changes in behaviour (Smith *et al*, 1982). The Behaviourists, on the other hand, seek to achieve organisational change solely by modifying the external stimuli acting upon the individual.

Both groups in the Individual Perspective school have proved influential in the management of change; indeed, some writers even advocate using them in tandem. This is certainly the case with advocates of the Culture–Excellence school, who recommend the use of both strong individual incentives (external stimuli) and discussion, involvement and debate (internal reflection) in order to bring about organisational change (*see* Chapter 3).

This combining of extrinsic and intrinsic motivators owes much to the work of the Human Relations movement, which (especially through the work of Maslow, 1943) stresses the need for both forms of stimuli in order to influence human behaviour. Though acknowledging the role of the individual, however, the Human Relations movement also draws attention to the importance of social groups in organisations, as do the Group Dynamics school.

The Group Dynamics school

As a component of change theory, this school has the longest history (Schein, 1969) and, as will be shown later in this chapter, it originated with the work of Kurt Lewin. Its emphasis is on bringing about organisational change through teams or work groups, rather than individuals (Bernstein, 1968). The rationale behind this, according to Lewin (1947a, 1947b), is that because people in organisations work in groups, individual behaviour must be seen, modified or changed in the light of groups' prevailing practices and norms.

Lewin (1947a, 1947b) postulated that group behaviour is an intricate set of symbolic interactions and forces that not only affect group structures, but also modify individual behaviour. Therefore, he argued that individual behaviour is a function of the group environment or 'field', as he termed it. This field produces forces, tensions, emanating from group pressures on each of its members. An individual's behaviour at any given time, according to Lewin, is an interplay between the intensity and valence (whether the force is positive or negative) of the forces impinging on the person. Because of this, he asserted that a group is never in a 'steady state of equilibrium', but is in a continuous process of mutual adaptation which he termed 'quasi-stationary equilibrium'.

To bring about change, therefore, it is useless to concentrate on changing the behaviour of individuals, according to the Group Dynamics school. The individual in isolation is constrained by group pressures to conform. The focus of change must be at the group level and should concentrate on influencing and changing the group's norms, roles and values (Cummings and Huse, 1989; French and Bell, 1984; Smith *et al*, 1982).

Norms are rules or standards that define what people should do, think or feel in a given situation. For the Group Dynamics school, what is important in analysing group norms is the difference between implicit and explicit norms. Explicit norms are formal, written rules which are known by, and applicable to, all. Implicit norms are informal and unwritten, and individuals may not even be consciously aware of them. Nevertheless, implicit norms have been identified as playing a vital role in dictating the actions of group members.

Roles are patterns of behaviour to which individuals and groups are expected to conform. In organisational terms, roles are formally defined by job descriptions and performance targets, though in practice they are also strongly influenced by norms and values as well. Even in their work life, individuals rarely have only one role. For example, a production manager may also be secretary of the company's social club, a clerical officer may also be a shop steward, and a supervisor may also be the company's safety representative. A similar situation exists for groups. A group's main role may be to perform a particular activity or service, but it might also be expected to pursue continuous development, maintain and develop its skills, and act as a repository of expert knowledge for others in the organisation. Clearly, where members of a group and the group itself are required to conform to a number of different roles, the scope for role conflict or role ambiguity is ever-present. Unless roles are both clearly defined and compatible, the result can be sub-optimal for the individual (in terms of stress) and for the group (in terms of lack of cohesion and poor performance).

Values are ideas and beliefs that individuals and groups hold about what is right and wrong. Values refer not so much to what people do or think or feel in a given situation; instead they relate to the broader principles that lie behind these. Values are a more problematic concept than either norms or roles. Norms and roles can, with diligence, be more or less accurately determined. Values, on the other hand, are more difficult to determine because group members are not always consciously aware of, or can easily articulate, the values that influence their behaviour. Therefore, questioning people and observing their actions is unlikely to produce a true picture of group values. Nevertheless, the concept itself is seen as very important in determining, and changing, patterns of behaviour.

The Group Dynamics school has proved to be very influential in developing both the theory and practice of change management. This can be seen by the very fact that it is now usual for organisations to view themselves as comprising groups and teams, rather than merely collections of individuals (Mullins, 1989).

As French and Bell (1984: 127–9) pointed out, the importance given to teams is reflected in the fact that:

> ... the most important single group of interventions in OD [Organization Development] are team-building activities, the goals of which are the improved and increased effectiveness of various teams within the organization. ... The ... team-building meeting has the goal of improving the team's effectiveness through better management of task demands, relationship demands, and group processes. ... [The team] analyzes its way of doing things, and attempts to develop strategies to improve its operation.

In so doing, norms, roles and values are examined, challenged and, where necessary, changed.

Nevertheless, despite the emphasis that many place on groups within organisations, others argue that the correct approach is one that deals with an organisation as a whole.

■ The Open Systems school

Having examined approaches to change that emphasise the importance of groups and individuals, we now come to one whose primary point of reference is the organisation in its entirety. The Open Systems school (as mentioned in Chapter 2) sees organisations as composed of a number of interconnected sub-systems. It follows that any change to one part of the system will have an impact on other parts of the system, and, in turn, on its overall performance (Scott, 1987). The Open Systems school's approach to change is based on a method of describing and evaluating these sub-systems, in order to determine how they need to be changed so as to improve the overall functioning of the organisation.

This school does not just see organisations as systems in isolation, however; they are 'open' systems. Organisations are seen as open in two respects. Firstly, they are open to, and interact with, their external environment. Secondly, they are open internally: the various sub-systems interact with each other. Therefore, internal changes in one area affect other areas, and in turn have an impact on the external environment, and vice versa (Buckley, 1968).

The objective of the Open Systems approach is to structure the functions of a business in such a manner that, through clearly-defined lines of coordination and interdependence, the overall business objectives are collectively pursued. The emphasis is on achieving overall synergy, rather than on optimising the performance of any one individual part *per se* (Mullins, 1989).

Miller (1967) argues that there are four principal organisational sub-systems:

- **The organisational goals and values sub-system.** This comprises the organisation's stated objectives and the values it wishes to promote in order to attain them. To operate effectively, the organisation has to ensure that its goals and values are compatible not only with each other, but also with its external and internal environments.

- **The technical sub-system.** This is the specific combination of knowledge, techniques and technologies which an organisation requires in order to function. Once again, the concern here is with the compatibility and appropriateness of these in relation to an organisation's particular circumstances.

- **The psychosocial sub-system.** This is also variously referred to as organisational climate and organisational culture. In essence, it is the fabric of role relationships, values and norms that binds people together and makes them citizens of a particular miniature society (the organisation). It is influenced by an organisation's environment, history and employees, as well as its tasks, technology and structures. If the psychosocial sub-system is weak, fragmented or inappropriate, then instead of binding the organisation together, it may have the opposite effect.

- **The managerial sub-system.** This spans the entire organisation. It is responsible for relating an organisation to its environment, setting goals, determining values, developing comprehensive strategic and operational plans, designing structure and establishing control processes. It is this sub-system that has the responsibility for consciously directing an organisation and ensuring that it attains its objectives. If the managerial sub-system fails, so does the rest of an organisation.

The Open Systems school is concerned with understanding organisations in their entirety; therefore, it attempts to take a holistic rather than a particularistic perspective. This is reflected in its approach to change. According to Burke (1980), this is informed by three factors:

1 Sub-systems are interdependent. If alterations are made to one part of an organisation without taking account of its dependence or impact on the rest of the organisation, the outcome may be sub-optimal.

2 Training, as a mechanism for change, is unlikely to succeed on its own. This is because it concentrates on the individual and not the organisational level. As Burke (1980: 75) argues, 'although training may lead to individual change and in some cases to small group change, there is scant evidence that attempting to change the individual will in turn change the organisation'.

3 In order to be successful, organisations have to tap and direct the energy and talent of their workforce. This requires the removal of obstacles which prevent this, and the provision of positive reinforcement which promotes it. Given that this is likely to require changes to such things as norms, reward systems and work structures, it must be approached from an organisational, rather than individual or group, perspective.

Though the Open Systems perspective has attracted much praise, attention has also been drawn to its alleged shortcomings. Butler (1985: 345), for example, while hailing it as a major step forward in understanding organisational change, points out that, 'Social systems are extremely dynamic and complex entities that often defy descriptions and analysis. Therefore, one can easily get lost in attempting to sort out all the cause-and-effect relationships.' Beach (1980: 138), in a similar vein, argues that Open Systems theory:

> ... does not comprise a consistent, articulated, coherent theory. Much of it constitutes a high level of abstraction. To be really useful to the professional practice of management, its spokesmen and leaders must move to a more concrete and operationally useful range.

Despite these criticisms, the level of support for this approach, from eminent theorists such as Burns and Stalker (1961), Joan Woodward (1965) and Lawrence and Lorsch (1967), is formidable. This is why, as explained in Chapter 2, it has proved so influential.

■ Summary

In looking at the three schools that form the central planks of change management theory, three major points stand out. Firstly, with the exception of the Behaviourists, not only do these schools of thought stand, generally, in sharp contrast to the mechanistic approach of the Classical school towards organisations and people, but also, in their approach to individuals, groups and organisations as a whole, form a link to the emerging organisational paradigms that were discussed in Chapter 3. Indeed, it might be possible to go further and say that these three schools provide many of the core concepts of the new paradigms, especially in respect to teamwork and organisational learning. If this is so, the claim (by Kanter, 1989; Senge, 1990; and others) that these new forms of organisation are a radical break with the past may have to be reconsidered.

Secondly, the three theoretical perspectives on change focus on different aspects of organisational life and, therefore, each has different implications for what change takes place and how it is managed. It follows that any approach to managing change should be judged by whether or not it is applicable to all or only some of the types of change covered by the Individual, Group and Systems schools.

Thirdly, though each school puts itself forward as the most effective, if not the only, approach to change, they are not necessarily in conflict or competition. Indeed, it could well be argued that they are complementary approaches. The key task, which will be examined in more detail later in this and the next two chapters, is to identify the circumstances in which each is appropriate: does the problem or the objective of change lie at the level of the organisation, group or individual? Can any of these levels be tackled in isolation from the others?

The Open Systems perspective may be correct: change at one level or in one area should take into account the effect it will have elsewhere in the organisation. However, whether the perspective adopted is organisation-wide, or limited to groups and individuals, in the final analysis, what is it that is being changed? The answer, surely, is the behaviour of individuals and groups, because organisations are, as the proponents of these perspectives admit, social systems. To change anything requires the cooperation and consent, or at least acquiescence, of the groups and individuals who make up an organisation, for it is only through their behaviour that the structures, technologies, systems and procedures of an organisation move from being abstract concepts to concrete realities. This is made even plainer in the remainder of this chapter and in the next two chapters, where we examine the main approaches to managing organisational change.

The Planned approach to organisational change

Change has always been a feature of organisational life, though many argue that the frequency and magnitude of change are greater now than ever before. Planned change is a term first coined by Kurt Lewin to distinguish change that was consciously embarked upon and planned by an organisation, as averse to types of change that might come about by accident, by impulse or that might be forced on an organisation (Marrow, 1969). However, just as the practice of change management is dependent on a number of factors, not least the particular school of thought involved, so, not surprisingly, even amongst those advocating Planned change, a variety of different models of change management have arisen over the years. Though these were devised to meet the needs of particular organisations, or arose from a specific school of thought, nevertheless, the Planned approach to change is now most closely associated with the practice of Organization Development (OD) and indeed lies at its core. According to French and Bell (1995: 1–2):

> Organization development is a unique organizational improvement strategy that emerged in the late 1950s and early 1960s. ... [It] has evolved into an integrated framework of theories and practices capable of solving or helping to solve most of the important problems confronting the human side of organizations. Organization development is about people *and* organizations and people *in* organizations and how they function. OD is also about planned change, that is getting individuals, teams and organizations to function better. Planned change involves common sense, hard work applied diligently over time, a systematic, goal-oriented approach, and valid knowledge about organizational dynamics and how to change them. Valid knowledge derives from the behavioral sciences such as psychology, social psychology, sociology, anthropology, systems theory, and the practice of management.

Underpinning OD is a set of values, assumptions and ethics that emphasise its humanistic orientation and its commitment to organisational effectiveness. These values have been articulated by many writers over the years (Conner, 1977; Gellerman *et al*, 1990; Warwick and Thompson, 1980). One of the earliest attempts was by French and Bell (1973), who proposed four core values for OD (*see* Exhibit 8.2).

Exhibit 8.2   French and Bell's core values of OD

- The belief that the needs and aspirations of human beings provide the prime reasons for the existence of organisations within society.
- Change agents believe that organisational prioritisation is a legitimate part of organisational culture.
- Change agents are committed to increased organisational effectiveness.
- OD places a high value on the democratisation of organisations through power equalisation.

Source: French and Bell (1973)

In a survey of OD practitioners, Hurley *et al* (1992) found these values were clearly reflected in the five main approaches they used in their work:

1 empowering employees to act;
2 creating openness in communications;
3 facilitating ownership of the change process and its outcomes;
4 the promotion of a culture of collaboration; and
5 the promotion of continuous learning.

Within the OD field, there are a number of major theorists and practitioners who have contributed their own models and techniques to its advancement (e.g. Argyris, 1962; Beckhard, 1969; Blake and Mouton, 1976; French and Bell, 1973). OD also shares some common concepts with, and sits easily alongside, the Human Relations movement. Indeed, Douglas McGregor, a key figure in the Human Relations movement, also played a significant role in the early stages of OD (*see* McGregor, 1967). However, despite this, there is general agreement that the OD movement grew out of, and became the standard bearer for, Kurt Lewin's pioneering work on behavioural science in general, and his development of Action Research and Planned change in particular (Cummings and Worley, 1997).

Kurt Lewin and Planned change

Though there has been an increasing tendency in recent years to play down the significance of his work for contemporary organisations, few social scientists can have received the level of praise and admiration that has been heaped upon Kurt Lewin (Ash, 1992; Bargal *et al*, 1992; Dent and Goldberg, 1999; Dickens and Watkins, 1999; Tobach, 1994). As Edgar Schein (1988: 239) enthusiastically commented:

There is little question that the intellectual father of contemporary theories of applied behavioural science, action research and planned change is Kurt Lewin. His seminal work on leadership style and the experiments on planned change which took place in World War II in an effort to change consumer behaviour launched a whole generation of research in group dynamics and the implementation of change programs.

For most of his life, Lewin's main preoccupation was the resolution of social conflict and, in particular, the problems of minority or disadvantaged groups. Underpinning this preoccupation was a strong belief that only the permeation of democratic values into all facets of society could prevent the worst extremes of social conflict. As his wife wrote in the Preface to a volume of his collected work published after his death:

> Kurt Lewin was so constantly and predominantly preoccupied with the task of advancing the conceptual representation of the social-psychological world, and at the same time he was so filled with the urgent desire to use his theoretical insight for the building of a better world, that it is difficult to decide which of these two sources of motivation flowed with greater energy or vigour.   (Lewin, 1948b)

To a large extent, his interests and beliefs stemmed from his background as a German Jew. Lewin was born in 1890 and, for a Jew growing up in Germany, at this time, officially-approved anti-Semitism was a fact of life. Few Jews could expect to achieve a responsible post in the civil service or universities. Despite this, Lewin was awarded a doctorate at the University of Berlin in 1916 and went on to teach there. Though he was never awarded tenured status, Lewin achieved a growing international reputation in the 1920s as a leader in his field (Lewin, 1992). However, with the rise of the Nazi Party, Lewin recognised that the position of Jews in Germany was increasingly threatened. The election of Hitler as Chancellor in 1933 was the final straw for him; he resigned from the University and moved to America (Marrow, 1969).

In America, Lewin found a job first as a 'refugee scholar' at Cornell University and then, from 1935–1945, at the University of Iowa. Here he was to embark on an ambitious programme of research, which covered topics such as child-parent relations, conflict in marriage, styles of leadership, worker motivation and performance, conflict in industry, group problem-solving, communication and attitude change, racism, anti-Semitism, anti-racism, discrimination and prejudice, integration–segregation, peace, war and poverty (Bargal *et al*, 1992; Cartwright, 1952; Lewin, 1948a). As Cooke (1999) notes, given the prevalence of racism and anti-Semitism in America at the time, much of this work, especially his increasingly public advocacy in support of disadvantaged groups, put Lewin on the political left.

During the years of the Second World War, Lewin did much work for the American war effort. This included studies of the morale of front-line troops and psychological warfare, and his famous study aimed at persuading American housewives to buy cheaper cuts of meat (Lewin, 1943a; Marrow, 1969). He was also much in demand as a speaker on minority and inter-group relations (Smith, 2001). These activities chimed with one of his central preoccupations, which was how Germany's authoritarian and racist culture could be replaced with one imbued with democratic values. He saw democracy, and the spread of democratic values throughout society, as the central bastion against authoritarianism and despotism. That he viewed the establishment of democracy as a major task, and avoided simplistic and structural recipes, can be gleaned from the following extracts from his article on 'The Special Case of Germany' (Lewin, 1943b):

> ... Nazi culture ... is deeply rooted, particularly in the youth on whom the future depends. It is a culture which is centred around power as the supreme value and which denounces justice and equality ...   (p. 43)

> To be stable, a cultural change has to penetrate all aspects of a nation's life. The change must, in short, be a change in the 'cultural atmosphere,' not merely a change of a single item.
>
> (p. 46)
>
> Change in culture requires the change of leadership forms in every walk of life. At the start, particularly important is leadership in those social areas which are fundamental from the point of view of power.   (p. 55)

With the end of the War, Lewin established the Research Center for Group Dynamics at the Massachusetts Institute of Technology. The aim of the Center was to investigate all aspects of group behaviour, especially how it could be changed. At the same time, he was also chief architect of the Commission on Community Interrelations (CCI). Founded and funded by the American Jewish Congress, its aim was the eradication of discrimination against all minority groups. As Lewin wrote at the time, 'We Jews will have to fight for ourselves and we will do so strongly and with good conscience. We also know that the fight of the Jews is part of the fight of all minorities for democratic equality of rights and opportunities ...' (quoted in Marrow, 1969: 175). In pursuing this objective, Lewin believed that his work on Group Dynamics and Action Research would provide the key tools for the CCI.

Lewin was also influential in establishing the Tavistock Institute in the UK and its Journal, *Human Relations* (Jaques, 1998; Marrow, 1969). In addition, in 1946, the Connecticut State Inter-Racial Commission asked Lewin to help train leaders and conduct research on the most effective means of combating racial and religious prejudice in communities. This led to the development of sensitivity training and the creation, in 1947, of the now famous National Training Laboratories. However, his huge workload took its toll on his health, and on 11 February 1947 he died of a heart attack (Lewin, 1992).

Lewin's work

Lewin was a humanitarian who believed that only by resolving social conflict, whether it be religious, racial, marital or industrial, could the human condition be improved. Lewin believed that the key to resolving social conflict was to facilitate learning and so enable individuals to understand and restructure their perceptions of the world around them. In this he was much influenced by the Gestalt psychologists he had worked with in Berlin (Smith, 2001). A central theme of much of his work is the view that '... the group to which an individual belongs is the ground for his perceptions, his feelings and his actions' (Allport, 1948: vii). Also, despite the fact that his work covered many subjects and fields, as Gold (1999: 295) states, 'It is quite clear that Lewin thought of his professional activities as a piece, seamless and integrated.' Therefore, though field theory, Group Dynamics, Action Research and the Three-Step model of change are often treated as separate themes of his work, Lewin saw them as a unified whole with each element supporting and reinforcing the others, and all of them necessary to understand and bring about Planned change, whether it be at the level of the individual, group, organisation or even society (Bargal and Bar, 1992; Kippenberger, 1998a, 1998b; Smith, 2001). As Allport (1948: ix) states: 'All of his concepts, whatever root-metaphor they employ, comprise a single well-integrated system.' This can be seen from examining these four aspects of his work in turn.

Field theory

This is an approach to understanding group behaviour by trying to map out the totality and complexity of the field in which the behaviour takes place (Back, 1992). Lewin maintained that to understand any situation it was necessary that: 'One should view the present situation – the *status quo* – as being maintained by certain conditions or forces' (Lewin, 1943a: 172). Lewin (1947b) postulated that group behaviour is an intricate set of symbolic interactions and forces that not only affect group structures, but also modify individual behaviour. Therefore, individual behaviour is a function of the group environment or 'field', as he termed it. Consequently, any changes in behaviour stem from changes, be they small or large, in the forces within the field (Lewin, 1947a). Lewin defined a field as 'a totality of coexisting facts which are conceived of as mutually interdependent ...' (Lewin, 1946: 240). Lewin believed that a field was in a continuous state of adaptation and that 'Change and constancy are relative concepts; group life is never without change, merely differences in the amount and type of change exist' (Lewin, 1947a: 199). This is why Lewin used the term 'quasi-stationary equilibrium' to indicate that, whilst there might be a rhythm and pattern to the behaviour and processes of a group, these tended to fluctuate constantly owing to changes in the forces or circumstances that impinge on the group.

Lewin's view was that if one could identify, plot and establish the potency of these forces, then it would be possible not only to understand why individuals, groups and organisations act as they do, but also what forces would need to be diminished or strengthened in order to bring about change. In the main, Lewin saw behavioural change as a slow process; however, he did recognise that under certain circumstances, such as a personal, organisational or societal crisis, the various forces in the field can shift quickly and radically. In such situations, established routines and behaviours break down and the status quo is no longer viable; new patterns of activity can rapidly emerge and a new equilibrium (or quasi-stationary equilibrium) is formed (Lewin, 1947a; Kippenberger, 1998a).

Despite its obvious value as a vehicle for understanding and changing group behaviour, with Lewin's death, the general interest in field theory waned (Back, 1992; Gold, 1992; Hendry, 1996). In recent years, however, with the work of Argyris (1990) and Hirschhorn (1988) on understanding and overcoming resistance to change, Lewin's work on field theory has once again begun to attract interest. According to Hendry (1996), even critics of Lewin's work have drawn on field theory to develop their own models of change (see Pettigrew *et al*, 1989, 1992). Indeed, parallels have even been drawn between Lewin's work and the work of complexity theorists (Kippenberger, 1998a). Back (1992), for example, argued that the formulation and behaviour of complex systems as described by Chaos and Catastrophe theorists bear striking similarities to Lewin's conceptualisation of field theory. Nevertheless, field theory is now probably the least understood element of Lewin's work, yet, because of its potential to map the forces impinging on an individual, group or organisation, it underpinned the other elements of his work.

Group Dynamics

> ... the word 'dynamics' ... comes from a Greek word meaning force. ... 'group dynamics' refers to the forces operating in groups. ... it is a study of these forces: what gives rise to them, what conditions modify them, what consequences they have, etc.
>
> (Cartwright, 1951: 382)

Lewin was the first psychologist to write about 'group dynamics' and the importance of the group in shaping the behaviour of its members (Allport, 1948; Bargal *et al*, 1992). Indeed, Lewin's (1939: 165) definition of a 'group' is still generally accepted: '... it is not the similarity or dissimilarity of individuals that constitutes a group, but interdependence of fate.' As Kippenberger (1998a) notes, Lewin was addressing two questions: What is it about the nature and characteristics of a particular group that causes it to respond (behave) as it does to the forces which impinge on it, and how can these forces be changed in order to elicit a more desirable form of behaviour? It was to address these questions that Lewin began to develop the concept of Group Dynamics.

Group Dynamics stresses that group behaviour, rather than that of individuals, should be the main focus of change (Bernstein, 1968; Dent and Goldberg, 1999). Lewin (1947b) maintained that it is fruitless to concentrate on changing the behaviour of individuals because the individual in isolation is constrained by group pressures to conform. Consequently, the focus of change must be at the group level and should concentrate on factors such as group norms, roles, interactions and socialisation processes to create 'disequilibrium' and change (Schein, 1988).

Lewin's pioneering work on Group Dynamics not only laid the foundations for our understanding of groups (Dent and Goldberg, 1999; Cooke, 1999; French and Bell, 1984; Marrow, 1969; Schein, 1988) but has also been linked to complexity theories by researchers examining self-organising theory and non-linear systems (Tschacher and Brunner, 1995). However, understanding the internal dynamics of a group is not sufficient by itself to bring about change. Lewin also recognised the need to provide a process whereby the members could be engaged in and committed to changing their behaviour. This led Lewin to develop Action Research and the Three-Step model of change.

Action Research

This term was coined by Lewin (1946) in an article entitled 'Action Research and Minority Problems'. Lewin stated in the article:

> In the last year and a half I have had occasion to have contact with a great variety of organizations, institutions, and individuals who came for help in the field of group relations.
>
> (Lewin, 1946: 201)

However, though these people exhibited ...

> ... a great amount of good-will, of readiness to face the problem squarely and really do something about it. ... These eager people feel themselves to be in a fog. They feel in a fog on three counts: 1. What is the present situation? 2. What are the dangers? 3. And most importantly of all, what shall we do?   (Lewin, 1946: 201)

Lewin conceived of Action Research as a two-pronged process which would allow groups to address these three questions. Firstly, it emphasises that change requires action, and is directed at achieving this. Secondly, it recognises that successful action is based on analysing the situation correctly, identifying all the possible alternative solutions and choosing the one most appropriate to the situation at hand (Bennett, 1983). To be successful, though, there has also to be a 'felt-need'. Felt-need is an individual's inner realisation that change is necessary. If felt-need is low in the group or organisation, introducing change becomes problematic. The theoretical foundations of Action Research lie in Gestalt psychology, which stresses that change can only successfully be achieved by helping individuals to reflect on and gain new insights into the totality of their situation. Lewin (1946: 206) stated that Action Research '... proceeds in a spiral of steps each of which is composed of a circle of planning, action, and fact-finding about the results of the action.' It is an iterative process whereby research leads to action, and action leads to evaluation and further research. As Schein (1996: 64) comments, it was Lewin's view that '... one cannot understand an organization without trying to change it ...'. Indeed, Lewin's view was very much that the understanding and learning that this process produces for the individuals and groups concerned, which then feeds into changed behaviour, is more important than any resulting change as such (Lewin, 1946).

To this end, Action Research draws on Lewin's work on field theory to identify the forces that focus on the group to which the individual belongs. It also draws on Group Dynamics to understand why group members behave in the way they do when subjected to these forces. Lewin stressed that the routines and patterns of behaviour in a group are more than just the outcome of opposing forces in a forcefield. They have a value in themselves and have a positive role to play in enforcing group norms (Lewin, 1947a). Action Research stresses that for change to be effective, it must take place at the group level, and must be a participative and collaborative process which involves all of those concerned (Allport, 1948; Bargal *et al*, 1992; French and Bell, 1984; Lewin, 1947b).

Lewin's first Action Research project was to investigate and reduce violence between Catholic and Jewish teenage gangs. This was quickly followed by a project to integrate black and white sales staff in New York department stores (Marrow, 1969). However, Action Research was also adopted by the Tavistock Institute in Britain, and used to improve managerial competence and efficiency in the newly-nationalised coal industry. Since then it has acquired strong adherents throughout the world (Dickens and Watkins, 1999; Eden and Huxham, 1996; Elden and Chisholm, 1993). However, Lewin (1947a: 228) was concerned that:

A change towards a higher level of group performance is frequently short lived; after a 'shot in the arm,' group life soon returns to the previous level. This indicates that it does not suffice to define the objective of a planned change in group performance as the reaching of a different level. Permanency at the new level, or permanency for a desired period, should be included in the objective.

It was for this reason that he developed his Three-Step model of change.

Three-Step model

This is often cited as Lewin's key contribution to organisational change. It needs to be recognised, however, that when he developed his Three-Step model Lewin was not thinking only of organisational issues. Nor did he intend it to be seen separately from the other three elements which comprise his Planned approach to change (i.e. field theory, Group Dynamics and Action Research). Rather Lewin saw the four concepts as forming an integrated approach to analysing, understanding and bringing about change at the group, organisational and societal levels. A successful change project, Lewin (1947a) argued, involved three steps:

Step 1: Unfreezing. Lewin believed that the stability of human behaviour was based on a quasi-stationary equilibrium supported by a complex field of driving and restraining forces. He argued that the equilibrium needs to be destabilised (unfrozen) before old behaviour can be discarded (unlearnt) and new behaviour successfully adopted. Given the type of issues that Lewin was addressing, as one would expect, he did not believe that change would be easy or that the same approach could be applied in all situations:

> The 'unfreezing' of the present level may involve quite different problems in different cases. Allport ... has described the 'catharsis' which seems necessary before prejudice can be removed. To break open the shell of complacency and self-righteousness it is sometimes necessary to bring about an emotional stir up.   (Lewin, 1947a: 229)

Enlarging on Lewin's ideas, Schein (1996: 27) comments that the key to unfreezing '... was to recognise that change, whether at the individual or group level, was a profound psychological dynamic process.' Schein (1996) identifies three processes necessary to achieve unfreezing: disconfirmation of the validity of the status quo, the induction of guilt or survival anxiety, and creating psychological safety. He argued that: '... unless sufficient psychological safety is created, the disconfirming information will be denied or in other ways defended against, no survival anxiety will be felt, and consequently, no change will take place' (Schein, 1996: 61). In other words, those concerned have to feel safe from loss and humiliation before they can accept the new information and reject old behaviours.

Step 2: Moving. As Schein (1996: 62) notes, unfreezing is not an end in itself; it '...creates motivation to learn but does not necessarily control or predict the direction.' This echoes Lewin's view that any attempt to predict or identify a specific outcome from Planned change is very difficult because of the complexity of the forces concerned. Instead, one should seek to take into account all the forces at work and identify and evaluate, on a trial and error basis, all the available options (Lewin, 1947a). This is, of course, the learning approach promoted by Action Research. It is this iterative approach of research, action and more research that enables groups and individuals to move from a less acceptable to a more acceptable set of behaviours. However, as noted above, Lewin (1947a) recognised that, without reinforcement, change could be short-lived.

Step 3: Refreezing. This is the final step in the Three-Step model. Refreezing seeks to stabilise the group at a new quasi-stationary equilibrium in order to ensure that the new behaviours are relatively safe from regression. The main point about refreezing is that new behaviour must be, to some degree, congruent with the rest of the behaviour, personality and environment of the learner or it will simply lead to a new round of disconfirmation (Schein, 1996). This is why Lewin saw successful change as a group activity, because unless group norms and routines are also transformed, changes to individual behaviour will not be sustained. In organisational terms, refreezing often requires changes to organisational culture, norms, policies and practices (Cummings and Huse, 1989).

Like other aspects of Lewin's work, his Three-Step model of change has become unfashionable in the last two decades (Dawson, 1994; Hatch, 1997; Kanter *et al*, 1992). Nevertheless, such is its continuing influence that, as Hendry (1996: 624) commented:

> Scratch any account of creating and managing change and the idea that change is a three-stage process which necessarily begins with a process of unfreezing will not be far below the surface.

Lewin and change: a summary

Lewin was primarily interested in resolving social conflict through behavioural change, whether this be within organisations or in the wider society. He identified two requirements for success:

1 To analyse and understand how social groupings were formed, motivated and maintained. To do this, he developed both field theory and Group Dynamics.
2 To change the behaviour of social groups. The primary methods he developed for achieving this were Action Research and the Three-Step model of change.

Underpinning Lewin's work was a strong moral and ethical belief in the importance of democratic institutions and democratic values in society. Lewin believed that only by strengthening democratic participation in all aspects of life and being able to resolve social conflicts could the scourge of despotism, authoritarianism and racism be effectively countered. Since his death, Lewin's wider social agenda has been mainly pursued under the umbrella of Action Research, though in recent years there has been an increasing interest in applying Action Research to organisations (Darwin *et al*, 2002; Dickens and Watkins, 1999; McNiff, 2000). It is also in the wider social arena where Lewin's Planned approach has been most closely followed. For example, Bargal and Bar (1992) described how, over a number of years, they used Lewin's approach to address the conflict between Arab-Palestinian and Jewish youths in Israel through the development of inter-group workshops. The workshops were developed around six principles based on Lewin's work:

> (a) a recursive process of data collection to determine goals, action to implement goals and assessment of the action; (b) feedback of research results to trainers; (c) cooperation between researchers and practitioners; (d) research based on the laws of the group's social life, on three stages of change – 'unfreezing,' 'moving,' and 'refreezing' – and on the principles of group decision making; (e) consideration of the values, goals and power structures of change agents and clients; and (f) use of research to create knowledge and/or solve problems.
>
> (Bargal and Bar, 1992: 146)

In terms of organisational change, Lewin and his associates had a long and fruitful relationship with the Harwood Manufacturing Corporation, where his approach to change was developed, applied and refined. Coch and French (1948: 512) observed that, at Harwood: 'From the point of view of factory management, there were two purposes to the research: (1) Why do people resist change so strongly? and (2) What can be done to overcome this resistance?' Therefore, in both his wider social agenda and his narrower organisational agenda, Lewin sought to address similar issues and apply similar concepts. Since his death, it is the organisational side of his work that has been given greater prominence by his followers and successors, mainly through the creation of the Organization Development (OD) movement (Cummings and Worley, 1997; French and Bell, 1995). However, whilst attempting to remain true to his participatory philosophy, and being greatly influenced by Lewin's work on group dynamics, OD tends to equate Planned change with Lewin's Three-Step model, rather than treating it as an integrated package that also requires the use of field theory, Group Dynamics and Action Research. As a stand-alone approach to change, the Three-Step model is rather underdeveloped, so OD practitioners have sought to develop it further.

Phases of Planned change

In attempting to elaborate upon Lewin's Three-Step model, writers have expanded the number of steps or phases. Lippitt *et al* (1958) developed a seven-phase model of Planned change, whilst Cummings and Huse (1989), not to be outdone, produced an eight-phase model. As Cummings and Huse (1989: 51) point out, however, 'the concept of planned change implies that an organization exists in different states at different times and that planned movement can occur from one state to another.' Therefore, in order to understand Planned change, it is not sufficient merely to understand the processes that bring about change; there must also be an appreciation of the states that an organisation must pass through in order to move from an unsatisfactory present state to a more desired future state.

Bullock and Batten (1985) developed an integrated, four-phase model of Planned change based on a review and synthesis of over 30 models of Planned change (*see* Exhibit 8.3). Their model describes Planned change in terms of two major dimensions: change phases, which are distinct states an organisation moves through as it undertakes Planned change; and change processes, which are the methods used to move an organisation from one state to another.

According to Cummings and Huse (1989), this model has broad applicability to most change situations. It clearly incorporates key aspects of many other change models and, especially, it overcomes any confusion between the processes (methods) of change and the phases of change – the sequential states that organisations must go through to achieve successful change.

The focus of Bullock and Batten's model, just as with Lewin's, is change at individual and group level. However, OD practitioners have recognised, as many others have, that 'Organizations are being reinvented; work tasks are being reengineered; the rules of the marketplace are being rewritten; the fundamental nature of organizations is changing', and, therefore, Organization Development has to adapt to these new conditions and broaden its focus out beyond individual and group behaviour (French and Bell, 1995: 3–4).

| Exhibit 8.3 | Bullock and Batten's (1985) four-phase model of Planned change |

1. **Exploration phase**. In this state an organisation has to explore and decide whether it wants to make specific changes in its operations and, if so, commit resources to planning the changes. The change processes involved in this phase are becoming aware of the need for change; searching for outside assistance (a consultant/facilitator) to assist with planning and implementing the changes; and establishing a contract with the consultant which defines each party's responsibilities.

2. **Planning phase**. Once the consultant and the organisation have established a contract, then the next state, which involves understanding the organisation's problem or concern, begins. The change processes involved in this are collecting information in order to establish a correct diagnosis of the problem; establishing change goals and designing the appropriate actions to achieve these goals; and persuading key decision-makers to approve and support the proposed changes.

3. **Action phase**. In this state, an organisation implements the changes derived from the planning. The change processes involved are designed to move an organisation from its current state to a desired future state, and include establishing appropriate arrangements to manage the change process and gaining support for the actions to be taken; and evaluating the implementation activities and feeding back the results so that any necessary adjustments or refinements can be made.

4. **Integration phase**. This state commences once the changes have been successfully implemented. It is concerned with consolidating and stabilising the changes so that they become part of an organisation's normal, everyday operation and do not require special arrangements or encouragement to maintain them. The change processes involved are reinforcing new behaviours through feedback and reward systems and gradually decreasing reliance on the consultant; diffusing the successful aspects of the change process throughout the organisation; and training managers and employees to monitor the changes constantly and to seek to improve upon them.

The changing nature of Organization Development

In the USA at least, OD has become a profession with its own regulatory bodies, to which OD practitioners have to belong, its own recognised qualifications, a host of approved tools and techniques, and its own ethical code of practice (Cummings and Worley, 1997). The members of this profession, whether employed in academic institutions, consultancy practices or private and public organisations, exist to provide consultancy services. As with any profession or trade, unless they provide their customers with what they want, they will soon go out of business. Therefore, to appreciate the current role and approach of Planned change, it is necessary to say something of how OD has responded to the changing needs of its customers.

As stated earlier, Organization Development is a process that applies behavioural science knowledge and practices to help organisations achieve greater effectiveness. The original focus of OD was on work groups within an organisational setting rather than organisations in their entirety, and it was primarily concerned with the human processes and systems within organisations. However, as French and Bell (1995) and Cummings and Worley (1997) have noted, in recent years there has been a major shift of focus within the OD field from the group to the organisation setting, and even beyond. Three developments in particular caused it to broaden out its perspective:

- With the rise of the Job Design movement in the 1960s (*see* Chapter 2), and particularly the advent of Socio-Technical Systems theory, OD practitioners came to recognise that they could not solely concentrate on the work of groups and individuals in organisations but that they needed to look at other systems. Gradually, OD has adopted an Open Systems perspective which allows it to look at organisations in their totality and within their environments.

- This organisation-wide perspective has caused OD practitioners to broaden out their perspective in two interrelated ways. Firstly, and not surprisingly, they have developed an interest in managing organisational culture. Given that, when working with groups, OD consultants have always recognised the important of group norms and values, it is a natural progression to translate this into an interest in organisational culture in general. Secondly, they have developed an interest in the concept of organisational learning. Once again, as derived from Lewin's work, OD practitioners tend to stress that their interventions are as much about learning as change. Therefore, it is a natural extension to move from group learning to organisational learning. In both cases, however, these developments have tended to reflect and follow on from a general interest in such issues by organisations and academics rather than necessarily being generated by the OD profession itself.

- The increasing use of organisation-wide approaches to change (e.g. culture change programmes), coupled with increasing turbulence in the environment in which organisations operate, have drawn attention to the need for OD practitioners to become involved in transforming organisations in their totality rather than only focusing on changes to their constituent parts.

Therefore, as can be seen, OD has attempted to move considerably away from its roots in group-based and Planned change and now takes a far more organisation- and system-wide perspective on change. This has created something of a dilemma for proponents of OD. As Krell (1981) pointed out, much of what can be conceived of as traditional OD (e.g. Action Research, t-groups, etc.) had become accepted practice in many organisations by the early 1980s. Even some of the newer approaches, such as job design and self-managed work teams, have become mainstream practices in many organisations (Beer and Walton, 1987). By and large, these tried-and-tested approaches still tend to focus on the group level rather than on the wider organisation level. However, the more organisation-wide transformational approaches, which are seen as crucial to maintaining OD's relevance for organisations, are less clear, less well-developed and less well-accepted (Cummings and Worley, 1997; French and Bell, 1995). In addition, the more that OD becomes focused on macro issues, the less it can keep in touch with and involve all the individuals affected by its change programmes and the less able it is to promote its core humanist and democratic values.

It would indeed be an irony if at this time, in pursuit of what is perceived as continued relevance, OD lost sight of its core values. This is because, as Wooten and White (1999) argue, the core values of OD – equality, empowerment, consensus-building and horizontal relationships – are ones that are particularly relevant to the postmodern organisation. If this is the case, rather than loosening its ties with its traditional values in order to retain its relevance, OD should be strengthening them in order to create the 'framework for a postmodern OD science and practice' (Wooten and White, 1999: 17).

Planned change: summary and criticisms

Planned change, as developed by Kurt Lewin, comprised four elements: field theory, Group Dynamics, Action Research and the Three-Step model. It is an iterative, cyclical, process involving diagnosis, action and evaluation, and further action and evaluation. It is an approach that recognises that once change has taken place, it must be self-sustaining (i.e. safe from regression). The original purpose of Planned change was to resolve social conflict in society, including conflict within organisations. In organisational terms, it has come to focus on improving the effectiveness of the human side of the organisation. Central to Planned change in organisations is the emphasis placed on the collaborative nature of the change effort: the organisation, both managers and recipients of change, and the consultant jointly diagnose the organisation's problem, and jointly plan and design the specific changes. Underpinning Planned change and indeed the OD movement is a strong humanist and democratic orientation and an emphasis on organisational effectiveness.

Nevertheless, as OD practitioners have developed Planned change over the years, although the emphasis on organisational effectiveness has remained, a difference has emerged with regard to the participatory and democratic nature of its approach. This is particularly the case with the role of the change consultant. Lewin stressed the need to solve problems through social action (dialogue). He believed that successful change could only be achieved through the active participation of the change adopter (the subject) in understanding the problem, selecting a solution and implementing it. Lewin, and the early OD practitioners, saw the change agent as a facilitator, not a director or a doer. More important even than the solution to the problem, Lewin believed that the consultant's real task was to develop those involved, and to create a learning environment that would allow them to gain new insights into themselves and their circumstances. Only through this learning process could people willingly come to see the need for and accept change.

Bullock and Batten's model, as with other more recent variants of Planned change, gives the consultant a more directive and less developmental role. Their model seems to place a greater emphasis on the consultant as an equal partner rather than as a facilitator; the consultant is as free to direct and do as the others involved. Those involved are more dependent on the change agent, not just for his or her skills of analysis but also for providing solutions and helping to implement them. Therefore, the focus is on what the change agent can do for those involved, rather than on seeking to enable the subjects to change themselves. This tendency for consultants to have a more directive role, and for employees to have a less participatory one, has become even more pronounced as OD practitioners have shifted their focus from individuals and groups to organisations in their entirety.

Lewin's approach to change was greatly influenced by the work of the Gestalt-Field theorists, who believe that successful change requires a process of learning. This allows those involved to gain or change insights, outlooks, expectations and thought patterns. This approach seeks to provide change adopters with an opportunity to 'reason out' their situation and develop their own solutions (Bigge, 1982). The danger with Bullock and Batten's approach, and certainly later developments in OD, is that they appear to be moving more in the Behaviourist direction. As French and Bell (1995: 351) observed, from the 1980s onwards, there has been a growing tendency for top managers to focus less on people-orientated values and more on 'the bottom line and/or the price of stock ... [consequently] some executives have a "slash and burn" mentality'. Clearly, this tendency is not conducive to the promotion of democratic and humanistic values. Instead, the emphasis is on the consultant as a provider of expertise that the organisation lacks. The consultant's task is not only to facilitate but also to provide solutions. The danger in this situation is that the learner (the change adopter) becomes a passive recipient of external and, supposedly, objective data: one who has to be directed to the 'correct' solution. Reason and choice do not enter into this particular equation; those involved are shown the solution and motivated, through the application of positive reinforcement, to adopt it on a permanent basis (Skinner, 1974). This appears to be especially the case with the newer, organisation-wide and transformational approaches about which even supporters of OD admit there is some confusion (Cummings and Worley, 1997).

Therefore, the move away from its original focus and area of expertise, i.e. the human processes involved in the functioning of individuals and groups in organisations, coupled with a more hostile business environment, appear to be eroding the values which Lewin and the early pioneers of OD saw as being central to successful change.

As might be expected, these developments in OD, as well as newer perspectives on organisations, have led many to question not only particular aspects of the Planned approach to change but also the utility and practicality of the approach as a whole. The main criticisms levelled against the Planned approach to change are, according to Burnes and Salauroo (1995) as follows.

Firstly, as Wooten and White (1999: 8) observe, 'Much of the existing OD technology was developed specifically for, and in response to, top-down, autocratic, rigid, rule-based organizations operating in a somewhat predictable and controlled environment'. Arising from this is the assumption that, as Cummings and Huse (1989: 51) pointed out, 'an organization exists in different states at different times and that planned movement can occur from one state to another'. An increasing number of writers, however, especially from the complexity perspective, argue that, in the turbulent and chaotic world in which we live, such assumptions are increasingly tenuous and that organisational change is more a continuous and open-ended process than a set of discrete and self-contained events (Arndt and Bigelow, 2000; Bechtold, 1997; Black, 2000; Brown and Eisenhardt, 1997; Garvin, 1993; Kanter *et al*, 1997; Peters, 1997a; Stacey, 2003).

Secondly, and on a similar note, a number of writers have criticised the Planned approach for its emphasis on incremental and isolated change and its inability to incorporate radical, transformational change (Dawson, 1994; Dunphy and Stace, 1993; Harris, 1985; Miller and Friesen, 1984; Schein, 1985; Pettigrew, 1990a, 1990b).

Thirdly, the Planned change approach is seen as being based on the assumption that common agreement can be reached, and that all the parties involved in a particular change project have a willingness and interest in doing so (Dawson, 1994; Hatch, 1997; Wilson, 1992). This assumption appears to ignore organisational conflict and politics, or at least assumes that problem issues can be easily identified and resolved. However, given what was said of organisational power, politics and vested interests in Chapter 5, such a view is difficult to substantiate. Also, as Stace and Dunphy (1994) have shown, there is a wide spectrum of change situations, ranging from fine-tuning to corporate transformation, and an equally wide range of ways of managing these, ranging from collaborative to coercive. Though Planned change may be suitable to some of these situations, it is clearly much less applicable to situations where more directive approaches may be required, such as when a crisis, requiring rapid and major change, does not allow scope for widespread involvement or consultation.

Fourthly, it assumes that one type of approach to change is suitable for all organisations, all situations and all times. Dunphy and Stace (1993: 905), on the other hand, argue that:

> Turbulent times demand different responses in varied circumstances. So managers and consultants need a model of change that is essentially a 'situational' or 'contingency model', one that indicates how to vary change strategies to achieve 'optimum fit' with the changing environment.

In supporting and adding to this list of criticisms, many writers have drawn attention to the increasing frequency and magnitude of change and, whilst the Planned approach may be applicable to incremental change, it is less relevant to larger-scale and more radical transformational changes that many organisations have undergone or are experiencing (Brown and Eisenhardt, 1997; Hayes, 2002). The same can be said in relation to the three schools of thought which provide the heoretical underpinnings of organisational change that were discussed at the beginning of this chapter. Planned change is certainly applicable to the individual and group context, but seems less appropriate for system-wide change.

Leading OD advocates, as might be predicted, dispute these criticisms and point to the way that Planned change has tried to incorporate issues such as power and politics and the need for organisational transformation (Cummings and Worley, 1997; French and Bell, 1995). Also, as Burnes (1998b) argues, there is a need to draw a distinction between Lewin's original analytical approach to Planned change and the more prescriptive and practitioner-orientated variants that have been developed by the OD profession subsequently. In defence of Lewin, Burnes (2004) points out that Lewin did not ignore the importance of power and politics, nor did he fail to recognise that change could be fast and dramatic. In particular, Burnes argues that Lewin did not see organisations as stable and changeless entities, but that his view was not dissimilar to that of many of his critics. As already mentioned, a number of proponents of complexity theory have also made similar observations. This is a point which will be returned to towards the end of the next chapter. Nevertheless, even taking these points into account, it has to be recognised that Lewin never saw Planned change as being applicable to all change situations, and it was certainly never meant to be used in situations where rapid, coercive and/or wholesale change was required. Nevertheless, from the late 1970s onwards, the incremental, small-group view of change favoured by Lewin and his supporters began to be replaced by one which saw change as being more frequent and of greater magnitude.

The frequency and magnitude of organisational change

As has been mentioned often in this book, the view which many leading commentators take is that organisations are changing at a faster pace and in a more fundamental way than ever before (Kanter *et al*, 1997; Kotter, 1996; Peters, 1997a). These commentators judge the present level of organisational change to be unprecedented, although –

as Chapter 6 noted – the history of the past 200 years could well be characterised as successive periods of unprecedented change. Obviously, an appreciation of whether organisational change is to be a continuing feature or a one-off event and whether it is on a small or large scale play a key role in judging the appropriateness of particular approaches to managing change. It is, therefore, important to go beyond the tabloid-like headlines thrown up by writers such as Tom Peters and to examine the main models of organisational change that are currently being promoted and, also, to recognise that there are strong disagreements about the nature and pace of change that organisations experience. In this respect, there are three current models that are prominent in the literature.

■ The incremental model of change

Advocates of this view see change as being a process whereby individual parts of an organisation deal incrementally and separately with one problem and one goal at a time. By managers responding to pressures in their local internal and external environments in this way, over time, their organisations become transformed. As Miller and Friesen (1984: 222) state:

> The incrementalist perspective on change has been around a, relatively, long time. It stems from the work of Lindblom (1959) and Cyert and March (1963), and was further developed by Hedberg et al (1976) and especially Quinn (1980b and 1982). Quinn argues that strategic change is best viewed as 'muddling through with purpose,' using a continuous, evolving and consensus building approach.

As Pettigrew et al (1992: 14) note, 'The received wisdom therefore is that change will take place through successive, limited and negotiated shifts'. Though Quinn (1980b, 1982) and others have marshalled considerable support for the incrementalist perspective from Western sources, and though Planned change sits very comfortably with this view, in recent years the pre-eminent exemplars of incremental change have been Japanese companies (Hamel and Prahalad, 1989). As described in Chapter 3, Japanese companies have an enviable track record of achieving fierce competitiveness through pursuing incremental change year in, year out. Dunphy and Stace (1992) also advocated this approach for Western companies, arguing for a form of managed incrementalism that avoids both the stagnation engendered by fine-tuning and the brutality associated with rapid corporate transformations. However, as Mintzberg (1978) argued, though organisations do go through long periods of incremental change, these are often interspersed with brief periods of rapid and revolutionary change. Indeed, given the turbulence of the last 20 years, some writers have argued that it is now the periods of stability which are brief and the revolutionary change periods which are long, at least in Western firms (Handy, 1989). Not surprisingly, this has led to an increased interest in how organisations move between periods of stability and instability.

■ The punctuated equilibrium model of organisational transformation

This somewhat inelegantly-titled approach to change:

> ... depicts organizations as evolving through relatively long periods of stability (equilibrium periods) in their basic patterns of activity that are punctuated by relatively short bursts of fundamental change (revolutionary periods). Revolutionary periods substantively disrupt established activity patterns and install the basis for new equilibrium periods.
>
> (Romanelli and Tushman, 1994: 1141)

The punctuated equilibrium model is associated with the work of Miller and Friesen (1984), Tushman and Romanelli (1985), and Gersick (1991). The inspiration for this model arises from two sources: first, from the challenge to Charles Darwin's gradual-ist model of evolution in the natural sciences: Steven Jay Gould (1989), in particular, mounted a case for a punctuated equilibrium model of evolution; and second, from the assertion that whilst most organisations do appear to fit the incrementalist model of change for a period of time, there does come a point when they go through a period of rapid and fundamental change (Gersick, 1991). Though this view began to take hold in the 1980s, it is by no means new. In the 1970s, Greiner (1972) observed that as organisations grow, they go through long periods of evolutionary change and short, sharp bursts of revolutionary change. Indeed, Lewin made a similar observation in the 1940s (Lewin, 1947a; Kippenberger, 1998a). However, as even Romanelli and Tushman (1994: 1142) admit, 'Despite the growing prominence and pervasiveness of punctuated equilibrium theory, little research has explored the empirical validity of the model's basic arguments.' This has led some to reject both the incremental and punctuated models of change (Brown and Eisenhardt, 1997).

■ The continuous transformation model of change

The argument put forward by proponents of this model is that, in order to survive, organisations must develop the ability to change themselves continuously in a fundamental manner. This is particularly the case in fast-moving sectors such as retail where, as Greenwald (1996: 54) notes, 'If you look at the best retailers out there, they are constantly reinventing themselves.' Brown and Eisenhardt (1997: 1) maintain that:

> For firms such as Intel, Wal-Mart, 3M, Hewlett-Packard and Gillette, the ability to change rapidly and continuously, especially by developing new products, is not only a core competence, it is also at the heart of their cultures. For these firms, change is not the rare, episodic phenomenon described by the punctuated equilibrium model but, rather, it is endemic to the way these organizations compete. Moreover, in high-velocity industries with short product cycles and rapidly-shifting competitive landscapes, the ability to engage in rapid and relentless continuous change is a crucial capability for survival ...

The underpinning rationale for the continuous transformation model is that the environment in which organisations operate is changing, and will continue to change, rapidly, radically and unpredictably. Only by continuous transformation will organisations be able to keep aligned with their environment and thus survive. Though this view has many adherents, there are two groups who are its main promoters. The first is the Culture–Excellence school. This group, especially Tom Peters (1997a, 1997b) and Rosabeth Moss Kanter *et al* (1997), have been arguing for a continuous transformation model of change since the early 1980s. However, as noted in Chapter 3, they provide little solid empirical evidence to support their view. The second group are those who seek to apply complexity theories to organisations. As described in Chapter 4, complexity theories are concerned with the emergence of order in dynamic non-linear systems operating at the edge of chaos: in other words, systems that are constantly changing and where the laws of cause and effect appear not to apply (Beeson and Davis, 2000; Haigh, 2002; Wheatley, 1992b). Order in such systems manifests itself in a largely unpredictable fashion, in which patterns of behaviour emerge in irregular but similar forms through a process of self-organisation, which is governed by a small number of simple order-generating rules (Black, 2000; MacIntosh and MacLean, 2001; Tetenbaum, 1998). Many writers have argued that organisations are also complex systems which, to survive, need to operate at the edge of chaos and have to respond continuously to changes in their environments through just such a process of spontaneous self-organising change (Hayles, 2000; Lewis, 1994; Macbeth, 2002; MacIntosh and MacLean, 1999, 2001; Stacey, 2003; Stickland, 1998).

The problems with this perspective, as Stickland (1998) shows, are that (a) it is not clear that one can readily apply theories from the physical sciences to the social sciences, as is demonstrated by the fact that even proponents of its use in the social sciences are equivocal on this point; and (b) there is little strong evidence to support the complexity view.

Nevertheless, as the next chapter will show, there is growing support for both the continuous transformation and punctuated-equilibrium models. In turn this has led to a search for what are seen as more appropriate approaches to change than the one offered by Lewin and the OD movement.

Conclusions

This chapter began by examining the theoretical foundations of change management and it was argued that in judging the applicability of approaches to managing change, one should assess whether they apply to individual, group or system-wide change.

The chapter then proceeded to examine the origins and development of the Planned approach to change, which dominated the theory and practice of change management from the 1940s to the 1980s. It was shown that the foundations of Planned change were laid by Kurt Lewin. After his death, however, it was taken up, and over time significantly modified, by the Organization Development movement in the USA. In terms of organisational change, the Planned approach focused upon resolving group conflicts and improving group performance by bringing together managers, employees and a change consultant. Through a process of learning, those involved gain new insights into their situation and are thus able to identify more effective ways of working together. Advocates of Planned change, especially the earlier ones, believe that group learning and individual development are at least as important as the actual change process itself. This, in part, arises from the humanist and democratic values that underpin Planned change and which derive from Kurt Lewin's background and beliefs.

Under the auspices of Organization Development, however, the influence of these values has lessened. The focus of Planned change has moved from conflict resolution to performance enhancement, as Organization Development has grown into a thriving consultancy industry aimed almost exclusively at resolving problems within client organisations. Therefore, as was the case with the approaches to strategy discussed in Chapters 6 and 7, it is possible to draw a distinction between those proponents of Planned change, especially Lewin and early OD pioneers, who take an analytical approach, and those who take a more prescriptive approach, especially those whose livelihood depends upon their selling their services as change consultants.

In the 1960s and 1970s, Planned change, with its increasing array of tools, techniques and practitioners, became the dominant approach to managing organisational change. From the 1980s onwards, however, Planned change has faced increasing levels of criticism, the main ones relating to its perceived inability to cope with radical, coercive change situations or ones where power and politics are dominant. In its defence, as described earlier, there are proponents of Planned change who would argue that these criticisms are not valid, that it is a more flexible and holistic approach than its detractors would acknowledge, and that it is capable of incorporating transformational change (Cummings and Worley, 2001; French and Bell, 1995; McLennan, 1989; Mirvis, 1990). There are also those who believe that many of the criticisms of Lewin's work are misplaced (Burnes, 2004). Nevertheless, partly as a consequence of these criticisms of the Planned approach, and partly in the context of newer perspectives on change such as the punctuated-equilibrium and continuous transformation models, new approaches to change have been gaining ground in recent years, one of which in particular has come to dominate the literature. Though aspects of it have been given a number of different labels, such as continuous improvement or organisational learning, it is more often referred to as the *Emergent* approach to change. The Emergent approach tends to see change as driven from the bottom up rather than from the top down; it stresses that change is an open-ended and continuous process of adaptation to changing conditions and circumstances; and it also sees the process of change as a process of learning, and not just a method of changing organisational structures and practices (Dawson, 1994; Mabey and Mayon-White, 1993; Wilson, 1992). Therefore, the next chapter will examine the principles and merits of the Emergent approach to change.

Test your learning

■ Short answer questions

1   What are the main theoretical foundations of change management?

2   What are the key differences between the main theoretical foundations of change management?

3   How did Kurt Lewin define the term 'Planned change'?

4   How do contemporary OD practitioners define Planned change?

5   What are the ethical principles which underpin Planned change?

6   What are the main criticisms of the Planned approach?

7   Evaluate the validity of the main criticisms of Planned change.

8   Discuss the implications of the Planned approach for managerial behaviour.

■ Essay questions

1   What was Kurt Lewin's main contribution to change management?

2   How has the OD movement sought to update its approach to organisational change? To what extent has it been successful?

Suggested further reading

1   Burnes, B (2004) Kurt Lewin and the Planned approach to change: a re-appraisal. *Journal of Management Studies*, **41**(6).
     Marrow, AJ (1969) *The Practical Theorist: The Life and Work of Kurt Lewin*. Teachers College Press (1977 edition): New York.
     Taken together, the article and the book provide a comprehensive examination of Lewin's life and work.

2   Cummings, TG and Worley, CG (2001) *Organization Development and Change* (7th edition). South-Western College Publishing: Mason, OH, USA.
     French, WL and Bell, CH (1995) *Organization Development* (5th edition). Prentice Hall: Englewood Cliffs, NJ, USA.
     These two books provide a comprehensive guide to the origins and practices of OD.

Chapter 9

Developments in change management

The Emergent approach and beyond

Learning objectives

After studying this chapter, you should be able to:

- list the reasons for the decline in popularity of the Planned approach to change;
- discuss the main elements of the Emergent approach to change;
- describe the processualist approach to change;
- explain the implications of complexity theories for organisational change;
- state the strengths and weaknesses of the Emergent approach;
- understand how Emergent change can be applied in practice;
- appreciate the role of the change agent.

Exhibit 9.1	Continuous change at Citigroup

Weill wields his power at Citigroup: revamp represents ongoing structural changes

Citigroup has proved itself an earnings powerhouse since the company was formed by the 1998 merger between Sandy Weill's Travelers and John Reed's Citicorp. However, Citigroup's announcement this week of a management reshuffle – the latest in a series of such exercises – is a reminder that for all the company's success, it remains a work in progress in a structural sense. The upheaval is not necessarily a bad thing. Mr Weill, the chairman and chief executive, is famously unsentimental about his businesses and he has shown an ability over the decades to redeploy capital – and executives – to increase profits. But the repeated changes in the chain of command at Citigroup also underscore the difficulty of running such a vast enterprise and are sure to reinforce anxieties about what will happen to the company when Mr Weill, 69, finally leaves. 'They have had several restructurings in a not very long period,' said Michael Mayo, Prudential Securities banking analyst. 'With a firm this complex, I think we are finding that the need for more management reorganisations goes up.' Making sense of the latest reshuffle is tricky because Mr Weill is doing several things at the same time. Broadly speaking, the revamp represents a fine-tuning of Citigroup's efforts to create a workable 'matrix' structure – allowing for management along product and geographical lines. As arcane as that sounds, it is a crucial issue for Mr Weill. A big reason he merged his company with Mr Reed's was to find ways to sell more Travelers products outside the US, using Citicorp's wealth of overseas connections. This week's changes were described by Mr Weill as an attempt 'to create a more open matrix', giving product executives more global power and pushing geographical managers to help identify opportunities. In the process, Mr Weill is addressing a more recent concern – the admitted failure of Citigroup's risk management systems to anticipate the severity of the Argentine financial crisis. The emerging markets group is being dismantled as part of the latest revamp and Victor Menezes, its leader, is being shifted into a strategic role. At the same time, Mr Weill is making often subtle changes in the roles of several other executives who occupy positions just below his in the Citigroup structure. Analysts said the changes were less indicative of a shift in the balance of power – or the anointment of a successor – than a demonstration of Mr Weill's continuing command. For example, Deryck Maughan, who negotiated the sale of Salomon Brothers to Travelers in 1997 and has since become a close aide to Mr Weill, will be given oversight of all five of Citigroup's international regions. But Mr Maughan's authority could be tempered by the greater global role assigned to the leaders of Citigroup's product lines – Bob Willumstad, consumer banking; Michael Carpenter, investment banking; and Tom Jones, investment management. Mr Willumstad, who was named president in January – filling a post that has been left open since Jamie Dimon, Mr Weill's heir apparent, was fired in 1998 – will also gain power in some areas and lose it in others. As a product leader, Mr Willumstad will have greater global responsibilities. But at the same time he will cede authority for finance and human resources to Chuck Prince, Mr Weill's trusted chief operating officer, who is also being given the crucial job of looking after risk management. At Citigroup, in other words, the situation is still status quo: Mr Weill giveth and Mr Weill taketh away.

Source: Gary Silverman, *Financial Times*, 13 June 2002, p. 30.

Introduction

As the case of Citigroup shows (*see* Exhibit 9.1), organisations today are seen less and less as stable and enduring institutions, and more and more as 'work in progress' subject to continuing and continuous change. Chapter 8 described how the Planned approach to change dominated the theory and practice of change management from the late 1940s to the early 1980s. Since then, however, the Emergent approach, which starts from the assumption that change is a continuous, open-ended and unpredictable process of aligning and re-aligning an organisation to its changing environment, has taken over from the Planned approach as the dominant approach to change. Advocates of Emergent change argue that it is more suitable to the turbulent environment in which firms such as Citigroup operate because, unlike the Planned approach, it recognises that it is vital for organisations to adapt their internal practices and behaviour in real-time to changing external conditions. Furthermore, and just as importantly, it sees change as a political process whereby different groups in an organisation struggle to protect or enhance their own interests.

This chapter begins by presenting the case against the Planned approach. It then goes on to examine the main arguments for, and characteristics of, Emergent change, including those put forward by complexity theorists. This will show that, although they do not always agree with each other, the advocates of Emergent change are united by the emphasis they place on organisational structure, culture and learning, and their perspective on managerial behaviour and the role of power and politics in the change process. Following this, the chapter presents the recipes for change put forward by proponents of Emergent change. It then goes on to examine the different perspectives on and the role of change agents. In summarising the Emergent approach, it is argued that, though it has a number of distinct strengths, like Planned change it is a flawed and partial approach to change. In conclusion, it is argued that despite the large body of literature devoted to the topic of change management, and the many tools and techniques available to change agents, there is considerable debate and little agreement regarding the most appropriate approach. Though it is clear that neither the Emergent approach nor the Planned approach is suitable for all situations and circumstances.

The case against the Planned approach to organisational change

As was shown in Chapter 8, the Planned approach to change has been, and remains, highly influential. It is still far and away the best developed, documented and supported approach to change. This is because of the custodianship of the Organization Development movement in the USA. OD has taken Kurt Lewin's original concept of Planned change and turned it into a thriving consultancy industry with its own standards, accreditation procedures and membership (Cummings and Worley, 1997). In doing so, Lewin's conception of Planned change as applying to small-group, human-centred change has been extended to include organisation-wide change initiatives. This has led to some confusion between Planned (participative) change as promoted by the OD movement and Planned (transformational) change as promoted by some elements of the strategic planning movement (Beer and Nohria, 2000; Mintzberg et al, 1998).

This section, following on from the previous chapter, is concerned with the Planned approach to change as promoted by Lewin and the OD movement and which, from the late 1940s to the early 1980s, was the dominant approach to change, especially in the USA. Nevertheless, as shown in Chapter 8, from the early 1980s onwards, it has faced increasing levels of criticism as to its appropriateness and efficacy, especially in terms of its ability to cope with continuous change, its emphasis on incremental change, its neglect of organisational conflict and politics, and its advocacy of a 'one best way' approach to change.

It was the rise of Japanese competitiveness and the apparent eclipse of Western industry in the late 1970s that precipitated the questioning of existing approaches to structuring, managing and changing organisations (e.g. Pascale and Athos, 1982; Peters and Waterman, 1982). The proponents of Culture–Excellence were the most vociferous critics of the existing order, arguing that Western organisations were bureaucratic, inflexible and stifled innovation. Their view of Planned change is, probably, best summed up by Kanter et al's (1992: 10) scathing comment that:

> Lewin's model was a simple one, with organizational change involving three stages; unfreezing, changing and refreezing ... This quaintly linear and static conception – the organization as an ice cube – is so wildly inappropriate that it is difficult to see why it has not only survived but prospered. ... Suffice it to say here, first, that organizations are never frozen, much less refrozen, but are fluid entities with many 'personalities'. Second, to the extent that there are stages, they overlap and interpenetrate one another in important ways.

In place of Lewin's 'wildly inappropriate' model of change, the Culture–Excellence proponents have called, as described in Chapter 3, for organisations to adopt flexible cultures that promote innovation and entrepreneurship and encourage bottom-up, flexible, continuous and cooperative change. However, Culture–Excellence advocates recognised that top-down coercion, and rapid transformation, might also be necessary to create the conditions in which this type of approach could flourish.

At the same time, other new perspectives on organisations, especially concerning the role of power and politics in decision-making, were also coming to the fore. As Chapter 5 argued, writers such as Jeffrey Pfeffer (1981, 1992) maintained that the objectives, and outcomes, of change programmes were more likely to be determined by power struggles than by any process of consensus-building or rational decision-making. This paved the way for the development of a processual approach to organisational change, which highlights the continuous, unpredictable and political nature of change (Dawson, 1994; Pettigrew, 1985, 1993; Wilson, 1992). Looking at Planned change versus a processual approach, Dawson (1994: 3–4) comments that:

> Although this [Lewin's] theory has proved useful in understanding planned change under relatively stable conditions, with the continuing and dynamic nature of change in today's business world, it no longer makes sense to implement a planned process for 'freezing' changed behaviours. Implementing stability and reinforcing behaviour which conforms to a rigid set of procedures for new work arrangements does not meet the growing requirements for employee flexibility and structural adaptation to the unfolding and complex nature of ongoing change processes. ... The processual framework ... adopts the view that change is a complex and dynamic process which should not be solidified or treated as a series of linear events. ... central to the development of a processual approach is the need to incorporate an analysis of the politics of managing change.

For the postmodernists (*see* Alvesson and Deetz, 1996; Foucault, 1983; Gergen, 1992), power is also a central feature of change, but it arises from the socially-constructed nature of organisational life:

> In a socially-constructed world, responsibility for environmental conditions lies with those who do the constructing. … This suggests at least two competing scenarios for organizational change. First, organization change can be a vehicle of domination for those who conspire to enact the world for others … An alternative use of social constructionism is to create a democracy of enactment in which the process is made open and available to all … such that we create opportunities for freedom and innovation rather than simply for further domination.
>
> (Hatch, 1997: 367–8)

As can be seen, from the early 1980s, a powerful consensus built up against the Planned approach to change. It is a consensus, however, that criticises Planned change from very different perspectives: ranging from the free market neo-liberalism of Tom Peters to the neo-Marxism of some of the postmodernists. Therefore, they are certainly a much less coherent group than the advocates of Planned change and, rather than being united by a shared belief, they tend to be distinguished by a common disbelief in the efficacy of Planned change. Nevertheless, they do share at least two common beliefs: firstly, instead of seeing change as a phenomenon that can be pre-planned and has a finite end point, they see change as an 'emerging' and ongoing process of organisational adaptation and transformation. Secondly, they adopt an open systems perspective. That is, they see individual organisations as interdependent parts or subsystems of a much larger environment, though they disagree about whether the environment is a concrete reality or a socially constructed phenomenon. The environment impacts upon and affects the actions and decisions of organisations, but they also impact on the environment. Proponents of the Emergent approach see change as emerging from the day-to-day actions and decisions of members of an organisation. In this sense, change can emerge from attempts by members of organisations to align the organisation with its environment, or as the result of different groups battling for domination, or even from attempts to construct a new, or challenge an old, social reality.

Having identified what separates it from the Planned approach to change, we can now move on to examine the Emergent approach in more detail.

The Emergent approach to change

For proponents of the Emergent approach, change is a continuous, dynamic and contested process that emerges in an unpredictable and unplanned fashion. As Weick (2000: 237) states:

> Emergent change consists of ongoing accommodations, adaptations, and alternations that produce fundamental change without a priori intentions to do so. Emergent change occurs when people reaccomplish routines and when they deal with contingencies, breakdowns, and opportunities in everyday work. Much of this change goes unnoticed, because small alternations are lumped together as noise in otherwise uneventful inertia …

The rationale for the Emergent approach stems, according to Hayes (2002: 37), from the belief that:

> ... the key decisions about matching the organisation's resources with opportunities, constraints and demands in the environment evolve over time and are the outcome of cultural and political processes in organisations.

In terms of Emergent change, a process is 'a sequence of individual and collective events, actions, and activities unfolding over time in context' (Pettigrew, 1997: 338). For Wilson (1992), it is the increasingly dynamic and uncertain nature of the business environment that undermines the case for Planned change and underlines the appropriateness of the Emergent approach. Wilson (1992) also believes that the Planned approach, by attempting to lay down timetables, objectives and methods in advance, is too heavily reliant on the role of managers, and assumes (perhaps rashly) that they can have a full understanding of the consequences of their actions and that their plans will be understood and accepted and can be implemented. In addition, Dawson (2003) contends that even in stable situations, change is emergent, messy and unpredictable. Similarly, Buchanan and Storey (1997: 127) maintain that the main criticism of those who advocate Planned change is:

> ... their attempt to impose an order and a linear sequence to processes that are in reality messy and untidy, and which unfold in an iterative fashion with much backtracking and omission.

One of the main strands of the Emergent approach is provided by processual analysts, deriving from the work of Andrew Pettigrew (1973, 1979, 1985, 1990a, 1990b, 1997, 2000). Processualists reject prescriptive, recipe-driven approaches to change and are suspicious of single causes or simple explanations of events. Instead, when studying change, they focus on the interrelatedness of individuals, groups, organisations and society (Dawson, 2003; Pettigrew and Whipp, 1993). In particular, they claim that the process of change is a complex and untidy cocktail of rational decision processes, individual perceptions, political struggles and coalition-building (Huczynski and Buchanan, 2001). Within this complex and untidy cocktail, processualists recognise 'the importance of planning for change' and the presence of 'processes of continuity'; they also recognise, however, that these are constrained and influenced by 'the complex untidy and messy nature of change' (Dawson, 2003: 25). The elaborateness of their view of change is shown by Pettigrew (1997: 340) who states that processualists pursue their work through five internally-consistent guiding principles, as follows:

1 embeddedness, studying processes across a number of levels of analysis;
2 temporal interconnectedness, studying processes in past, present and future time;
3 a role in explanation for context and action;
4 a search for holistic rather than linear explanations of process; and
5 a need to link process analysis to the location and explanation of outcomes.

For Pettigrew, change cuts across functions, spans hierarchical divisions, and has no neat starting or finishing point; instead it is a 'complex analytical, political, and cultural process of challenging and changing the core beliefs, structure and strategy of the firm' (Pettigrew, 1987: 650).

The Emergent approach, therefore, stresses the developing and unpredictable nature of change. It views change as a process that unfolds through the interplay of multiple variables (context, political processes and consultation) within an organisation. In contrast to the pre-ordained certainty of Planned change, Dawson (2003) in particular adopts a processual approach to change that is less prescriptive and more analytical and, he argues, better able to achieve a broader understanding of the problems and practice of managing change within a complex environment.

This processual approach to change is akin to the processual approach to strategy discussed in Chapter 6. Advocates of Emergent change who adopt this perspective tend to stress that there can be no simple prescription for managing organisational transitions successfully, owing to time pressures and situational variables. Neither, as Dawson (1994: 181–2) argued, can change be represented as 'the results of objective rational decision-making on the part of managers. ... [nor] as a single reaction to adverse contingent circumstances'. Therefore, successful change is less dependent on detailed plans and projections than on reaching an understanding of the complexity of the issues concerned and identifying the range of available options. Processualists also stress the central role played by power and politics in initiating and managing change (Pettigrew, 1997). This point is further emphasised by the postmodernists, for whom the struggle for power and domination is the central feature of change in organisations (Hassard, 1993; Hatch, 1997). As Finstad (1998) notes, however, the difference is that, for the processualists, the political nature of change tends to close off options, whereas for the postmodernists, the presence of conflicting interests gives people a range of new possibilities and ideas to choose from.

Despite their difference in emphasis, proponents of the Emergent approach do agree that power and politics play an important role in the process of organisational change. This is a major point of departure between them and proponents of Planned change. In commenting on the failure to incorporate the political nature of change into the traditional and more prescriptive literature on change, Hardy (1996) argues that this 'aversion' to discussing power has restricted our understanding of change and impeded our ability to manage it effectively. Pugh (1993) makes a similar point by emphasising that organisations are occupational systems and political systems as well as systems for allocating resources through rational decision-making. He also argues, however, that members of an organisation operate in all three systems simultaneously and, therefore, the rational and occupational systems need to be considered alongside, and not subordinate to, the political system. This clearly conflicts with the processualists who see the political system as being paramount.

Moving on to examine the change process itself, the Emergent perspective rejects both simple taxonomies of change, and approaches such as TQM and BPR, which promise success through following a series of laid-down steps and stages (Beer and Nohria, 2000; Collins, 1998). According to Stace and Dunphy (2001: 5):

> The appealing aspect of the promises held out for these change technologies is that they can absolve the manager from the onerous task of critically reviewing the full range of other competing approaches or devising a custom-made program. They cut through complexity. However, the offer is often illusory, for particular change approaches usually apply to particular situations, and simple solutions sometimes ignore the complexity of real life.

Dawson (2003) sees change as:

> ... a complex ongoing dynamic in which the politics, substance and context of change all interlock and overlap, and in which our understanding of the present and expectations of the future can influence our interpretation of past events, which may in turn shape our experience of change.

From this perspective, even when changes are operational, they will need to be constantly refined and developed in order to maintain their relevance. Genus (1998: 51) uses an 'interpretive' perspective to explain the messy nature of organisational change, arguing that the ' ... various political, symbolic and structural factors [involved in the change process] condition the perceptions of individuals or groups ... '. Finstad's (1998) view of organisational change, whilst being consistent with the perspectives of Dawson and Genus, does, however, appear to adopt a realist perspective on change by drawing an important distinction between the concrete elements of change, such as structures and practices, and the more symbolic elements, such as people's basic understandings and assumptions about their organisations. He maintains, though, that it is the symbolic aspects that dominate the change process rather than the more concrete changes. The importance of symbolism and ritual in the change process is also emphasised by Schuyt and Schuijt (1998), who argue that the management of these is not only central to achieving successful change, but also plays a crucial role in reducing the uncertainty which change generates.

It is because change is so complex and multifaceted that Carnall (2003) suggests that mastering the challenge of change is not a specialist activity to be facilitated or driven by an expert but an increasingly important part of every manager's role. Carnall (2003: 125–6) proposes four core managerial competences that are essential for the effective management of change: decision-making; coalition-building; achieving action; and maintaining momentum and effort. Stace and Dunphy (2001), on the other hand, identify a range of approaches to change and argue that these each require different sets of managerial competences. This view fits better with McCalman and Paton (1992) who suggest that, to be effective in creating sustainable change, managers will need an extensive and systemic understanding of their organisation's environment, in order to identify the pressures for change and to ensure that, by mobilising the necessary internal resources, their organisation responds in a timely and appropriate manner. Similarly, Dawson (1994) claims that change must be linked to developments in markets, work organisation, systems of management control and the shifting nature of organisational boundaries and relationships. He emphasises that, in a dynamic business environment, one-dimensional change interventions are likely to generate only short-term results and heighten instability rather than reduce it. This is a point emphasised by many other writers (Beer and Nohria, 2000; Graetz *et al*, 2002; Hartley *et al*, 1997; Senior, 2002).

As can be seen, though they do not always openly state it, advocates of Emergent change tend to adopt a Contingency perspective, arguing that approaches to change need to be tailored to the situation of the individual organisation. Implicit in their argument is the assumption that if organisations operated in more stable and predictable environments, the need for change would be less and it might be possible to conceive of it as a process of moving from one relatively stable state to another. Consequently, for advocates of Emergent change, it is the uncertainty of the environment that makes Planned change inappropriate and Emergent change more pertinent. This is a point emphasised by Stickland (1998: 14), who draws on systems theory to emphasise the way that organisations are separate from but connected to their environment:

> A system has an identity that sets it apart from its environment and is capable of preserving that *identity* within a given range of environmental scenarios. Systems exist within a *hierarchy* of other systems. They contain subsystems and exist within some wider system. All are interconnected ...

From this systems perspective, Stickland (1998: 76) raises a question that many of those studying organisational change appear not to acknowledge: 'To what extent does the environment drive changes within a system [i.e. organisation] and to what extent is the system in control of its own change processes?' Finstad (1998: 721) puts this issue in a wider context by arguing that 'the organization is ... the creator of its environment and the environment is the creator of the organization.' Though this has a postmodernist sound to it, realists would also recognise that organisations do contribute to the creation or the maintenance of their environment, but they see this as a long-term and largely unconscious process.

This reciprocal relationship between an organisation and its environment clearly has profound implications for how organisations conceptualise and manage change. It also serves to emphasise that a key competence for organisations is the ability to scan the external environment in order to identify and assess the impact of trends and discontinuities (Graetz *et al*, 2002; McCalman and Paton, 1992; Pettigrew and Whipp, 1993). This involves exploring the full range of external variables, including markets and customers, shareholders, legal requirements, the economy, suppliers, technology, and social trends. This activity is made more difficult by the changing and arbitrary nature of organisation boundaries: customers can also be competitors; suppliers may become partners; and employees can be transformed into customers, suppliers or even competitors for scarce resources.

To cope with this complexity and uncertainty, Pettigrew and Whipp (1993) maintain that organisations need to become open learning systems, with strategy development and change emerging from the way the company as a whole acquires, interprets and processes information about its environment. Carnall (2003) and Hayes (2002) take a similar view, arguing that an organisation's survival and growth depend on identifying environmental and market changes quickly, and responding opportunistically. This is in line with the discussion on organisational learning covered in Chapter 3. However, as Benjamin and Mabey (1993: 181) point out:

> ... while the primary stimulus for change remains those forces in the external environment, the primary motivator for how change is accomplished resides with the people within the organization.

Changes in the external environment, therefore, require organisations to make choices over how and when to respond. Such responses, the supporters of the Emergent approach state, should promote, throughout the organisation, an extensive and deep understanding of strategy, structure, systems, people, style and culture, and how these can function either as sources of inertia that can block change, or alternatively, as levers to encourage an effective change process (Dawson, 2003; Pettigrew, 1997; Wilson, 1992). A concomitant development is the adoption of a 'bottom-up' rather than 'top-down' approach to initiating and implementing change. After all, there is little point in encouraging staff to identify change opportunities unless they are also encouraged to implement them. The case in favour of this move is based on the view that the pace of environmental change is so rapid and complex that it is impossible for a small number of senior managers effectively to identify, plan and implement the necessary organisational responses. The responsibility for organisational change is therefore of necessity becoming more devolved. As described in Chapter 2, this is very much what the advocates of Contingency theory would expect in such a situation.

Nevertheless, the need for a bottom-up approach does not just arise from external pressures. As Stickland (1998: 93) notes, organisations are continually experiencing 'natural changes', i.e. the unintended consequences of deliberate decisions and actions:

> Within any organisation at a given point in time there are a number of continual shifts and changes playing out at various levels. These are not planned changes with a defined beginning and end, but rather reflect the natural dynamics which take place internally.

Such events may present organisations with unexpected and unlooked for opportunities, such as new product ideas, but may also present unwelcome threats, such as the departure of key staff. Given that such changes are continually happening at all levels and across all functions, organisations would quickly become paralysed if it was left solely to senior managers to identify and resolve them. Therefore, if they are to be dealt with speedily, these local problems or opportunities have to be dealt with locally. As Senior (2002) comments, this requires organisations to empower their employees to make changes at a local level. This follows from Mintzberg's (1994) assertion that it is from these local and bottom-up actions that the direction of the organisation emerges and is given shape.

Therefore, a bottom-up approach requires a major change in the role of senior managers. Instead of controlling employees, they have to empower people. Instead of directing and controlling change, they have to ensure that the organisation's members are receptive to, and have the necessary skills, motivation and power to take charge of, the change process. There is a distinction here between those who take a narrow view of empowerment, seeing it mainly as devolving some limited managerial responsibility, and those, *à la* Lewin, who see it as an emancipatory process that aims to create genuine organisational democracy, though it must be pointed out that even the former has a poor track record of success (Eccles, 1993; Foegen, 1999; Graetz *et al*, 2002; Huczynski and Buchanan, 2001; Lawler *et al*, 1998; Lee, 1999; Pfeffer, 1996; Stohl and Cheney, 2001; Wetlaufer, 1999). Nor is this just an issue of managers changing. Wilson (1992) believes that to achieve effective empowerment, senior managers must not only change the way they perceive and interpret the world, but achieve a similar transformation amongst everyone else in the organisation as well. Pettigrew and Whipp (1993) contend that the degree to which organisations can achieve such a difficult task, and create a climate receptive to change, is dependent on four conditioning factors:

- the extent to which key players in the organisation are prepared to champion methods for gathering and assessing information on the organisation's position that increase openness;
- the degree to which such information-gathering occurs and how effectively it is integrated with central business operations;
- the extent to which environmental pressures are recognised;
- the structural and cultural characteristics of the organisation.

As was described in Chapter 4, a wide range of organisational theorists and practitioners have argued that organisations are complex, non-linear systems in which change emerges through a process of spontaneous self-organisation, which is underpinned by a set of simple order-generating rules (Arndt and Bigelow, 2000; Bechtold, 1997; Black, 2000; Fitzgerald, 2002a; MacIntosh and MacLean, 2001; Stacey, 2003). The concept of self-organisation, as well as its implications for organisations, is very similar to the concept of Emergent change, especially in terms of the link between the emergent or self-organising nature of change and the need for greater organisational democracy.

Complexity theorists argue that the best-run companies survive because they operate at the edge of chaos by relentlessly pursuing a path of continuous innovation brought about by a process that resembles self-organisation in nature (Brown and Eisenhardt, 1997; Frederick, 1998; Jenner, 1998). However, Beeson and Davis (2000) make the point that whilst it might be fruitful to see organisations as non-linear systems, to do so will require a fundamental shift in the role of management. Like many others (e.g. Boje, 2000; Stacey *et al*, 2002; Sullivan, 1998; Tetenbaum, 1998; Wheatley, 1992b), they point out that self-organising principles explicitly reject cause-and-effect, top-down, command-and-control styles of management. Brodbeck (2002) suggests that the belief by managers that order and control are essential to achieve their objectives should be rejected. For Tetenbaum (1998), the move to self-organisation will require managers to destabilise their organisations and develop the skill of managing order and disorder at the same time. Managers will need to encourage experimentation, divergent views, even allow rule-breaking, and recognise that '... people need the freedom to own their own power, think innovatively, and operate in new patterns' (Bechtold, 1997: 198). Beeson and Davis (2000) echo this point and argue that, in such situations, change becomes an everyday event undertaken by all in the organisation.

The implication of this for Bechtold (1997) is that organisations seeking to adopt a complexity approach will need to have a balanced distribution of power, strong customer focus, a strategy of continuous learning and an orientation towards community service. A further strand in this argument is provided by Kiel (1994), who argues that because small actions can have large and unpredictable consequences, individual human activity assumes great importance. Similarly, Jenner (1998) claims that for self-organisation to work, authority must be delegated to those who have access to the broadest channels of information that relate to the issue or problem concerned. Therefore, to all intents and purposes, the complexity approach to change lies firmly within the Emergent camp.

As can be seen, the advocates of Emergent change come from a wide variety of backgrounds and each offers their own distinct view on how organisations should and should not manage change. As the following section will show, however, there are some core similarities which link them.

The Emergent approach to successful change

Though the proponents of the Emergent approach reject the concept of universally-applicable rules for change, the guidance they do provide tends to stress five features of organisations that either promote or obstruct success: structures, cultures, organisational learning, managerial behaviour, and power and politics.

Organisational structure

This is seen as playing a crucial role in determining where power lies, in defining how people relate to each other and in influencing the momentum for change (Carnall, 2003; Dawson, 2003; Hatch, 1997; Huczynski and Buchanan, 2001; Kotter, 1996). Crucially, as Galbraith (2000: 154) notes: 'The theory of organization has always identified some types of [organisational structures] as being more easily changeable than others.' Therefore, an appropriate organisational structure, in both its formal and informal elements, can be an important facilitator of change.

The case for developing more appropriate organisational structures in order to facilitate change very much follows the arguments of the Contingency theorists (discussed in Chapter 2) and the Culture–Excellence school (discussed in Chapter 3), i.e. that dynamic and chaotic environments require organisations to adopt more flexible, less hierarchical structures. Those favouring an Emergent approach to change point out that the 1990s witnessed a general tendency to create flatter organisational structures in order to increase responsiveness by devolving authority and responsibility (Senior, 2003). As Kotter (1996: 169) remarks, the case for such structural changes is that:

> An organization with more delegation, which means a flat hierarchy, is in a far superior position to manoeuvre than one with a big, change-resistant lump in the middle.

A similar point is made by proponents of the complexity approach. For Jenner (1998: 402), the key issue is that:

> ... enterprise must be organized into flexible basic units that permit new organizational structures to be identified and to emerge, and which promote efficient exchanges of information.

In studying innovating organisations, Brown and Eisenhardt (1997: 29) refer to such flexible structures as 'semistructures', which they claim:

> ... are sufficiently rigid so that change can be organized, but not so rigid that it cannot occur. ... sustaining this semistructured state is challenging because it is a dissipative equilibrium and so requires constant managerial vigilance to avoid slipping into pure chaos or pure structure.

A similar point is made by Galbraith (2000: 155), who refers to the 'reconfigurable' organisation, which:

> ... consists of a stable part and a variable part. The stable part consists of 'homes' for specialists in functions, which also host generalists on rotating assignments. ... The variable part of the structure consists of integrating mechanisms and networks across the functions.

Brown and Eisenhardt (1997) claim that such structures are essential for ensuring organisational survival in highly-competitive environments because they facilitate continuous innovation and improvisation and allow intensive, real-time communication within a structure of a few, very specific rules.

A common aspect of these new structures is the move to create customer-centred organisations with structures that reflect, and are responsive to, different markets rather than different functions (Galbraith, 2000; Hamel and Prahalad, 1994; Stace and Dunphy, 2001). Customer responsiveness places greater emphasis on effective horizontal processes and embodies the concept that, whether one is looking internally or externally, everyone is someone else's customer (Dale, 2003; Jenner, 1998).

One result of attempts to respond rapidly to changing conditions by breaking down internal and external barriers, disseminating knowledge and developing synergy across functions is the emergence of network organisations (Morgan, 1997; Wisdom, 2001). Network organisations have been defined in a number of ways and given a number of names – Handy (1989) refers to them as federal organisations, Robbins (1997) uses the term virtual organisation, after the Internet on which many of them either rely or are based, and Senge (2000: 77) writes of 'living human communities'. For Cummings and Worley (2001: 291) the purpose of a network-based structure is that it:

> ... manages the diverse, complex, and dynamic relationships among multiple organizations or units, each specializing in a particular business function or task.

Birchall and Lyons (1995) stress that networks can be in a constant state of flux as they adjust to the changing needs of their dynamic customer base. They also comment that in some cases, customers are even part of the network. For Snow et al (1993), a major benefit of network structures is that the semi-autonomous nature of each part of a network reduces the need for and erodes the power of centrally-managed bureaucracies, which, in turn, leads to change and adaptation being driven from the bottom up rather than from the top down. They further argue that the specialisation and flexibility required to cope with globalisation, intense competition and rapid technological change, especially the challenge of the Internet, can only be achieved by loosening the central ties and controls that have characterised organisations in the past (Genus, 1998; Hardaker and Graham, 2001; Kanter et al, 1997; Kotter, 1996; Wisdom, 2001). However, is it clear that every organisation will have to adopt such structural changes in order to survive? The premise that they will have to is based on the assumption that all organisations experience similar levels of environmental turbulence and cannot do anything other than adapt their internal arrangements to these external conditions. As argued in previous chapters, there are three flaws to this argument. Firstly, environmental instability is not uniform; it varies from industry to industry and organisation to organisation. Secondly, even where instability is present, organisations can choose to take action to reduce it rather than merely having to adapt to it. Lastly, as Child's concept of equifinality discussed in Chapter 6 suggests, there are a range of internal arrangements that are compatible with external turbulence, of which flattened hierarchies are only one.

Organisational culture

There can be few people who now doubt the important role culture plays in the life of organisations, especially when it comes to change (Allaire and Firsirotu, 1984; Brown, 1995; De Witte and van Muijen, 1999; Hirschhorn, 2000). Johnson (1993: 64) suggested that the strategic management of change is 'essentially a cultural and cognitive phenomenon' rather than an analytical, rational exercise. Clarke (1994) states that the essence of sustainable change is to understand the culture of the organisation that is to be changed. If proposed changes contradict cultural biases and traditions, it is inevitable that they will be difficult to embed in the organisation. Kotter (1996) takes a similar view, arguing that for change to be successful it must be anchored in the organisation's culture.

Dawson (2003) echoes this theme. He suggests that attempts to realign internal behaviours with external conditions require change strategies that are culturally sensitive. Organisations, he points out, must be aware that the process is lengthy, potentially dangerous, and demands considerable reinforcement if culture change is to be sustained against the inevitable tendency to regress to old behaviours. Pointing to Pirelli's attempt to implement TQM in two of its Australian plants, Dawson (2003: 33) comments that:

> Management had a plan and a timeframe for the 'successful' management of change, but they were not prepared for the very different contextual conditions and local operating cultures of the two adjacent plants in South Australia. The cultural socio-political aspects of change turned out to be far more important and influential than had been anticipated, or could be accommodated for, in planning the process of change.

Likewise, Pettigrew (1997) stresses that organisational processes are embedded in an organisation's context, of which culture forms an important part. Pettigrew also points out that, because of this embeddedness, change can be slow. From the complexity perspective, Stacey (2003) similarly points to the importance of having an appropriate culture and the difficulty involved in changing an existing one. Cummings and Worley (2001) likewise recognise that culture can hinder the speed of change, especially when it is the culture that needs to change. In such cases, they point out, it is necessary to challenge mechanisms that reinforce old or inappropriate behaviour, such as reward, recruitment and promotion structures – all areas where resistance can be expected. In addition, if these reinforcement mechanisms are complemented by managerial behaviour which promotes risk aversion and fear of failure, it is unlikely to create a climate where people are willing to propose or undertake change. Accordingly, as Clarke (1994: 94) suggests, 'Creating a culture for change means that change has to be part of the way we do things around here, it cannot be bolted on as an extra.'

Therefore, for many proponents of the Emergent approach, an essential factor in successful change is for organisations to possess or to be able to develop an appropriate organisational culture. However, Senior (2002) notes that many writers and researchers take a different view. Beer *et al* (1993), for example, suggest that the most effective way to promote change is not by directly attempting to influence organisational behaviour or culture. Instead, they advocate restructuring organisations in order to place people in a new organisational context which imposes new roles, relationships and responsibilities upon them. This, they believe, forces new attitudes and behaviours upon people. This view, as discussed in Chapter 3, is also shared by Tom Peters (1993) who advocates rapid and complete destruction of existing hierarchical organisation structures as a precursor to behavioural change.

In Chapter 5 we discussed the difficulty and relevance of achieving cultural change, by whatever means. It was argued that many writers are highly sceptical about seeing culture as a promoter of change. This view is, perhaps, best summed up by Wilson (1992: 91), who claims that:

> ... to effect change in an organization simply by attempting to change its culture assumes an unwarranted linear connection between something called organizational culture and performance. Not only is this concept of organizational culture multi-faceted, it is also not always clear precisely how culture and change are related, if at all, and, if so, in which direction.

Organisational learning

This was examined in Chapter 3. For advocates of the Emergent approach, learning plays a key role in preparing people for, and allowing them to cope with, change (Bechtold, 1997; Senge, 2000). Put simply, learning means '... the capacity of members of an organization to detect and correct errors and to seek new insights that would enable them to make choices that better produce outcomes that they seek' (Martin, 2000: 463). A willingness to change often only stems from the feeling that there is no other option (Argyris, 1999; Pettigrew *et al*, 1992). Therefore, as Wilson (1992) suggests, change can be precipitated by encouraging dissatisfaction with current systems and procedures or making impending crises real to everyone in the organisation. Kotter (1996) even advocates engineering a crisis in order to build the momentum for change. Whatever the spur for change, however, staff are unlikely to recognise the need for change unless managers create mechanisms which allow them to become familiar with the company's performance, market place, customers, competitors, legal requirements, etc. (Fiol and Lyles, 1985; Probst and Buchel, 1997). Pettigrew and Whipp (1993: 18) also contended that 'collective learning' is one of the main preconditions for sustainable change. They argue that 'collective learning' ensures that the full implications of an organisation's view of its environment can then inform subsequent actions over the long-term and, in turn, the way in which future shifts in the environment are tackled.

Clarke (1994) and Nadler (1993) suggested that individual and organisational learning stem from effective top-down communication and the promotion of self-development and confidence. In turn, this encourages the commitment to, and shared ownership of, the organisation's vision, actions and decisions that are necessary to respond to the external environment and take advantage of the opportunities it offers. Additionally, as Pugh (1993) points out, in order to generate the need and climate for change, people within organisations need to be involved in the diagnosis of problems and the development of solutions. Carnall (2003) takes this argument further, arguing that:

> The effective organization is one which encourages and supports learning from change. This means that an open management style, encouraging initiative and risk, is needed.

Likewise, Clarke (1994: 156) maintains that involving staff in change management decisions has the effect of 'stimulating habits of criticism and open debate', which enables them to challenge existing norms and question established practices.

Clarke points out that although this can create the opportunity for innovation and radical change, challenging the status quo is also akin to challenging managerial judgment and authority. As Benjamin and Mabey (1993) maintain, though the questioning of the status quo is the essence of bottom-up change, it also leads to a form of role reversal whereby, rather than managers pressuring staff to change, the reverse occurs. Therefore, a new, open management style can result in staff putting pressure on managers to address fundamental questions about the purpose and direction of the organisation which previously they might have preferred to avoid. Consequently, as Easterby-Smith *et al* (2000) and Tsang (1997) suggest, organisational learning is neither an easy nor an uncontentious option for organisations. There is also a great diversity of opinion as to what it is and how it can be promoted, which makes organisational learning a more difficult concept to apply than many of its supporters acknowledge (Burnes *et al*, 2003).

Managerial behaviour

Chapter 1 showed that the traditional view of managers sees them as directing and controlling staff, resources and information. It sees managers as being the only ones with the expertise, knowledge and legitimate authority to decide how and when change should take place. However, the Emergent approach to change, as with the Culture–Excellence approach to managing organisations, requires a radical change in the role of managers (Dawson, 2003; Kanter *et al*, 1997; Kotter, 1996; Peters, 1997a; Weick, 2000). Instead of directing change from the top, managers are expected to operate as facilitators and coaches who, through their ability to span hierarchical, functional and organisational boundaries, can bring together and empower teams and groups to identify the need for, and achieve, change (Bennis, 2000; Carnall, 2003; Mabey and Mayon-White, 1993; Weick, 2000). Crucial to this, according to Kotter (1996), is for managers to develop leadership skills. Drawing on the work of Burns (1978), Kotter argues that management concerns a set of processes, such as budgeting and planning, for ensuring that organisations run smoothly. Leadership, on the other hand, is a set of processes for creating or transforming organisations: 'Leadership defines what the future should look like, aligns people with that vision, and inspires them to make it happen ... ' (Kotter, 1996: 25).

To be effective in this new role, managers require knowledge of and expertise in strategy formulation, human resource management, marketing/sales and negotiation/conflict resolution, and much more (Beer and Nohria, 2000; Clarke, 1994; Hayes, 2002). But the key to success, the decisive factor in creating a focused agenda for organisational change is, according to many observers, managers' own behaviour (Graetz *et al*, 2002; Kanter, 1989; Kotter, 1999; Pfeffer, 1996). If managers are to gain the commitment of others to change, they must first be prepared to challenge their own assumptions, attitudes and mindsets so that they develop an understanding of the emotional and intellectual processes involved (Buchanan and Boddy, 1992; Burns, 1978; Harrison, R, 2002; Sosik and Megerian, 1999).

For supporters of the Emergent approach, the essence of change is the move from the familiar to the unknown, from the certain to the uncertain (Jones *et al*, 2000). In this situation, it is essential for managers to be able to tolerate risk and cope with paradox and ambiguity (Weick, 2000; Stacey *et al*, 2002). Pugh (1993) took the view that, in a dynamic environment, open and active communication with those participating in the change process is the key to coping with risk and ambiguity. This very much follows the view expressed by many that top-down, unilaterally-imposed change doesn't work and that bottom-up change, based on devolved responsibility and genuine empowerment, is the way forward (Brown and Eisenhardt, 1997; Clarke, 1999; Harung *et al*, 1999; Styhre, 2002). This in turn requires managers to facilitate open, organisation-wide communication via groups, individuals, and formal and informal channels (Hayes, 2002; Kanter *et al*, 1992; Senior, 2002).

An organisation's ability to gather, disseminate, analyse and discuss information is crucial for successful change, from the perspective of the Emergent approach. The reason for this, as Wilson (1992) argues, is that to effect change successfully, organisations need consciously and proactively to move forward incrementally. Large-scale change and more formal and integrated approaches to change (such as Total Quality Management) can quickly lose their sense of purpose and relevance for organisations operating in dynamic and uncertain environments. However, if organisations move towards their strategic vision by means of many small-scale, localised incremental changes, managers must ensure that those concerned, which could potentially be the entire workforce, have access to and are able to act on all the available information. Also, by encouraging a collective pooling of knowledge and information in this way, a better understanding of the pressures and possibilities for change can be achieved, which should enable managers to improve the quality of strategic decisions (Boddy and Buchanan, 1992; Quinn, 1993).

Proponents of complexity take a slightly different view. They reject both small-scale incremental change and large-scale radical-transformational change in favour of 'a third kind' which lies between these two, and which is continuous and based on self-organisation at the team/group level (Brodbeck, 2002; Brown and Eisenhardt, 1997). To a certain extent, part of this difference is about terminology: how big is incremental change? Perhaps the issue to concentrate on is that, by and large, there is general agreement among proponents of emergent change that large-scale, top-down change programmes, whilst sometimes being necessary, rarely succeed (Beer and Nohria, 2000). This does not mean that there is not a crucial role for managers in identifying issues to be addressed or in developing an organisational vision which can guide Emergent change (Bennis, 2000; Dunphy, 2000). It does mean, however, that successful change is seen as coming from bottom-up initiatives which emerge from local responses to issues, threats or opportunities in the environment (Bennis, 2000; Pettigrew, 2000). It follows that the size of such responses will vary but, because they are local responses, they can never be large-scale.

Whatever the scale of the change, however, the potential for resistance will always be present. Resistance to change can arise from a number of sources, including middle and senior managers, and for a number of reasons ranging from different perspectives on what is best for the organisation to sectional or individual self interest (Hayes, 2002; Huczynski and Buchanan, 2001). To cope effectively with resistance, managers will need to acquire and develop a range of interpersonal skills that enable them to deal with individuals and groups who seek to block or manipulate change for their own benefit (Boddy and Buchanan, 1992; Kotter, 1996). Promoting openness, reducing uncertainty, and encouraging experimentation can be powerful mechanisms for over-coming resistance and promoting change (Mabey and Mayon-White, 1993). In this respect, Coghlan (1993) and McCalman and Paton (1992) advocated the use of Organization Development (OD) tools and techniques (such as transactional analysis, teamwork, group problem-solving, role-playing, etc.), which have long been used in Planned change programmes. However, there is an enormous and potentially confusing array of these; Mayon-White (1993) and Buchanan and Boddy (1992) argue that man-agers have a crucial role to play in terms of identifying and applying the appropriate ones. The main objective in deploying such tools and techniques is to encourage shared learning through teamwork and cooperation. It is this that provides the framework and support for the emergence of creative and innovative solutions and encourages a sense of involvement, commitment and ownership of the change process (Carnall, 2003; Kanter *et al*, 1997; McCalman and Paton, 1992; Peters, 1997a).

Nevertheless, it would be naïve to assume that everyone will want to work, or be able to function effectively, in such situations. The cognitive and behavioural changes necessary for organisational survival may be too large for many people, especially managers (Ghoshal and Bartlett, 2000). An important managerial task will, therefore, be to identify sources of inertia, assess the skill mix within their organisation and, most of all, consider whether their own managerial attitudes and styles are appropri-ate. It needs also to be recognised that there are different types of change, and that these often require different approaches (Stace and Dunphy, 2001). Proponents of Emergent change tend to see the world from one perspective but, as will be discussed in Chapter 10, there are other ways of viewing change and other ways of bringing it about (Beer and Nohria, 2000).

Power and politics

The importance of power and politics in organisational life, especially change situa-tions, was explored in Chapter 5. Though the advocates of Emergent change tend to view power and politics from differing perspectives, they recognise their importance and that they have to be managed if change is to be effective. Dawson (1994: 176), for example, concluded that 'The central argument is that it is important to try and gain the support of senior management, local management, supervisors, trade unions and workplace employees.' According to Weick (2000: 236) gaining support requires 'con-siderable linguistic skills to capture and label the flow of events [and] resequence and relabel that sequence'. Pettigrew *et al* (1992: 293) take a similar view, stating that 'The significance of political language at the front end of change processes needs emphasiz-ing. Closures can be labelled as redevelopments. Problems can be re-coded into opportunities with ... broad positive visions being articulated to build early coalitions ... '. Kanter *et al* (1992: 508) argue that the first step to implementing change is coalition-building: ' ... involve those whose involvement really matters ... Specifically, seek support from two general groups: (1) power sources and (2) stakeholders.' In a similar vein, Nadler (1993) advocates the need to shape the political dynamics of change so that power centres develop that support the change rather than blocking it. Senior (2002), drawing on the work of Nadler (1988), proposes four steps that organi-sations need to take to manage the political dynamics of change (*see* Exhibit 9.2).

Important though power and politics are in the change process, as Hendry (1996) and Pugh (1993) argue, they are not the be-all and end-all of change and it is impor-

Exhibit 9.2	Managing the political dynamics of change

Step 1 Ensure or develop the support of key power groups.

Step 2 Use leader behaviour to generate support for the proposed change.

Step 3 Use symbols and language to encourage and show support for the change.

Step 4 Build in stability by using power to ensure that some things remain the same.

Source: Senior (2002)

tant not to focus on these to the exclusion of other factors. Nevertheless, the focus placed on the political dynamics of change does serve to highlight the need for those who manage change to be aware of and control this dimension of the change process. To this end, Carnall (2003: 133) offered a model of the political skills that can be utilised to manage change (*see* Table 9.1). As Table 9.1 shows, Carnall identifies three basic types of political skill: the ability to utilise resources, such as formal authority and information; the aptitude to understand and manage political processes, such as negotiation and mobilising support; and the capacity to recognise and engage in the various forms of political activity, such as battles over budgets and organisational structures. Carnall's argument is not that one individual will possess all these skills, but that those managing change will have to gain the support of those who do.

Table 9.1 Political skills and the management of change

Resources	Process	Form
Formal authority	Negotiation	Politics of:
Control of resources	Influencing	Budgets
Control of information	Mobilising support	Careers
Control of agenda	Mobilising bias	Succession
Control of access symbols	Use of emotion	Information
	Ceremony and rituals	Organisational structures
	Professional 'mystery'	Appraisal

As can be seen, therefore, there are a number of core issues on which the advocates of Emergent change share similar views. Having identified the beliefs which distinguish them as a group, it is equally important to understand what advice they offer for putting their approach into practice.

■ Recipes for Emergent change

Pettigrew and Whipp (1993: 6) maintain that there are no universal rules with regard to leading change; rather it involves 'linking action by people at all levels of the business'. However, this has not prevented most of the advocates of Emergent change from suggesting sequences of actions which organisations should follow. Pettigrew and Whipp (1993), for example, propose a model for successfully managing strategic and operational change that involves five interrelated factors (*see* Exhibit 9.3).

Exhibit 9.3	Managing change successfully

- **Environmental assessment** – organisations, at all levels, need to develop the ability to collect and utilise information about their external and internal environments.

- **Leading change** – this requires the creation of a positive climate for change, the identification of future directions and the linking together of action by people at all levels in the organisation.

- **Linking strategic and operational change** – this is a two-way process of ensuring that strategic decisions lead to operational changes and that operational changes influence strategic decisions.

- **Human resources as assets and liabilities** – just as the pool of knowledge, skills and attitudes possessed by an organisation is crucial to its success, it can also be a threat to the organisation's success if the combination is inappropriate or managed poorly.

- **Coherence of purpose** – this concerns the need to ensure that the decisions and actions that flow from the above four factors complement and reinforce each other.

Source: Pettigrew and Whipp (1993)

For his part, not to be outdone by Pettigrew and Whipp's five factors, Dawson (1994: 179) puts forward 15 'major practical guidelines which can be drawn from a processual analysis of managing organizational transitions'. These guidelines range from the need to maintain an overview of the dynamics and long-term process of change, to the need to take a total organisational approach to managing transitions. On the way, he makes the case for understanding and communicating the context and objectives of change, and ensuring managerial and employee commitment. Wilson (1992: 122) also draws attention to the complex and long-term nature of change, writing that:

> This book has deliberately taken a particular stance towards the question of organizational change. The argument has largely been against skill-based approaches, ready-made models of good organizational practice (for example, the 'excellence' models) and reliance upon analysing change as primarily the outcome-oriented pursuit of great and charismatic individuals. The arguments have, rather, favoured the potency of organizational structures, of economic determinism, of institutionalization within which the manager must operate. To operate successfully (and in the long term) he or she must understand and learn from the wider context or organization. This is not to say that individual skills are unimportant, only that they cannot be considered in isolation from the wider factors of strategic change.

Unfortunately, the problem with much of the advice for managing change offered by advocates of the Emergent approach is that it tends to be too general or cursory in nature and thus difficult to apply. It can sometimes also appear almost as an afterthought. However, there are those whose work offers much more substantial guidance to managers and organisations. Inevitably, as one might expect, these tend to come from the prescriptive camp rather than the analytical camp and are more concerned with telling organisations what they should do than in providing detailed analyses of what they do do. The two leading exponents of change in this respect are Rosabeth Moss Kanter and John P Kotter. Kanter's work has already been discussed extensively in Chapter 3, but to recap briefly, as shown in Exhibit 9.4, she proposes 'Ten Commandments for Executing Change' (Kanter *et al*, 1992).

Exhibit 9.4	Ten commandments for executing change

1. Analyse the organisation and its need for change.
2. Create a shared vision and a common direction.
3. Separate from the past.
4. Create a sense of urgency.
5. Support a strong leader role.
6. Line up political sponsorship.
7. Craft an implementation plan.
8. Develop enabling structures.
9. Communicate, involve people and be honest.
10. Reinforce and institutionalise change.

Source: Kanter *et al* (1992: 382 –3)

Looking at approaches to change, Kanter *et al* (1992) distinguished between 'Bold Strokes' and 'Long Marches'. The former relate to major strategic decisions or economic initiatives, usually of a structural or technological nature. These, they argue, can have a clear and rapid impact on an organisation, but they rarely lead to any long-term change in habits or culture. The Long March approach, on the other hand, favours a host of relatively small-scale and operationally focused initiatives, each of which can be quickly implemented but whose full benefits are achieved in the long term rather than the short term. However, the Long March approach can, over time, lead to a change of culture. Bold Strokes are initiatives taken by a few senior managers, sometimes only one; they do not rely on the support of the rest of the organisation for their success. In contrast, the Long March approach requires widespread commitment throughout an organisation. Without the involvement and commitment of the majority of the workforce, Kanter *et al* argue, such initiatives cannot succeed. They do maintain that Bold Strokes and Long Marches can be complementary, rather than alternative, approaches to change; though in practice companies appear to favour one or the other. Nevertheless, companies may need both if they are to succeed in transforming themselves.

Like Kanter, Kotter is a professor at the Harvard Business School and runs his own highly successful consultancy – Kotter Associates. He is the author of a wide range of books and articles on management and change, including his highly influential 1995 *Harvard Business Review* article, 'Leading change: why transformation efforts fail'. This article jumped to first place among the thousands of reprints sold by the *Review*, which, considering the quality of the articles in its reprint base, is a considerable achievement. Spurred on by the reception of his views on change, Kotter went on to write his 1996 book, *Leading Change*. This elaborates and expands on the ideas in his *Harvard Business Review* article. The book begins by identifying eight key errors that Kotter believes cause transformation efforts to fail (*see* Exhibit 9.5).

Exhibit 9.5	Why change initiatives fail

Error 1 Allowing too much complacency.

Error 2 Failing to create a sufficiently powerful guiding coalition.

Error 3 Underestimating the power of vision.

Error 4 Undercommunicating the vision by a factor of 10 (or 100 or even 1000).

Error 5 Permitting obstacles to block the new vision.

Error 6 Failing to create short-term wins.

Error 7 Declaring victory too soon.

Error 8 Neglecting to anchor changes firmly in the corporate culture.

Source: Kotter (1996)

Kotter (1996: 16) maintains that the consequences of these errors are that:

– New strategies aren't implemented well.
– Acquisitions don't achieve expected synergies.
– Reengineering takes too long and costs too much.
– Downsizing doesn't get costs under control.
– Quality programs don't deliver hoped-for results.

In order to eliminate these errors and their consequences, the book then proceeds to present Kotter's Eight-Stage Process for successful organisational transformation (*see* Exhibit 9.6).

Exhibit 9.6	Kotter's eight steps to successful change

Step 1 Establishing a sense of urgency.

Step 2 Creating a guiding coalition.

Step 3 Developing a vision and strategy.

Step 4 Communicating the change vision.

Step 5 Empowering broad-based action.

Step 6 Generating short-term wins.

Step 7 Consolidating gains and producing more change.

Step 8 Anchoring new approaches in the culture.

Source: Kotter (1996)

Kotter (1996: 23) stresses that his eight stages are a process and not a checklist, and that 'Successful change of any magnitude goes through all eight stages ... skipping even a single step or getting too far ahead without a solid base almost always creates problems.' He also points out that most major change efforts comprise a host of small and medium-sized change projects which, at any one point in time, can be at different points in the process. Kotter (1996: 24–5) cites the example of a telecommunications company where:

> The overall effort, designed to significantly increase the firm's competitive position, took six years. By the third year, the transformation was centred in steps 5, 6 and 7. One relatively small reengineering project was nearing the end of stage 8. A restructuring of corporate staff groups was just beginning with most of the effort in steps 1 and 2. A quality program was moving along, but behind schedule, while a few small initiatives hadn't even been launched yet. Early results were visible at six to twelve months, but the biggest payoff didn't come until near the end of the overall effort.

As can be seen, there is a reassuring similarity between Kanter *et al*'s Ten Commandments and Kotter's eight-stage process. Taken together, they provide detailed guidance for implementing change. However, there is one area where both they and the other advocates of the Emergent approach seem strangely imprecise. Though advocates of Emergent change place a great deal of emphasis on leadership and the ability to manage change, what most of them put to one side is the role of the change agent. Indeed, as the next section will show, though there are a number of different models of change agency identified in the literature, there is a tendency to assume there is a 'one best' model or set of skills/competences which fits all situations (Caldwell, 2001, 2003).

The role of the change agent

Whether one is dealing with change at the individual, group or organisational level, whether one perceives change as incremental, punctuated or continuous, or whether one is viewing it from a Planned or Emergent perspective, change has to be managed; someone has to take responsibility for ensuring that change takes place. Whether this person is a team leader, facilitator, coach or even a dictator, there is usually one individual who bears the responsibility of being the change agent. The previous chapter showed that the concept of the change agent originated with Kurt Lewin and has been extensively developed by the OD movement. However, over the last two decades, as different perceptions of change have emerged, so different views of the role of the change agent can also be perceived. As Caldwell (2003) notes, we have seen eulogies to the 'heroic' change leader capable of transforming organisations, calls for line managers and functional specialists to become change agents, and the growth of internal and external management consultants as 'catalysts' for change. However, rather than clarifying the role and competences of the change agent, these developments appear to have made the picture more confused.

One of the strengths of the Planned approach is that it not only offers a well-developed change process, but it also provides a blueprint for the behaviour and attributes of change agents who, in turn, are buttressed and supported by a host of tools and techniques for analysing organisations and managing change (Cummings and Worley, 1997). The Emergent approach, whilst stressing the issue of process, takes the view that change is not a specialist activity driven by an expert, but an increasingly important part of every manager's role (Clarke, 1994). The drawback with this perspective is that it deflects attention from or even ignores the specialist skills necessary to manage the different types of change, whether this is being done by a manager or by a change specialist. It may also be one reason why, as Hartley *et al* (1997) observe, there has been relatively little empirical research on the roles played by change agents. However, Buchanan and Boddy (1992: 27) sought to redress the balance by analysing the skills needed to be a successful change agent and, in particular, by drawing attention to the change agent's need to:

> ... support the 'public performance' of rationally considered and logically phased and visibly participative change with 'backstage activity' in the recruitment and maintenance of support and in seeking and blocking resistance. ... 'Backstaging' is concerned with the exercise of 'power skills', with 'intervening in political and cultural systems', with influencing and negotiating and selling, and with 'managing meaning'.

Buchanan and Boddy suggest a model of the expertise of the change agent which identifies the skills and competences necessary to achieve successful change. Their model begins by listing the diagnostic skills required to identify the organisation type; change category; personal vulnerability; agenda priorities; and public performance and backstage skills. The model then goes on to list 15 competences under five clusters: goals; roles; communication; negotiation; and managing up. The last two elements of their model relate to process outcomes and personal and organisational outcomes. What emerges from their work is a picture of the change agent as a highly skilled and well-trained political operator who has not only an in-depth knowledge of change processes and tools, but also the personal qualities and experience to use them both in the open and, especially, behind the scenes. In contrast to this, the Planned approach sees the change agent's role as being mainly an up-front 'public performance' activity and working with a transparent agenda to help those involved to identify the options and make their own choices (French and Bell, 1995).

For proponents of Emergent change, the change agent is not a neutral facilitator, but an active manager of the change process with his/her own agenda which they seek to promote or impose by managing and shaping the perceptions of those concerned (Pettigrew, 2000; Weick, 2000). Buchanan and Boddy (1992: 123) also draw attention to the social construction of the process of change which, they argue, is a creative activity:

> Expertise does not simply involve the mechanical deployment of diagnostic tools, competences and stereotyped solutions, but involves also the innovative and opportunistic exploitation of other dimensions of the organizational context.

Mirvis (1988) is another who focuses on the crucial role played by innovative and creative skills of change agents in achieving successful change. In an article entitled 'Grace, magic and miracles', Lichtenstein (1997) investigated this side of the change agent's role further by examining the work of three leading change practitioners: Peter Senge, William Torbert and Ellen Wingard. In the article, the three consultants described their approach to change and the theories which underpin it. They also described how, in applying their approaches, it was insufficient just to follow the steps laid down. Success required the consultants to overcome major obstacles, and, in so doing, to adopt novel and experimental methods. Senge, Torbert and Wingard use terms such as 'grace', 'magic' and 'miracles' to describe the moment of breakthrough; the point where serious obstacles were overcome and genuine progress made. In fact, what they describe is the ability of the change agent to recognise the need to depart from the 'script' and to experiment with the unknown in order to make progress. Just as Buchanan and Boddy (1992) identified the need for change agents to be able to present and utilise the rational face of change, whilst being adept at the less rational 'backstage' skills, so Lichtenstein (1997: 407) also concludes that:

> ... there is a logical framework that produces rational actions in the first stages of an intervention effort. However, at a critical threshold it is non-linear logic and spontaneous felt action – grace, magic and miracles – that actually supports organizational (and personal) transformation.

Drawing on the work of cultural anthropologists, Schuyt and Schuijt (1998) use the analogy of the change agent as a magician. They point out that magicians, witch doctors and medicine men in non-Western cultures use symbols and rituals to smooth the various transitions in life cycles: birth, puberty, marriage and death. In the same way, Schuyt and Schuijt (1998: 399) pose the following question: are not consultants and change agents 'also, in a certain sense, magicians who guide and structure important transitions through the use of rituals and symbols?' These rituals and symbols have a number of key functions: to establish the change agent's credentials, to prepare the participants mentally for change, to guide them through the transition, and to reinforce the 'participants' feeling that they are taking part in a controlled and well-managed process of change ... but ultimately the crux is to reduce the client's uncertainty' (Schuyt and Schuijt, 1998: 405).

The argument of many in the Emergent school is that the complexity and multi-level nature of change mean that it cannot be left to a few experts or a few managers but is the responsibility of everyone in the organisation. However, if this is so, what skills and competences do they need and how are they to get them? What the work of Buchanan and Boddy, Lichtenstein, Schuyt and Schuijt, and, indeed, the Organization Development movement would seem to argue is that the more complex the change process, the more difficult it is to achieve, and the greater the need to utilise the skills and experience of a specialist change agent. The conclusion they draw from this is that there is a 'one best' type of change agent who possesses a generic set of high-level competences that can be employed in any situation.

Caldwell (2003) takes issue with Buchanan and Boddy *et al*. Just as Dunphy and Stace (1993: 905) called for a 'situational' or 'contingency model' of change, so Caldwell calls for a contingency model of change agency which recognises that different change situations require different types of change agent. From an extensive literature review, Caldwell identifies four groups of models of change agent (*see* Exhibit 9.7). These four different types of change models highlight the difficulty, not to say impossibility, of attempting to construct a generic change agent who can operate in any situation.

The type of change agent identified by Buchanan and Boddy may fit into some of these models but not all of them. Similarly, the OD type of change agent may fit into some of these models, but not all of them. What Caldwell has done is to direct academics and practitioners away from both the 'it's everyone's responsibility' and the 'one best way' schools and towards identifying the behaviours and competences necessary for each type of change situation.

Exhibit 9.7	Models of change agents

- Leadership models where change agents are senior managers responsible for identifying and delivering strategic/tranformational change.
- Management models where change agents are seen as middle-level managers/functional specialists who have responsibility for delivering or supporting specific elements of strategic change programmes or project.
- Consultancy models where change agents are external or internal consultants who can be called on to operate at any level.
- Team models where change agents are seen as teams that operate at various levels in an organisation and which are composed of the requisite managers, employees and consultants necessary to accomplish the particular change project set them.

Source: Caldwell (2003)

Emergent change: summary and criticisms

The proponents of Emergent change are a somewhat disparate group who tend to be united more by their scepticism regarding Planned change than by a commonly agreed alternative. Nevertheless, there does seem to be some agreement regarding the main tenets of Emergent change, which are as follows:

- Organisational change is a continuous process of experiment and adaptation aimed at matching an organisation's capabilities to the needs and dictates of a dynamic and uncertain environment.
- Though this is best achieved through a multitude of (mainly) small- to medium-scale incremental changes, over time these can lead to a major re-configuration and transformation of an organisation.
- Change is a multi-level, cross-organisation process that unfolds in an iterative and messy fashion over a period of years and comprises a series of interlocking projects.
- Change is a political-social process and not an analytical-rational one.
- The role of managers is not to plan or implement change *per se*, but to create or foster an organisational structure and climate which encourages and sustains experimentation, learning and risk-taking, and to develop a workforce that will take responsibility for identifying the need for change and implementing it.
- Though managers are expected to become facilitators rather than doers, they also have the prime responsibility for developing a collective vision or common purpose that gives direction to their organisation, and within which the appropriateness of any proposed change can be judged.
- The key organisational activities that allow these elements to operate successfully are information-gathering – about the external environment and internal objectives and capabilities; communication – the transmission, analysis and discussion of information; and learning – the ability to develop new skills, identify appropriate responses and draw knowledge from their own and others' past and present actions.

Though not always stated openly, the case for an Emergent approach to change is based on the assumption that all organisations operate in a turbulent, dynamic and unpredictable environment. Therefore, if the external world is changing in a rapid and uncertain way, organisations need to be continuously scanning their environment in order to respond in a timely and appropriate manner. Because this is a continuous and open-ended process, the Planned approach to change is inappropriate. To be successful, changes need to emerge locally and incrementally in order to respond to environmental threats and take advantage of opportunities.

Presented in this manner, there is an apparent coherence and validity to the Emergent approach. However, it is a fragile coherence and a challengeable validity. As far as coherence is concerned, some proponents of Emergent change, especially Pettigrew (1997) and Dawson (2003), clearly approach it from the processual perspective on organisations. However, it is not clear that Buchanan and Boddy (1992) and Wilson (1992) would fully subscribe to this view. In the case of Carnall (2003), Clarke (1994), Kanter *et al* (1992) and Kotter (1996), it is clear that they do not take a processual perspective. They do not doubt the importance of power and politics in the change process, but for them the issue is one of legitimacy and pragmatism. Managers and change agents have the legitimate right to introduce changes, but to do so they must use political skills in a pragmatic way to build support and overcome or avoid resistance. For the processualists, like the postmodernists, change is about dominant coalitions, and smaller groupings, trying to impose their will on all or part of an organisation in order to maintain or improve their position. Partly, this is explained by the fact that some of these writers (especially Dawson, 2003; Pettigrew, 1997; Wilson, 1992) are attempting to understand and analyse change from a critical perspective, whilst others (notably Kanter *et al*, 1992; Kotter, 1996) are more concerned with prescribing recipes and checklists for successful change. Therefore, though the advocates of Emergent change have a number of common bonds, their differing objectives and perspectives do put a question mark against the coherence of the Emergent approach.

An assessment of the validity or general applicability of the Emergent approach to change depends to a large extent on whether or not one subscribes to the view that all organisations operate in a dynamic and unpredictable environment to which they have to adapt continuously. The issue of the nature and uniformity of the environment in which organisations operate has been discussed extensively in previous chapters. The conclusion reached was that not all organisations face the same degree of environmental turbulence and that, in any case, it is possible to manipulate or change environmental constraints. This does not invalidate the Emergent approach, but it does indicate that some organisations, by accident or action, may find the Planned approach to change both appropriate and effective in their particular circumstances.

Obviously, the above raises questions over the universal applicability of the Emergent approach; even without reservations regarding its coherence and validity, however, there would still be serious criticisms of this approach. For example, many of its supporters seem to advocate the same approach to organisations as the Culture–Excellence school and are, therefore, open to the same criticisms (*see* Chapter 3). Given this link to Culture–Excellence, not surprisingly, a great deal of emphasis is placed on the need for appropriate organisational cultures. But, as the writers on Emergent change seem to sway between advocating the need for culture change (Kanter *et al*, 1992) and advocating the need to work with existing cultures (Kotter, 1996), it is not clear what they perceive the role of culture to be. In any case, as is noted in Chapter 5, the whole issue of the role and the manipulability of organisational culture is a veritable minefield. Indeed, as mentioned earlier, even Wilson (1992), who supports the Emergent perspective, was sceptical about the case for culture. Similar points can be made regarding the 'learning organisation' approach. As Whittington (1993: 130) commented:

> The danger of the purely 'learning' approach to change, therefore, is that ... managers [and others] may actually recognize the need for change, yet still refuse to 'learn' because they understand perfectly well the implications for their power and status. Resistance to change may not be 'stupid' ... but based on a very shrewd appreciation of the personal consequences.

A variant of this criticism relates to the impact of success on managerial learning. Miller (1993: 119) observed that, whilst managers generally start out by attempting to learn all they can about their organisation's environment, over time, as they gain experience, they 'form quite definite opinions of what works and why' and as a consequence tend to limit their search for information and knowledge. So experience, especially where it is based on success, may actually be a barrier to learning, in that it shapes the cognitive structures by which managers, and everyone else, see and interpret the world. Nystrom and Starbuck (1984: 55) observed:

> What people see, predict, understand, depends on their cognitive structures ... [which] manifest themselves in perceptual frameworks, expectations, world views, plans, goals ... myths, rituals, symbols ... and jargon.

This brings us neatly to the topic of the role of managers. Though this will be discussed extensively in Chapter 16, for now it should be noted that managers are the ones who appear to have to make the greatest change in their behaviour. As the above quotations indicate, however, they may neither welcome nor accept such a change, especially where it requires them to challenge and change their own beliefs, and where it runs counter to their experience of 'what works and why'. Also, if the possibility exists (as mentioned above) to manipulate environmental variables and constraints rather than having to change their behaviour, managers may perceive this as a more attractive or viable option.

Though the above reservations regarding the coherence and validity of the Emergent approach are fairly serious, there are three further criticisms that are equally serious. The first relates to the difference between their approach and the Planned approach. The Planned approach is attacked because of its reliance on Lewin's Three-Step model of unfreezing, moving and refreezing. It is argued that in a turbulent environment, organisations are in a constant state of change and that, therefore, to speak of unfreezing and refreezing is nonsense (Kanter *et al*, 1992). However, if one examines the process of change advocated by, for example, Dawson (1994), Kotter (1996) and Pettigrew *et al* (1992), though they argue to the contrary, they do speak of change as a 'transition' process with a beginning, middle and end. Indeed, Hendry (1996: 624) comments:

> Scratch any account of creating and managing change and the idea that change is a three-stage process which necessarily begins with a process of unfreezing will not be far below the surface.

There are others who strongly support Hendry's view that the Three-Step model has greater validity and wider usage than its critics acknowledge (Burnes, 2004; Elrod and Tippett, 2002). It should also be noted that there are a number of Lewin supporters amongst proponents of the complexity approach to change (Back, 1992; Tschacher and Brunner, 1995) and that MacIntosh and MacLean (2001) advocate the use of the Three-Step approach to identify and change order-generating rules.

The second criticism concerns the emphasis placed on the political and cultural aspects of change. Advocates of the Emergent approach have undoubtedly provided a valuable contribution to our understanding of change by highlighting the neglect of these important issues in the past. However, they have also been criticised from a number of perspectives for perhaps going too far the other way. Hendry (1996: 621) argues that 'The management of change has become ... overfocused on the political aspects of change', whilst Collins (1998: 100), voicing concerns of his own and of other researchers, argues that:

> ... in reacting to the problems and critiques of [the Planned approach], managers and practitioners have swung from a dependence on under-socialized models and explanations of change and instead have become committed to the arguments of, what might be called, over-socialized models of change.

This very much fits in with those who take a realist perspective on organisations; they argue that whilst the social world, including organisations, is a product of human action, it is not necessarily a product of conscious human design but exists independently of human beings (Connelly, 2000; Easton, 2000).

Lastly, though the Emergent approach undoubtedly raises key issues, and offers valuable insights and guidance, it does not appear to be as universally applicable as its advocates imply. In Chapter 8, we identified three different perspectives on change: the individual, group and system perspectives, and three categories of change: incremental, punctuated equilibrium and continuous transformation. The Emergent approach is specifically founded on the assumption that organisations operate in a dynamic environment where they have to transform themselves continuously in order to survive. It is, then, by its own definition, not applicable to organisations operating in environments which require disjointed incremental, or perhaps even punctuated equilibrium change programmes. The focus of Emergent change tends to be the organisation and its major sub-systems and, consequently, it is less suitable for situations requiring change at the individual and/or group levels. It is also the case that, both implicitly and explicitly, the Emergent approach advocates cooperative change rather than coercive or confrontational change, though it sees political manipulation and the deployment of power as essential to achieving this. However, as Dawson (2003) notes, it is also clear that there are many situations where managers prefer to push change through in a rapid and confrontational manner (see Stace and Dunphy, 2001; Edwardes, 1983; Franklin, 1997; Grinyer et al, 1988). Therefore, like Planned change, Emergent change has much to recommend it but, again like Planned change, it also has a number of significant shortcomings.

Conclusions

Organisations come in all shapes and sizes, provide a vast variety of products and services, and face an enormous array of challenges. Perhaps the only factor common to all organisations is change. Organisations never stand still, though the speed and magnitude of change does vary from organisation to organisation and over time. It is now generally accepted that the ability to manage change effectively is a crucial component of an organisation's ability to compete successfully. As Chapter 8 demonstrated, for many years, the Planned approach was considered as the best way of managing change. However, as was shown at the beginning of this chapter, from the early 1980s onwards, the Planned approach has faced a torrent of criticisms as to its suitability in a world of rapid and unpredictable change. In particular, its detractors claim that the notion that organisations operate in stable environments and can move from one fixed state to another is, to quote Kanter *et al* (1992: 10), a '... quaintly linear and static conception ... [and] ... wildly inappropriate.' In the light of these criticisms of the Planned approach, the chapter went on to describe the Emergent approach and make the case for it, being the best way to manage change. The Emergent approach sees organisational change as an ongoing process of adaptation to an unpredictable and ever-changing environment. For proponents of this view, change is a messy, unpredictable, open-ended and political affair. In such a situation, it is impossible for a few managers at the top of an organisation to identify and implement all the changes necessary to keep the organisation aligned with its environment. Consequently, successful change is a bottom-up, emergent, response to events. However, just as the Planned approach to change can be criticised as limited and flawed, similar criticisms can be made of the Emergent approach. In particular, it seems less a coherent approach to change and more a label for a collection of approaches critical of Planned change. Its proponents appear to disagree about key elements of Emergent change such as culture, organisational learning and the role of managers. In addition, the Emergent approach is criticised for its over-emphasis on the political dimension of change and its view that all organisations operate in a dynamic and unpredictable environment. It is also clear that Emergent change is limited in terms of both the types of organisational change to which it can be applied, and how it can be applied. Therefore, though it has apparent advantages over the Planned approach, or rather it is applicable to situations for which Planned change is not suitable, an examination of the Emergent approach reveals that there are serious question marks over its coherence, validity and general applicability.

From this and the previous chapter, it is clear that, even taken together, neither the Planned nor Emergent approach cover the broad spectrum of change events organisations encounter. Though both Planned and Emergent change have important theoretical and practical benefits, their dominance of the change literature appears to have led to a neglect of other approaches to change. In order to address this neglect, the next chapter will examine the change situations faced by organisations, and will construct *A Framework for Change* that identifies the range of change situations and a matching range of approaches to change.

Test your learning

Short answer questions

1 Briefly discuss the Processual approach to change.

2 List the main attributes of the Emergent approach to change.

3 How do proponents of the Emergent approach view the nature of the environment in which organisations operate?

4 What are the reasons for considering the complexity approach to change as part of the Emergent approach?

5 From the Emergent perspective, what are the five features of organisations that promote or hinder successful change?

6 List the main criticisms of the Emergent approach.

7 What are the implications of the Emergent approach for managerial behaviour?

Essay questions

1 Discuss and evaluate the following statement: Emergent change does not offer a coherent alternative to Planned change but merely provides an umbrella for those who oppose it.

2 To what extent and how do Caldwell's four models of the change agent undermine Buchanan and Boddy's generic model of the expertise of the change agent?

Suggested further reading

1 Dawson, P (2003) *Organizational Change: A Processual Approach*. Routledge: London. Patrick Dawson's book is an excellent guide to the processual approach to change which raises some important questions about both Planned and Emergent change.
2 Kotter, JP (1996) *Leading Change*. Harvard Business School Press: Boston, MA, USA. John Kotter's work represents the more prescriptive and pragmatic wing of Emergent change.

Chapter 10

A framework for change

Approaches and choices

Learning objectives

After studying this chapter, you should be able to:

- recognise that, even taken together, the Planned and Emergent approaches do not cover all change situations;
- list the range of change situations that organisations face;
- appreciate the variety of approaches to change;
- understand the situations in which the various approaches to change are most appropriately used;
- describe how organisations can increase their degree of choice when undertaking change.

Exhibit 10.1   Learning from others

Why companies have much to learn from charities

Conventional wisdom says the voluntary sector has much to learn from the commercial world. But our work suggests the opposite: voluntary organisations often display precisely those management skills that leading companies are struggling to acquire, particularly in managing change.

Both sectors face similar forces for change. In the 'market' for donations, voluntary organisations, just like businesses, face increasing consumer choice. While competing outlets for discretionary spending proliferate, the voluntary sector's income has remained more or less static in real terms. This intensifies pressure to compete for funds and to keep costs down.

Prices, too, are squeezed. Government-funded social services, important customers for the voluntary sector, increasingly set prices at the level of the lowest-cost provider, limiting what voluntary organisations may charge.

Consumers of charitable and commercial services alike demand continually improving standards. Stakeholders in both voluntary and commercial organisations want more accountability for performance. Donors, end-users, volunteers and members all require that charitable funds are demonstrably well managed, just as shareholders require of corporate capital. And success in a voluntary organisation, as in a business, depends on success in the market for talent. Competition to hire the best people is equally strong.

In society too, charities and businesses see the same emerging trends, though charities seem instinctively better at adapting to them.

First, all organisations are under pressure from stakeholders to be more socially responsible. Voluntary organisations handle this effectively – after all, they exist mainly to serve social needs and usually involve local communities in delivering services.

Second, government regulation has greatly increased during the past 15 years, yet voluntary services have always been 'regulated' by their explicit codes of ethical standards. They use compliance with these standards to measure success, in the absence of a profit motive.

Third, people are seeking better quality of life – more meaningful work and increased leisure time.

Again, a voluntary organisation's objective is to improve the quality of its target groups' lives, and to provide a worthwhile means for volunteers to participate in the community.

Voluntary organisations often cope better with change than businesses. We believe this is because they are, as Henry Mintzberg said, 'pioneers in the motivation and productivity of knowledge workers'. They are particularly good at:

- Changing, but staying the same. Voluntary organisations change with the times, but hold on to their history. They steep new staff in their traditions and values, by induction courses and apprenticeships. But precedent does not bind their people. Useful new practices and ideas spread fast by informal networks. The need to do more with less encourages initiative and creativity.
- Thinking big, acting small. A voluntary organisation may have a nationally or internationally recognised name but it will often be rooted in local operations. Fuzzy organisational structures help charities to think big and to act small. At first glance, they may look sclerotic: reporting lines abound; decisions are often taken by large groups of elected frontline representatives. But there are benefits. The lack of central executive power means local managers can act on their own initiative.
- Managing multiple stakeholders. Voluntary organisations are used to managing multiple stakeholders with disparate interests. Their techniques include involving people from different stakeholder groups in their decision-making bodies, and pursuing different objectives to satisfy different groups. They thank stakeholders for their interest by such means as personalised marketing or donor receptions. And they listen carefully to stakeholders when setting their goals.
- Getting everyone to own organisational goals. Most voluntary organisation staff are unusually dedicated. That is partly because they are so committed to the organisation's goals. Staff commitment to organisational policy is reinforced by their membership of frontline forums that take important policy decisions.

Exhibit 10.1 *continued*

■ Making values matter. In voluntary organisations, it is not only what gets done that is important but also how it is done. Staff feel they can challenge senior managers if they fall short of the organisation's values.

Should companies try to emulate the voluntary sector? There are two reasons executives should take the challenge seriously.

First, the benefits are real and realisable. Business managers already know they can tap extraordinary employee motivation in a crisis. How much better to tap these reserves every day. Businesses could achieve the involvement and commitment to corporate values we see in the voluntary sector if they do what the voluntary organisations do: for example, encourage and reward staff for mentoring, for building and maintaining institutional knowledge, for tending networks, for creating involving events.

Second, the differences between voluntary and private sector organisations are more apparent than real. Certainly, volunteers are motivated to work for nothing while businesses must pay people to do work they otherwise would not do. But 'wage slaves', too, get personal fulfilment from their work. And if volunteers are demotivated by poor management, they can quit in an instant. Commercial employees may not be able to leave so quickly, but the best of them usually can, and will, run frighteningly fast.

Businesses and voluntary organisations need better capabilities to manage their environments. Businesses would do well to work with voluntary organisations, to bring them commercial rigour, but – more importantly – to learn their skills in helping employees to manage change.

Source: Keith Leslie, Vaughan Lindsay, Helen Mullings and Neville Salkeld, *Financial Times*, 9 February 1999, p. 16.

Introduction

Since the Industrial Revolution, the conventional wisdom has been that the private sector is better at managing and changing organisations than either the public or voluntary sectors. This view is based on the belief that only free-market competition will drive organisations and individuals to innovate and change. However, as the article by Leslie *et al* (1999)(Exhibit 10.1) shows, the voluntary sector faces considerable competitive and other pressures which require innovative responses. Similarly, as will be described in case studies 4 and 10 in Part 3 of this book, the public sector has come under increasing pressure over the last 25 years to find new and more cost-effective ways to provide services. Therefore, as the Leslie *et al* article also shows, the notion that the private sector is always the leader and the other sectors always the followers when it comes to managing and changing organisations is something of a misconception. It must be recognised, however, that different sectors and different organisations face widely-differing challenges, and what is appropriate for one organisation or sector is not necessarily appropriate for another. This is particularly the case when considering organisational change. As Stickland (1998: 14) remarks:

> ... the problem with studying change is that it parades across many subject domains under numerous guises, such as transformation, development, metamorphosis, transmutation, evolution, regeneration, innovation, revolution and transition to name but a few.

The last two chapters have reviewed the two dominant approaches to managing change, identifying their strengths, weaknesses and the situations they are designed to address. It has become clear that, even taken together, neither the Planned nor

Emergent approach covers the broad spectrum of change events that organisations encounter. Pettigrew (2000: 245–6) observes that:

> There is a long tradition in the social sciences and in management and organization theory of using bipolar modes of thinking: dichotomies, paradoxes, contradictions and dualities. ... The duality of planned versus emergent change has served us well as an attention director but may well now be ready for retirement.

Though both Planned and Emergent change have important theoretical and practical benefits, their dominance of the change literature has led to a neglect of other approaches. In order to address this neglect, this chapter will seek to identify the range of change situations organisations face and match these to a wider group of approaches. This will enable the construction of a framework that will allow different change situations to be matched to appropriate approaches to managing change. It will then be argued that, by manipulating key variables in this framework, it is possible for organisations to have genuine choices in what to change, how to change and when to change.

Varieties of change

As noted in Chapter 8, types of change can be categorised as to whether their primary focus applies to individuals, groups, or systems and sub-systems. As far as models of change are concerned, once again as noted in Chapter 8, the three main ones are the incremental model; the punctuated equilibrium model; and the continuous transformation model. Figure 10.1 brings these together to create a change matrix that, as the examples illustrate, appears to cover most situations. However, there are other types, models and forms of change that expand on, cut across or are not included in this matrix. Senior (2002), drawing on the work of Grundy (1993), identifies three categories of change: *smooth incremental*, covering slow, systematic, evolutionary change; *bumpy*

	Incremental	Punctuated	Continuous
Individuals	Learning	Promotion	Career development
Groups	*Kaizen*	Team building	Changes in composition and tasks
Systems	Fine tuning	BPR	Culture

Figure 10.1 Varieties of change

incremental, pertaining to periods where the smooth flow of change accelerates; and *discontinuous change*, which is similar to the punctuated equilibrium model. Kanter *et al* (1992), addressing the issue of transformational change, noted that it can be achieved either by a Bold Stroke approach (rapid overall change) or a Long March approach (incremental change leading to transformation over an extended period of time).

In a similar vein, Beer and Nohria (2000) identify two basic archetypes, or theories of change: Theory E, which is similar to Kanter *et al*'s Bold Stroke, and Theory O, which is similar to Kanter *et al*'s Long March. The main objective of Theory E change is to maximise shareholder value. It is applied in situations where an organisation's performance has diminished to such an extent that its main shareholders demand major and rapid change to improve the organisation's financial performance. Typically this is a 'hard' approach based on downsizing, divestment of non-core or low-performing businesses, and the heavy use of financial incentives. Theory O is also aimed at improving an organisation's performance, but this is more a 'soft' approach based on incrementally developing the organisation's culture and its human capabilities, and promoting organisational learning.

Beer and Nohria (2000) believe that both of these are valid models of change but that both have their flaws. Theory E can achieve short-term financial gains but at the cost of denuding an organisation of the human capabilities and organisational culture necessary for long-term survival. Theory O, whilst focusing on people and culture, falls into the trap of not restructuring to concentrate on core activities, thus failing to deliver shareholder value. To achieve the gains of both these approaches, whilst avoiding the pitfalls, Beer and Nohria advocate using these in tandem by focusing on the rapid restructuring elements of Theory E but following this with the human capability development offered by Theory O.

Cummings and Worley (2001: 30) identify a 'continuum ranging from incremental changes that involve fine-tuning the organization to quantum changes that entail fundamentally altering how it operates'. Stace and Dunphy (2001), in a like but more detailed way, identify a four-stage change continuum that comprises the following: fine-tuning, incremental adjustment, modular transformation and corporate transformation. Looking at the latter, Stace and Dunphy argue that corporate transformations can take four forms: developmental transitions; task-focused transitions; charismatic transformations; and turnarounds. For Peters (1989), rapid, disruptive and continuous change is the only appropriate form of change there is. With echoes of Peters, Quinn (1996) differentiates between incremental change, which he sees as leading to slow death, or deep, radical change leading to irreversible transformation. Pettigrew *et al* (1992) distinguish between types of change by their scale and importance. Their change continuum spans operational change (small-scale, relatively unimportant) and strategic change (major and important structural changes). Buchanan and Boddy's (1992) classification is almost the same as Pettigrew *et al*'s, but they use two dimensions: incremental change to radical change; and changes that are of central importance to the organisation to those that are peripheral to its purpose. Kotter (1996) ignores the notion of a continuum of change as such and, instead, argues that organisations need to be continuously transforming themselves through a series of large and small interlinked change projects spanning different levels and functions and having different timescales.

One could of course extend this review further by including other writers (e.g. Dawson, 2003; Strickland, 1998; Wilson, 1992); however, the end product would be the same: change can be viewed as running along a continuum from incremental to transformational. Incremental or fine-tuning forms of change are geared more to changing the activities/performance/behaviour/attitudes of individuals and groups, whereas transformational change is geared towards the processes/structures and culture of the entire organisation. Obviously, there are differences in how these writers construe these concepts. Some writers see fine-tuning or incremental change as being relatively isolated and/or relatively unimportant (i.e. Stace and Dunphy, 2001; Pettigrew *et al*, 1992), whilst others see it as being part of an overall plan to transform an organisation (e.g. Kanter *et al*, 1992; Senior, 1997). In contrast, all seem to view transformational change as being strategic and important; though there are those who see it as being a relatively slow process (Kotter, 1996), those who see it as being a relatively rapid one (Peters, 1989), and those who argue that it can take both forms (Kanter *et al*, 1992; Stace and Dunphy, 2001).

Regardless of these differences, the overall view as shown by Figure 10.2 is that change can be seen as running along a continuum from small-scale incremental change to large-scale transformational change. This of course is no surprise; intuitively, one would expect change to range from small-scale to large-scale and from operational to strategic. The important consideration is perhaps not the type of change but how it should be conceived and managed. Implicit in the arguments of the Emergent approach is the view that Planned change stands at the left-hand end of this spectrum and Emergent change at the right-hand end, and that what separates them is the nature of the environment (*see* Figure 10.3). Planned change is considered suitable for (relatively) stable environments, with Emergent change being better suited to more turbulent environments. As shown in Chapters 7 and 8, however, these two approaches to change are more limited than their advocates claim. In particular, both the Planned and Emergent approaches tend to stress the collaborative and consultative approach to managing change. Stace and Dunphy (2001), however, identify four approaches to managing change based on the degree to which employees are involved

Figure 10.2 Change continuum

Figure 10.3 Approaches to change

in planning and executing change, as follows: collaborative, consultative, directive and coercive. They also argue that consultative and directive approaches tend to dominate, except where rapid organisational transformations are required, when more coercive approaches come into play. Kotter (1996) takes a different view, seeing the overall direction of change as being decided by senior managers, but its implementation being the responsibility of empowered managers and employees at all levels. Boddy and Buchanan (1992) believe that the way in which a change should be managed will be viewed differently, depending on whether it is central or peripheral to the organisation's purpose. Davenport (1993) expands on these two issues by constructing a list of five principal factors that influence how a project will be managed: the scale of change; the level of uncertainty about the outcome; the breadth of change across the organisation; the magnitude of change in terms of attitudes and behaviour; and the timescale for implementation. Storey (1992), taking a slightly different tack, begins by identifying two key dimensions. The first concerns the degree of collaboration between the parties concerned: varying from change that is unilaterally constructed by management, to change brought about by some form of joint agreement with those involved. The second dimension concerns the form that change takes: ranging from change that is introduced as a complete package, to change comprising a sequence of individual initiatives. From these two dimensions, Storey constructs a fourfold typology of change:

1 **Top-down systemic change** aimed at transforming the organisation.
2 **Piecemeal initiatives** devised and implemented by departments or sections in an unconnected fashion.
3 **Bargaining for change** where a series of targets are jointly agreed between managers and workers, but are pursued in a piecemeal fashion.
4 **Systemic jointism** where managers and workers agree a total package of changes designed to achieve organisational transformation.

As with the earlier review of the types of change, to make sense of this review of the nature of change and how it should be managed, we need to find a way of categorising and tabulating the various viewpoints. However, this is a far from straightforward exercise. Stace and Dunphy's (2001) fourfold categorisation of approaches to change, ranging from cooperative to coercive, is useful in that it appears to cover most of the managerial approaches on offer. However, it is the circumstances in which each of these might best be used that is perhaps of most concern. Boddy and Buchanan's categorisation of central–peripheral is interesting but, in most instances, this appears to boil down to an issue of project size. Almost by definition, all major projects can be considered as central by virtue of their size and, for a similar reason, most smaller projects are, relatively speaking, peripheral. Davenport's five factors are perhaps more useful in helping us to categorise change, especially those concerning uncertainty, behaviour and attitudes, and timescale. As we have noted frequently in this book, uncertainty tends to be present when the environment is changing in a rapid and unpredictable fashion. This requires organisations to respond quickly; advocates of the Emergent approach believe this is best done by small- to medium-scale local or cross-functional or process changes. The ability to do this, however, is dependent on having appropriate structures, attitudes and cultures in place. If this is not the case, then change will be delayed or not quick enough and, as

Stace and Dunphy (2001) showed, will be likely to require rapid transformational change undertaken in a directive or coercive fashion. Nevertheless, both Kanter *et al* (1992) and Beer and Nohria (2000), as well as the review of culture in Chapter 5, argue that changes in attitudes and culture cannot be achieved in a rapid and coercive manner. That type of approach tends to be effective in changing structures and processes, but achieving attitudinal and/or cultural change is a much slower process.

A framework for change

If we summarise the above views, we can create yet another change continuum. At one end is slow change, where the focus is on behavioural and cultural change. At the other end of the continuum is rapid change, where the focus is on major changes in structures and processes. If we merge this together with Figures 10.2 and 10.3, what we get, as Figure 10.4 shows, are four quadrants, each of which has a distinct focus in terms of change. The top half of the figure, Quadrants 1 and 2, represents situations where organisations operating in a turbulent environment need to make large-scale, organisation-wide changes to either their culture or structure. The bottom half of the figure, Quadrants 3 and 4, represents situations where organisations operating in a stable environment need to make small-scale, piecemeal and localised adjustments to attitudes and behaviours or tasks and procedures. As can be seen, the left-hand side of the figure, Quadrants 1 and 4, represents situations where the main focus of change is the human side of the organisation, i.e. cultural and attitudinal/behavioural change. As argued above, these sorts of changes are likely to be best achieved through a relatively slow, participative approach, rather than a rapid

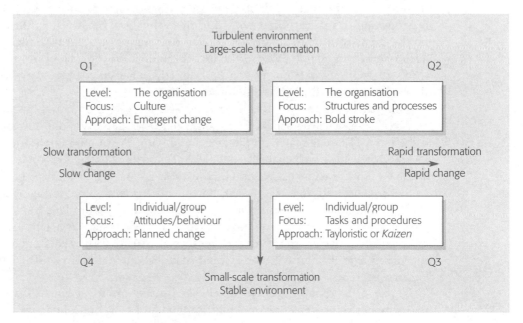

Figure 10.4 A framework for change

and directive or coercive one. The right-hand side of Figure 10.4 represents situations where the primary focus is on achieving changes to the technical side of the organisation, i.e. structures, processes, tasks and procedures. These types of changes tend to be less participative in nature and relatively more rapid in their execution.

Taking each of the quadrants in turn: Quadrant 1 identifies situations where the culture of an organisation operating in a turbulent environment is no longer appropriate. For such relatively large-scale initiatives, where the main focus is culture change at the level of the entire organisation or large parts of it, the Emergent approach (e.g. Kanter *et al*'s Long March), which emphasises both the collaborative and political dimensions of change, is likely to be most appropriate. As argued in Chapter 5, attempts to change culture through top-down, directive or coercive initiatives are liable to fail. Therefore, where they are to be successful, such forms of change are less likely to be consciously embarked on and more likely to 'emerge' from a host of initiatives that arise in response to changes in the environment, though this does not necessarily exclude some elements of deliberation and guidance from senior managers. Although the organisation may be operating in a turbulent environment and, therefore, individual elements of the cultural change may be rapid, the overall cultural transformation is likely to be a slow process.

Quadrant 2 relates to situations where the focus is on achieving major changes in structures and processes at the level of the entire organisation (e.g. Kanter *et al*'s Bold Stroke). Situations where such changes are required arise for a variety of reasons. It may be that an organisation finds itself in serious trouble and needs to respond quickly to realign itself with its environment. Alternatively, it may be that an organisation is not experiencing a crisis, but that it perceives that it will face one unless it restructures itself to achieve a better fit with its environment. In such cases, it may not be possible or advisable to change the structure slowly or on a piecemeal basis and, therefore, a major and rapid reorganisation is necessary. Because it involves the entire organisation or major components of it, this is likely to be driven by the centre and to be the focus of a political struggle, given that major structural changes are usually accompanied by major shifts in the distribution of power. Therefore, the new structure will be imposed from the top in a directive or even coercive way, depending on the balance between winners and losers.

Quadrant 3 presents a different picture. This represents organisations operating in a relatively stable environment where changes to the technical side of the organisation tend to be relatively small-scale and piecemeal and with few (if any) implications for behaviour and attitudes. Such changes take place at the individual and group level rather than at the level of the entire organisation. How these are managed will depend on the culture of the organisation. In a traditional, bureaucratic organisation, a Tayloristic approach may be adopted, i.e. specialist managers and engineers will identify the 'best way of working' and impose it. In a more participative culture, such as a Japanese company, a more collaborative approach may be appropriate, such as a *Kaizen* initiative that brings together a team comprising workers and specialists. But either is possible and it should be possible to achieve either in a relatively speedy fashion.

Finally, Quadrant 4 covers relatively small-scale initiatives whose main objective is performance improvement through attitudinal and behavioural change at the individual and group level. Once again, organisations in this situation tend to be operating in a relatively stable environment and, therefore, the Planned approach, with its emphasis on collaboration and participation, is likely to be most appropriate. However, because such changes focus on behavioural and attitudinal change, they tend to be relatively slow.

Of course, it could be argued that, at the organisational level, it is difficult to identify situations that involve solely cultural changes or involve solely structural changes. A similar comment could be made with regard to attitudinal/behavioural change and changes to tasks and procedures at the individual/group level. Such comments are valid to an extent, but the real issue is to identify the main focus of the change. Chapter 3 examined the work of the Culture–Excellence approach. Here it was shown that writers such as Tom Peters and Rosabeth Moss Kanter were arguing for structural change in order to promote the values and behaviours necessary for organisations to survive in an increasingly complex world. Therefore, though significant structural changes were recommended, these were part of the process of culture change and not an end in themselves. John Kotter, as noted in the previous chapter, advocates the need for organisations to restructure themselves on a continuous basis in order to meet the challenges of the future. At different times and in different areas, he believes that this can involve all of the types of change shown in Figure 10.1. There are also many cases, as Kotter argues, where an organisation already has an appropriate culture and where changes to its overall structure, and piecemeal changes to its component parts, are seen as working with and reinforcing the existing organisational culture rather than leading to its replacement.

Therefore, the question of whether changes can be labelled as mainly structure-orientated or mainly people-orientated is partly a matter of sequencing: what does the organisation need to do first? It is also partly concerned with the extent to which environmental turbulence has a uniform effect across an organisation. As shown in Chapter 2, in the 1960s, James Thompson (1967) identified that different sections of an organisation, by accident or design, could experience different levels of uncertainty. On this basis, it would be perfectly feasible for some parts of an organisation to be experiencing relatively low levels of uncertainty and concentrating on small-scale, piecemeal changes whilst at the same time the overall organisation was going through a process of rapid transformation.

Where does this leave us? Drawing on the work of Davenport (1993), we need to distinguish between initiatives that focus on fundamental attitudinal change and those aimed at fundamental structural change. As mentioned by Allaire and Firsirotu (1984) and as argued in Chapter 5, there is a strong relationship between organisational structures and organisational cultures, and so changes in one may require corresponding changes in the other. As was also argued earlier, however, it is much easier and quicker to change structures than to change cultures. Consequently, we need to take into account the timescale for change. Culture change, to be effective, is likely to be slow and involves incremental changes to the human side of the organisation. Also, because of its nature, it is likely to be participative and collaborative. Rapid change is only likely to be effective or necessary where the main changes are structural changes, or where the organisation is in such trouble that delay is not an option. In the case of structured change, this may involve some consultation but is likely to have a large element of direction from the centre. In the latter case, where the organisation is in trouble because of the urgency of the situation, change is likely to be directive and, probably, coercive.

There is one further point that needs to be noted, and that relates to how these various approaches can be used in combination. In a manner reminiscent of Mintzberg's (1994) definition of 'umbrella' strategies, Pettigrew *et al* (1992: 297) write of instances where change is both 'intentional and emergent'. Storey (1992) identifies the need for change projects whose outlines are decided at corporate level with little or no consultation, but whose implementation comprises an interrelated series of change initiatives, some or all of which could be the product of local cooperation and consultation. Kotter (1996) takes a similar perspective. He sees strategic change as comprising a series of large and small projects aimed at achieving the same overall objectives but which are begun at different times, which can be managed differently and which vary in nature. Buchanan and Storey (1997) also hint at this when criticising Planned change for attempting to impose order and a linear sequence to processes that are untidy, messy, multi-level and multi-function, and that develop in an iterative and backtracking manner. This is also identified by Kanter *et al* (1992) when speaking of Long Marches and Bold Strokes. They argue that Bold Strokes often have to be followed by a whole series of smaller-scale changes over a more extended timescale in order to embed the changes brought about by the Bold Stroke. Beer and Nohria (2000) are even more explicit in arguing for the use of Theory E and Theory O in tandem. Therefore, when considering major change projects, one should not see them as being managed solely in a cooperative fashion or solely in a coercive fashion. Instead, they may have elements of both but at different levels, at different times and managed by different people. They may also, indeed probably will, unfold in an unexpected way which will require rethinking and backtracking from time to time.

A framework for choice

As can be seen from Figure 10.4, what appears to be on offer is a menu approach to change whereby organisations, or more accurately those who manage them, can choose the approach which fits their circumstances. This conception of a multiplicity of approaches is in line with the call by Dunphy and Stace (1993: 905) for 'a model of change that is essentially a "situational" or "contingency model", one that indicates how to vary strategies to achieve "optimum fit" with the changing environment'. If we were to stop at this point, it might be considered that we had indeed made significant progress in our understanding of change; yet there would still be one essential question outstanding: what about choice? We have identified situations where these various approaches seem appropriate or not, but does that mean they cannot be used in other situations and does that mean that the context cannot be changed? Supposing organisations, whose management prefer a cooperative approach, find themselves seriously out of alignment with their environment: is their only option rapid and coercive structural change? Or, alternatively, where managers prefer a more directive, less participative style, are they compelled to adopt a more participative style and culture?

These questions revolve around two issues. The first issue concerns the extent to which an organisation can influence the forces driving it to change in one direction or another. If we accept that the speed and nature of the changes that organisations are required to make are dependent upon the nature of the environment in which they are operating, then choice will relate to the extent that organisations can influence, manipulate or recreate their environment to suit their preferred way of working. This is a subject that has been examined a number of times so far, especially in Chapters 5 and 6. The conclusion reached was that organisations could influence their environment, either to stabilise or to destabilise it. If this is the case, then the important question is not just how organisations can do this, but whether, finding themselves in trouble, they have the time to influence their environment?

This leads on to the second issue: to what extent and for how long can an organisation operate with structures, practices and cultures that are out of line with its environment? The answer to this question revolves around Child's (1972) concept of equifinality. As discussed in Chapter 6, equifinality 'quite simply means that different sorts of internal arrangements are perfectly compatible with identical contextual or environmental states' (Sorge, 1997: 13). This does not imply that any structure is suitable for any environment. What it does suggest, though, is that total alignment between structure and environment is not always necessary. The duration for which this non-alignment is sustainable will clearly vary with the degree of non-alignment and the circumstances of the organisation in question; at the very least, however, it does offer organisations the potential to stave off realignment for some time during which they can influence or change their circumstances. It follows that Figure 10.4 depicts not only a framework for change but also a framework for choice.

In summary, therefore, what we can see, as Pettigrew (2000) suggested, is that the debate between Planned change and Emergent change is too narrow. It is too narrow in the sense that there are other approaches to change that organisations have available to them; in particular, it tends to ignore the more coercive and directive approaches to change that, in many organisations, may be more prevalent than more cooperative ones. It is also too narrow in the sense that it assumes that change is uni-directional, i.e. is driven by the environment. Organisations do have the opportunity to make choices about what to change, how to change and when to change. This does not mean that all organisations will exercise such choices or that those which do will be successful. Nor, as Chapter 6 argued, does it mean that choice is not severely constrained. It does mean, however, that those who do not recognise that choice exists may be putting themselves in a worse competitive position than those who do.

Conclusions

The previous two chapters examined the Planned and Emergent approaches to change, which have successively dominated the theory and, to a large extent, the practice of organisational change over the past 50 years. Chapter 8 was devoted to the Planned approach to change. It was argued that, though elaborated upon and supported by a considerable number of very useful tools and techniques, it has remained essentially true to Kurt Lewin's original 'unfreezing', 'moving' and 'refreezing' approach. In the increasingly dynamic and unpredictable business environment of the 1980s, writers began to question the appropriateness of a top-down approach that saw the process of change primarily in terms of a 'beginning, middle and end' framework. In place of the Planned approach, as was shown in Chapter 9, the Emergent approach began to gain support. With its emphasis on bottom-up and open-ended change, it appeared to offer a more appropriate method of accomplishing the stream of adaptations organisations believed they needed to make in order to bring themselves back into line with their environment. However, Chapter 9 also showed that Emergent change may have as many shortcomings as Planned change.

Nevertheless, the two approaches appear to have some striking similarities, especially the stress they place on change as being a learning process. They also share a common, and major, difficulty, which is that whilst both claim to be universally applicable, they were developed with particular change situations, organisation types and environments in mind. The Planned approach appears to be predicated on the assumptions that organisations operate in stable or relatively predictable environments, that managers can identify where change is required, that change projects are concerned primarily with group attitudes and behaviours, and that change is about moving from one fixed point to another fixed point and that the steps or phases in between are relatively clear and realisable. The Planned approach also appears to assume that organisations, managers and employees are open and frank, they welcome involvement, and are willing to change, or that these attributes can be achieved with the application of the appropriate tools and techniques.

The Emergent approach, on the other hand, assumes that organisations are open and fluid systems that operate in unpredictable and uncertain conditions over which they have little control. It further assumes that change is a continuous process of adaptation and transformation which, because of its speed and frequency, managers can neither fully identify nor effectively control centrally. Therefore, from the Emergent perspective, identifying and managing change has to be the responsibility of everyone in the organisation. This view portrays managers, who are seen as highly competent and adaptable, as capable of changing themselves from outmoded controllers and coordinators to new-style facilitators and partners; and employees are seen as willing to take responsibility for identifying deficiencies and implementing change. Above all, and perhaps somewhat contradictorily, change is seen as being a political process whereby different groups and individuals strive to protect or enhance their power and position. As mentioned earlier, it is on this last point – the overriding importance of power and politics in the change process – that postmodernists are most in agreement with the Emergent approach and realists most in disagreement.

As Chapter 8 showed, the Planned approach has had a considerable impact on organisation practice since its inception in the 1940s. However, despite its undoubted merits, as argued earlier, it does appear limited in terms of the situations in which it can successfully be applied. In particular, the Planned approach has been criticised for its lack of suitability to situations requiring large-scale change and/or ones where political and power considerations are prevalent. However, as was demonstrated in Chapter 9, the Emergent approach, which is seen as being suitable to such situations, also has major drawbacks, especially its heavy emphasis on the political dimension of change and its contradictory tendency, both implicitly and explicitly, to characterise change as a slow and cooperative process. It has also been argued that, even taken together, the Planned and Emergent approaches do not cover all change situations. In particular, neither approach seems suitable for situations where the primary focus is rapid and radical structural change.

Instead of portraying the argument regarding the most appropriate approach to change as a contest between the merits of the Planned and Emergent approaches, the

Framework for Change (Figure 10.4) provides an overview of the range of change situations organisations face, and the approaches they are offered and the types of situations in which they can best be applied.

Though this Contingency-type approach to change appears to have some merit, it is subject to the same sort of criticisms levelled at Contingency Theory in Chapter 2. However, this chapter has also argued that, if we adopt the perspective developed in previous chapters and see the environment and other organisational constraints as potentially manipulable or subject to managerial choice, many of these criticisms can be answered and new possibilities opened up. It has to be recognised that there is dispute between the realists and postmodernists as to what can be manipulated and the degree of choice which exists. However, this is a matter of degree; both acknowledge the existence of choice. Therefore, some organisations will find that the organisational adjustments required to accommodate their position on the environment continuum coincide with the dominant view in the organisation of how it should operate. In that case, whether the approach to change adopted is Planned or Emergent, directive or cooperative, it will fit in with both how the organisation wishes to operate and the needs of the environment. Some organisations will, obviously, find that the dominant view internally of how they should operate is out of step with what is required to align or re-align them with their environment. Such organisations face a number of choices ranging from whether to attempt to change their structure, culture or style of management to accommodate the environment, or whether to attempt to manipulate the environment and other constraints so as to align them more closely with the dominant view within the organisation of how it should operate. Still further, there will be other organisations who face severe problems either because they failed to respond quickly enough or in an appropriate manner to changes in their environment, or because the environment moved too rapidly for an incremental approach to respond adequately. Nevertheless, by showing that a more conducive environment can be brought about, the framework also provides those who wish to promote more cooperative approaches to change with the means to argue their case in situations where previously more directive and coercive measures appeared to be the only option.

The concept of a *Framework for Change* that allows approaches to change to be matched to environmental conditions and organisational constraints is clearly attractive. The fact that it incorporates the potential for managers, and others, to exercise some choice or influence over their environment and other constraints allows the model to move beyond the limitations of mechanistic and rational perspectives on organisations, and into the heartland of organisational reality. In addition, though not by accident, it is in harmony with the approach to strategy developed in Chapters 6 and 7.

Nevertheless, though such a model of change has its attractions, its usefulness depends on how well it accommodates the reality of organisational life. To investigate this, the next part of the book (Chapters 11–13) presents ten case studies of strategy development and change. This is then followed, in Chapter 14, by a comparison of the case studies with this and the previous four chapters (6, 7, 8 and 9) dealing with change management and strategy. The intention in Chapter 15 is to present a model of change management that incorporates both theory and practice.

Test your learning

■ Short answer questions

1   To what extent can we say that Kanter *et al*'s (1992) 'Bold Stroke' and 'Long March' approaches to change are the same as Beer and Nohria's (2000) 'Theory E' and 'Theory O' approaches?

2   Using the headings in Figure 10.1, identify your own 'varieties of change'.

3   Describe Storey's (1992) fourfold typology of change. Give a real-life example of each type of change.

4   What are the main components of the *Framework for Change* shown in Figure 10.4?

5   Evaluate the following statement: At the organisation level, change can either be structure-orientated or culture-orientated but it cannot be both at the same time.

6   To what extent and how does Child's (1972) concept of 'equifinality' indicate that organisations may be able to control the pace at which they change?

7   Summarise the case presented in Chapters 5 and 6 that organisations can manipulate or change the contingencies they face.

■ Essay questions

1   What are the arguments for and against Pettigrew's (2000: 245–6) comment that: 'The duality of planned versus emergent change has served us well as an attention director but may well now be ready for retirement.'

2   Use the Framework for Change, Figure 10.4, to analyse change in one of the case studies in Part 3 of this book or for a case of your own choosing. In particular, identify the type of change or changes involved, the selection and suitability of the approach to change and the degree to which the approach was aligned with the management style of the organisation.

Suggested further reading

1   Beer, M and Nohria, N (eds) (2000) *Breaking the Code of Change*. Harvard Business School Press: Boston, MA, USA.
This edited collection contains contributions by many of the leading thinkers on organisational change. It covers the main approaches to change, including the Planned and Emergent.

Part Three

Case studies in strategy development and change management

Chapter 11

Case studies in strategic change

Learning objectives

After studying the case studies in this chapter, you should be able to:

- appreciate how small changes can have large impacts on an entire industry;
- understand how real-life organisations develop and implement strategy;
- describe how organisations can reinvent themselves;
- discuss the traps that organisations can fall into when seeking to bring about strategic change;
- show how staff can be motivated or demotivated by different approaches to strategic change;
- appreciate that managers can exercise considerable choice in terms of their organisation's strategy;
- identify the positive and negative roles played by managers in developing and implementing strategy;
- discuss the implications of internationalisation and globalisation on organisation strategy.

Introduction

The five chapters in Part 2 of this book examined approaches to strategy development and change management by leading theorists and practitioners. Chapters 6 and 7 described the origins and development of strategic management, showing how it had moved from being considered as a rational perspective solely concerned with product–market issues, to a situation where there are radically differing perspectives on its purpose, function and efficacy. The quantitative rationality of the Classical approach is still very much in evidence, but it has been challenged by the fatalism of the Evolutionists, the pragmatism of the Processualists and the societal perspective of the Systemicists – though no one now appears to doubt the need to view organisations in their entirety, rather than being merely concerned with external variables. In a similar way, Chapters 8 and 9 described the development of change management, showing that many theorists and practitioners see it as having moved from being a planned, predictable and rational process to one that is inherently unpredictable and where politics and power have a major role to play. In Chapter 10, the concluding chapter of Part 2, however, it was argued that the various approaches to strategy development and organisational change all have their drawbacks as well as benefits. It was also argued that none of these approaches has universal applicability; all are situation-dependent. Successful change, therefore, requires organisations to choose the most appropriate approach for their circumstances or, as was emphasised, to change their circumstances to accommodate their favoured approach.

This chapter presents four case studies that focus on strategic change at the industry and organisational levels. In particular, the case studies draw attention to the challenges that new technologies, especially the Internet, and internationalisation and globalisation are having on organisations.

Case Study 1 looks not at an individual organisation but at an entire industry – the music industry. This shows how rapidly the Internet is transforming the industry and the difficulties faced by existing companies in maintaining their competitive position. It also shows that there is a deep division between those who see the Internet as another way of making money and those who see it as a way of creating sharing communities.

Case Study 2 focuses on the disastrous experience of Marconi. This was a company that, as GEC, had been primarily focused on the heavy electrical industry, consumer goods and defence. At the end of the 1990s, new managers tried to transform it into a telecoms equipment company that could take advantage of the Internet age. Within a space of two years, most of the old businesses had been sold, billions of pounds were borrowed and spent on new telecoms businesses and, when the dotcom bubble burst, the company was left virtually bankrupt and its shareholders penniless.

Case Study 3 examines the experiences of the Danish hearing-aid manufacturer, Oticon, which reinvented itself literally overnight. This is a company singled out as an outstanding example of transformational change by no less a person than Tom Peters (1992: 206): ' ... the transition at Oticon to a radically new form of organization has been smoother than almost anyone would have imagined'. Unlike Marconi, Oticon's story is one that highlights that visionary leadership can be successful, and that organisations can break out of the industry standard approach and, *de facto*, change the rules of the game.

Case Study 4 focuses on the privatisation of the Public Power Corporation (PPC) of Greece. This shows the various steps that were taken to privatise the company and concomitant organisational changes. It also shows the influence of the European Union in setting the ground rules for how the company should operate and, in effect, how it should be structured.

The chapter concludes by discussing the implications of the case studies in the light of the constraints on managerial choice identified in Chapter 6. It is argued that breaking out of constraints and exercising choice, especially where this challenges the status quo, requires special qualities from a manager.

Case Study 1

The Internet and the P2P Revolution in the music industry[1]

Background

Though the creation of music is as old as mankind itself, in its commodity form, as a saleable product, it is a relatively recent phenomenon. The market for music began with the sale of sheet music in the nineteenth century. In the twentieth century, with the emergence of and demand for recorded music in the form of vinyl records, cassettes, CDs, etc., the market expanded enormously to become a global industry (Gillett, 1996). Whether in Moscow or Miami, Paris or Peking, London or Lusaka, the same records are being listened to and the same companies are supplying them. However, though the physical product itself may have changed, the distribution channels and the division of labour within the industry have remained relatively stable: artists create music, record labels promote and distribute it and the fans consume it. As this case study will show, however, the advent of the Internet, and related software developments, is causing a seismic shift in the way music is distributed, and is threatening to sweep away the dominance of the big five record labels. The credit or blame, depending on whether you are a music industry executive or a music fan, will go to Shawn Fanning. Fanning is the classic American computer geek who dropped out of college because he wanted to spend his time developing a computer program which would make it easier to find and swap music via the Internet. He called the program, and the company he launched, Napster after his school nickname. Napster quickly became one of the legends of the Internet. As Alderman (2001a: 4) commented:

> The program launched in June 1999 and took off with unprecedented speed. For many, using Napster was an epiphany. One would fire it up, type in a song and instantly be connected with possibly thousands of other users who had what you wanted. Sure, you could get the studio version of Led Zeppelin's Whole Lotta Love. But if you were on at the right time, you could also get live versions of the song recorded in LA in 1977, San Francisco in 1975 or Tokyo in 1972. You might also get the new Radiohead or Eminem album weeks before their official release dates. Millions did. Using Napster was easier than going to a record store, and easier than ordering records online, and it allowed the discovery of music in ways that had not existed before. Record stores, for instance, didn't give you the opportunity to identify the cool people and investigate what else they were listening to. If there was another Napster user whose songs you liked, you could check what other music they had on their hard drive and send them instant messages. As a bonus, the whole Napster experience (excluding the computer and net costs) was free. The industry's response was incredulity and, initially, inaction.

As will be described below, there are two competing views of the Internet. One is that it will allow companies to increase their service provision and make greater profits. The other is that it will allow individuals to create a community of equals where they can exchange ideas, products and services on a no-cost, Peer-to-Peer (P2P) basis. With Napster, idea of P2P song-trading took off in a big way. The Napster software was very simple to use. You installed it, you placed your favourite music files in a folder on your hard disk and then connected to the Internet. Immediately, through Napster's centralised indexing system, MusicShare, you had access to every other Napster user's MP3 files (and they to yours). All the files were automatically catalogued on the Napster server and, through its search engine, anyone could connect to anyone else's drive and download their music.

What Napster really did was to index and manage distributed data resources. Napster was essentially an index site. The company compiled a list of Napster software users and the songs they possessed and made the list available to other users when they installed the Napster software. A user simply searched for the music they wanted and then downloaded it directly from the computer

1   This case study is based on work carried out with Gary Graham of the Manchester School of Management and Glenn Hardaker of Huddersfield University Business School. A fuller version of this case can be found in Graham *et al* (2002).

on which it was located. The search and download were free to the user, and Napster did not have to touch the file.

What's the big deal? After all, it is just a computer program. True – but at its height in 2000, more than 80 million users per month were treating themselves to free music (Gibson, 2003a). Not surprisingly, the industry was not inactive for long. Whilst Napster might seem a cool idea to its millions of users, to the big record labels it meant piracy on a scale that could eventually lead to their bankruptcy.

The music industry and the Internet

Record-making is economically as well as technically a complex process. Like books, films, television and other art forms, music is rarely just a product. Not only is it difficult to identify, develop and manage successful artists, the artistic value (and therefore the commercial value) of records depends upon their consumers' aesthetic preferences, which are neither stable nor predictable. Just because an artist has sold millions of records in the past does not mean they will in the future. The reverse is also the case. Before getting a record contract, even the biggest-selling artists, such as the Beatles, have usually been turned down by a number of record companies who failed to spot their sales potential. Over the last 50 years or so, the music industry has been dominated by five big record labels. Even though they may own or heavily influence the distribution and promotional channels for music, such is the competition between artists that only a few become successful, and then often only for a short period of time. Therefore, though the record labels are often accused of exploiting artists and taking the lion's share of the profits from their work, the labels also have to bear the main financial risks for the 90 per cent of artists who are not successful (Alderman, 2001a; Caves, 2001). However, the potent combination of the Internet and programs like Napster are changing all that.

For organisations involved in any form of distribution, the Internet offers the opportunity to replace 'bricks' with 'clicks' and thus improve their competitiveness (profitability) by removing stages in the distribution process. For example, developments such as on-line banking, insurance and bookshops are already calling into question the need for their high street, physical equivalents. In terms of the music industry, the 'clicks' versus 'bricks' issue is particularly acute in that the on-line delivery of music is transforming the industry's supply chain and could lead to the elimination of its physical manifestations such as CDs, record shops, etc.

Therefore, for many organisations, the Internet as a distribution channel is seen as a way of improving their profit margins (Mintzberg et al, 1998; Porter, 2001). As mentioned above, however, the value-creating, profit-centred model of the Internet was not how it was originally envisaged and is not the only way of looking at its potential. The World Wide Web was created in the 1990s by British scientists to allow academics and scientists to share knowledge more easily, not as a mechanism for businesses to make more profits (Alderman, 2001b). Table 11.1 shows that there are two very distinct approaches to using the Internet. Approach 1 sees the Internet as a Value System. Proponents of this view see it as just another means for organisations and individuals to gain competitive advantage and pursue profit-making activities. Approach 2 is more in line with the intentions of the Internet's originators. This Network-Based view rejects the idea that profit-making is, or should be, the most important motivation of interacting parties in virtual markets. Commenting on this, Markus et al (2000: 14) give the example of the 'virtual open source software movement' as individuals and organisations who are motivated more by altruism, reputation and the personal benefit of using and sharing an improved software product than by the pursuit of profit.

Table 11.1 Differing perspectives on the Internet

Approach 1: Value System	Approach 2: Network-Based
Cost and value approaches based on the individual firm as a competitive unit	Cooperative perspectives based on multi-firm integration
Value chain framework	Multi-agent modelling
Virtual value	Supply chain networks
Virtual markets	Architecture sharing
Building a virtual chain	B2B hub
Enterprise technology	Virtual communities
Virtual organisation	Open sourcing
Virtual organising	On-line communities
Virtual integration	Vertical nets
Value webs	Functionality
Value creation	e-Procurement
	P2P exchange

Source: adapted from Graham *et al* (2002)

As Table 11.1 shows, the terms used by proponents of the competitive, profit-centred, value system approach to the Internet and those used by proponents of the network-based, cooperative approach are significantly different. Table 11.1 shows that the key themes for proponents of the value-system approach tend to be economic and related to value creation (profit-making) at the organisation level. The network proponents, on the other hand, appear to be much more concerned with using the Internet to develop sharing communities rather than profit-making organisations. The various initiatives to use the Internet for more cooperative and less profit-centred activities can be encompassed under the broad heading of a supply chain networks (SCN) approach. A supply chain network is a series of processes (also called tiers, states or phases) owned by one or more enterprises in order to promote information-sharing through the construction of a 'virtual organisation' (Strader *et al*, 1998). The use of P2P technology to swap music files on the Internet is a classic SCN, and the fact that it might contravene copyright law appears not to trouble its originators or users one jot.

It would be an overstatement to see all proponents of the value-system approach as being solely driven by the profit motive and all proponents of the network approach as being selfless idealists. As Table 11.1 shows, however, there is a distinct tension between those who see the Internet as just another mechanism for enabling organisations to develop their profit-making activities, and those who see it as an opportunity to create communities in which sharing rather than profit-making is the prime rationale for their existence. As will be seen with the following discussion of the music industry, these very different approaches have significant implications for existing businesses.

The changing nature of the supply chain for music

Prior to the advent of the Internet, the supply chain for popular music comprised three main activities: the creation of music; the marketing of music; and the distribution of music (Parikh, 1999). It is the record labels that dominate the supply chain for music rather than the artists who actually create the music. This is because it is the record labels who control access to, and in some cases actually own, the major distribution and marketing channels. According to Parikh, it is the dominant position of the labels that prevents artists from independently distributing their own material, and it is this dominant position that explains why the labels collect approximately 85–90 per cent of the profit from music sales.

Parikh (1999) also argues that the current structure works against the interests of consumers. This is because the number of intermediaries and elements between the artist and the consumer make it relatively inefficient. Whilst each stage in the chain adds costs, it is not clear to what extent they provide any added value for the consumer. It is this potential to remove cost, without necessarily removing value to the final consumer, that makes the supply chain for music ripe for transformation by the Internet. Mougayar (1998) maintains that one of the key driving forces behind the growth of electronic commerce is the potential to reduce both distribution costs and value system inefficiencies. He contends that the greater the number of intermediaries between those who make a product and those who consume it, the greater the mark-up on the final price paid by the consumer. It can, therefore, be assumed that fewer intermediaries would result in a reduction of 'mark-up' pricing. Consequently, in the case of the music industry, the removal of some or all of the intermediaries should result in more of the profits flowing to the artists and less costs flowing to consumers.

As Amazon.com has shown with books, and latterly with music, the Internet does offer the potential to remove some layers and elements in the distribution channel for music. As with books, the need physically to produce and distribute music, in the form of CDs and cassettes, has nevertheless limited the extent to which intermediaries can be eliminated and costs reduced. However, the advent of digital technology in the 1980s, which enabled music to be recorded and stored digitally in the form of CDs and minidiscs, also allows it to be transmitted digitally via the Internet. This development is taking layers out of the supply chain for music, and thus threatening the livelihood of those involved in manufacturing and distributing physical products such as CDs. But, as such, it does not threaten or challenge the dominance of the record labels, who still retain control over production and distribution. By itself, so long as consumers download and pay for copyrighted musical content through legitimate online trading organisations, this would not be a problem for the record companies. Indeed, the Internet offers enormous scope for the music industry to bring music to a wider public, afford niche artists access to their audiences, and distribute old, new and unusual music at affordable prices.

What does threaten the dominance of the labels, however, is the advent of P2P music-swapping technologies such as Fanning's Napster. These developments enable consumers to bypass the record labels by swapping music files directly between themselves without any money flowing to the record labels. P2P offers enormous scope to music pirates. Music piracy is not new; however, according to Magex (2000a) what really scares the music industry is the sheer scale and ease of the piracy allowed by the Internet. P2P technologies, in theory and increasingly in practice, make it possible to download (i.e. pirate) any piece of music without paying for the privilege of doing so.

Magex (2000b), relates that Napster users could access between 500,000 and 800,000 individual tracks of music. It is easy to see what scares the music industry about this type of P2P swapping of music: in theory, if one person buys a recording and places it on their hard drive, they can then make it available, free of charge, to everyone else in the world. This means that there is virtually no way to guarantee that record companies, artists, or the distribution chains get paid for the music. Certainly, since the advent of programs such as Napster and similar ones, music sales have declined significantly (Gibson, 2003a, 2003b). The US music industry's income fell from $14.6bn in 1999 to $12.6bn in 2002. The industry blames Internet piracy for most of this drop in sales (Teather, 2003).

Therefore, on the one hand, the Internet offers an enormous potential to reduce the complexity and the cost of music production and distribution by eliminating the need for CD manufacturers, music shops, transportation, etc. On the other hand, it facilitates piracy on a scale previously unknown, which threatens to have a significant and adverse impact on the income of the record labels. The music industry is responding to the challenge of the Internet in two ways. Firstly, in an attempt to stop Napster and similar organisations from facilitating music-swapping, it took Napster to court for copyright infringement (Greenberg and Erios, 2001). Though this led to the closure of Napster, it does not appear to have diminished the growth in music piracy. This is why the music industry in the US is also threatening to take the individuals who use such music-swapping facilities to court as well (Teather, 2003).

The second form of response by the industry has been for the big labels to set up their own online subscription services for music (Gibson, 2003a, 2003c). However, this in itself is not without perils. For example, it could even aid piracy by making it easier to obtain the 'first' copy of a music file, which can then be passed on to anyone. In addition, in January 2002, a judge, presiding over a case brought by Napster against the Recording Industry of America, gave Napster leave to explore whether the record labels were working together, i.e. conspiring, to prevent Napster from licensing music for online distribution (Hammersley, 2002).

Nevertheless, research undertaken by Hardaker and Graham (2001) concluded that the combination of technological developments, consumer preferences and industry economics means the record labels have no choice but to adopt a subscription-based, as averse to a product-sales-based, model for supplying and being paid for music. The subscription-based approach envisages that, for a monthly fee, customers can download a set number of recordings directly to their PCs, portable devices, home stereos and even their cars. Therefore, in theory, the music industry can benefit from and should welcome the technology promoted by Napster and other similar organisations. However, the key practical problem for the music industry is getting people to pay a subscription for something they can already download for free from the Internet.

Summary

As a means of transforming the supply chain for the purchasing and delivery of products and services, the Internet is becoming, and in some industries has already become, a dominant force (Hardaker and Graham, 2001). As the above discussion shows, the ability of the Internet to remove cost-adding activities whilst retaining those that add value is enormous. Nor is it just an issue of cost: the Internet also significantly increases the speed and convenience of doing business, and it allows consumers much greater access to products and service than ever before. Even distance is no longer the obstacle that it once was, especially in those industries supplying information-based products. It does not necessarily follow, however, that those who have been the dominant forces in traditional supply chains will remain so in the virtual era. The record labels have been the dominant forces in the supply chain for music for most of the last 100 years. Their preferred option for the virtual music chain is for them to remain as the intermediary between artists and consumers, retaining control over the artists who create the music, and distributing music digitally through the Internet on a subscription basis. For the labels, this would have the benefit of eliminating cost-adding activities, such as CD production and music shops, whilst still allowing them to retain control over value-adding activities and so ensuring they continue to receive the lion's share of the profits.

The emergence of P2P technology, however, represents a second option, one which challenges the role and dominance of the record labels. As Hammersley (2002: 4) observed: 'For something that sounds like so much technology jargon and hype, peer-to-peer technology (P2P) is the fastest growing idea in the history of computing.' With or without the aid of organisations such as Napster, P2P technology is available to anyone and everyone on the Internet. It is now possible for anyone to swap music files with anyone else in the world without any payment either to the record labels or to the recording artists. This may not be a life-and-death issue for the artists who have other income streams, who only receive a small percentage of profits from their record sales, and whose loyal fans may, in any case, be willing to pay them directly for their music. However, for the labels, who take 85–90 per cent of the profits from record sales, it could well signal the end. This sort of development is, of course, in line with the more egalitarian, more cooperative view of the Internet advocated by supporters of the supply chain network approach. Although this piracy of music is illegal, given the unregulated nature of the Internet, it may be unstoppable.

There is a third option, which could also lead to the record labels being bypassed in the virtual supply chain: this is that artists could take control over the production and distribution of their own music, completely cutting out the 'middle man'. Many leading artists are highly critical of the role of the record labels, believing that it is the labels, through their contractual arrangements, who are the real pirates stealing money from the artists (Alderman, 2001a). The Internet offers the opportunity for successful, and even not so successful, artists to distribute their music directly to their fans. Indeed, some artists have already experimented with this mode of delivery. Whilst this is perfectly legal, it is likely to prove no more popular with the record labels than the P2P option, though both artists and fans might welcome it.

The potential for the Internet to transform the music supply chain has been heralded for a number of years (Gillett, 1996). What we can now see is that the potential has become a reality. What we can also see is that the Internet is not just cutting out costs and increasing the speed of transactions, it is also challenging the traditional power relations in the music industry. Underpinning this is the clash of two very different views of the Internet which was discussed earlier. P2P technology and the possibility of artists using the Internet to distribute their own music, either on a no-cost or low-cost basis, fits in well with the network-based view. On the other hand, the provision of an Internet subscription service by the record labels fits in more with the value systems approach to the Internet. In theory the two are not incompatible, but as the case of the music industry shows, in practice they may well be so. Where this will lead is difficult to predict but one thing is clear – now the P2P genie is out of the Internet bottle, the music industry will never be the same again.

Case Study 2

The rise and fall of Marconi

Background

There can be few who are not aware of the spectacular crash of Marconi, which, in the space of two years, went from a share value of £12.50 to under 2p, a stock market valuation of £35bn to just a few million pounds, and a profit of £750m to a loss of some £5.6bn, one of the biggest in UK corporate history.

Marconi grew out of GEC, the giant industrial conglomerate built by Arnold Weinstock. In a period when the UK's industrial competitiveness, and its base, declined, GEC was one of the UK's leading and most successful industrial enterprises. Weinstock, who died in 2002 at the age of 77, created GEC and was the UK's leading industrialist for over 30 years.

Weinstock graduated from the London School of Economics in 1944. He worked for the admiralty for three years before moving into property development. In 1954, he joined his father-in-law's firm, Radio and Allied Industries, where he built a strong reputation for his managerial abilities. In 1961, the firm made a reverse takeover of the larger but struggling GEC. Weinstock became GEC's Managing Director, a post he held for over 30 years until he retired in 1996. In his period as Managing Director, he turned GEC into one of the great British success stories, through a combination of acquisition and organic growth. In 1961, GEC took over AEI, and in 1968 they bought English Electric, the owners of Marconi. GEC's acquisitions continued into the 1970s and 1980s. Under Weinstock, GEC acquired a portfolio of solid, well-regarded and profitable companies, including Hotpoint, Avery, Metropolitan Vickers, Yarrow Shipbuilders and Marconi. GEC's last purchase under Weinstock was the VSEL shipyard at Jarrow, reflecting its commitment to maintaining the strength of its defence businesses, which accounted for some 50 per cent of sales and profits.

Weinstock had a knack for running businesses profitably where others had failed. This was down to his famously intimidating management style, which produced profits and, in the early years at least, gained him much praise from financial markets. For their time, his methods were revolutionary, at least in the UK. He was legendary for tight control of cash and focus on financial measures. He moved cash out of the separate GEC businesses and held it in the centre. He drove and monitored each business on their financial performance. Budgets became key growth mechanisms that put managers under enormous pressure to deliver on their forecasts. By ruthlessly cutting out overheads, introducing tight financial controls and forcing managers to think intelligently about their businesses, GEC grew in size and increased shareholder value.

Throughout his period in charge, GEC profits grew. Indeed, in 1990–1992, when the UK economy was undergoing one of its worst recessions, GEC broke the £1bn profit barrier. Despite this, however, in the 1990s, GEC and particularly Weinstock became increasingly unpopular with investors in the City of London. GEC was a massive, sprawling industrial conglomerate when these were hugely unfashionable. Driven by academics and consultants such as Tom Peters and Rosabeth Moss Kanter, and break-up specialists such as Lord Hanson, managers were told that they had to identify their core business, 'stick to the knitting' and sell off non-core activities to release shareholder value. This went against Weinstock's business philosophy. He was not particularly interested in whether there was synergy between the various GEC businesses. In GEC, he had created a company composed of businesses that were leaders in their fields, made steady and consistent profits and which were, to an extent, insulated from wilder economic fluctuations. It was anathema to him to sell a business that had a profitable future or to buy one that was overpriced or unlikely to perform. In the early 1990s, he looked at many companies, but bought few. This approach did not please the markets, which seemed enamoured of companies that sold, spent and borrowed. However, the performance of the companies he turned down appeared to justify Weinstock's parsimonious approach (Owen, 2002). It also enabled the company to build up a cash stockpile of over £2bn, but strangely enough, this also attracted criticism.

Two of the City of London's main ways of making money are to lend it or to charge for their services in mergers and takeovers. GEC's stockpile of cash meant it did not need to borrow money, and Weinstock's insistence that he would not buy companies that were either overpriced or did not fit into GEC's portfolio appeared to enrage the City money men. There was also a common view in the City that GEC had missed the high-tech boat and that it was stuck in the 'old economy' when the smart money was moving into the 'new economy'. Certainly, as Heller (2002) commented, there was a downside to Weinstock's tough financial, risk-averse regime in that it appeared to discourage inter-company working in the GEC empire. Though GEC had a toe-hold, and sometimes a lot more, in the various technologies and markets that would allow companies such as Nokia, Intel and Dell to become giants of the Internet era, it never quite managed to link them together or develop them enough to establish itself in the new economy.

Having passed the age of 70, Weinstock was finally pressured into resigning as GEC's Managing Director in 1996 and became its President Emeritus. Under pressure, he recruited George Simpson as a replacement. However, he saw this as an interim measure until his son Simon was ready to take over. Simon Weinstock's sudden death in late 1996 changed these plans and George Simpson became undisputed head of GEC. Simpson had run and sold both Rover and Lucas, was much admired in the City of London, and was considered to have the entrepreneurial qualities needed to reinvigorate GEC.

Whatever criticisms there were of Weinstock in his later years, his legacy was huge. Not only had he built an enormously successful industrial conglomerate in a period when British industry was in decline but also, as Brummer (2002: 1) commented:

> The fact that Britain is still a leading player in the global power industry, and has a world-class research-based defence industry, can largely be attributed to his precocious skills.

The rise and fall of Marconi

Simpson bought into the popular view that GEC needed to get out of the old economy, characterised by its involvement in defence and heavy engineering, and into the new, high-tech world of telecoms and the Internet. He believed it also needed to stop being a UK/European company and become a global player. As he later said:

> What else were we going to do? The old GEC had had it and everyone told us that focus was what was needed. Telecoms was the obvious industry to expand into. (quoted in Harrison, M, 2002: 24)

He began to bring in his own people, notably John Mayo as Finance Director. Mayo had been an investment banker before moving to Zeneca as Finance Director, from where he was recruited by Simpson. It was Simpson and Mayo who charted GEC's push into the new dotcom economy through a whirlwind series of sales and acquisitions. The crucial period was 1999 to 2001. In 1999, GEC divested itself of its defence business to BAe. This halved the size of GEC and sold off its most consistently profitable elements. To mark this momentous step, GEC was renamed Marconi to signal its intention to become a leading telecoms company, and began a process of acquiring new businesses in the then growing international market for high-capacity telecoms networks. Simpson and Mayo believed, like many more, that the future lay with dotcom companies, and they wanted a big share of it. Not only did they spend the proceeds from selling businesses they did not want and the money that Weinstock bequeathed them, but they borrowed over £4bn as well. In the three years up to the middle of 2001, they sold off almost all of Marconi's non-telecoms business, i.e. the vast majority of the old GEC, and purchased over 20 telecoms businesses, for prices ranging from a few hundred million to a few billion pounds. Mayo stated that:

> The common theme between our [new] core businesses is the ability to securely capture, manage and communicate enormous amounts of data. The 'data wave' is turning into a tidal wave and we have positioned ourselves to ride the wave. (quoted in Gow, 1999c: 25)

At another time, the speed of Marconi's transformation into a rapidly-growing telecoms equipment provider might have been a cause for concern. But this was taking place at the height of the dotcom bubble. It seemed that everyone wanted to have a slice of the telecoms/Internet cake and was not too concerned how much they paid. Rather than worrying the financial markets, Marconi's splurge of buying, selling and borrowing seemed to please them enormously. The share price soared to £12.50 and Marconi were the darlings of the financial markets. However, this was short-lived. By late 2000, whilst Simpson and Mayo were still issuing optimistic forecasts of what was to come, other telecoms companies such as Nortel, Alcatel, Nokia and Ericsson began issuing sales and profit warnings as the telecoms recession, and the dotcom collapse, began to bite. Almost to the last, Marconi denied there were any problems, but in July 2001 it asked for its shares to be suspended ahead of a profits warning, a highly unusual move for a FTSE 100 company.

Though Marconi's profits warning was clearly going to damage the company's standing, the lateness and severity of the warning led to a disastrous fall in the share price, a rapid exit from the Board of senior staff and the virtual destruction of the company. Indeed, such was the concern for the way the Board handled the profits warning that the UK's financial watchdog, the Financial Services Authority (FSA), conducted a lengthy investigation into it. Its report was issued in April 2003. The FSA pointed out that the company had a legal obligation to keep the market informed of price-sensitive information in a timely manner, and that, in this instance it had not, and had therefore broken the FSA's rules. Treanor and Wray (2003) reconstructed the events leading up to and just after the profits warning:

17 May 2001   Marconi says the first six months of 2001 are unlikely to show an improvement on the previous year's figures.

12 June   Trading figures show a 10 per cent decline for April and May. No public statement is made.

21 June   Accounts for April and May show a loss of £180m, £156m more than the previous year. No public statement is made.

26 June   The financial forecast for the six months to September 2001 show a loss of £47m, as averse to the £320m profits that analysts had predicted. The forecast also shows that profits for the year to March 2002 will be £491m as against the predicted £807m. The Board disputes these figures and asks for them to be recalculated. No public statement is made.

28 June   A Board meeting is called for July 4.

30 June   The revised financial forecasts are even worse than those presented to the Board on June 26. Full-year profits are projected to be only £272m, and half-year losses have risen to £121m. No public statement is made.

| 4 July | At 7.40 am, Marconi asks for its shares to be suspended pending a meeting of the Board at 4 pm. At 6.41 pm, the Board issues a statement saying that profits are likely to halve, with sales down 15 per cent. |
| 5 July | When the markets open, Marconi's shares fall by nearly 50 per cent. John Mayo tells investors that business will recover in 2002 when the telecom networks 'will be running so hot they'll fall over' and that there will be no change in Marconi's management. Marconi's share price continues to collapse. At 9.40 pm John Mayo resigns. |

Two months later, George Simpson also resigned. Both men received substantial payoffs. As a Leader in the *Financial Times* (2003: 20) stated, 'we can only speculate whether more could have been saved had directors been quicker to acknowledge that their headlong rush into telecoms oblivion was flawed.' Regardless of this, the events of June and July meant that, for Marconi, the dotcom bubble had burst with a vengeance. From then on, it was downhill all the way. In May 2002, Marconi announced one of the biggest yearly losses in UK corporate history: some £5.6bn. Its share price plunged to below 2p (down from £12.50 at its height), making the company in effect bankrupt and its shares worthless. It then began a long process of trying to stay alive by negotiating with its creditors. In May 2003, Marconi finally agreed a debt restructuring deal with its creditors. In return for writing off over 90 per cent of the approximately £4.5bn they were owed, Marconi's creditors received 99.5 per cent of the company's equity. The refinanced company would be valued at just over £600m. The previous shareholders would own just 0.5 per cent, thus reducing the value of their holding to £3m from £35bn at its peak, always assuming that anyone would want to buy the shares.

Summary

Simpson and Mayo argued that they were taking GEC through a much overdue reinvention. However, there is a world of difference between reinventing a company around its core business and spending billions to construct a new one from scratch. What Simpson and Mayo did was to sell off most of what was GEC and to use the money from the sale, and much more besides, to create a new telecoms company that could rival established companies such as Alcatel, Siemens and Lucent. Unfortunately for them, their vision of creating a leading telecoms company came at a time when the dotcom bubble was about to burst. They made one of the classic business mistakes – they bought at the top. In the space of three years they bought some two dozen companies for billions of pounds that very quickly became almost worthless as their markets collapsed. The US company Fore Industries is a prime example of this. Marconi bought the company for £2.8bn in 1999. In 2002, a financial analyst commented that: 'The business has very little value. If Marconi tried to dispose of it, there may even be costs associated with it' (quoted in Hirst, 2002: 1). Marconi was brought low by the combination of massive overcapacity in the industry, a worldwide economic slowdown and the enormous financial drain on telecom operators of paying for third-generation mobile phone licences. This led Marconi's customers, especially its biggest customer, BT, to cut their purchasing of telecoms equipment quickly and savagely. In effect, Marconi's market collapsed.

Simpson and Mayo also made another key mistake. Neither had much experience of the telecoms industry. Simpson had made his reputation on running, and selling, Rover and Lucas, both firmly established in the 'old economy'. Mayo was an investment banker turned finance director. They were both deal-makers with little experience of the telecoms industry. As Weinstock commented, 'They knew nothing about the business they were in, and nothing about the businesses they were buying' (quoted in Aris, 2002: 8).

It is difficult to exaggerate the disaster that happened at Marconi. Whatever the criticisms of the old GEC, when Weinstock handed over power in 1996, it was a strong and profitable company. The parts that were sold off by Simpson and Mayo still appear profitable. On the other hand, by 2002, the new Marconi was bankrupt and worthless. When he stepped down, Weinstock was the biggest private investor in GEC, with some 45 million shares valued at over £400m. At the time of his death in 2002, these were practically worthless. Simpson and Mayo, who were both forced out, received handsome payoffs, and appeared not to accept that they bore any personal responsibility for the Marconi debacle, preferring to cite bad luck, poor timing and other people for the collapse of Marconi (Harrison, M, 2002; Hirst, 2002). Hardly surprising, therefore, that Weinstock commented: 'I'd like to string them up from a high tree and let them swing there for a long time' (quoted in Aris, 2002: 8).

Case Study 3

Oticon – the disorganised organisation[2]

Background

Oticon, a Danish company founded in 1904, was the first hearing instrument company in the world. In the 1970s, it was the world's number one manufacturer of 'behind the ear' hearing aids. However, as the market for 'in the ear' products grew in the 1970s and 1980s, its fortunes plummeted and it lost money and market share. In 1987, so poor was the company's performance that it lost half of its equity. The basic problem was that Oticon was a very traditional, departmentalised and slow-moving company. It had a distinguished past but it was a small company operating in a global market. Though it had 15 sites around the world and 95 distributorships, the Head Office, its largest site by far, only employed 145 people. Yet it was operating in a market which had come to be dominated by Siemens, Phillips, Sony, 3M and Panasonic. More importantly, it had the wrong products. Oticon manufactured the standard 'behind the ear' hearing aid, but customers increasingly preferred the 'in the ear' variety. Also, Oticon was strong in analogue technology, whilst the market and its customers were moving towards digital technology. In addition, though the company was strong in the state-subsidised markets of Scandinavia and Northern Europe, it was weak in the more buoyant markets of America and the Far East.

This began to change with the appointment of Lars Kolind as President of the company in 1988. The fact that he was only the third person to hold this post in the company's history helps to explain its strong attachment to tradition. In his view the company had 'been sleeping for ten years'. In the next two years, he worked hard to turn the situation round through cost-cutting measures: he pared the company down, cut staff and increased efficiency, and reduced the price

2   I am grateful for the help of Ronnie Stronge of Transform People International Communications in preparing this case study. Further information on Oticon can be obtained from its website (www.oticon.com).

of a hearing aid by 20 per cent. By 1990, Oticon made a profit of some £16 million on a turnover of £400 million with sales growing at 2 per cent per annum. However, the market was growing at 6 per cent. More importantly, Kolind did not think the company had a future. He had been searching for a sustainable competitive advantage for Oticon: 'I looked at technology, audiology. I looked at distribution strength. I looked at everything, but there was nothing we could do better than the competition'. That he arrived at this view is hardly surprising. When competing against the world's leading electronics companies, it is very difficult to see how a small Danish company could, for example, design a better microchip for digital sound processing than Sony.

Nevertheless, he did not give up. Instead, Kolind resolved to 'think the unthinkable'. On New Year's Day 1990, the solution came to him:

> Maybe we could design a new way of running a business that could be significantly more creative, faster, and more cost-effective than the big players, and maybe that could compensate for our lack of technological excellence, our lack of capital, and our general lack of resources.

The vision – a knowledge-based organisation

Kolind realised that the industry was totally technology-focused, and that the main thrust was to make hearing aids smaller. He, on the other hand, thought this exclusive focus on technology was short-sighted. He believed Oticon was not in the hearing-aid business *per se*; they were in the business of 'making people smile' – restoring the enjoyment of life that hearing impairment can destroy. Making people smile, he reasoned, means not only giving them a wonderful piece of technology but actually changing people's lives for the better. To this end, the company adopted a new mission statement:

> To help people with hearing difficulties to live life as they wish, with the hearing they have.

To achieve this requires a knowledge of people's lifestyle and how hearing impairment affects this, and an understanding of the social stigma associated with hearing impairment and the use of hearing aids. He saw that what would allow Oticon to compete and thrive was not selling hearing aids, but providing a new holistic approach to customer care – a system that would allow a hearing clinic to assess hearing loss, to discuss the lifestyle needs of the person concerned, to select the appropriate hearing aid, to programme it, and to interpret the feedback from the user in order to fine-tune the hearing aid. The intent would be to allow people with hearing difficulties to lead the sort of life they wanted in their situation, whether they preferred classical music or rock music, whether they worked in a noisy environment or a quiet one, whether sound was central to their work or peripheral.

Kolind had the vision for Oticon's role in meeting customers' needs, but he still had to find a way of implementing it. He believed the key lay in the mix of expertise necessary to provide each customer with an effective hearing aid: micro-mechanics, microchip design, audiology, psychology, marketing, manufacturing, logistics, and all-round service capability. If Oticon were to move away from merely making hearing aids and instead provide a total package of support for people with hearing difficulties, it would have to develop a whole new concept in hearing-aid service. It would need to combine this expertise in a new way and add new areas of expertise to the organisation. In short, they would have to move from a technological orientation to a knowledge orientation, from a technology-based manufacturing company to a knowledge-based service business. They had to build a learning organisation where experts put aside their expertise and work as a team to 'make people smile'.

For Kolind, a knowledge-based or learning organisation:

... should not work like a machine, it should work like a brain. Brains do not know hierarchies – no boxes – no job descriptions; what there is is a very chaotic set of thousands of relationships tangled in with each other based on certain knowledge centres, with an interaction which may seem chaotic. It is the reflection of the brain into the organisation that creates companies that are able to manage that knowledge process.

Kolind began by redefining his role as CEO. Instead of seeing himself as the captain that steers the ship, he saw himself as the naval architect who designs it. He believed that it was more important to design the organisation to act in a clever and responsible way than to control every action. On this basis, he drafted plans for the company's future which he first presented in April 1990. He wanted to create 'the spaghetti organisation' – a chaotic tangle of relationships and interactions that would force the abandonment of preconceived ideas and barriers to innovation and competitiveness.

The strategy

Having identified the vision for the organisation, the next step was to set about fleshing out and implementing his strategy for change. Beginning with the Head Office, which comprised the finance, management, marketing and product development functions, he decided to abandon the concept of a formal organisation; instead he wanted to create a 'disorganised organisation'. Formal structures, job descriptions and policies were seen as creating barriers to cooperation, innovation and teamwork rather than facilitating it. Kolind's new disorganised organisation would be founded on four principles:

- Departments and job titles would disappear and all activities would become projects initiated and pursued informally by groupings of interested people.
- Jobs would be redesigned into fluid and unique combinations of functions to suit each employee's needs and capabilities.
- All vestiges of the formal office would be eradicated and replaced by open space filled with workstations that any one could use.
- Informal, face-to-face dialogue would replace memos as the acceptable mode of communication.

Therefore, Oticon got rid of departments, departmental heads and other managerial and supervisory positions. Job descriptions and titles and anything else that created a barrier between one member of staff and another were also eliminated. The company wanted to get rid of everything associated with traditional organisations, including budgets. The intent was to see what happened when staff were 'liberated' to do what they thought best. Kolind wanted everyone in the organisation, from secretaries to technical experts, to work much more closely together to make things happen more creatively, faster and more cost-effectively.

After 15 months of preparation, the change to the new way of working took place at 8 am on 8 August 1991. Two old buildings were abandoned and the Head Office moved into a refurbished former factory in the northern part of Copenhagen. The heart of the new Head Office was a state-of-the-art electronic infrastructure, costing nearly £30 million.

The reason for beginning with the Head Office was relatively simple: this was not just where the largest percentage of Oticon's costs were but, more importantly, where the core of its competence lay. The belief was that if it could get the Head Office functioning effectively, the rest of Oticon's somewhat scattered organisation would follow.

The concept of creating chaos out of organisation and expecting anything other than a disaster to follow seems far-fetched, if not downright lunatic. Oticon also recognised the dangers in the course it was embarking upon. The company realised that if success was to follow, above all else, there were two elements it needed to get right: direction and human values.

Direction

Oticon's management was convinced that without a clear direction that everyone understood and believed in, the company would fragment and collapse into a disorientated mass of individuals each pursuing their own course of action. To avoid this, the management and staff openly and at length discussed and debated the new strategy for the company, and the implications for how Oticon would be structured and operate. Kolind commented that:

> ... the entire staff discussed not only where we were going but why we were doing so, and we created a consensus among staff that not only made them know why we were doing it and what we were doing, but we also got as far as having everybody think that this fundamentally made a lot of sense ... so there was consensus on the strategy.

Human values

As well as a consensus about the strategy, Oticon realised it also needed to get a 'fundamental consensus about the basic human values' of its business. After much debate, these were summed up in one sentence:

> We build this company on the assumption that we only employ adults, and everything we do will rest on that assumption, so we will not treat our staff as children – we will treat them as responsible adults.

Underlying this simple statement was a view that adults do not have to be told when to come to work and go home or that those dealing with, for example, the Japanese market will come in later and go home later than those servicing the American market. In a similar way, Oticon's management believed that staff would not overspend or misspend budgets and, therefore, there was no need continually to remind them of this fact or harp on about other company rules or practices.

Implementing the strategy

Oticon now operates on a project basis. Anyone can start a project, provided they have the permission of one of five senior managers. Some projects are also initiated by management. Whomsoever the idea comes from, the main criterion for acceptance is that a project is customer-focused. Anyone can join a project, provided they have the agreement of the project leader. The basic idea, going back to the concept that Oticon treats everyone as an adult, is that it is the individual's responsibility to fill their day usefully. If people do not have anything to do, it is their job to find something useful to do – either by starting a project or by joining one.

Kolind's view of Oticon would send shivers down the spine of most traditional CEOs: 'Hearing aids are not the core of what this company is about. It's about something more fundamental. It's about the way people perceive work. We give people the freedom to do what they want.' This is perhaps why, as well as the 100 or so 'authorised' projects, as Kolind comments, 'We have a lot of skunk work going on that's not in any official priority.' There is a saying in Oticon that 'It's easier to be forgiven than to get permission.' Basically, this means, 'If in doubt do it. If it works, fine. If it doesn't, we forgive you.'

Communication is at the centre of this new approach to work. Partly this is facilitated by computer. Each desk has a computer, and these list all the projects 'on offer' and the team leader's name along with the tasks involved. Usually the team leader will try and 'recruit' the skills he or she needs, but individuals are also expected to seek out opportunities as well. There are no demarcation lines; if an R&D specialist or a secretary wants to work with a marketing group, then all they have to do is have a chat with the project leader in order to sign on.

The physical embodiment of this new 'structureless' structure is the workplace. Gone are individual offices, gone are corridors – all the walls were taken out and everyone works in the same open-plan office. Staff gather where they wish to work. Instead of individual offices, everyone has a little filing cabinet on wheels. Staff come in each morning, pick up their mobile office and trundle it to where they are working that day. Oticon is also a genuinely 'paperless office'. All incoming mail is scanned into the computer and then shredded. The reason for this is simple: Oticon wants staff to move around from project group to project group as work requires. It does not want this process hindered by staff having to transport masses of paper as happens in most offices – the solution is to get rid of the paper.

This requires everyone to have access to and to be able to use a computer. However, the emphasis at Oticon is on face-to-face, informal communication (although, for example, e-mail is used but not extensively). This is why the office is littered with stand-up coffee bars to encourage small, informal (but short) meetings. Three or four people will meet to discuss an issue or exchange ideas and information and then return to where they are working that day and follow up ideas and suggestions. These are usually fed straight into the computer and are available to everybody else. There is also an expectation not only that all information is open to staff in this manner, but that staff actually want to know the information. Therefore, rather than putting up barriers or operating on a need-to-know basis, Oticon tries to be transparent about all aspects of its business, whether it be new products, staff salaries or finance in general. The view is that the more a person knows, the more valuable they are to the company.

Staff did not take to this radically new way of working overnight. This is perhaps not surprising. Staff were not originally recruited for their teamworking and project management skills, and some found it hard to come to terms with these new arrangements. Nor did they welcome the loss of routine and clear authority relationships or find the resultant uncertainty easy to adjust to. This was especially the case with managers for whom the loss of their power base, information monopoly and status symbols was difficult to accept.

In addition, under the new arrangement, managers were reclassified as project leaders and had to compete for the best staff, rather than having their own dedicated subordinates. Some groups of staff also found it difficult to find a role in the project team environment; for some time, receptionists, for instance, still answered the telephone. It was also some years before this new approach was adopted outside the Head Office, though the Danish manufacturing operation, which is on a different site, did show some interest quite early.

Kolind anticipated resistance and sought to overcome this by involving staff in planning the transformation of the company. Small groups of staff were selected to handle such projects as designing the new electronic infrastructure, locating a site for the new Head Office and selecting an architect. Also, all staff were given IT skills training. Indeed, they were all given a home PC and encouraged to identify their own training needs. One result of this was that staff formed their own PC club to work together to develop their skills. Despite this, prior to the move to the new building, Kolind found it necessary to issue an ultimatum to staff: accept the new arrangements or leave.

Regardless of this carrot and stick approach, the biggest boost to the new arrangements came when staff could see they actually worked better than the old ones. One immediate benefit was that Oticon 'found' that it had already developed the industry's first automatic, self-adjusting hearing aid in the 1980s. However, owing to technical problems (the solution to which was given a very low priority), lack of communication between the R&D and sales staff, and a lack of imagination, nobody seemed to have realised that they had developed a potentially world-beating product. In the transformed Oticon, this new type of hearing aid quickly resurfaced, the technical problems were rapidly ironed out, and the

MultiFocus hearing aid, as it became known, was launched in late 1991. In the next two years, three more powerful variants of the MultiFocus were developed and its size reduced by half.

To set the seal on this transformation, in December 1994, after a seminar with staff, Oticon (1994: 6) published a statement of fundamental human values (see Table 11.2).

Table 11.2 Oticon's statement of fundamental human values

Oticon's fundamental human values	How do we implement them?
We assume that Oticon employees want to take responsibility if they get the opportunity.	Whenever possible (especially within a project), an employee chooses his task, work hours and place of work.
We assume that Oticon employees want to develop and grow in their jobs and experience new challenges within the company.	We make it possible for an employee to assume several tasks at the same time, if he is interested and qualified – possibly with the support of colleagues.
We assume that Oticon employees want the greatest possible freedom …	This freedom is possible because Oticon has the fewest rules practicable, and because we encourage staff to use their common sense instead of slavishly complying with rules.
We assume that Oticon employees want to have qualified and fair feedback to their work and a salary corresponding to their contribution.	All levels of management – technical, staff and project managers – should give honest feedback to their employees – negative as well as positive.
We assume that Oticon employees want to be partners in Oticon, and not adversaries.	At intervals, we offer staff in Oticon shares at favourable rates so that they benefit financially from the success to which they have contributed.
We assume that Oticon employees want the security that derives from improving themselves in their current jobs so that they are able to get another job if they – for one reason or another – should leave Oticon.	We make it possible for staff to improve themselves in their jobs and assume other tasks in the company wherever relevant.
We assume Oticon employees want to be treated as grown-up, independent people.	Oticon's entire way of operating is based on this.
We assume that Oticon's employees want to understand how their tasks fit into the context of the whole company.	Oticon is an open company where all employees have access to as much information as possible.
We assume that Oticon employees are more interested in challenging and exciting tasks than in formal status and titles.	We have a minimum of titles and no formal career planning. We seek, however, to give each employee the possibility of personal and professional development through varied and ever more challenging tasks.

Sustaining and extending change

The changes to – or rather the transformation of – Oticon started at 8 am on 8 August 1991. At the beginning, all was chaos. It took months before everyone understood their new roles, and for the organisation to cast off its old ways and begin to operate in the manner Kolind had envisaged. By 1994, however, the results were impressive:

- 15 new products had been launched (twice as many as the company had previously);
- new product lead time had been halved;
- the company's sales were growing at 20 per cent per year, after a period of 10 years without real growth and at a time when the market had begun shrinking by 5 per cent per year;
- Oticon's market share increased from 8 per cent in 1990 to 12 per cent in 1993.

Nor did the progress stop there. In 1995, Oticon launched the world's first digital hearing aid, the DigiFocus. This is, in effect, a four-gram computer that fits in the ear but has the processing power of a desk-top machine. Not only was this a technological breakthrough for which Oticon has won a number of major innovation awards, but it also allowed Oticon to regain its position as one of the world's top three hearing aid producers. Also, by 1995 turnover had increased by 100 per cent on 1990 and profits had increased tenfold.

For some, this would have been a time to sit back and feel satisfied. Yet Kolind was becoming increasingly dissatisfied. The launch of the DigiFocus had dominated 1995 and the long-standing project teams created to develop and launch the product had taken on an air of permanency. He believed the company was in danger of slipping back into a traditional departmental organisational form. His response to this was to 'explode the organisation'.

In an uncharacteristically directive way, Kolind instructed people and teams to relocate within the Head Office. Teams devoted to short-term business goals (such as sales, marketing, and customer service) were moved to the top floor. People working on medium-term projects (upgrading existing products, for example) and long-term research were put on the second floor. Those dealing with technology, infrastructure and support were located on the first floor. In Kolind's words, 'It was total chaos. Within three hours, over 100 people had moved.' He justified this new bout of chaos by arguing that 'To keep a company alive, one of the jobs of top management is to keep it dis-organised.'

As can be seen, Oticon went through major and substantial changes in the 1990s; nor were these solely restricted to its Head Office. In the early 1990s, Oticon began to extend the new working arrangements to its two factories in Denmark, and laid plans for their extension to its sales operations throughout the world. By 1997, all of its major subsidiaries in Europe, the USA and the Pacific Rim had moved into purpose-built offices designed to replicate the arrangements in its Danish HQ. The intention was to:

> ... set the standard for the knowledge-based sales company of the future ... [through the] concept of a flat organisation, which stimulates openness, flexibility and informal communication ...

Though Oticon believes that its approach can be replicated in other countries, it is not blind to cultural differences. The company realised that Denmark, with a culture characterised by equality and lack of formality, provided fertile ground for its approach to work. Therefore, in extending this approach to its operations in other countries, Oticon recognised the need for cultural sensitivity.

In addition to its own organisation, Oticon also developed partnership-style arrangements with both its component suppliers and the 5000 or so hearing care centres who distribute its products throughout the world.

Such has been its perceived success that Oticon's approach has been copied by many other organisations in Denmark, including a government ministry.

In 1998, after 10 years at the head of Oticon, Lars Kolind decided it was time to move on. He left the company in a far, far stronger position than it had been when he first arrived. In almost every sense, whether financial, technological, structural and most of all philosophical, he transformed the company. His leaving was very amicable. As he said:

> I am quitting Oticon now because I feel that both the company and I will benefit from a change. There is a whole new generation of young people who are ready to run with the ball – and why shouldn't I let them?

Kolind's departure highlights the dilemma of transformational managers: what do you do when you have transformed the company? For Oticon, success did not end with Kolind's departure, nor does it appear to have led to any rethinking of his approach to work. Rather the reverse. Oticon is now more than ever stressing the wider ethical and social role it wishes to play. As his successor, Niels Jacobsen, stated when receiving the prestigious Employee Empowerment Pioneer Award in New York in 1998:

> Our goal is to do business in a manner that positively contributes to society in every country where we do business. We support the principle that industry has a responsibility for society and that we have a collective responsibility to the environment.

Summary

Quite obviously, Oticon must be doing something right, but what? The key to its success appears to lie in seven factors:

- *Changing the rules of the game*. Oticon created a vision of where it wanted to be. Like Japanese companies such as Cannon and Honda, this was based not only on ambition but also on a deep understanding of the nature of the market in which it operates. This allowed Oticon to spot the chink in the armour of the big players, and in effect to change the rules of the game – recognising that service delivery in total, and not technological development in isolation, is what customers really want.
- *Moving to a project-type structure that fits the strategy and vision of the business*.
- *Creating a whole-hearted commitment from everyone to working cooperatively and proactively*. In effect, there appears to have been a wholesale cultural change at Oticon, from the senior management down.
- *Creating a learning organisation*. The restructuring (or rather, de-structuring) of Oticon removed hierarchical, horizontal and cultural barriers to information flows, and created a situation where people genuinely want to exchange ideas and learn from each other. This is supported by the emphasis on informality, experimentation, innovation and risk-taking.
- *Leadership*. The Oticon story appears to be one of those rare cases of genuine visionary leadership that transformed an organisation over a relatively short space of time and then continued to support, drive and reinforce the transformation.
- *Consistent vision*. Lars Kolind had a vision of what he wanted Oticon to become. He pursued this consistently and with passion. Nor, after the new Oticon had been working for some years, and was very successful, did he hesitate to take decisive action when he felt that the company was slipping back into old ways.

■ *Societal values*. As has been mentioned previously, Scandinavia has a long history of industrial and social democracy. Denmark in particular has led the way with the creation of a strong cooperative movement. The changes that have taken place at Oticon appear to be a classic, if somewhat extreme, form of Scandinavian industrial democracy. As such, Oticon's new way of working fits in with the societal values espoused by Denmark and other Scandinavian countries.

Case Study 4

Privatisation and the European Union: the case of the Public Power Corporation of Greece[3]

Background

In the three decades from 1945, across the world, there was an enormous increase in the size and range of activities undertaken by the public sector. This expansion included traditional public service activities, such as health and education, and embraced some traditional private sector activities, such as banking and car production. Since the mid-1970s, however, privatisation, not nationalisation, has been the order of the day. The contraction of the public sector has also been a global phenomenon. Led by right-of-centre governments in the UK and USA, the move to roll back the state has been driven by ideological and economic concerns (Hutton, 1995; Osborne and Gaebler, 1992; Talbot, 2001). Ideologically it was argued that the competition-based nature of the private sector meant that it would always provide services more efficiently and achieve greater customer satisfaction than public sector bureaucracies. The economic argument concerned the need to cut rising public sector deficits, and the accompanying tax bills, by reducing the size and cost of the public sector.

As the 1980s and 1990s progressed, more and more countries joined the privatisation movement. From the early 1990s, Greece became one of the most enthusiastic privatisers. In 2000 it announced the privatisation of the country's sole electricity supplier, the Public Power Corporation (PPC). The PPC was established in 1950 to provide low-cost electricity to support the expansion of the Greek economy. As a state monopoly and the country's largest employer, it was a prime target for privatisation. However, the PPC's privatisation was driven by the European Union (EU), which, with the creation of the European Single Market in 1992, had the responsibility for creating a level, competitive, playing field across all EU countries.

---

3 This case is based on work carried out with Michael Katsouros and Trefor Jones of the Manchester School of Management. A fuller version of this case can be found in Burnes *et al* (2004).

What is privatisation?

For such a ubiquitous term, 'privatisation' is not easy to define. Peacock (1984) defines it as the complete transfer of ownership from the public to the private sector. For Beesley and Littlechild (1983), privatisation takes place when a minimum of 50 per cent of an enterprise's shares are sold to the private sector. Talbot (2001) emphasises the transfer of ownership but notes that, in the case of 'natural monopolies', governments usually retain regulatory control. The need for and effectiveness of regulation are contentious issues. Ayres (1995) described privatisation in Brazil as a process of converting public monopolies into private oligopolies with no beneficial impact for the public.

Vickers and Yarrow (1991) identified three types of privatisation:

1 The transfer of state enterprises operating in competitive product markets to the private sector, e.g. state-owned car and aircraft companies.
2 The privatisation of public monopolies such as water and electricity utilities.
3 The contracting out of in-house services to the private sector, e.g. IT and facilities management.

An important difference between the first and second types of privatisation is that, with the second type, governments frequently retain some rights of control, in the form of regulation. In the third case, contracting out, the public sector is even more directly involved, in that it is the customer for the contracted-out service and needs to ensure that it is getting value for money. Contracting out, therefore, widens the definition of privatisation to include the transfer of responsibility for service provision. In the USA, contracting out has tended to be the main form of privatisation. The USA has also championed the introduction of what Talbot (2001) refers to as 'market-type mechanisms' into the public sector. Writing of the UK, he states that:

> Where public services could not be privatised for structural and/or political reasons there were a number of attempts to introduce market-type mechanisms (MTMs). These included: internal contracting or quasi-contracting ... internal markets ... competitive sourcing ... and 'market testing' ... MTM reforms were designed to introduce some elements of 'competition' into public services that would in turn, it was assumed, lead to improvements in economy, efficiency, effectiveness and customer services. (Talbot, 2001: 291)

It was developments such as these that led Adams et al (1996) to offer a much broader definition of privatisation, to include an array of actions designed to widen the scope of private sector market activity, or the assimilation by the public sector of efficiency-enhancing techniques generally employed by the private sector.

The privatisation of the Public Power Corporation (PPC)[4]

The PPC generates 97 per cent of Greece's electricity needs and is responsible for the transmission and distribution of all the country's electricity. It provides electricity to 6.7 million customers; it is the country's largest employer with 35,000 staff; and had a turnover of €3bn in 2001/2.

The PPC was created in 1950 when the Greek government nationalised the electricity industry, which comprised a wide variety of private companies and municipal entities. The service provided by these was unreliable, geographically patchy, expensive and suitable only for domestic lighting purposes. The Greek government saw the provision of a country-wide, low-cost and reliable electricity supply for both domestic and industrial users as fundamental to economic growth. It

---

4   Unless otherwise stated, the statistics given in this section are taken from either the PPC's website, www.dei.gr, or the website of the Greek Regulatory Authority for Energy, www.rae.gr.

established the PPC as a 'not-for-profit' organisation whose prime responsibility was to provide an infrastructure that could meet the growing needs of both domestic and industrial users throughout Greece, including the remotest villages and far-flung islands.

Since its creation, the PPC has provided essential support to the development of the industrial, commercial and service sectors of the economy. Its expansion of electricity generating and distribution facilities not only provided direct employment for large numbers of people, but also aided the economic and social development of rural as well as urban areas. It also owns and operates the mines that produce the lignite which fuels 67 per cent of electricity production. In addition, its use of indigenous lignite and its promotion of renewable energy sources substantially reduced the need to import expensive oil, thus considerably aiding the country's balance of payments.

The PPC was much more than a supplier of electricity: it was an extension of the government's economic and social policies. However, the combination of huge capital projects, a large workforce, and the lowest tariff structure in the EU, meant that the PPC consistently ran up heavy losses. By the 1990s, political support for loss-making state monopolies had dwindled in Greece, and the PPC's position was also being challenged by EU competition policy.

The privatisation process

In the late 1990s, the Greek government began the process of privatising the PPC. This was influenced by a change of political climate within Greece, and driven externally by EU competition rules. Internally, the PPC found itself operating in an environment which looked to economic liberalisation and the free market for economic growth. The Greek government was trying to shrink the size and cost of the public sector, which included banks, industrial and commercial concerns, and even the Athens Stock Exchange, because it was considered too big, too costly, overstaffed and inefficient. Therefore, privatisation became a key policy objective of the Greek government. This led to three successive waves of privatisation, which by 1999 were generating receipts for the government totalling some 5.5 per cent of GDP (Stournaras, 1999). The first wave of privatisation covered banks, Duty Free Shops, the Hellenic Telecommunications Organisation and the Athens Stock Exchange. The second wave included the Corinthian Canal, the Athens Water and Sewerage Company and the Hellenic Vehicle Industry. The third wave, which began in 1999, involved the Agricultural Bank, the Commercial Bank, the Hellenic Aerospace Industry and the Public Power Corporation (PPC). The PPC's privatisation, however, appears to have been driven more by external pressures from the EU than by internal ones.

With the creation of the EU Single Market in 1992, the European Commission became responsible for harmonising and liberalising markets across the EU, with electricity generation and distribution being a priority (Barnard and Scott, 2002; Parker, 1998). In 1998, the EU issued a European Electricity Directive (96/92/EC) designed to guarantee security of supplies; open up markets to competition; allow large consumers the right to choose their own supplier; prevent cross subsidies between the different activities of an electricity supplier, e.g. mining, generation, transmission and distribution; and promote environmentally friendly sources of energy (European Commission, 1998).

In 1999, the government passed the Liberalisation Law, which incorporated the Directive into Greek law. It also provided for third party access to the PPC's transmission and distribution facilities, through the creation of the Hellenic Transmission System Operator (HTSO), and the establishment of the Regulatory Authority for Energy (RAE) responsible for regulating the electricity market.

Though the EU Electricity Directive did not require the Greek government to sell off the PPC, the government began the process of transferring the PPC to the private sector. The main stages in this process were as follows:

- In November 2000, the Greek government announced that the PPC was to be privatised.
- On 1 January 2001, the PPC was transformed into a société anonyme (i.e. a limited company) and became the PPC SA, though the government still owned 100 per cent of the company's issued share capital.
- In December 2001, the PPC was listed on both the Athens and London Stock Exchanges.
- In June and July 2002, 15% of the PPC's shares were sold.

These changes evoked a great deal of opposition. There was considerable resistance from the PPC's workforce, who feared that privatisation would lead to job losses for some and worse terms and conditions for the rest. Employees also complained about the lack of information. As one employee in the Distribution Division stated:

> There is a total absence of communication between management and staff. As no part of the decision-making process takes account of the employees' claims and wishes, employees increasingly feel that they have been marginalised by the company's top management …

This was echoed by the Employees' Representative on the Board of Directors:

> It seems that this privatisation process will only benefit a small elite of managers, whilst the majority of staff will have no financial or other benefits and, as well as that, we will have to face all the negative consequences of this privatisation. … resistance to change, even when expressed in a more extreme manner, is the only way for our employees to attract the top managers' attention and be taken more seriously.

Public opinion was also against the sale of the PPC and other state assets (Financial Times, 2000). Even the government was split over the privatisation of the PPC. As one senior manager in the Generating Division observed:

> Until now, the privatisation process has been a very lengthy process. It has been much longer than it was originally intended to be, let alone the fact that it's not finished yet. The reasons for this delay are twofold: first, the lack of strategic vision that characterises those most closely involved with the process and second, the internal conflicts among government members about future privatisation scenarios.

Nevertheless, by July 2002, to all intents and purposes the PPC was operating as a private sector, profit-making company. This can be seen from the changes to its organisational structure and orientation.

The restructuring and reorientation of the PPC
The creation of the new PPC was accompanied by a redefinition of its mission. Out went the notion that it was there to facilitate economic and social developments in Greece; in its place the company stated that its objectives were to:

> … maintain leadership in the Greek electricity market, improve the efficiency of its operations, rationalize its   capital expenditure and explore growth initiatives. (Public Power Corporation, 2001: 6)

The first steps towards achieving these objectives involved restructuring the company to comply with the Liberalisation Law's requirement to provide separate accounts for the different areas of the PPC's business, and to prevent cross subsidies between them. Restructuring also involved changes in personnel to ensure that the company was managed by competent staff who were orientated towards private sector values. As an employee in the Distribution Division commented:

> The organisation had a very convoluted hierarchy in the past. Even promotions, as in every public sector company, were based on hierarchical rank rather than individual performance, let alone the fact that the only way to survive was never to be responsible for any of your actions … Now it's the exact opposite.

However, some appear to question whether all managerial posts were filled on the basis of competence and orientation. There had been considerable trade union resistance to the PPC's privatisation but, as one Assistant Director commented:

> Many of these [new] General Managers were previously the most opinionated unionists. Suddenly, they lost their voice as they got offered prestigious job positions. Indeed, this must be the biggest change in the organisation from this privatisation process.

Restructuring also included job losses and changes in employment conditions and job security. One of the first acts of the new PPC was to announce that 6,000 jobs would be shed through natural wastage by 2005 – some 20 per cent of the workforce. A Director of the Generating Division remarked:

> The company was overstaffed and this was one of our major problems in the past. Today, we cannot afford to have three people doing a job which our European peers have one person doing. Thus, we are currently pursuing a policy of workforce rationalisation, through a combination of natural wastage and restrictions on recruitment …

The Director of Human Resources was very clear where the blame lay for overstaffing:

> Throughout the pre-privatisation period, all previous governments mismanaged our operations and they even exploited our company and sacrificed its well-being in order to solicit votes and win the elections, by hiring superfluous staff.

The Director of Human Resources believes that there has also been a transformation in the company's culture:

> PPC SA has been transformed into a learning organisation, which is now based on values rather than rules, whilst its employees behave as knowledge workers, and not as typical civil servants.

However, an employee in the Distribution Division took a different view:

> … the increasing job insecurity and the new entrepreneurial practices inevitably urged employees to compete with each other for the sake of their own career development and promotion and always at the expense of their colleagues. Therefore, we witnessed the phenomena of fierce internal competition and lack of co-operation.

As part of the restructuring of the PPC, three new subsidiaries were created. Kozen SA will develop joint ventures with small companies to generate electricity from heat produced as a by-product of their normal business activities. PPC Renewables SA will enter into joint ventures to develop renewable, environmentally friendly, energy sources. PPC Telecommunications SA is a joint venture with Greece's two largest banks and the Italian company WIND. Its purpose is to create a new telecoms network capable of winning 17 per cent of the Greek market over the next decade.

Therefore, the PPC appears to have moved a long way from its role as a public monopoly, though the Greek government still owns 85 per cent of its shares.

What next for the PPC?

The PPC's main objectives over the next few years are to maintain its dominant position in the Greek electricity market and to expand into the Balkans and Turkey. To achieve this, it intends to form a strategic alliance with a leading EU electricity company to gain their expertise. The government has begun the process of selecting a strategic partner for the PPC with a view to its taking a 10–15 per cent stake in the company.

At a later date, the government plans to sell a second tranche of shares (approximately 20 per cent) to the strategic partner. However, this will depend on whether the alliance allows the PPC successfully to expand its activities and show that it is capable of becoming one of the top five or six firms in the European electricity market over the next two decades.

As can be seen, the PPC has an ambitious, three-pronged strategy. First, in the short-term, it is attempting to protect its domestic market through cost-cutting and joint ventures. Second, in the medium to long term, with its strategic partner's expertise, it intends to expand on a regional basis and then throughout the rest of the EU. Third, drawing on its transmission and distribution networks and its large customer base, over the next decade, it intends to become a significant player in the Greek telecoms sector.

So far, the PPC appears to be making good progress with its plans. Its new structure, new profit-seeking orientation and job cuts seem to be producing significant financial benefits for shareholders. After its first year of operating as a private company, the PPC announced that its profits had increased by over 50 per cent to _399m. Whether it can maintain this type of performance over the medium term, or – like other privatised electricity companies – it will find that once the easy gains from job cuts have been achieved, the twin pressures of competition and regulation will squeeze profits, remains to be seen (Macalister, 1999).

Summary

In examining the privatisation of the PPC, there are three issues that seem particularly pertinent: the process of privatisation; future plans for the operation of the PPC; and whether or not there was an alternative to privatisation. Taking the first of these, the process: as many writers have noted, privatisations are not the nice, neat events that their proponents would wish to believe (Coram and Burnes, 2001; Parker, 2000; Young, 1990). The PPC's privatisation evoked arguments in government, resistance from the trade unions and some concern from the general public. To date, only 15 per cent of its shares are in private hands, so privatisation has not been particularly rapid. However, like most state monopolies, it had had no experience of operating in a competitive market. As Dudley (1999) maintains of such organisations, they have to take charge of their own destiny, develop new relationships both internally and externally, satisfy the expectations of different stakeholders and develop or acquire new market-orientated skills and competencies. Nevertheless, the PPC has been restructured, it is operating as a private sector concern, it is making significant profits and, more to the point, no one seems to doubt that this is a permanent change. Therefore, at least in the short term, the PPC privatisation appears to have been successful. However, what about its longer-term prospects?

In terms of the second issue the PPC has followed a well-trodden privatisation path of restructuring, cost-cutting and the introduction of commercial practices. This is the relatively easy part of privatisation, however: the difficult part comes when competition and regulation start to bite. The PPC's strategy is to defend its existing electricity markets, expand its core electricity business internationally and expand its domestic activities into telecoms. The problem with the defensive strategy is that if it is successful, and the PPC retains its dominant position, the Regulatory Authority for Energy, driven by the EU, will take action to make life easier for the PPC's competitors. The purpose of the EU Energy Directive is to open up the market to new entrants in order to stimulate competition. If this does not happen then, as elsewhere, the Regulator, or the EU, will change the rules to favour new entrants (Parker, 2003). For example, as in other countries, the Regulator could break up the company by separating electricity generation from distribution.

The experience elsewhere is that it is very difficult for utilities to hold on to their dominant position and, in the short term at least, markets tend to become fragmented as lots of new players enter (Parker, 2003). Consequently, the PPC's defensive strategy may fail and it could be forced to sell, close or downsize the less profitable areas of its business.

Nor do the PPC's expansion plans seem any surer of success. The move into telecoms seems risky. The telecoms market in Europe is extremely competitive, costly to break into and also highly regulated (Parker, 2003). The likelihood of a new player succeeding appears to be very small. Similar points can be made about the PPC's intentions to become one of the leading electricity companies across the EU, albeit with a strategic partner. Market liberalisation has made the EU electricity market a very competitive place inhabited by a plethora of competing companies from across the globe. Therefore, the PPC and any strategic partner would have to be very good and, perhaps, very lucky to succeed.

There is also the point as to whether the Greek government has done the PPC any favours by privatising it as a single entity rather than breaking it up, as was the case in the UK electricity industry. Newly-privatised companies tend to lack key managerial competencies necessary to survive in the private sector. By attempting to be competitive in all of its old activities, as well as expanding into new businesses domestically and internationally, the PPC's management may be spreading itself too thinly.

This brings us to the last issue, was there an alternative to privatisation? it was the EU's European Electricity Directive (96/92/EC) that compelled the government to open up the Greek electricity market to competition and to restructure the PPC so that it operated on a commercial basis (European Commission, 1998). The Electricity Directive did not compel the government to sell the PPC and, indeed, the government intends to retain a 51 per cent stake in the company. Consequently, if we take the 'narrow' definition of privatisation discussed earlier, it has not privatised the PPC because it has not sold the company or even a majority holding in the company. However, quite evidently, the new PPC is not a state enterprise in which the private sector has a minority shareholding; it is a private sector company in which the government has a majority stake, so to all intents and purposes it is now a privatised company. For that reason, it clearly meets Adams et al's (1996) 'broader' definition of privatisation, i.e. it is a profit-orientated concern run on commercial lines. Therefore, whilst it can be argued that the Greek government had an alternative as to whether it chose privatisation according to the narrow or broad interpretation, the EU Electricity Directive did not allow the government the choice to reject privatisation altogether.

Conclusions

In Parts 1 and 2 of this book, it was argued that the potential exists for managers to exercise a wide degree of choice with regard to almost all aspects of their business, whether that be products, structures, personnel policies or culture. This potential freedom, however, is constrained by societal, environmental, industry-specific and organisational constraints, not to say managerial preferences and competences, many of which may conflict with each other.

This chapter has demonstrated that organisations do indeed face formidable constraints and pressures on managerial freedom of action. The case study of the music industry shows how powerful these are. For the big companies in the industry, it is essential that they maintain their control over the production and distribution of music, but the Internet has changed the rules of the game in a big way. Music is a global business and the Internet offers the potential for record companies to provide a quicker, better and cheaper service to their customers. However, because the Internet is enabling music piracy on an unprecedented scale, it is also a major threat to the dominance, or even the existence, of the big record labels. It is not clear how the big record labels can or will respond successfully to this industry-wide transformation, but whatever the outcome, managers cannot rely on old ways of working and old ways of doing business if they are to survive. The second case study, Marconi, is one where the company's new management believed that they had seen the writing on the wall for the old GEC and that the company had to move into the Internet era as a major telecoms equipment provider if it was to survive. They were encouraged in this by investors in the City of London and the prevailing dotcom euphoria. Senior managers constructed and pursued a vision of a brave new telecoms world for the company. The company sold off the vast majority of its existing business, changed its name to Marconi, and went on a spectacular spending spree which saw both its share price and debts rise spectacularly. When the dotcom bubble burst, the company went with it.

If Marconi shows the dangers of a company trying to reinvent itself rapidly, the Oticon study shows that it is possible for a determined manager to break out of the standard patterns of competition that exist in an industry and rewrite the competitive rule book to his company's advantage. This is a company that operates in a global market and faces competition from larger and technologically more advanced companies. The CEO believed that Oticon could not compete technologically but could provide a better service to customers than its competitors. Unlike Marconi, the company did not try to reinvent itself by selling its assets and buying new ones. Instead, it radically changed its structures, ways of working and culture to unleash the human potential of the company, and in so doing regained its competitive edge.

The last case study, the privatisation of the PPC, shows two different dimensions of internationalisation. On the one hand, the Greek government was heavily influenced in its industrial policies by the neo-liberal political and economic agenda that has swept through much of the world over the last 20 years or so. This led Greece to follow the same privatisation route as many other countries. On the other hand, Greece is also a member of the EU and as such is bound by its rules. In this case, the liberalisation of the European electricity market forced Greece to restructure its electricity industry and open it up to competition. It was the twin pressures of a neo-liberal ideology and the EU's competition rules for the electricity industry that encouraged the privatisation of the PPC and greatly influenced the structure and operation of the post-privatised PPC.

The case studies raise a number of important issues regarding strategic change in general and managerial choice in particular:

- The particular strategic approach that an organisation (or rather its management) adopts is limited by, and to an extent must accommodate, societal, environmental, sectoral and organisational constraints. It must also be recognised that, in an increasingly globalised world, even apparently small events can have a major impact on industries and organisations. In the case of the music industry, the creation of a small piece of software by a 19-year-old computer geek has thrown the industry into turmoil.

- Nevertheless, it must also be recognised that because the various societal, environmental, sectoral and organisational constraints can conflict with each other – can pull organisations in different directions, or be manipulated or changed for more favourable conditions – managers do have a degree of freedom to adopt a strategic approach that is more in keeping with their own interests or beliefs. That is to say, under certain conditions and certain circumstances, the world in which they operate can be shaped by their views, rather than vice versa. This certainly appears to be one interpretation of events at Oticon. The implications of the constraints faced by Oticon were that it could no longer compete with its big, technologically advanced competitors. Oticon showed that by reinventing itself it could.

- Marconi, on the other hand, showed the fallacy of believing that anything is possible. Indeed, it could be argued that rather than questioning the received wisdom, as Oticon did, it appeared to accept it at face value. George Simpson sounded much less of a visionary and more of a fatalist when, in justifying his failure, he asked:

> What else were we going to do? The old GEC had had it and everyone told us that focus was what was needed. Telecoms was the obvious industry to expand into.
>
> (quoted in Harrison, M, 2002: 24)

The privatisation of the PPC is another example of where managers, and politicians, appeared to accept that the constraints they faced were immutable, and proceeded to work within the perceived rules of the game. This pushed them to adopt a strategy of holding onto its domestic market, expanding internationally and diversifying into other industries. Whilst this might have been the obvious course to take, it is also one which others have found very difficult to navigate successfully.

- A clear vision of the future appears to be an essential attribute for managers seeking to secure their organisation's future survival and success. This is certainly something that many in the music industry are seeking. However, it has to be coupled with the strength of character to challenge existing norms and received wisdom. The CEO of Oticon had both and succeeded. Senior managers at Marconi, arguably, had the strength of character to challenge the Weinstock inheritance, but their vision for the company's future was seriously flawed, and the outcome was disastrous. As far as the PPC is concerned, only time will tell if they were right or wrong not to challenge the received wisdom.

- As well as a realisable vision, managers also need to win over the rest of the organisation. In Oticon this took approximately 18 months (though much remained to be done after this). Marconi does not appear to have tried to win over staff because the intention was to get rid of most of them. The PPC do appear to have embarked on a programme to win over staff, though how effective this has been is disputed.

■ In implementing strategy, it is not necessary to work out all the details in advance, but the first few steps must be clear and consistent with the vision. It also helps if they are seen to succeed! This appears to have been the situation for Oticon and, initially at least, for Marconi and the PPC. Where strategies are radical, as in these three cases, their implementation is usually accompanied by a degree of chaos as old certainties are discarded and new ones have yet to be established. In Oticon's case, the initial degree of chaos may well have been deliberate. For Marconi, however, the chaos increased and turned into panic as it became clear that its strategy was failing.

Test your learning

■ Short answer questions

1   List the main ways in which it could be said that Shawn Fanning changed the rules of the music industry.

2   What are the main strategic options facing the big record labels in coping with the challenges posed by the Internet?

3   What was Marconi's vision?

4   In what ways did Marconi's vision challenge the rules of the game?

5   Identify three ways in which it could be said that Oticon reinvented itself.

6   List three ways in which it could be said that Oticon changed its culture.

7   What were the main pressures faced by the PPC when considering its future?

8   List three advantages and three dangers of the PPC's strategy for its future.

■ Essay questions

1   To what extent does the case of the music industry support the arguments of complexity theorists?

2   In what ways does the Marconi study support the realist perspective on organisations?

3   Evaluate whether or not the Oticon case study supports the argument for managerial choice.

4   Is the PPC case an example of Planned or Emergent strategy?

CHAPTER 12

Case studies in changing internal relationships and attitudes

Learning objectives

After studying the case studies in this chapter, you should be able to:

- list the main pressures on organisations for change;
- understand how real-life organisations manage change;
- appreciate that individual change projects can be viewed either as isolated and finite events or as one of a stream of events that can, over time, shape and reshape an organisation;
- identify different approaches to managing change;
- discuss the strengths, weaknesses and suitability of different approaches to change;
- show the respective roles of managers and staff in planning and executing change;
- describe how environmental uncertainty influences the process of change;
- understand why employees might resist change and how this can be avoided or coped with;
- show how managers can exercise choice in what to change, when to change and how to change.

Introduction

This chapter presents three case studies of organisations who, for varying reasons of efficiency, effectiveness and competitiveness, attempted to change internal relationships and attitudes across functions and between hierarchical levels. Drawing on the arguments developed in Part 2, the case studies examine why and how the particular decisions relating to change were taken and, especially, whether the resultant implementation programmes could be described as Planned or Emergent.

Case Study 5 recounts the attempts by Volvo, over a period of more than 30 years, to break with the assembly-line approach to car production and move to a more human-centred approach. The study shows that it is unclear to what extent the move to Job Design precepts could be construed as part of a vision or concerted strategy for the organisation. Other strategic developments within Volvo were certainly in tune with and helped to encourage the move to Job Design. It is nevertheless apparent that, both in its conception and execution, the move to reorganise work at Volvo was Emergent rather than Planned. Subsequent job redesign initiatives were obviously informed by, and built on, what went before to the extent that a general orientation towards group work and the creation of more satisfying jobs appears to have become embedded in Volvo. The particular form of work reorganisation varied from case to case, however, and was heavily influenced by local circumstances and the orientation of the parties involved; the same applied to implementation and development. Though much effort went into planning the actual changes, it does not appear as though a settled pattern of working arrangements developed on any of the sites. Rather, as circumstances changed, and perhaps the balance of forces shifted, so too did the actual characteristics of jobs and relationships between groups and individuals, groups and other functions, and groups and management. Therefore, the move to Job Design at Volvo, though driven by a general predisposition, can be characterised as a process of development, experimentation and learning.

The XYZ Construction study, Case Study 6, describes how the company went about changing its organisational structure from a hierarchical and functional-based one to a flatter, more teamwork-based matrix-style structure. The company adopted a participative and open approach to change that set out to build a wide consensus around the need for change and type of structure required. Through a series of stages, it moved from auditing the readiness for change, planning the change, implementing it and evaluating the progress made. Though the development and implementation of a new structure at XYZ was not without its difficulties, it was planned and working effectively remarkably quickly. As with any major structural change in an organisation, there were many possible and actual losers, some of them at a senior level. Therefore, the potential for resistance and disruption was high. The participative and open nature of the change process, however, coupled with the recognition that change was required, and the strong commitment from the top, meant that the process was relatively free from disruption by individuals or groups.

The XYZ study seems to turn some of the literature on change on its head. As shown in Chapter 10, Kanter *et al* (1992) see structural change (Bold Strokes) as a precursor to cultural change (Long Marches). In this instance, however, changes in culture and attitudes were achieved prior to the structural change which, in some senses, can be seen as a reinforcing mechanism to the cultural and attitudinal changes. The explanation for this is relatively simple. When the new Managing Director of XYZ took over, he saw the main priority as improving the company's performance through a combination of attitudinal/cultural change and management and staff development at all levels. For him, major structural change was not a priority at this stage; it could come later. Instead, he embarked on a series of Emergent changes that, over time, worked towards his goal of improving the performance of the company. By 1999, he saw that the company was ready for and needed structural change. Because of the nature of the change and the situation in the organisation, the approach adopted was Planned rather than Emergent. Therefore, in this instance, as in most, the issue of what comes first, Bold Strokes or Long Marches, was primarily a tactical one. Similarly, the issue of whether change should be approached in a Planned way or not was also tactical. A Planned approach was seen as being the best way to achieve the necessary improvements at this time given the situation in the company.

GK Printers, Case Study 7, is now an efficient and forward-looking company, but is a prime example of an organisation that so nearly 'snatched defeat from the jaws of victory'. The company put a great deal of collective effort into turning around its fortunes, only to see the gains threatened by inertia and conflict between managers. Fortunately, it managed to rescue the situation in time, but it could so easily have been different. In many respects, it is a company where only in a crisis can existing norms and concepts be challenged and new strategies emerge. The actual implementation process tended towards Planned rather than Emergent or open-ended change. GK operates in a changing and highly competitive environment, and though it was inclined to view change as a one-off activity rather than a process of continuous improvement, this view has been evolving. GK is also showing that it can be innovative, and has extended the range of its capabilities to develop a lucrative business in developing and designing websites for its customers.

The chapter concludes by arguing that in modern organisations, facing uncertain and changing environments, it is not just strategy that is Emergent but also, in many cases, the implementation process. This does not invalidate the Planned approach to change, and certainly not the many tools and techniques associated with it. However, it does mean that, for change projects which are rather experimental in nature and/or open-ended, the concept of some form of settled pattern being established, and thus the process of change being concluded, is not valid.

Case Study 5

Volvo's approach to Job Design[1]

Background

In Chapter 3, we examined the emergence of new organisational paradigms. In reviewing the Culture–Excellence school, the Japanese approach and organisational learning, the emphasis placed on team or group work was striking. Though the importance of group work for individual well-being, organisational performance and collective learning has been a central feature of the Job Design literature for many years (see Chapter 2), its actual influence on work and organisational design in Western companies has been relatively small. One of the few exceptions to this has been Volvo, the Swedish motor vehicle manufacturer, which has been seen as a leader in innovations in work organisation since the 1970s. Indeed, it is probably not an exaggeration to say that in the 1970s, when it began moving away from traditional methods of car assembly, Volvo was more famous for its commitment to work humanisation than for the actual vehicles it manufactured (Blackler and Brown, 1978).

As will be described below, Volvo's approach to reorganising vehicle production has evolved through a number of distinct phases: the abandonment of the assembly line in favour of group-based static assembly; the extension of group roles to include more collective responsibility and some decision-making autonomy; and the introduction of self-paced assembly work (Pontusson, 1990). It is also worth noting that the process of change was initially entirely management-driven (though the unions were involved or consulted on some aspects). The Swedish Co-determination Law, which came into effect in 1976, obliged firms to involve unions more but, in this instance, it may also have encouraged Volvo to be more radical in extending group work than might otherwise have been the case. However, through the 1980s in particular, the trade unions took a more proactive role.

The move to more flexible forms of work organisation at Volvo went hand-in-hand with its move away from corporate bureaucracy and to more decentralised, localised management of its various vehicle operations. In addition, the last 30 years have seen repeated attempts at diversification and alliances by Volvo, aimed at spreading the risks and costs of operating in a highly cyclical and very capital-intensive industry. In 1993, Pehr Gyllenhammar, Volvo's long-serving Chief Executive, attempted to merge Volvo with Renault, the French state-controlled car company. This move was defeated by a coalition of shareholders and managers with the result that Gyllenhammar resigned from the company. With his departure in 1994, Volvo tried to construct a new direction for itself. It began selling off its interests in other industries and businesses in order to concentrate on vehicle production (Done, 1994). However, as the wave of takeovers and mergers that swept the industry in the 1990s showed, as far as car production is concerned, size matters. In 1999, Volvo finally recognised that it did not have the financial resources to operate as an independent car company. In what must be one of the industry's great ironies, after rejecting a merger with Renault five years earlier, Volvo sold its car division to the Ford Motor Corporation.

Although Ford's takeover does not invalidate Volvo's unique approach to building cars, it does potentially threaten it. Despite the benefits of good design and leading-edge technologies, vehicle producers tend to stand or fall by the effectiveness and efficiency of their assembly operations (Womack et al, 1990). Ford's opinion of the efficiency of Volvo's assembly operations will be crucial in determining whether the Volvo approach survives or is replaced by more traditional Fordist ways of work. So far, both Ford and Volvo appear to have benefited from the takeover. Volvo have been able to produce a range of new models that have sold very well, especially in North America, and Volvo is the most profitable part of Ford's Premier Automotive Group, which includes Jaguar, Land Rover and Aston Martin.

---

1   The term Job Design is explained in Chapter 2. In essence it is the antithesis of Taylorism and involves designing work to fit human needs and abilities.

Nor does this seem to have been at the expense of the Volvo culture. As Hans-Olov Olsson, Volvo Cars Chief Executive, stated: 'They [Ford] cannot touch the soul of Volvo. They have to protect Volvo's Swedishness in product development and managing the business'(quoted in Burt, 2002: 13).

What this highlights, though, is that Volvo's move to end assembly-line production was not and is not a marginal activity – it has become embedded in the culture, or to use Olsson's word, the 'soul'of the company. The decision to adopt Job Design at Volvo was and remains driven by management, regardless of later union and legislative encouragement, though to what extent they foresaw how extensively it would develop is not known. What is clear is that, in the 1960s, Volvo was as committed as any car company to the Classical approach to work organisation espoused by Taylor and embodied in the assembly-line approach to car production devised by Henry Ford. Yet, in the 1970s, it chose to break away from this industry-standard approach and embark on (what has turned out to be) a long-term programme of increasingly radical work reorganisation.

There are two complementary explanations for Volvo's actions. The first is the explanation given by Pehr Gyllenhammar (1977: 73), until 1994 Volvo's Chief Executive, identifying the need to reduce labour turnover, which the company believed was caused by boring and monotonous jobs:

> The company has to bear the costs of recruiting labour and training employees. The absenteeism and turnover rates also increase the costs for quality control, for maintaining buffer stocks of semifinished goods and components, and for adjustments, tools and machinery. Administrative costs go up when a company must maintain pools of reserve labour to fill requirements during peak periods of absenteeism.

To flesh Gyllenhammar's explanation out a little, Pontusson (1990) pointed out that Volvo's freedom of manoeuvre in tackling its recruitment and retention problems was limited by the labour market conditions of the time. There was full employment, which made it easier for workers to move jobs; and very effective wage bargaining by unions, establishing industry and sectoral pay rates, which made it very difficult for Volvo to offer higher wage rates than other employers. In the presence of full employment and the absence of wage flexibility, Volvo chose to tackle labour turnover and absenteeism by attempting to create more satisfying and varied jobs.

The second explanation was offered by Karlsson (1973). He pointed out that Volvo was one of Sweden's largest and most successful companies. As such, its actions and practices were always in the public eye. With the increasing interest in Job Design in Scandinavia in general and Sweden in particular in the 1960s and 1970s, it was hardly surprising that Volvo's work organisation methods were the subject of much attention. In particular, Karlsson (1973: 34) pointed out that the company was heavily criticised for its 'inhuman principles of organisation' based 'entirely on the scientific management method'.

So it appears that Volvo's conversion to Job Design was inspired by commercial considerations relating to the costs of absenteeism and labour turnover, allied to pressure from public opinion in Sweden for it to embrace a less 'inhuman' form of work organisation. Although these appear to be the principal reasons for Volvo's management embarking on its commitment to Job Design, since then the process has developed its own momentum, to the extent that (as noted by Auer and Riegler, 1990: 14): 'group work is the basic concept for all changes in the organisation of production work at Volvo'. This did not come about overnight, without hesitation and backtracking, however, or in a fully planned and coordinated fashion; rather it has evolved or emerged through a number of distinct phases.

Phases of change

Volvo's adoption of Job Design principles began over 30 years ago. It has now reached a stage where group work has become the standard approach to work design, and assembly-line working is not considered appropriate for any new Volvo plant. When dealing with events spanning such a long period, it is often difficult to form an accurate picture of what has taken place and why; particularly when, as in this case, these events have been played out on different sites by different groups of managers and workers. Nevertheless, as Auer and Riegler (1990) and Pontusson (1990) pointed out, by examining major change programmes involving large investments in new or remodelled plants, it is possible to identify a number of distinct phases in the evolution of Volvo's approach to Job Design.

These phases are related to major investment projects that occurred in the 1970s, 1980s and 1990s, namely:

■ **Kalmar** – this plant opened in 1974 and was the company's first, and most cited, attempt to move away from assembly-line work.
■ **Torslanda** – this is Volvo's main car plant, which, since the late 1970s, has seen a number of increasingly radical attempts to move away from the traditional assembly-line approach to car production.
■ **Uddevalla** – this new assembly plant opened in 1990, and exemplifies Volvo's decisive break with traditional motor industry jobs.
■ **Gent and Born** – the introduction of new cars in these existing plants in the late 1980s allowed Volvo the opportunity to introduce the methods developed in its other plants, thus showing Volvo's commitment to extending its Job Design philosophy across all areas of its operations.

Phase one – Kalmar

Those committed to challenging the 'inhuman' approach to work, epitomised by the Classical school in general and Henry Ford's moving assembly line in particular, came to look on Volvo's Kalmar car plant as a sort of promised land – a blueprint for the future of work. This was not only because Kalmar was seen as a model of human-centred work organisation, but also because it struck at the very heart of the industry, which, through its use of the moving assembly line with its severe division of labour and short cycle times, had taken Taylorist work practices to their ultimate extremes. In addition, and just as importantly, it was heralded as a commercial success. Indeed, Kalmar was famous throughout the world for its 'revolutionary' approach to Job Design even before it opened (Blackler and Brown, 1978).

Perhaps the main reason for the perception that Kalmar was making a decisive break with the past was due to the way Volvo approached its design. The original management concept for Kalmar attempted to incorporate many of the progressive Job Design ideas circulating in the early 1970s. A project team composed of managers, engineers and architects was given responsibility for designing and building the plant. Each decision of this team had to be approved by a committee that included trade union representatives, health and safety experts, doctors and outside Job Design experts, including colleagues of Einar Thorsrud, the noted Norwegian work psychologist.

The 'revolutionary' image of Kalmar also owed much to the efficiency of Volvo's own publicity machine. This can be seen from statements about the ethos of the plant made by Pehr Gyllenhammar, Volvo's former Chief Executive, before it opened:

> The objective of Kalmar will be to arrange auto production in such a way that each employee will be able to find meaning and satisfaction in his work.

This will be a factory which, without any sacrifice of efficiency or the company's financial objectives, will give employees opportunities to work in groups, to communicate freely among themselves, to switch from one job assignment to another, to vary the pace of their work, to identify with the product, to be conscious of a responsibility for quality, and to influence their own working environment.

When a product is made by people who find meaning in their work, it must inevitably be a product of high quality. (All quotes are from Aguren *et al*, 1984: 13)

Opened in 1974, Kalmar was Volvo's second largest final assembly plant (the much bigger Torslanda being the largest). It had been planned for an annual capacity of 30,000 cars with around 600 employees. In 1976, it produced 22,000 cars but production fell to 17,000 when demand slumped after the second oil shock in 1977. Production rose again in 1979 but fell back in 1980, when a four-day week was briefly introduced. In 1985, Kalmar produced 32,500 cars, representing about 16 per cent of Volvo's Swedish output of cars. In 1988 the plant had around 960 employees (Aguren *et al*, 1984; Auer and Riegler, 1990).

The differences between Kalmar and a traditional car plant are that, in the latter, the pace of work is determined by the moving assembly line, jobs are extremely fragmented and have cycle times of a few minutes or less, and workers are dedicated to one task only. At Kalmar there was no assembly line, workers operated in teams, with each team having its own dedicated area of the factory. Within the team, workers could move between tasks, and each task had a cycle time of between 20 and 30 minutes. In place of the assembly line, cars were mounted on automated carriers which moved around the plant and served both as a means of transport and as a work platform. This arrangement allowed Kalmar originally to operate two alternatives to the moving assembly line:

- **Straight-line assembly**. Work within each team area is split up into four or five work stations placed in a series along the production flow. Two team members work at each station, following the carrier through all the stations and carrying out all the necessary assembly operations.
- **Dock assembly**. This is where one carrier at a time is guided into the 'dock' assembly areas where all of the team's tasks are carried out on the stationary carrier by two or three people.

The main difference between the two approaches is that the first, straight-line assembly, still bears some relation to the moving assembly line in that the car carriers move automatically from station to station thus determining the pace of work. In the second approach, the dock system, the car is stationary all the time giving workers more control over the pace of work. Nevertheless, both forms revolve around teamwork and offer variety and task completeness.

There can be very little doubt that, for its time, Kalmar represented a significant break with the past. There were those, however, who questioned whether the original high hopes for the plant, in terms of the humanisation of work, had been met. Pontusson (1990) argued that the economic consequences of fluctuations in output levels led the plant management to retreat from its original ambitions and, in the latter part of the 1970s, to tighten managerial control over the work process. It was certainly the case that, compared to its conventional plants, there was no significant improvement in output. Also, as Berggren (1992: 123) noted, the ability of work teams to change the pace of work led to some 'mischief', and a team might change the pace of work of another team 'for fun'. For these reasons, according to Pontusson (1990), dock assembly was abandoned, and the potential for workers to influence the pace of work by taking automated carriers out of the main flow was ended.

Blackler and Brown (1978) argued that, with the abandonment of dock assembly, and despite longer cycle times, some fundamental elements of the assembly line (i.e. machine-paced work) were maintained. Auer and Riegler (1990) made a similar point. They argued that, over time, changes such as new work evaluation methods, the removal of time buffers between stages and the general speeding up of the carriers (which are controlled by a central computer) intensified the pace of work and returned the production process much closer to the assembly-line concept than was originally intended.

Before it opened, Kalmar was being hailed as a revolution in Job Design. The reality is that Kalmar does not appear to have represented the dramatic break with the Fordist–Taylorist production process that many had hoped for (Auer and Riegler, 1990; Blackler and Brown, 1978; Pontusson, 1990). This does not mean that Kalmar was a failure, however. Given that Volvo, hitherto very much a traditional car company, were trying to invent a new concept in car assembly, it would have been surprising if they had managed to rewrite the rules of car production at the first attempt. It must be remembered that, although Kalmar was a social experiment, it was also expected to be an economic success. If the social dimension appeared to threaten financial performance, it was the former rather than the latter that would be sacrificed. The true measure of Kalmar's success lies not in the degree to which it achieved its 'revolutionary' goal, but in the extent to which it encouraged Volvo's management to continue with and accelerate the move away from Fordist–Taylorist approaches to work. As Auer and Riegler (1990: 27) concluded, despite some disagreement among managers over the effectiveness of the organisation of Kalmar plant, there were sufficient supporters for Volvo to proceed with the development of 'far more progressive' and 'radical' attempts to distance itself from the traditional assembly-line approach to car production. This is a point also made by Gyllenhammar:

> Volvo Kalmar is no final solution. It is the first step on the road. But much remains to be done in the field of work organisation. I could imagine much greater freedom and independence at work. (Quoted in Berggren, 1992: 127)

Nevertheless, in 1992, at the time of a major recession in the European car industry, Kalmar was closed.

Phase two – Torslanda

As well as Kalmar, the late 1970s and early 1980s saw Volvo experimenting with alternatives to the traditional assembly line at a number of plants. In the main, these were small-scale, and tended to concentrate on bus or truck production rather than car assembly. From the late 1970s onwards, however, a series of increasingly radical attempts were made to transform work organisation at Torslanda, Volvo's main car assembly plant. In 1976, at the central assembly plant, Torslanda management experimented with the use of large, autonomous work groups to assemble an entire car using a dock-assembly approach similar to that being attempted at Kalmar. Owing to poor productivity, this was abandoned within six months. Management believed that the workforce lacked the necessary skills to make such an approach work, whilst the metal workers' trade union felt the experiment was too risky.

In 1979/80, with the opening of the TUN facility at Torslanda to assemble the new 700 series car, management attempted to revive group-based assembly. The TUN workforce was selected from the existing production personnel at Torslanda. The original plan for TUN, initially drawn up without union involvement, envisaged car assembly being carried out by autonomous work groups who would be responsible for their own quality and pace of work. It was planned that work groups would also have responsibility for job rotation, managing material supplies and some maintenance tasks.

The reality though was somewhat less ambitious than originally conceived. The unions, who – when eventually involved – played a larger part in the design of TUN than they had at Kalmar, were highly sceptical of the original concept and this, together with certain practical difficulties in trying to mix indirect tasks, such as maintenance and material control, with direct production work, led to the scaling-down of the original proposals. TUN is still organised around group-based assembly, and job rotation is still practised, but the pace of work is centrally controlled and workers no longer perform indirect tasks. Nevertheless, workers at TUN see it as being a clear improvement on the traditional approach to car assembly (Auer and Riegler, 1990).

In 1986, once again management began to consider major changes to the organisation of work at Torslanda's central assembly plant. At this time, the plant employed 4,000 workers and was mainly organised around Fordist–Taylorist principles. This time the trade unions were involved much earlier and played a more central role. In February 1986, management and unions agreed on an 'action plan' that emphasised the transformation of car assembly into an 'attractive alternative' to the traditional methods of car manufacture. In particular, learning from the earlier failure, the plan stressed the need for high-quality training and continuing education to allow workers to gain the skills necessary for effective group work. The action plan appeared to revive many of the original plans for TUN (including the provision for direct production workers to carry out indirect tasks). In addition, it envisaged working time being adjusted to employee needs.

Though the reorganisation of Torslanda is a continuing process, some of the individual sections, such as motor and axle assembly, have been operating along new lines for some time. The changes envisaged in the action plan have been introduced, especially those relating to workers controlling the pace of work and undertaking indirect tasks. Staff turnover and absenteeism is very low at Torslanda, which reflects both the work environment and the rigorous recruitment methods designed to select well-educated staff who are team-orientated. It is a very clean plant with good recreational facilities, such as a gym and swimming pool, and also provides a creche for the children of all staff. At Torslanda, upward and downward communication is considered vital, and staff are encouraged to show initiative through formal and informal discussion groups.

As might be expected, there have been some difficulties in implementing these new working arrangements at Torslanda. The main problem appears to relate to trade union attempts to protect traditional demarcations between direct and indirect tasks and between work groups and supervisors. Maintenance staff still work outside the work group structure, and the foremen's trade union successfully resisted their partial replacement by rotating team leaders. The metal workers' union also wanted to maintain a more hierarchical structure in order to preserve a job ladder between the shopfloor and management.

By the late 1990s, the workforce at Torslanda had increased to 5,500 and the plant was producing 580 vehicles a day. Multi-skilling was a fact of life and, in some parts of the factory, jobs were rotated every hour. Such was the perceived success of the factory that it was given responsibility for assembling Volvo's C70 car, which was launched in 1997. Therefore, progress has been made and, though the final form that Torslanda will take is still uncertain, it does appear to promise a more radical break with tradition than occurred at Kalmar (Auer and Riegler, 1990; Pontusson, 1990).

Phase three – Uddevalla

This was the first all-new car assembly plant built by Volvo in Sweden since Kalmar. It was designed to employ 1,000 people and have the capability to produce 40,000 cars per year. Many observers believe the plant goes far beyond Volvo's previous attempts at Job Design: 'the only one [car plant] in the world where workers build cars from start to finish rather than on an assembly line' (McIvor, 1995: 37). The design of the plant was the result of a 'modernisation pact' between the plant's management and the metal workers' union, many of whose extensive demands were incorporated into the plant's design (Auer and Riegler, 1990). In accordance with Sweden's Co-determination Law (and Volvo's practice at Torslanda), the unions were involved in the steering group responsible for designing and building the Uddevalla plant. Indeed, three union officials worked full-time on the project between 1985 and 1987.

The completed plant comprised six mini-factories, each containing eight dock assembly areas, each with its own autonomous work group. Therefore, in total, there were 48 assembly groups. Each work group has ten fully-trained assembly workers, each of whom can, again in theory, perform all the tasks necessary to assemble an entire car. The work groups are responsible for determining their own pace of work and internal job rotation. In addition, the groups have responsibility for maintenance, administration and quality control. The role of group leader rotates among the members of each group. The incorporation of so many functions within each group resulted in a very flat hierarchy; there are no layers between the groups and the factory managers. To facilitate these working arrangements, the process of car assembly had to be re-thought in order to refine and simplify it. The plant also adopted an equal opportunities policy that reserved at least 40 per cent of production jobs for women and at least 25 per cent for workers over 45 years old.

The plant is clearly at the leading edge of Job Design, at least as far as the car industry is concerned. As Karlsson (1996: 11) remarked:

> What was created was an extremely horizontal organisation, but also some vertical integration. This included responsibilities for quality and some integration with sales, because in the result-oriented team the idea was that the worker should be able to experience what he delivered to the customer. Hence the members of the assembly group could meet and talk directly to the customer.

Nevertheless, as other such initiatives by Volvo have shown, economic and operational concerns can lead to its more radical elements, especially self-paced work, being modified over time. Indeed, the original plan for the plant very much followed the practices adopted at Kalmar. It was only with considerable pressure from the trade unions, and the intervention of Volvo's top management, that more radical ideas were eventually adopted, though even the unions took some convincing that machine-paced assembly might be abandoned altogether (Pontusson, 1990).

Unfortunately, the plant opened at a time when car demand was falling dramatically. Despite attempts to keep it open, along with the Kalmar plant, Volvo closed Uddevalla in 1992 in the face of mounting losses, and notwithstanding the fact that, in productivity terms, it was the most efficient of Volvo's Swedish plants (Cressey, 1996). In 1995, however, the plant was reopened as a joint venture. Though operating on a smaller scale than originally envisaged, Uddevalla's new Chief Executive appeared determined to stick to its original Job Design concept (McIvor, 1995).

Phase four – Gent and Born

By the late 1980s, Volvo's approach to Job Design was widely accepted and practised throughout the company, especially wherever new developments were taking place. When Volvo's Gent plant was chosen to build the 850 series (known internally as the VEC – Volvo European Car), it was natural for Volvo to adopt team-based assembly. The VEC teams operated very much as at the Uddevalla plant but with even greater emphasis on continuous improvement. There was also a great deal of emphasis on the teams to carry out their own maintenance as well as other support tasks. Indeed, so successful was this that Gent became the first plant outside Japan to gain the Total Productive Maintenance Award. In 1996, similar developments took place in Volvo's Dutch plant at Born. The plant was chosen as the site of a joint venture between Volvo and Mitsubishi called Nedcar. The objective was to make cars for both companies that share the same chassis, and have one-third of the parts in common. In essence, it was an attempt to blend Japanese lean production techniques with Volvo's Job Design approach. The aim was to achieve world class efficiency, and the plant quickly became one of Europe's most efficient car plants.

Both Gent and Born demonstrate Volvo's ongoing commitment to develop, extend and experiment with alternative forms of Job Design to those used elsewhere in the car industry. As Karlsson (1996) suggests, Volvo is continually looking for new and different ways to organise production, in the case of Gent and Born by adopting a lean production philosophy, but ensuring that group work lies at the heart of any new developments.

Summary

The progress of redesigning jobs at Volvo has been remarkable in comparison with the Tayloristic–Fordist nature of the company in the 1960s. The fact that it has continued and intensified over a period of 30 years, and that any organisational changes at Volvo are expected to revolve around group work, speaks volumes for the degree to which it has become embedded in the culture of the company. This is not to say that the result is perfect. It must be remembered that assembling cars and trucks will always be a physically demanding job. Also, Volvo are not an altruistic organisation; they exist to make a profit, and the way they organise work must reflect and facilitate this (regardless of pressures from trade unions, government legislation and public opinion). Nevertheless, as Pontusson (1990: 315) observed of Volvo, the 'stages of workplace reform involve a cumulative process of innovation, with a trajectory which adds up to a more or less definitive break with Fordism'. This conclusion, of course, makes the takeover of Volvo's car division by Ford in 1999 all the more ironic.

Some might also point out that though Volvo have led the way, many other companies have followed – including much of the car industry. However, this would be to miss two important points. Firstly, Volvo's approach is not a copycat or 'flavour of the month' one. Rather, it is long-standing and still developing approach which appears to be fundamental to the way the company operates. Secondly, though most other car companies have adopted, to a lesser or greater extent, the autonomous/semi-autonomous work group concept, especially the Japanese, no one else has abandoned the assembly line or gives workers the degree of autonomy and control that Volvo do, especially over the pace of work. Indeed, given the output of the leading car plants, if anything the pace of work on assembly lines, and rigid control over what assembly workers do, seemed more intense in the 1990s than in the supposedly bad old days of the 1960s and 1970s (Milner, 1998)

The changes at Volvo have taken place over an extended timescale, at different sites and under different conditions and, therefore, have been influenced by a wide range of factors. Despite the subsequent advent of the Culture–Excellence approach and the Japanese approach, what has successfully taken place at Volvo is the adoption of practices and principles associated with the Human Relations school as operationalised by the Job Design movement. The key factors that appear to have influenced Volvo to adopt this approach are as follows:

- For sound economic and business reasons, Volvo needed to reduce absenteeism and high labour turnover.
- Full employment and a lack of wage flexibility precluded more traditional 'stick and carrot' measures for dealing with absenteeism and labour turnover. Therefore, Volvo had to look at

alternative methods of reducing absenteeism and labour turnover and, instead of trying to alleviate the symptoms, they chose to tackle the boredom and dissatisfaction that gave rise to labour problems in the first place. The decision by Volvo's management to adopt a Job Design approach appears to have come about owing to a combination of intense public pressure on the company to move to a more human-centred approach to assembly work, and managerial preference. It should be noted, though, that Volvo's management have never been unanimous in supporting the more radical aspects of Job Design, as was demonstrated by the disagreement over the success of Kalmar and the need for senior managers to intervene to ensure a more radical approach at Uddevalla.

■ The parallel move by Volvo to adopt a strategy of decentralising control to plant level (as averse to its previous centralised, bureaucratic control procedures) gave local management some freedom to experiment with new ways of working, and also allowed management to experience the lessening of control that they were advocating for workers.

■ Though originally the move away from Fordist–Taylorist work practices was entirely management-inspired, trade unions came to play an increasingly active role in encouraging its adoption. In this, they were aided by both the Co-determination Law, which came into effect in 1976, and the generally favourable climate towards Job Design in Sweden. However, as Torslanda demonstrated, the trade unions – like Volvo's management – are capable of exhibiting conservative tendencies and need to be convinced that some of the more radical elements of group work should be adopted.

■ Whilst these changes have taken place on different sites and at different times, both management and workers appear to have found a way of capturing the knowledge gained at other plants and lessons learnt for future projects. This process of organisational learning appears to be fundamental to understanding how Volvo has moved (not always in an easy or deliberate fashion) from the limited, though significant, structural changes at Kalmar to the genuine expansion of workers' control seen at Uddevalla. Auer and Riegler (1990: 52), who carried out a comprehensive review of work organisation changes at Volvo, commented that:

Interviews with managers, representatives of trade unions and researchers all confirmed ... Volvo is one of the few companies where management, employees, and trade unions have found broad opportunities for gathering experience in changing the organisation of work and that the company is a place of learning ...

Evidently, the case of Volvo's attempts to move to a radical change in its internal relationships, one which passes significantly greater control of production to workers than had hitherto been considered wise and efficient, is by no means straightforward. Though the intent was there from the start, though we can argue about why the move to Job Design came about, the actual details have been subject to a process of pragmatism, revision and trial and error over more than 30 years. The new approach to work organisation coincided with Volvo's granting of greater autonomy to plant-level managers, the introduction of the Co-determination Law, and considerable public support for Job Design in Sweden; clearly, these were all influential in what happened at Volvo. It should be remembered, however, that Volvo was, at the time, a large and relatively successful private company. If it had wanted to, it could have chosen another course of action; indeed, Volvo's management itself disagreed about the need for and extent of Job Design. The fact that Volvo chose to break the car industry mould at Kalmar, and to keep breaking it at other plants, shows that no matter how powerful or dominant a particular paradigm is, alternatives are always possible. It is also true that, if the move to new ways of working had not allowed the company to develop its competitiveness, the initiative would not have flourished. It may well have been the case that in the atmosphere of the 1970s, Volvo was under great pressure from a number of sources to develop a more human-centred approach to work. With the easing of this pressure in the 1980s and 1990s, however, the company could have chosen quietly to abandon this approach. That it did not clearly demonstrates the belief, especially by Volvo's management, that job redesign works. So far, this commitment has survived the Ford takeover; whether it will continue to do so, only time will tell.

Case Study 6

XYZ Construction

Background

XYZ Construction employs 500 staff and is part of a European-based multinational enterprise. Its main business is the provision of specialist services to major construction projects. As is typical for the construction industry, XYZ operates in a highly competitive and at times hostile and aggressive environment. Disputes between contractors and subcontractors can become bitter and frequently end in litigation, though there have been a number of attempts over the last decade to create better relationships. Just as relationships between organisations tended to be hostile, so relationships within organisations were also less than friendly. Up to 1996, XYZ had been run by an autocratic Managing Director who was feared by his colleagues and who treated the company as his own personal fiefdom. His style of management was not liked and many felt that it was counterproductive but, as one manager commented, 'You didn't challenge him, you didn't put your head above the parapet, or he'd make life hell for you'. When he retired, the parent company took the view that XYZ was underperforming and that much of this was due to poor management and a lack of cooperation within the company. His replacement was appointed with the remit to improve the performance of the company and develop its managerial competency. This he did to great effect. Over a four-year period, he transformed the operation, culture and structure of the organisation.

Focusing on people and performance

The new Managing Director was appointed in 1996. He had trained as an engineer at XYZ but had then left and worked for a number of other companies in the construction industry. Construction is a close-knit industry, however, and he still knew XYZ and its staff quite well. He came with a reputation as an enlightened manager who could deliver performance improvements. The construction industry was notorious for the antagonistic relations between the main contractors and subcontractors such as XYZ, who specialise in one aspect of the construction process. The Managing Director recognised, however, that the industry was attempting to change, and conflict was being replaced by 'partnership' initiatives – contractors and subcontractors working in a more cooperative and team-based manner (Burnes and Coram, 1999). The Managing

Director also recognised that external partnerships needed internal partnerships and teamworking if they were to be successful. In turn this would require a new style of participative management in XYZ. Therefore, the Managing Director set out not just to upgrade XYZ's management but to undertake a root and branch overhaul of the company's operations and culture.

As a signal of his way of working, as a first step in creating better relationships amongst managers, he broadened out the Senior Management Team to include key staff who were not directors. In what had been a very hierarchical and status conscious company, this was a significant change. The Managing Director knew that the staff in the company, particularly at a senior level, were experienced and competent people. He believed it was in the company's interest to retain staff rather than replace them. However, he also believed that they would need to change their attitudes and behaviours and upgrade their managerial skills if the company was to achieve the changes he believed were necessary. His strategy for transforming the company rested on carrying out two crucial activities in parallel: to introduce new practices and techniques into the company in order to provide a better service to customers (and thus improve the company's overall performance), and to change attitudes and behaviours within the company, especially those of managers. He did not see these as being separate activities or programmes: he saw them as being linked. New practices, such as customer care and customer partnering, were not mere technical exercises. They required behavioural changes and new managerial skills. Therefore, the Managing Director wanted to create a change programme whereby any change designed to improve the organisation's performance, whether it be new skills, new techniques or whatever, also had to promote and reinforce behavioural and culture change. The converse was also the case: any effort designed to change culture or behaviour also had to have the objective of improving the organisation's performance.

Between 1996 and 2000, the company undertook a series of organisational, management and staff development initiatives designed collectively to transform the organisation's performance and culture. The main initiatives are shown in Table 12.1.

Table 12.1 Key changes at XYZ

Date	Event
June 1996	New Managing Director appointed
August 1996	*Kaizen* Phase 1
October 1996	Customer Care Programme launched
March 1997	Investors in People launched
April 1997	*Kaizen* Phase 2
September 1997	Customer Care Programme extended to construction sites
January 1998	Construction Supervisors' new role launched
June 1998	New Senior Management Team formed
November 1998	*Kaizen* Phase 3
March 1999	Site-based trainers appointed
June 1999	XYZ culture redefined
July 1999	Leadership and behaviours review
September 1999	Begin to develop Team XYZ
March 2000	Team XYZ up and running

The Managing Director's first initiative was to introduce a small-scale *Kaizen* programme. *Kaizen* is a Japanese technique for achieving small-scale improvements through teamwork (Witzel, 2002). The Managing Director saw his *Kaizen* initiative as delivering four benefits: it would show the organisation that improvements could be achieved on a quick low-cost/no-cost basis; it would promote teamworking; it would give managers confidence to delegate to and empower their staff; and it would allow both staff and managers to acquire new skills. In a traditional company such as XYZ, it was not easy to introduce new ideas and new ways of working, especially where managers might perceive them as a threat. But the Managing Director made it clear he was committed to this initiative and that it had to work. Over the next few years the *Kaizen* approach was rolled out throughout the organisation.

The next initiative, in October 1996, was a customer care programme. This was designed to engender a positive view of customers by promoting joint teamworking. In an industry where antagonism between customers and suppliers (contractor and subcontractors) was the order of the day, where settling disputes through the courts was almost a standard practice, it was never going to be easy to promote customer care. The Managing Director knew, however, that the future of the company depended on working with customers to understand what they wanted and to give it to them. Once again, this initiative was a combination of organisational change and management development; but, much more than the *Kaizen* initiative, it was also central to changing the culture of the organisation. It began with a few key customers and a few key managers, but such was its perceived success that a year later it was extended to the actual construction sites.

Other initiatives were introduced over the next few years, including Investors in People, and a redesigning of the Construction Supervisors' role to ensure that the post-holders possessed the skills, competencies and behaviours necessary to work closely with customers and staff under the new regime. Once again this was designed to achieve a combination of aims, including changes to working practices, the upgrading of managerial competency on the construction sites, and the promotion and development of a more team-based culture in the organisation.

In 1999, XYZ decided it was time to redefine its culture and change its structure. As a number of writers have emphasised, structure and culture need to be aligned, but it takes much longer to change the latter than the former (Allaire and Firsirotu, 1984; Burnes, 1991; Handy, 1993). However, the company had already made sufficient changes to its behaviour and practices to believe its culture was very much different from when the Managing Director took over in 1996. It went through a company-wide process of identifying and redefining its culture. This then led into a process of reviewing each manager's leadership abilities and behaviours. With these activities underway, the scene was set for redrawing the company's structure in order to promote and reflect its new ways of working and its developing culture.

Towards Team XYZ

By 1999, the company was a much more cohesive, open and efficient organisation. However, its basic structure remained the same as when the new Managing Director had taken over. There was Head Office, which dealt with large, national projects, and five regional offices that dealt with smaller, local projects. Each of these offices was organised on a functional basis; they each had separate departments for Finance, Estimation, Design and Engineering. In addition, the Head Office had a Human Resources function which covered the entire company. This structure gave rise to a number of problems: rivalry between the Head Office and the regional offices; and rivalry and lack of communication within the various offices between departments and functions. A particular problem was the relationship between Estimation and Design in the Head Office. The former were responsible for dealing with customers and setting the price for a job. The cost of a job, however, was based on the design provided by the Design Office. Though based in the same building, there was friction between the two functions, with each seeking to second-guess the other. The large jobs were often very complex and even within the two functions of Estimation and Design there could be disputes about the best way to carry out a job. However, there was much more dispute between the two functions. Estimation felt that Design sometimes made jobs too complex and costly, and Design felt that Estimation did not understand the technical aspects of what they were suggesting to customers. This caused problems for Engineering, which was responsible for the actual construction process. The engineers sometimes found themselves starting jobs where there were still disagreements between Estimation and Design over what had been quoted for and what was required. Nevertheless, the general view was that the company was more efficient, better-run and a friendlier place than it had been four years earlier.

In 1999, the Managing Director and his Deputy began to have discussions in the company over restructuring. Their basic aim was to remove functional barriers and create a more teamwork-based, process-focused organisation. However, they did not underestimate how difficult this would be. It would need a complete reorganisation within and between the offices. It would reduce the power of the regional managers and amalgamate the Head Office empires of some directors. The Managing Director recognised that such changes could and probably would create friction and resistance. He also recognised that XYZ lacked the skills to plan and implement such a change. He, therefore, brought in a change consultant to assist with the exercise. After discussions with the consultant, a five-stage change process was agreed comprising the following activities:

1 Change readiness audit
2 Evaluation and planning workshops
3 Communication
4 Implementation and team-building
5 Evaluation

Stage 1

The consultant undertook a change readiness audit to identify key issues and concerns which needed to be addressed. This consisted of face-to-face interviews with all senior managers, and interviews and discussions with other staff from all levels of the company. It also involved a SWOT [2] exercise to assess the company's competitive position. Some 70 people, at all levels, were involved in the SWOT. The interviews showed that there was a general recognition of the problems brought about by the existing structure, but little agreement about any new structure, and some concern over potential loss of status and career opportunities if a flatter, less functional structure was adopted. However, the audit also showed that managers and staff alike had faith in and respect for the Managing Director. They also felt that the changes that had taken place over the previous three years had been positive. In addition, there was a strong sense of self-belief in the company that whatever the changes required, they could achieve them. Nevertheless, there was also concern by some individuals that changes in structure would affect their career progression or status, especially if the new structure involved multi-function teams and reduced the number of departments. The SWOT exercise showed that there was considerable agreement that the company had a strong technical base but

2   See Exhibit 15.1 in Chapter 15 for a description of a SWOT analysis.

concerns about lack of team-working and entrepreneurial flair. In particular, staff in the regional offices felt that opportunities for new business were being missed. They also felt that their skills were under-utilised by being devoted to mainly small jobs rather than having an opportunity to participate in the larger contracts. The finding from the change audit were used to structure and begin the second stage of the change process, the evaluation and planning workshops.

Stage 2

There were five one-day workshops spread over a two-month period. The purpose of these workshops was to establish a set of criteria for evaluating alternative structures, identify what alternatives existed, test these against the evaluation criteria, select a preferred structure and develop plans for implementing it. This was seen as an iterative process. Even when the evaluation criteria had been agreed, it was expected that further discussions about alternative structures and planning would lead to some of these being questioned, challenged and amended. Similarly, once a preferred structure had been agreed, it could still be amended if the planning process threw up issues that had not been considered. At the end of each workshop, participants had an agreed set of actions which they had to undertake, a key one being to go out and discuss what had emerged from the workshops with their colleagues in the rest of the company. A newsletter was also issued from each workshop.

The first two workshops were for the senior management team (SMT) only and the remaining three for the SMT plus the next layer of managers down, an additional 15 to 20 people. The results of the audit were presented to the first workshop, which began the process of developing a set of evaluation criteria and generating alternative structures. At the end of Workshop 1, a consensus seemed to be emerging with regard to a preferred structure. At the end of Workshop 2, it was agreed that the new structure should be built around the three core activities of the company, which were labelled: Get Work; Do Work; and Get Paid. It was also agreed that whilst it was important to keep the regional offices, their staff should be merged into the new structure. In effect, what emerged was a process-orientated flat, matrix structure with staff in the regional offices being responsible both to the Regional Manager and the Process Manager in Head Office. For the Head Office staff, in the main, their line manager and process manager would be the same person. As might be expected, this new structure did not emerge without much discussion, debate and in some cases soul-searching. The SMT also recognised that this was probably the most radical of the proposals they had looked at, and the one likely to meet the most resistance both from regional managers, whose power would be much reduced, and functional specialists in Estimation and Design who would have to be merged to create the 'Get Work' group. In addition, it was clear that some Directors were not happy to see their own department dismantled and their own position threatened.

The first of the remaining three workshops was devoted to presenting the proposed structure to the new participants, testing it and in some cases agreeing to amend it. The remaining two workshops concentrated on the details of implementing the new structure. This covered everything from where people would sit, to whom they would report to, new job descriptions, communication and team-building. This latter exercise was seen as vital to ensuring that staff in the reorganised structure worked as teams and cooperated with other teams rather than merely creating another set of functional barriers. It was at this point that it was agreed that the new structure be named 'Team XYZ' to emphasise that the intention was to create a company where everyone felt they were members of one team. There was also much discussion and consultation between the Workshops with staff in the rest of the company. At the end of Stage 2, almost all managers and supervisors in the company and a great number of the workforce had been involved in the process and by November 1999, the company was ready to communicate the new structure both internally and externally (to their parent company and customers).

Stage 3

The communication stage was both short and intense. Members of the SMT were given the task of visiting all areas of the company and briefing them on the new structure and how it would impact on them. Though there were also newsletters and information on the company's intranet, it was these face-to-face briefings with small groups of staff which generated the most debate. They also raised some questions, mainly of a detailed nature, which had not been addressed. In general, however, the new structure received a positive welcome and the implementation stage then began.

Stage 4

The new structure was rolled out over a three-month period. Ideally everything would have changed overnight, but the logistics of moving staff around from one group to another, physically altering office accommodation, and training managers for their new roles took time. Also, the intention was to ensure that all managers and supervisors, including those on sites, went through Team XYZ team-building workshops. Although, as expected, there were some hiccups and some unanticipated problems, by the end of March 2000 the new structure was fully up and running with remarkably little difficulty.

Stage 5

In April, a two-day meeting of all the company's senior and middle managers was held to evaluate the change that had taken place, identify issues that needed to be addressed, and ensure that the momentum was maintained and that staff did not fall back into old ways of working. As part of this process, each manager was asked to identify two steps that they personally would take to develop the new structure further and promote teamworking. These were all written on flip charts and pinned to the walls for everyone to see. At the beginning of the two days, there was something of an air of exhaustion about the managers; they had been through a period of major upheaval and, as one said, 'We need a period of consolidation'. At the end of the two days, they left not only having agreed that the new structure was working remarkably well, but also with a whole host of new changes they wanted to make to improve the structure further.

Summary

Though the development and implementation of a new structure at XYZ was not without its difficulties, it was achieved remarkably quickly and with relatively little disruption. There was significant potential for those who might lose out from the changes to try to prevent, or at least slow down, their implementation. All the regional managers and a number of the directors saw their areas of responsibility, and thus power, reduced. Many of the functional specialists found themselves operating in multi-function teams where their promotion prospects depended less on their technical abilities *per se* and more on their ability to work and manage as a team player. There was also the fact that people who did not like each other suddenly found that they were working side by side. One explanation as to why the potential dangers to the change process did not emerge is clearly a result of the way it was managed. It was an open process that involved a great number of people either directly or indirectly. At some point, all the issues that needed to be considered, even personality issues, were brought out on the table and discussed, sometimes quite often. There was also a tenacity and momentum to the process. It was clear from the start that the Managing Director wanted to see a new structure and would not be fobbed off with a sub-optimal compromise. It was also clear from the change audit that many other people in the company recognised that its structure needed changing, even if they were nervous about such a change. In essence, the company was ready for such a change, even if some were uncomfortable with the outcome. This of course raises the question: Why were they ready?

For organisations to work effectively, it is necessary for structure and culture to be aligned, but whilst structure can be changed quickly, changing culture is a much slower and less certain process (Allaire and Firsirotu, 1984; Handy, 1993). As mentioned in Chapter 10, Kanter *et al* (1992) identify two basic approaches to change: Bold Strokes and Long Marches. The former refer to rapid and major structural transformation initiatives. The latter covers slow, incremental change programmes that run over a number of years and which are geared to achieving changes in culture and behaviour. The received wisdom is that when companies need to transform themselves, they should change their structures first because this is the quickest and easiest change to make. They should then embark on a process of developing a culture to support and align with the new structure. This is why Kanter *et al* (1992) note that Bold Strokes often need to be followed by Long Marches in order for organisations to seek to develop a culture and behaviours suitable for their new structure. In the case of XYZ, this logic was turned on its head. As Table 12.1 shows, the Bold Stroke, the new structure, followed the Long March to create a new culture in the company, and this is why it could be implemented so quickly, so successfully and with relatively little resistance. XYZ already possessed the culture to go along with its new structure. It already possessed a management and workforce orientated to working in a team-based environment. The new structure was necessary both to formalise and facilitate the new teamworking ethos of the organisation, and to reinforce the new culture itself. Therefore, the development and implementation of the new structure at XYZ can be seen as much more a case of Planned change rather than Emergent change. However, it also needs to be viewed within the context of a series of changes that had emerged in XYZ since 1996 as the company, under the leadership of the new Managing Director, sought to transform itself.

Case Study 7

GK Printers Limited – changing systems and attitudes

Background
GK Printers Limited is a small, family-run printing business. It was established just after the Second World War by the present Managing Director's father. The company was originally a jobbing printers; which is to say they would print anything. 'No job too large or too small' might well have been their motto, although in fact, the mainstay of their business was producing stationery, business cards and publicity brochures for local companies.

This work was moderately profitable and provided a reasonable living for the owners and their workforce, some 20 people. By the beginning of the 1980s, however, this situation was beginning to change. Firstly, the recession at this time had a strong negative effect on their traditional customer base, and orders began to fall off dramatically. Secondly, the advent of newer, computerised printing techniques, which GK had not adopted, meant that rivals could offer a quicker, cheaper and often better-quality service. Thirdly, the advent of small printing bureaux (such as Prontaprint), often situated in prime city centre locations, and portraying an up-to-date image, further eroded GK's business. Lastly, it was clear that many of their customers were no longer going to a printer directly. Instead, in the image-conscious 1980s, they were putting their work out to graphic designers who, having finalised the design, would then subcontract out the printing. In such a situation, there was no guarantee that the work from their traditional customers would eventually end up with them. It depended upon the preference of the particular graphic designers concerned.

All these factors combined to threaten the financial viability of GK and, for the first time ever, the company lost money. The loss was only small (£20,000), but it came as a major shock to a company that had grown used to making a reasonable, if not spectacular, profit. The result of this was that the Managing Director and the company's Printing Manager, along with other members of the owning family, formed a 'crisis committee' to review the future of the business.

Phase One: developing a strategy

It rapidly became clear to the committee that to do nothing was not an option; the result would be to go out of business. The two main options considered were whether to sell the business, or, in some way, to change it to secure a viable future. Without exception, the crisis committee preferred the second option, if only because it was clear that it would be very difficult to find a buyer for the company. However, no one was sure what it was that they needed to do to change the fortunes of the business.

In desperation, almost, they approached a lecturer at the local polytechnic who was a friend of the Printing Manager. His suggestion was that one of his business studies students should undertake a project to examine the company's options. This took two months, during which the Managing Director and Printing Manager worked closely with the student.

The student's final report had a dramatic impact on the company. Its main findings were as follows:

- The printing market was expanding rather than contracting. This was mainly due to companies recognising the need to promote themselves more and in a better way than in the past.
- The market expansion was mainly at the higher value-added end of the market, in the area of high-class, glossy promotional material.
- The newer print bureaux were not as strong competitors as the company had thought. Their product quality was both variable and, at best, no better than GK's. Also, their costs appeared to be higher.
- GK's existing customer base would prefer to continue to do business with them, but perceived them as old-fashioned, lacking in key capabilities (mainly graphic design), slow, and not particularly flexible.
- GK's printing equipment was not capable of producing the higher value-added products that customers were increasingly demanding.

These findings were met with some astonishment and a great deal of relief by the crisis committee. Without exception they had steeled themselves for a report that would be doom-laden. Instead, they could see that a future did exist, and possibly a very profitable one. But some major changes would be required. Before making any decisions, however, the Managing Director and Printing Manager insisted that the findings should be discussed with the workforce.

Employee relations were very good in the company and, whilst not being paternalistic, the tendency was to see the company almost as an extended family. The print workers, who made up the majority of the workforce, were all union members, and two of them were prominent activists in their local union branch. The workforce knew that a review was taking place; it would have been almost impossible to keep it from them, given the nature of the company, but in any case the management had been very open about it. Like the crisis committee, the workforce were relieved that the findings were more optimistic than many had believed possible. They wanted to know, however, what the management intended to do to change the company in order to take advantage of the opportunities that appeared available.

The Managing Director was slightly taken aback by the workforce's apparent eagerness for change; he had expected some resistance, especially from the print workers. Instead, the reverse was the case: the two union activists were the strongest advocates of new equipment. As one later said: 'We knew what was happening elsewhere; skilled workers were being replaced by glorified typists. But we also knew that we needed new equipment. The deal we struck with management was that we would accept anything they bought, but we would be trained for it and we would operate it'. Indeed, they went beyond this – they actually told the management what to buy and from whom.

On the basis of the report from the student, the management constructed a strategy for rejuvenating the company. The strategy had three main elements:

1 The appointment of a Marketing and Design Manager to develop the company's customer base and provide a graphic design capability.
2 Upgrading the company's image. The above appointment was part of this process, but it also involved remodelling the company's frontage and reception areas, redesigning its stationery and creating a company logo.
3 Progressively replacing old printing machines with newer, more capable equipment.

Though the company never formally created a 'vision'of its future, the Managing Director later said:

> After the student's report I began to see a picture in my own mind of what I would like the company to be. I wanted it to be a one-stop shop for all our customers' printing needs. In the past, if we could not do it ourselves, or if we were too busy, we turned people away. Not any more. If we could not do it, we subcontracted, just like the graphic designers. But we would ensure that we could do the money business in-house (the high value-added business) and eventually only subcontract out the cheap stuff.

Therefore, the company began its transformation by the appointment of a Marketing and Design Manager and upgrading its image. Initially, it did not buy any new equipment, but took the decision to subcontract work they could not do until such time as the volume of work necessitated new investment. This allowed them to turn round the business without having to borrow large sums of money.

Nevertheless, within 12 months, such was the success of the strategy that the company began buying new equipment. After that, as the economy grew in the 1980s, the company's fortunes also grew. By the late 1980s, GK employed 40 staff (double its previous number) and had quadrupled its turnover to £4 million. In the process, it had managed to improve its profitability substantially.

In 1989, however, it grew concerned that the increased volume of business, made more complicated by the need both to design as well as print, and to coordinate their subcontracting activities, was having an adverse effect on customer service. The main problems were controlling paperwork (especially orders and invoices), the company's costing system, and production scheduling. Therefore they undertook a review of these activities to see how they could be improved. Thus began the second phase of the transition of GK into a highly competitive printing company.

Phase Two: changing systems

Reasons for change

As mentioned above, market, product and operational changes meant that the company needed to provide a faster and better service to its customers. While much had been done to achieve this, in 1989 it was also realised that better business systems were required, especially in the area of costing, invoicing and production control.

Given that GK is only a small company, it was relatively easy for the Managing Director to bring together the six people who were responsible for these activities and, in effect, to state the problems and give them the authority to come up with a solution.

The people concerned agreed to meet for two hours each Friday afternoon to review the issues involved and come up with options. They were clear that they did not want to rule anything out, but set out instead to identify all the available alternatives, and choose the one that suited them and the company best.

After three weeks they had reached a consensus on the root cause of their problems: they were all being asked to do more and more without any additional resources. Not only did this mean that backlogs occurred, but also that the greater need to communicate across functions, which the company now required, was not taking place.

Given this analysis, their first inclination was to ask for more staff. They also looked at other options, however, the main one being to introduce better systems – ones that reduced duplication. This raised the additional question: manual or computer systems?

Eventually they agreed a number of key objectives that any option must be tested against. These were that any new system should provide the following:

- a faster and better response to customers' requests for quotations;
- speedier invoicing and improved debtor control;
- better record-keeping and a reduction in duplication;
- an increase in productivity of clerical staff;
- better control of production, resulting in reduced lead times, and quicker and more reliable service to customers;
- system integration.

Having decided upon these criteria, the people involved then asked the Printing Manager if he would approach his contact at the local polytechnic for assistance. This he did, and once again the assistance came in the form of a student project. The student evaluated the company's existing operations and looked at alternatives. Her report stated that it was possible to improve the existing systems but that this would not allow them to achieve their objectives. Instead, she advocated introducing computer-based systems.

As they had witnessed the successful introduction of computerised printing equipment during recent years, staff were neither overawed nor complacent about computerising their systems. They discussed with the local polytechnic how best to approach an evaluation of the benefits of computer systems, and selection of a system.

The group then prepared a written report for the Managing Director that detailed their investigations, their initial objectives, and the advice they had received. Their recommendation was that the company should invite a number of computer companies to visit them to discuss their needs. A long discussion took place between the Managing Director and the group, which resulted eventually in their report being accepted. However, the Managing Director did add one proviso. This was that the group should be responsible for deciding whether to computerise, and, if so, what system to select and from whom to purchase it. The Managing Director said he would sit in on any negotiations that took place with computer companies, but that he would not take the decision away from them; rather he would bolster their authority by his presence.

So a number of computer companies were invited to discuss the company's requirements with them. In total, some 20 companies visited them. The upshot of these visits was that the company became convinced that their needs could best be met by purchasing a computerised business system that could perform the necessary work and integrate their existing manual systems. However, the cost of this was likely to be between £20,000 and £30,000, which – for a company of GK's size – was significant. The Printing Manager, and others, pointed out that such an amount spent on printing equipment would greatly extend their capabilities. Nevertheless, after much discussion, the decision was taken to go ahead with the purchase of a computerised business system (CBS).

Though it took a number of meetings to reach this decision, which was subject to much discussion throughout the company, the final decision was almost unanimous. The reason for this was that the company was performing well on all fronts except in the areas covered by the proposed changes. Late and inadequate quotations, poor debtor control and erratic delivery performance were all causing the company problems. These were not as yet major problems, but could be expected to get worse as the company expanded.

Introduction and development of CBS

Once the decision had been made, the original group were given the responsibility, as the Managing Director had earlier stated, for specifying and deciding which equipment to purchase. Their task was made difficult because, whilst it was clear that standard software packages were suitable for such tasks as sales ledgers, wages and invoicing, special software would need to be written to accommodate the company's production control needs. The CBS steering group, as they jokingly referred to themselves, spent a number of months identifying and writing a specification of their exact requirements from a production control system. They then asked the computer companies to quote for a CBS on the basis of this specification. However, of the original companies who had shown interest, only two were prepared to provide the bespoke software the company required. The company wished to ensure that both the hardware and software were supplied by the same vendor, not only to avoid any incompatibility problems, but also to have only one organisation responsible for any problem that might arise. Further discussions took place with the two companies, during which the software specification was further refined, and eventually a supplier was chosen. The entire process, from the Managing Director raising the issue, to actually placing the order, took over a year.

The computer for running the systems, and the standard packages, were delivered almost immediately, but it was another six months before the production control package was installed. This was because it had to be specially written. The company ensured that it closely monitored the writing of the software and that the final package met the specification. It then took some three months to bring the production control package on line. During this period, manual records were still kept in parallel to the computerised system. After this, it took a further three months before the total CBS package was up and running satisfactorily. Therefore, in total, it took two years from the inception to the completion of the project. Nevertheless, no one regretted the time spent. As the Managing Director said:

> If you'd told me at the beginning it would take so long I'd have laughed at you. But now we've ended up with a system that gives us all we want – and more. It's a system that 'belongs' to the people who work it – it's not my system, it's theirs.

Though the company only bought one workstation initially, it had specified that the CBS should be capable of networking. This was done with the intention that once the CBS had proved itself, further workstations would be acquired. Subsequently, three more workstations were purchased and the company also doubled the memory capacity of the system. In total, some £35,000 was spent on the CBS.

As with other aspects of the CBS, the company was careful to ensure that adequate training was provided to those who would use the system. Once again, this was made easier because it was the users who had selected the system, so they knew what it could do and what training they required. This ranged from three days to a week, depending upon the users' requirement. The training was provided by the equipment supplier. Training took place in stages, allowing users to become familiar with one aspect of the system before being trained on another aspect of it. Training was provided for clerical staff who would use and maintain the system, and also to managers who needed to access it for information.

Staff appeared to take to the CBS very well. Though initially there was an additional workload for them in terms of inputting information into the system, they found that it was better and faster than the previous manual system. Their workload was no less than before, but they took satisfaction from being more effective by using 'their' system. Obviously, the system had a knock-on effect elsewhere in the company, both in the collection and use of information. This adjustment appears to have been accomplished with little or no difficulty.

The benefits

The CBS did not transform the fortunes of GK; no single system will do that for any company. In the areas covered, however, it made a significant contribution to improving the service GK provided to its customers and meeting its own requirements.

The company believed that computerising its business systems brought the following benefits:

- better and more accurate records;
- quicker access to information;
- better control of resources;
- a speedier and more accurate response to quotation requests;
- higher productivity from clerical staff;
- reduced lead times;
- faster and more reliable deliveries;
- a greater integration of business functions;
- an improvement in staff morale and skills.

Though this looks like an example of successful technical change, it would be wrong to perceive it exclusively in this light. Certainly, that is not how those involved saw it. Rather they believed that the main benefit gained was the ability to work together more effectively. The CBS assisted this by automating some of the more routine elements of their work, thus allowing them to put their skills to better use. However, they are the ones who know what customers and the company require, not the CBS. Whether their perception is true or not may not matter: the real issue is that they believed it to be so. This clearly had a substantial effect on their effectiveness, self-esteem and morale.

Reasons for success

To the outsider, at least, this appears to be an almost textbook case of how to manage change. However, the staff involved, whilst clearly pleased with their role, were also not uncritical of their performance. With hindsight, they said that they should have completed the process in a year rather than two years. They also believed that they should have included additional features in the CBS.

Whilst these criticisms may be true, they are only so from the vantage point of having gone through the process of change and having gained confidence and experience from it. They also reflect a key reason for the success of the process: a willingness to be open and critical about themselves and their requirements, and a belief that they all needed to be convinced of what was required before proceeding.

Nor should the role played by the Managing Director be undervalued. In a company where – a few years earlier – change, of any sort, was very rare indeed, it took considerable courage for a senior manager to delegate authority to users. Indeed, at one point he openly told the group that 'if you succeed, it's your success – not mine. If you fail, I carry the can – not you.' This created the climate of trust and responsibility that made those involved determined to succeed.

Nevertheless, it would be remiss not to draw attention to several other factors that contributed to successful change in this instance:

- The company had a strategy for its future development (or at least a general view of what it wanted to become) and therefore was able to take an overview of all areas of its business in relation to future objectives.
- Because the company was strategy-driven, it was able to establish not only where problems lay in the company, but also whether the problems were high, low or medium priority. This meant that the company could establish that there was a need to improve business systems and that this was the priority.
- The company did not rush into making a decision about what exactly was the problem, what solution to adopt or what equipment to purchase.
- The company clearly documented its requirements, and identified where standard packages were sufficient and where bespoke software was required.
- It carefully selected a supplier in whom it had confidence and with whom it could work closely.
- It constructed a timetabled implementation plan with clear objectives for the introduction of the CBS.
- It ensured that the appropriate training was provided.

Two further points should be stressed about the introduction of the CBS. Firstly, the company was attempting to move from being an organisation where change was the exception, to one where it becomes the norm. In such a situation, it is impossible for change to be controlled exclusively by management or 'experts'. The sheer volume of work would overwhelm them. Without devolving the responsibility to those affected, change either would not take place or would be unsuccessful. Nor would it be possible for senior managers to concentrate on the longer-term strategic aspects of their business. Therefore, sustaining the changes in managerial behaviour that promote involvement and team work was essential to GK's prosperity.

Secondly, devolving responsibility in this way ensures that those who have to live with the change take ownership of the process, and are committed to it. It allows those involved to develop their skills and confidence. It also ensures that once the changes do take place, they become fully operational as rapidly as possible. It should have the additional advantage that it encourages those concerned to continue to search for improvements.

Unfortunately, as business increased, thanks to the changes at GK, there was a tendency to concentrate on output rather than development, and to revert back to old patterns of behaviour. This was particularly the case with the Managing Director, who felt that the priority was to meet customers' requirements rather than to involve other managers in decisions that had always been his responsibility.

When an organisation is operating successfully, as GK appeared to be, it is difficult to argue that time should be spent improving what already, apparently, works well. Similarly, though teamworking had proved its usefulness in facilitating major decisions and changes, it was more difficult for managers, especially the Managing Director, to appreciate its effectiveness on a day-to-day basis.

Therefore, though major organisational changes had taken place at GK, changes in managerial behaviour were not sustained. By 1993, it was apparent that the pace of improvement was slowing down under the pressure of work. This situation continued until the beginning of 1994 when, once again, the company recognised that it faced serious problems.

Phase Three: changing attitudes and behaviour

Accelerating the pace of change

Unlike many companies, GK's business continued to grow throughout the early 1990s. Though its existing customers were being hit by the recession, it was winning new business that more than compensated for this. Nevertheless, in 1993, GK started to become aware that its customers, old and new, were becoming increasingly demanding with regard to price and delivery. In addition, there were signs that its competitors were beginning to win back some of the work they had lost to GK.

By the beginning of 1994 it was clear that GK was losing a significant amount of business. This was partly due to increased competition, but mainly it was because its customers, in seeking to cut their own costs, were reducing the size and frequency of their orders (though when orders were placed, they were often required far faster than previously). This presented a double threat to GK. Firstly, the fall in overall volumes was having an adverse effect on turnover and profit. Secondly, the reduction in size of individual print runs was having an adverse effect on costs because, though the actual volume was smaller, the design, order processing and set-up costs remained constant. In effect, as volumes decreased, the cost of each printed item increased. In addition, there were worrying signs that some customers were using word-processing packages and colour printers to produce their own publicity material instead of going to a printer.

At a time when its customers were facing severe pressure to cut their costs, GK were faced with the dilemma of whether to increase its prices to offset rising costs (and risk customers going elsewhere or developing their own facilities), or to maintain or reduce prices and see its profits plunge. This was not a situation unique to GK; practically every company in the UK was experiencing a similar dilemma. This knowledge, however, did not make it any less painful or any easier to resolve.

The knee-jerk reaction of many in the company was, 'If customers want smaller runs, the price goes up'. However, the Managing Director and the other managers in GK came reluctantly to accept that, whilst the logic was impeccable, the result could be disastrous. After much seemingly futile discussion, it was the Marketing and Design Manager who eventually came up with a suggestion that, though laughed at initially, later turned out to be the key to GK's survival. He pointed out that to maintain its existing volume of business, and perhaps even increase it, GK needed to improve on its already good level of service. In particular, it needed to cut costs in order to cut prices and improve the efficiency of its internal operations to cut delivery times. The initial reaction to these suggestions was, perhaps predictably, very negative. After all, if volumes decrease, unit costs must increase because set-up costs are constant; also, an increase in the number of smaller print runs actually extends turnaround times for a similar reason – more set-ups are required. So the Marketing and Design Manager was attempting to turn the conventional wisdom regarding printing on its head. In addition, in some people's eyes, he was still a newcomer to GK and consequently he was believed to lack an in-depth knowledge of the printing industry. Finally, GK had made significant strides in improving efficiency and cutting costs, and there was some doubt as to the scope for any real improvements in these areas.

A false start

Despite the initial adverse comments, the Managing Director began to wonder if it might be possible to reduce set-up times and costs. If it could, he reasoned, the company would be able to attract more business, prevent customers seeking in-house solutions, and undermine their competitors. He considered asking for outside assistance again, but instead asked the Marketing and Design Manager to put forward some suggestions for reducing costs and set-up times. This was for two reasons. Firstly, he wanted to give him a chance to prove himself to the rest of the team who, to an extent, thought he still had to learn the ropes. Secondly, the Managing Director wanted to demonstrate that they now had the managerial talent to dispense with outside assistance.

The Marketing and Design Manager quickly responded and within a fortnight presented his proposals to the Managing Director and other senior staff. He began by identifying what he saw as the main problem the company faced:

1 Though there had been a slight decline in the number of individual orders, the actual reduction in the volume of business was much greater because customers were ordering shorter print runs.
2 The result of this was that, whilst office staff, marketing, design, administration, etc., were as busy as ever, the print shop was short of work, and it was not unusual to see printers sitting reading the paper with nothing else to do.
3 However, though the printers were underworked, this did not provide much scope for reducing delivery times, because most of GK's lead time was accounted for by non-printing activities – especially design, which could take anything up to two weeks.

Having laid out what he saw as the problem, the Marketing and Design Manager went on to offer a solution. He argued that the key to solving the company's problems lay in speeding up design time. He pointed out that there was always a backlog of design work ranging from one to two weeks. Given that everything, even repeat orders, went through design, total lead time could be anything from three to five weeks. Whilst this was considerably better than in the 1980s, it was no longer acceptable as customers were cutting stock to a minimum. Many customers were asking to have their printing back within seven days, sometimes even sooner where promotional material was concerned. The solution, therefore, he argued, was to have more design staff. If one extra designer was employed and another design workstation purchased, the Marketing and Design Manager believed that design lead time could be reduced to two or three days.

The Managing Director and other managers, especially the Printing Manager, who had been arguing unsuccessfully for new equipment for some time, were taken aback by this proposal. The analysis, they believed, was correct but the solution, they felt, was an outrageous piece of opportunism. The case for more design staff had been raised and rejected in the recent past. The Marketing and Design Manager's colleagues felt that he was blatantly using the company's current problems to empire-build. Not surprisingly, he vigorously denied this. Nevertheless, the meeting ended acrimoniously and no decision was taken.

The Managing Director was particularly infuriated, as he had genuinely been expecting an acceptable solution to emerge from the meeting. Instead, the friendly working atmosphere he valued, and which he felt he did much to promote, had been shattered. Nor did he see an easy way to bring his managers back together to seek a cooperative solution. He was also annoyed because he realised that he had made a mistake in asking only one person to put forward their view. Not only would a team have avoided favouring one area rather than another; it would not even occur to anyone to make the accusation. Having made the mistake, however, he was not sure how to remedy it. If a team was set up to examine the options that did not include the Marketing and Design Manager, he would rightly see it as a snub and probably attack any solution that was put forward. If he was included, it was likely that he would continue to push his proposal and the other managers would react badly. His inclination was to impose a solution and tell everyone to get on and implement it. Unfortunately, he did not have a solution to impose.

Towards a new way of working

After several weeks of indecision, during which tensions within the management team continued to rise, the Managing Director decided once again to seek outside assistance. He approached GK's contact at the local polytechnic and, at length and with some passion, explained the situation. However, rather than proffering help, as expected, the lecturer stated that the situation was outside his area of expertise. He explained that there seemed little point in offering a 'technically appropriate' solution, because relations were so bad in the company that, whatever it was, it would be met by hostility from some quarters. He pointed out that the success of earlier interventions was due to achieving unanimity about both the problem and the solution; at present, this was unlikely. He did, though, refer the Managing Director to a colleague at the polytechnic who was skilled in team-building. Though the Managing Director was sceptical, the lecturer pointed out that, working together, there was enough experience in GK to solve its current dilemma. Therefore, the issue was how to bring people together, rather than seeking outside solutions.

The Managing Director met with the team-builder, who impressed him not only with his general demeanour of professionalism but also with the impressive array of organisations he had worked with. The team-builder said that the process he used was straightforward. Firstly, all the relevant managers had to be involved. Secondly, he would meet each of them individually and then, as a group, would take them away from the company for two days to work on the problem. Thirdly, each member of the team would have to agree to operate in an open and constructive fashion during the two days. This meant not only responding positively to each other's ideas, but also being honest. Lastly, the team would agree to reach a commonly-agreed solution by the end of the two days.

It was on this basis that the team-building exercise went ahead. Though the GK management later admitted that the first day had been decidedly uncomfortable, they also agreed that the two days had been a success. The proceedings began with the team-builder reporting on his findings from the individual interviews. Though he did not reveal who said what, in a small organisation such as GK, it was relatively easy for managers to make a good guess as to the source of particular comments. This was one of the reasons why they found the first day uncomfortable.

The team-builder's report was split into positive and negative findings. On the positive side, there was a strong commitment to making the company a success, and common agreement regarding priorities for change (primarily, cost reduction and increasing responsiveness to customers). On the negative side, there was considerable tension between the managers, especially the Printing Manager and the Marketing and Design Manager. Underlying this, however, was the style of the Managing Director.

Though on a number of occasions the Managing Director had used teams to make crucial decisions and had been prepared to consult widely, this was not his normal mode of operation. He tended to make decisions either by himself or in consultation with one other manager. He justified this on the grounds that most decisions were not related to overall policy but to particular areas of the business. If new printing equipment was to be purchased, then this concerned him and the Printing Manager. If the issue was customers, then the Marketing and Design Manager would be involved. Decisions concerning finance were, the Managing Director felt, mainly his responsibility. The counter-argument to this, identified and articulated by the team-builder, was that it inevitably created suspicion among managers excluded from decisions, and led to accusations of favouritism. All the managers, other than the Managing Director, favoured a more open and collective style of management.

The Managing Director was very upset and said so. He believed he had always acted to promote teamwork and good relations in the company. To be accused of the reverse came as a shock. He wanted, he said, to 'clear the air' there and then. However, the team-builder suggested, and agreement was eventually reached, that they should all reflect on what had been said, and return to the issue at the end of the second day. They then moved on to discuss the immediate problems facing GK: how to reverse the decline in turnover and profitability. With the delicate matter of the Managing Director's approach to decision-making out in the open but put to one side, everyone seemed happy to focus on these problems. For the rest of day one and most of day two, they alternated between working in two groups and working as one team. The result was that they reached an agreement on the way forward which they all accepted.

The main areas of action were very straightforward:

1   GK should meet with its main customers to identify what their needs were and discuss how these could best be met. It was felt that not all of a customer's requirements were urgent, and that what was necessary was to identify those that were and agree that they would be dealt with in a speedy fashion.
2   The company's CBS – computerised business system – was much more efficient than the previous manual system, but all orders, large or small, urgent and non-urgent, were dealt with in the same manner and at the same speed. The same applied to design: though the actual design time varied between orders, they were all scheduled and dealt with in the same fashion. This meant that they all tended to take between one and two weeks, depending on the design office's workload. It was also a similar story when it came to printing and dispatch: everything was in the same queue. It was agreed that the entire process from order intake to dispatch be examined, with the intention of either reducing it for all orders, or possibly shortening it for specific categories of orders.

These actions were to be carried out by two groups comprising managers and employees from the areas involved, who would report directly to the management team.

This then left the thorny issue of the Managing Director's role. Since the issue had been raised on the first day, he had spoken to the team-builder and his colleagues informally, and had come to recognise the strength of feeling on the issue, though he did not fully accept their interpretation of his actions. Nevertheless, he was prepared to amend his management style. He agreed that there would be regular management team meetings which would deal with all major decisions. He also agreed that he would not seek to impose a decision on the team unless the managers themselves could not reach agreement.

Six months later

The investigation of customer requirements and the order-to-dispatch process resulted in changes that brought significant improvements in the service GK could offer to its customers, and a reduction in lead times and costs.

The company now offers its customers a choice of lead times and prices: normal – a two-week delivery and a 5 per cent reduction on the standard prices; accelerated – a one-week delivery charged at standard prices; and urgent – a one working day delivery charged at 10 per cent above standard prices. GK was able to achieve these improvements owing to three factors:

1 Understanding what its customers wanted and were prepared to pay for. In speaking to customers, GK also identified what its competitors were offering in terms of prices and deliveries.
2 In examining the order-to-dispatch process, GK came to appreciate that there was a large amount of wasted time involved that could be eliminated with better cooperation between functions, especially design and printing, and a greater awareness of the need to reduce lead times. In examining the entire process in detail and involving everyone in this, some very glaring examples of wasted time emerged. For convenience, incoming orders were processed in batches. So an order could sit for two days just waiting to be entered on the system. Similar delays were identified in dispatch, with completed orders sitting for one or two days waiting either for collection or for GK to make a delivery in that part of the city where the customer was located. As the dispatch clerk commented, 'No one told me it was a problem'. Once staff realised it was a problem, there was almost a competition to see who could come up with the best suggestion.

   Most of this did not require additional expenditure, merely better communication and a willingness to help each other. Reducing set-up time on the printing presses did require some modest expenditure, but this led to reductions in set-up times of between 50 and 80 per cent. Some small expenditure was also required to modify the computer system to cope with the new three-tier delivery price system.
3 The design office made a number of changes to the way it operated which speeded up its activities. Nevertheless, it was recognised that there was also a capacity shortage: they simply had more work than they could cope with. Much of the work was simple and did not need a fully-qualified designer; and only about 50 per cent of a designer's time was actually spent on the computer. Therefore, it was decided to employ someone else to perform the more simple design tasks.

   At first, GK was going to recruit a new member of staff for this post, but the printers, who had always wanted to be involved in design, suggested that they might do this. When the suggestion was discussed, a number of possibilities opened up, including that simple but urgent jobs be given straight to a printer who would undertake the entire design and printing process at one go. The actual mechanics of this were difficult to work out, and many practical obstacles were apparent, but GK nonetheless decided to undertake a trial with one printer in order to identify the difficulties and evaluate the benefits.

In addition to these changes, the management team, after some initial difficulties (such as identifying what constituted a major decision), found that working together and having all information out in the open reduced the tension, not only between individual managers but between the individual functions as well.

Going online

For the most part, GK's fortunes rose steadily throughout the latter half of the 1990s, despite much talk of an imminent recession. They developed strong partnerships with key customers and attracted new ones. They acquired a reputation as a forward-looking company that was responsive to its customers' needs. However, they developed one area of their business that grew much faster than the rest and which promised much for the future: developing and designing websites for its customers.

As with so much of GK's development, there seemed to be an almost accidental element to its website business. In the mid-1990s, one of its main customers decided to conduct much of its business, especially in terms of orders and invoices, electronically. GK had no alternative but to accommodate this. The Managing Director gave the task of developing electronic communications to one of the graphic designers who was very keen on computing; not only did he have his own website, but he had also developed one for his local athletics club.

Consequently, as well as allowing them to receive and send information electronically, he also constructed a website for GK. Being a graphic designer, and an enthusiast, what he produced was a state-of-the-art website that provided an excellent showcase for GK's capabilities. Almost before most people in the company realised they had a website, or understood what one was, its customers were asking GK to do the same for them. At first, the Managing Director thought that this was something of a diversion from the company's main activities. However, when he saw what customers were prepared to pay, and he realised that, in essence, it was a logical extension of printing publicity material, he created a separate department under the graphic designer to develop the website business. It became the fastest-growing part of GK and by far its most profitable.

Summary

After the first two phases of changes at GK, the company felt it could rightly take pride in how it had responded to the situation in which it had found itself. Rather than falling into a spiral of decline, as seemed possible, it had reinvigorated itself. It had introduced new equipment and, initially at least, developed a new sense of cooperation. However, its own success began to eat away at some of its gains. The pressures of day-to-day business began to take precedence over both improvement activities and cooperation. In particular, the Managing Director went back to taking decisions either without consulting anyone else or only in consultation with the 'appropriate' manager. In effect, though the company had maintained the operational changes, it had failed to maintain behavioural changes, especially those associated with teamwork, cooperation and delegation. Therefore, the first two phases of the company's turnaround can be characterised by successful operational changes but less successful behavioural changes.

The results of the failure to sustain behavioural changes were as follows:

- GK failed to adopt a continuous improvement approach.
- Poor coordination and cooperation led to inefficiencies in the processing and dispatch of work.
- Most importantly, an undercurrent of discontent and fighting for position arose among managers, which made it difficult to reach agreement about how the organisation should respond to its changed circumstances.

For these reasons, the key action in the third phase of the transformation of GK was not any of the operational changes, but the changes in attitudes among managers and other staff regarding cooperation, and in particular, the Managing Director's belated conversion to team-based decision-making. It was the new element of cooperation that allowed GK successfully to identify what to change and how to change it. The greater teamwork, and trust, also created the environment that allowed the company's website business to be developed by making people more open to new ideas and less suspicious of others' motives.

Conclusions

In the review of strategy and change management in Chapters 6–10, it was argued that whilst approaches to strategy and change needed to be matched to the constraints under which an organisation operated, these constraints were themselves amenable to change and in any case could conflict with each other. This means that the freedom of action or manoeuvre of managers is potentially very significant. It was also argued that whilst organisations might have a preference for a particular approach to change, in practice they used a variety of approaches, often at the same time. In the three case studies we have examined in this chapter, we can see managerial choice in action both in what they chose to do and how they chose to do it.

In the Volvo study, we can see that managers made a determined and apparently successful attempt to break away from the industry standard approach to car assembly. However, in challenging and changing a powerful constraint on their freedom of manoeuvre, they were very much in tune with societal, environmental and, at least in some instances, their own orientations. Also, there were parallel changes in the structure of the organisation towards decentralisation and flexibility, which supported and made more appropriate the emergent and open-ended approach to strategy used by Volvo. However, Volvo Car's takeover by Ford does pose a serious challenge to Volvo's approach to work organisation. Given that Volvo's approach represents a clear and decisive break with Fordist methods, it will be interesting to see whether or how the two can coexist over the long term.

The XYZ study is another case where an organisation made significant changes to its culture, operation and structure over a number of years. The impetus for the changes came with the appointment of a new Managing Director. The new Managing Director, supported by the parent company, saw the need to transform radically how XYZ worked if it was to improve its performance. The Managing Director saw that the changes he believed were necessary within the company paralleled changes that were being attempted across the construction industry as whole. Therefore, to an extent, he was trying to align the company to the changing nature of the industry. In order to do that, however, he had to overcome significant cultural and structural constraints within the company and saw that the former needed to be tackled before the latter could be effectively changed. Therefore, he embarked on a stream of Emergent, open-ended and, to an extent, experimental changes aimed at changing the company's culture and improving both managerial and staff competencies. Within this stream of Emergent change, however, there was also a significant role for Planned change, as the case study shows.

The case of GK Printers is somewhat different. It is much more difficult to perceive any distinct societal or industry constraints on the organisation. Both environmental and organisational constraints were clearly apparent, however, and the changes that took place were to a greater or lesser extent aimed at both changing and harmonising these constraints. One reason for the internal changes in the company was to tie customers closer to the company, and thus reduce the uncertainty present in the environment. As with Volvo and XYZ, GK's strategy emerged rather than being pre-planned, but it seems to have been much more stop–go than either of the other companies. Also, its approach to change appears to be more in line with the Planned approach than the Emergent.

Therefore, as far as managerial choice, strategy development and change management are concerned, the case studies provide some interesting and thought-provoking insights:

- Managerial freedom is clearly constrained but this does not mean that managers cannot break out of or change these constraints. In so doing, however, the tendency appears to be to resolve or reduce conflict between constraints rather than necessarily to rewrite the managerial rule book completely.
- The process of strategy development and change management in these cases was mainly Emergent, open-ended, and in some instances opportunistic. However, significant examples of Planned change were also evident. In addition, it can be seen that managerial conflict and politics played a part in decision-making and, in the case of XYZ, the change of Managing Director appeared to be a necessary precondition for wider organisational changes.
- The case studies show that there is a role for both Planned and Emergent change. Planned change as such, however, appears to be less effective than Emergent change in achieving sustained organisational transformation over time. Planned change programmes tend to have a finite duration and are aimed at achieving a particular and specific objective. Emergent change, on the other hand, is open-ended both in terms of timescale and objectives.

Test your learning

Short answer questions

1   Briefly describe the main reasons for Volvo's original move to Job Design.

2   What were the trade unions' main concerns regarding Volvo's move to Job Design?

3   List the main benefits XYZ expected to gain from changes to its structure.

4   Identify the main factors which contributed to XYZ's success in changing its organisational structure.

5   Briefly discuss one example of employee involvement at GK Printers.

6   Identify three ways in which the managers at GK can be seen to have changed their style from autocratic to participative.

Essay questions

1   Discuss the following statement: the stages of workplace reform at Volvo involve a cumulative process of innovation, with a trajectory which adds up to a more or less definitive break with Fordism.

2   To what extent does the XYZ study show that Emergent and Planned change are complementary rather than competing approaches to change?

3   Does the GK case study represent an example of emergent change, or of *ad hoc* and reactive management?

Chapter 13

Case studies in changing external relationships

Learning objectives

After studying the case studies in this chapter, you should be able to:

- recognise the pressures that have led to the growth in outsourcing by both private and public sector organisations;
- understand why private sector organisations find it easier to work more closely with their customers and suppliers than do public sector bodies;
- appreciate that changing external relationships can require significant changes in internal relationships;
- describe some of the mechanisms used by organisations to bring about changes in their external relationships;
- discuss how changes at one level between two firms may not always result in changes at other levels;
- show how customers and suppliers can overcome suspicion and achieve mutual gains;
- appreciate the need for outsourcing to be viewed as a strategic activity requiring strong and consistent management.

Introduction

The previous two chapters have presented examples of strategies and initiatives that have resulted in new internal relationships within organisations through structural, operational, cultural and behavioural change. It is not only the relationships within organisations that are changing, however, but also the relationships between organisations. There is a great deal of evidence to show that the outsourcing of activities previously done in-house is increasingly taking over from vertical integration as the preferred approach to organising the provision of many goods, processes and services (Domberger, 1998; Gay and Essinger, 2000; Takac, 1993). In the private sector, as Chapter 3 showed, the upsurge in outsourcing over the last 20 years has been fuelled by arguments from management gurus and leading academics that an organisation's competitive advantage stems from its ability to identify, concentrate on and develop its core competences and activities, and out-source anything that is non-core. In the public sector, the pressure to outsource has grown alongside the pressure to privatise. As Case Study 4 in Chapter 11 argued, the rising tide of privatisation over the last 20 years or so has been led by both ideological and practical concerns, both of which have focused on reducing the cost of providing public services through the greater use of market mechanisms.

In the private sector, the greater emphasis on outsourcing has led companies to review their relationships with both suppliers and customers in order to develop closer and more effective links. As Case Studies 8 and 9 in this chapter will show, this is usually accompanied or preceded by internal changes within either the supplier, the customer or both. These changes are taking place due to a growing climate of opinion that customers, suppliers and even rivals working cooperatively have considerable advantages over the more traditional adversarial relationships (Hines, 1994; Lamming, 1993; Saunders, 1997). Though this move has been led by the automotive and electronics industries, the concept has spread into many other sectors as well (Burnes and New, 1997; Christopher, 1998; New and Burnes, 1998).

Though there is no universally-agreed definition of customer–supplier partnerships, Partnership Sourcing Ltd (1991b: 2), the UK body established by government and industry to promote the concept, appears to have captured its essence by defining it as a situation:

> ... where customers and suppliers develop such a close and long-term relationship that the two work together as partners. It isn't philanthropy: the aim is to secure the best possible commercial advantage. The principle is that teamwork is better than combat. If the end-customer is to be best served, then the parties to a deal must work together – and both must win. Partnership sourcing works because both parties have an interest in each other's success.

The move to more cooperative and stable relationships between customers and suppliers is not merely a case of adjustments at the organisational interface. Rather, to be successful, it requires more fundamental changes in both customers and suppliers. The three case studies in this chapter reveal how such partnerships work in practice and, in particular, illustrate how the concept requires not only changes in the relationships between organisations but also attitudinal, behavioural and structural changes within them.

As Case Study 10 will show, outsourcing is as popular in the public sector as the private sector. However, whilst in the private sector it is seen as a strategic initiative designed to allow organisations to become more competitive by concentrating on their core competences, in the public sector, it is seen more as a cost-cutting measure. Most public bodies in the UK are now required by law to outsource their activities where to do so would lead to cost savings. They are also constrained in how they carry this process out and the sort of relationships they develop with their suppliers. The result of this is that outsourcing in the public sector is more an operational than a strategic activity. Nor is outsourcing leading to notable changes in internal relationships or external relationships with suppliers, which still tend more towards the adversarial than partnership.

Each of the three studies relates to a different aspect of the partnership process. Case Study 8 deals with the consequences of Rover's decision to outsource the assembly of suspension modules to TRW. It demonstrates that such initiatives, through closer operational integration, can bring great benefits but that these can be jeopardised if they are not also accompanied by closer strategic relationships. Case Study 9 shows that the move to develop new relationships is not just driven by customers. In this instance a supplier, Speedy Stationers, took the first step. It recognised that, in its case, the partnership approach was not just a means of providing a better service to its customers; it could also be an effective mechanism for securing increased business. The case study recounts how Speedy came to this conclusion, the steps it took to convince one of its customers to enter into a partnership and to cooperate, and the resulting changes and benefits. Case Study 10 looks at the approach to outsourcing of a UK police force, and shows the process it is required to undertake to evaluate whether or not its activities should be outsourced. It also shows that its relations with suppliers are constrained by the outsourcing rules and regulations laid down by government to the extent that it appears to be treated as a relatively low-grade administrative activity.

The chapter concludes by arguing that though much attention has been given to the creation of new internal relationships and structures as a mechanism for coping with environmental turbulence and uncertainty, changes in external relationships can also play an important role in this process. Consequently, partnerships can help organisations to restore, to an extent, a degree of stability and predictability to their lives. However, as far as the public sector is concerned, the constraints under which it operates may instead mean that outsourcing is creating greater uncertainty rather than being used as a means of reducing it.

The conclusion also points out that, as the case of PoliceCo shows, it is possible to quantify the short-term, narrow cost-cutting benefits of outsourcing; on the other hand, as the Rover–TRW case illustrates, it is very difficult for organisations to quantify in advance the longer-term benefits of developing partnerships. The Rover and Speedy examples show that early benefits can also accrue. Therefore, the move to new customer–supplier relations is not driven by rational and quantitative decision-making. Rather, the move to partnership requires an act of faith based on an instinctive and philosophical belief that the old methods do not work and that the game requires new rules, rules which cannot be written in advance but which emerge as the game unfolds. This, of course, may be why public sector organisations, which are rightly obliged to demonstrate openly that their suppliers are providing the best value for money, have difficulty in adopting more partnership-based approaches to purchasing.

Rover–TRW – operational integration[1]

Background
This case study concerns the relationship between Rover Group and one of its largest suppliers, TRW. The case study focuses on Rover's decision to outsource the assembly of front suspension modules to TRW and the benefits and difficulties which ensued. It shows that outsourcing sub-assemblies can bring great operational benefits when managed effectively by both parties, but that these may be jeopardised if this cooperation fails to extend to a more strategic level.

Details of Rover's history are relatively well known. It should be noted, however, that from the early 1980s, Rover was developing more cooperative internal working relationships and that it gradually began to extend this approach to its suppliers (see Grove, 1998, for further details). Though it has now been split into separate businesses, during the 1990s, TRW was one of the world's largest manufacturing companies. Founded in 1901, and with its Headquarters in Cleveland, Ohio, TRW was an American-owned company with a turnover of some $12 billion and a workforce in excess of 80,000 people by 1999. TRW was organised into two divisions: Space, Avionics, Defence and Communications; and Automotive. The automotive business was the largest division, accounting for over 60 per cent of sales and employees.

TRW Automotive's European sales were well over $1 billion in 1999. Some 23 per cent of this came from its UK business (TRW Steering Systems Ltd) which operated on five sites, the main one being at Resolven in Wales, employing 1,400 people and, as its name states, manufactures steering systems. Its main customers were Rover, Honda, Nissan, Ford and Volvo. Though TRW had a close working relationship with all these companies, it enjoyed a particularly strong and long-standing relationship with the Rover Group and was Rover's second biggest supplier.

TRW's steering systems business began supplying the forerunners of Rover over 60 years ago. A major milestone in the relationship came in 1959 when it was awarded the contract to supply the rack-and-pinion steering for the then revolutionary Mini. This was the first time rack-and-pinion steering had been fitted as standard on any mass-produced vehicle. During the 1960s and 1970s, British Leyland (as Rover were then called) had its own in-house facility for manufacturing both power-assisted and manual rack-and-pinion steering. In 1980, however, this was closed down and TRW took over responsibility for supplying all British Leyland's steering requirements.

In 1989, this relationship was further strengthened when Rover decided to outsource the assembly of front suspension modules, of which the steering gear was the key component. TRW was asked to bid for this work, was awarded the contract and began supplying the suspension modules in May 1989. In order to meet Rover's exacting standards, TRW set up a new assembly facility located at Frankley, about two miles from Rover's Longbridge plant.

The origins of Frankley
The main reason for Rover's decision in 1988 to outsource the assembly of front suspension modules, and consequently for TRW to establish a new facility at Frankley, was quite straightforward: Rover needed the space. The introduction and success of new models meant that Rover no longer had the space to carry out this assembly operation at its Longbridge plant. A subsidiary reason was that Rover, like most car companies at the time, believed that modular assembly of cars, from

1 The research on which this case study is based was funded by AT Kearney Ltd and carried out jointly with Dr Steve New of Hertford College, Oxford University (see Burnes and New, 1996, for further details).

outsourced sub-assemblies, was a strong possibility for the future, and this initiative with TRW gave the company the opportunity to assess the benefits of this approach.

Rover invited TRW and one other existing supplier to put forward proposals for running the new facility to assemble front suspension modules. TRW saw this as a major opportunity and responded in a very positive way. The main reasons for this were as follows:

- They wanted to continue to supply direct to Rover rather than through another supplier.
- TRW in the USA had (unsuccessfully) bid for a similar initiative with Ford, and could see the benefits it could bring to the business in terms of future growth and becoming 'essential' to the customer. In addition, TRW also thought that modular assembly was the future for the car industry.

Therefore, not only was TRW responsive to Rover's suggestion, but it could draw on its experience with Ford in preparing its proposal. TRW showed Rover the proposal they had put to Ford in the United States and prepared a business plan for the new operation. A succession of increasingly detailed meetings ensued with both Rover and their (then) partner, Honda.

Rover moved very quickly in making a decision and awarded the contract to TRW. This was mainly because Rover were impressed with TRW's plans and proposals, but also because they felt that its size and resources (of both expertise and money) made it a suitable partner in this instance. An additional factor was that TRW's steering gear was by far the most complex and expensive part of the suspension modules.

Planning and proposing was one thing; getting started was quite another. Rover were working to a very tight timetable and needed both the space and the suspension modules for a range of new cars it was introducing. One of the conditions of the contract was that TRW had to establish an assembly operation within a few miles of the Longbridge Plant. Therefore, in late 1988–early 1989, TRW found itself pursuing two major activities simultaneously:

1 developing its own approach to suspension module assembly;
2 finding a site and recruiting staff for the new facility.

Developing its own approach to suspension module assembly

After a rigorous selection process, three supervisors were recruited from TRW's Cleveden plant to run the new operation. One of the supervisors was appointed as manager for the new facility; in essence, however, the three were jointly responsible for the new product and new facility, and operated very much as a team. This cooperative approach was new to TRW but it was clear that everyone needed to work closely together if the project was to be successful. TRW had no previous experience of assembling suspension modules and, to a large extent, the manager and two supervisors were thrown in at the deep end. As one of the three put it, 'We were given a bag of parts and told to assemble them.' Initially based at TRW's main UK site at Resolven, they worked closely with an engineer from Rover to learn what Rover's requirements were in terms of the suspension modules and then they began to experiment with different approaches to assembly.

All three had previously been on TRW's First Line Supervisors course, and the Rover work gave them the opportunity to utilise some of the ideas they had learnt. In particular, they chose to adopt a 'greenfield' approach (starting from scratch) rather than building on existing TRW/Rover practices. Despite the tight timetable, they were allowed to experiment, and through a process of trial and error began to see how the assembly process could be best organised. The essence of their approach was to focus on continuous improvement by developing teams, encouraging initiative and ensuring that change was driven by and with the full support of the people on the assembly line. Since it began production in 1989, the Frankley operation has been transformed out of all recognition. Manual assembly has given way to semi-automation, they have achieved zero defects, costs and assembly times have been reduced considerably and, regardless of the inherent instability of customer schedules, they always deliver what the customer wants, when it wants it and in the correct order.

Finding a site and recruiting staff

At the same time that TRW were undertaking trial assemblies at Resolven, it located a site at Frankley, near Longbridge, that was ideal for their requirements, and the assembly operation was moved there in May 1989. Though they had tried to recruit from within, the only TRW staff who transferred to Frankley were the manager and the two supervisors. All the rest (some 30 staff initially) were recruited locally. The recruitment procedures were very structured and rigorous. They wanted skilled and flexible staff who would fit into a teamworking environment and who were prepared to contribute ideas and give commitment. Above all, they wanted to build an operation that was dedicated to meeting the customer's requirements fully, no matter how demanding or difficult these might be.

Though they had the advantage of starting out with a greenfield site and a workforce that had few preconceptions or restrictions, it also meant that everyone had to be trained from scratch.

Frankley – the early years

Mainly drawing on their own ideas and resources but working hard to understand Rover's needs, Frankley began to develop itself into a world-class assembly plant. The Frankley operation started out with two shifts and eventually moved to three in order to match Rover's own assembly operation. In order both to understand the customer's needs and to develop an effective working relationship, a great deal of time (by all concerned) was spent at the Rover plant. Indeed, it became compulsory for all new recruits to Frankley to spend a period working at Rover before taking up their appointment at Frankley.

Year on year, Frankley has consistently and diligently reduced costs and lead times, and improved quality. The essence of its ability to do this revolves around three core principles:

- understanding what Rover wants and giving it to them;
- teamwork and involvement;
- continuous improvement.

The biggest difficulty Frankley faced was in matching what it produced to Rover's actual build requirements. The steering assembly has 39 derivatives, and it is far from easy to ensure that the mix of derivatives TRW dispatches matches the mix of cars Rover is assembling at any one time. Rover did and does provide Frankley with a monthly schedule and a ten-day rolling programme (five days firm and five tentative). This allows TRW to schedule its suppliers. However, the key information, originally at least, was the mix of cars going into the paint shop (the step immediately prior to assembly). This provided TRW with only 12 hours' notice of the model mix that Rover planned to assemble.

Initially, therefore, Frankley had to gear itself to working on 12 hours' notice. Owing to damage during painting, however, what went into the paintshop was not always what went down the assembly line. Therefore, in the first year of operation, though Frankley delivered to the pre-paint shop schedule, it found that what it delivered was not always what Rover was actually assembling.

In many instances, the customer and supplier would have argued about whose fault this was. Instead, Frankley and Rover worked to resolve the problem. It was eventually agreed that instead of informing Frankley of the mix that went into the paint shop, they should tell them what undamaged cars came out. This represented a major step forward in terms of Rover trusting its suppliers. Rover, like most car companies, had been reluctant to give too much information to its suppliers. This was not only because information was seen as power, but also because it would be Rover's line managers who would have to take responsibility if the information was wrong. Nevertheless, Rover did provide the information. It did mean that Frankley only had $4\frac{1}{2}$ hours' notice of Rover's requirements rather than the 12 hours previously, but at least the schedule was much more accurate. Even this was not foolproof, however, and eventually they moved to a system whereby Rover would notify them of the build mix just $2\frac{1}{2}$ hours before the parts were required.

Working in this way does give Frankley exact information on what is required and they now know that if they build a particular suspension module it will be used. To get to this position has required two major efforts, however:

- building trust between Rover and Frankley, so that both have faith in each other and are prepared to provide information and make commitments without feeling that either is leaving itself open to abuse;
- establishing an assembly operation that is not only capable of building a wide product range in an efficient and effective manner, but which can also do so at very short notice. To achieve this required a major effort by Frankley staff.

Though this approach has obvious advantages to Rover, it also has considerable advantages to Frankley. Firstly, it means that it must run a lean and efficient operation which operates with a 'right first time' approach. Secondly, it has no finished stocks and only two days' worth of component stocks (down from eight days in 1994).

The Frankley site has clearly developed an approach to assembly and customer satisfaction that owes more to Japanese than Western methods. One recent Japanese visitor, however, was heard to remark that Frankley was not as good as Japanese plants … it was better!

TRW has not achieved this overnight, and in some instances has had to modify its initial ideas. Originally, TRW looked on the Frankley site merely as an assembly plant. Most of the support services were dealt with by Resolven. Though this made Frankley a very 'lean' enterprise, it also meant that the lack of on-site, dedicated resources restricted its ability to improve, especially in the areas of process improvement and supplier development. Over time, therefore, Frankley came to acquire its own support staff rather than having to rely on Resolven.

The benefits of this are clear in terms of the efficiency of the Frankley assembly operation. Though less visible, the benefits of materials management being based at Frankley have also been substantial; this was forced on them by the necessity of having to build the same type of relationship with its suppliers that it enjoys with Rover. Nevertheless, originally this did not look as though it would be necessary.

Developing suppliers

Taking over an operation from another company and re-creating it from scratch is never going to be easy, but when it also involves managing that company's suppliers on their behalf, some difficulty can be anticipated, to say the least. TRW had few illusions that suppliers selected by and working for Rover, and who would continue to see Rover as their customer, would welcome being managed by an 'intermediary'. The reality, however, was even more difficult than TRW anticipated.

Though communication and cooperation between TRW and Rover was constructive from the outset, the one area Rover seemed most reluctant to discuss with TRW was the handover and management of the other suspension module component suppliers. Consequently, when TRW began assembling the suspension modules at Frankley, none of the suppliers had been informed of the change. TRW found that not only had Rover not informed them, but that some companies did not even know who TRW was. The suppliers still considered themselves as working directly for Rover, and were more than somewhat resentful of TRW's new role.

Initially, TRW managed the suppliers from its main site at Resolven, but it soon became apparent that if the supplier–Frankley interface was to operate effectively, responsibility for suppliers would have to reside at Frankley. To achieve this, one of the original Frankley supervisors was made responsible for managing suppliers. His first task was to visit all the suppliers and explain the new arrangement to them. Though some began to adopt a more cooperative attitude to TRW, others still tended to ignore it and liaised with Rover instead. However, with Rover's assistance, Frankley gradually came to build a working relationship with the Rover-nominated suppliers. Nevertheless, when it came to know the suppliers better, two issues emerged:

1 Though Frankley was tailoring its production and deliveries to Rover's assembly programme, suppliers still tended to operate on a 'boom or bust' basis, i.e. they would deliver too much or too little.

2 A number of the suppliers did not meet TRW's quality standards.

Given that the suppliers were nominated by Rover, TRW was not in a position to change them. Therefore, it had no alternative but to work with the suppliers to improve them. Frankley set out to build the same relationship with the suppliers that it was developing with Rover. Initially, presentations were made to all the suppliers explaining who TRW was, what Rover required of the Frankley operation, and what Frankley required of the suppliers. This was followed by reviews of each supplier's performance with action plans being agreed to resolve any problems and concerns. Though no one would pretend that everything always ran smoothly or that continuous improvement was not expected, supplier performance became far better than it was in 1989.

The new contract

Up to 1994, the relationship between Rover and TRW continued to improve and there were very few operational concerns. In 1994, however, Rover began to discuss the replacement of the 200/400 series cars for which Frankley supplied the suspension modules. Though TRW expected stiff bargaining over the terms of the new contract, it did not expect Rover to question whether TRW should get the contract or not. From TRW's perspective, it had more than exceeded Rover's expectations when the original contract was awarded in 1989. In the intervening period, however, there had been a number of intense and not always good-tempered negotiations regarding the pricing of the contract and TRW had, reluctantly, made a number of downward adjustments to the original contract price.

It should also be said, though Rover did not appear to be fully aware of this, that TRW had made better profits from the Frankley operation than it originally expected. In the main, this was because Frankley was much more efficient than Rover had been at assembling the suspension modules, the volume of products was greater than originally assumed, and the overhead charges were generous. For its part, Rover was more concerned with the latter issue rather than the first two. It felt that TRW's costing system exaggerated the true cost of the Frankley operation. TRW's procedure was to add a management fee to the direct cost of the Frankley operation and so arrive at what they believed was a true cost to themselves. Rover, however, disputed the size of this fee and though, as mentioned, TRW did reduce the price it originally agreed with Rover, when the contract came up for renewal, some senior Rover managers were so concerned at the situation that they wanted to take the work back in-house.

TRW found itself in a position where it had to justify its accountancy system (which was standard throughout TRW), and also convince Rover that it could continue to offer it a better service than could be achieved by taking the work back in-house. Though the latter was not difficult to do, the former took some hard negotiations to achieve. In the end, TRW made a considerable reduction in its Frankley management fee and the new contract was awarded to TRW.

The difficulties did not end there, however. As Rover introduced new vehicles, it redesigned the suspension modules, which necessitated changes to component suppliers. As was the case originally, Rover would not let TRW enter a dialogue with suppliers until actual assembly began. Nevertheless, building on its earlier experience, TRW has become extremely proficient at overcoming any resistance amongst new suppliers and is able rapidly to inculcate them in the TRW approach.

Summary

The Rover–TRW case study clearly shows that the outsourcing of major sub-assemblies can bring important benefits to both customers and suppliers, particularly at an operational level. It also shows that the process is far from easy, and that even after many years major misunderstandings can occur which can threaten the relationship. The Rover–TRW experience can be judged at two levels – operational and strategic. At the operational level, it can be viewed as follows:

- The Frankley staff were given a clear, though by no means simple, task: they had to meet Rover's needs for suspension modules. In so doing, they were allowed, and encouraged, to use their own initiative.
- Though Frankley met some initial scepticism from Rover's assembly staff, whose cooperation they needed, it consistently and with real determination set out to identify what Rover needed, to establish where the obstacles lay and to overcome these.
- This was neither a one-off effort nor limited to a few managers. Instead, it was a process of continuous improvement by all concerned.
- There were three key factors in this: (a) the selection and training of staff; (b) allowing staff to interface directly with their customer, thus ensuring rapid performance feedback; and (c) establishing a 'greenfield' mentality, which meant that they all started from scratch and without preconceptions regarding how best to organise assembly or the nature of relations with their customer.

At the strategic level, however, a different picture emerged:

- Though one of the original objectives – albeit of secondary importance – was for both parties to assess the benefits of and approach to contracting out major sub-assemblies, this appears to have been quickly forgotten. Instead, the initiative came to be seen as a purely operational matter.
- As the relationship developed, it was clear that neither partner had had any real idea of how to cost such an operation. Originally, Rover had felt that it had negotiated a good deal because it was getting better supplies at lower cost. Likewise, TRW were happy to win the contract and felt that it would make a profit because it would be more efficient than Rover.
- Neither party anticipated that the Frankley operation would be able to make the large performance improvements that it did. When Rover realised how much more efficient Frankley was than it had been itself, however, it began to question the price it was paying. TRW, for its part, was extremely pleased by the return on its investment, though reluctant to reduce its prices.

■ This led to a series of acrimonious confrontations, culminating in Rover seriously considering taking the work back in-house. Fortunately for both parties, the issue was resolved. Nevertheless, it demonstrated that though operationally Rover and TRW were working closely in partnership, at a more senior level they were not. Yet, if they had been, not only might they have avoided much acrimony, but they would also have learned more about how to run such collaborations in the future.

In this instance, it is important to note that neither Rover nor TRW set out to achieve strategic and high-level cooperation *per se*. Rather, Rover were motivated, primarily, by operational considerations and though TRW did see strategic advantage, its main aim was to maintain first-tier supplier status. This may explain why both parties made enormous strides forward in operational integration but failed to make similar progress in terms of strategic integration and trust.

Case Study 9

Speedy Stationers Ltd and UTL (Turbines) Ltd – supplier-driven change[2]

Background

In the vast majority of cases, it is customers who take the initiative to change relationships rather than suppliers. This is for quite obvious reasons to do with power (it is the customer who has the money and who decides what to purchase and from whom) and experience (there are very few examples of how suppliers can influence customers). Unlike the Rover study, however, where it was the customers who made the first move, this case study deals with organisational change driven by a supplier.

This case examines the development of a partnership between Speedy Stationers Ltd and UTL (Turbines) Ltd, whereby the former took responsibility for the provision and in-company management of all UTL's stationery requirements.

Speedy Stationers was founded in 1953, and in 1994 had a turnover of roughly £50 million. Originally the firm acted just as a wholesaler selling to distributors and retailers. In the mid-1980s, almost by accident (an acquaintance of the Managing Director happened to be appointed to the same position in UTL), it began dealing directly with a small number of large industrial companies. Typically, these companies' total stationery bill might be over £200,000 per year. However, because Speedy did not deal with printed stationery, letterheads, etc., it rarely did more than £50,000 worth of business with any of these customers. Nevertheless, the Managing Director, whose pet project this was, had high hopes for direct selling.

---

2 This case study is based on original research by Dr Steve New of Hertford College, Oxford University.

Partly influenced by the possibility of selling directly to large companies, Speedy embarked on an expansion programme in the late 1980s that doubled its number of distribution centres from three to six. This geographical spreading of risk allowed the company to weather the recession of the early 1990s without any significant loss of business – though its profit margins were squeezed. Nevertheless, by 1993, senior managers came to recognise that the possibilities of continued expansion through the establishment of more distribution centres was limited, as well as expensive. Also, selling stationery directly to end users, whilst potentially attractive, had failed to live up to its initial promise. This was partly because there was a limited number of companies whose stationery bills made it worthwhile dealing with them directly, and partly due to the fact that even the ones they did deal with tended to shop around pursuing, in some cases, extremely small savings. A continuing bone of contention was also the amount of the Managing Director's time taken up with servicing the direct customers. Orders had originally been won on the basis of his contacts, and he felt that they could only be maintained on this basis.

A strategy emerges

It was in 1993, after much heated debate, that senior managers took the decision to set up the direct sales business as a distinct entity within Speedy. It was given its own manager, and a small team of staff was assembled to run the operation. The intention was to allow the rest of the company to focus on its core business, the provision of stationery to distributors and retailers, whilst giving the direct sales operation one last chance to prove itself. Though this was something of a 'sink or swim' approach, Speedy was not abandoning direct sales to its fate. As a concession to the Managing Director's strong commitment to direct sales, the person given responsibility for its development was a board member who, it was felt, would eventually succeed the present Managing Director.

Before informing its customers of this change, the Direct Sales Division (to give it its official title) set about establishing its strategy. Though this was mainly the work of the Director for Direct Sales, he was careful to involve all his staff and to ensure the continued support of the Managing Director. The strategy that emerged had three objectives:

- to offer a complete stationery service to its existing customers, including printed letterheads, forms, etc.;
- to develop partnerships with its customers whereby the Direct Sales Division would supply and manage their stationery stock;
- to triple turnover in three years whilst maintaining its profit margin.

The thinking behind this strategy stemmed from four characteristics of its present business:

1 The turnover of the direct business was £750,000 (out of Speedy's total turnover of £50 million) from 15 customers. The profit margin on this business was 7.5 per cent (as opposed to 5 per cent on Speedy's main business).
2 Direct customers were mainly located near its headquarters in Birmingham and therefore could easily be serviced by one group of staff. A geographical expansion would be proportionately more costly owing to distance.
3 Speedy only accounted for some 20–25 per cent of direct customers' stationery requirements, because it did not provide printed stationery. Once this was on offer, doubling or tripling business with each customer seemed quite possible.

4 In the early 1990s, the concept of partnerships between suppliers and customers began to take off. Already, the wholesale business was discussing managing the inventory for a number of medium-sized distributors, so it did not seem totally unfeasible to offer a similar service to direct customers – especially if Speedy were likely to be supplying the majority of their stationery needs in any case.

In developing the strategy, it was agreed that the first two priorities were to establish a partnership with a printer, and to identify the first customer to approach regarding partnering. The first part of this was relatively easy: they approached the printer who had dealt with all Speedy's own printing requirements over the past 20 years, and with whom they had a very close relationship already. The printer readily agreed to the arrangement – apart from anything else, it did not entail any major cost for them, but did promise additional lucrative business.

Identifying a customer for partnership was more problematic, but eventually they decided to approach UTL (Turbines) Ltd. Not only had UTL been Speedy's first direct customer (thanks to the relationship between the two Managing Directors), but it was well known that it wanted to develop partnerships with its suppliers. Therefore, it was decided to make an approach to them.

UTL (Turbines) Ltd

In 1992, UTL spent some £200,000 per annum on stationery, but this was small compared to the £30 million it spent on buying components for its turbines. It had a very traditional, distrustful and arms-length approach to purchasing, which it applied to all its purchases. It had at least five suppliers for each commodity and, with some exceptions, it purchased purely on price. Not surprisingly, it had over 1,500 suppliers, and the main contact most of these had with UTL was in response to written requests for quotations. Owing to the friendly relations at senior level, Speedy was one of the few suppliers who ever met purchasing staff.

The company is part of a large multinational group, and serves markets worldwide. UTL (Turbines), as its name implies, is the division responsible for the design and manufacture of turbines, which are supplied to a wide range of industrial users.

Like many manufacturing operations in the UK, the plant had experienced severe reductions in the number of people employed. From over 1,500 in 1987, the number working at the factory by 1994 had shrunk to about 900. In recent years, purchasing activities had undergone significant reorganisation. In 1992, two different aspects of the business – export and domestic turbines – merged their operations. Purchasing was one of the first functional groups to combine, and a new manager was brought into the company to take charge of the combined department.

As noted above, the company had a very traditional purchasing orientation. With the creation of the new purchasing function, however, a number of important changes were introduced to encourage staff to take a wider view of their role. In particular, the new manager wanted to focus attention on the total cost of doing business with a particular supplier, rather than just favouring those who submitted the lowest tender. The manager recognised that he needed to change staff attitudes towards suppliers, and indeed the Purchasing Department's view of its role in general. As a starting point, several innovations were introduced, including a series of lunchtime seminars, which the manager saw as a vehicle for both team-building and idea generation. The seminar programme consisted of outside speakers (including suppliers), presentations from staff in the department who had been on training courses, and videos.

When vacancies in the department arose, these were generally filled from outside the company, with appointments favouring youth and enthusiasm over age and experience. The new manager was keen that the importance of the purchasing group should be recognised in the organisation, and wanted to develop a team with a clear professional focus. He believed that the traditional perceptions of purchasing as merely a bureaucratic support activity had to be challenged.

As might be imagined, most of the Purchasing Department's attention was focused on suppliers of production components. Nor did this change under the new manager; indeed, as far as he was concerned, the less he had to do with non-production suppliers the better. It was this that gave Speedy Stationers its opportunity for building a partnership with UTL.

Speedy takes the initiative

By 1993, the reorganisation and reorientation of UTL's Purchasing Department was well under way. In particular, the seminar series, which at first attracted some adverse comment within the company, was proving a key vehicle for introducing new ideas and generating fresh thinking. When the Director for Direct Sales at Speedy heard about the seminar programme, he offered to come and talk about its new approach to working with customers. The Purchasing Manager was at first resistant, as were many of his staff, because this was not the area on which he wished to focus attention. Nevertheless, he finally agreed when the Speedy Director told him that the title of his presentation would be 'Contract Out Stationery Management and Reduce Costs by 10 Per Cent'.

Under the existing system, ordering stationery was a slow, complicated process. When individual departments required stationery, a requisition would be raised that was then translated by the Purchasing Department into a purchase order. On arrival, items would be inspected – which, for stationery, meant that the contents of each delivery would be counted and checked against the delivery note and original order. The items would then be booked into the stores, from which they could be withdrawn to departmental stores after more paperwork. As there were many stationery suppliers, problems with shortages were sometimes difficult to resolve. Each supplier would send invoices, which needed to be checked against orders and delivery notes. In addition, there was a particular problem with printed stationery; it was not unusual for the wording that the originating department thought it had specified to be incorrect when the stationery finally arrived with them. Tracing where the fault lay could be a tortuous process, however. It was also the case that departments ordered, and kept, far more stationery than they needed in order to avoid shortages. It was clear to the Direct Sales Division at Speedy, if not to UTL's own purchasing staff, that inefficiencies were rife, and that a 10 per cent reduction in costs should be achievable.

Speedy's proposal for managing all UTL's stationery needs was to establish two or three stationery bunkers in each department, close to the point of use (one for general stationery, e.g. photocopying paper; one for specialist items, e.g. printed forms; and one for consumables, e.g. pens and pencils, printer cartridges, etc.). These bunkers were to be clearly labelled; the average requirement for each type of stationery would be calculated and two week's worth of inventory was to be held in each. Speedy staff would visit weekly and top up the bunkers to the agreed level. Each delivery would be signed for by a designated manager for that area and, at the end of each month, all the supplies would be consolidated onto a single invoice. None of the incoming stationery would go through goods inwards or inspection, and there would be no need to raise individual orders. Indeed, the only work required of the Purchasing Department would be to pay the monthly invoice.

Though the Director for Direct Sales presented a very well-argued case, he met with some incredulity, not to mention hostility. Some staff thought the plan simply would not work. Others felt that UTL would be swindled. Yet another group feared for their jobs if this type of approach spread from stationery to other purchased items. Nevertheless, the prospect of getting rid of stationery purchasing, plus all the complaints it generated, and thus releasing staff for what he considered more important activities, proved too tempting for UTL's Purchasing Manager. The estimated 10 per cent saving, and informal encouragement from his Managing Director, also assisted the decision. In addition, Speedy pointed out that, for the first time, UTL would have accurate and regular figures for stationery consumption broken down by area and type of stationery.

Towards the end of 1993, Speedy and UTL signed a two-year contract covering the provision of all stationery requirements from the beginning of 1994. Though the contract included certain specific details (especially regarding auditing the new system), it was acknowledged that most of the mechanics of the arrangements would only emerge as the system was implemented.

Implementing the new system

Under the new system, UTL was divided into 20 separate stationery zones, each with three stationery bunkers. The initial target was to set up this system for two of these zones from the beginning of 1994, with the remainder in place by March 1994. Speedy promised a maximum three-hour response time to resolve problems.

The new system entails significant reductions in the bureaucracy of supplying stationery, but also challenges many traditional approaches to buyer–supplier relationships, especially in relation to trust. Firstly, in the absence of direct checks, UTL has to have complete confidence in the quality of the products supplied by Speedy and the reliability of its operation. Secondly, UTL has to trust that Speedy is actually delivering what it is invoicing for. Finally, UTL has to be sure that a single-source supplier will not exploit its position and introduce opportunistic price rises.

Managers from different functions within UTL needed to be reassured that the system was going to work, and that Speedy were capable of providing the new style of service. Presentations were held at which reservations could be expressed, and the new approach explained. It was not only managers within UTL who had some concerns, however, so did some of the workforce. To set up the new system, Speedy had up to five staff carrying out the initial analysis and making the arrangements for the new stocking locations. It became clear that UTL employees were suspicious and wary of what was going on. A major source of this unease was a fear that a system for delivering items direct to departments and zones would threaten the jobs of those in the goods inward, the incoming inspection and stores activities.

To help overcome these doubts, representatives from all areas concerned, including trade unions, were included in the series of presentations organised jointly by Speedy and UTL. Many of the questions raised related to the logic of the planned arrangement from UTL's point of view, and the potential vulnerability of being dependent on a single source. Other objections reflected the more immediate fear about the loss of jobs. Despite his earlier reservations, UTL's Purchasing Manager became the main champion for the Speedy initiative. In essence, he pointed to the need for all UTL employees and resources to focus on improving the competitiveness of their core business, rather than 'messing about trying to find an envelope'. This, together with a promise that no one's job was threatened by the initiative, seemed to overcome most of the reservations.

Despite winning staff over to the new arrangements, the practicalities still had to be worked out. One of the major obstacles in implementing the new delivery system was the amount of stationery already held at UTL. The problem was not just the inventory held centrally and in each department's own store, but also the large quantities of stationery 'hidden' in various locations around the factory. These had arisen because staff, especially those working on the shopfloor, frequently took more from the stores than they actually needed in order to avoid 'shortages'.

As part of the implementation programme Speedy staff scoured UTL for these 'private' stationery cupboards. The office of one supervisor on the night shift became known as 'WH Smith' because of the large collection of stationery, much of it years out of date, that was held there. He had been unable to draw stationery from the stores at night, and so had assembled his own supply. In some cases, the unofficial inventory amounted to a year's worth of a particular item.

UTL had estimated that they held about two months' worth of stationery overall. In order to integrate this with the new system, Speedy began sorting this by type into agreed quantities. It transpired, however, when all the existing stationery had been accounted for, that in fact existing stocks were nearer four months' worth of inventory. This meant that for the first few months of the relationship, Speedy delivered relatively little of its own material, and so had little to invoice for. Like many aspects of the new stationery management system, this factor was not covered by the written contract; episodes like this were dealt with on the basis of mutual understanding and trust.

By the end of 1994, the new system was fully up and running. Despite a number of hiccups, the change appears to have been much smoother than anyone really imagined possible. Also, both parties felt that they had obtained major benefits from the change. The benefits to Speedy were as follows:

■ It increased its business with UTL from approximately £50,000 per year to over £200,000, and actually improved its profit margin to 8.5 per cent.
■ It proved that the new arrangements could work, and had three other customers keen to develop similar arrangements.

For UTL, the benefits were also significant:

■ It made a 20 per cent saving on its annual stationery bill – twice as much as anticipated, even taking account of using up old stock.
■ Consumption of stationery declined significantly in some areas, partly thanks to better stock control, and partly owing to a decline in 'home usage' – as one manager put it.
■ The number of complaints relating to stationery dwindled almost to zero.

However, UTL managers felt there was a more important, if less quantifiable, benefit, which was that managers at UTL (not just in Purchasing) had seen the possibilities for new ways of conducting and organising business. In particular, managers now had a more favourable view of the prospects for achieving change in the company. As one manager commented:

> We've had our eyes opened. No one suspected some of our people would so easily accept such radical changes, especially ones driven by a supplier. The improvements we've made in handling stationery are really secondary to the confidence it's given us in our ability to manage change and make improvements.

One clear sign of this new confidence was that UTL began to examine seriously how it could develop similar links with other suppliers and its own customers.

Summary
Though the new direction proved profitable and effective for both Speedy and UTL, it also has important implications for customer–supplier relations in particular, and change management in general:

■ Whilst it has been recognised since the 1960s that customers and suppliers can impact on each other's internal operations, the general view has been that this occurs in an unintended and unplanned fashion. What this case study shows is that customers and suppliers can link together consciously to change the nature of the environment in which they operate to their mutual benefit.

- The study also shows the serendipitous and unplanned nature of much of business life. Speedy only moved into the direct sale of stationery because of a friendship between its Managing Director and UTL's. It was only by chance that Speedy's decision to extend its operations into printed stationery and to develop partnerships occurred at a time when UTL were receptive to such an approach. A year earlier, and the approach would undoubtedly have been rejected; a year later, and UTL might have moved away from the idea, or might have been busy developing partnerships with production suppliers.

- The manner in which suspicion and resistance were overcome is also worth noting. From the start, Speedy approached the project in an open and frank manner – it raised the suggestion of a partnership in an open seminar attended by all purchasing staff, and open to all other UTL managers. UTL for their part chose to hide nothing from its workforce; both parties took account of worries and suspicions, and did their utmost to resolve these before embarking on change. Furthermore, UTL gave an assurance that the changed arrangements would not lead to any job losses.

- Another major point is that both parties were prepared to set aside the distrust that permeates so many business relationships, and attempt to establish a partnership based on trust. Nevertheless, the trust was based on adequate checks and a belief, subsequently proved correct, that such an approach was mutually beneficial.

Since 1994, the contract between Speedy and UTL has been renewed a number of times, and now runs for a four-year period. The benefits to UTL have been considerable. It has dispensed with the need to manage its own stationery requirements and, therefore, can concentrate more effectively on its core business and its core suppliers. In addition, instead of the original 10 per cent savings it expected, it is now making a 20 per cent saving on stationery costs. Speedy has also achieved significant benefits by building on its experience with UTL. It has developed similar relationships with another ten large organisations. The turnover from its Direct Sales Division is now over £2 million and the profit margin is well in excess of that from its other activities. Since 1998, however, this area of Speedy's activities has stood still. To develop it further would take a considerable effort in terms of time and money because, having exhausted the possible customers in the Birmingham area, it would need to offer it on a national basis. The current Managing Director, whose original idea this was, is opposed to this; he believes that the time and money would be better spent developing other aspects of Speedy's business. Nevertheless, he is to retire shortly and is expected to be replaced by the Director of Direct Sales. If this is the case, the Director is determined that direct sales will be offered on a national basis.

Case Study 10

PoliceCo – outsourcing in the public sector

Background

Though outsourcing is one of the fastest-growing and arguably most important areas of business activity, there is a tendency to assume that it is predominantly a private sector activity and that that is where the expertise lies. This case study will show that outsourcing is at least as prevalent in the public sector as it is in the private sector. As Case Study 4 in Chapter 11 argued, the rising tide of privatisation over the last 20 years or so has been led by both ideological and practical concerns. The former expresses the belief that the competition-based nature of the private sector means it will always provide services cheaper and more efficiently than the public sector. In terms of practical concerns, the need to cut rising public sector deficits, and the accompanying tax bills, led to a search for more cost-effective ways of providing public services. Though these arguments were deployed in order to promote privatisation, where this was not feasible, the outsourcing or contracting out of public services became seen as the alternative. In the USA, with its lack of state enterprises, outsourcing, rather than the selling off of state assets, has tended to be the main way of transferring activities from the public to the private domain (Osborne and Gaebler, 1992). Indeed, as Cant and Jeynes (1998) point out, the US government has been using private companies to provide public services since the early 1900s. For this reason, it is the USA that has pioneered the introduction of what Talbot (2001) refers to as 'market-type mechanisms', such as outsourcing and market testing, into the public sector (*see* Case Study 4 in Chapter 11).

It is not just the UK that has followed the USA's lead. Domberger (1998) collected data from the USA, UK, France, Germany, Japan and Australia. This shows that in all these countries, the outsourcing of public sector activities was a significant and increasing practice. Domberger concluded that outsourcing was permeating the public and private sectors in these countries with equal force, and that in both sectors the prevailing belief is that best value is achieved through the use of competitive, market solutions for service provision. However, just because something is popular does not mean it is always effective. In examining outsourcing studies conducted in the UK and USA, Gay and Essinger (2000) found that outsourcing failed to measure up to expectations in some 28 per cent of cases.

Nevertheless, there is an increasing and significant trend towards outsourcing, in the public sector in the UK and many other countries. The motivating factors tend to focus on cost savings and service improvements brought about by the involvement of private sector know-how in public sector activities. Though there are similarities between the public and private sectors, there are also marked differences. Private sector organisations have to deliver a profit for their shareholders but are relatively unconstrained in how they achieve this. Public sector bodies have to demonstrate that they are achieving value for the taxpayers' money but how they achieve this is constrained by a host of legal and policy requirements. Therefore, though it may be the case that the public sector bodies can benefit by adopting private sector practices, they may be constrained by legal and policy requirements from doing so, as the following examination of PoliceCo's experience of outsourcing will show.

PoliceCo

PoliceCo is one of the largest Police Forces in the UK. It has over 6,000 employees and is responsible for policing an area of 2,200 square miles with a population of 2.1 million. As with all public bodies in the UK, it operates under a legal framework which obliges it to demonstrate in an open and auditable manner that, in spending public funds, it is providing value for money (Talbot, 2001). In addition, successive governments have required all police forces to show, usually by market testing, that the services provided in-house cannot be provided more cheaply and/or better by the private sector (Johnson and

Scholes, 2001). This began in 1994 with the introduction of Compulsory Competitive Tendering (CCT) (Day *et al*, 1998). CCT required PoliceCo to open up a range of activities to outside competition in order to test whether or not an outside provider could offer better value for money. If it was shown that an outsider provider was cheaper, PoliceCo had to outsource the activity, whether it wished to or not.

CCT was superseded in 1999 by the government's 'Best Value' initiative. According to the Local Government Act 1999, police authorities are obliged to produce a Best Value Performance Plan (Doherty and Horne, 2002). This requires local authorities, including police services, to carry out 'Fundamental Performance Reviews' of each of their services over a five-year rolling period (Speller, 2001: 119). These reviews cover the economy, efficiency and effectiveness of the service provided and seek to address four key questions, which are known as the four 'Cs': Challenge, Compare, Consult and Compete (Speller, 2001).

As part of the government's Best Value initiative, PoliceCo's funding is conditional on achieving a 2 per cent year-on-year efficiency improvement. This 2 per cent improvement may be achieved by efficiency savings (achieving the same output with less resources) and efficiency gains (achieving greater output with the same resources). Therefore, PoliceCo is required by law to test its in-house service provision against outside competition.

When CCT was introduced in 1994, catering at PoliceCo had already been outsourced. In subsequent years, other activities were outsourced. These included some parts of IT, finance, human resources and legal work. The first activity to be outsourced under CCT, however, was building cleaning. Building cleaning was outsourced for the first time in 1995 under the CCT legislation. Prior to this, PoliceCo had employed its own cleaners. It was decided that the contract should be split into four parts. This decision was taken for several reasons, including the size of the geographical area that PoliceCo covers, to ensure that each supplier would have the capacity to manage such a contract and also because the CCT legislation required the size of the contract to be appropriate to the size of the supplier. An additional reason was that PoliceCo believed that splitting the contract between different suppliers would encourage competition and lead to a better quality of service.

European Union legislation obliges PoliceCo to undertake a Europe-wide tender process when seeking to appoint outside suppliers or contractors. This clearly makes the outsourcing process longer, more complex and costly than it might be if PoliceCo had a free hand as to the selection of contractor. Neither the Best Value legislation nor European legislation would have prevented PoliceCo from submitting a bid to continue running the cleaning services itself. However, PoliceCo decided not to make an in-house bid because it felt it lacked the administrative structure and bidding expertise to make a successful bid, though it was keen to ensure that its existing employees were transferred to the new cleaning service providers.

In awarding the contract, PoliceCo went through a rigorous process of assessing each bidder's capability to deliver the contract, including visits to some of their existing customers. Nevertheless, the final selection was made on the basis of lowest overall cost judged against a tender document drawn up by PoliceCo. The core of the tender document is a detailed output specification for the activity concerned. In terms of the cleaning contract, this was a lengthy and difficult document to draw up because of both the number of sites involved and the difficulty in defining output measures that could be easily monitored and understood. However, PoliceCo considered that this approach was necessary to be able to demonstrate whether or not value for money was being achieved. The contracts were for five years at a fixed price, though there was provision for price increases arising from factors such as increases in labour costs.

The four cleaning contracts were awarded to two separate companies who received two contracts each. Once the companies began the contracts, conformance to the specification was monitored through regular visits to the various sites and reports from the business managers of the sites. Regular meetings are held with the contract companies, which were more frequent at the early stages (even on a weekly basis in some cases). This close monitoring helped PoliceCo identify serious problems with one of the contractors, and their two contracts were terminated and re-advertised. These contracts were awarded to the other cleaning contractor, which resulted in their having sole responsibility for all cleaning contracts (this company also belongs to the same group as PoliceCo's catering contractor). When a new site was built, however, the cleaning contract for that site was awarded to another company. Though this restored a degree of comparison and competition, it also doubled the number of companies PoliceCo had to liaise with. When the contracts were re-advertised in 2000/1, the competitive tendering process resulted in both retaining their existing contracts.

Evaluating outsourcing at PoliceCo

When a private sector company decides to outsource an activity, it is relatively free to please itself as to what to outsource, who to award the contract to and how it makes the selection, although ultimately it does have to show that its overall approach to managing the business is providing the shareholders with value for money. Public sector bodies such as PoliceCo also have to demonstrate that they are delivering value for money, but have to operate under far more stringent rules and regulations than private sector companies. These rules and regulations specify what they cannot do, what they have to do and how they have to do it. If we examine the decision to outsource, the selection of the contractor, the contractual arrangement and the way the relationship with the contractor is managed, we can see how these rules and regulations impact on PoliceCo's approach to outsourcing.

The decision to outsource

PoliceCo was originally obliged by Compulsory Competitive Tendering legislation to put certain activities out to tender. In 1999, this was superseded by 'Best Value', which obliges PoliceCo to undertake a periodic review of all its activities. Where the review indicates that PoliceCo might save money by doing so, it has to put that activity out to tender. It is also subject to external audit and inspection to ensure that it undertakes this review in the manner prescribed by government legislation.

Supplier selection

PoliceCo, like the rest of the public sector in the UK, is obliged by legislation to undertake a rigorous and open supplier selection process. This involves drawing up tender documents that clearly specify what is required and the form and timetable for tendering and making a decision. PoliceCo is also obliged to advertise across the European Union and must, providing the tender specification is met, award the contract to the lowest (total cost) bidder. Even where a contractor fails, as in the cleaning contract, PoliceCo cannot just pass the work over to another contractor who is performing well; the contract must go through the tendering process again. Similarly, even when an existing contractor is seen to be performing well, they must still tender against everyone else for any new work and, as the cleaning contract for the new site demonstrated, they may not be awarded the contract.

This is different from how many private sector companies operate. Often they do not advertise for suppliers. Instead, they may seek to identify the 'best in class' suppliers and approach them directly. They may also enter into negotiations with each potential supplier in order to see who can offer the best service, rather than asking them to bid against a specific tender document. Even when choosing a supplier, issues of cost, etc, may not be paramount – track record and confidence that they can deliver may be seen to be more important. Also, even when a supplier has been finally selected, this is more likely to signify the beginning of a new stage of negotiations rather than signalling the end of the process. This forms a contrast with the public sector; because it is something of a regulatory minefield, PoliceCo and most public sector organisations are reluctant to enter into further negotiations once the tender process has been completed and the supplier selected. Even during the contract period, in the private sector, developments and changes will continue. In the public sector, however, once a contract specification has been agreed, it is very difficult for either partner to change it.

Contractual arrangements

In general, it appears that the public sector tends to offer longer and more formal contracts than the private sector. The main reason is that public sector contracts are usually of a larger scale. For example, there are very few private sector organisations that have the number of buildings requiring cleaning that PoliceCo does. Contracts of a large scale imply large set-up costs for the supplier, which have to be spread over a wider time span in order to make the contract proposition more economical. In terms of performance monitoring, as is common in the public sector, PoliceCo decided to use output specification measures for its cleaning contracts. They found, however, that output specifications can be very difficult to put in writing for such simple tasks as cleaning an office, and the process can turn out to be very time-consuming. Nevertheless, the downside of not devoting sufficient time to specifying what is required, as many private companies have found, is that problems, disagreements and additional costs can arise during the contract period.

The use of 'gain-share' clauses in the outsourcing contract, whereby both parties benefit from any savings above and beyond those specified in the contract, is common in the private sector. This is because gain-share clauses are seen as encouraging suppliers to seek improvements that benefit both themselves and their customers. Public sector organisations tend to be more wary of these, however, because of the need to demonstrate that value for money is being achieved. If it became public knowledge that a supplier was achieving gains above and beyond those specified by a contract, this could be portrayed as incompetence, or even corruption, on the part of the public sector organisation involved.

A structured and clear procedure for conflict resolution is written into all PoliceCo's contracts. Indeed, it does appear that the public sector as a whole does have the best conflict resolution practices in terms of transparency, structure, consistency and fairness. This is a consequence of both the legal framework within which the public sector operates and also the need to be aware of public scrutiny, especially by the media.

Managing the relationship

As far as relationship management is concerned, though PoliceCo personnel speak of adopting a partnership approach, the use of mechanisms such as competitive tendering, even where a contractor has performed well, do seem somewhat adversarial. Of course, PoliceCo is obliged by public sector regulations to behave in this manner. The lack of a genuine partnership orientation may also be inevitable, given the number of activities it outsources and the uncertainty as to whether a contract will be renewed. In the private sector, companies often use a portfolio approach in dealing with suppliers. That is to say, they try to place a number of related activities with the same supplier, even where the supplier may not always offer the lowest price. This allows them to have fewer but more significant relationships to which they can devote more time and resources. It also seems to ensure that senior managers are involved in developing and monitoring the relationships and that problems which might threaten contract renewal are dealt with effectively. Obviously, public sector regulations make it very difficult for PoliceCo to operate portfolio practices. Indeed, public sector purchasing regulations seem to have almost the opposite effect, in that they can even result in organisations having more than one supplier for the same activity, such as PoliceCo's cleaning contracts.

Supplier development is another area that appears to be hampered by public sector regulations. For PoliceCo, and other public sector organisations, working with suppliers to improve their performance can lead to accusations of favouritism in that it might be seen to give the supplier an unfair advantage when it comes to re-tendering. Indeed, PoliceCo's contract for radio maintenance deliberately forbids the introduction of new technologies, despite the fact that communication technologies are changing rapidly. This is because any new communications technology would require different maintenance procedures, which would in turn require changes to, or even the re-tendering of, the maintenance contract. Therefore, in the public sector there is a tendency to manage by the book and hold suppliers to the contract, rather than working with them to improve on what was specified.

This emphasis on contract monitoring and compliance, rather than performance improvement, may account for why, in PoliceCo, outsourcing is seen as an administrative task to be undertaken by relatively junior staff rather than a strategic priority involving senior managers.

Summary

This case study has shown that outsourcing is a substantial activity in the public sector, driven by government regulations that oblige bodies such as PoliceCo to adopt market mechanisms in order to reduce the cost of providing public services. These government regulations do not *per se* force PoliceCo and other public bodies to outsource activities. If an activity is to be retained in-house, however, the contract has to be won through an open, competitive bidding process which demonstrates that the in-house provider offers 'Best Value' over external competitors. To do this, however, PoliceCo would need to have the skills required to put together such a bid. As was shown with the cleaning contract, PoliceCo felt they did not have these skills. Nor is this just an issue of preparing a bid document: PoliceCo would have needed to reorganise the cleaning operation into a separate cost/profit centre and restructure its management. Faced with this, it was easier to outsource the service rather than providing it itself. This does not mean that PoliceCo has not benefited from outsourcing. CCT, and subsequently Best Value, have enabled PoliceCo to outsource many activities to which it previously had to devote management time, and left it to concentrate on its core activity of law enforcement. However, the way that outsourcing operates in the public sector does mean that PoliceCo and other public bodies may not be getting the full benefit of outsourcing, and that, in some cases, activities are outsourced that might be better provided in-house. As Erridge and Nondi (1994) note, there is a tendency in the public sector for the pursuit of economy, efficiency and effectiveness to result in a predominantly cost-cutting approach to outsourcing.

It does appear that the public sector purchasing requirements do constrain PoliceCo's ability or willingness to adopt some of the practices which are beneficial to private sector companies. For example, it would seem to make sense to have one cleaning contractor rather than two, especially as the second is only responsible for one facility. Similarly, its radio contract, which prevents the introduction of new communications technologies, seems to be counter-productive. Likewise, PoliceCo's inability to adopt a portfolio approach to purchasing or to engage in supplier development seems to encourage a proliferation of contracts whilst at the same time turning the purchasing activity into a relatively low-grade administrative task. After all, PoliceCo could have decided to offer cleaning as one contract rather than four, and it could have linked cleaning to other activities, such as catering, which the main cleaning company also provides. It felt, however, that splitting contracts would encourage greater competitiveness. It is not always easy to see whether or not the failure to adopt such practices is driven by the public sector purchasing requirements or by innate risk aversion. Certainly, Burnes and Coram (1999) found that even senior public sector managers were very risk-averse in their dealings with outside contractors. In PoliceCo, this seems even more the case given the level of managers involved.

On the other hand, just as the public sector might benefit from some of the practices of the private sector, so the reverse may also be the case. Certainly, the private sector could learn lessons from the more structured approach of the public sector in terms of rigorously reviewing which activities might best be outsourced, the tender process and contract specification. In the private sector, choosing an activity to outsource often seems a somewhat *ad hoc* process, often tied to political concerns. The requirement for public sector bodies to review all their activities in an open, and auditable, manner means that it is very difficult for poorly-performing ones to hide or be hidden. Similarly, whilst the private sector's ability to continue to negotiate and refine a contract specification after a contract is awarded can be useful, it can also be a sign that the purchaser has been lazy in the first place. Also, by not having to go out to public tender, a company may miss the opportunity of attracting an innovative bid for its work. In addition, the public sector does appear to have a more structured and formal approach to conflict resolution that allows problems to be dealt with in a fair and effective manner.

In summary, therefore, it can be seen that outsourcing decisions and practices in the public sector are driven and constrained by governmental and EU legislation and regulations. The removal of freedom of action from public bodies in this way appears to turn outsourcing into an operational rather than a strategic activity. The constraints under which PoliceCo operates may also reduce its ability to adopt practices from which their private sector organisations derive benefit. In particular, there is little evidence that the public sector is developing the sort of partnerships with its suppliers that seem to prove beneficial to organisations in the private sector. On the other hand, the more structured approach to outsourcing in the public sector may in some aspects be superior to the approach adopted by many private sector organisations.

Conclusions

The three case studies in this chapter amply demonstrate the extent to which both private and public sector organisations are outsourcing significant aspects of their activities. Outsourcing appears to be equally prevalent in both sectors, but the manner in which it is conducted and the resulting changes, and possibly benefits, are different. For the private sector, the purpose of outsourcing is to allow customers to concentrate on their core competences. In the public sector, it is seen as a cost-cutting measure based on the assumption that, because they operate in a competitive market, private-sector companies will always provide a lower-cost service than the public sector can. In the private sector, outsourcing is leading to changes in both companies' internal and external relationships. Though the move towards closer relationships between customers and suppliers clearly makes for a more harmonious atmosphere in which to conduct business, this is almost a side-effect and not the main reason for the change. Increasingly, companies have come to recognise the need to make major improvements in their performance but, as anything up to 70, 80 or even 90 per cent of the value of their products comprises bought-in goods and services, this cannot be achieved solely on the basis of internal performance improvements. Rather, what is required is that their suppliers also improve their business. As Ford found out in the car industry, seeking to impose improvements has its limitations. Suppliers have to be keen to improve and willing to work with customers. The argument for adopting a partnership approach to purchasing in the UK, and other Western countries, was that it was one of the cornerstones of Japan's success and, therefore, must be beneficial (Womack *et al*, 1990).

Whilst in the private sector the move to outsourcing can be the beginning of a process of sustained and continuing attempts to improve the service provided by the supplier, in the public sector, it is almost the end of it. In the public sector there are legal, and possibly cultural, barriers to using outsourcing as a strategy for continuous improvement. Instead of a close working relationship aimed at service improvement, the public sector opts for a formal relationship whose aim is to monitor what is being provided and to ensure that the supplier sticks to the letter of the contract.

Therefore, as this chapter shows, outsourcing is providing private sector organisations with the potential for continuous service improvement through close and mutually beneficially relationships, whereas for the public sector it offers a onc-off opportunity to cut costs. However, it would be unwise to see this as an example of the private sector being efficient and the public sector being less so. Rather, the two sectors operate under different rules and have different degrees of freedom. PoliceCo is a publicly-accountable body that has a statutory and regularly-monitored duty to demonstrate that it is providing value for money and awarding contracts in a fair and open manner. Its freedom of action in choosing a supplier and how it works with that supplier is severely constrained by this. Contrast that with Case Study 8, Rover–TRW. This showed that close working relationships at an operational level, based on openness and trust, can bring great benefits to both customers and suppliers. It also showed, however, that in a situation where continuous improvements are being made, it is sometimes difficult to judge who is benefiting the most financially. Even in the private sector, as this case study shows, this puts a strain on customer–supplier relationships. In the public sector, managers would be severely censured if they allowed a situation to arise where the suppliers appeared to be making gains above and beyond what was envisaged in the contract.

The Rover–TRW case also illustrates the emerging, and to an extent unplanned, nature of partnership developments. The close operational-level relationship could not have prospered unless both companies, especially TRW, had not broken with traditional, Tayloristic, approaches to managing people and allowed their staff the freedom to experiment with and develop new ways of working.

Case Study 9, Speedy Stationers, also offers an example which the public sector would find almost impossible to follow. Normally, it is the customer who takes the lead in promoting changes in purchasing behaviour. This is for the obvious reason that the customer is usually the one with the power in the relationship (they can generally choose where to purchase and on what terms). In this instance, however, Speedy took the initiative and approached their customer with a suggestion for change. This was for basic commercial reasons: they needed to win additional business and saw partnerships as being the prime vehicle. They believed that the partnership approach would not only be commercially beneficial but would also give Speedy a competitive edge over its rivals. Speedy were fortunate in that they were able to approach a customer responsive to this type of initiative. The process of building the relationship led to many changes, both at Speedy and particularly in its customer. Much information only came to light as the new arrangements were developed and implemented, and it was only by actually putting the new approach into practice that sceptics could come to appreciate its benefits. For both Speedy and its customer, this new approach was something of a leap into the unknown which appeared to succeed, though only time will tell to what extent. It is difficult to see PoliceCo or other public bodies being legally able, let alone willing, to take such a leap of faith.

Yet it must not be assumed that PoliceCo did not benefit from its outsourcing activities. In an era when police forces operate under considerable operational and financial pressures, and where their activities receive unprecedented media scrutiny, to be able to concentrate more on direct policing issues and less on managing services such as cleaning, catering, etc., is clearly a benefit, as are any cost savings that this brings. Nevertheless, a greater freedom of manoeuvre, and a less risk-averse culture, might increase the benefits that PoliceCo achieved from outsourcing. From the procedural point of view, it should be recognised that many of PoliceCo's outsourcing practices are exemplary and might beneficially be adopted by the private sector.

As Part 1 of this book showed, we live in an era when all organisations, whether public, private or voluntary, recognise that they have to change their internal operations and relationships in order to increase their effectiveness and competitiveness. What the three case studies in this chapter show is that for private sector organisations, these improvements do not necessarily stop at their own office or factory door. Most see the full potential for performance improvement will only be realised when there are also similar developments within their suppliers and customers, and when they develop better working relationships with them. For the public sector, what happens outside their doors, so long as it does not affect their contract with a supplier, does not appear to be of concern.

In considering the developing nature of relationships between customers and suppliers, three points stand out from the case studies. The first is that private sector companies are changing the rules of the game; they are challenging the prevailing orthodoxy in the UK and the rest of Europe with regard to commercial relationships between customers and suppliers. Public sector organisations are working within the existing rules and not seeking to challenge them.

The second point is that, although the move to greater partnership working is based on others' successful experiences, it nevertheless requires a considerable act of faith by the parties concerned. It is not possible in advance to spell out either the exact form of the new relationships or the specific measurable benefits they might bring. Yet dissatisfaction with traditional relationships, and the potential for commercial advantage, have spurred the private sector companies described in this chapter to take such decisions. As can be seen, the decision to move towards partnerships cannot be judged solely on the basis of rational analysis and the pursuit of quantified and clear commercial objectives. Actually establishing a partnership may constitute a leap in the dark, requiring boldness, initiative and trust. It is difficult to see how individual public sector bodies could adopt this approach given the constraints under which they work.

The last point to note relates to one of the major benefits or consequences of partnerships. One reason why private sector companies are seeking to develop new ways of working is to help them to cope with the competitive pressures and uncertainty of the modern world. Partnerships appear not only to allow companies to strengthen their competitive position, but also to reduce a major source of environmental uncertainty, by making the actions of customers and suppliers more predictable and transparent. This goes against those, such as Tom Peters, who argue for the benefits of increasing chaos rather than reducing it. It also shows that one of the major constraints or contingencies organisations face, environmental uncertainty, can be managed in such a way that the ability to plan for the future, in terms of product development and production, is increased. In the public sector, outsourcing practices may be having the opposite affect. They can be destabilising for the public sector body because they can give rise to uncertainty about who will be supplying a service when a contract comes up for renewal. It can also lead to increased uncertainty for their employees, who do not know whether their jobs will be outsourced in future, and if so what impact that will have on their employment prospects and terms of employment. For suppliers and their employees, the competitive bidding process creates even greater levels of uncertainty, because no matter how well they have performed, they can always lose a contract if somebody else undercuts their price.

As the Contingency Theorists, described in Chapter 2, argued some four decades ago, the external environment does affect the internal workings of an organisation, but an organisation's internal arrangements can also affect the environment. Therefore, if a turbulent environment leads to changed internal relationships, then given that organisations are open systems, we can expect these to be mirrored in changed external relationships. So although internal changes are often seen as mechanisms for coping with environmental uncertainty, the move by suppliers and customers in the private sector to develop closer links externally can go one step further, actually reducing uncertainty. Conversely, the public sector's purchasing practices may be having the effect of increasing uncertainty.

Test your learning

■ Short answer questions

1 Identify the key reason why Rover developed its partnership with TRW.

2 List the two main benefits that each party gained from the Rover–TRW partnership.

3 To what extent can the Speedy case study be seen as supporting the Emergent approach to change?

4 What was the decisive factor in persuading UTL to enter into partnership with Speedy?

5 What are the main factors behind PoliceCo's policy of outsourcing?

6 What are the barriers to PoliceCo adopting a partnership approach to outsourcing?

■ Essay questions

1 To what extent does the Rover–TRW case study show the limitations of continuous improvement?

2 In moving towards partnerships, how did Speedy overcome potential resistance to change from both its own staff and those of its customers?

3 Discuss the following statement: The PoliceCo study shows the limits to which private sector practices can be adopted by public sector bodies.

Part Four

Managing choice

Chapter 14

Managing change

Lessons from theory and practice

Learning objectives

After studying this chapter, you should be able to:

- analyse the ten case studies in Part 3 in relation to the following:
    - (a) how each organisation's strategy developed;
    - (b) the constraints on choice;
    - (c) managerial behaviour;
    - (d) the way change was managed;
    - (e) the approach or approaches to change adopted;
    - (f) the objectives pursued;
- describe the main lessons from each of the ten case studies in relation to the above issues;
- understand the factors that determine the level of employee involvement necessary to bring about successful change;
- appreciate that there are a multiplicity of approaches to change that can be used separately, sequentially or in combination.

Introduction

In the previous three parts of this book, we examined the theory and practice of how organisations develop and change. From the Industrial Revolution to the present day, we can see that the history of organisations is one of change and upheaval. In the light of this, the idea that organisations have ever operated in a stable state or a predictable environment, other than for relatively brief periods, is difficult to sustain. Whether because of economic fluctuations, the development of new products and processes, social and political change or war, organisations and entire industries tend to face recurrent bouts of upheaval. Some industries still remain strong, though their products and leading players have changed significantly. One clear example of this is the computer industry, which has moved from being dominated by IBM's mainframes to being dominated by Microsoft's operating systems.

Other industries though, such as the UK coal industry, have shrunk to a shadow of their former size and importance, and appear doomed to be relegated to the role of bit player on the industrial stage.

Not surprisingly, given the rise and fall of industries and technologies over the last two decades, many writers argue that organisations and society at large are in a period of rapid and unprecedented change: a period where old certainties no longer hold good, and new ones have yet to emerge. An alternative view is that the pace and uncertainty of change varies from company to company, industry to industry and even country to country. As a consequence, at any one point in time, some organisations will be experiencing extreme turbulence whilst others appear to operate in a relatively stable environment. However, whether either of these views offers a suitable explanation of the stability–turbulence question is perhaps irrelevant. The pertinent issue is how organisations can cope with both the environment in which they operate and the constraints, challenges and threats they face. In undertaking this task, one thing is perfectly clear: the amount and diversity of information and advice on offer is certainly greater than ever before.

No longer is business analysis and advice confined to a few specialist publishers and journals, or locked up in business school libraries. Books, magazines and videos on 'how to' management can be found in airports and railway stations as well as almost any bookshop. Newspapers, radio and television also play their part in popularising the latest panacea or giving a platform to business gurus or practitioners. In addition, the ubiquitous management consultant can always be relied upon to offer the latest approach, at a price. Therefore, managers cannot claim to lack advice or offers of assistance. The problem, as this book has shown, is that no two approaches appear to be exactly the same and in some cases they may almost entirely contradict each other. Almost in despair, many managers must ask themselves the simple question: 'If the experts can't agree, what hope is there for me?'

This question illustrates the powerlessness some managers feel when faced with issues that, quite wrongly, appear to have become the territory of the specialist. Though there are managers who adopt an almost fatalistic attitude to their situation, believing that events are beyond their control, others, fortunately, adopt a more positive stance. However, even these managers often give the impression that their job is to implement the particular approach to strategy and change that the specialists recommend, or which other more successful organisations have adopted. This book has sought to argue that this is not only incorrect, but a potentially dangerous notion.

Though many 'experts' claim some sort of universal applicability for their favoured approach or theory, as argued in the first two parts of this book, the reality is that such approaches are developed in particular circumstances, at particular times and often with particular types of organisations in mind. It follows that a key role for organisations and their managers is to understand the approaches on offer, identify their own circumstances and needs, and choose the approach that is most appropriate for their circumstances. By doing this, in effect, as this book has attempted to show, managers can cease to be prisoners of circumstances and experts, and begin to make their own choices about the future operation, direction and nature of their organisations.

This chapter draws on the review of the literature on organisations, strategy and change presented so far in this book to shed light on the ten case studies presented in the last three chapters. The chapter begins by reviewing Chapters 6–10 and identifying a number of key common points, especially with regard to managerial choice. These are then used to examine the case studies presented in Chapters 11–13. This is followed by a discussion of the nature of and rationale for employee involvement, particularly in cases of rapid transformational change. The chapter concludes by contending that organisations and theorists need to reject the notion that Planned and Emergent approaches to change necessarily stand in opposition to each other, or that they cannot be used in tandem. Instead, it is argued that there are a multiplicity of approaches to change and that managers have genuine choice in how and when they are used, and what to change and when to change it.

Lessons from theory and practice

Chapters 6–10 began to develop a model of managerial choice and change management. The ten case studies that followed showed how organisations dealt with these issues. The case studies will now be compared with the findings from Chapters 6–10. First, the five chapters will be briefly reviewed and key issues identified; these issues will then be used to examine the case studies. The intention is to combine theory and practice in order to lay the basis for the Choice Management–Change Management model for understanding and implementing organisational change that is presented in Chapter 15.

■ Issues from Chapters 6–10

Chapters 6 and 7 examined the origins and development of approaches to strategy. They showed that strategy was originally conceived of as a rational, quantitative process concerned with an organisation's external environment, especially its products and markets. The key role for managers was to identify trends, establish future objectives or targets, and then implement them. It was shown that as the concept of organisational strategy developed, a distinction emerged between the Prescriptive school of strategy and the Analytical school. The former was and is primarily concerned with telling managers what they should do and, in the main, promoting a planned, quantitative and rational approach to strategy. On the other hand, the Analytical school tends to focus on what organisations actually do when formulating and implementing strategy, rather than what the experts say they should do. For the Analytical school, strategy is a messy, complex, less rational and more emergent affair than the picture painted by the Prescriptive school.

Though over the last 20 years, the Prescriptive school has still tended to dominate the practice of strategy, the insights of the Analytical school have had a significant impact. In particular, there has been a growing recognition of the importance of intuition, creativity, and power and politics in shaping an organisation's strategy. The implications of this for managers have been that instead of being required to construct detailed and elaborate plans for their organisation's future, they are increasingly being seen as primarily responsible for creating a vision or strategic direction for their organisations, which is pursued, often in a bottom-up fashion, through day-to-day decisions concerning such matters as resource allocation, product/market development and a host of, often, small-scale organisational changes. From this standpoint, an organisation's strategy is not set in advance, but emerges from the decisions taken at all levels in the organisation. Therefore, as Chapters 6 and 7 demonstrated, the Analytical school of strategy, as opposed to the Prescriptive school, draws no distinction between strategy development and implementation – an organisation's decisions are informed by its visions or intent, but the nature and details of the strategy they pursue emerge from the decisions they take. Nevertheless, despite the growing interest in the Analytical school, more rational and quantitative approaches to strategy have not been replaced. Rather, as Chapters 6 and 7 show, the situation is that a number of more or less competing perspectives on strategy are now available to organisations, particularly the Competitive Forces, Resource-Based and Strategic Conflict models.

In Chapter 6, it was argued that none of the competing perspectives on strategy were necessarily true or false. Instead, they tended to be appropriate to given situations. The main elements determining their appropriateness were national characteristics, the business environment, industry-specific factors, and the internal characteristics of the organisation in question. Rather than arguing that the role of managers was merely to choose the appropriate approach to strategy for their organisation's circumstances, however, the chapter concluded by arguing that managers could choose to amend these circumstances to fit in with their preferred approach to strategy.

Chapters 8 and 9 moved from examining strategy to reviewing change management. Chapter 8 began by describing the main theories which underpin approaches to change management. These concerned the behaviour and importance of individuals, groups and systems within organisations. This was followed by a review of what had been the dominant approach to change management – Planned change. The Planned approach tends to concentrate on individuals and groups, but has less to say about the overall organisation and its environment, though there have been attempts by its promoters to rectify this. This approach, as its name implies, regards change very much as a conscious process of moving parts of organisations from one relatively stable state to another. It is an approach that seeks to improve organisational effectiveness by changing individual and group beliefs and behaviour through a process of participation and learning. The Chapter concluded by looking at three models dealing with the pace and nature of organisational change – the Incremental, Punctuated Equilibrium and Continuous Change models. These drew attention to the spectrum of change events ranging from small-scale, localised ones to large-scale events designed to transform or reinvent an organisation in its totality. It was argued that whilst Planned change might be suitable in some of these situations, a wider range of approaches were required to cover all of them.

Alternative, and newer, approaches to change management were assembled and reviewed in Chapter 9 under the collective title of the Emergent approach. This approach conceives of organisations as operating in a continuous state of flux and turbulence. Though its proponents recognise that change can take many forms, Emergent change tends to be characterised as a bottom-up, unpredictable, messy and politically-driven process. From this perspective, it is argued that the role of managers is to develop a climate in which everyone in the organisation has a responsibility for identifying the need for and implementing change. The objective is not to achieve a fixed outcome but continuously to align and realign the organisation with the changing needs of an unpredictable environment. In particular, the Emergent approach identifies five features of organisational life that either promote or block change: structure, culture, organisational learning, managerial behaviour, and power and politics. The Chapter also showed that though the Emergent approach may have some advantages over the Planned approach, it has drawbacks and does not cover all change situations.

In Chapter 10, it was argued that despite the support for these two approaches, neither the Planned nor the Emergent approach provided a comprehensive picture of organisational change. Rather, there are a wide variety of approaches that are suited to different situations. The suitability of any one approach is determined by a range of factors, especially the stability, or otherwise, of an organisation's environment. From this perspective, as Chapter 10 maintained, a key role for managers is to make sense of the complexity of their organisation's situation and choose an approach to change which best aligns with this. Nevertheless, it was also argued that, though constraints such as the nature of the environment in which their organisations operate place limitations on managers' freedom of choice, managers can often, but not always, influence, moderate or alter these constraints to make them better suited to their and their organisations' own preferences and needs.

Therefore, the evidence and arguments from Chapters 6–10 can be summarised:

- There are a wide and diverse range of change situations, ranging from small-scale change to the complete transformation or reinvention of organisations. These are not, however, mutually exclusive. They can occur, whether consciously or unconsciously, simultaneously within the same organisation, though not necessarily to achieve the same objectives.
- Though there are a number of valid and well-supported approaches to strategy development and change management available to organisations, there is a tendency for managers, and academics, to focus on and advocate a limited range. Whilst not always explicitly stated, underpinning these approaches to strategy development and change management is a Contingency perspective that makes assumptions about the degree of stability present in the environment in which organisations operate.
- The dominant view is that managers have to adopt the approach that appears to fit in with the constraints, especially environmental ones, they face.
- An alternative perspective, however, is that it is often, though not always, possible for managers to influence these constraints, in effect to change the rules of the game, to make them more appropriate to the particular approach to strategy and change management which suits them and their organisations.

In order to examine the above points further, the ten case studies from Part 3 will now be reviewed to see to what extent the experience of real life organisations supports or contradicts them. In particular, drawing on Chapters 6–10, for each case study the following key issues will be explored:

1 **Strategy.** How was the organisation's strategy developed?
2 **Constraints.** What were the constraints the organisation faced, and did the strategy seek to work within or influence these?
3 **Managerial behaviour.** What role did managers play in strategy development and change management?

4 **Change management**. How were change projects managed and who was involved?

5 **Planned, Emergent or combined change**. To what extent can the change projects be classed as Planned, Emergent or exhibiting a combination or variety of approaches?

6 **Objectives**. Was the focus of strategy development and/or change projects to alter individual and group behaviour or to change or reinvent an organisation in its entirety?

Reviewing the case studies – Chapters 11–13

In examining the 10 case studies against the above six issues, it should be borne in mind that Case Studies 1–4 (Chapter 11) deal specifically with strategy development, and Case Studies 5–10 (Chapters 12 and 13) concentrate on change management projects. Nevertheless, all the case studies, to a lesser or greater extent, contain elements of strategy development and all contain elements of change management. With that proviso in mind, we can now move to a brief examination of the individual case studies. Each case will be reviewed under the six headings listed above.

Case Study 1: The music industry

1 **Strategy**. In this instance we are not considering the actions of one or two companies but of an entire industry, and a global one at that. It is an industry that has been dominated by the big five record labels for over 50 years. The managers of these companies have developed what appears to be a common strategy to ensure that their organisations retain their dominant position in the industry. It basically revolves around signing the artists who will sell the most recordings, shaping and marketing them and their output to maximise sales, and ensuring that the vast proportion of the revenues generated go to the label rather than the artists or anyone else. The advent of the Internet threatens the income and dominance of the big labels. It can offer them many advantages in terms of cutting the costs of record distribution; however, these may pale into insignificance in terms of the threat posed by peer-to-peer music swapping (P2P). Those managing the big labels appear be taking a reactive rather than proactive and strategic response to this. They are attempting, not very successfully, to use the law to stop the free downloading of music whilst at the same time attempting to copy and adapt the Napster approach by developing subscription services which charges for the downloading of music.

2 **Constraints**. The ease with which the Internet now allows recorded material to be pirated is clearly a major constraint on the actions of the record companies. Shawn Fanning opened the Pandora's Box of the Internet and it is difficult to see how the big labels can hold on to their iron grip on production and distribution and continue to take the lion's share of the revenues. Though this is partly a case of people taking advantage of changes in technology to get free records, it is also about the nature of the Internet. In essence it is a clash of philosophies between those who see the Internet as a vehicle for making money and those who see it as a way of creating communities where sharing takes precedence over profit-making. This means that there are many talented and committed computer-literate people who, as a matter of principle, are working to make it as easy as possible to access material free via the Internet, regardless of any technological or legal obstacles that are put in their way. Nor is this just about the music industry. Piracy is spreading to

any industry whose output is in, or can be turned into, a digital format whether this be records, films, television or books. Chapter 4 discussed the implications of complexity theories for organisations. One of the key arguments of complexity theorists is that even small changes can transform an entire system, overthrowing existing constraints and laws and creating new ones. It could well be that the case of Shawn Fanning and the music industry is an example of complexity theories in action.

3 **Managerial behaviour.** Music industry executives tend to be powerful individuals who have risen through the creative side of the industry and who take a hands-on role in running their companies. They know the music industry inside out, and follow tried-and-tested approaches to developing, promoting and taking profit from artists. The situation created by Fanning's Napster was beyond their experience. Their response was reactive rather than strategic. They sought to use the courts to stifle Napster and similar bodies, whilst at the same time attempting to turn the Napster approach into a subscription-based service. Neither initiative appears to have stemmed the rising tide of piracy.

4 **Change management.** This case study does not deal with change management *per se*. So far, however, the changes that have taken place appear to be in the hands of the lawyers and senior managers, and have revolved around stifling and copying rather than seeking wider organisational involvement and looking for more creative solutions.

5 **Planned, Emergent or combined change.** Despite the fact that the music industry is based on a creative process, much of its past ways of working have tended towards the dictatorial and formulaic and have been designed to ensure that the big companies retain control over the artists. The P2P revolution has created an unprecedented level of uncertainty in the industry, however. It is unlikely that the changes that this is bringing about can be managed by a few senior managers trying to keep control of the situation. Therefore, the reshaping of the music industry is likely to arise from a host of local responses and initiatives, many of which may come from smaller and more entrepreneurial companies rather than the big labels. Indeed, it is not yet clear that the big labels can survive in the new P2P era, at least in their present form.

6 **Objectives.** So far, the main objective of the big labels has remained unchanged; they want to retain their dominant position in the industry. They have attempted both to stop and to copy the Napster model. In essence, they have tried to change the behaviour of those who seek to promote a more community-based approach to the Internet by threatening them with the law. In this, they have signally failed. The technology that enables piracy now seems to be built into most computers or can be purchased or downloaded free from the Internet. Nor have they succeeded in their attempt to get consumers to change their behaviour and pay for music through Internet subscription services rather than downloading it free. Once people discover that they can easily get something for free, it is very difficult to persuade them that they should pay for it. Rather than tinkering round the edges, the big labels need to ask themselves some very awkward questions about the nature of the music industry in future and their role within it.

Case Study 2: Marconi

1 **Strategy**. Though on the face of it, Marconi's strategy was the product of its CEO, George Simpson, and Finance Director, John Mayo, its origins lay in the general belief by institutional investors in the City of London that GEC, as it was, had missed the Internet/telecoms boat and needed to swim very fast to catch up. It is not clear whether either Simpson or Mayo ever questioned this belief. It is clear, however, that their entire strategy for selling off most of GEC and going on a telecoms buying spree was based on it.

2 **Constraints**. It could be argued that the view of investors that GEC was no longer viable was a constraint on the strategy that Simpson and Mayo could adopt. Certainly, they chose to align GEC/Marconi's strategy with this view. There were other constraints on the viability of such a strategy that they appeared to ignore, however. Firstly, Marconi's senior managers were seeking to create a global Internet/telecoms equipment company rapidly by buying up other companies rather than by growing one organically. This is a very risky strategy which has seldom been successful in any industry. Secondly, Marconi had put itself in a position where it had to buy fast in a booming market, even though questions were already being asked about the very high price and viability of dotcom-orientated companies. Lastly, it was buying into a sector where the competition was stiff and the main customers, the big telecoms companies, were few. Any downturn in the market could and did prove disastrous. However, even when its competitors were taking action to tackle the prospect of falling demand, Marconi ignored the indications and continued to act on the assumption that demand for the products and services of its new businesses would grow and grow.

3 **Managerial behaviour**. The strategy was developed by Simpson and Mayo, who took a very hands-on role in selling the various parts of GEC and stitching together the new parts of Marconi. In doing so, they were hailed almost as heroes by institutional investors and commentators. What criticism Marconi did receive appeared to come from the departing 'old guard' of GEC, whose comments could be interpreted as sour grapes.

4 **Change management**. The main changes that took place in transforming GEC into Marconi were the selling and buying of companies. In both cases, because of the pace at which the new Marconi was being created, the transactions seemed almost to take the form of an auction rather than the sort of slow and deliberate evaluation that the old GEC was used to. To create Marconi, it was necessary to dispose of most of the old GEC, which did not fit with the new Internet/telecoms world. Therefore, it was a case of selling the old businesses for whatever was the best price that could be obtained in order to raise the money to buy new businesses with. The same applied when buying. In a booming market, Marconi had to pay the going price if it wanted a slice of the action. In the 1970s, when OPEC controlled the world's supply of oil, the then Head of OPEC, Sheihk Yamani, was asked what was a fair price for oil, his response was, 'Anything you can get plus 10%'. This seemed to be the attitude of those who owned the companies Marconi was seeking to purchase. Having set itself on this path, however, Marconi's management clearly felt that it had no option but to buy at the going rate. Managers appeared to be the prisoners of investors and lenders who expected, indeed, demanded, that the company behave in

this fashion. Indeed, the more money Marconi borrowed and spent, the higher its standing and share price rose, and the more praise its management received.

5 **Planned, Emergent or combined change**. This case study does not focus on change management *per se*, but on the strategic issues involved in dismantling one company and building another. Simpson and Mayo had a vision of turning GEC into a high technology Internet/telecoms equipment company. They clearly had a view of what bits of GEC they needed to sell off (most of it) and what parts of the telecoms sector they needed to buy. Though it could be argued that both sales and purchases were undertaken on an opportunistic basis, the strategy itself never wavered or was changed, until it failed spectacularly. Therefore, Marconi's approach to change as such can best be described as a top-down structural transformation carried out in a directive manner.

6 **Objectives**. The intention of Marconi's strategy was to create an entirely new company. Indeed, it seemed to go beyond the concept of transformation, because that implies that the old organisation is in some ways being reinvigorated and refocused. Marconi set out to sell off the old GEC and to purchase a new organisation with new staff, new products and markets, and new customers.

Case Study 3: Oticon

1 **Strategy**. The company's strategy was developed and driven by one person (its then President, Lars Kolind). He created a vision of a service-based organisation and pursued it by, in effect, razing the existing organisation to the ground and starting again.

2 **Constraints**. Though there is no clear evidence that existing constraints influenced the strategy, the new flexible structure that emerged was certainly compatible with Danish norms or expectations regarding job design. As far as industry norms were concerned, Oticon was at a disadvantage in that competition was based on the technical sophistication of products, and Oticon's capability in this respect was falling behind that of other companies. To counter this disadvantage, Oticon chose to rewrite the rules of competition in the industry by moving the focus from technology to service. The business environment in which Oticon operated had been and still remained very turbulent. Indeed, by attempting to change the basis of competition in the industry, Oticon can be seen as adding to rather than reducing uncertainty. In terms of organisation characteristics, Lars Kolind was again attempting to rewrite the rule book. The existing structure was demolished, its culture was challenged and the style of management changed drastically. Kolind appeared to face very little overt resistance but, in introducing the changes initially, and taking corrective action when he thought they were failing, he did use the power of his position in a very directive and, perhaps, coercive manner.

3 **Managerial behaviour**. The strategy was developed by Oticon's President and, though he explained it to other managers, it is clear that he neither expected nor wanted them to modify it. Their role was to support him and to help sell and implement the idea, rather than necessarily to be part of the process of its development. However, in helping to sell the new vision to the rest of the organisation, both managers and staff changed their views of how the company should be run and their roles in it. As a more cooperative atmosphere developed in the company, managers moved away from their previous directive style of management and developed a more facilitative role.

4 **Change management**. The approach taken was to prepare the ground carefully but then to change overnight. This part of the approach was, in effect, to use Kanter *et al*'s (1992) phrase, a Bold Stroke. Employees left the company and its old systems and practices on a Friday night, and on Monday walked into a completely different organisation. What followed, however, was months of chaos as everyone tried to work out what they were doing and how they should do it. Nor did Kolind appear to wish for more settled internal arrangements to prevail. When he felt that the company was in danger of, as Kurt Lewin would say, refreezing, he 'exploded' the organisation again.

5 **Planned, Emergent or combined change**. Though we can see some evidence of Planned change in the way that employees were involved in projects, it was the Emergent approach to change that was dominant. Lars Kolind had a vision of the organisation's future but the actual details and nature of the change process emerged as the company struggled to implement it. Also, change was open-ended and, given the nature of the new organisation, it is not clear if it will ever settle down into a fixed state. There is also a great emphasis on collective learning, and using this learning to keep the company on the move. To use Kanter *et al*'s (1992) analogy, again, it was a Bold Stroke followed by a Long March.

6 **Objectives**. The aim was no less than a total transformation or reinvention of the organisation in all its aspects, and to move from being a traditionally-structured technology-driven organisation to a learning organisation focused on service delivery. However, central to this was the need to change the attitudes and behaviour of individuals and groups.

Case Study 4: The Public Power Corporation (PPC) of Greece

1 **Strategy**. The PPC's strategy was created by its Board of Directors in response to the Greek government's decision to privatise it and in the light of the European Union Electricity Directive.

2 **Constraints**. The main constraint under which the PPC developed and is implementing its strategy is the EU Electricity Directive. This to a large extent determines or constrains the PPC's structure and behaviour. However, the PPC has sought to mitigate this constraint by moving into the electricity markets in other countries and by linking up with other providers so that it is not dependent solely on the Greek market or its own lack of experience of operating as a commercial concern. However, where this international expansion takes it into other EU countries, it will still have to abide by EU regulations. Also, the international energy market is very competitive. It is also attempting to move into the telecoms business, but this is also regulated by the EU and is even more competitive than the electricity market.

3 **Managerial behaviour**. The PPC's Board seems to have taken the lead in determining its strategy. However, it was and still is predominantly owned by the Greek government. The Board had to produce a strategy that, on the one hand, met EU and Greek government competition laws, and on the other does not threaten the government's income from the PPC nor its eventual price when it is sold.

4 **Change management**. The PPC says that it wants to create a participative learning organisation based on a committed and skilled workforce imbued with an entre-

preneurial culture. However, the changes which have taken place so far appear to be structural, both in terms of the reorganisation of the company into a number of divisions and the decision to reduce the size of the workforce by some 20 per cent. These changes appear to have been decided upon and implemented with little or no consultation with the workforce or their representatives. If they are to lead to the sort of organisation the PPC says it wants, then this 'Bold Stroke' approach will need to be succeeded by a 'Long March'.

5 **Planned, Emergent or combined change**. The PPC has laid out a clear strategy for its future. Its plan is to turn the PPC from a bureaucratic public service into a private, market-orientated company. So far, this plan has been implemented by imposition rather than cooperation. If the plan is to be realised, however, the PPC needs to change the behaviour of its employees in order to create a more participative and proactive organisation. Therefore, imposition will need to give way to participation if the necessary behavioural changes are to be achieved. Given the various obstacles and constraints it faces, not least the twin threats of regulation and competition, future changes and developments at the PPC are more likely to be based on an Emergent than a Planned approach to change.

6 **Objectives**. The PPC's main objective appears to be to reinvent itself as a highly competitive private sector electricity and telecoms company. This will require it both to restructure itself, which to a large extent it has achieved, and to develop a more entrepreneurial culture, which still seems some way off. The measure of success will be whether or not it can hang onto its dominant position in the Greek electricity market. However, this is where there seems to be a contradiction at the heart of the PPC's objectives. If it is successful in holding on to its market share, then the various competition regulators at national and EU levels will step in to change the rules of the game to reduce the PPC's dominance, probably by breaking up the business. If on the other hand the PPC is not successful, it is likely that it will have to sell off the less successful parts of the business, thus breaking itself up. Therefore, despite its objective of holding onto a unified electricity business, it is not clear how it can do this given the constraints it faces.

Case Study 5: Volvo

1 **Strategy**. Volvo's strategy for Job Design was to reorganise its plants to eliminate the moving assembly line, and replace it with group-based assembly. The strategy originated from a need both to reduce labour turnover and absenteeism, and to respond to societal pressures to eliminate dehumanised forms of work organisation. However, even when these were no longer an issue, the company continued to pursue the move away from assembly-line working. The strategy was driven, and continuity provided, by Volvo's long-serving Chief Executive, Pehr Gyllenhammar. However, even after his somewhat acrimonious departure, the commitment to Job Design survived, though it is difficult to imagine that, had he stayed, Gyllenhammar would have sold Volvo's car business to Ford with all the risks to the Job Design strategy that this implies.

2 **Constraints**. Though public opinion in Sweden favoured a move away from the assembly line, it was and remains the car industry's established mode of operation. Therefore, Volvo was clearly aiming to change industry constraints whilst aligning

itself with societal ones. From the perspective of the business environment, Volvo's move to 'humanise' car assembly appeared to bring them much valuable publicity and its approach to building cars was seen as a selling point. In the early years, however, internal constraints and resistance (both attitudinal and technical) acted to limit the radicalness of the initiative. One point to note is that, at least in the early years, there was perhaps more open suspicion and resistance from Volvo's trade unions than from its managers.

3   **Managerial behaviour.** All the change projects involving Job Design were driven by senior managers. Outside experts in Job Design were also involved at the planning stage, and so were trade union representatives, whose enthusiasm grew over the years. Nevertheless, the outcome of successive waves of Job Design was to devolve power from Volvo's headquarters to the individual plants, and in the plants to give the shopfloor teams more authority and control. This led to the elimination of middle management layers, the creation of a flatter organisation structure and the progressive development of a much more empowered workforce.

4   **Change management.** Each project was planned in great detail in advance. This involved not only managers, but also trade union representatives and outside experts. Once in operation, however, the actual arrangements were modified, in order, so it was argued, to meet business needs and cope with operational difficulties. In most cases these modifications appear to have reduced the ability of workers to set their own pace of work and to expand their range of activities. Nevertheless, whether in new or existing plants, each change project built on the last, and each project resulted in greater levels of shopfloor control. Central to this was organisational learning: the ability collectively to capture and transmit, from one plant to another, the experience of making radical Job Design work. It is also clear that with each project, the confidence of managers, workers and trade unions that Job Design could work grew.

5   **Planned, Emergent or combined change.** Though Volvo's strategy for Job Design was driven by a clear intent, it was implemented on different sites and in different ways over a considerable period of time using a combination of approaches. Though driven from the top, Volvo sought to involve staff and managers in developing, implementing and amending projects. In terms of the individual Job Design projects, the Volvo case shows that even where changes are planned in detail in advance, the final outcome emerges through a process of iteration, modification and negotiation once the new practices are put into operation. Therefore, it is this combination of Planned and Emergent change, linked to willingness by senior managers to experiment and an organisational commitment to continuous improvement for over 30 years, which makes the Volvo experience unique.

6   **Objectives.** The objectives were twofold. The first was financial – to reduce absenteeism and labour turnover. The second was social – to humanise the assembly of cars. These were pursued through a combination of structural and behavioural change, which led to major changes both in the overall shape of the company and in the attitudes of individuals and groups. However, the social objectives were modified, though not superseded, by the need for the company to operate profitably in a highly competitive market. Despite the takeover of Volvo's car division by Ford, the company still appears to be committed to continuing with its human-centred approach to car assembly.

Case Study 6: XYZ Construction

1 **Strategy.** It can be seen that XYZ had a relatively clear and consistent strategy that aimed to transform the culture, practices and structure of the company. The strategy began with and was driven by the new Managing Director. He had come with a remit for change from XYZ's parent company, which believed that it had fallen behind the competition and needed to be reinvigorated if it was to survive. In developing the strategy, the Managing Director sought to expand the senior management team, and win them and the rest of the organisation over to the need for and type of change. In this and the strategy itself, he appears to have been very successful.

2 **Constraints.** The new Managing Director had to contend with two opposing sets of constraints. On the one hand, the parent company wanted to see changes that would create a more cooperative and team-based organisation that could cope better with the changing nature of the construction industry. On the other hand, XYZ was a hierarchical company where the previous Managing Director had behaved in a dictatorial and heavy-handed fashion that inhibited challenge, cooperation and change. Also, though the construction industry was attempting to change, it was still riddled with conflict and mistrust. Therefore, the new Managing Director had to change the company quickly enough to satisfy the parent company but not so fast that he failed to win over staff, managers and customers.

3 **Managerial behaviour.** The strategy and changes were led by the new Managing Director, but he was careful from the start to involve managers and staff in identifying and implementing the changes, thus winning them over. The various changes shifted the balance of power in the company and, in particular, the organisational restructuring reduced the influence and standing of the Regional Managers and some directors. The Managing Director expected that there would be some resistance to the changes from these and others who might lose out. However, his clear support for the changes, the widespread recognition of the need for change, and an open and transparent change process where it was difficult for individuals to block change, prevented any major obstructions occurring.

4 **Change management.** Though change was driven from the top, increasing numbers of managers and staff became involved in the process of identifying and implementing change. In the more open-ended change projects, the responsibility for maintaining the momentum was given to staff and lower-level managers. This is not to say that senior managers did not take an interest, or did not give the process a shove or tweak if they thought it was necessary. The Managing Director recognised that he could not be everywhere at once, however, and that if changes were to become embedded within the organisation, they had to be owned by those concerned.

5 **Planned, Emergent or combined change.** Overall, XYZ's approach to change can be characterised as Emergent and in many cases experimental. A series of relatively small changes were made that, taken collectively over a period of time, led to a significant change in the culture and operations of XYZ. However, when it came to the change of organisational structure, this appeared to be conducted in a more Planned fashion. This shows, as argued elsewhere in this book, that organisations tend to use a variety of approaches to change depending on what is to be changed and the circumstances of the organisation at the time. In this instance, within a predominantly emergent strategy, we can see many instances of Emergent change and a significant example of Planned change.

6 **Objectives**. The objective of the new Managing Director was to reinvigorate the company by changing its culture, structure and practices. His first priority, however, was to change the behaviour of managers and staff and to develop their competence. He was also keenly aware that in doing this he must also improve the performance of the company. Therefore, most of the changes which took place had two equal objectives: one was to change how managers and staff worked with and behaved towards each other and the company's customers; the other was to improve the performance of staff and managers and so offer a better service to customers and achieve an overall improvement to XYZ's performance. Only when the cultural and behavioural changes were embedded in the organisation, and its performance improved, did the Managing Director begin to focus on the overall structure of the company. He saw these structural changes as an important element in facilitating the effective working of the company and removing barriers to teamworking. However, he also felt that without the prior cultural and behavioural changes, the structural changes would have little impact.

Case Study 7: GK Printers

1 **Strategy**. GK's strategy tended to develop in response to potential crises, or latterly opportunities, rather than being proactively led by its management. The company, mainly on a reactive basis, appears to be reinventing itself as a modern, service-orientated company by aligning its internal arrangements with the changing needs of its environment and customers. However, this was not and is not part of any conscious plan or vision; rather it is being revealed by the pattern of actions the organisation has taken over the last decade. Originally, this pattern began to emerge through technological changes within GK, but over time it has become more pronounced by attitudinal and behavioural change, especially among managers.

2 **Constraints**. External considerations, such as societal pressures, business environment and industry-specific factors did not appear to constrain the freedom of action of GK's managers. Indeed, the turbulence and increased competition in the external environment seemed to assist GK with its internal changes. GK's main constraints were internal and related to existing attitudes, technology and practices. Increasingly, however, as the need arose to develop a more collective leadership, it was the directive style of the Managing Director that was seen as a key constraint on progress. Nevertheless, his directive style, and his tendency to play managers off against each other, gradually changed.

3 **Managerial behaviour**. Though originally it was the Managing Director who was responsible for strategy development and change, it became clear over time that a more collective and cooperative style of management was required if GK was to overcome the obstacles it faced and seize the opportunities on offer. Therefore, gradually, all the company's managers became involved in and took responsibility for strategy development, and they even devolved responsibility for some change projects to staff in the areas concerned.

4 **Change management**. A mixture of approaches to managing change projects can be seen at GK. In most instances, managers took responsibility for identifying the need for change, and in some instances actually directed it. However, with the comput-

erised business system, for example, the company left selection and implementation to the staff concerned. Also, in terms of the website business, GK allowed a staff member who was a web enthusiast to develop this area. This demonstrates how far the company has progressed in developing a climate of trust and involvement.

5 **Planned, Emergent or combined change.** A mixture of both Planned and Emergent approaches can be seen at GK. In the early days, the company tried to adopt a more Planned approach, especially when introducing new technology. However, new developments or improvements to existing arrangements have tended to be both open-ended and reactive in nature. Also, the Managing Director has tended to oscillate between a directive and a participative approach to change. Overall the pattern of change at GK appears to be reactive and Emergent, but within this pattern there have been certain proactive and Planned elements. Therefore, change at GK can be characterised as *ad hoc*, reactive or opportunistic rather than being part of any consistent approach.

6 **Objectives.** The original aim was to survive. To this end, GK changed its technology and image in order to improve its competitiveness. As events unfolded, however, it became clear that the key to competing effectively was to change people's attitudes and behaviour, especially at management level, and create a greater commitment to teamwork and collective decision-making. This has created a climate where managers and staff are more receptive to new ideas, and responsive to new opportunities, than before. Therefore, a pattern of change can be seen at GK, though it is by no means a well-articulated or even conscious one, which seems to be leading in the direction of organisational transformation.

Case Study 8: Rover–TRW

1 **Strategy.** This particular initiative between Rover and TRW did not form part of a strategic plan, or contribute towards a vision. In essence, the objective was an operational one, not a strategic one: to outsource the assembly of suspension modules owing to lack of space. At TRW, those in charge focused on the steps necessary to have the new operation up and running on time, and able to meet Rover's requirements. There was a strategic element to this initiative in that both organisations wished to find out more about modular assembly, but this sub-objective very quickly vanished from sight.

2 **Constraints.** The main constraints tended to be attitudinal and organisational. To be successful, TRW needed to ensure that staff at the Frankley site had the motivation, initiative and ability to develop a new operation remote from the main TRW site in Wales. There was also a requirement to build a good working relationship with Rover's assembly line personnel. In organisational terms, a new factory and workforce needed to be established, new equipment installed, new practices learned and new skills developed. At an operational level, both in terms of the relationship and the performance, this worked better than anyone had anticipated. However, the persistence of old, less trusting relationships at a more senior level between the two companies did threaten the gains made at the operational level.

3 **Managerial behaviour.** At Frankley, supported by their superiors within TRW, managers created a genuine atmosphere of cooperation that allowed staff to work closely with their counterparts at Rover, and to improve their performance continuously. At

a more senior level, though, a less cooperative and more guarded atmosphere prevailed between Rover and TRW.

4 **Change management**. Frankley was created from scratch and, once established, was committed to continuously improving and developing its performance. From the outset, and in contrast to established practices within TRW, the Frankley management sought to ensure that everyone was involved in and could contribute to change. It was only a small organisation, with some 30 to 40 staff initially, and this obviously made it easier to create a team spirit. Nevertheless, the key was the attitude of the management at Frankley, who set out to involve all staff.

5 **Planned, Emergent or combined change**. This was clearly a case where one could see both Emergent and Planned change going on side by side. Originally, there was a clear set of objectives that Frankley had to achieve and a fixed timescale within which to achieve them; these revolved around setting up the new plant and beginning deliveries to Rover. Beyond that, though, was a process of learning, experimentation and development that was central to the major performance improvements made by Frankley.

6 **Objectives**. The original objectives were basically structural and revolved around establishing a new assembly operation capable of meeting Rover's requirements. Though these objectives were met, staff at the Frankley site did not rest on their laurels. Instead, motivated by the desire to improve the service to Rover, they set themselves, and achieved, ever more ambitious targets.

Case Study 9: Speedy Stationers

1 **Strategy**. To the extent that it had any conscious vision or strategy, it tended to be driven by opportunism or force of events rather than necessarily being proactive. Each time a major threat or opportunity arose, Speedy examined its options and chose the one that appeared to be more favourable to the survival and development of its business. Also, as the Direct Sales initiative showed, 'gut instinct' rather than rational analysis tended to drive decisions.

2 **Constraints**. The degree to which external or internal factors affected Speedy's strategy is unclear. Certainly, the company did not appear to have faced great restrictions on its freedom of manoeuvre. Nor, except in one case, did it appear to have sought to change or influence the constraints it faced. The big exception is its attempt to develop a partnership approach to customers. In this instance it was attempting to change industry practice. Though this met with some resistance internally, it also had to overcome a large degree of scepticism in the customer concerned.

3 **Managerial behaviour**. It was Speedy's Managing Director who originally developed its partnership strategy. Subsequently, and rather reluctantly, he handed responsibility for its continuing development to another director of the company, who established his own plans and then convinced his colleagues, and Speedy's customers, to accept them. Later, however, when it came to convincing his fellow directors that they should expand direct sales nationally, he was less successful and even the project's original champion, the Managing Director, rejected the suggestion. Therefore, overall, though Speedy wanted to promote more cooperative relationships with customers, this does not appear to signal any company-wide move towards more cooperative working within Speedy.

4 **Change management**. The actual implementation of the partnership approach required not only the involvement of Speedy's own staff, but also, as the UTL instance shows, cooperation from its customers' managers and staff at all levels. Though there was resistance to the partnership approach in both Speedy and UTL, the commitment of senior managers, the involvement of staff, and some early gains, helped to overcome this.

5 **Planned, Emergent or combined change**. The development of the strategy itself, the partnership with UTL, and the further expansion of this approach, constituted an open-ended process. Initial implementation of the partnership was carefully thought through, but from then on the form and content of the changes tended to be more *ad hoc* and reactive. For this reason, the process of change can be seen to be Emergent.

6 **Objectives**. The objective of Speedy's strategy was to grow its business by developing a new type of relationship with its customers. Implementing this led to changes within both Speedy, though these tended to be limited to its Direct Sales Division, and within the ten customers with whom it developed partnerships. Though some of these changes were structural, most changes concerned the attitudes and behaviour of individuals and groups, especially in terms of greater openness and trust. There is little evidence, however, that these have led to any wider cultural changes within Speedy.

Case Study 10: PoliceCo

1 **Strategy**. It does not appear that PoliceCo had a strategy for outsourcing or thought it necessary to have one. Rather, successive governments had a strategy for improving public services by compelling them to adopt the practices, and use the services, of the private sector. Government legislation, by introducing Compulsory Competitive Tendering (CCT) and Best Value, compelled PoliceCo to market-test its activities by putting them out for tender. The way activities were selected and the process of asking for tenders and selecting contractors was laid down by government regulations, and, to an extent, European Union legislation. Therefore, for PoliceCo, outsourcing was an administrative issue rather than a strategic choice.

2 **Constraints**. The main constraint faced by PoliceCo was government legislation. This compelled them to act in a certain fashion, i.e. to outsource, whether they liked it or not. A secondary constraint was the risk-aversive culture that appears to pervade the public sector in terms of awarding contracts and working with suppliers. For example, PoliceCo could have packaged all its cleaning needs into one contract and awarded them to one contractor. However, it felt that by splitting them it would reduce risk, and better demonstrate, through competition between the contractors, that value for money was being achieved. For similar reasons, it chose to go through the full re-tendering process when the contracts came up for renewal, even though they might have been able to use a more truncated process designed to test whether the existing contractor was still offering Best Value. The fact that they did not do either of these is related to the nature of public scrutiny under which they operate. They can be held to account locally, nationally and, most worryingly for them, through the media. Decisions in terms of the nature, duration and renewal of contracts, which would be unremarkable were they taken

by a private organisation, can be labelled as incompetence or even potentially corrupt if taken by a public service.

3 **Managerial behaviour.** The role of senior managers in PoliceCo was simply to ensure that the legislation was complied with. The actual execution of the legislation, the operation of CCT and later Best Value, became a lower-level administrative task.

4 **Change management.** As mentioned, outsourcing became treated as an administrative, almost routine process in PoliceCo. Where consultations needed to be conducted with staff and trade unions, i.e. when jobs as well as activities were being outsourced, PoliceCo tried to be as helpful as it could in smoothing the transition process and ensuring that staff retained their jobs under the new regime. However, where it was shown that an activity could be provided cheaper from outside than inside, it was outsourced, and that decision was not negotiable.

5 **Planned, Emergent or combined change.** It is difficult to characterise outsourcing at PoliceCo as either Planned or Emergent. It could be argued that because it was responding to outside changes on an incremental basis, i.e. activity by activity, there was an emergent aspect to it. However, it might be better described as a process of administrative coercion.

6 **Objectives.** PoliceCo's main objective was to comply with the legislation in as efficient and painless fashion as possible. Though outsourcing has led to significant behavioural changes in private sector organisations, as far as PoliceCo was concerned, the main changes were structural. Activities which had previously been performed in-house were transferred to outside bodies, leaving the rest of the organisation unaffected and free to continue with their own activities.

Having examined the ten case studies, we are now in a position to discuss the implications of the above for the way in which strategy and change are conceived and executed. Before doing so, however, there are two interrelated issues raised by the case studies that need to be clarified. These concern the degree to which employee involvement is a necessary factor in successful change, and whether or not wholesale organisational transformation, including attitudes and behaviour, can be achieved rapidly.

Employee involvement and organisational transformation

The received wisdom in the literature on organisational change is that employee involvement is crucial to successful change, especially in situations that require attitudinal and cultural change. However, both the Planned and Emergent perspectives stress that this is a slow, learning process. For this reason, it is argued, rapid organisational transformations can only be successful if they focus on structural as averse to cultural change. This is a conclusion that can certainly be drawn from the literature on both Planned and Emergent change. It is also something stressed by Kanter *et al* (1992), who believe that an organisation's structure can be changed relatively quickly through a 'Bold Stroke' but that cultural change can only be achieved by a 'Long March' requiring extensive participation over time. The Oticon study in Chapter 11 appears to offer a different perspective on culture change, however. This was a case of rapid organisational transformation, which was based on a vision imposed on the company in a mainly directive fashion by its CEO, but which led to a widespread change of attitudes and behaviours in the company. This change in organisational culture both preceded and paved the way for a more participative approach to the planning, execution and subsequent development of the vision. It was the CEO's imposed vision that appeared to bring about the rapid change in attitudes across the company. The change in attitudes facilitated a more Planned approach that was used to achieve the rapid structural change. In turn, this was followed by a period of Emergent change where staff had to develop and adjust to new ways of working with, and behaving towards, each other.

Though this shows how Planned and Emergent change can be used in combination, it still leaves the question of how the change in organisational culture that preceded these phases at Oticon was achieved rapidly and without the full cooperation and involvement of the people concerned. In addressing this question, the work of Schmuck and Miles (1971) is particularly useful. They argue that the level of involvement required in any change project is dependent on the impact of the change on the people concerned. Huse (1980) developed this distinction further. Building on earlier work by Harrison (1970), Huse categorised change interventions along a continuum based on the 'depth' of intervention, ranging from the 'shallow level' to the 'deepest level'. The greater the depth of the intervention, Huse argues, the more it becomes concerned with the psychological make-up and personality of the individual, and the greater the need for the full involvement of individuals if they are to accept the changes.

The argument, therefore, is that it is necessary to link levels of involvement to the types of change proposed. The key is that the greater the effect on the individual, especially in terms of psychological constructs and values, the deeper the level of involvement required if successful behaviour change is to be achieved. This appears to explain why in some cases, such as the PPC and PoliceCo, involvement can be dispensed with or minimised, whilst in other cases, such as XYZ, it is vital. It does not, though, explain why major and rapid attitudinal changes at Oticon were successful without a great deal of initial involvement.

In seeking to understand and explain such apparent contradictions, Burnes and James (1995) draw on the theory of cognitive dissonance. This theory states that people try to be consistent in both their attitudes and behaviour. When they sense an inconsistency either between two or more attitudes or between their attitudes and behaviour, people experience dissonance; that is, they feel frustrated and uncomfortable with the situation, sometimes extremely so (Jones, 1990). Therefore, individuals will seek a stable state where there is minimum dissonance. This latter point is important. It is unlikely that dissonance can ever be totally avoided, but where the elements creating the dissonance are relatively unimportant, the pressure to correct them will be low. Where the issues involved are perceived by the individual to be significant, however, the presence of such dissonance will motivate the person concerned to try to reduce the dissonance and achieve consonance, by changing either their attitudes or behaviour to bring them into line (Robbins, 1986; Smith et al, 1982). This may involve a process of cognitive restructuring, which is unlikely to be free from difficulties for the individual concerned (Mahoney, 1974). However, as Festinger (1957), one of the originators of the concept, pointed out, in addition to trying to reduce the dissonance, people will actively avoid situations and information that would be likely to increase the dissonance. Since the emergence of the theory of cognitive dissonance in the 1950s, it has been developed and refined (see Cooper and Fazio, 1984; Fazio et al, 1977; Jones, 1990).

Applying principles of cognitive dissonance to organisational change, it can be seen that, if an organisation embarks on a change project that is decisively out of step with the attitudes of those concerned, it will meet with resistance unless those concerned change their attitudes. On the other hand, where the level of dissonance occasioned by proposed changes is low, attitudinal adjustments will be minor and potential resistance negligible. Therefore, the level and type of involvement should be geared to the level of dissonance that any proposed changes may provoke.

Up to this point, cognitive dissonance supports the work of Schmuck and Miles (1971) and Huse (1980). However, if we apply the theory to situations, such as Oticon's, where old certainties proved inadequate and the very survival of the organisation is at stake, a different picture emerges. The crisis (or potential crisis) raises the level of dissonance in the organisation as it becomes apparent that existing practices are no longer viable and change is required. Not only does this make individuals and groups more receptive to radical change, but, in addition, change can be one of the main ways of reducing dissonance. At Oticon, fundamental attitudinal change was achieved relatively quickly because management and employees recognised the need for major change and saw the new vision as their only hope for the company's survival. Arguably, this was the reason why the new vision met with so little resistance at Marconi. Therefore, in such instances, the dissonance is occasioned not by the change, but by the condition of the organisation leading up to the change. This perspective also helps to explain cases, such as Rover–TRW, GK and UTL, where, initially, managers and others were resistant to changes or were only prepared to move slowly. In such situations, the absence of a sense of deep crisis prevents existing certainties being successfully challenged. Only when more severe threats arise are these old certainties challenged, and those involved become more prepared to accept and promote radical solutions that had previously been rejected.

A similar and complementary explanation for the involvement or non-involvement of employees is offered by the notion of the psychological contract. Though this concept has been around since the 1950s (*see* for example Argyris, 1960), it was only in the 1980s and 1990s that it became widely used by organisation theorists, especially in America (Arnold *et al*, 1998). As Schein (1988: 22–3) explains:

> The notion of a psychological contract implies that there is an unwritten set of expectations operating at all times between every member of an organization and the various managers and others in that organization. ... The psychological contract implies further that each role player, that is, employee, also has expectations about such things as salary or pay rate, working hours, benefits and privileges ... and so on. Many of these expectations are implicit and involve the person's sense of dignity and worth. ... Some of the strongest feelings leading to labor unrest, strikes, and employee turnover have to do with violations of these aspects of the psychological contract, even though the public negotiations are often over the more explicit issues of pay, working hours, job security, and so on.

We can certainly see why the employees of the PPC, who had joined a public sector organisation with a public sector ethos, might feel as though their psychological contract had been violated when they were suddenly told they were to be transferred to the private sector – particularly as the change represented a considerable threat to their job security. However, why was there not a more adverse reaction from XYZ's staff or GK's employees? The reason offered by proponents of the psychological contract would be that they recognised the need and justification for the changes and therefore the legitimacy of the need to change their psychological contracts.

Consequently, in understanding the employee involvement/non-involvement question, we need to draw on the complementary ideas of levels of involvement, cognitive dissonance and the psychological contract. What these show us is that in many cases where change is proposed, it is necessary to convince staff, through a process of constructive engagement, of the need to challenge their existing beliefs, behaviours and expectations and to renegotiate their 'contracts' with the organisation. However, this questioning of beliefs, behaviours and expectations can also arise in situations of crisis without the need for elaborate involvement techniques, because those concerned can see that the old attitudes and ways of behaving have had their day and, unless major or radical changes are made, their jobs or even the entire organisation may cease to exist.

Having addressed the issue of employee involvement and organisational transformation, we can now move on to present the conclusions drawn from the analysis of the case studies.

Conclusions: merging theory and practice

One should be wary of drawing any firm conclusions about either theory or practice from such a small number of case studies. However, the case studies presented in Part 3 do illustrate a range of change situations, are rich in detail, cover an extended time period, and do raise some important issues that it would be unwise to ignore. These are as follows.

Strategy

Though in some cases this was driven by a clear vision, more often it was triggered by perceived opportunities, problems or crises. The actual form of each organisation's strategy emerged from attempts to pursue visions or respond to events. In addition, we should note that there were instances where senior managers, individually or collectively, tried to reinvent their organisations. Whether we refer to this as creating a vision, as the Japanese might, or trying to impose a new reality, as the postmodernists might, is perhaps irrelevant. What is important is that some managers, as the Oticon and XYZ cases show, do have the will and the ability to reshape their organisations and to overcome or modify the constraints they face. However, it is also important to note, as the Marconi example shows, that a vision by itself is not enough. The vision needs to be achievable, though managerial judgement and competence are required to construct an achievable vision. Managers also need the skills to implement the vision and, most importantly, to ensure that the constraints they face can be modified or overcome.

Constraints

As one might expect, the case studies reveal that external and internal constraints do affect the degree of choice managers have or perceive themselves to have. In addition, the case studies show that managers respond to constraints in a variety of ways. In some instances, such as the PPC and PoliceCo, managers take action to change their organisations to accommodate external demands and constraints. In other instances, such as Volvo, Marconi, XYZ and Speedy, managers sought to influence or change the constraints they faced to suit their personal preferences and beliefs. The case studies also show that whilst some constraints appear to be amenable to change or influence, others, such as those faced by Marconi and PoliceCo, were much more resistant. Interestingly, in terms of internal constraints, despite what many writers believed, overtly political behaviour did not feature in most of the case studies, though there were some power struggles and some political battles. There are a number of possible explanations as to why politics did not appear to play a more significant role in most of these cases. These include the presence of dominant individuals or coalitions, the widely-recognised need for change in some of the organisations, which gave legitimacy to managerial initiatives, and the openness and transparency of the change process, which was especially the case in XYZ.

Managerial behaviour

In most of the instances examined, managers played a central role in initiating or developing visions and strategies. The exceptions were the music industry study and PoliceCo. In the former, music industry executives still seem unsure how to proceed in the new world of the Internet, and in the latter, PoliceCo are treating outsourcing as an administrative task rather than a strategic issue. With the exception of these two cases, managers played a leading role in implementing strategies or attempting to create the conditions for their implementation. In some cases they also led change projects. There were, though, instances, as with GK, where managers had to change their behaviour or managerial style in order to achieve successful change. In addition, there were instances where one of the strategic objectives was to change managerial behaviour, such as in XYZ. One crucial point to note is that successful change does not appear to be related to a change of manager. Oticon changed CEOs and successfully changed; GEC/Marconi changed Managing Directors and failed miserably; whereas GK and Volvo kept their existing Managing Directors and still achieved successful change. Therefore, for an organisation in trouble, though changing senior managers may be an easy option, it may not always be a successful one.

Managing change

A variety of approaches to change management can be seen in the case studies. These range from instances where all the major decisions were taken by one manager, to others where staff in the areas concerned led and planned change projects. The general tendency was for managers to involve employees in planning and implementing smaller, more short-term projects, often of a technical nature, and in some cases even to devolve such responsibility to them. Larger, more strategic and longer-term projects, though, especially those concerned with attitudinal or behavioural change, were very much initiated and under the control of senior managers. However, as the XYZ example showed, this does not mean that there cannot also be widespread managerial and employee involvement.

Planned, Emergent or combined change

Once again, the picture is mixed. Longer-term and larger projects were usually open-ended, with diffuse objectives, and involved large numbers of people; whereas smaller projects, where clearer objectives could be set, were inclined to be more tightly controlled and, in some instances, aligned more with the Planned approach to change. However, others appeared to be undertaken in a more directive and Tayloristic fashion. Perhaps the main distinction was between those projects aiming to change attitudes and behaviour, which in general tended to be more participative and flexible, and those concentrating on structural or technical change, especially at the operational level, which tended to have clearer objectives and required more fixed timescales. Nevertheless, some organisations appeared to use a combination of approaches to change consciously and appropriately, e.g. XYZ, whilst others, such as GK, tried a variety of different approaches, though not always consciously, appropriately or successfully. Yet again, some of the other organisations tried to stick to one approach to change even where it did not appear to be working, e.g. Marconi.

Underpinning the case study companies' preferences as far as change is concerned appear to be two dominant factors. The first concerns their preferred or dominant style of management. The use of a combination of change approaches seems to have been more prevalent and successful in those companies where there was, or there developed, a participative style of management. An example is XYZ, who favoured working cooperatively both internally and externally. This explains not only their wish to develop team working internally, but also their commitment to developing a partnership approach to working with their customers. Though XYZ's approach to changing its organisational structure can be seen as an example of Planned change, this needs to be seen within XYZ's overall style, which favoured the Emergent approach and which promoted employee involvement and learning. In the cases of the PPC and PoliceCo, on the other hand, managers preferred a much more command-and-control, top-down approach with little involvement from staff. Therefore, their dominant approach to change was mechanistic and directive. Oticon and Volvo, though, represent different aspects of managerial style again. In these instances, managers set out to change the dominant managerial style of their companies. Initially, in all the companies, managers began to make these changes by imposition rather than through employee involvement. Nevertheless, over time, more quickly in some cases than others, as the changes began to work, a more participative form of management emerged and there was less need for changes to be imposed from above instead of emerging from below. Therefore, what we can see is that a variety and combination of approaches to change were used by the more successful companies.

The second factor concerns the degree to which organisational change was seen as a series of one-off events, or a continuous process. In some of the companies, e.g. GK, each change project arose and was dealt with on its own merit. Indeed, at GK, each new project seemed to involve reinventing the wheel as far as choosing an approach to change was concerned. Consequently, and not surprisingly, there were a number of false starts before an effective approach was chosen. In other companies, however, e.g. XYZ, where change was considered as – or became – the norm, a battery of approaches, tools and techniques were developed that could be used as and when appropriate.

Therefore, if we take these two factors together, participative managerial style and the need to see change as a continuous process, they not only account for the successful use of a combination of change techniques but also for the successful outcome to change projects.

Objectives

A variety of objectives could be discerned, ranging from localised structural change to organisation-wide cultural change. In most of the cases, however, either at the outset or over time, changes to the behaviour and attitudes of individuals and groups came to be considered as more important than either technical or structural adjustments.

Therefore, we can see that, depending on the circumstances or constraints, strategy development and change management can take many forms. In the case studies, there are examples of deliberate and conscious attempts to shape strategy as well as more unconscious and accidental approaches. We can also see cases where an organisation's strategy or change programme, by design or accident, resulted in the reshaping or realignment of the constraints the organisation faced. In terms of change management, there were cases where the process of change and the process of strategy development, because of their emergent nature, coincided. However, there were also cases where Planned change followed on from and was determined by a pre-set strategy.

In conclusion, the case studies illustrate the arguments regarding managerial choice, strategy and change developed in Part 1 and Part 2. They show that whilst the Planned and Emergent approaches to change are important, they are not the be-all and end-all of change, or even mutually exclusive. The case studies also show that managers can exercise a high degree of choice about what to change, when to change it and how to change it. They also show that real and considerable constraints on an organisation's freedom of action do exist, as in Marconi and PoliceCo, which may be beyond the managers' power to change or even mitigate. In addition, it can be seen that where decisions are taken in an open manner, when those concerned are genuinely listened to and involved, and where serious attempts are made to identify and resolve reservations and resistance, there is less likelihood that political behaviour, individual interests or bias will be able to subvert the process.

Having now reviewed the ten case studies in the light of Parts 1–3, the next chapter will present the Choice Management–Change Management model for strategy development and organisational change.

Test your learning

Short answer questions

1   In what way does the Music Industry study support the case for adopting a complexity approach to organisations?

2   What are the main implications for vision-building and strategy development that can be drawn from the Marconi study?

3   What are the key lessons that other companies can learn from the way the relationship between Rover and TRW developed?

4   In what way can it be said that Speedy Stationers failed to overcome the constraints it faced?

5 List three of the main differences between the behaviour of senior managers within Oticon and the behaviour of senior managers in the PPC.

6 What lessons can be learned by comparing change management at XYZ with that at GK?

7 Discuss the case for seeing Volvo as an example of combined change.

8 What did Huse (1980) mean by the 'depth' of intervention?

9 What is cognitive dissonance?

10 What is a psychological contract?

Essay questions

1 Given that its initial approach to change was somewhat autocratic, explain the level of cooperation and commitment which Oticon received from its staff.

2 Compare and contrast the different approaches of Speedy and PoliceCo to outsourcing.

3 What advice would you offer to the big record labels for coping with the changes being brought about by the Internet?

Chapter 15

Organisational change and managerial choice

Learning objectives

After studying this chapter, you should be able to:

- understand the rationale underlying the Choice Management–Change Management model;
- discuss the three organisational processes which make up the Choice–Change model;
- describe how organisations can manage change effectively;
- identify the range of choices that organisations have when considering change;
- appreciate how organisations can influence their circumstances to align them with their preferred way of working;
- understand the need for managers to play a proactive role in the change process.

Introduction

From Chapter 14, we can see that whilst organisational change can be a complex, ambiguous and open-ended phenomenon, it can also be relatively straightforward with understandable and limited objectives. This in itself is not a new or radical finding – anyone who works in or studies organisations will have noted that change comes in a wide variety of shapes and sizes. It was argued in Chapter 10, however, that in order to cope with the wide variety of types of change, there is a need for a corresponding variety of approaches to strategy development and change management.

This point, the need to match types of change with appropriate approaches to managing change, is not as prominent in the literature on organisational change and behaviour as one might expect. As Part 2 showed, despite the widespread influence of Contingency Theory, the majority of writers and practitioners are committed to a 'one best way' approach to strategy and change. The call by Dunphy and Stace (1993) for a situational or contextual approach to these issues has still been taken up by few others. Though there are writers on strategy, such as Mintzberg *et al* (1998a) and Whittington (1993), who identify the various approaches to strategy, in most cases they tend, eventually, to opt for one as their preferred approach. This is even more pronounced in the change literature, where there is a clear distinction between those who support the Planned approach (such as Cummings and Worley, 1997; French and Bell, 1995) and those who adhere to a more Emergent approach (such as Kotter, 1996; Pettigrew, 1997; Weick, 2000; Wilson, 1992).

Many of those arguing for their own favoured approach to strategy and change do so, either explicitly or implicitly, on the basis of their perception of the nature of the environment in which organisations operate. Those arguing for a Planned approach to strategy and/or change appear to assume that the environment is relatively stable and predictable. Those who take a more Emergent approach to both seem to operate on the assumption that the environment is turbulent and unpredictable.

Furthermore, most writers seem to assume that the principal role of managers and the ultimate objective of strategy and change is to align or realign an organisation with its environment. In the preceding chapters, a case has been built for rejecting this argument and adopting a different stance. Rather than accepting the view that managers are prisoners of the circumstances in which their organisations operate or find themselves, it was argued that managers can and do exercise a considerable degree of choice. It was further argued, however, that the scope and nature of the choices managers face and make are constrained by a range of external factors (national characteristics, the business environment and industry norms) and internal organisational characteristics (especially structure, culture, politics and managerial style). This argument goes much further than many by challenging the assumption that managers are in some way the passive agents of forces beyond their control, but it still leaves them as prisoners of circumstances – although the prison in this case is much roomier than many of the writers we have discussed would acknowledge.

The arguments in Chapters 5, 6 and 10 challenged even this definition of managerial choice, however. It was suggested that many of the constraints on choice are themselves amenable to managerial actions – in effect, organisations can influence or change the constraints under which they operate. This possibility was first suggested when examining Contingency Theory in Chapter 2; it was further developed in subsequent chapters and shown to be more than a possibility. In particular, some managers are even capable of reinventing their organisations or, as the postmodernists would have it, creating a more preferable reality for them. The ten case studies in Part 3 reveal that, though organisations do try to align and realign themselves with their environment, they also attempt to influence and restructure the environment and other constraints in their favour. Sometimes, by accident or design, this results in a reconfiguration of the accepted rules by which the industry in which they operate competes; whilst in other instances, it prevents organisations being forced to undertake more radical internal upheavals.

In the case of Oticon (Chapter 11), it can be seen that the company deliberately set out to change the basis on which it competed by reinventing itself as a service-based rather than a technology-driven organisation. Lacking the technological strength of its competitors, which was the accepted cornerstone of competition in its industry, it proposed to offer a superior level of service instead. By changing the rules of the game in its industry, Oticon hoped to steal a march on its competitors. In the case of XYZ, the new Managing Director sought to change the internal constraints in the company, in terms of its culture, management style and structure, in order to improve its performance and align it with the changing nature of the construction industry and the desires of its parent company. In essence, the new Managing Director was attempting to reinvent the company, based on more cooperative internal relationships, in order to create more stable relationships with customers and establish a less uncertain external environment.

So, as the case studies show, organisations can and do influence and change the constraints under which they operate. On the other hand, though, the case studies give some support to those, such as proponents of the realist perspective discussed in Chapter 4, that there are some types of constraint that are not amenable to change. This can be seen from the Marconi example, where no amount of effort on behalf of its management could alter the situation that they had borrowed too much money to buy overpriced assets at the top of the dotcom boom that, when the demand for telecoms equipment went into freefall, were found to be virtually worthless. Similarly, though PoliceCo might have had more room for manoeuvre than they used, there was no way that they could change the basic situation that they were forced by government legislation to outsource activities and that this had to be undertaken in a prescribed manner.

Therefore, we can see that organisations do have considerable scope for changing or influencing the constraints they face but that, despite what the postmodernists may claim, there are some constraints that appear beyond the scope of individual organisations or, in the case of the record companies, even entire industries to change. Nevertheless, this still leaves most organisations with considerably more freedom of choice than many commentators on strategy and change would acknowledge. The implications of this wider perspective on managerial choice for the nature and focus of change management are, as the above shows, significant. Change management need not be seen as a mechanism for achieving a specified and predicted outcome (the Planned approach). Nor need it be conceived of as a continuing process of aligning and realigning the organisation with its environment (the Emergent approach). Instead, as this chapter will show, by linking managerial choice to the management of change, organisations can open up a much wider spectrum of options. These range from focusing on achieving radical internal change to align an organisation with its external constraints, doing the same in an attempt to restructure such constraints, to influencing or changing external constraints in order to avoid internal upheavals. In such a situation, not only are managers trying to make sense of their situation for themselves and others, but they are also seeking to construct a more favourable environment as well.

Building on this insight into managerial choice, the next section in this chapter will present an overview of the Choice Management–Change Management model for understanding and implementing organisational change. This is followed by a detailed description of the three components of the model: the choice process, the trajectory process, and the change process. The chapter concludes by maintaining that though organisations may choose to restructure their internal operations and practices in order to align them with the external circumstances they face, they can also choose to change or modify external and internal conditions and constraints in order to avoid extensive internal upheaval and/or to bring the constraints into line with their preferred *modus operandi.* Whatever choices are made, it is the role of managers consciously to explore and identify all the available options, however improbable they seem, rather than assuming that they have no, or only limited, choice in the matter.

The Choice Management–Change Management model

As the Choice Management–Change Management model in Figure 15.1 shows, organisational change can be viewed as the product of three interdependent organisational processes:

- **The choice process** – which is concerned with the nature, scope and focus of organisational decision-making.
- **The trajectory process** – which relates to an organisation's past and future direction and is seen as the outcome of its vision, purpose and future objectives.
- **The change process** – which covers approaches to, mechanisms for achieving, and outcomes of change.

These processes are interdependent because, as Figure 15.1 shows, the change process is itself an integral part of the trajectory process and this, in turn, is a vital part of the choice process. Within each of these processes there are a group of elements, or forces, which interact, clash with and influence each other in subtle and complex ways. It is this interaction of elements or forces which prevents decision-making and

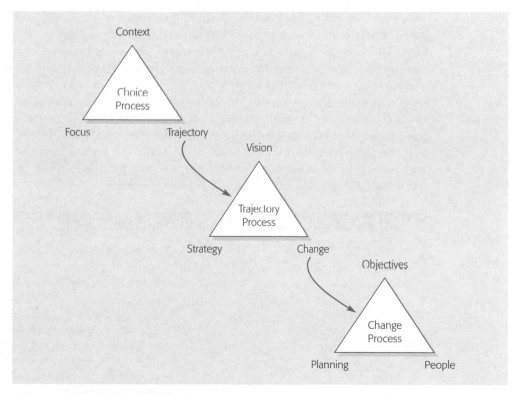

Figure 15.1 **The Choice Management–Change Management model**

change management from being a totally, or even predominantly, rational-mechanical process, and ensures that they are based on subjective and imperfect judgment.

Each of these three processes will now be described, not only to show their complexity and interdependence, but also to provide a guide to putting the Choice Management–Change Management model into practice. For this latter reason, the description of the change process, in particular, will dwell on the steps necessary to accomplish change successfully.

The choice process

The choice process comprises three elements:

- Organisational context
- Focus of choice
- Organisational trajectory

Organisational context

One of the standard prescriptions for successful organisations is that they should know their own strengths and weaknesses, their customers' needs and the nature of the environment in which they operate. As the case studies show, however, many organisations appear only to begin collecting this sort of information when they are in trouble. Yet how can organisations hope to understand and appreciate the options open to them unless they develop mechanisms for collecting and analysing information on their performance and general situation?

No one would suggest that assembling information on past, present and anticipated future performance is easy or that understanding the nature of the constraints faced by an organisation is simple. However, there are relatively well-established methods for benchmarking an organisation's performance against a range of internal and external comparators (Camp, 1989). There are also a number of tried-and-tested tools that organisations can use for gathering information on and evaluating the main internal constraints, such as structure, culture, politics and management style, and the main external constraints, such as national characteristics, industry and sector norms, and the business environment. Exhibits 15.1 and 15.2 show two of the tools most widely used by organisations for this purpose, the SWOT analysis and the PESTEL framework (Johnson and Scholes, 2002; Lynch, 1997).

Exhibit 15.1   SWOT analysis

What is a SWOT analysis?

SWOT stands for :

Strengths (internal)
Weaknesses (internal)
Opportunities (external)
Threats (external)

What does it do?

A SWOT analysis enables managers to identify the key internal and external issues they need to take into account in order to understand the context in which the organisation operates. Also, by identifying key issues, it begins to focus managers on the areas where they need to make choices, and helps to identify some of the constraints and risks involved.

Exhibit 15.2	PESTEL framework

What is the PESTEL framework?

PESTEL stands for:

Political
Economic
Sociocultural
Technological
Environmental
Legal

What does it do?

The PESTEL framework is a rigorous approach to identifying and understanding the main external environmental factors which affect an organisation. As with the SWOT analysis, it also plays a role in focusing organisations on the choices open to them and the constraints and risks involved in these choices.

As in the XYZ case study, one advantage of adopting such well-understood tools, which are easily explained and do not require expert assistance, is that organisations can use them to promote openness and reduce, though probably not eliminate, political behaviour and conflict. Nevertheless, some organisations will find that owing to the context in which they operate, teamwork, cooperation and openness are very difficult to achieve without first changing those factors which hinder or prevent these. Perhaps the prime consideration in this respect is the prevalent style of management. The issue of management style will be covered in Chapter 16; however, as Exhibit 15.3 shows, different styles of management can have significantly different implications for the way managers see, run and change their organisations.

Exhibit 15.3	Styles of management

Strengths	Weaknesses
Traditionalist management	
■ Practical common sense	■ Makes snap decisions
■ Attentive to facts	■ Lacks responsibility for change
■ Systems focus	■ Poor at relationships
■ Steady worker	■ Concerned with difficulties
■ Super dependable	
■ Realistic about time scales	
Catalyst management	
■ Charisma and commitment to staff	■ Can be drawn into pleasing others
■ Communicates well	■ Has difficulties with rules and conventions
■ Comfortable with changing environment	■ May spend too long on issues
■ Comfortable with diversity	■ Takes over problems and responsibilities
Visionary management	
■ Strong on intellectual vision	■ May be insensitive to others
■ Creative and progressive	■ Devalues others who are not intellectual
■ Enjoys problem solving	■ Expects too much of people
■ Outspoken	■ Restless and easily bored

Source: from Maddock (1999:40), based on Vinnecombe (1987)

Though others can exert pressure, managers are really the only group who can initiate change and will rarely (as a group) voluntarily adopt changes which adversely affect them. It follows that, faced with a mismatch between their organisation and its environment, some managers will seek to achieve realignment by influencing the environment rather than pursuing an internal upheaval that may involve changes in management style and personnel.

An organisation's management style will also influence how and by whom information is gathered and discussed. If an accurate picture of an organisation's context is to be constructed, it will require the involvement of a wide range of people. Not only should this provide a robust basis for decision-making, it can also develop a sense of teamwork, cooperation and mutual understanding amongst those concerned. If only a few managers are involved, however, it is likely to result in a skewed and biased picture of the organisation. Nevertheless, it should also be recognised that no matter how rigorously information is collected, analysed and argued over, there will always be a large element of subjectivity in this process. This is why, as a number of writers have commented, one of the key tasks managers perform is 'sensemaking' (Weick, 1995). As Weick (1995: 13) commented:

> ... sensemaking is about the ways people generate what they interpret. Jury deliberations, for example, result in a verdict. Once jurors have that verdict in hand, they look back to construct a plausible account of how they got there.

For managers in organisations, sensemaking is about understanding, interpreting and explaining, making sense of, their organisation's world for themselves and others in such a way that it provides a rationale and justification for past, present and future actions. Sensemaking is also the process by which managers attempt or can attempt to impose their view of reality on others. The Oticon case is a prime example of where a CEO first made sense of the world for himself and then imposed this sense on others in such a way that it allowed the organisation to move successfully forward. Marconi is another example where a senior manager attempted to impose his 'sense' on others in order to justify and guide actions. In this case, however, the outcome was far from successful.

Focus of choice

Many organisations can find themselves in a situation where they appear to be constantly reacting to events and indulging in 'fire-fighting' rather than being proactive. Certainly, this seems to be the current position in the music industry. One of the benefits of sensemaking, as successful organisations show, is that it allows managers to identify and focus their attention on the narrow range of short-, medium- and long-term issues that are generally agreed to be crucial to the organisation's success. Some of these will relate to the organisation's performance, whilst others may be more concerned with building or developing particular competences or technologies. In some cases, the issues may be of passing interest only, whilst in other cases they may be fundamental to the organisation's survival. Certainly, in most instances, organisations will in one way or another focus on aligning themselves with or even influencing or changing the constraints under which they operate.

How an organisation decides upon which issues to focus, and whether this is done in a concerted way (as at XYZ), or in a way which allows different groups and individuals to pursue their own agenda, is a fundamental factor in any organisation's decision-making process. Certainly, the received wisdom is that a concerted and coordinated approach, which focuses upon a small number of issues at any one time, is more effective than a fragmented one (Kay, 1993; Senge, 1990). It is interesting to note that Weick (1995) appears to consider the Japanese approach to decision-making as an example of sensemaking in action. This may explain why Japanese organisations are particularly good at identifying the key aspects of their strategy on which they need to focus. The particular technique they use is called *Hoshin Kanri* (*see* Exhibit 15.4). *Hoshin Kanri*, or Policy Deployment as it is often termed in the West, was developed in Japan to communicate a company's policy, goals and objectives throughout its hierarchy in a structured and consistent fashion (Lee and Dale, 2003). Its main benefit is that it focuses attention on key activities for success. It is a process that is undertaken annually to ensure that everyone on the company is conscious of and addressing the same objectives and that these inform actions and decision-making at all levels in the organisation (Akao, 1991).

Exhibit 15.4	*Hoshin Kanri*

The word hoshin can be broken into two parts. The literal translation of *ho* is *direction*. The literal translation of *shin* is *needle*, so the word hoshin could translate into *direction needle* or the English equivalent of *compass*. The word kanri can also be broken into two parts. The first part, *kan*, translates into control or channeling. The second part, *ri*, translates into reason or logic. Taken altogether, hoshin kanri means management and control of the organization's direction needle or focus.

Source: Total Quality Engineering Inc (2003)

Organisational trajectory

An organisation's trajectory or direction is shaped by its past actions and future objectives and strategies. As such it provides a guide or framework within which to judge the acceptability, relevance or urgency of issues, concerns and proposed actions. The trajectory process encompasses the determination of and interplay between an organisation's vision, strategies and approach to change. This can be seen from Volvo's strong commitment to Job Design, which has arisen from the interplay of events over more than 30 years. Any attempt by Ford to reverse this commitment would surely face strong opposition at all levels in Volvo.

Nevertheless, the concept of trajectory comprises not only an organisation's 'memory' of past events but also its intent in terms of future ones. For some organisations, such as Volvo with its commitment to Job Design, the trajectory will be clear and unambiguous, unless there is some major disturbance which throws into question past practice. In others, making sense of past events and agreeing proposals for future actions will be the subject of dispute and uncertainty. Certainly, since its crash, one might assume that there has been much rewriting of history in the Marconi boardroom, especially with regard to the supposed failure of GEC and the attractiveness of telecoms. In the light of the reappraisal of its past, one might also assume that Marconi would be faced with serious disagreements about how it should proceed in the future; if it cannot go back to the days of GEC, and if becoming a telecoms giant is no longer viable, where does it go?

It will also be the case that some organisations will deliberately and consciously attempt to plot their trajectory in minute detail, such as PoliceCo, whilst others, such as Oticon, may adopt a more global and distant set of objectives from which their trajectory emerges. Whatever the approach, as Mintzberg (1994: 25) observes:

> ... few, if any, strategies can be purely deliberate, and few can be purely emergent. One suggests no learning, the other, no control. All real-world strategies need to mix these in some way – to attempt to control without stopping the learning.

Therefore, an organisation's trajectory can be seen as a blend of, or clash between, the deliberate and emergent elements of its strategy. Whether or not this blend or clash produces the intended or expected outcomes for the organisation appears to depend partly on the quality of its sensemaking and partly on the degree of control it can exert, or chooses to exert, over events. Furthermore, as the case studies show, it is also dependent on an organisation's ability to learn from, deal with and take advantage of unexpected events as they emerge. For Oticon, TRW and above all Volvo, the ability to learn and successfully move on was crucial. For Marconi, the inability to do so was disastrous. Therefore, it is the interplay between the interpretation of past actions and future intent coupled to the ability of organisations to shape developing events to their advantage that makes decision-making so complex.

Each of the three elements of the choice process, context, focus and trajectory, is complex in itself, but they also interact with each other in an intricate and unpredictable way. An organisation's trajectory, whether it is seen as successful or not, can influence both the focus of its decision-making, and the context within which the organisation operates. Likewise, the context provides a framework within which the trajectory is developed. Similarly, the focus of choice will influence which aspect of the organisation's context its trajectory will be directed towards, not only in the short term but also in the medium and long term.

The case studies show that decision-making is a complex and multifaceted process. One reason for this is the type of decisions that have to be addressed when organisations deal with major questions. Decisions can be classed on a spectrum that runs from 'bounded' to 'unbounded'. Bounded decisions are usually small, have relatively easily-defined parameters, and tend to be relatively separable from the environment or context in which they arise. Unbounded decisions usually concern large and important issues, have difficult-to-define parameters, are ambiguous and are intertwined with other issues and factors in the environment or context in which they arise (Rollinson, 2002). Obviously, most, if not all, of the major strategic issues an organisation has to address tend to lie at the unbounded rather than bounded end of the spectrum. Given the unbounded nature of such decisions, it is not surprising, as models of decision-making described in Exhibit 15.5 show, that managers tend to adopt a less rational and more haphazard approach to decision-making than they themselves would often openly acknowledge. However, as the case studies revealed, and as writers have pointed out for many years, there is a tendency for managers to 'muddle through' rather than attempt an exhaustive and exhausting examination of all the available options (Lindblom, 1968). Nor is it surprising that some managers prefer 'fire-fighting' to tackling fundamental issues (Burnes, 1991) – at least the objective is immediate and clear, and a favourable outcome can be achieved (though it is usually short-lived).

Exhibit 15.5	Decision-making models

Model	Assumptions
The Rational Choice model of decision-making	■ Decision-makers have knowledge of all possible alternative solutions. ■ They have complete knowledge of the consequences of all these alternatives. ■ They have a robust set of criteria for evaluating these alternatives. ■ They have unlimited resources, including time, money and abilities. ■ They follow a systematic and orderly sequence of decision steps.
The Bounded Rationality model of decision-making	■ Decision-makers do not have complete knowledge. They rely on hunches and intuition. ■ Decision-makers do not have fixed and consistent preferences. ■ Decision-makers do not have unlimited resources. ■ An optimal solution may not exist or even be necessary. ■ Decision-makers do not optimise or seek a solution that maximises the expected benefits. ■ They 'satisfice' – they seek a solution or decision option which is 'good enough' rather than ideal. ■ They do follow a systematic and orderly sequence of steps.
The Garbage Can model of decision-making	■ Decisions involve four elements: problems, solutions, participants and choice opportunities. ■ Some decisions will only be made when all four elements come together. ■ Political motives can lead to these elements being manipulated. ■ Decision-making is volume-sensitive – managers cannot be everywhere at once or deal with all issues at once. ■ As the number of problems increase, decision opportunities decrease. ■ Novel problems are likely to attract more attention than mundane ones. ■ Decision-makers do not follow an orderly sequence of steps. ■ Chance plays a large part in what decisions get made and when.

Source: adapted from Rollinson (2002)

Appreciating the complexity of decision-making also casts the Japanese *ringi* system (discussed in Chapter 3) in a favourable light. Only by an exhaustive analysis of the issue concerned and the options available is the most appropriate decision likely to be arrived at. Moreover, the *ringi* system is usually aided by and carried out within the framework of a strong corporate vision and clear strategies for its pursuit, which make it easier to identify which decisions and actions are appropriate. By embracing decisions within such a framework, Japanese companies ensure that they do not have to explore all the available possibilities when taking decisions – merely those that are in harmony with their vision/strategy/intent. In this way, the entire choice process is simplified and made more achievable. Japanese companies have shown themselves to be masters of developing visions and strategies that not only make them successful but also, and not incidentally, reduce the uncertainty in their environment, alter the basis of competition in their favour, and narrow the focus of decision-making (Hamel and Prahalad, 1989). The result is that though the choice process remains complex, not only does it have a greater degree of consistency between the elements and people involved, but it is also more focused in the range of issues and decisions required.

Therefore, what can be seen is that whilst the choice process is uncertain, complex and time-consuming, there are approaches that do reduce these factors and can make the process more transparent and effective. Nevertheless, the degree of transparency and the efficacy of the choice process is heavily influenced by an organisation's ability to turn choices into workable strategies and to turn strategies into successful actions. The success of these, in their turn, will influence future choices. In order to understand the choice process further, we shall now examine the trajectory process and then go on to examine the change process.

The trajectory process

Like the choice process, the trajectory process comprises three elements, namely vision, strategy and change.

Vision

As described in Chapter 7, many organisations now use scenario-building and 'visioning' techniques. The purpose of these techniques is to generate different organisational futures, or realities, in order to select the one that seems most favourable or appropriate. The ten case studies in Part 3 showed that not all companies have visions, not all visions find favour with the managers and employees who have to implement them, and not all visions lead to success. Nevertheless, the concept of organisations driving themselves forward by creating an ambitious vision (or intent or scenario) of where they wish to be in the long term has become increasingly influential over the last 15 years (Cummings and Worley, 2001; Johnson and Scholes, 2002; Mintzberg *et al*, 1998a & b), though it has also generated increasing levels of cynicism (Collins, 1998; Watson, 1994). The argument, in brief, for this approach is that previous attempts to plan the future have either fallen foul of the difficulty of accurately translating past trends into future projections, or have not been ambitious enough because they have allowed future plans to be constrained by present resources (Hamel and Prahalad, 1989). The process of developing an organisation's vision attempts to overcome this by encouraging senior managers to think freely, without considering present resource constraints, about possible futures for their organisation in the long term.

This can produce very ambitious objectives, such as Honda's declaration in the 1960s (when it was barely more than a motorcycle producer little known outside Japan) that it wanted 'to become the second Ford'. As the Marconi case study in Chapter 11 shows, however, the possession of an ambitious vision is, by itself, no guarantee of success, though the rigour with which a vision is developed may help to overcome or avoid some of the more obvious pitfalls. As Exhibit 15.6 shows, Cummings and Huse (1989) argue that visions comprise four elements: *mission*; *valued outcomes*; *valued conditions*; and *mid-point goals*.

Exhibit 15.6 Constructing a vision

The four elements of a vision

1. **Mission**. This states the organisation's major strategic purpose or reason for existing. It can indicate such factors as products, markets and core competencies.
2. **Valued outcomes**. Visions about desired futures often include specific performance and human outcomes the organisation would like to achieve. These can include types of behaviour and levels of skill as well as more traditional outcomes such as turnover and profit. These valued outcomes can serve as goals for the change process and standards for assessing progress.
3. **Valued conditions**. This element of creating a vision involves specifying what the organisation should look like to achieve the valued outcomes. These valued conditions help to define a desired future state towards which change activity should move. Valued conditions can include issues relating to structure, culture, openness and managerial style as well as external issues such as relations with customers and suppliers.
4. **Mid-point goals**. Mission and vision statements are by nature quite general and usually need to be fleshed out by identifying more concrete mid-point goals. These represent desirable organisational conditions but lie between the current state and the desired future state. Mid-point goals are clearer and more detailed than desired future states, and thus, they provide more concrete and manageable steps and benchmarks for change.

Source: Cummings and Huse (1989)

The creation of visions should be an iterative process whereby options are identified, an initial vision is created, and the gap between this and the present circumstances is identified. Then the organisation considers its strategic options to bridge the gap, and in so doing refines the vision itself. This refining process serves partly to ensure that the vision is discussed widely within the organisation, and to gain employees' commitment to its objectives, thus using the vision as a motivating and guiding force for the organisation. Over time, by this process of revisiting and refining the vision, loose and intangible ideas become transformed into achievable medium-term goals that people can relate to and pursue. The process can, and in some cases does, eventually encompass everyone in the organisation. Nevertheless, the vision is usually driven, not to say created by, a few senior managers who use the power of their position and strength of their personalities to get others to accept the vision as a beneficial and achievable reality.

The organisational vision can best be described as a beacon shining from a faraway hillside at night that guides travellers to their destination. Travellers can usually only see a few feet ahead but are prevented from getting lost by the beacon. Occasionally the traveller will have to make a detour, or sometimes even reverse course, but this is done in the certain knowledge that they still know where it is that they are travelling to. The concept of the beacon is a useful analogy, in that it highlights one of the main differences between vision-building and other forms of long-range planning. Normally it is only the leadership of an organisation that has a clear view of where the organisation is going in the long term. The vision, like the beacon, should shine clearly for everyone in the organisation to see, however, so that they can all know where they are heading for, and use it to judge the appropriateness of their actions.

By constructing a vision in this manner, the organisation not only has a picture of what it wishes to become but also some concrete targets to aim for. In the case of Oticon, (Chapter 11), its vision of becoming a knowledge-based organisation sprang from the mind of its CEO, Lars Kolind. However, to give it flesh and to be able to construct his 'disorganised organisation' required the involvement of everyone else in the organisation. It was an iterative process of trial and error. Above all, it was a process of experimentation. He and they knew how they wanted to operate, what they wanted to achieve, but the actual details had to be worked out. Kolind could also recognise when things were going wrong, however, and acted to 'explode the organisation' when he felt that it was becoming too rigid.

The Marconi vision, on the other hand, seemed both to start and end with two senior managers. The extent to which they required the commitment and understanding of others, as opposed to their compliance, appears to be small. Also, unlike Kolind, they seemed unable to adapt their strategy to save their vision. When the downturn in demand for telecoms equipment became evident to other companies, who took action to protect themselves, Marconi did not. Instead, it continued its strategy of selling profitable companies and borrowing money to buy ones which fitted its vision but whose viability declined with the decline in demand for telecoms equipment. The point is that visions (and components of visions such as Oticon's Statement of Fundamental Human Values) identify the intent, and mid-point goals are then needed to help identify a way forward. As the vision is implemented, these goals will periodically have to be renewed and revisited in the light of changing circumstances, usually within the context of the vision, as was the case with Oticon. As the Marconi example shows, however, the possibility always exists that changing circumstances, or the process of implementation, can raise serious questions about the viability of the vision itself. It is through the development of strategy that visions are implemented, brought to life and, if necessary, changed.

Strategy

In the context of a vision, strategy can be defined as a coherent or consistent stream of actions which an organisation takes or has taken to move towards its vision. This stream of actions can be centrally planned and driven, they can be delegated and distributed throughout the organisation, and they can be either conscious actions in pursuit of the vision, or unconscious or emergent ones resulting from past patterns of decisions or resource allocations, or from current responses to problems and opportunities. In reality, an organisation's strategy tends to be a combination of, and be pursued through, a mixture of formal and informal plans and actions.

As Chapter 7 showed, formal strategies usually cover marketing, product development, manufacturing, personnel, purchasing, finance, information technology and quality. The characteristics of conscious strategies are that they generally look five years or more ahead, but only contain firm and detailed plans for the next 12 to 18 months (this is because changing circumstances usually prevent most companies from being firm about their intentions for any longer than this). These strategies are put together in one strategic plan that is, usually, formally reviewed annually, but is frequently reviewed informally and when major and unexpected events occur. Because the strategies are not ends in themselves, but means to an end (the vision), they are by necessity both flexible and pragmatic. They should be constructed and pursued only to the extent that they facilitate the pursuit of the vision. Indeed, even when their strategies appear to fail, the more successful organisations seem to have an innate ability to turn failure into success, as the Microsoft example in Exhibit 15.7 shows. Microsoft established MSN in 1995 in order to become an Internet content provider. It quickly saw that this was not where its core competences lay, but what it also saw was that MSN gave it a direct link to an enormous customer base. The original strategy of adding content provision to its software activities was abandoned in favour of a much more ambitious strategy of delivering its services over the Internet directly to customers, something on which Bill Gates says he has 'bet the company'. It is also something that contributes directly to Microsoft's vision of remaining the world's dominant software company.

Exhibit 15.7   The development of MSN

Microsoft's direct connection to the customer

Sometimes it seems that even when Microsoft loses, it wins. ... take MSN, the company's internet portal. This unit of Microsoft has lost money ever since it was set up ... But to Microsoft that does not really matter. The real point of MSN is not to make money at all. Instead, the division serves a peculiar mixture of purposes including research and development, testing the company's software, advertising its services and even product distribution. What is more, these capabilities set Microsoft apart from its rivals.

In the next phase of Microsoft's plans, its .Net vision, in which software becomes a service delivered over the internet – a vision on which Bill Gates admits he has 'bet the company' – the site will become even more vital. MSN is quietly emerging as the centrepiece of the whole .Net strategy. This is a far cry from the original MSN, named for the Microsoft Network. The website was initially set up as a media play in

1995, the early days of the dotcom boom. It produced content including news and sport, horoscopes, and e-commerce offers. For a while it looked as if Microsoft had serious ambitions in media ...

That phase did not last long. The career of Geoff Sutton, now Managing Director of MSN in the UK, illustrates the change of heart. Mr Sutton was originally brought into the company in 1997 to run a team of journalists writing news for the portal. In 1998, the news team was scrapped and Mr Sutton found himself working in a software company.

'It quickly became apparent that Microsoft shouldn't try to be a content player,' he says. Judy Gibbons, vice-president of MSN for EMEA, agrees: 'Microsoft is a software company, that's what we do, and we shouldn't stray away from our core competences.'

With its foray into content, however, Microsoft had managed to gather up something very useful: an

Exhibit 15.7 *continued*

audience. Through MSN, Microsoft found it had a direct line with consumers that it had never experienced before. People visited the site regularly, ... in the process being exposed to Microsoft branding and services.

Today, MSN is one of the world's top three internet destinations, along with yahoo and AOL, receiving some 270m visitors a month, while its Hotmail has 110m users.

Once this kind of connection with customers was in place, all kinds of things became possible. Microsoft could start marketing services to its customers direct. It could even start giving them software direct, over the internet.

This interactive and instant relationship with customers even gave Microsoft a testing ground for new software products, as people could be asked to download beta software, software still in the process of development, from the site for comments and suggestions.

The .Net strategy neatly takes advantage of all these aspects of Microsoft's portal. ... Users will plug

into a web of services running across a wide variety of devices, including PCs, handheld computers, phones, television sets, and even games consoles.

'MSN will provide the entry point for consumers to .Net services, as you will be able to go up to the site and sign on and get access to all the pieces you want,' says Ms Gibbons.

Microsoft estimates that the market for such services could run into trillions of dollars by 2010, in what it terms the 'digital decade'.

No other internet portal can yet offer anything similar. And no other software company boasts its own internet portal through which to dispense rival versions of these web services. The huge MSN user base forms a ready-made audience to which Microsoft can market its services with ease. The fact that all the visitors attracted to the portal by this range of services can be 'monetised' by charging advertisers to market them is just the icing on the cake. If MSN can reach break-even from these advertising dollars, so much the better, if not, it scarcely matters.

Source: Fiona Harvey, *Financial Times*, 31 December 2001, p. 7.

Therefore, in pursuit of its vision, an organisation can have a central strategy and a number of sub-strategies and, influenced by the vision and circumstances, a general awareness of the need to act or respond in a particular way to opportunities and threats, or successes and failures. From this perspective, one way of viewing strategy is to see it as a series of links in a chain which stretch from the present to the indeterminate future where the vision lies. Each link in the chain represents particular strategies or groups of decisions that organisations pursue to move themselves forward, in the light of both their eventual target and the prevailing circumstances of the time. The links (strategies) are continually having to be forged and reforged (to use Mintzberg's, 1987, term, 'crafted') over time as events develop and circumstances change. For Microsoft, MSN was a link forged for one purpose which became reforged for another purpose but with the same end in sight: to bolster Microsoft's dominance of the software market. So an organisation's strategy is likely to comprise both pre-defined and emergent elements – the exact balance being determined by the circumstances of the particular organisation in question rather than any intrinsic merit of either the planning or emergent approaches to strategy.

One final point: it follows from this that organisations do not need to be able to see all the links in the strategic chain: merely those that will guide them over the next few years. Nor do they need to dictate centrally or identify in detail what should be done and when. Instead, they need to establish both a climate of understanding and a general willingness to pursue certain courses of action, as the opportunity arises or circumstances necessitate. It is only when a course of action is pursued, however, that organisations begin to change and move towards their vision.

Change

Just as an organisation's trajectory is both an important element of the choice process and a process in its own right, the same applies to change. The change process will be discussed below, but in the context of the trajectory process it is necessary to note that, though visions and strategies can be crucial in shaping the life of organisations, it is only when some facet of the organisation is changed or changes that visions and strategies advance from being mere possibilities to become reality. This is also a two-way street. On the one hand, visions and strategies shape and direct change. They indicate what needs to change and where. They also create the conditions and climate within which change takes place. On the other hand, because visions and strategies only become reality through the actions of the organisation, it is these changes, these actions which shape visions and strategies.

In summary, we can see that the trajectory process, whilst playing a key role in shaping choice, is also itself a complex process comprising vision, strategy and change. Though it is difficult to conceive of any organisation that does not possess some elements of all three, the degree to which they are held in common or are consistent with each other or are part of a conscious effort clearly varies. Partly this relates to the circumstances of the organisation. Under conditions of stability and predictability, even without prompting from senior managers, it is much easier for people to develop a common view of how an organisation should operate, what its future should be and what changes need to be made. In rapidly-changing circumstances, however, where certainties and fixed points of reference are few and far between, a common understanding is unlikely to arise automatically. Where a common understanding does exist, in such situations, it is likely to be outmoded and inappropriate. This is why senior managers more and more are trying consciously to use visions to create a common cause. They want to reduce uncertainty, make sense of what is happening, and create a broad understanding of what needs doing, and how. For many organisations, the merit of this approach is not only that it makes change easier, but that it also allows staff to judge for themselves what changes need to be made and what approach to adopt. In order to explore this further, we can now examine the change process itself.

The change process

Change can be viewed as a one-off event, an exception to the normal running of an organisation and, therefore, something to be dealt on an issue-by-issue basis as it arises. On the other hand, some organisations see change not as an exception but as a norm, a continuous process that forms part of the organisation's day-to-day activities. As the case studies in Part 3 illustrated, where change is seen as the exception, such as in GK, organisations tend to have difficulty in choosing the most appropriate approach and there also tends to be no structured, or even informal, procedure for capturing the lessons from one change project and making them available for future projects. Each change is seen as a unique event, and seems to involve an element of reinventing the wheel as the organisation struggles to determine how best to deal with it. However, in organisations where change is seen as a continuous process, such as

Oticon, they appear to be able not only to treat each project as a learning opportunity, but to capture this learning and pass it on. This allows them to select the most appropriate approach for each situation. In such organisations, not only is change seen as an everyday event, but the management of it is also seen as a core capability that needs to be developed and in which all staff need to become competent.

The change process itself, like the choice and trajectory processes, comprises three interlinked elements:

- Objectives and outcomes
- Planning the change
- People

Objectives and outcomes

There is now much evidence and a general acceptance, at least amongst those studying it, that a high proportion of change efforts end in failure (Beer and Nohria, 2000; Burnes, 2003; Huczynski and Buchanan, 2001). Though there are numerous reasons for this, Burnes and Weekes (1989) found that, in many cases, change projects failed because their original objectives or desired outcomes were ill-thought-out and inconsistent. In addition, as noted in Chapter 5, organisational change, because it often affects the distribution of power and resources in an organisation, is an inherently political process which can be driven by sectional interests rather than organisational needs.

Though it is difficult to envisage a situation where political interests are not present, Burnes (1988) suggested an approach to assessing the need for and type of change that attempts to make the process of establishing objectives and outcomes more rigorous and open. Openness and rigour not only make it harder to disguise political considerations, they also allow assumptions regarding the merits (or lack of them) of particular options to be tested. Burnes' approach has four elements – the trigger, the remit, the assessment team and the assessment.

The trigger

Organisations should only investigate change (other than relatively minor projects that can be easily accommodated) for one of the following reasons:

- The company's vision/strategy highlights the need for change or improved performance.
- Current performance or operation indicates that severe problems or concerns exist.
- Suggestions or opportunities arise (either from the area concerned or elsewhere) that potentially offer significant benefits to the organisation.

If one or more of the above arises, then this should trigger the organisation to assess the case for change, which leads to the next phase.

The remit

This should state clearly the reasons for the assessment, its objectives and timescale, and who should be involved and consulted. The remit should stress the need to focus as much on the people aspects as the technical considerations involved. In addition, it must make clear that those who will carry out the assessment must look at all options rather than merely considering one or two alternatives. Organisations need to be clear who draws up such remits and who has the final say on the assessment team's recommendations. As was shown by Burnes and Weekes (1989), this responsibility is often unclear. In traditional organisations, this responsibility would lie with senior managers. In many of today's organisations, the responsibility for such activities is devolved. There is usually a requirement to inform senior managers of change, however, and certain types of major change remain the responsibility of senior managers. Also, where change affects more than one area or activity, coordination between areas will be essential. The important point is that there must be clarity and agreement about who has the responsibility and authority to initiate change before an assessment begins.

The assessment team

This is the body who will assess the need for change. In most cases, this should be a multi-disciplinary team consisting of representatives from the area affected (both managers and staff), specialist staff (e.g. finance, technical and personnel), and, where appropriate, a change specialist, either an internal facilitator or external consultant who is a specialist in organisational change. It may also require the involvement of senior managers.

The assessment

The first task of the assessment team is to review and if necessary clarify or amend its remit. Only then can it begin the assessment, which should comprise the following four steps:

1 **Clarification of the problem or opportunity**. This is achieved by gathering information, especially from those involved. In some situations it might be found that the problem or opportunity is redefined, or does not exist, or can be dealt with easily by those most closely concerned. If so, this is reported back and probably no further action needs to be taken. If the clarification reveals that a significant problem or opportunity does exist, however, then the remaining steps need to be completed.

2 **Investigate alternative solutions**. A wide-ranging examination should take place to establish the range of possible solutions. These should be tested against an agreed list of criteria covering costs and benefits, in order to eliminate those solutions that are clearly inapplicable and to highlight those that appear to offer the greatest benefit. Companies will usually seek to define benefits in monetary terms. It should be recognised, however, that not all changes, particularly those of a behavioural or strategic nature, can be assessed on purely financial criteria, e.g. Oticon's restructuring and XYZ's move to teamworking. In any case, changes rarely have single benefits. For example, a change in technology that brings financial benefits may also offer opportunities to increase teamworking and to develop the skill and knowledge base of the organisation. Therefore, organisations need to develop ways of defining and assessing non-monetary benefits. Also, where there are benefits there are usually disbenefits. Where new skills are gained, old ones are discarded. For example, a partnership approach to customer–supplier relations can lead to a loss of negotiating and bargaining skills; greater teamworking can undermine the authority of line managers and middle managers. If such disbenefits are to result from change, it is better to recognise this in advance and prepare for them rather than finding out later when the damage is done. This then leads on to the next step.

3 **Feedback**. The definition of the problem or opportunity and the range of possible solutions should be discussed with interested or affected parties, particularly those from whom information was collected in the first place. This helps to counter the tendency to fit solutions to problems, i.e. it makes it more difficult for people to promote their favoured solution regardless of its suitability. It also helps to prepare people for any changes that do take place. In addition, the response to feedback can provide an important source of information on the advantages and disadvantages of the possible solutions on offer and, thus, it helps to establish the criteria for selecting the preferred solution or solutions.

4 **Recommendations and decision**. The team should present their recommendations in a form that clearly defines the problem/opportunity, identifies the range of solutions, establishes the criteria for selection and makes recommendations. These recommendations should include not only the type of change, but also the mechanics and timescale for making such changes and the resource implications, as well as performance targets for the new operation.

This then leaves those responsible for making the final decision in a position to assess, modify, defer or reject the assessment team's recommendations in the light of the vision and strategic objectives of the organisation. Indeed, some change programmes and projects are so complex that it is only possible to judge their worth in relation to an organisation's long-term intent. For example, in the 1990s, one of the UK's largest biscuit makers established an assessment team to determine whether the company should build a new factory solely dedicated to the production of chocolate biscuits (the biggest growth area for the company). The team recommended that one should be built next door to an existing factory in the north of England. The Board accepted the recommendation for the new factory but decided, because of its long-term ambitions to develop in Europe, to locate the new factory in France. Though this decision could be justified as being in the long-term interests of the company, such decisions are more an act of faith than a racing certainty, though managers may choose to present them as closer to the latter in order to garner support. Nevertheless, if the decision is to proceed with the proposed changes, then it becomes necessary to begin planning the implementation process.

Planning the change

Whether the need for change arises from an organisation's strategy or emerges in some other way, once it has been established that it should take place and what form it should take, it is then necessary to plan how this will be achieved and then to implement the plan. As argued in Chapter 10, there are many different approaches to change, and their appropriateness depends on what is to be changed. As the case studies in Part 3 showed, small-scale and relatively technical or structural changes can usually be planned and executed relatively quickly, and may not require extensive consultation with or the involvement of all the staff affected. Similarly, changes which are isolated to one part of the organisation and seen as 'inevitable', may also be relatively straightforward, as was the case at PoliceCo. However, unless the need for radical change is already accepted, as it was at Oticon, it can be dangerous to adopt a rapid-change/low-involvement approach to larger-scale changes, particularly where people's attitudes and behaviours are the prime object of the change process. Therefore, as the XYZ case shows, planning and execution, and consequent development, in such cases can be extensive, span hierarchical levels and horizontal processes and include a high degree of ambiguity. For these reasons, the success of large-scale changes will depend, to a significant extent, on the involvement and commitment of all those concerned with and affected by them. The range of change situations and approaches, therefore, needs to be borne in mind when considering the following six interrelated activities that make up the planning and change process:

1 **Establishing a change management team**. To maintain continuity, the team should include some, if not all, of those responsible for the original assessment of the need for change. However, it will usually also have a greater user input, especially at the implementation stage. When the Labour government was first elected in the UK in 1997, the Inland Revenue was asked to undertake a review as to whether the Contributions Agency, then a semi-autonomous body, should become part of the Inland Revenue. The man who led the assessment team, and who recommended that the Contributions Agency should become part of the Inland Revenue, was also made responsible for leading the change management team. In the case of XYZ, all the original assessment team became members of the change management team, along with a much wider spectrum of middle and line managers. For large change projects, it is usual to establish sub-groups responsible for discrete elements of the change programme. These will generally comprise those most closely affected by the changes, both managers and others. Their role is to handle the day-to-day implementation issues. It must be recognised that all the people in the change management team, and its sub-groups, are in effect 'change agents'. Nevertheless, as was the case at XYZ, change specialists should also be involved, i.e. people whose primary input is their experience in managing change. As was discussed in Chapter 9, the role of change agents is not just a technical one concerned with establishing plans and ordering their implementation. Change agents need a wide range of skills, not least of which is what Buchanan and Boddy (1992: 27) refer to as the ability to deploy 'backstage activity':

> 'Backstaging' is concerned with the exercise of 'power skills', with 'intervening in political and cultural systems', with influencing and negotiating and selling, and with 'managing meaning'.

Change agents also need the ability to deal with the unexpected. 'Expect the unexpected' might well be the motto of most change agents. In discussing the role of change agents in Chapter 9, the article on 'Grace, magic and miracles' by Lichtenstein (1997) was cited. This showed that whilst a structured approach to change is necessary, it is often, by itself, not sufficient to ensure success. Success, Lichtenstein (1997: 393) argued, also requires change agents to have the ability and experience to recognise and take advantage of 'intuitive, unexpected, and serendipitous' situations. Therefore in choosing members of the change management team, it is necessary to have the right blend of skills for the change being undertaken, including the ability to deal with the unexpected.

2 **Management structures**. Because larger change projects, especially organisational transitions, are wide-ranging, have multiple objectives and can involve a high degree of uncertainty, existing control and reporting systems are unlikely to be adequate for managing them. For example, the more that a change project challenges existing power relations and resource allocation procedures, the more it is likely to

encounter managerial resistance. In such cases, unless the change management team has a direct line to, and the public support of, senior managers or the CEO, the change process is likely to become bogged down or even abandoned. For example, one of the main reasons why Regional Managers did not block the organisational changes at XYZ was because the Managing Director was closely involved in the change process. He was aware that the Regional Managers might try to block changes that threatened their interests and standing, and he was prepared to take action if they did so, and he made sure the Regional Managers knew this. Where senior managers are less directly involved, effective reporting and management structures need to be put in place in advance in order to provide direction, support, resources, and where necessary decisive interventions.

3 **Activity planning.** Beckhard and Harris (1987: 70–1) refer to this as a process of 'getting from here to there'. They state that: 'The activity plan is the road map for the change effort, so it is critical that it is realistic, effective and clear. Exhibit 15.8 describes Beckhard and Harris's five key characteristics of an effective activity plan. Activity planning involves constructing a schedule for the change programme, citing the main activities and events that must occur if the transition is to be successful. It must be recognised, however, that not all the elements of a large change programme can be planned in detail in advance. Such programmes are by their nature multi-level, multi-stage, can stretch over an extended time-frame, and can involve elements of backtracking and rethinking. However, as a change programme proceeds, it becomes possible for successive levels and stages to become clearer and for plans to become more detailed. It follows that, in order to stay on course, activity planning should clearly identify and integrate key change events and stages and ensure they are linked to the organisation's change goals and priorities. Activity planning should also gain top management approval, should be cost-effective, and should remain adaptable as feedback is received during the change process. Activity planning therefore comprises the final and intermediate objectives, and ensures that where and when possible these are tied to a specific timetable in order to avoid uncertainty amongst those who have to carry out the changes.

Exhibit 15.8	Activity planning

The five characteristics of an effective activity plan

- **Relevance** – activities are clearly linked to the change goals and priorities
- **Specificity** – activities are clearly identified rather than broadly generalized
- **Integration** – the parts are closely connected
- **Chronology** – there is a logical sequence of events
- **Adaptability** – there are contingency plans for adjusting to unexpected forces

Source: Beckhard and Harris (1987: 72)

4 **Commitment planning.** This activity involves identifying key people and groups whose commitment is needed, and deciding how to gain their support. Beckhard and Harris (1987: 92) observe that, '... in any complex change process, there is a

critical mass of individuals or groups whose active commitment is necessary to provide the energy for change to occur.' Designating someone as a key person is concerned less with their nominal position or level of authority in an organisation than with their ability to block or promote particular changes. This may be because they have power to dispense or withhold specific resources or information, or because, as Exhibit 15.9 shows, others look to them for guidance or leadership, even though they may have no formal role in this respect.

Exhibit 15.9	The importance of commitment

Getting rid of the bonus

Northern Engineering is a very efficient and progressive manufacturing company which has successfully introduced many Japanese techniques for improving its business. However, it did operate a shopfloor bonus system based on individual output. It recognised that this was detrimental to quality but felt that the workforce would strongly resist any effort to change it. Eventually though, the company decided it would offer the workforce a very tempting financial package to buy out the bonus. The Operations Director was the man responsible for selling the idea to the workforce. He did this through a series of presentations, to each of the company's three shifts.

The group he was most concerned about were the night shift. These were the people he seldom met and who had shown the least commitment to change in the past.

The Operations Director described his experience with the night shift:

They work ten while six, four nights a week. I went to brief them at the beginning of their shift. The presentation took about 20 minutes and then I opened it up for questions. All through my presentation, this big bloke on the front row had been staring at me with a disgruntled look on his face. When I finished he stood up and everybody looked at him in an expectant fashion. When he began talking, I thought, 'I'm sunk'. He said, 'It's the same as usual. You only see the bosses when they want to take something off you.' Others on the shift nodded in agreement at this. He then went on, 'Once they take the bonus off us, we won't get it back. Some might be OK, but others'll lose money. But, this is not a bad company, so I think we should give them a chance.' He sat down, nobody else said anything, and it was agreed, the bonus would go. I was totally flummoxed. The bloke's body language, his tone, his first words, all indicated that he was against it. I was very, very lucky; if he'd gone against the idea, I could see that everybody would have gone with him. What I learned that night was a very valuable lesson. The next time I have to talk to the night shift, I'll get hold of that bloke first and win him over.

The case of the PPC in Chapter 11 is an example of where the organisation does not appear to have recognised the importance of commitment planning, whereas the case of XYZ in Chapter 12 is an example of where the company recognised it needed to gain the commitment of key staff in planning and implementing change.

Exhibit 15.10 shows the main steps in developing a commitment plan. Beckhard and Harris (1987) note, however, that even where the commitment of an individual or group is necessary, it is not necessary to gain the same level of commitment from all. They identify three kinds of commitment:

Let it happen – i.e. do not obstruct the change.
Help it happen – i.e. participate in the change process.
Make it happen – i.e. drive the change.

Exhibit 15.10	Commitment planning

A *commitment plan* is a strategy, described in a series of action steps, devised to secure the support of those [individuals and groups] which are vital to the change effort. The steps in developing a commitment plan are:

1. Identify target individuals or groups whose commitment is necessary.
2. Define the critical mass needed to ensure the effectiveness of the change.
3. Develop a plan for getting the commitment of the critical mass.
4. Develop a monitoring system to assess the progress.

Source: Beckhard and Harris (1987: 93)

For most kinds of change, success depends on winning the commitment of key staff. Without this support, it will be impossible to mobilise the energy necessary to start the change process and keep it moving to a successful conclusion. However, whilst most managers, with some encouragement, might be able to identify the critical mass, many would lack the skills and motivation to win them over. This is why the participation of experienced change agents, with the necessary 'backstage' expertise, is crucial to the change process.

5 **Audits and post-audits**. It is important to monitor progress and see to what extent objectives are being met. This allows plans to be modified in the light of experience. It also allows for opportunities to improve on the original objective to be identified or created. The more uncertain and unclear the change process, the greater the need for periodic review. After the change, or when a particular milestone has been passed, a post-audit should be carried out (a) to establish that the objectives have really been met, and (b) to ascertain what lessons can be learned for future projects. In addition, periodic reviews give senior managers the chance to praise, support and encourage those carrying out the change.

Though the auditing process sounds straightforward, it rarely is. Large projects, in particular, are collections of a number of relatively smaller sub-projects and, as Kotter (1996: 25) remarks, 'Because we are talking about multiple steps and multiple projects, the end result is often complex, dynamic, messy, and scary.' These 'multiple projects' start at different times and operate at different levels and in different areas of an organisation. Some of these sub-projects will run concurrently, some consecutively and a few may even be largely free-standing. By their nature, they will also be geared to different sub-objectives, which may need to be monitored and measured in different ways. Seen in this way, it becomes easier to understand why conducting audits and post-audits, and even day-to-day monitoring of progress, can be exceedingly difficult but is also exceedingly necessary. Nor is the post-audit the end of the line: a chance for people to rest on their laurels. It can be another opportunity for improvement. The post-audit at XYZ, as shown in Chapter 12, was turned into an opportunity for continuing to drive the change process forward, by the simple expedient of asking each manager to identify two initiatives they would personally take to reinforce and enhance the benefits from the company's new organisational structure. This is an example of what Kotter (1996: 21) refers to as 'consolidating gains and producing more change.'

6 **Training and development**. This is a key part of any change project and takes a number of forms. The obvious one is in relation to new skills and competences that might be necessary. Furthermore, as the case studies show, training and development can have a number of other purposes. They may aim to give staff the skills to undertake the change themselves. It may be the intention to leave them with the ability to pursue continuous improvement, once the change has been substantially achieved, or training and development may be intended to make them aware of the need for change and to win them over. Also, there is a need to give general awareness training to those in the organisation who might be indirectly affected. Even where the primary objective is to enhance skills, training can also contribute to other objectives, such as culture change, by structuring it in such a way that training promotes teamworking or inter-departmental cooperation. To ensure that the various types of training are targeted at the right people or groups, a training programme – starting before implementation and continuing after completion – should be established, showing who needs training, the form of the training and when it will take place. Looking wider than just individual change projects and programmes, as Burnes (2003) has argued, there are many benefits to formally linking an organisation's overall management and staff development programme with its various change initiatives. Burnes comments that many of the skills and competences that organisations wish to develop in staff and managers are the same ones necessary for bringing about successful change. Therefore, management and staff development programmes can provide the human resources necessary for managing change, and change projects can provide the real learning opportunities that staff and managers need to develop their skills and competences. The link between management development and change will be returned to in Chapter 16.

There is often a tendency to portray the planning element of change as a technical exercise involved with timetabling and resource allocation. Though planning change is in some ways a 'technical' issue, as the above six activities show, it is also very much a people issue. The success of any change effort is always likely to hinge on an organisation's ability to involve and motivate the people concerned and those whose support is necessary.

People

Chapter 10 showed that organisational change takes many forms. It can be of a predominantly structural or technical nature which requires little of individuals in terms of behavioural or attitudinal change. On the other hand, as the case studies in Part 3 have shown, increasingly the objective of change is to modify the attitudes and behaviours of individuals and groups, sometimes radically so. People are being required to reconsider their attitudes towards how work is performed, how they behave towards their colleagues internally, and their attitudes to their counterparts externally. Whatever form it takes, however, if it is to be successful, there are three people-related activities that need to be undertaken: creating a willingness to change; involving people; and sustaining the momentum.

Creating a willingness to change
Even where change is purely of a technical or structural form, there has to be willingness amongst those concerned to change: to accept the new arrangements. In an ideal

world, organisations would want everyone to buy into a change project. However, as mentioned above, the important issue is to win over what Beckhard and Harris (1987: 92) refer to as the '*critical mass* of individuals or groups whose active commitment is necessary to provide the energy for change to occur.' There are organisations who have put, and are continuing to put, a great deal of effort into creating a climate where change is accepted as the norm and the critical mass is already present or needs little effort to assemble. As described in Chapters 11 and 12, Oticon and XYZ are examples of this. Most organisations, however, are still at the stage where they have to convince staff of the need for change. This is especially the case in those organisations, such as GK in Chapter 12, where each change project is perceived to be a one-off event, almost an exception to the 'normal' flow of organisational life.

For many people, organisational change involves moving from the known to the unknown, with the possibility of loss as well as gain. In such situations, it is often the case that those who fear they will lose out will vociferously oppose any change, whilst those who believe they will gain from the change will keep quiet for fear of antagonising the losers. This was a point most famously made by Niccolo Machiavelli (1515: VI–1):

> And it ought to be remembered that there is nothing more difficult to take in hand, more perilous to conduct, or more uncertain in its success, than to take the lead in the introduction of a new order of things. Because the innovator has for enemies all those who have done well under the old conditions, and lukewarm defenders in those who may do well under the new.

Organisations, therefore, in seeking to create a willingness and a readiness for change, need to be aware that stressing the positive aspects of any proposed change may have much less impact than they might imagine. This point was recognised by Lewin (1947a) when he argued that the *status quo* needs to be destabilised before old behaviour can be discarded (unlearnt) and new behaviour successfully adopted. He referred to this process as 'unfreezing' (*see* Chapter 8). Drawing on his work on Field Theory, Lewin recognised that the *status quo* occurred when the forces for change and the forces for stability were equal (*see* Figure 15.2). To bring about change, one had to increase the strength of the former and reduce that of the latter. Like Machiavelli, however, he also recognised that making proposed changes seem attractive had less effect on increasing the pressure for change than making the current situation less attractive, i.e. it is often easier to create a readiness for change by

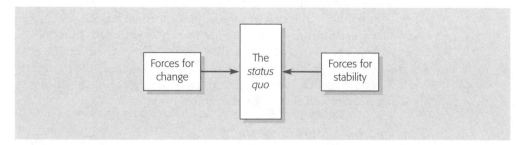

Figure 15.2 **Maintaining the *status quo***

making people dissatisfied with their current situation, and thus prepared to consider alternatives, than to try to paint a rosy picture of the future. Kotter (1996: 36) echoed this point when he stated that: 'Establishing a sense of urgency is crucial to gaining needed cooperation'. For Kotter (1996: 42):

> Increasing urgency demands that you remove sources of complacency or minimize their impact: for instance, eliminating such signs of excess as a big corporate air force; setting higher standards both formally in the planning process and informally in day-to-day interactions; changing internal measurement systems that focus on the wrong indexes; vastly increasing the amount of external performance feedback everyone gets; rewarding both honest talk in meetings and people who are willing to confront problems; and stopping baseless happy talk from the top.

In order to create a willingness for change, a sense of urgency, a feeling of dissatisfaction with the present, there are four steps an organisation needs to take:

1 **Make people aware of the pressures for change.** The organisation should inform employees on a continuous basis of its plans for the future, the competitive/market pressures it faces, customer requirements and the performance of its key competitors. This should be a participative process where staff have opportunity to question, make comments and make suggestions. Many companies now encourage staff at all levels to spend time meeting and working with customers. Customers are also increasingly being invited to come and give direct feedback to staff and managers. The aim is to make staff aware of what customers want and do not want and, particularly, to highlight the organisation's shortcomings. This seems to be a development that is common to both private and public sector organisations (Crawford et al, 2003; Kotter, 1996). Obviously, promoting the vision and explaining the strategic plan are also vital components in this. Through this approach, members of the organisation come to appreciate that change is not only inevitable, but is being undertaken to safeguard rather than threaten their future. It is also necessary to use informal as well as formal channels of communication. In any organisation, department or team there are individuals who are opinion-formers: people to whom others look for guidance. They may not hold any position of power or authority but, as the example in Exhibit 15.9 shows, they do have influence. Therefore, to get the message across successfully, managers must identify who these people are and seek to ensure that they not only understand the message being transmitted, but will also pass a favourable judgment on it.

2 **Give regular feedback on the performance of individual processes and areas of activity within the organisation.** This allows a company to draw attention to any discrepancy between actual performance and desired present and future performance. The feedback has to be in a form that people can relate to and act on. Telling a team that it is losing money is less useful than giving them feedback on productivity and quality. Feedback also has to be timely. Discussing yesterday's performance is useful in getting staff to identify and address problems; discussing last year's performance is rarely so. Also, giving people the skills and authority to undertake improvement activities, as XYZ did with its *Kaizen* initiatives, is likely to make people more receptive to feedback because they can do something to

improve the situation. In addition, it makes a difference who provides and delivers the feedback. A quarterly or annual meeting led by the CEO may have little impact. However, as mentioned above, direct and timely feedback from customers and product and service users, whether internal or external, is likely to have a much greater impact. Once again, the form of this and the recipient's ability to act upon it is also important. Feedback can encourage those concerned to begin to think about how their performance can be improved, and prepare them for the need for change. In looking at the case study companies, it is noticeable that there was a greater readiness to change in those organisations where management was open about its objectives and the company's or function's current performance than in those organisations where information was guarded. This can clearly be seen in Oticon, XYZ and TRW. Conversely, in the PPC, suspicion over the organisation's objectives led to resistance to change. In GK, suspicion over the objectives of some individuals led to resistance to change. Therefore, openness helps people to understand the need for change, which is an essential step on the road to achieving change.

3 **Understand people's fears and concerns**. One of the major mistakes companies can make when introducing change is to fail to recognise, and deal with, the real and legitimate fears of the managers and staff. Though people's concerns tend to focus on the proposed change, they will also be strongly influenced by the outcome of previous change initiatives. In the case of Volvo and XYZ, where past changes had been successful, this appeared to act to reduce concerns. In the case of the PPC, however, the employees' experience of privatisation is likely to increase fears and suspicion in the future. This is partly to do with the fact that they saw privatisation as threatening their jobs and careers, which it did, but also to do with the way it was managed: they felt that they were not consulted or informed about changes. This led to a lack of cooperation from staff and trade unions. Similarly, the failure by senior managers at TRW to recognise or anticipate the concerns of their counterparts at Rover created a history of mistrust between the two companies that nearly led to the termination of a highly beneficial alliance. The new Managing Director at XYZ, on the other hand, understood that people had to be won over and their concerns addressed. This appears to be a key lesson that can be drawn from the success achieved by XYZ in introducing its many change initiatives. Organisations need to recognise that change does create uncertainty and that some individuals and groups may resist, or may not fully cooperate with it, if they fear the consequences. In this respect, resistance can be seen as a signal that there is something wrong with the change process or its objectives rather than with those who are opposing or questioning it. From this perspective, resistance can be viewed as positive: it reminds the organisation that it has not considered all the consequences of its actions, and forces it to review its plans. It follows that those championing change need to pay special attention to the potential for resistance, both in terms of the adverse consequences it can bring and the underlying problems it may indicate. They also need to pay close attention to the organisation's past history of change and the extent to which this reduces or enhances people's fears and concerns.

4 **Publicise successful change**. In order to reduce fears and create a positive attitude towards change, companies should publicise the projects that are seen as models of how to undertake change, and the positive effects change can have for employees. This does not mean that mistakes should be hidden or poor outcomes ignored; these should be examined, explained and lessons learned. Staff should, however, be

encouraged to expect and set credible and positive outcomes for change programmes. Once again, the experience of the case study companies illustrates this
point. At Volvo, there have now been three decades of successful change, which
have produced a positive attitude amongst employees and managers alike. It is also
change that has been well publicised both inside and outside the company, and has
been praised by independent academics who have examined it. Staff and managers
can see the effects of Volvo's commitment to Job Design; they can see that Job
Design has led to improvements for all concerned. Therefore, the wide publicity
given to, and the rigorous examination of, its past Job Design initiatives have
helped Volvo to reduce their employees' fears of future changes. The Rover–TRW
partnership described in Chapter 12 is an example of successful change that was
not well publicised. The later problems with Rover's senior managers could have
been avoided if TRW and Rover's operational managers had explained to their
senior colleagues what they were doing and why. This would have allowed issues
to be explored and a positive attitude developed.

As the above four steps show, in order to create a willingness for change, an effective two-way flow of information is vital. Even where this is the case, however,
organisations should not take for granted the willingness of staff and managers to
undertake every change that is proposed. It is noticeable that even after XYZ had
spent a number of years creating a willingness and readiness for change, it undertook
a change readiness audit before embarking on the project to change its organisation
structure. Not only did this allow it to estimate the degree of readiness for change,
but it also formed part of the second people-related activity, involving people in the
change project.

Involving people

Chapter 14 reviewed the three main theories that underpin our understanding of
employee involvement, i.e. cognitive dissonance, the 'depth' of intervention and the
psychological contract. In summary, the argument from these theories is that the more
a change challenges a person or group's existing norms of behaviour, beliefs or
assumptions, the more resistance it is likely to meet. It follows from this that the
appropriateness of an involvement strategy needs to be judged less by the type of
change being considered and more by how people will react to it. Changes that may
readily be accepted in some organisations may be strongly resisted in others.
Likewise, some major changes may meet with much less reaction than much smaller
ones. For example, over the last decade it has become the norm for staff in public
services to give their name on the telephone and wear name badges when meeting
members of the public. Previously, staff were not encouraged to give their name or to
wear a name badge. When this was first introduced, it met with a level of hostility
from staff that appeared to be greatly out of proportion to what was being suggested.
The reason for this was that many staff felt threatened, exposed to public scrutiny, by
having to give their name.

In developing an involvement strategy, it is also important to remember Beckhard
and Harris' (1987) advice regarding levels of commitment. They argued that the key
objective was for organisations to gain the active support of the *critical mass* of
people necessary to bring about the change. This is not all, or even necessarily a
majority, of those affected. Nor is the same level of support necessary from all of the

critical mass. Instead it can be split into three groups: those who let it happen, those who help it to happen and those who make it happen.

In addition, an involvement strategy needs to take account of the size and duration of the proposed change project. Though some change projects can be short-lived and, possibly, easily achieved, many are not. In some cases, achieving a successful change can be a long and complex task. There will be difficult obstacles to overcome, not all of which can be anticipated in advance. To gain and maintain the active involvement of the *critical mass*, and to develop the momentum necessary to ensure that the project is successful, is not a one-off occurrence but an ongoing activity stretching over the lifetime of the change project. There are two main activities that help secure and maintain this level of involvement:

■ **Communication.** As well as being key to gaining people's involvement, communication is an essential element of all the above change activities. In terms of involvement, the establishment of a regular and effective communications process can significantly reduce people's levels of uncertainty. In turn, this eliminates one of the major obstacles to people's willingness to get involved in the change process. The purpose of communication is not just to inform staff that change is being considered, but by drawing them into the discussions and debates about the need for and form of the change, and allowing them the freedom to discuss the issues involved openly, to get them to convince themselves of the need for change. The evidence that this is one of the most effective ways of gaining support goes back to the work of Kurt Lewin in the 1940s (Lewin, 1999a). During the Second World War, he was asked by the American government to find an effective way of getting people to change their eating habits. Through a series of now classic experiments, he demonstrated that the most effective method of convincing people to change their behaviour was by providing groups with information for them to evaluate and discuss, and letting the group come to its own decision. Once the decision had been made by the group, it exerted a strong pressure on all the individuals concerned to adhere to the group's decision.

  Communication should be a regular rather than a one-off exercise. Nor should it be pursued through one or two channels, such as newsletters or team briefings. As mentioned above when discussing the need to make people aware of the need for change, organisations have a wide range of formal and informal channels for communication. They should consciously use all of these. As a rule of thumb, it should be recognised that, whilst people are often willing to believe the wildest rumour from unofficial sources, anything from management has to be stated at least six times in six different ways before people start giving it credence.

  In some cases, where all those concerned become directly involved in the change process, communication is less of an issue. An example of this is the first phase of change at GK Printers, where all those affected were involved. Another example was Speedy's Stationery Management initiative. However, the small size of the groups concerned in these instances makes them something of an exception. In most cases, it is impractical to give everyone this level of involvement; therefore, as at XYZ and Volvo, it is important to communicate proposals from the outset. This involves not only providing information, but also listening to the response and taking it seriously. This has a number of benefits. The change management team will very quickly pick up any worries and concerns and can respond to these; they will also be made aware of aspects that need to be taken into consideration which have been overlooked; and assumptions that have been made will be tested and sometimes challenged. In addition, this will assist in identifying issues, individuals and groups who might obstruct change. In terms of the three target groups for commitment, i.e. those who let it happen, those who help it to happen and those who make it happen, communication can secure the commitment of the first but, by itself, is unlikely to secure the commitment of the other two groups. Their commitment will come through and be tested by their involvement in the change process.

■ **Getting people involved**. One of the most vital initiatives an organisation can take with staff is not to treat them as objects of, or obstacles to, change, but to involve them in it and make them responsible for it. There are good examples of this in Oticon, XYZ, GK, TRW and Speedy. Particularly where large-scale projects are concerned, not everyone can be involved in all aspects of planning and execution. However, as mentioned above, it is important to identify and enrol those whose assistance is necessary and those who are essential to make change happen. This should be the main criterion for selecting who will be involved. Obviously, where it is possible, it is a good idea to ensure that all those most closely affected are involved in some, if not all, aspects. Similarly, again where possible, responsibility for aspects of the change project should be given to those who will be directly affected by the result. In many cases, however, the numbers involved will prevent all those affected being involved and, consequently, managers will need to select those to involve. Sometimes, volunteers will be asked for. Sometimes, people who are perceived to have 'the right attitude' will be chosen. On the other hand, as the GK case showed, the presence of sceptics, people prepared to challenge assumptions and ask awkward questions, can be useful. This not only ensures that awkward questions are asked but can also, if the sceptic is won over, create a powerful advocate for the change. Likewise, it is useful to consider involving key opinion-formers: people to whom their colleagues look for guidance.

As the above shows, communication and involvement are essential to gaining people's understanding of the need for change. Change can be a slow and difficult process, however, and commitment can diminish unless steps are taken to maintain it. This leads on to the third and last people-related activity, sustaining the momentum.

Sustaining the momentum

Even in the best-run organisations, it sometimes happens that initial enthusiasm for change wanes and, in the face of the normal day-to-day pressures to meet customer needs, progress becomes slower and can grind to a halt. When the CEO in Oticon thought that its change effort was running out of steam, he 'exploded the organisation' in order to breathe fresh life into the change process. In some less well-run organisations, however, the momentum may not even be present in the beginning. In such situations, people will return to the methods and types of behaviour with which they are familiar. Given that momentum does not arise of itself nor continue without encouragement, organisations need to consider how to build and sustain it. The points already made above regarding planning and implementation, and especially involvement, are clearly part of this. In addition, organisations should also:

■ **Provide resources for change.** Kotter (1996: 35) states that:

> In an organization with 100 employees, at least two dozen must go far beyond the normal call of duty to produce a significant change. In a firm of 100,000 employees, the same might require 15,000 or more.

For a one-off change project of short duration, it might be acceptable to ask staff to 'go far beyond the normal course of duty'. However, for many organisations, as Part 3 demonstrated, change is a way of life. Also, in many organisations, staff and managers have to work long hours merely to get their normal work done. In cases such as these, and indeed in most cases, it is probably difficult, and certainly unwise, to ask staff to undertake change initiatives without some additional resources, whether these be financial or human. In cases where staff are required to keep up the same level of output during the transition phase, it may require considerable additional resources to achieve this. The 1999 case of the UK's Passport Office, which failed to provide sufficient extra staff during the introduction of a new computer system, is a case in point. Not only did this result in inexcusable delays in issuing passports, but the Passport Office eventually had to provide the extra staff anyway. It is important, therefore, that the need for any extra resources is identified and extra resources allocated, whether for the provision of temporary staff, the training of existing staff, senior management time or whatever. As the example of the Passport Office showed, nothing is guaranteed to be more demoralising than having to make changes without some additional resources or support.

■ **Give support to the change agents.** As Buchanan and Boddy (1992) noted, an enormous responsibility falls upon the change management team. They have not only to plan and oversee the change project, but also to motivate others and deal with difficulties, sometimes very personal problems. However, just as they have to support others, so too must they receive support themselves. Otherwise they may be the ones who become demoralised and lose their ability to motivate others. Sometimes this can be done by offering them financial rewards, sometimes by the promise of future advancement but often the most effective method is through public praise of the individuals concerned. In Chapter 2, we drew attention to Chester Barnard's (1938) observation that monetary rewards are often less effective than non-monetary ones, such as praise. This does not mean that monetary rewards should be avoided, but it does mean that too great a reliance on them may be counter productive.

■ **Develop new competences and skills.** This reiterates the point made when discussing 'planning the change' above. Change frequently demands new knowledge, skills and competences. Increasingly, managers are having to learn new leadership styles, staff are having to learn to work as teams, and all are expected to be innovators and improvers. This requires more than just training and re-training. It may also include on-the-job counselling and coaching. Therefore, organisations need to consider what is required, who requires it and – the difficult part – how to deliver it in a way that encourages rather than threatens staff. XYZ is a good example of a company who recognised that managerial and staff development go hand-in-hand with organisational change. This can be an expensive process, however, both in terms of staff time and the cost of training and development. This, once again, emphasises the need to provide additional resources for change.

■ **Reinforce desired behaviour.** In organisations, people generally do those things that bring rewards or avoid criticism. Consequently, one of the most effective ways of sustaining the momentum for change is to reinforce the kinds of behaviour required to make it successful. Sometimes this may be monetary, such as increased pay or bonuses for particular types of activity or progress. Sometimes it may be symbolic, such as Oticon's tearing down of walls and elimination of personal desks. Sometimes it may be through recognition, whereby senior managers openly or privately single out individuals or groups for special praise. Such activities are particularly important during the early stages of change, when achieving an identifiable and openly-recognised success helps participants develop a positive attitude about the change project. In XYZ, it could be argued that the change in organisational structure was a method of reinforcing the behavioural changes that had already taken place. Alternatively, it could be said that they reinforced the new organisational structure. However one views XYZ, the key point is that the behavioural changes might have been difficult to sustain without the new structure and, certainly, the new structure would have been much less effective without the prior behavioural changes.

In looking at the three interlinked elements that make up the change process – objectives and outcomes, planning the change, and people – we can see why change is so complex and why so many initiatives fail. Though there are technical aspects that must be accomplished, no matter what type of change is involved, it can never be a purely technical exercise. Establishing objectives involves testing assumptions and challenging preconceived ideas. It also involves gathering both fact and opinion, and making judgments about which is the most important. Similarly, planning change often involves an impressive and daunting array of challenges and activities, some of which are amenable to straightforward techniques of analysis and decision, many of which are not. The final element, though, is the most complex: people. People are not just important because they are often the 'object' of change, but also because they are the ones who have to carry it out. In a real sense, they are the glue that holds it together. They can influence the choice of objectives and the way change is planned. In turn, objectives and planning can also affect their willingness to accept or become involved in change.

One final point: even after a change project has been 'completed', the story does not end there. As the Japanese have shown, even when change has resulted in a stable state being achieved, there always remains scope for improvement. Furthermore, as is clear from the case studies, many change projects are open-ended. Change will continue to take place. Therefore, both in planning a project and evaluating its outcomes, it is necessary to identify the open-endedness of it, and the degree to which the final outcome will require a continuous improvement approach or a continuing change approach. As mentioned earlier, there is a marked difference, however, between organisations where change is seen as an everyday occurrence and those where it is seen as a one-off event. In the latter, it is very difficult to develop the capabilities and commitment necessary to achieve continuous improvement; whereas in the former, continuous improvement and continuous change, and the capabilities, skills and commitment required of both, go hand in hand.

Conclusions

This chapter has sought to merge the theory and practice of strategy development and change management as presented in Chapters 6–14. In doing so, it has also drawn on many of the arguments and insights into the behaviour, operation and rationality of organisations presented in Chapters 1–5. Based on these 14 chapters, this chapter introduced and elaborated on the Choice Management–Change Management model for understanding and managing organisational change. This comprised three interrelated organisational processes: the choice process, the trajectory process and the change process (*see* Figure 15.1). It was argued that not only did this model incorporate and go beyond both the Planned and Emergent approaches to strategy and change, but it also demonstrated how managers could attempt to change their organisation's circumstances to fit them to the approach that best suited them and their organisation.

It was asserted that the Choice Management–Change Management model incorporates the full scope of the various approaches to strategy and change, including the Planned and Emergent approaches, and that it also accommodates and explains the use of more directive approaches. However, one of the fundamental differences between this model and many other approaches to strategy and change is that it recognises that managers are active players rather than passive spectators in the development of their own organisations. The model is based on the assumption that not only can managers choose to align their organisation with the external conditions and constraints it faces, but they can also do the reverse and align these external conditions and constraints to their preferred way of structuring and running their organisation. Whether they choose to attempt to influence, alter or align their organisation to the circumstances it faces will depend on a range of issues, not least their own views about whether they or the organisation are better suited by a stable, planned situation or whether more turbulent, emergent conditions are preferable.

Though the Choice Management–Change Management model appears to offer significant theoretical avenues for understanding how organisations and managers operate, it also offers considerable practical benefits as well. In Chapter 3, we examined the Culture–Excellence perspective on organisations. The proponents of this view, especially Tom Peters, argue that organisations have no choice but to change radically if they are to survive. The Culture–Excellence theory is based on a particular view of the environment and other constraints organisations face. Assuming that this view is accurate, the Choice Management–Change Management model indicates that organisations need not radically restructure themselves, but could seek to influence the constraints they face to bring them more in line with their existing organisational arrangements. Even if, in the long term, organisations did have to structure themselves along the lines advocated by Peters, Kanter and Handy, they could still seek to influence the conditions under which they operated to achieve this over a longer timescale than might otherwise be assumed. Indeed, as Chapter 3 revealed, this is just the approach the Japanese take. Between the 1950s and the 1980s, Japan's leading organisations transformed themselves. This was achieved by slow and gradual transformation rather than by rapid shock tactics. Japanese companies achieved this gradual transformation by a combination of long-term vision allied to the ability to influence and restructure the constraints under which they operate, especially, as argued by Hamel and Prahalad (1989), their ability to change the rules of competition in their particular industries. In so doing, they provide much support for Kanter *et al*'s (1992) view that a Long March is more effective than a Bold Stroke for building competitive organisations.

Therefore, the Choice Management–Change Management model, in conjunction with the Change Framework presented in Chapter 10, potentially at least, resolves the dispute between proponents of Planned and Emergent approaches to strategy development and change. It also raises fundamental questions, however, about what managers *can* do and what they *do* do in terms of running and shaping their organisations. In particular, it raises questions about the way that managers can make sense of their situation for themselves and others and, in so doing, construct alternative scenarios or realities for their organisation's future. Many writers, especially from the Culture–Excellence perspective, have made a case for visionary leadership being the key to an organisation's success. Certainly, the transactional, steady-as-she-goes type of manager is very much out of favour (Kotter, 1996; Peters, 1997a; Senge, 1990). The case for transforming managers, as well as organisations, however, tends to be based on a biased view of what managers need to do and, often, only a shallow understanding of what they actually do. In order to come to grips with the nature of managerial work and the extent to which the Choice Management–Change Management model requires a rethink of how managers operate, the concluding chapter of this book will examine the role of managers.

Test your learning

■ Short answer questions

1   Briefly describe the choice process.

2   How might a SWOT or PESTEL analysis help an organisation to understand better the context in which it operates?

3   What are the key features of the trajectory process?

4   Describe how an organisation might construct a vision for itself.

5   List the key components of the change process.

6   What does commitment planning involve?

7   Discuss the role of the change agent in planning and implementing change.

■ Essay questions

1   Critically evaluate the key linkages between the three processes that make up the Choice Management–Change Management model.

2   Use the Choice–Change model to assess one of the ten case studies from Part 3.

Chapter 16

Management – roles and responsibilities

Learning objectives

After studying this chapter, you should be able to:

- define globalisation and understand the importance of sustainability, workforce diversity and business ethics;
- list the key duties of managers;
- understand that much of what managers do is reactive and driven by expediency;
- describe the three main perspectives on leadership;
- identify the primary approaches to managerial development and education;
- appreciate the differences between management and leadership and the different skills required for each;
- explain the relationship between management, leadership and organisational change;
- appreciate the need for managers to identify and examine the full range of choices facing them;
- understand the impact of managers' decisions on society as a whole, and their wider and longer-term responsibilities.

Exhibit 16.1   A lesson in leadership

Manage with mother

FT

As a lesson in leadership, the residential course I have been on for the last four months has been quite something. Requiring 24-hour commitment seven days a week, it has been more gruelling than the toughest Outward Bound exercise. There has been no 'facilitator' to show the way, nor any schedule at all. Instead, I have been assigned a group of four young people to manage, and left to get on with it.

My group is aged between nought and seven, but despite their young age they have much in common with top executives. Each is equipped with a towering ego, an agenda all of their own and a disturbing mixture of friendliness and outright hostility towards each other. They have awesome will-power, yet are strikingly incompetent at everyday tasks, needing help with eating, sleeping, crossing roads and so forth. Rational behaviour is also a problem for most of them; indeed the youngest shows scant sign of rationality at all. My task, then, has been similar to that facing every leader: how to get a group of difficult people to work happily together.

A little time spent with my four team members and you start to understand why senior managers behave as they do. When you have witnessed a seven and a five-year-old fighting over the sharing of a bedroom, the failure of the merger between Glaxo Wellcome and SmithKline Beecham becomes a lot easier to comprehend. Sir Richard Sykes and Jan Leschly could not agree on who was going to have control of the bedside light nor on where their favourite teddies were going to go, so it turned out to be impossible for them to share a bedroom after all.

My course had hardly begun before I realised that command and control was the only way forward. In the corporate world this model has sadly fallen from favour. But in my company rules and rigid structures are essential. As chief executive I make sure that everyone knows that 7pm is bedtime. I have also come to see that choice is my enemy. To start the day by offering Cheerios, Coco Pops, Frosties or Honey Nuts is to ask for trouble. I offer Bran Flakes or nothing, and breakfast is faster and smoother as a result.

A second problem is the non-executive director I have been saddled with. Periodically he will pop in, flagrantly disregard all the rules and then have the cheek to offer advice in the fond belief that he understands the business.

I have also discovered that both rewards and punishments are poor motivational tools. Give a strawberry Chewit to one team member and before you know it you find inflation has taken hold and you are handing out Chewits as a reward for getting dressed. Punishments are even worse.

The first time you lose your temper you get results; but to achieve the same effect on subsequent occasions requires ever increasing quantities of violence. Understanding this is one thing. Living by it is another. On bad days I do nothing other than bribing and bollocking.

Like most chief executives, I have found that I get little feedback, and what I do get is inadequate. 'I hate you, you're poo,' is not exactly constructive. I am at the top, and it can be lonely up here. Not to say stressful. The boss of a big company may lay awake fretting about his share price – being woken up every three hours by the youngest member may be nearly as bad.

So what is the answer? Surprise, surprise, it turns out to be complicated, exhausting and quite impossible to bring off. You have to be firm, but also nice and approachable. You need to keep your temper and motivate people by making them want to do the job in hand.

Source: Lucy Kellaway, *Financial Times*, 2 March 1998, p.14.

Introduction

Lucy Kellaway's article, Exhibit 16.1, on the similarities between managing children and managing organisations will strike a chord with most parents and managers. Though written in a way that amuses, it raises serious questions concerning the nature of management: How can we control organisations? How can we motivate staff? How can we win over colleagues? The answer, as Kellaway states, ' ... turns out to be complicated, exhausting and quite impossible to bring off'. Not all people have the same needs or can be motivated in the same way. Also, people's needs change over time; what motivates them one day may have little effect the next. Neither do organisations, or their customers, suppliers and competitors, stand still. Faced with the vast array of present challenges, organisations must also look to the future. Over the past few years, with the advent of a new millennium, many writers and commentators have felt the urge to provide us with their views on the future. Sometimes these have a postmodern rosy glow about them, whilst often, in the wake of the dotcom collapse, they present a gloomy, doomsday picture of the future. As Kellaway's article indicates, it is unlikely that the challenges facing managers in the future will get any easier but, one thing we do know about attempts to predict the future, as Exhibit 16.2 shows, is that they usually fall very short of the mark.

Exhibit 16.2	Predicting the future

This 'telephone' has too many shortcomings to be seriously considered as a means of communication. (Western Union internal memo, 1876)

Airplanes are interesting toys, but of no military value. (Marshal Foch, 1911)

Who the hell wants to hear actors talk? (HM Warner of Warner Brothers, 1927)

I think there is a world market for maybe five computers. (Thomas Watson, Chairman IBM, 1943)

This is unfortunately no excuse for ignoring the many serious and daunting challenges that organisations and those who manage them, not to mention the world at large, have to face in the coming decades. The globalisation of world trade may open up new markets and create new opportunities, but it also brings with it new competitors and new uncertainties. The same holds true for scientific advance. The beneficial effects of computers are there for all to see, with the range of applications expanding daily. However, advances such as genetically modified crops and even genetically modified human beings are much more controversial and unpredictable. For most of the developed world, the spectre of an increasingly ageing population looms large. Then there is the reality of global warming, the dwindling of natural resources, the growing gap between rich and poor countries, and the threat to the natural world of indiscriminate industrialisation; we are reminded of these almost daily (Dunphy *et al*, 2003; Paton *et al*, 1996).

Nevertheless, nothing is inevitable until it actually happens, and even then it may be reversed. Individual consumers and pressure groups have some influence, and governments can pass laws; but in an age where organisations dominate our lives, where they appear to be more powerful then ever before, the role and performance of managers will be crucial. Managers will need to recognise that in the future, as in the past, regardless of the particular issues involved, the environment in which their organisations operate will continue to change. They will also have to recognise that the appropriateness of their decisions will be judged by a wider set of criteria and a wider range of stakeholders than in the past. At the same time, managers will continue to have to find ways of ensuring that their organisation and its environment, and the other constraints under which it operates, are, as far as possible, kept aligned. As pointed out in previous chapters, this does not mean that each and every organisation has to change rapidly and radically, though many will. Instead, managers can seek to influence the constraints under which their organisation operates, and the pace and timing of change, to make them more favourable to their preferred way of working. However, as in the past, over time, both organisations and their environments will change.

As the case studies in Part 3 have shown, and as most people's everyday experiences confirm, change is neither easy nor necessarily always successful. Regardless of this, organisations do change, either by design or default, and managers do play a crucial role in determining whether the outcome is success or failure. Managers are the ones who have the responsibility for ensuring that options are identified, choices made and action taken. They are also the ones who have the responsibility for making sense, presenting a coherent picture, of the events and developments that make up an organisation's past, present and potential future. Therefore, in concluding this book, it is only right that we look at how well or not managers are equipped, or can be equipped, for this task.

The chapter begins by examining the implications of globalisation, especially in terms of sustainability, workforce diversity and business ethics. This highlights the need for managers not just to acquire appropriate skills and competences but also to adopt appropriate behaviours. This leads on to a review of the literature on what managers are supposed to do and what they really do. This shows that, despite what leading thinkers such as Fayol and Weber believed and advocated, most managers are driven by expediency and operate in a responsive mode. The chapter then moves on to discuss the importance and nature of leadership in organisations. In particular, it seeks to identify the characteristics and contexts that make for effective leadership. Arising from this, the leadership role played by managers in the case studies is explored. This is followed by an examination of the education and development of managers, which leads on to a discussion of the relationship between management, leadership and change. The chapter and the book conclude by arguing that managers have an important responsibility to identify and exercise choice, when faced with situations which require change. Though choice can be determined on a very narrow basis of short-term financial return, increasingly managers will have to take into account wider organisational and societal factors. Especially important in this respect is that managers should be prepared to question trends and advice that seem designed to increase organisational and societal instability and fragmentation. The interests of society in general and their own organisations in particular may be better served by seeking stability rather than promoting instability.

Globalisation and the challenge of change

Arguably, the biggest single challenge facing managers today is globalisation: the creation of a unified world market place. Allied to globalisation, however, are three other challenges: how to achieve sustainability in a world of dwindling natural resources and increasing environmental pollution; how to manage an increasingly diverse workforce; and, at a time when business leaders are considered less trustworthy than ever before, how to manage ethically.

Trade between different parts of the world has been taking place for thousands of years. In the last 20 to 30 years, however, and particularly since the fall of communism in Eastern Europe, the integration of the global economy appears to have gone through a step change. Whereas in the 1970s and 1980s it was common to talk about international brands such as Coca Cola and McDonald, it is now equally common to speak of global, transnational corporations that dominate their industries and gobble up the smaller companies. Examples of these include General Electric, Toyota, Mitsubishi, Microsoft, Merck, News International, Vodafone and Time Warner. One of the prime examples is Ford, which, as well as being a global brand, also owns Mazda in Japan, Volvo Cars in Sweden, and Aston Martin, Jaguar and Land Rover in the UK, not to mention having joint ventures in the world's two most populous nations, India and China. One obvious manifestation of globalisation is that, in the developed world, we take for granted that our supermarkets will be stocked with our favourite foods from every part of the world all year round. Nor is globalisation merely an issue for large companies; it is affecting smaller organisations as well, whether through the threat of increased competition and takeover, or the promise of new markets.

Like many hot topics that attract a great deal of attention, it is difficult to find an agreed definition of globalisation. For some, it is primarily an economic phenomenon, concerned with the integration and convergence of economic systems through the growth in international trade, investment and capital flows (Jones, 1995; Deresky, 2000). Others, though, see it as a much wider phenomenon involving social, cultural and technological exchanges that will '... transform our world into the beginnings of a global civilization, a new civilization of civilizations, that will blossom through the coming century' (Schwartz and Leyden, 1997: 1). For Giddens (2002), the advent of new communications technologies is leading to the 'death of distance' and making it possible to share knowledge and culture across the globe instantaneously and simultaneously. Some argue that globalisation may also be sounding the death knell of the nation state, as large trading blocks, based on Europe, North America and Asia and overseen by the World Trade Organisation, take over from the nation state (Deresky, 2000). Reich (1998), in an attempt to make sense of these differing perspectives, identifies the four main definitions of globalisation: a historical epoch; a confluence of economic phenomena; the hegemony of American values; and a technological and social revolution.

Despite these different views as to what globalisation is, as Reich (1998) shows, there is some agreement amongst commentators as to what is driving it: the intensification of international competition, the fall of communism, economic liberalisation, the removal of trade barriers, and the advent of new communication technologies such as the Internet. It is these very real developments which make globalisation a key issue for managers rather than a passing fad. Globalisation is also a highly contentious issue which has given rise to a great deal of bitter conflict between those who see it as a force for global good and those who see it as the oppression of poor nations by rich ones (*Economist*, 2002; Klein, 2001). To a great extent, much of the pro and anti argument revolves around the size and behaviour of the large, transnational corporations that are coming to dominate the global economy. For example:

■ more than half of the 1,000 largest economies in the world are private corporations;
■ the sales of Ford and General Motors combined are greater than the combined GDP of sub-Saharan Africa;

- the combined turnover of the six largest Japanese trading companies is almost as big as the national incomes of all the nations in Latin America (Globalisation Guide.org, 2003).

For the pro-globalisation camp, this provides the rationale for the creation of global institutions such as the World Trade Organisation (WTO) and the World Bank that can set the rules for and police such organisations. For the antis, this shows that big business is the dominant force in globalisation and the WTO and the World Bank exist to do their bidding.

Regardless of whether one see globalisation as a force for good or ill, organisations have to come to terms with the changing nature of domestic and international trade. They have to live with a situation where the rules that govern their behaviour are set by supra-national bodies such as the EU and WTO. In addition, as mentioned above, they need to come to terms with three other issues whose importance has been intensified by globalisation, namely sustainability, workforce diversity, and business ethics.

Sustainability

Globalisation both derives from and is driving economic development across the globe; the greater the level of economic integration across the planet, the greater the level of consumption. As we can see around us every day, however, the result of this rush for ever greater levels of economic growth and consumption is the dwindling and depredation of natural resources, increasing levels of pollution and rapid global warming (Paton *et al*, 1996). As Lines (2002: 126–7) argues:

> The regenerative and assimilative capacities of the biosphere cannot support even the current levels of consumption, much less the manifold increase required to generalize to higher standards of living worldwide. Still less can the planet afford an ever-growing human population striving to consume more per-capita.

It would be good to think that the sustainability of the planet will be secured by cooperation between governments. However, as the failure of the USA to sign up to the Kyoto Protocol on achieving reductions in the emissions of greenhouse gases shows, this does not seem likely. Even if such accords are signed, we also know that organisations, driven by market forces, will have a major influence on how they are formulated and will have the major responsibility for their implementation. As Dunphy and Griffiths (1998: 183) argued in their book *The Sustainable Corporation*:

> There is a widespread view that governments must solve environmental problems. However, the major multinationals outstrip many of the world's national economies in terms of wealth and power, and their global coverage allows them to escape the requirements of particular governments seeking to place severe environmental restrictions on them. They can simply move their operations across national borders. The world's multinationals are in fact more powerful than most national governments.

Nevertheless, Dunphy and Griffiths do believe that it is possible for these large organisations to change their ways. They point out that those who run organisations live in the same world as the rest of us, and, to a large extent, experience the consequences of their actions in the same way everyone else does. Therefore, they argue, managers cannot divorce their actions from the wider impact they have on society; nor can they ignore the fact that a sustainable future for their organisations requires a sustainable future for the world. This presents a major challenge for managers, particularly at the senior level. Whilst operating in competitive and hostile markets, they have to marry the desire of their shareholders for increased profit with the need to act in the wider and longer-term interests of society as a whole. They will not achieve this without pressure and support from governments and the force of public opinion. Nor, as Dunphy *et al* (2003) show, will managers be able to create sustainable organisations unless they have the change management skills to do so. Dunphy *et al* argue that both incremental and transformational approaches can be used to create sustainable organisations. However, the appropriateness of either depends on the circumstances of the organisation in question. Therefore, the role of managers is not just to lead change but to develop the skills necessary to identify which approach to change, is suitable for their organisation.

Furthermore, as Docherty *et al* (2002: 12) maintain, sustainability is not just about the relationship of organisations to their environment, or the depletion of natural resources:

> Sustainability … encompasses three levels: the individual, the organizational and the societal. Sustainability at one level cannot be built on the exploitation of the others. These levels are intimately related to the organization's key stakeholders: personnel, customers, owners and society. An organization cannot be sustainable by prioritizing the goals and needs of some stakeholders at the expense of others … Thus sustainability has a value basis in the due considerations and balancing of different stakeholders' legitimate needs and goals.

Therefore, as Dunphy *et al* (2003) argue, life cannot be sustained on earth unless we create sustainable organisations. However, Docherty *et al* (2002) point out that creating sustainable organisations cannot be achieved unless all stakeholders, including the organisation's own members, are treated in an equitable and ethical manner. This is why the issues of workforce diversity and business ethics are so important.

■ Workforce diversity

Jones *et al* (2000: 166–7) observe that:

> Diversity is dissimilarities – differences – among people due to age, gender, race, ethnicity, religion, sexual orientation, socioeconomic background, and capabilities/disabilities … Diversity raises important ethical issues and social responsibility issues as well. It is also a critical issue for organizations, one that if not handled well can surely bring an organization to its knees, especially in our increasing global environment.

Ever since the Industrial Revolution ushered in the age of the organisation, the workforce has become increasingly diverse, though faster in some industries and countries than others. Globalisation is intensifying workforce diversity in three key ways. The first and most obvious is that the growth of the transnational corporations means that, increasingly, companies are being owned and managed by people from different countries and cultures. The fact, given above, that Ford runs Volvo in Sweden, Mazda in Japan and Land Rover in the UK is a typical example. However, there are also many examples of Japanese and South Korean companies, such as Honda and Hyundai, establishing factories in Europe and the USA. Companies are also increasingly buying products and services from overseas. The epitome of German manufacturing, Mercedes Benz, now purchases car components from India, and many big UK companies, such as BT and Aviva, have relocated Call Centres to India. The second effect of globalisation concerns the migration and recruitment of workers from other countries. Richer countries have always been a magnet for workers from poorer countries. The emigration from Europe to the USA in the nineteenth century is a case in point. It offered the potential for a better life for immigrants and met the severe shortage of workers the USA was experiencing. The last 50 years has seen the mass migration of people from South America to the USA. In some American cities, Hispanics are now the largest ethnic grouping and by 2050 will make up some 25 per cent of the population of the USA (Deresky, 2000). The transportation and communications infrastructures that have made globalisation possible also make it easier to move from one country to another, whether legally or illegally, to seek a better life. Also, with globalisation, the need to move skilled labour from where it is plentiful to where it is scarce, or where it can be better rewarded, is an increasingly important factor of competitiveness. In recent years, for example, the UK government has sought to recruit medical staff from across the world to compensate for staff shortages in the National Health Service.

The third effect of globalisation on diversity has been to increase the participation rate of women and minority groups in the workforce. As economies develop, they require greater amounts of labour. The tendency is first of all to recruit male workers, and often to give preference to ones from particular groups, whether these be based on grounds of race, tribe, religion, age or sexual orientation. As demand for labour grows, other groups are drawn into the workforce. In the twentieth century, for example, the participation of women in the workforce of most developed countries probably accounted for the biggest increase in diversity.

It has always be the case that the USA tends to exemplify workforce diversity. Jones *et al* (2000: 167) recommend their readers to consider the following statistics:

> Thirty percent of the residents of New York City were born in foreign countries. 33 percent of the residents of San Francisco are Asian, 70 percent of the residents of Washington, D.C., are African-American, and approximately 70 percent of the people currently entering the workforce are either women or minorities. Between 1979 and 1992, the number of women in the workforce increased at twice the rate of men, and currently 1 out of 10 U.S. workers is employed in a company owned by women. ... There are many more women and minorities – including people with disabilities and gays and lesbians – in the workforce than ever before, and most experts agree that diversity is steadily increasing.

Cummings and Worley (2001: 429–30) echo this point stating that:

> ... contemporary workforce characteristics are radically different from what they were just twenty years ago. Employees represent every ethnic background and color; range from highly educated to illiterate; vary in age from eighteen to eighty; may appear perfectly healthy or may have terminal illness; may be single parents or part of dual-income, divorced, same-sex or traditional families; and may be physically or mentally challenged.

Diversity would not be an issue if we all reacted to the same things in the same ways and treated everybody else as we would wish to be treated ourselves. In his entertaining and enlightening book *Blunders in International Business*, Ricks (1999) catalogues the blunders made by businesses in trying to sell their products in other countries or trying to establish businesses in other countries. As he points out (Ricks, 1999: 4):

> Cultural differences are the most significant and troublesome variables encountered by the multinational company. The failure of managers to comprehend fully these disparities has led to most international business blunders.

Hofstede (1980, 1990) sought to identify the similarities and differences between national cultures and the implications of these for the management of different groups (*see* Chapter 5). From the work of Hofstede and that of other researchers (*see* Trompenaars, 1993, for example) it is clear that approaches which might be effective when managing, say, Japanese workers might be considerably less effective when managing ones from the USA. Jones *et al* (2000: 175) comment that:

> When American and Japanese managers interact, for example, the Americans often feel frustrated by what they view as indecisiveness in the Japanese, and the Japanese are often frustrated by what they perceive as hasty, shortsighted decision making by the Americans.

Managing diversity is not just about how to manage effectively relationships between people with different national cultures. Managing diversity is also concerned with developing appropriate approaches to managing differences in gender, age, abilities, sexuality, ethnicity, etc. For instance, in the West, it is argued that male and female workers have different strengths and weaknesses and different preferences in how they prefer to manage and be managed (Maddock, 1999; Thomas, 2003). Alimo-Metcalfe (1995a, 1995b) maintains that women tend to be more motivated by organisational goals than their male counterparts and more amenable to change. Women also appear to have different work-life balance priorities, especially in terms of childcare, as BA found to its cost in 2003. An attempt by the airline to impose a new clocking-on arrangement on its check-in staff at Heathrow Airport turned out disastrously when the predominantly female workforce went on unofficial strike. This cost BA some £40 million in lost revenues and an incalculable amount in bad publicity (Harrison, 2003). The company failed to understand its staff's priorities and concerns, as Phillips (2003: 17) comments:

> Currently, shifts are organised three months at a time and women can arrange childcare around their working hours. What they fear is a system in which a computer will decide on a day-to-day, or hour-to-hour, basis when they should come into work. ... BA, and the unions too, have been caught on the hop because they failed to understand that, for these relatively low-paid, often part-time, women workers, the welfare of children comes first – above money.

Despite the evidence that women have different preferences and priorities to men, studies have shown that if women are to progress up the managerial hierarchy, they are expected to conform to male characteristics such as decisiveness, competitiveness and playing by the rules (Schein and Mueller, 1992). Workforce diversity is not just about gender, however, or even cultural or ethnic differences, as Cummings and Worley (2001: 429–30) point out:

> Such a definition is too narrow and focuses attention away from the broad range of issues that a diverse workforce poses. Diversity results from people who bring different resources and perspectives to the workplace and who have distinctive needs, preferences, expectations and lifestyles. Organizations must design human resource systems that account for these differences if they are to attract and retain a productive workforce and if they want to turn diversity into a competitive advantage.

That people who are different are treated less well than those who conform to whatever the prevailing stereotype is in organisations and society is well known. Most countries now have laws that seek to prevent or punish discrimination. This of course can provide a powerful incentive for organisations to recognise and manage workforce diversity. In raising the issue of competitive advantage, however, Cummings and Worley draw attention to the positive side of diversity. In a fiercely competitive world where markets are expanding and customers are increasingly rejecting standardised products and services in favour of ones tailored to their needs, workforce diversity can bring substantial benefits. It offers the possibility of more creativity, innovation, and flexibility, it provides a heightened sensitivity to different customer groupings and a wider pool of talent to draw from. Only by attracting, retaining and motivating workers effectively, including recognising and promoting the benefits of diversity, can organisations expect to prosper or even survive in an increasingly competitive global economy. This means that organisations have to achieve the difficult but essential task of treating workers differently because of their diversity but treating them all fairly. This is a task that can only be achieved if those in positions of power and authority in organisations are also prepared to manage ethically.

Business ethics

It is commonplace, as the following quotations show, for most books on organisations and management to make some reference to business ethics:

> Ethics are moral principles or beliefs about what is right or wrong. These beliefs guide people in their dealings with other individuals and groups (stakeholders) and provide a basis for deciding whether behavior is right and proper.   (Jones *et al*, 2000: 183)

> Managers today are usually quite sensitive to issues of social responsibility and ethical behavior because of pressure from the public, from interest groups, from legal and government concerns, and from media coverage. It is less clear where to draw the line between socially responsible behaviour and the corporation's other concerns, or between the conflicting expectations of ethical behaviour among different countries.   (Deresky, 2000: 56)

There is certainly no shortage of advice about what ethics are or how they should be applied to business. The problem, as the last quotation shows, is that, in an increasingly complex, diverse and competitive world, applying an ethical approach to business is not straightforward. This is why many companies and governments, even those who profess to have ethical policies, have difficulty bridging the gap between rhetoric and reality, as the following extracts show:

> The [UK] government's own arms sales department is directly implicated in bribery abroad, according to documents obtained by the Guardian. Such bribery has supposedly been out-lawed since 2001. Current Ministry of Defence files show that DESO, the defence exports services organisation, officially authorises what it calls 'special commissions' paid by arms firms. Payment arrangements are even written by civil servants into the secret contracts on government-to-government arms deals. Firms which pay the bribes, described as 'common-place in certain parts of the world', are, it is explained, exempt from normal MoD rules banning corruption.
>
> (Evans *et al*, 2003: 1)

> Swiss investigators have joined the US in the biggest bribery investigation ever into foreign deals where millions of pounds of apparently legitimate payments by BP, Shell and others allegedly ended up in the hands of Kazakhstan officials.
>
> (Macalister, 2003: 1)

> Workers at nine Nike plants in Indonesia have been found to suffer from sexual and verbal abuse, lack of medical attention and compulsory overtime. ... The company has issued a remediation plan to placate its critics. Nike's healthy corporate image has been battered in recent years by allegations that it employs underage workers in its Asian factories and asks all employees to work long hours for low pay in conditions that would never pass US inspections.
>
> (Left, 2001: 1)

> A chill must have swept through many a City [of London] boardroom yesterday after Louise Barton won her appeal in a high-profile sex discrimination case. The case has shone a spot-light on the secretive pay structures of investment banks, which are known for paying large discretionary bonuses. ... Statistics show that women earn on average 19 per cent less per hour than men across all professions. But for women working in the City, the disparity can be even greater. Typically, those on six-figure salaries earn an average of almost 60 per cent less than their male counterparts.
>
> (Saigol, 2003: 8)

Though these ethical shortcomings can be viewed as examples of corporate management valuing the interests of one group of stakeholders above those of other groups, that is not the end of the story. The last decade has also shown that in many instances, senior and even junior managers have put their own personal interests above those of everybody else, even to the extent of breaking the law. There can be few people unaware of the Enron scandal, where a number of senior managers conspired to line their own pockets at the expense of everyone else and, in the process, ruined the company and destroyed its accountants, Arthur Andersen (Bryce, 2002). As Partnoy (2003: 1) observed, however, this was not an isolated incident:

> The 1990s were a decade of persistently rising markets – 10 years of economic expansion, with investors pouring record amounts into stocks and pocketing double-digit returns year after year. ... The decade was peppered with financial debacles, but these faded quickly from memory even as they increased in size and complexity. The billion dollar-plus scandals included Robert Citron of Orange County, Nick Leeson of Barings and John Meriwether of Long-Term Capital Management, but the markets merely hiccoughed and then started going

> up again. When Enron collapsed in late 2001, it shattered some investors' beliefs and took a few other stocks down with it. Then Global Crossing and WorldCom declared bankruptcy, and dozens of corporate scandals materialised as the leading stock indices lost a quarter of their value. … Companies' reported earnings were a fiction and financial reports chock-full of disclosures that would shock the average investor if they ever even glanced at them – not that anybody ever did.

In the USA, the finger has been pointing very sharply at the practices of Wall Street analysts who aggressively oversold shares, as Tran (2003: 1) observed:

> … analysts hoodwinked investors by hyping up the prospects of internet and other hi-tech companies, while privately dismissing them. Former star internet analyst Henry Blodget once privately described as a 'piece of shit' a stock he was publicly touting, according to previously disclosed emails.

According to Teather (2002), the hyping or 'ramping' of shares was central to the operation of Wall Street's financial institutions and not just limited to a few rogue analysts. In May 2003, in an attempt to draw a line under the crimes of the boom years, leading Wall Street financial institutions agreed to pay fines totalling $1.4 billion (Tran, 2003). Nevertheless, corporate greed was not limited to Wall Street, and much of it was quite legal. Across America, executive salaries rose dramatically in the 1990s. In 1980, the average CEO salary was 42 times than that of the average hourly-paid worker, by 1990 it was 85 times greater, but by 2000 it had grown to 531 times greater (AFL-CIO, 2003). A similar phenomenon, though on a lesser scale, could be seen in the UK where, in the 1990s, basic executive salaries rose four times faster than inflation, and additional rewards, such as bonuses and share options, far outstripped even that (Business Notebook, 2003). However, what really seems to have annoyed UK investors is not that executives are rewarded for success, but that they also get rewarded for failure. As noted in Chapter 5, amongst FTSE-100 companies the pay of directors rose 84 per cent in the three years to 2003 but the stock market value of these companies fell by 50 per cent (Finch and Treanor, 2003). In the UK, 2003 will go down as the year of the shareholder revolt. At AGM after AGM, shareholders in leading companies, such as HSBC, Shell and, most spectacularly of all, GlaxoSmithKline voted in large numbers to reject salary packages that they saw as too generous or which promised to reward failure (Stewart, 2003). It is no wonder, therefore, that opinion polls show that the vast majority of people in the UK think executives are untrustworthy and overpaid (Caulkin, 2003).

Though in the West the 1990s was the decade when the rich got seriously richer, for the world's poorest countries, the reverse was the case. In the 1990s, 54 countries saw their average income decline, and 21 went backwards in terms of human development – a measure of income, life expectancy and literacy; the number of people in sub-Saharan Africa living on less than $1 a day increased from 47 to 49 per cent, and in eastern and central Europe it increased from 7 to 20 per cent (Elliott, 2003).

In public at least, there are two aspects of business ethics that business leaders agree upon: all businesses should have them, and all businesses have difficulty abiding by them. Difficult though they are to implement and maintain, if organisations fail to adopt an ethical approach, the result can be disastrous. Managers can put their own interests above those of shareholders, staff and the law, as the collapse of Enron demonstrated. Entire industries can become corrupt, as the Wall Street example shows. Above and beyond that, however, we create societies and a world where there are increasing divisions between the few 'haves' and the many 'have-nots'.

Globalisation is often couched in terms of the competitive challenge it poses for individual organisations, i.e. how can an organisation, whether in the public, private or voluntary sectors, survive and prosper in a borderless world that is increasingly dominated by a few giant, transnational corporations? As the discussion of sustainability, diversity and ethics shows, however, globalisation also raises crucial questions about the role and impact of organisations on and in a global society. These questions go beyond traditional business concerns such as profit and loss, value for money or market share; they are concerned with fundamental issues of the role of organisations in sustaining life on Earth, respect for human diversity and dignity, and the ethical rules by which we live. These issues are not new, but globalisation has accentuated and brought them to the fore as never before. Governments, international bodies and individual organisations have responded by adopting policies that supposedly promote responsible and ethical behaviour. All big organisations and many small ones now have policies on minimising their environmental impact, promoting and managing diversity, and on behaving in an ethical fashion. Nevertheless, the gap between ethical rhetoric and the reality of unethical behaviour seems to be getting wider rather than narrower. The real challenge for organisations is to change managerial behaviour so that business ethics become business practices. Policies, skills and good intentions are clearly not enough. The fundamental point is that managers need to behave differently. They need to put the policies and skills into practice. Therefore, in examining the role and development of managers in the rest of this chapter, one of the key issues to be addressed will be what determines managerial behaviour and how can we change it.

The manager's role

It has never been easy to define the role of managers, though this has not prevented a great number of attempts over the years (*see* Barnard, 1938; Brewer and Tomlinson, 1964; Carlson, 1951; Constable and McCormick, 1987; Golding and Currie, 2000; Griffin, 2002; Handy *et al*, 1987; Horne and Lupton, 1965; Kotter, 1982, 1990; Mintzberg, 1973, 1975; Nahavandi, 2000; Silverman and Jones, 1976; Sjöstrand, 1997; Stewart, 1976; Yukl, 2002). As Hales (1986) found when he reviewed many of these studies, the information available presents the reader with a confusing and conflicting picture of what managers should do and how they should do it.

Definitions of the role of managers have ranged from attempts to list basic tasks:

[The manager] plans, organises, directs and controls, on proprietors' or own behalf, an industrial, commercial or other undertaking, establishment or organisation, and co-ordinates the work of departmental managers or other immediate subordinates.

(Quoted in Dakin and Hamilton, 1990: 32)

to more ambitious attempts to define the essence of the manager's role:

> [The manager has the] task of creating a true whole that is larger than the sum of its parts, a productive entity that turns out more than the sum of the resources put into it.
>
> (Drucker 1985: 53)

Drucker (1985) also likened the manager to the conductor of a symphony orchestra. As conductor, the manager is the one through whose effort, vision and leadership the various instrumental parts, that are so much noise by themselves, become the living whole of music. In this instance, the manager is also the composer as well as the conductor.

Handy (1986), on the other hand, likened the manager to a doctor: the manager is the first recipient of problems. The manager's role is, therefore, to identify the symptoms in any situation; to diagnose the disease or cause of the trouble; to decide how it might be dealt with, through a strategy for health; and to start the treatment.

Such analogies are useful in that they create a concrete picture of the manager's role, but they can also be misleading. Conducting is an art form; is management an art form? Or, as Handy's analogy implies, is it a science in the same way that medicine is a science? As Part 1 of this book showed, the clash between those who see management as a rational, science-based process, and those who believe it to be more intuitive and less rational, is not new.

Duncan (1975) tried to resolve this conflict by taking a holistic view of the job of the manager. He identifies three distinct levels of management activity: *philosophical* (goal formation); *scientific* (goal accomplishment and evaluation); and *art* (implementation of decisions). At the philosophical level in forming goals, the manager – Duncan argues – is mainly concerned with the effects of the actions and reactions of other individuals and groups within the wider economic and social context within which the organisation is set. At this level, managers and their associates formulate clear and precise strategies that will encompass all envisaged effects that can result from the set goals, not only on the various pressure groups within its internal and external environment, but also on competitors and regulatory agencies. It is also at this level that the ethics of managerial behaviour, values and priorities of the organisation are formulated and established. At the scientific level, management develops plans, methods and techniques for achieving set goals, and establishes procedures for monitoring and evaluating progress.

The art level is concerned with the implementation of decisions; this is the level at which tactical and administrative decisions are made to deploy the organisation's resources and attain the optimum degree of operational efficiency. This level is an 'art' because, according to Duncan, there appears to be a particular talent necessary to persuade others that management-generated goals and decisions should be accepted.

Whilst one might not necessarily agree with his definitions, especially in terms of strategy formulation, Duncan's three-level approach is extremely useful in that it shows, as Mullins (1989) argued, that management is both a science and an art. By its very nature, management is forced to deal with both rational, science-based activities, such as the design and operation of manufacturing and administrative systems, and less rational, more intuitive activities, especially those concerning managing and motivating people. The extent to which a manager is involved in any of these activities will depend on the kind of organisation the manager works for, the type of job the manager has, and – crucially – the manager's level in the organisation's hierarchy (Hales, 1986). Position in the hierarchy, formally at least, is likely to exert the greatest influence on the role given to and expected of a manager. The three main hierarchical levels are as follows:

- **Top management** – the policy-making group responsible for the overall direction of the company.
- **Middle management** – responsible for the execution and interpretation of policies throughout the organisation and for the successful operation of assigned divisions or departments.
- **First level or supervisory management** – directly responsible to the middle management group for ensuring the execution of policies by their subordinates. They are also responsible for the attainment of objectives by the units they control, through practices and procedures approved and issued by top or middle management.

Superficially, at least, these three categories appear to mirror Duncan's three levels. On a closer examination, however, it becomes more difficult to match them because each category can encompass all three levels. This can be seen more clearly by examining what it is that managers actually do, as averse to what academics say they should do.

There have been a number of important studies conducted to determine how managers spend their time (*see* for example Brewer and Tomlinson, 1964; Child and Ellis, 1973; Kotter, 1982). Perhaps the most widely known and replicated work in this area is by Mintzberg (1973, 1975). Synthesising his results and the previous research on the role of managers, he concluded as follows:

- Although much managerial work is unprogrammed, all managers do have regular, ordinary duties to perform.
- Rather than being systematic, reflective thinkers and planners, managers simply respond to the pressures or demands of their jobs.
- Managerial activities are characterised by brevity, variety and discontinuity.

Some 30 years after Mintzberg's work, Yukl (2002), in reviewing the literature on management, came to similar conclusions:

- The content of managerial work is varied and fragmented.
- Many activities are reactive.
- Interactions often involve peers and outsiders.
- Many interactions involve oral communications.
- Decision processes arc disorderly and political.
- Most planning is informal and adaptive.

Yukl (2002: 22) also found that the pace of managerial work was hectic and unrelenting:

> During the typical workday there is seldom a break in the workload. Managers receive almost continuous requests for information, assistance, direction, and authorization from a large number of people, such as subordinates, peers, superiors, and people outside the organization.

Yukl's work confirms Mintzberg's (1973) finding that managers' jobs are remarkably similar, and that their work can be described in terms of ten very important roles that could be categorised under three headings: interpersonal, informational and decision-making.

Interpersonal roles

One of the most time-consuming and important aspects of most managerial jobs is to work with, direct and represent people. The three key roles in this respect are as follows:

- **figurehead** – as the formal representative of the organisation;
- **liaison** – forming connections with other organisations;
- **leader** – in relation to members of a group within the organisation.

Informational roles

Those in managerial positions have unique opportunities to obtain and disseminate information. The three key roles involved are given below:

- **monitor** – as monitors, managers seek, receive and store information that can be used to the advantage of the company;
- **disseminator** – the manager must broadcast this useful information to the organisation;
- **spokesperson** – on behalf of the organisation, the manager communicates information to other relevant groups and bodies, both internal and external.

Decision-making roles

One of the main parts of any manager's job is to take decisions. In this respect, there are four key roles involved:

- **entrepreneur** – looking for ways to improve the operation of the organisation or for new product/market opportunities;
- **disturbance-handler** – managers must handle crises effectively;
- **resource allocator** – responsible for constructing budgets and allocating resources;
- **negotiator** – according to Mintzberg, managers spend a great deal of their time as negotiators, because only they have the necessary information and the authority to carry out this role.

As Yukl (2002) notes, though these roles are common to most managerial jobs, the emphasis and importance of these roles varies between managers depending on a range of factors such as organisation size, level of management, level of managerial independence, and the stage the organisation had reached in its life cycle. Mintzberg (1975) argued that the lack of uniformity within managerial jobs can be accounted for by hierarchical and functional differentiation. He contended that chief executives, for example, focus considerable attention on external roles, such as liaison, spokesperson and figurehead, which link the organisation to its environment. At lower levels, work is more focused, more short-term in outlook, and the characteristics of brevity and fragmentation are more pronounced. As a result of this, the external managerial roles are less important, and real-time internal roles (disturbance-handler and negotiator) concerned with daily operating problems and maintaining the work flow become relatively more important. Furthermore, he argued that interpersonal roles are more important to sales managers, that staff managers give more attention to informational roles, and production managers focus on decisional roles. Mintzberg's observations have been supported by a number of other studies (Kotter, 1982; Silverman and Jones, 1976).

Stewart (1976, 1982) drew particular attention to demands, constraints and choices in shaping managerial roles:

- **Demands** – these are the expectations that those in positions of power have for a role holder.
- **Constraints** – these are factors peculiar to the organisation and its environment that limit a manager's freedom of manoeuvre.
- **Choices** – though managers are limited in what they can do by the demands and constraints of their jobs, all managers have a degree of discretion (choice) in what to do and when to do it.

One key area where managers are called on to make choices is when faced with role conflicts. For example, managers are often caught between subordinates' expectations that managers will protect their interests and provide resources, and superiors' expectations that managers will act in the best interests of the organisation and minimise costs. Another example of conflict between roles is where managers are expected to spend considerable time, in their figurehead role, dealing with the external world whilst at the same time colleagues expect them to be present internally carrying out their leadership role.

Nevertheless, despite the presence of conflicts and choices, Hales (1986: 102), in reviewing the research on the manager's role, concluded that:

> Much of what managers do is, of necessity, an unreflective response to circumstances. The manager is less a slow and methodical decision maker, more a 'doer' who has to react rapidly to problems as they arise, 'think on his feet', take decisions in situ and develop a preference for concrete activities. This shows in the pace of managerial work and the short time span of most activities ...

Therefore, in examining the role of managers, it can be seen that there is a discrepancy between what the literature says managers should do and what the managers actually do. Indeed, as Mintzberg (1975: 49) pointed out, this discrepancy even extends to managers' own observations on their role:

> If you ask a manager what he does, he will most likely tell you he plans, organizes, co-ordinates and controls. Then watch what he does. Don't be surprised if you can't relate what you see to those four words.

Important as it is to understand the manager's role, it is just as important, if not more so, to understand what constitutes effectiveness. Despite the very many books and articles on management and the role of the managers, most writers seem to shy away from defining either organisational or managerial effectiveness. Part 1 of this book reviewed organisation theory and behaviour. What this showed is that the promoters of these theories, either implicitly or explicitly, state that effectiveness is defined by the extent to which managers adopt their 'one best way'. From this perspective, however, effectiveness is something of a moving target; the 'best way' for Frederick Taylor is not the best way for Douglas McGregor or Tom Peters or Peter Senge. Nahavandi (2000: 5) made a similar point when commenting that '... leadership effectiveness depends on the point of view of the person who is evaluating the leader.' In an attempt to cut through the idea that effectiveness is defined by adherence to a particular approach or theory, or lies solely in the eye of the beholder, Burnes (1998: 101) defined effectiveness as '... the ability or power to have a desired effect ...'. In terms of managerial effectiveness, this means that an effective manager is one who achieves what is required of them, whether that be to transform an organisation or merely to ensure that services continue to be delivered on time, at the right cost and to the right quality. If this is the definition of managerial effectiveness, the next question is: 'What determines managerial effectiveness?' Are there key attributes, skills or competences that managers need to possess in order to 'have a desired effect'? As the next section will show, there are three main perspectives on what makes an effective manager.

Management and leadership

Regardless of the difficulty in identifying what managers do or how they should do it, there has been a long-held belief that the major factor which distinguishes successful organisations from their less successful counterparts is the presence of dynamic and effective leadership (Jones *et al*, 2000). However, as Yukl (2002: 5) observes, '... there is a continuing controversy about the difference between leadership and management.' For some writers, such as Nahavandi (2000) – *see* Table 16.1, management and leadership are seen as being distinctly different activities. Nahavandi sees the process of management as essentially concerned with achieving stability. On the other hand, he sees leadership as essentially being concerned with bringing about change. Nahavandi (2000: 13) comments that:

> Whereas leaders have long-term and future-oriented perspectives and provide a vision for their followers that looks beyond their immediate surroundings, managers have short-term perspectives and focus on routine issues within their own immediate departments or groups.

Bennis and Namus (1985: 21) take this argument further by associating management and leadership with different types of people: '... managers are people who do things right and leaders are people who do the right thing'. Though it is conceptually appealing to separate people into one of two mutually exclusive types, managers or leaders, there is little empirical evidence for this view (Yukl, 2002). It is also a view that, in a rapidly-changing world, tends to imply that visionary leaders are superior to their stick-in-the-mud managerial counterparts. On the other hand, there are many writers who, whilst distinguishing between management processes and leadership processes (as in Table 16.1), do not assume that leaders and managers are different types of people (Bass, 1990; Hickman, 1990; Mintzberg, 1973; Rost, 1991; Yukl, 2002). Indeed, Vroom and Jago (1988) specifically argue that managers can and do possess both managerial and leadership skills, which they swap between depending on the situation.

Table 16.1 **Management v leadership**

Managers	*Leaders*
Focus on the present	Focus on the future
Maintain status quo and stability	Create change
Implement policies and procedures	Create a culture based on shared values
Remain aloof to maintain objectivity	Establish an emotional link with followers
Use the power of their position	Use personal power

Source: adapted from Nahavandi (2000)

Though the topic of leadership, its definition, promotion and difference from management, has dominated the management literature for over 40 years, it still remains an elusive concept. Even in the 1950s, when there had been much less research on the subject than now, Bennis (1959: 259) commented:

> Always it seems that the concept of leadership eludes us or turns up in another form to taunt us again with its slipperiness and complexity. So we have invented a proliferation of terms to deal with it ... and still the concept is not sufficiently defined.

Now, at the beginning of the third millennium, we are faced with a greater proliferation of articles and books on the subject than ever before, yet the topic appears more fragmented and confusing than ever. As Thomas (2003: 25) comments in relation to the question 'What is management?':

> The inquisitive reader seeking an answer to this question will find not only differences but complete contradictions and may well be inclined to beat a hasty retreat ...

Nevertheless, it is possible to divide researchers on leadership and management into three main groups: those who focus on the personal characteristics and process of leadership; those who concentrate on the leader–follower situation; and those who attempt to relate leadership and management styles to the overall organisation context and climate.

■ The personal characteristics–trait approach to effective leadership

Early investigations into leadership tended to concentrate on such factors as personal qualities (intelligence, age, experience), or personality traits (extroversion, dominance). Consequently, regardless of the task or situation, if a person did not possess the appropriate personal attributes, then he or she was deemed unlikely to be a good manager. The numerous studies of leadership failed, however, to reveal any consistent pattern of traits or characteristics related to leadership (Arnold *et al*, 1998; Gibb, 1969; Yukl, 1994).

In an effort to breathe new life into this approach, attempts were made to view leadership as a process, and the focus moved to examining the interaction between leaders and followers, and how leaders influence individuals and groups to pursue the achievement of a given goal. This view, that leadership behaviour rather than attributes may more effectively predict leadership success, has been advanced in a variety of approaches. Fleishman (1953, 1969) identified two separate classes of behaviour as important in determining effective leadership:

1 **Consideration** – the quality of the interpersonal relationship between the leader and his or her subordinates, and in particular the degree to which a leader shows trust of subordinates, respect for their ideas and consideration for their feelings.
2 **Initiating structure** – the degree to which leaders define and structure their own and their subordinates' roles towards achieving set goals. It also covers the extent to which a leader directs group activities through planning, communication, information, scheduling, trying out new ideas, and praise and criticism.

Another related dimension of leadership behaviour that received much attention in the 1950s and 1960s was participation – whether the leader leans towards an autocratic or democratic style of management. As was noted in Chapters 2 and 8, both the Human Relations school and proponents of Planned change believed that, in the aftermath of the Second World War, participation and democracy would prove to be essential components of organisational effectiveness. It was not a coincidence that those studying leadership and those studying organisational change should develop similar views on participation and democracy. Much of the work on leadership at this time was influenced by a series of ground-breaking studies into leadership styles by Kurt Lewin, Ronald Lippitt and Ralph White (Marrow, 1969). These studied three styles of leadership – democratic, autocratic and laissez faire, and found that democratic leadership produced the best results (Lewin, 1999b; Lippitt and White, 1960). According to Gastil (1994), there are three key elements of democratic leadership:

- maximising participation and involvement of group members;
- empowerment;
- facilitating group decision-making.

In the 1950s and 1960s, this stress on leadership characteristics gave rise to a number of 'universal theories' of effective leader behaviour – which is to say, researchers began to argue for a 'one best way' approach to leadership (see for example Argyris, 1964; Likert, 1967; McGregor, 1960). These theories postulated that the same style of leadership is optimal in all situations (Yukl, 1994).

Perhaps the best known and most influential of these 'universal theories' is Blake and Mouton's (1969, 1985) Managerial Grid – later re-named the Leadership Grid (Blake and McCanse, 1991). The Grid has two critical dimensions: *concern for people* – similar to *consideration*; and *concern for production* – similar to *initiating structure*. By examining how these two dimensions interact, in both their strong and weak states, Blake and Mouton identified five different styles of management, which they labelled as follows:

- **Team management**. This arises from a high concern for people and a high concern for production. The objectives are to achieve high levels of both performance and job satisfaction by gaining subordinates' willing commitment to achieving their assigned tasks.
- **Country club management**. This occurs when concern for production is low but concern for people is high. The main concern of this approach is to achieve the harmony and well-being of the group in question by satisfying people's social and relationship needs.

- **Middle-of-the-road management.** This situation comes about where there is moderate concern for production and moderate concern for people. Managers who follow this approach tend to have a 'live and let live' philosophy and tend to avoid difficult or contentious issues.
- **Task management.** This can be defined as a high concern for production but a low concern for people. The objective is to achieve high productivity by planning, organising and directing work in such a way that human considerations are kept to a minimum.
- **Impoverished management.** This ensues from a low concern for both production and people. This form of managerial behaviour centres on exacting the minimum effort from subordinates in order to achieve the required result.

Though Blake and Mouton (1985) identify these five styles of management, for them the most effective is team management, where leaders are both task- and people-orientated – the so-called 'high–high' leader. They also argue that whilst managers have a dominant or preferred style of leadership, many managers are capable of switching from one style to another or of combining styles if they encounter a situation where their preferred style does not work. In a significant departure from other adherents of the personal characteristics approach, Blake and Mouton also argue that a person's dominant style is influenced not only by their personal values and personal history but by the nature of the organisation in which they are operating, and chance – the types of management situations and styles they have encountered in their career.

Despite the wide number of studies seeking to test and elaborate the Managerial Grid approach, however, the evidence in support of it, or for any of the universal theories, is limited (Evans, 1970; Filley *et al*, 1976; Larson *et al*, 1976; Wagner, 1994; Yukl, 1994, 2002). Because of the difficulty of relating leadership traits and behaviours to effectiveness, many writers turned to investigate the nature of the relationship between leaders and their subordinates.

The leader–follower situation approach to effective leadership

In response to the inability of researchers to make a convincing case for a 'one best way' approach to leadership, attention began to focus on identifying the situations in which leaders were effective. In particular, researchers began to examine how a leader's behaviour varies between subordinates. This leader–follower approach, or leader–member exchange as it is sometimes called, is concerned with how the two parties develop an interpersonal relationship over time. It focuses on how the leader and the follower influence each other and negotiate the subordinate's role in the organisation. The basic premise of the theory is that a leader develops a different relationship with each subordinate. These relationships take one of two forms: the leader will develop a close and trusting relationship with a small number of people, and a much more distant and formal relationship with the rest. In the first type of relationship, both parties have high expectations of each other. The leader expects loyalty and commitment and the follower expects preferment and advancement. In the more distant types of relationship, both parties have relatively low expectations. The leader expects the subordinate to comply with rules and perform their allocated duties. In turn, the subordinate expects to receive the rate for the job and be treated fairly (Graen and Cashman, 1975; Yukl, 2002).

In examining leader–follower relations, Kerr *et al* (1974) took the two forms of leadership behaviour identified by Fleishman (1969) – consideration and initiating structure – and applied these to a framework that included three situational variables or contingencies:

1 **Subordinate considerations** – such as the subordinates' experience and abilities, and their expectations of the leader.
2 **Superior considerations** – in particular, the amount of influence subordinates have over the behaviour of their superiors.
3 **Task considerations** – including factors such as time urgency, amount of physical danger, permissible error rate, presence of external stress, degree of autonomy and scope, importance and meaningfulness of work, and degree of ambiguity.

Kerr *et al* (1974) argued that the effectiveness of the two forms of leadership behaviour (consideration and initiating structure) in promoting high levels of performance from subordinates is moderated by the above three situational variables. For example, if the task to be performed is characterised by time pressure, subordinates will be more amenable to a higher level of initiating structure (i.e. direction by superiors) and there will be a stronger relationship between job satisfaction, performance and initiating structure. Alternatively, when a task is seen as intrinsically very satisfying to a subordinate, a leadership style with high consideration will not significantly increase satisfaction or performance. Support for the central premises of Kerr *et al*'s (1974) model has been limited. Research by Schriesheim and Murphy (1976) produced mixed results. There was evidence that high levels of initiating structure did increase performance in high-pressure situations and reduce it under low levels of pressure. Different levels of pressure, however, did not appear to impact on subordinates' satisfaction with their superiors. Nor, where tasks were viewed as having higher clarity, were either consideration-based or initiating structure-based styles significantly related to satisfaction.

The most influential situational theory of leadership has been Fiedler's (1967) Least Preferred Co-worker (LPC) model. Based on a decade of research, Fiedler argued that leaders have relatively stable personal characteristics that, in turn, leave them with a particular set of leadership behaviours which they cannot change. Therefore, there is no point in trying to train or educate managers to adopt different behaviours towards their subordinates. Instead, both they and their subordinates have to learn to live with the leader's behaviour. For Fiedler, the key personal characteristics involved in leadership concern how positively or not the leader views his or her Least Preferred Co-worker. Fiedler developed a questionnaire to determine a leader's LPC measure. The questionnaire is built around a scale of 16 bi-polar adjectives (e.g. pleasant–unpleasant, distant–close, efficient–inefficient) that attempts to measure whether a person is 'task' or 'relationship' orientated. As Arnold *et al* (1998) note, there is some dispute about exactly what a leader's LPC score means and how it relates to other leadership dimensions such as consideration and structure. In general, leaders with a high LPC are often seen as being people- or relationship-orientated, whilst those with a low LPC are seen as being task-orientated. From his work, Fiedler concluded that the effectiveness of particular leadership traits or behaviours, as measured by a high or low LPC score, are moderated by the situation in which they are deployed. Therefore, it is important to match the leader to the situation (Fiedler and

Chemers, 1984). Fiedler identified three key aspects of a work situation, which taken together, he argued, determined the effectiveness or not of particular leadership characteristics. In descending order of importance, these are as follows:

1 **The leader–follower relationship** – friendliness and loyalty from subordinates increases the leader's influence over them.
2 **Task structure** – the greater the degree of standardisation, detailed instructions and objective measures of performance, the more favourable the situation for the leader.
3 **The leader's formal position and power** – the more discretion and authority the leader has regarding the reward and punishment of subordinates, the more influence he or she will be able to exert.

By attributing a high or low score to each of these three aspects, Fielder constructed eight (i.e. $2 \times 2 \times 2$) types of work situation. He maintained that the most favourable situation is where leader–follower relations are good, the task is well-defined and highly structured, and the leader has a high level of formal authority. In contrast, the least favourable situation is where leader–follower relations are poor, the task structure is ill-defined, and the leader has only a low level of formal authority.

Although (or perhaps because) it is the most influential and widely-utilised situational theory of leadership, it is also the most widely-criticised. The main criticisms are that it lacks empirical support, that it fails to explain how particular leadership behaviour affects subordinates' performance, and that the measures used by Fiedler are arbitrary and lack any explicit rationale (Ashour, 1973; Shiflett, 1973; Vecchio, 1983). Fiedler's model has also been subjected to the same type of criticism as other contingency-situational approaches (*see* Chapter 2). In particular, critics maintain that it ignores a manager's ability to change or influence factors such as task structure to favour their style of leadership. In this respect, a number of writers have pointed out that Fiedler treats structure, an important component of his model, as a given, whereas in many instances, determining and changing organisation and job structures is a major component of a manager's role (O'Brien and Kabanoff, 1981). In any case, as the following shows, there are those who believe that managers can and do change their leadership behaviours (Vroom and Jago, 1988).

■ The contextual approach to effective leadership

One of the weaknesses of the leadership literature is, as the above demonstrates, that it tends to concentrate on the traits of individual managers and their relations with subordinates. The assumption, both explicit and implicit, is that effectiveness is an attribute of the individual manager, moderated by the leader–subordinate situation; a good manager in one organisation will be a good manager in all organisations. Yet, as many writers have observed, a manager's effectiveness may be determined as much by the nature of the organisation in which he or she operates as by the qualities of the individual manager (*see* Burnes, 1991; Griffin, 2002; Hales, 1986; Nahavandi, 2000; Sjöstrand, 1997).

It is out of and in response to such observations that the contextual approach to leadership developed. This approach is a variant of the leader–follower approach to leadership; however, instead of concentrating on leadership behaviour, it focuses on leadership style, and instead of the narrow leader–follower situation, it focuses on the overall organisation context and climate. In addition, it is the only one of the three approaches to leadership that incorporates change as a variable. One of the most influential contingency approaches to leadership was developed by Vroom and Yetton (1973). This was later extended by Vroom and Jago (1988). In contrast to Fielder, this approach suggests that leaders can and do change their behaviour from situation to situation. The theory identifies five styles of leader decision-making, ranging from the most autocratic to the most democratic. To complement these, Vroom and Jago (1988) also identified some key features of problem situations that leaders have to take into account, such as the need to resolve conflict or achieve goal congruence. By combining leadership styles with problem situations, Vroom and Jago developed a computer package to help managers to identify how suitable or not their style is for particular situations. Unfortunately, the package has proved very complex to use, which has limited its efficacy. Nevertheless, Vroom and Jago have expressed the hope that knowledge of its general principles may be sufficient for most situations. To this end, as Arnold *et al* (1998) note, Vroom and Jago's model has been used to provide some general 'rules of thumb' for leaders, including advice such as:

■ Where subordinates' commitment is important, a more participative style of leadership is better.
■ Where subordinates do not share the organisation's goals, group decision-making should be avoided.

However, advice couched in such general terms is usually too general to be of much use. Even if they were not so general, these rules of thumb are still subject to being overridden by factors such as time constraints, organisational policies and the ability and preferences of managers and subordinates. This is perhaps why other contextual approaches have also been put forward.

One of the most interesting and influential of these was developed not by a social scientist but by a political scientist, James MacGregor Burns, in his 1978 Pulitzer Prize winning book, *Leadership*. Burns' book combines biography, history and political theory to produce a major study of the nature of leadership. Primarily, he identifies two basic organisation states or contexts, convergent and divergent; and two matching management-leadership styles, transactional management and transformational leadership. Most writers tend to use the terms management and leadership interchangeably. Burns was the first to draw a distinction between what he called transactional management (which focuses on maintaining the *status quo*) and transformational leadership (which focuses on overthrowing the *status quo*). However, Burns was primarily concerned with management and leadership in the political context. Bass (1985, 1995) refined Burns' concepts and applied them to organisations.

A *convergent* state occurs when an organisation is operating under stable conditions; where there are established and accepted goals and a predictable external and internal environment (Case Study 10, PoliceCo, is an example of an organisation operating in a convergent state). The most appropriate style of management in such a situation, it is contended, is *transactional*. The concept of transactional management stems from the notion that the manager–subordinate relationship is based on a transaction between the two, whereby managers exchange rewards for subordinates' performance. Transactional managers focus on task completion, goal clarification and optimising the performance of the organisation through incremental changes within the confines of existing policy, structures and practices – basically, they seek to work within and maintain the status quo (*see* Table 16.2). Transactional managers motivate followers to perform the tasks expected of them by appealing to their self-interest through the use of incentives and rewards such as pay and promotion.

A *divergent* state occurs when environmental changes challenge the efficiency and appropriateness of an organisation's established goals, structures and ways of working (Case Study 3, Oticon, is an example of an organisation operating in a divergent state). The most appropriate style of leadership in this situation, it is argued, is *transformational*. Transformational leaders are often portrayed as charismatic or visionary individuals who seek to overturn the status quo and bring about radical change (*see* Table 16.2). Transformational leaders use the force of their personality to motivate followers to identify with the leader's vision and to sacrifice their self-interest in favour of that of the group or organisation. Transformational leaders seek to gain the trust and emotional commitment of their followers by appealing to higher moral and ethical values.

Table 16.2 **Management v leadership**

	Transactional management	*Transformational leadership*
Creating the agenda	Planning and budgeting: developing a detailed plan of how to achieve the results.	Establishing direction: developing a vision that describes a future state along with a strategy for getting there.
People	Organising and staffing: which individual best fits each job and what part of the plan fits each individual.	Aligning people: a major communication challenge in getting people to understand and believe the vision.
Execution	Controlling and problem-solving: monitoring results, identifying deviations from the plan and solving the problems.	Motivating and inspiring: satisfying basic human needs for achievement, belonging, recognition, self-esteem, a sense of control.
Outcomes	Produces a degree of predictability and order.	Produces changes – often to a dramatic degree.

Source: adapted from Kotter (1990)

The compatibility between organisational state and leadership style is seen as essential for successful leadership. Where the organisation is required to face new challenges and develop new ways of adapting to these for the sake of survival, then a purely transactional approach would be counter-productive – the phrase 'fiddling while Rome burns' springs to mind. However, transformational leadership is just as likely to be counter-productive during periods where maintenance of the current operational systems would be most appropriate.

Since its publication in 1978, Burns' work has been taken up and cited by a wide range of organisation theorists who subscribe to the view that managers need to, and can, match or adapt their style and approach to the circumstances of the organisation in which they operate (Arnold *et al*, 1998; Bass, 1985, 1995; Beatty and Lee, 1992; Burnes and James, 1995; French and Bell, 1995; Gibbons, 1992; Yukl, 1994). As argued in Chapter 3, however, the late 1970s and early 1980s, the period when Burns' book was published, was a time of crisis for many Western organisations. It was a period when organisations and entire industries and sectors were going through massive changes. Not surprisingly, therefore, there was a tendency for those in the leadership field to focus on Transformational leadership, and downplay or even denigrate Transactional management (Yukl, 2002). However, Bass (1985, 1995), whilst seeking to develop the concept of the Transformational leader, argued that Transformational leadership and Transactional management are distinct but not mutually exclusive processes. Transformational leaders may be more effective at motivating their followers but, Bass maintains, effective leaders need to have both transformational and transactional tools in their armouries. In situations where radical change is required, however, as Alimo-Metcalfe and Alban-Metcalfe (2000: 27) found when studying leadership in the UK National Health Service (NHS), '… the transactional competencies of managers, while crucial, are simply not sufficient on their own.' The argument from Bass (1985, 1995) and Alimo-Metcalfe and Alban-Metcalfe (2000) is that someone with purely transactional skills would struggle to deal effectively with the many changes that are an ever-present part of organisational life. On the other hand, someone with purely transformational skills would not be able to cope with the day-to-day, routine activities that need to be accomplished even where radical change is taking place. The key issue, therefore, is to identify the optimum balance of transactional-transformational skills in any given circumstances.

Kanter (1989) offers a different perspective on the balance issue by maintaining that good leaders need to incorporate both transactional and transformational characteristics. She argues that archetypal images of managers tend to derive from two basic models: the 'corpocrat' (i.e. the transactional manager) and the 'cowboy' (i.e. the transformational leader). The former is the corporate bureaucrat, the conservative resource-preserver who lives by, and controls the organisation through, established and detailed rules. The latter, the 'cowboy', is a maverick who challenges the established order, who wants to seize every opportunity, question every rule and who motivates and controls through personal loyalty. However, instead of seeking to relate the balance of these two sets of characteristics to their appropriate organisational setting, Kanter (1989: 361) argues that, in future, organisations will require managers who combine the best of both the corpocrat and cowboy:

> Without the bold impulses of the take-action entrepreneurs and their constant questioning of the rules, we would miss one of the most potent sources of business revitalization and development. But without the discipline and coordination of conventional management, we could find waste instead of growth, unnecessary risk instead of revitalization. … Our new heroic model [of leadership] should be the athlete who can manage the amazing feat of doing more with less, who can juggle the need to both conserve resources and pursue growth opportunities. This new kind of business hero avoids the excesses of both the corpocrat and the cowboy. … the business athlete has the strength to balance somewhere in the middle, taking the best of the corpocrat's discipline and the cowboy's entrepreneurial zeal.

Exhibit 16.3	Characteristics of the business hero

Skills and sensibilities of the business athlete

1. Learn to operate without the might of the hierarchy.
2. Compete in a way that enhances rather than undercuts cooperation.
3. Operate with the highest ethical standards.
4. Have a dose of humility.
5. Develop a process focus.
6. Be multifaceted and ambidextrous.
7. Gain satisfaction from results.

Source: Kanter 1989: 361–4

As Exhibit 16.3 shows, Kanter maintains that there are seven skills and sensibilities that this 'new heroic' type of leader needs to possess. Kanter's model avoids the issue of how to determine the optimum balance of transactional and transformational skills in a given set of circumstances. Instead, she argues that there is a basic set of transactional and transformational skills or characteristics that all effective leaders need to possess and which can be applied successfully in any situation. In effect, she is attempting to turn the leadership debate full circle and make the case for a universal – one best way – approach to leadership. Her argument, as mentioned in Chapter 3, is basically that all organisations operate in the same turbulent context, face the same challenges and, consequently, require the same style of management.

Though there are different perspectives on the contextual approach to leadership, taken as a whole, the approach does not seek to invalidate either the characteristics or situational approaches; rather it tries to incorporate them within and link them to the wider organisational context. It explicitly recognises that a manager's personal characteristics are an important component of leadership style, and consequently, effectiveness. In addition, it acknowledges the crucial importance not just of the relationship between leaders and followers, but also of the overall context within which this takes place (Yukl, 2002). In particular, as Gibbons (1992: 5) remarked, 'organizational survival and success are dependent on the ability of leader–follower relations to resolve the problems of internal integration and external adaptation'. Many writers argue, however, that (despite its attractiveness) there is little evidence to support the case for the contextual approach to leadership or to show that is a more suitable approach to running organisations than either the personal characteristics or leader–follower models (Arnold *et al*, 1998; Hinkin and Tracey, 1999; Yukl, 2002).

Just as a review of the role of managers produced a confusing and conflicting picture, so too does an examination of the three approaches to leadership. Nevertheless, the idea of considering context and style together does fit in, partly at least, with the argument developed in the previous parts of this book: namely that there is a need to match the approach to change to the context of the organisation. That argument was developed further to include the possibility that managers could reverse this process and match the organisation's context to their preferred style of working. However, one major factor needs to be remembered when considering approaches to management: most of the research and writing on leadership is set in Western, and particularly American, organisations, and addresses their concerns (Alimo-Metcalfe and Alban-Metcalfe, 2000). Also, the majority of research studies have tended to focus on male managers and their characteristics (Maddock, 1999; Thomas, 2003). Therefore, before moving on, we need to return to the issue of diversity raised earlier when discussing globalisation.

To recap, Jones *et al* (2000: 166–7) explain that:

> Diversity is dissimilarities – differences – among people due to age, gender, race, ethnicity, religion, sexual orientation, socioeconomic background, and capabilities/disabilities ...

Diversity is not just about differences 'among people', however, it is also about differences between people. According to Ricks (1999: 4):

> Cultural differences are the most significant and troublesome variables encountered by the multinational company.

In terms of differences among people, the posited differences in managerial style between men and women have attracted a great deal of attention (Loden, 1986; Macdonald *et al*, 1999; Maddock, 1999; Mullins, 2002; Thomas, 2003). Davies (1995) for example, found significant differences between masculine and feminine approaches to management. In particular, she found that the masculine approach valued self-esteem, abstract thinking, control and loyalty to superiors. The feminine approach, on the other hand, valued selflessness, contextual thinking, experience and accommodation. It is findings like these that have led writers such as Alimo-Metcalfe (1995a, 1995b) to argue that women prefer to use a more transformational style of leadership whilst men tend to be more transactionally-orientated. Differences in management style are not just gender-related, however, they can also come about due to age, ethnicity, religion, or simple differences in personality (Deresky, 2000; Jones *et al*, 2000). To complicate the picture, these preferences are not stable between countries and cultures. Much of the work on gender and management has tended to focus on the USA and Europe. It is not clear, however, that men and women managers in, for example, Japan and China have the same style preferences as their Western counterparts. Indeed, as Trompenaars' (1993) ten-year study of management in 28 countries covering 47 national cultures showed, the differences between countries is as great as the differences within. His work showed, for example, that managers as a whole, male and female, in Japan and China tended to fit the characteristics attributed to women managers in the West. For example, they favoured relationships as against rules, they promoted interpersonal trust as against contracts, and they tended to avoid rather than welcome confrontation. This, of course, confirms, Hofstede's (1980, 1990) earlier work on cultural differences, which showed that organisational culture, and the values and behaviours of managers, do vary from country to country. Arnold *et al* (1998) maintain that there is also sufficient evidence to show that leader behaviour is interpreted differently in different cultures. Consequently, managerial behaviour that might be considered supportive in one society may be seen as threatening in another. Therefore, we have to be very wary of taking work on managerial styles and behaviour developed in one setting, and assuming it applies to all organisations and all societies.

The implications of these findings for management and leadership are significant. Firstly, there are no universal rules for what is an effective manager or leader. An effective manager in one country, company or situation may be less so in others. Secondly, therefore, effectiveness is situation-dependent. In judging what is or is not an effective approach, managers and leaders need to take into account the nature of the organisation and the diversity of its workforce. Lastly, in training and developing managers, there is a need to recognise that whilst there are some generic skills, competences and behaviours, there will also be a need to tailor development programmes to the person and their situation. The issue of management development will be examined in more detail later. Before doing so, however, we will first examine the behaviour of the managers in the ten case studies in Part 3. By establishing whether their approach was transactional or transformational and the context convergent or divergent, it becomes possible to judge not only the appropriateness of their behaviour in the situation in which they were operating, but also the usefulness of the contextual approach to leadership.

Management and leadership in action

If we examine the case studies in Part 3, we find that managers and the context within which they operated varied enormously. Merely analysing what managers did in each situation, interesting though it would undoubtedly prove, is likely to generate more heat than light. However, using the transactional–transformational and convergent–divergent categorisations discussed above allows a clearer picture to emerge. Taking the case studies in order:

The music industry

For most of the last 50 years, the music industry has operated under a relatively stable set of conditions: artists made music, the big labels recorded and distributed it, and the consumers paid for it. The big record labels recruited the artists and controlled them ruthlessly, often dropping them the minute sales dipped, and took the lion's share of the revenues. It was often the case that artists could earn big money for the labels and end up penniless themselves. Therefore, the industry existed in a convergent state and was managed in a transactional manner. The Internet, however, with the aid of Shawn Fanning, changed all that. Consumers are finding that they do not have to pay for their favourite records; they can download them free from the Internet. The power of the big labels is dependent on their controlling distribution and collecting the sales revenues. Therefore, the industry is entering unknown territory. It is now in a divergent state; the old rules no longer apply, but the new ones have not yet emerged. In such a situation, the key players – the labels – have two choices: they can either try to re-establish their control by fighting Internet piracy, or they can embrace the Internet and seek new and more innovative ways of running the industry. At the moment, they have chosen the former, but this seems destined to fail. No one has yet found a way of controlling the Internet, and if they did, a new Shawn Fanning would come along and find a way round it. Consequently, though the record labels have chosen to tackle a divergent context by continuing with their transactional approach to management, it seems unlikely to succeed.

Marconi

As GEC, Marconi was a company which had been very successful. When George Simpson took over, however, there was great concern by the big, city investors that it had missed out on the Internet/telecoms boom. Arnold Weinstock, in the years leading up to his retirement, had also recognised the need for change but had pursued this through joint ventures. Under Weinstock, GEC operated in a mainly convergent context and was managed in a transactional manner. When Simpson took over, he decided to pursue transformational change through buying and selling companies. In effect, he wanted to exchange those GEC companies who were operating in the old economy, the majority of them, for ones operating in the new economy. This he did at great expense. Unfortunately, the strategy failed and the company, now re-named Marconi, went bust. When a person who has dominated a company for over 30 years retires, a period of change and uncertainty will follow. If the retirement coincides with the emergence of major new technologies, the level of uncertainty will be considerable. Therefore, George Simpson took over GEC at a time when it was operating in a divergent context. He made the assumption, as did the people who controlled the majority of the company's shares, that it needed to be transformed. His transformational style of management was a far cry from that advocated by Kotter (1990), however, as shown in Table 16.2. He did not attempt to motivate and inspire GEC's staff by the power of his vision. Instead, he chose to sell the companies that employed them. As transformational leadership goes, it appeared to be a very uncreative and mechanical example. It also proved to be spectacularly unsuccessful.

Oticon

This was a company that was being left behind as the rules of the game in its industry were being changed by technological advances. In effect, it was a company operating in an increasingly divergent context but which was run on transactional lines. The company was transformed by an inspired Chief Executive, Lars Kolind. He was an archetypical transformational leader who, through his vision and ability to inspire and motivate others, transformed Oticon. However, it should be noted that, for the first two years of his appointment, he operated within the same transactional mould as his predecessors. It was only then that he recognised the limitations of continuing to attempt to improve incrementally an organisation that was out of step with its environment and competitors. He did not attempt to sell the company or acquire other companies. Instead, he changed the internal organisation of the company, not to align it with the external environment, but in an attempt to change that as well, by changing the rules of the game in his industry. Kolind's transformational leadership, especially his vision of a new Oticon and his ability to inspire others, was clearly appropriate to the divergent needs of the company.

The PPC

For most of its life, the PPC was a company operating in a convergent context and managed in a transactional fashion. The decision to privatise the PPC and to turn it into a commercial concern changed all that. The PPC needed to be transformed both structurally and culturally to adapt to its new environment and strategic objectives. The privatisation of the PPC tended to focus on the structural aspects, however, and failed to address effectively the cultural dimensions of the change from a public to a private company. It appears to be a classic case of a situation requiring transformational leadership, tackled by managers who could rearrange the organisation's structure but did not know how to begin winning over and inspiring the human side of the organisation. This difficulty was compounded by the fact that staff were hostile to and suspicious of the changes. Therefore, like Marconi, it was a case where supposedly transformational leadership appeared to lack the creative skills necessary to transform the organisation's culture to match the changes they made to its structure. Whether the outcome will be more successful than in Marconi's case, only time will tell.

Volvo

Though there have been considerable changes at Volvo, it is not easy to place either the organisation or its leadership on the convergent–divergent, transactional–transformational scale. For example, in the early 1970s, Volvo diverged from the expectations of Swedish society in using assembly lines, but was very much convergent with the rest of the car industry. Similarly, though Volvo transformed the way it assembled cars and made other significant structural changes, it does not appear to have reinvented itself in the way that, for example, Honda or Toyota did. However, Volvo has transformed its production methods, and indeed the ethos of the company, but it has been a very slow transformation – very much a 'Long March' rather than a 'Bold Stroke' approach. For much of this period, the company was led by Pehr Gyllenhammar, who was certainly a visionary when it came to creating a human-centred approach to car assembly. Unlike Japanese car companies, however, he did not try to rewrite the rules for the rest of the industry, though he did see the marketing potential of his approach to assembly. Nor, as its sale to Ford showed, did this new approach transform Volvo's fortunes. The reality of the car industry is that the small players, like Volvo, find it increasingly difficult to generate the vast amounts of money necessary to launch new models. Nevertheless, the Volvo approach to assembly is firmly embedded in the company and it will be interesting to see if Ford attempts to change it.

XYZ Construction

This was a company that had been run along transactional lines by an authoritarian figure for a number of years. When he retired, its parent company decided his management style was no longer appropriate for a company operating in an industry that was trying to develop partnerships between customers and suppliers. In effect, it decided that a transactional approach was no longer appropriate in a situation where the construction industry was beginning to move away, diverge, from its past practices and behaviours. XYZ's new Managing Director was charged with the task of creating a more teamwork-based organisation which could develop effective partnerships with its customers, thus transforming the company. This is exactly what he did. Over a period of four years, through a series of often small-scale initiatives, he changed the management approach in the company and encouraged a more creative and teamwork-based approach to internal and external relationships. This culminated with the development of the new organisation structure which formalised the new, more cooperative and creative way of working.

GK Printers

The company can be characterised as one that was out of step with – diverging from – its environment. The Managing Director appeared to operate in a transactional mode, as did most other people in the organisation. He and they were aware, however, that the company could not survive if it persisted with the old ways of working. This was not a company where a new Managing Director with a transformational, style of management was appointed. Rather it was an emergent process where, on an issue-by-issue basis, both the company and the Managing Director were gradually, and not always willingly, transformed. Though the initial changes appeared to have elements of the transformational approach about them, it was only later, when the organisation came to tackle internal relationships and managerial behaviour, that a more genuinely transformational approach to the company began to emerge.

Rover–TRW

This was very much a case of operational transformation that was not matched by significant changes at more senior levels in either organisation. Undoubtedly, the way that the TRW managers at Frankley established and continuously improved the assembly operation, and the way they developed a new working relationship with Rover's assembly line personnel, was transformational. The behaviour of senior managers in both companies appeared to be very much fixed in a transactional and antagonistic mode, however, in part at least because the overall climate was more convergent than divergent. Therefore, this showed that, even within a predominantly convergent and transactional approach to management, there are occasions where transformational leadership is required to enable parts of an organisation to respond effectively to new challenges.

Speedy Stationers

In this case, the company was trying to develop a new business area which needed a new approach. The way the new business area needed to operate was divergent from the existing norms in both Speedy and its customers. It could not be run in the transactional way in which other parts of the business operated. Speedy eventually chose to isolate the new business from its existing activities. This allowed it to pursue a transformational approach to the new business, whilst allowing its existing business, which was operating in a more convergent climate, to be managed as before. It also enabled it to limit the transformation of external relationships to the new business customers, thereby allowing the different parts of their business to adopt their own preferred style of management.

PoliceCo

This was a case where the organisation operated in a predominately convergent state and was managed in a transactional fashion. Though PoliceCo was required to outsource parts of its operation, this was treated in a routine fashion and managed in a transactional manner. The pressure to outsource did not undermine or in any way appear to raise questions about the appropriateness of the convergent context in which PoliceCo existed. Therefore, this was an example where the management felt no need to reassess how it operated or whether the organisation needed to change fundamentally. The decision to embark on outsourcing was handed down from government as a bureaucratic edict that PoliceCo responded to in a like manner.

To summarise the evidence from the ten case studies, these show a very diverse range of approaches, situations and outcomes. They also show the limitations of attempting to apply simple definitions to complex situations. The categorisation of leadership types and organisational states are useful in situations where a clear and relatively unambiguous picture of events is possible, such as in the case of Oticon, the PPC and PoliceCo. In many of the cases, however – Volvo, GK Printers and Rover–TRW – the picture is less clear. Elements of divergence exist, but these appear to be limited to certain areas of their environment or to change over time. Because of this, managers can be required to exhibit both transactional and transformational qualities either at the same time or in turn. Certainly, in the case of XYZ, for example, even though the new Managing Director was attempting to transform the company, he still had to keep it working effectively on a day-to-day basis in an industry that was still predominantly transactional and with a workforce that was used to an authoritarian style of management. As the cases of the PPC and the Music Industry showed, even when there are strong pressures and reasons for adopting a new style of management, this does not always happen. Also, as was illustrated at GK, even where it does take place, it can be slow and painful to achieve. Nor, as was seen in PoliceCo, is it always appropriate to adopt a transformational style, even where significant changes are occurring. In addition, as the PPC's attempts to maintain its dominant market position showed, managers sometimes seek to influence their environment to limit the need for internal changes and to bring them more into line with their preferred style of management.

Though the evidence from the case studies fits in with the general literature on managers' activities, which sees these as fragmented, lacking in consistency and reactive, it gives less support to those leadership theorists who see managers and leaders having a preferred approach which is difficult to change. The picture that emerges from the case studies is one where effective managers are required to possess and utilise a wide range of skills and attributes depending upon the situation and context. Effective managers must be capable, often at the same time, of being both transactional and transformational, given that the environmental pressures and other constraints do not appear to affect all parts of an organisation in the same manner nor at the same time. In particular, as Thompson (1967) remarked in relation to Contingency Theory (see Chapter 2), some organisations do at least seem adept at sealing off the productive cores of their organisations from environmental uncertainty whilst other functions are more directly affected. The result is that managers can be required to adopt distinct approaches towards managing different parts of the same organisation. Despite what the contextual approach to leadership maintains regarding the ability of managers to change their leadership style, this 'Jekyll and Hyde' view of management raises important questions about how managers can be prepared and developed to cope with a wide variety of situations. These include ones where they might have to maintain some parts of their organisation on a transactional basis, whilst rebuilding other parts in a transformational style and, at the same time, be attempting to influence constraints either to prevent, reduce or even promote the need for transformational change. In order to address this question, the next part of this chapter will discuss management development.

Management development

■ Learning and flexibility

Like the literature on management and leadership, the case studies give support for the notion that different situations require different approaches to change. They also show that managers are, sometimes at least, able to change their style of management or leadership, and even exhibit different styles to different parts of their organisations at the same time. This is consistent with the arguments in Chapters 14 and 15 that managers can and do adopt both the Planned and Emergent approaches to change management either alternately or simultaneously as the situation requires. In addition, the case studies show that managers, not necessarily by conscious design, create situations where the context in which their organisations operate is changed to suit their preferred or existing approach to both management and change. As argued in Chapters 14 and 15, changing the situational context can be very important; yet in terms of leadership roles and managerial expectations, one of the main findings from the case studies is the apparent ability of some managers not only to adapt their style to the particular situation, but also to adopt transactional and transformational approaches at the same time. The case studies also show, however, that other managers have great difficulty in changing their leadership approach or influencing their circumstances.

In part at least, the argument that there are managers who can change their style of leadership runs counter to some of the literature on managerial learning discussed in Chapter 9. Miller (1993: 119) argued that as they gain experience, managers 'form quite definite opinions of what works and why'. This view was supported by earlier work from Nystrom and Starbuck (1984) who maintained that managers interpret the world through their own perceptions and expectations, which are built up over time. Yet, as the Oticon case study illustrated, some managers do seem capable under certain conditions – especially when faced with a crisis – of restructuring their mental models of how the world is and how they should respond. In Chapter 14, the concepts of Cognitive Dissonance, Depth of Intervention and the Psychological Contract were used to explain why it was that people could, in crisis situations, change deeply-held attitudes very quickly. This 'crisis mode' only partly helps to explain, however, how some managers, when faced with change situations, appear capable of switching from a transactional approach to a transformational one as the circumstances demand or, indeed, become capable of adopting both at the same time.

The work of Mintzberg (1976) offers some clues as to how managers might accomplish this mental juggling act. In studying brain functions and successful managers, he concluded that effective and proficient managers are 'whole thinkers' – they use both the left and the right hemispheres of their brain. That is, they can combine a rational–analytical approach to management with creativity and lateral thinking. Mintzberg argued, however, that, in general, Western managers tend to think on the left side of their brain – they tend to adopt a rational–analytical approach. Interestingly, this is compatible not only with a transactional approach to management, but also with a rational–planned approach to strategy and the directive approach to change.

In contrast, Nonaka (1991) argued that one of the great strengths of Japanese companies is their belief that creating new knowledge depends more on tapping the tacit and often subjective insights and intuitions of all their employees, whether managers or not. He maintains that traditional Western management, on the other hand, sees organisations as information processing machines with the only useful knowledge being formal, scientific, quantifiable and rational. He contends that such a perspective limits the creation of new knowledge which, in turn, makes it difficult for organisations to respond to changing and new situations. Nonaka argues that new knowledge always begins with the individual. One of the main foundations of the success of Japanese companies is, he states, managers' ability to gather and combine the insights and intuitions of individual employees and use them for the benefit of the entire organisation. The tendency of Japanese managers to use softer, more creative approaches and to involve staff in decision-making was also noted in Chapters 3, 6 and 7 when discussing approaches to management and strategy.

The case studies, and the success of many Western firms, particularly those concerned with creative processes (such as software development) and the performing arts (such as film-making), show that it is not inevitable that Western managers should operate solely in a rational–analytical mode. Nevertheless, as Hofstede's (1980, 1990) and Trompenaars' (1993) work on national cultures reveals, there is a predisposition in Western societies towards more rational–analytical ways of working, whereas in Japan and China managers tend to use more subjective decision-making processes. Also, as Miller (1993) points out, a manager's view of the world and what works is shaped by his or her previous work experience. If this has been in organisations that have operated on traditional Western principles, which are structured in a Classical way and give credence only to formal and scientific knowledge, then they undoubtedly will tend to operate on the left side of the brain. This does not mean that such managers cannot develop or access the right side of their brain, but it does mean it is unlikely to come about accidentally or without strong encouragement from the organisations in which they work. To this end, many organisations are seeking to construct management development programmes designed to broaden the outlook and develop the creative, inductive and questioning side of their managers' personalities (Harrison, R, 2002). However, this is unlikely to be achieved through traditional management development programmes, which offer standard packages delivered in classroom situations, because of their low success rate (Burnes, 2003; Lessem, 1998; Mullins, 2002; Mumford et al, 2000). If management development programmes are to be effective, in future, as Harrison, R (2002) contends on behalf of the UK's Chartered Institute of Training and Development (CIPD), they will have to be tailored to both the needs of the individual manager and the strategic objectives of their organisation.

In respect of developing managers' creativity, Kirton's (1989) Adaptation–Innovation theory, and subsequent work by Talbot (1993, 1997), provide useful insights. Kirton maintains that not only do people exhibit different degrees of creativity, but that they also express their creativity in different ways, along a spectrum which runs from *adaptors* to *innovators*. Those who tend towards the adaptor end of the spectrum prefer to work within the existing system to improve things. Adaptors are efficient, tend to conform to existing norms and like to deal with only a few ideas at a time. Innovators tend to ignore or challenge the system and to come up with radical proposals for change. Figure 16.1 shows how Kirton's ideas relate to transactional management and transformational leadership. As can be seen, transactional managers tend to have lower levels of creativity because they are dealing with changes at the group level, whereas transformational leaders need higher levels of creativity because they are involved in transformational activities at the organisation level.

However, as Figure 16.1 also shows, even within the transformational dimension of leadership, there will be situations which require a more adaptive approach, such as structural rather than cultural change. Similarly, transactional managers may be faced with situations where more innovative than adaptive solutions are required, such as when dealing with behavioural issues as averse to technical ones. Regardless of their levels of creativity, some managers may find it easier than others to switch between innovative and adaptive behaviour. There may also be many managers who can exhibit varying levels of creativity as the situation demands. This may be the reason why some people, as demonstrated by our case studies and the leadership literature, can change their style of leadership or even adopt different styles at the same time. The story does not end there. Talbot (1997) demonstrated that, regardless of the level of creativity a person possesses or where they are located on the adaptor–innovator spectrum, there are proven tools and techniques for increasing their level of creativity and flexibility. By so doing, transactional managers may find it easier to operate in a more transformational and innovative mode, or move between both as circumstances necessitate. Talbot (1993) also points out, though, that such tools and techniques can only overcome barriers to creativity that lie within the individual. Other barriers, he argues, such as the attitudes and behaviours of superiors and colleagues, and the way the organisation operates, can also block individual creativity. Therefore, in management development, as with so many other aspects of organisational life, we cannot consider the individual in isolation from the rest of the organisation.

Figure 16.1 Leadership, management and change

■ The management development process

Under different names, management training and education has been around since the Industrial Revolution. In the nineteenth century, it tended to be geared towards giving managers specific skills such as engineering, production control, etc., either through on-the-job training or self-help societies. In the twentieth century, more and more, employers took on the job of specifying and providing formal management training, but it still tended to be geared towards giving managers specific skills. Over the last 20 years or so, there has been a significant change in emphasis. Management development programmes are increasingly seeking to change managerial behaviour, especially to promote leadership and creativity, and to align managers' behaviour with the longer-term strategic objectives of their organisations and with society's wider social and ethical considerations (Harrison, R, 2002). Though management development is big business in all advanced countries, there is no universally-agreed definition of what it is. The following quotations give a flavour of the range of definitions on offer:

> ... a conscious and systematic decision-action process to control the development of managerial resources in the organisation for the achievement of organisational goals and strategies.
> (Ashton *et al*, 1975: 5)

> ... that function which from deep understanding of business goals and organisational requirements, undertakes: (a) to forecast needs, skill mixes and profiles for many positions and levels; (b) to design and recommend the professional, career and personal development programmes necessary to ensure competence; (c) to move from the concept of 'management' to the concept of 'managing'.
> (Beckhard, 1985: 22)

> ... an attempt to improve managerial effectiveness through a planned and deliberate learning process.
> (Quoted in Mumford, 1987: 29)

> Management development is concerned not only with improving the effectiveness of individual managers but also with an improvement in management performance as a whole and organisational effectiveness.
> Mullins (2002: 845)

In an age where organisations are often required to change rapidly and radically, management education and development is taken seriously in most advanced countries and entry into a managerial job often requires formal, university-level qualifications (Arnold *et al*, 1998; Jones *et al*, 2000; Lippitt, 1982; Marsh, 1986; Morgan, 1988; Mullins, 2002; Pearson, 1987; Storey, 1989). The nature of management development varies between countries, however (Keuning, 1998). In Japan, for example, it tends to be a very competitive process which begins by recruiting elite cohorts who have usually studied law or engineering at a top university. In Germany, there is a greater emphasis on a formal apprenticeship system which develops managers through a career path that often involves the attainment of higher degrees. France, like Japan, tends to be very elitist and managers are expected to have studied for a degree in business or law at one of the Grandes Ecoles (Harrison, R, 2002).

In the UK, management education tends to be more *ad hoc* and less well-regarded, even in large organisations. UK companies also spend a much lower percentage of their turnover promoting education and training than their counterparts in France,

Germany, Japan and the USA (Harrison, R, 2002; Keuning, 1998). This is probably why a number of studies revealed in the 1980s that the UK was particularly poor at providing the type of formal and structured education necessary for nurturing managerial creativity (Constable and McCormick, 1987). Partly in response to these findings, the 1980s and 1990s saw a growing interest in management development by government and organisations (OECD, 1996; Sissons and Storey, 1988; Storey, 1989, 1990; Worrall and Cooper, 1997, 1998). However, a 1997 survey of 258 chief executives carried out for the *Sunday Times* found that UK managers did not have the skills to obtain the full potential from their businesses (Hannagan, 2002). Likewise, the government sees poor management as the reason why UK productivity lags behind that of the US by 42 per cent, France by 14 per cent and Germany by 7 per cent (Paton, 2003). This continuing lack of management skills appears to be the main reason why the UK government has abandoned most of the management training and development schemes its predecessors launched in the 1980s and 1990s, such as the Management Charter Initiative, and in 2002 established a new body, the Council for Excellence in Management and Leadership. Certainly, the Council itself has concluded that most management and business leadership programmes are 'dysfunctional' and that the lack of appropriate leadership skills is detrimental to the UK's economic performance (Paton, 2003).

Regardless of the encouragement or not of governments, it is individual organisations who initiate such programmes. Given that organisations are different and face different challenges, if management development programmes are to be successful in producing effective managers and improving the performance of organisations, then it is self-evident not only that they will vary from company to company, but also that they will need to vary from individual to individual. Harrison, R (2002: 348) claims that, despite the differences between organisations, an effective management development process (MDP) has six basic features:

- a clear MDP mission, linked to the organisation's business strategy;
- specific programme objectives that relate to the external challenges that the organisation is facing;
- a focus on major internal organisational issues;
- programmes tailored to organisational and individual needs;
- the systematic assessment of management development needs, aims and outputs;
- a professional business-led approach to MDP.

Harrison's six basic features of an effective MDP represent a clear break with the standard management development programmes of the past that companies required all their managers to pursue, regardless of their individual needs, and which appear to have served them and their managers poorly (Arnold *et al*, 1998; Burnes, 2003; Mangham Working Party, 1987; Sissons, 1989; Storey, 1989; Thornberry, 1987; Yukl, 2002). The two main problems with such standard offerings is that, firstly, they tend to develop managers within an existing behaviour pattern and set of expectations. Therefore, traditional organisations will tend to continue to produce transactional managers, regardless of the presence or absence of formal training and education programmes. The second problem is that they fail to address the needs of individual managers. Whilst they might meet a manager's training requirements in terms of technical skills (such as accountancy, engineering, etc.), they rarely address how they could develop the attitudes and behaviours necessary to be an effective manager.

Though formal, classroom-based qualifications such as Management Diplomas and MBAs are still seen as having an important role in most management development programmes, they are now being balanced with more individual and experientially-based approaches. These approaches include the use of assessment and assessment centres, coaching and mentoring, self-development and, increasingly, Action Learning. Though such approaches have been around for a long time, their potential contribution to management development has been ignored (Burgoyne and Germaine, 1984; Harrison, R, 2002; Long, 1986; Mullins, 2002; Newstrom, 1985; Pedler, 1996; Stuart, 1986; Wilkinson and Orth, 1986; Willbur, 1987). More recently, with a greater emphasis being placed on individual development, especially in terms of aligning behaviour with the needs of the organisation and society, these techniques are finding increasing favour.

Changing managerial behaviour

In terms of challenging and changing managerial attitudes and behaviours, the use of Action Learning is particularly interesting. It was developed in the 1940s in the UK by Reg Revans and is based on small groups of managers tackling a set problem or case study. As Pedler (1996: 9) states:

> Action Learning is a method of problem solving and learning in groups to bring about change for individual, teams and organisations. It works to build relationships which help any organisation improve existing operations and learn and innovate for the future.

The aim is not only that managers learn how to approach problems together, but also that they learn about themselves and challenge the appropriateness of their own attitudes and behaviours. As Revans commented:

> The central idea of this approach ... is today that of the set, or small group of comrades in adversity, striving to learn with and from each other as they confess failures and expand on victories.   (Quoted in Crainer, 1996: 195)

Though Revans' ideas were out of fashion for many years, his emphasis on team-working and the power of groups to solve their own problems, linked with the potential for self-reflection and development, is making it an increasingly popular approach (Mullins, 2002). Contemporary approaches to Action Learning tend to be based on Kolb's cycle of experiential learning (Experience–Understanding–Planning–Action) with sets or groups being guided by a facilitator who acts as a catalyst for ideas (Darwin *et al*, 2002). Also, as its name implies, Action Learning has strong similarities with and can be seen as a derivation of Lewin's Action Research (McLaughlin and Thorpe, 1993). Action Research is one of the four elements of Lewin's Planned approach to change (*see* Chapter 8). Like Action Research, Action Learning places a heavy emphasis on self-reflection, behavioural change and learning. Whilst the latter tends to focus on developing the individual, however, Action Research focuses more on change at the group level. Nevertheless, Revans' statement that 'there is no learning without action and no (sober and deliberate) action without learning' (quoted in Pedler, 1996: 15) could have been written by Lewin.

Burnes (2003) links Action Learning with organisational change. He argues that change projects can double as Action Learning projects, and vice versa. Burnes maintains that there are clearly situations and times when organisational change and management development go hand-in-hand. These are not situations where it is either necessary or desirable for the objectives of one to become subservient to the other, or to be compromised by the needs of the other. Rather these are genuinely situations where the need to change an organisation and the need to develop managers are mutually supportive. Unfortunately, as Crainer (1998: 259) comments, though Action Learning is attracting much attention, its complexity makes it a 'daunting prospect'. Given that organisational change projects can, in themselves, be a 'daunting prospect', it is perhaps not surprising that many organisations choose not to link them to management development initiatives. Nevertheless, the benefits, Burnes argues, may be considerable.

As with all general developments, this move away from formal, off-the-job training programmes to more personalised and experiential, on-the-job programmes needs to be viewed critically. Storey (1989), in a major review of the management development literature, argued that drawing a distinction between on-the-job and off-the-job training may miss the main issue. This is the requirement to assess the development and training needs of individual managers accurately and to provide programmes that allow managers to develop a much more critical and intuitive approach to their situation. Argyris (1991) argues, however, that one of the main barriers to developing more critical and intuitive approaches is that, within the narrow confines of transactional behaviour, many managers do operate effectively, even though, looking at the wider picture, their organisation may be in trouble. This is akin to Peters and Waterman's (1982) concept of 'irrational rationality' – managers applying the 'right' solution even when the situation means that it is no longer appropriate. Argyris believes that managers need to experience failure or recognise the inappropriateness of their behaviour before they can begin questioning their assumptions and practices, and develop their ability to be critical and creative. Senge (1990) contends that the most important factor in developing such a questioning approach and achieving organisational success is the ability to comprehend in a critical way the overall organisational context. This takes us back to the point made by Talbot (1993, 1997), cited earlier, that it is insufficient to develop managers if the organisation as a whole – people, values and systems – does not also change, or perceive the need for change. The case studies in Part 3 support this argument. As was shown in Oticon and XYZ in particular, it was the need for transformational change that forced or enabled managers to break out of the transactional mould and think critically and creatively about solutions to the problems their organisations faced.

Therefore, whilst management development has increasingly come to be seen as a process that must address the needs of the individual managers, it must not lose sight of the need to develop management as a whole in organisations. Nowhere is this more apparent than when we look at the areas discussed earlier in this chapter covering sustainability, diversity and ethics. These are areas where organisations have failed significantly in the past, whether it be in terms of environmental depredations, racial and sexual discrimination and stereotyping, or the illegal 'ramping' of shares on Wall Street. Organisations often put such transgressions down to the failure of an individual or group to follow the organisation's guidelines and policies. The regular occurrence of illegal and unethical practices in business tends to show that these are a failure of management as a group in organisations, however, rather than the failure of individual managers.

Though it is necessary for individual managers to address issues of sustainability, diversity and ethics as part of their personal development, by itself this it is not sufficient. If organisations and those in them are to behave differently, it is also necessary that the management of an organisation as a whole should address these issues as part of its development. The question, of course, is how can this be done? If organisations are capable of systematically side-stepping the policies and guidelines that they have developed, how can a management development programme make them face up to the issues? One answer might be to utilise Action Learning where managers 'learn with and from each other as they confess failures'. Action Learning has a number of drawbacks, however, not least that its focus is on developing individual managers, albeit in a group setting (McGill and Beaty, 1995). It does not appear to be appropriate to situations where behavioural change and reflection needs to take place at the group rather than the individual level. Nor does it appear suitable for situations where the issue is the effectiveness of management at the organisational level, rather than the individual level.

There is an approach that was specifically established to enable groups to address the appropriateness of their behaviour, especially in terms of discriminatory activity, and which also has a strong ethical basis. It is, of course, Planned change as formulated by Kurt Lewin. Planned change was designed to enable groups, in this case management groups in an organisation, to understand the factors which make them act as they do, and to develop effective ways to change them and 'freeze' or institutionalise those changes. As described in Chapter 8, Planned change has four elements: field theory, Group Dynamics, Action Learning and the Three-Step approach to change. His critics maintain that Lewin's approach is not suitable for large-scale, rapid and coercive change situations, or situations where the focus is on structural rather than behavioural change. However, both Lewin's own work, and that of his successors, have shown that it is a highly effective process for achieving sustained behavioural changes in groups. It has been applied to a wide variety of situations, including the food habits of American housewives, teenage inter-racial gang warfare in American cities, conflict between Palestinians and Israelis, and management behaviour in organisations (Bargal and Bar, 1992; Cummings and Worley, 2001; Gold, 1999; Lewin, 1947a; Marrow, 1969). Lewin's approach to change was specifically developed to bring about changes in group behaviour, and it has had considerable success in achieving this in the years since his death (Day *et al*, 2002; French and Bell, 1995; Harvey and Brown, 2001; McNiff, 2000; Wheelan *et al*, 1990). Therefore, as an approach to tackling the failures of management as a group in an organisation, Planned change has a lot to recommend it. This does not undermine the case for other approaches which address the needs of managers as individuals, but does recognise that individual behaviour and effectiveness cannot be separated from group behaviour and effectiveness. Indeed, it may be one of the ironies of management development that, in order to equip managers to meet the challenges of the twenty-first century, it has to look back to the work of Kurt Lewin.

■ Summary

From the above examination of managerial learning, seven factors can be discerned as important in the ability of managers to operate effectively:

1 The managers' past experience, and whether this has reinforced their beliefs or, instead, led them to question their appropriateness.
2 The level of creativity of the manager. Does the manager have a preference for transactional management or transformational leadership, and to what degree can they move between the two?
3 His or her cognitive style: are they adaptors or innovators? Are they 'whole thinkers' or are they more left hemisphere–rational thinkers or right hemisphere–creative thinkers?
4 The managers' ability to perceive the whole picture. Can they see the organisation in its context? In particular, do they understand the choices available in terms of changing the organisation itself, its context, and their own approach to leadership, strategy and change?
5 The organisational context: is it amenable, or can it be made amenable, to a more critical, creative and ethical style of leadership?
6 The organisation's management team: does it have a commitment to promoting sustainability, diversity and ethical behaviour, and are the senior managers committed to ensuring that its statement and policies in these areas are implemented through the day-to-day actions of all its members?
7 The organisation's management development process: is it effective? Is it geared to developing individual managers and the management cadre of the organisation as a whole?

As far as the UK is concerned, as surveys by Worrall and Cooper (1997, 1998) found, the 1990s saw a considerable increase in the provision of education and training for managers. This was driven by a number of factors: individuals seeing the need to maintain their marketability; organisations recognising the importance to them of well-trained managers; and successive governments identifying the link between good management and the overall health of the UK economy. Nevertheless, Worrall and Cooper also found that some 20 per cent of managers still receive no formal training for their role. Furthermore, they found that many managers question the appropriateness of the training they do receive and feel the quantity is insufficient; in addition, the increasing pressure of work, and their longer working hours, are reducing their ability to take advantage of and apply the training and education that is available.

Management, leadership and change

The literature on management and leadership goes back many hundreds of years. Indeed, if one takes the view of some writers that *The Art of Warfare* by Sun Tzu, which was written in China around 400 BC, is pertinent to managing today's organisations, then the study of management goes back thousands of years (Michaelson, 2001). As was shown in Chapter 1, however, to all intents and purposes the systematic study of management can be said to have begun with the work of Frederick

Taylor at the beginning of the twentieth century. Since then, there have been more books and articles on management than anyone can possibly count. These have thrown up a plethora of theories, studies and terminology which, as Thomas (2003) comments, has probably caused more confusion than clarification. In this chapter, we have tried, as Karl Weick (*see* Chapter 15) might put it, to make sense of the literature on management. This 'sensemaking' began with an examination of the challenges posed to management by globalisation, especially in terms of sustainability, diversity and ethics. This was followed by a review of the literature on the manager's role which drew attention to the three main theories on leadership, i.e. the personal characteristics approach, the leader–follower approach, and the contextual approach. Next came a brief description of management and leadership in the ten case study companies described in Part 3. Finally, we investigated the role played by, or that could be played by, management development in shaping the behaviour of managers and leaders both at the individual and group levels. This attempt to make sense of management and the literature on management has shown the following:

- The incredible variety and complexity of the role of people who hold the title 'manager'. The title is applied to people in a wide range of hierarchical levels and functional specialisms. These 'managers' are presented with a myriad of responsibilities and challenges, ranging from the mundane, but vital, everyday tasks required to ensure that organisations operate efficiently, to the rarer and far more spectacular need to transform and reinvent organisations.
- The wide range of factors that impinge on managerial effectiveness, including managers' own personalities, those of their followers, superiors and peers, and the wider organisational context and objectives in which they operate.
- The ability or potential of managers to increase their level of creativity and change their style of management from transactional to transformational, and back, as situations require.
- The recognition that management development has a key role to play not only in developing individual creativity but also in changing the ethical behaviour of management as a group in organisations.

What conclusions can we draw from this review for the relationship between management, leadership and change in organisations? The first is that there does seem to be some terminological agreement, as shown in Tables 16.1 and 16.2, as to the differences between management and leadership. Management is about the present, it is about maintaining the *status quo*, and it is about objectivity and aloofness. Leadership is about the future, it is about change and it is about values and emotions. However, whilst management and leadership may be different, this does not mean that managers and leaders are or should be different people. This chapter has shown that most management and leadership roles require a mixture of transactional and transformational skills. In an ideal world, managers would be able to adjust the balance of transactional and transformational skills they deploy to the organisation's requirements at anyone time. In our less than ideal world, the balance is likely to be static rather than dynamic, and usually determined by the background, experience and personality of the individual manager. Nevertheless, it would be difficult to think of a manager who never had to deal with organisational change, even on a small scale, and who, therefore, did not possess some transformational skills. Similarly, it would also be difficult to think of a leader who, regardless of the size of the changes they were responsible for, did not have to possess some of the transactional skills necessary for ensuring that an organisation continued to satisfy its stakeholders. Therefore, the balance of management–leadership/transactional–transformational skills an individual needs to possess at any one time is related to the degree of change or stability they encounter.

The second conclusion we can draw, as Figure 16.1 showed, is that management and leadership focus on different types of change. Management tends to focus on small-scale, localised changes, whilst leadership tends to focus on more radical, organisation-wide changes. The former tend to require only low levels of creativity, whilst the latter require high levels. Even within these different types of change, however, there are some forms of change that appear to be more innovative and others more adaptive. Consequently, the ability of managers and leaders to deal effectively with different change situations will be related to the level of creativity they possess and the degree to which their creativity expresses itself in an innovative or adaptive manner.

Having drawn these two conclusions, we are now in a position to relate approaches to management and leadership to approaches to managing change. In Chapter 10, we developed a *Framework for Change* (*see* Figure 10.4). This related the types of changes organisations experienced, such as cultural or structural change, to the most appropriate approach to change, e.g. Emergent, Planned, etc. If we merge Figure 10.4 from Chapter 10 with Figure 16.1 from this chapter, we can construct a *Framework for Management, Leadership and Change* (*see* Figure 16.2).

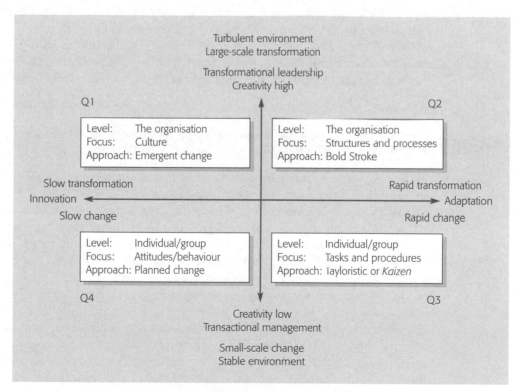

Figure 16.2 A framework for management, leadership and change

The four quadrants in Figure 16.2 show what form of management or leadership is best suited to each form of change and each approach to change management. For example, quadrant 3 shows that where changes to tasks and procedures are concerned, these can be achieved either by a Tayloristic or *Kaizen* approach and managed in a transactional manner which requires only a low level of adaptive creativity. Quadrant 1, on the other hand, presents a much more complex picture. It shows that where an organisation wishes to change its culture, this is best achieved by an Emergent approach to change led by someone with a transformational approach to leadership and who exhibits a high degree of innovation. Remembering, however, that Emergent change can encompasses a wide range of change initiatives spread over a period of time, which can include Planned change and Bold Strokes, such transformational leaders may also need to possess adaptive and transactional skills, or be able to call on others who possess such skills.

Figure 16.2 also allows us to understand better the obstacles and approaches to dealing effectively with issues of sustainability, diversity and ethics. As was shown in examining globalisation earlier in this chapter, these are issues that organisations are aware of and, at least in large organisations, have policies and procedures to address. Possessing the ability to put these policies and procedures into practice is a different matter, however. These are issues that, for most organisations, require a major change of culture, especially by management and leadership at all levels. If sustainability, diversity and ethics are treated merely as structural or policy issues, as in quadrant 2, this is unlikely to lead to any permanent or sustained changes in attitudes and behaviour. Similarly, if they are seen as issues that are primarily about individual behaviour and attitudes, as in quadrant 2, there is unlikely to be an organisation-wide and lasting change to the way that managers and leaders behave. If ethics, diversity and sustainability are treated as issues that need to be embedded in an organisation's culture, however, and if the required changes are managed and led as shown in quadrant 1, then changes in attitudes and behaviour at the overall level are likely to be achieved and maintained.

Summary and conclusions

In reading some of the literature on strategy and change, one might be forgiven for asking whether managers and what they do matter at all. If strategy is Emergent, often unrelated to conscious decisions, does an important role exist for managers? Or if, as the evolutionary perspective on strategy would have it, luck plays a greater part in success than conscious action, does the quality of the manager matter? However, as this chapter has shown, the way an organisation is managed and led can have profound implications not only for the organisation and its members but for society as whole.

On the negative side, managers can act to hold back organisations, prevent beneficial change and create a climate of blame and wrong-doing where in-fighting and discrimination are tolerated or even promoted. On the positive side, managers can identify opportunities for progress, promote ethical behaviour, recognise the opportunities that diversity brings, and create sustainable organisations which achieve harmony with their environment. Good managers and leaders can create the conditions for growth and prosperity. Effective managers are, therefore, for very positive reasons, important to an organisation. However, they do not operate in isolation or have a totally free rein.

The Chief Executives of Oticon and Marconi both wanted to transform their organisations. They both developed ambitious visions for their organisation's future. The Chief Executive of Oticon sought organisation-wide approval and support for his vision. All Oticon's employees were involved in developing and implementing the strategy to realise the vision. It was a vision that was seen as benefiting all Oticon's employees. It was a vision which succeeded. The vision for the new Marconi, on the other hand, was not seen as benefiting its employees, nor were they involved in developing or implementing it. With hindsight, the vision was badly flawed and it failed disastrously. There is a strand in the management literature which equates organisational success with strong, clear-sighted and charismatic leadership (Thomas, 2003). Certainly, there are leaders, such as Jack Welch in his time at General Electric, Pehr Gyllenhammar before his departure from Volvo, Richard Branson at Virgin, Bill Gates at Microsoft or Rupert Murdoch at News International, who through sheer force of personality dominated and transformed organisations. There are also others who have ruined their organisations. The successful charismatic leader appears to be in the minority. In any case, as the Arnold Weinstock example at GEC-Marconi shows, successful leaders may outstay their welcome, or radical surgery to fit their organisations for the future may become overdue.

Most managers, even of very large corporations, have to rely far less on their personality, important though this may be, and far more on their business knowledge, skills, creativity and experience. They are also called upon to perform a wide range of duties and activities. Though the theories and approaches to strategy and change appear to paint managers as either directing change or facilitating it, and the leadership literature tends to dwell on whether they are transactional or transformational managers, the reality is that they are often required to be all of these things, depending on the circumstances. As Figure 16.2 shows, in bringing about organisational change, there will be occasions when managers and leaders will need to devolve responsibility to subordinates; sometimes, though, they will need to encourage and support change projects; and, in other instances, they will have to lead the process themselves. Although the approach adopted will depend to a certain extent upon the size and importance of the change project, the timescale involved and the state of the organisation, in the final analysis it will rely on managerial judgment to make the appropriate choice. Changing organisations is a complex process fraught with more opportunities for failure than success. If managers are to accomplish and keep accomplishing this task, as this book has argued, they have to be aware of the choices and approaches available and be willing themselves to change their beliefs and attitudes.

Despite the views of some writers, there can never be any general recipes or formulas for organisational success. The vast variety of organisations, each with its own differing constraints and pressures, makes that impossible. What there is, however, is a large body of theories and associated advice which organisations can draw upon to assist them. As the quotation by George Box at the beginning of this book states: 'All models are wrong, some models are useful'. This book has shown that there is no such thing as an uncontested theory – all have their drawbacks. In particular, most tend to be situation-specific, even if they do not acknowledge this. Managers and organisations need to treat theories with a degree of scepticism. They also need to realise, however, that if they can identify the main theories for running and changing organisations, and they do understand the context in which they operate, they are in a position to identify choices and make changes.

Sometimes managers may choose or be required by circumstances to change their organisations radically and quickly; sometimes they may choose to influence the context to promote or reduce the need for such changes. In other cases, change may take place more slowly and over a long period, as both organisation and context are shaped and changed. The key factor in all this is to make conscious decisions rather than rely on untested assumptions. This will require those who manage and lead organisations to question and challenge their own and other people's assumptions. It will also require them to gather and be open to a wide variety of information – as Chapter 3 showed, the experience of more and more successful companies is that learning should be an organisation-wide and continuous process, rather than one limited to a few like-minded individuals at one point in time.

Even where choices are identified, managers should not assume that exercising choice is easy or that the results will be beneficial for all concerned, including themselves. For this reason, managers have a responsibility in making and implementing choices to consider the implications in the widest context: not just for themselves, not just for their organisation, but for society as well. In the West, especially the UK and USA, there is a tendency to think mainly in terms of short-term profitability, and ignore the longer-term organisational and social consequences of actions. We can see this in the context of the Classical school, whose concentration on narrow issues of control and efficiency leads to the creation of jobs that are both physically strenuous and mind-numbingly boring. The adverse consequences of organisation theory are not limited to the Classical school, however; in many ways, the policies and approaches advocated by the Culture–Excellence school could be considered even worse. Though both Handy (1997) and, to a lesser extent, Kanter (1997) are concerned about the impact of fragmented organisations and insecure jobs on society at large and family life in particular, neither appears to believe that these can be avoided.

Yet the consequences of this approach in creating instability and unpredictability in the job market are disastrous. As was noted in Chapter 3, the 1990s saw the UK become more socially divided than at any time since the Second World War, with some 60 per cent of the population either marginalised or living in very insecure circumstances (Hutton, 1995; Saul, 1997; White, 1999). Increasingly the rich are choosing to live behind security fences in elite communities (Arnot, 2002). The situation is even worse in the USA where the tendency for the better-off to retreat into walled compounds patrolled by armed guards is widespread and long-established (Dunphy and Griffiths, 1998; Elliott, 1997; Reich, 1997). Nevertheless, as the discussion on globalisation showed, in a borderless world, it will be impossible to escape the consequences of environmental depredation, a lack of business ethics and discriminatory behaviour merely by building walls. If this seems a somewhat apocalyptic vision, then bear in mind the reality of global warming. Bear in mind the millions of people who lost their savings and pensions in the dotcom boom. Also bear in mind that one of the most fashionable American gurus of the late 1990s, William Bridges, advocated the jobless organisation. He believes that there should no longer be any permanent jobs, not even for managers. Instead, he wants to see the labour force form one enormous pool of labour waiting for temporary employment – the just-in-time workforce to complement the just-in-time organisation (Bridges, 1996, 1998; Golzen, 1995). In support of his view that jobless organisations are the future, he points out that General Motors is no longer the largest employer in the USA; instead, it is the temporary employment agency, Manpower.

Some would argue that these developments are only the inevitable consequence of capitalism (Collins, 1998). However, as Crouch and Streeck (1997) and Whitley (1998) demonstrated, capitalism comes in many forms and guises. The fragmentation and insecurity of the labour market that was a growing characteristic of the USA and UK in the 1980s and 1990s was much less pronounced in some other countries. This was especially the case in those nations that, historically, had seen the objectives of individual organisations as subservient to national interests. In the 1990s for example, despite economic problems associated with reunification, Germany still had an enviable record of attempting to prevent job losses and reduce job insecurity, as did the Scandinavian states and Japan.

This, of course, emphasises that national governments as well as individual organisations have a major contribution to make when considering the wider context and implications of managers' decisions. In the West, led by the USA and UK, the last 20 years have seen an increasing move towards deregulation, privatisation and the introduction of market forces into the operation of the public sector. Whatever the merits of these policies in terms of efficiency, and they are debatable (Flynn, 1993; Ferlie *et al*, 1996), no one can doubt that they acted to increase instability both in the economy at large and in public sector bodies, as the cases of the Greek Public Power Corporation and PoliceCo showed. Whether such changes will eventually lead to a better deal for consumers or not is obviously an issue, but so is the effect on the social fabric. Post-1945, all Western governments used their public sectors both to provide services and as a means of creating employment and maintaining economic and social stability. These latter functions have now been abandoned in many countries, and the resulting insecurity is evident for all to see.

The point of mentioning this is not merely to show concern, but to argue that it need not be the case. The Culture–Excellence concept is only one of many approaches to running organisations. All have their downside, but not all result in job cuts and labour market instability. One alternative is for managers to choose to adopt approaches that reduce instability in their environment, rather than to implement policies that increase the use of short-term contracts, part-time and casual working. If followed widely, this would have two effects. Firstly, the result of many organisations seeking stability would be to reduce the overall level of turbulence in the environment. This is because, as Stickland (1998) maintains, organisations and their environment are not separate entities, but part of the same system. If organisations become more stable, so too does the environment. If organisations become more sustainable, so does the planet. Similarly, if, as recommended by Tom Peters, organisations adopt internal chaos to cope with external chaos, this merely acts to increase the overall turbulence in the system; in effect, a vicious spiral of increasing chaos is created which, instead of poising an organisation at the 'edge of chaos', may tear it apart. Also, if organisations focus solely on narrow profitability, environmental and ethical problems will grow. The second consequence of organisations seeking stability is that it increases the stability in society – jobs and communities become more stable and more sustainable.

Therefore, as a final note: organisations face many challenges and choices. Some organisations will find that their room for manoeuvre is very limited. Others may find that there is considerable scope for discretion. It is the role of managers and leaders to ensure that all available options and choices are identified, and that the choices made take account of both the short- and long-term interests of all their stakeholders – whether these be shareholders, employees, the managers themselves or the community at large. The worst managers may not be those who make poor choices; it may be those who fail to recognise that there are choices to be made.

Test your learning

■ Short answer questions

1   What is globalisation?

2   What is the link between sustainability, workforce diversity and ethics?

3   Describe Duncan's (1975) three levels of management.

4   Briefly discuss Mintzberg's (1973, 1975) description of managerial roles.

5   What is the personal characteristics approach to leadership?

6   State the key features of the leader–follower approach to leadership.

7   Describe the contextual approach to leadership.

8   How does Kirton's (1989) Adaptation–Innovation theory help us to understand managerial behaviour?

9   Describe two approaches to managerial development.

10   What is the difference between management and leadership?

11   How do management and leadership relate to organisational change?

12   List three ways in which managers' decisions can have a wider impact on society.

■ Essay questions

1   How can the *Framework for Management, Leadership and Change* (Figure 16.2) be used to guide organisational change? Illustrate your answer with reference to one of the case studies in Part 3 or by using an organisation of your choice.

2   How can the concept of managerial choice help managers to reconcile the needs of their organisation with the wider needs of society?

Suggested further reading

1 Yukl, G (2002) *Leadership in Organizations* (5th edition). Prentice Hall: Upper Saddle River, NJ, USA.
   Gary Yukl's book is an excellent guide to the literature and research on management and leadership.
2 Deresky, H (2002) *International Management: Managing Across Borders and Culture* (3rd edition). Prentice Hall: Upper Saddle River, NJ, USA.
   This book provides a well-researched and well-written guide to international management. It is especially strong in the areas of culture, diversity and ethics.
3 Dunphy, D, Griffiths, A and Benn, S (2003) *Organizational Change for Corporate Sustainability*. Routledge: London.
   This is an important book which does not just make the case for creating sustainable organisations but also provides illustrations of and guidance on managing the changes necessary to achieve this.

Bibliography

Abegglen, J (1958) *The Japanese Factory*. Free Press: Glencoe, IL, USA.

Abegglen, J and Stalk, G (1984) *Kaisha, the Japanese Corporation*. Basic Books: New York, USA.

Abell, DF (1977) *Using PIMS and Portfolio Analysis in Strategic Market Planning: A Comparative Analysis*. Intercollegiate Case Clearing House, Harvard Business School: Boston, MA, USA.

Abell, P (1975) Organisations as technically constrained bargaining and influence systems. In P Abell (ed): *Organisations as Bargaining and Influence Systems*. Heinemann: London.

Abodaher, D (1986) *Iacocca*. Star: London.

Ackroyd, S (2000) Connecting organisations and societies: a realist analysis of structures. In S Ackroyd and S Fleetwood (eds): *Realist Perspectives on Management and Organisations*. Routledge: London.

Ackroyd, S and Fleetwood, S (2000a) Realism in contemporary organisation and management. In S Ackroyd and S Fleetwood (eds): *Realist Perspectives on Management and Organisations*. Routledge: London.

Ackroyd, S and Fleetwood, S (2000b) *Realist Perspectives on Management and Organisations*. Routledge: London.

Ackroyd, S, Burrell, G, Hughes, M and Whitaker, A (1988) The Japanisation of British industry. *Industrial Relations Journal*, 19(1), 11–23.

Adams, C, Cavendish, W and Mistry, P (1996) *Adjusting Privatisation: Case Studies from Developing Countries*. Heinemann: London.

AFL-CIO (2003) *Trends in Executive Pay*. Available at www.aflcio.org.

Aglietta, M (1979) *A Theory of Capitalist Regulation: The US Experience*. NLB: London.

Aguren, S, Bredbacka, C, Hansson, R, Ihregren, K and Karlsson, KG (1984) *Volvo/Kalmar Revisited: Ten Years of Experience*. The Development Council: Stockholm, Sweden.

Aitken, H (1960) *Taylorism at the Watertown Arsenal: Scientific Management in Action 1908–1915*. Harvard University Press: Cambridge, MA, USA.

Akao, Y (ed) (1991) *Hoshin Kanri: Policy Deployment for Successful TQM*. Productivity Press: Cambridge, MA, USA.

Albrow, M (1970) *Bureaucracy*. Pall Mall Press: London.

Albrow, M (1997) *Do Organizations Have Feelings?* Routledge: London.

Alderman, J (2001a) *Sonic Boom: Napster, P2P and the Battle for the Future of Music.* Fourth Estate: London.

Alderman, J (2001b) Free for all. *Guardian*, August 4, available at www.guardian.co.uk.

Alimo-Metcalfe, B (1995a) Female and male constructs of leadership and empowerment. *Women in Management*, 10(2), 3–8.

Alimo-Metcalfe, B (1995b) Leadership and assessment. In S Vinnicombe and NL Colwill (eds): *The Essence of Women in Management*. Prentice Hall: Englewood Cliffs, NJ, USA.

Alimo-Metcalfe, B and Alban-Metcalfe, R (2000) *Heaven Can Wait*. Health Service Journal, 12 October, 26–29.

Allaire, Y and Firsirotu, ME (1984) Theories of organizational culture. *Organization Studies*, 5(3), 193–226.

Allaire, Y and Firsirotu, ME (1989) Coping with strategic uncertainty. *Sloan Management Review*, 30(3), 7–16.

Allen, FR and Kraft, C (1982) *The Organizational Unconscious. How to Create the Corporate Culture You Want and Need.* Prentice Hall: Englewood Cliffs, NJ, USA.

Allen, RW, Madison, DL, Porter, LW, Renwick, PA and Mayes, BT (1979) Organizational politics: tactics and characteristics of its actors. *California Management Review*, 22, 77–83.

Allport, GW (1948) Foreword. In GW Lewin and GW Allport (eds): *Resolving Social Conflict*. Harper & Row: London.

Alvesson, M and Deetz, S (1996) Critical theory and postmodern approaches to organizational studies. In SR Clegg, C Hardy and WR Nord (eds): *Handbook of Organization Studies*. Sage: London.

Amin, A and Robins, K (1990) The re-emergence of regional economics? The mythical geography of flexible accumulation. *Environment and Planning D: Society and Space*, 8, 7–34.

Amit, R and Schoemaker, PJ (1993) Strategic assets and organisational rents. *Journal of Management Studies*, 30, 31–49.

Anderson, C and Paine, F (1978) PIMS: a re-examination. *Academy of Management Review*, 3(3), 602–12.

Andrews, KR (1980) *The Concept of Corporate Strategy*. Irwin: Homewood, IL, USA.

Andrews, KR (1998) The concept of corporate strategy. In H Mintzberg, JB Quinn and S Ghoshal: *The Strategy Process*. Prentice Hall: London.

Ansoff, HI (1965) *Corporate Strategy*. McGraw-Hill: New York, USA.

Ansoff, HI (1987) *Corporate Strategy* (revised version). McGraw-Hill: New York, USA.

Appignanesi, R and Garratt, C (1995) *Postmodernism for Beginners*. Icon Books: Cambridge.

Argenti, J (1974) *Systematic Corporate Planning*. Nelson: London.

Argyris, C (1960) *Understanding Organizational Behavior*. Dorsey: Homewood, IL, USA.

Argyris, C (1962) *Interpersonal Competence and Organizational Effectiveness*. Irwin: Homewood, IL, USA.

Argyris, C (1964) *Integrating the Individual and the Organization*. Wiley: London.

Argyris, C (1970) *Intervention Theory and Method*. Addison-Wesley: Reading, MA, USA.

Argyris, C (1973) Peter Blau. In G Salaman and K Thompson (eds): *People and Organizations*. Longman: London.

Argyris, C (1977) Double-loop learning in organizations. *Harvard Business Review*, September–October, 115–25.

Argyris, C (1980) *Inner Contradictions of Rigorous Research*. Academic Press: New York, USA.

Argyris, C (1990) *Overcoming Organizational Defenses*: *Facilitating Organizational Learning*. Allyn & Bacon: Boston, MA, USA.

Argyris, C (1991) Teaching smart people how to learn. *Harvard Business Review*, May–June, 99–109.

Argyris, C (1992) *On Organizational Learning*. Blackwell: Oxford.

Argyris, C (1999) *On Organizational Learning* (2nd edition). Blackwell: Oxford.

Argyris, C and Schon, D (1978) *Organizational Learning: A Theory of Action Perspective*. Addison-Wesley: Reading, MA, USA.

Argyris, C, Putnam, R and McLain-Smith, D (1985) *Action Science: Concepts, Methods and Skills for Research and Intervention*. Jossey Bass: San Francisco, CA, USA.

Aris, S (2002) Weinstock: I wanted to string up Simpson. *The Sunday Times,* 28 July, 8.

Arndt, M and Bigelow, B (2000) Commentary: the potential of chaos theory and complexity theory for health services management. *Health Care Management Review*, 25(1), 35–38.

Arnold, J, Cooper, CL and Robertson, IT (1998) *Work Psychology* (3rd edition). Pitman: London.

Arnot, C (2002) Laager toffs. *The Guardian,* 30 January, 2–3.

Aronowitz, S (1989) Postmodernism and politics. In A Ross (ed): *Universal Abandon: the Politics of Postmodernism*. Edinburgh University Press: Edinburgh.

Ash, M G (1992) Cultural contexts and scientific change in psychology – Lewin, Kurt in Iowa. *American Psychologist*, 47(2), 198–207.

Ashforth, BE and Fried, Y (1988) The mindlessness of organizational behaviours. *Human Relations*, 41(4), 305–29.

Ashour, AS (1973) The contingency model of leadership effectiveness: an evaluation. *Organizational Behavior and Human Performance*, 9, 339–55.

Ashton, D, Easterby-Smith, M, and Irvine, C (1975) *Management Development: Theory and Practice*. MCB: Bradford.

Ashton, TS (1948) *The Industrial Revolution 1760–1830*. Oxford University Press: Oxford.

Ashworth, W (1987) *A Short History of the International Economy since 1850.* Longman: London.

AT Kearney (1989) *Computer Integrated Manufacturing: Competitive Advantage or Technological Dead End?* Kearney: London.

AT Kearney (1992) *Total Quality: Time to Take Off the Rose-Tinted Spectacles.* IFS: Kempston.

AT Kearney Ltd (1994) *Partnership or Powerplay?* AT Kearney: London.

Auer, P and Riegler, C (1990) *Post-Taylorism: The Enterprise as a Place of Learning Organizational Change – A Comprehensive Study on Work Organization Changes and its Context at Volvo.* The Swedish Work Environment Fund: Stockholm, Sweden.

Ayres, R (1995) Privatisation and distributional equity: the case of Brazil. *International Journal of Social Economics*, 22(12), 36–49.

Babbage, C (1835) *On the Economy of Machinery and Manufacture.* Knight: London.

Bachman, JG, Bowers, DG and Marcus, PM (1968) Bases of supervisory power: a comparative study in five organizational settings. In AS Tannenbaum (ed): *Control in Organizations.* McGraw-Hill: New York, USA.

Back, KW (1992) This business of topology. *Journal of Social Issues*, 48(2), 51–66.

Bargal, D and Bar, H (1992) A Lewinian approach to intergroup workshops for Arab-Palestinian and Jewish youth. *Journal of Social Issues*, 48(2), 139–54.

Bargal, D, Gold, M and Lewin, M (1992) The heritage of Kurt Lewin – introduction. *Journal of Social Issues,* 48(2), 3–13.

Barnard, C (1938) *The Functions of the Executive.* Harvard University Press: Cambridge, MA, USA.

Barnard, C and Scott, J (eds) (2002) *The Law of the Single European Market: Unpacking the Premises.* Hart Publishing: London.

Barratt, ES (1990) Human resource management: organisational culture. *Management Update*, 2(1), 21–32.

Barrie, C (1995) Saatchi loses accounts to new agency. *Guardian*, 16 February, 15.

Barrie, C (1999) It's a far cry from safe and secure. *Guardian* – Jobs Section, 2 January, 12–13.

Bass, BM (1985) *Leadership and Performance Beyond Expectations.* Free Press: New York, NY, USA.

Bass, BM (1990) *Handbook of Leadership: A Survey of Theory and Research.* Free Press, New York, NY, USA.

Bass, BM (1996) Transformational leadership redux. *Leadership Quarterly*, 6, 463–78.

Bateson, G (1972) *Steps to an Ecology of the Mind.* Ballantine: New York, USA.

Batten, JD and Swab, JL (1965) How to crack down on company politics. *Personnel*, 42, 8–20.

Baudrillard, J (1983) *Simulations.* Semiotexte: New York, USA.

Beach, SD (1980) *Personnel.* Macmillan: London.

Beatty, CA and Lee, GL (1992) Leadership among middle managers – an exploration in the context of technological change. *Human Relations*, 45(9), 957–89.

Bechtold, BL (1997) Chaos theory as a model for strategy development. *Empowerment in Organizations*, 5(4), 193–201.

Beckhard, R (1969) *Organization Development: Strategies and Models*. Addison-Wesley: Reading, MA, USA.

Beckhard, R (1985) Whither management development? *Journal of Management Development*, 4(2).

Beckhard, R and Harris, RT (1987) *Organizational Transitions: Managing Complex Change* (2nd edition). Addison-Wesley: Reading, MA.

Beer, M and Nohria, N (eds) (2000) *Breaking the Code of Change*. Harvard Business School Press: Boston, MA, USA.

Beer, M and Walton, RE (1987) Organizational change and development. *Annual Review of Psychology*, 38, 339–68.

Beer, M, Eisenstat, RA and Spector, B (1993) Why change programmes don't produce change. In C Mabey and B Mayon-White (eds): *Managing Change* (2nd edition). The Open University/Paul Chapman Publishing: London.

Beesley, ME and Littlechild, SC (1983) Privatisation principles, problems and priorities. *Lloyds Bank Review*, 149, 1–20.

Beeson, I and Davis, C (2000) Emergence and accomplishment in organizational change. *Journal of Organizational Change Management*, 13(2), 178–89.

Bell, D (1973) *The Coming of Post-Industrial Society*. Basic Books: New York, USA.

Bell, RM (1973) *The Behaviour of Labour, Technical Change, and the Competitive Weakness of British Manufacturing*. Technical Change Centre: London.

Benjamin, G and Mabey, C (1993) Facilitating radical change. In C Mabey and B Mayon-White (eds): *Managing Change* (2nd edition). The Open University/Paul Chapman Publishing: London.

Bennett, J and Jayes, S (1995) *Trusting the Team: The Best Practice Guide to Partnering in Construction*. Reading University, Centre for Strategic Studies in Construction: Reading.

Bennett, R (1983) *Management Research. Management Development Series, 20*. International Labour Office: Geneva.

Bennis, W (2000) Leadership of change. In M Beer and N Nohria (eds): *Breaking the Code of Change*. Harvard Business School Press: Boston, MA, USA.

Bennis, W and Namus, B (1985) *Leaders: The Strategies for Taking Charge*. Harper & Row: New York, USA.

Bennis, WG (1959) Leadership theory and administrative behaviour. *Administrative Science Quarterly*, 4, 259–301.

Bennis, WG (1966) The coming death of bureaucracy. *Think,* November–December, 30–5.

Bennis, WG and Nanus, B (1985) *Leaders: The Strategies for Taking Charge*. Harper & Row: New York, NY, USA.

Berggren, C (1992) *The Volvo Experience*. Macmillan: London.

Bernstein, L (1968) *Management Development*. Business Books: London.

Bessant, J (1983) Management and manufacturing innovation: the case of information technology. In G Winch (ed): *Information Technology in Manufacturing Processes*. Rossendale: London.

Bessant, J and Haywood, B (1985) *The Introduction of Flexible Manufacturing Systems as an Example of Computer Integrated Manufacture*. Brighton Polytechnic: Brighton.

Bhaskar, R (1979) *A Realist Theory of Science* (2nd edition). Harvester: Brighton.

Bhaskar, R (1986) *Scientific Realism and Human Emancipation*. Verso: London.

Bhaskar, R (1989) *Reclaiming Reality*. Verso: London.

Bhote, KR (1989) *Strategic Supply Management*. American Management Association: New York, NY, USA.

Biberman, J and Whitty, M (1997) A postmodern spiritual future for work. *Journal of Organizational Change*, 10(2), 130–8.

Bigge, LM (1982) *Learning Theories for Teachers*. Gower: Aldershot.

Birchall, D and Lyons, L (1995) *Creating Tomorrow's Organization: Unlocking the Benefits of Future Work*. FT/Pitman: London.

Black, JA (2000) Fermenting change: capitalizing on the inherent change found in dynamic non-linear (or complex) systems. *Journal of Organizational Change Management*, 13(6), 520–5.

Blackler, F and Brown, C (1984) Alternative models to guide the design and introduction of new information technologies into work organisations. *Journal of Occupational Psychology*, 59(4), 287–314.

Blackler, F and McDonald, S (2000) Power, mastery and organisational learning. *Journal of Management Studies*, 37(6), 833–51.

Blackler, FHM and Brown, CA (1978) *Job Redesign and Management Control: Studies in British Leyland and Volvo*. Saxon House: Farnborough.

Blake, RR and McCanse, AA (1991) *Leadership Dilemmas – Grid Solutions*. Gulf Publishing: Houston, TX, USA.

Blake, RR and Mouton, JS (1969) *Building a Dynamic Corporation Through Grid Organisation Development*. Addison-Wesley: Reading, MA, USA.

Blake, RR and Mouton, JS (1976) *Organizational Change by Design*. Scientific Methods: Austin, TX, USA.

Blake, RR and Mouton, JS (1985) *The Managerial Grid lll*. Gulf Publishing: Houston, TX, USA.

Blanchard, K (1994) Changing role of executives. *Executive Excellence*, 11(4), 7.

Blau, PM (1970) The formal theory of differentiation in organizations. *American Sociological Review*, 35, 201–18.

Blau, PM and Schoenherr, RA (1971) *The Structure of Organizations*. Basic Books: New York, USA.

Block, P (1981) *Flawless Consulting: A Guide to Getting Your Expertise Used*. Learning Concepts: Austin, Texas, USA.

Boddy, D and Buchanan, D (1992) *Take the Lead: Interpersonal Skills for Change Agents*. Prentice Hall: London.

Boje, D M (2000) Phenomenal complexity theory and change at Disney: response to Letiche. *Journal of Organizational Change Management*, 13(6), 558–66.

Borchardt, K (1973) Germany 1700–1914. In C Cipolla (ed): *The Fontana Economic History of Europe Vol. 4, The Emergence of Industrial Societies – Part 1*. Fontana: London.

Bower, T (1996) *Maxwell: The Final Verdict*. HarperCollins: London.

Bowers, DG, Franklin, JL and Pecorella, P (1975) Matching problems, precursors and interventions in OD: a systematic approach. *Journal of Applied Behavioural Science*, 11, 391–410.

Bowles, M (1989) Myth, meaning and work organisation. *Organization Studies*, 10(3), 405–23.

Bowman, C and Asch, D (1985) *Strategic Map*. Macmillan: London.

Bracker, J (1980) The historical development of the strategic management concept. *Academy of Management Review*, 5(2), 219–24.

Brandenburger, AM and Nalebuff, BJ (1996) *Co-opetition*. Doubleday: New York, USA.

Bratton, J (1992) *Japanization at Work: Managerial Studies for the 1990s*. Macmillan: London.

Breslin, J and McGann, J (1998) *The Business Knowledge Repository: Consolidating and Accessing Your Ways of Working*. Quorum Books: Westport, CT, USA.

Brewer, E and Tomlinson, JWC (1964) The manager's working day. *Journal of Industrial Economics*, 12, 191–7.

Bridges, W (1996) *Jobshift: How to Prosper in a Workplace Without Jobs*. Nicholas Brealey: London.

Bridges, W (1998) *Creating You & Co: Learn to Think Like the CEO of Your Own Career*. Perseus Books: New York, USA.

Brindle, D (1998a) Benefits payments in chaos: computer collapse wipes out records. *Guardian*, 10 September, 1.

Brindle, D (1998b) Gap between rich and poor widens again. *Guardian*, 16 October, 7.

Brindle, D (1999) Pensions computer upgrade hit by 1,900 bugs as deadline looms. *Guardian*, 26 January, 3.

Brodbeck, PW (2002) Implications for organization design: teams as pockets of excellence. *Team Performance Management: An International Journal*, 8(1/2), 21–38.

Brown, A (1995) *Organisational Culture*. Pitman: London.

Brown, DH and Jopling, D (1994) Some experiences of outsourcing: a systemic analysis of strategic and organisational issues. Paper presented to the British Academy of Management Annual Conference, University of Lancaster, September.

Brown, SL and Eisenhardt, KM (1997) The art of continuous change: linking complexity theory and time-paced evolution in relentlessly shifting organizations. *Administrative Science Quarterly*, 42, March, 1–34.

Bruland, K (1989) The transformation of work in European industrialization. In P Mathias and JA Davis (eds): *The First Industrial Revolutions*. Blackwell: Cambridge.

Brummer, A (1999) Weinstock's heirs look for an encore. *Guardian*, 20 January, 21.

Brummer, A (2002) Lord Weinstock. *Guardian*, 24 July, available at www.guardian.co.uk.

Brummer, A and Cowe, R (1998) *Weinstock*. HarperCollins: London.

Bryant, A (1998) Beyond BPR: confronting the organizational legacy. *Management Decision*, 36(1), 25–30.

Bryant, D (1979) The psychology of resistance to change. *Management Services*, March, 9–10.

Bryce, R (2002) *Pipe Dreams: Greed, Ego, Jealousy and the Death of Enron*. Public affairs: London.

Buchanan, DA (1984) The impact of technical implications and managerial aspirations on the organization and control of the labour process. Paper presented to the Second Annual Conference on the Control and Organisation of the Labour Process, UMIST/Aston, 28–30 March.

Buchanan, DA and Badham, R (1999) *Power, Politics and Organizational Change: Winning the Turf Game*. Sage: London.

Buchanan, DA and Boddy, D (1992) *The Expertise of the Change Agent*. Prentice Hall: London.

Buchanan, DA and Storey, J (1997) Role-taking and role-switching in organizational change: the four pluralities. In I McLoughlin and M Harris (eds): *Innovation, Organizational Change and Technology*. International Thompson: London.

Buckingham, L and Finch, J (1999) SmithKline bows to revolt over directors' pay. *Guardian*, 24 April, 22.

Buckley, PJ and Mirza, H (1985) The wit and wisdom of Japanese management. *Management International Review*, 25, 16–32.

Buckley, W (1968) *Modern Systems and Research for the Behavioral Scientist*. Aldine Publishing: Chicago, USA.

Bullock, RJ and Batten, D (1985) It's just a phase we're going through: a review and synthesis of OD phase analysis. *Group and Organization Studies*, 10, December, 383–412.

Burawoy, M (1979) *Manufacturing Consent: Changes in the Labour Process under Monopoly Capital*. University of Chicago Press: Chicago, USA.

Burgoyne, J (1995) Feeding minds to grow the business. *People Management*, 1(19), 22–6.

Burgoyne, J and Germaine, C (1984) Self development and career planning: an exercise in mutual benefit. *Personnel Management*, 16(4), April, 21–3.

Burgoyne, J, Pedler, M and Boydell, T (1994) *Towards the Learning Company*. McGraw-Hill: London.

Burke, W (1980) *Organisation Development*. Little, Brown and Co: Toronto, Canada.

Burke, W, Michael, RS, Luthems, F, Odiorne, S and Hayden, S (1981) *Techniques of Organisational Change*. McGraw-Hill: London.

Burnes, B (1988) *Strategy for Success: Case Studies in Advanced Manufacturing Technologies*. EITB: Watford.

Burnes, B (1989) *New Technology in Context*. Gower: Aldershot.

Burnes, B (1991) Managerial competence and new technology: don't shoot the piano player – he's doing his best. *Behaviour and Information Technology*, 10(2), 91–109.

Burnes, B (1996) No such thing as ... a 'one best way' to manage organizational change. *Management Decision*, 34(10), 11–18.

Burnes, B (1997) Organisational choice and organisational change. *Management Decision*, 35(10), 753–9.

Burnes, B (1998a) Recipes for organisational effectiveness: mad, bad, or just dangerous to know. *Career Development International*, 3(3), 100–6.

Burnes, B (1998b) The planned approach to change: come back Kurt Lewin – all is forgiven. Paper presented to the Second Maintaining Organizational Effectiveness Conference, Edge Hill University College, Ormskirk, June, 17.

Burnes, B (2003) Managing change and changing managers: from ABC to XYZ. *Journal of Management Development*, 22(7), 627–42.

Burnes, B (2004) Kurt Lewin and the planned approach to change: a re-appraisal. *Journal of Management Studies*, 41(6).

Burnes, B and Coram, R (1999) Barriers to partnership in the public sector: the case of the UK construction industry. *Supply Chain Management*, 4(1), 43–50.

Burnes, B and Dale, B (eds) (1998) *Working in Partnership*. Gower: Aldershot.

Burnes, B and James, H (1995) Culture, cognitive dissonance and the management of change. *International Journal of Operations and Production Management*, 15(8), 14–33.

Burnes, B and New, S (1996) *Strategic Advantage and Supply Chain Collaboration*. AT Kearney: London.

Burnes, B and New, S (1997) Collaboration in customer–supplier relationships: strategy, operations and the function of rhetoric. *International Journal of Purchasing and Materials Management*, 33(4), 10–17.

Burnes, B and Salauroo, M (1995) The impact of the NHS internal market on the merger of colleges of midwifery and nursing: not just a case of putting the cart before the horse. *Journal of Management in Medicine*, 9(2), 14–29.

Burnes, B and Weekes, B (1989) *AMT: A Strategy for Success?* NEDO: London.

Burnes, B and Whittle, P (1995) Supplier development: getting started. *Logistics Focus*, February, 10–14.

Burnes, B, Cooper, C and West, P (2003) Organisational learning: the new management paradigm? *Management Decision*, 41(5), 443–51.

Burnes, B, Katsouros, M and Jones, T (2004) Privatisation and the European Union: the case of the Public Power Corporation of Greece. *International Journal of Public Sector Management*, 18(1).

Burns, JM (1978) *Leadership*. Harper & Row: New York, USA.

Burns, T and Stalker, GM (1961) *The Management of Innovation*. Tavistock: London.

Burrell, G (1988) Modernism, post modernism and organisational analysis 2: the contribution of Michel Foucault. *Organization Studies*, 9(2), 221–35.

Burrell, G (1997) Organization paradigms. In A Sorge and M Warner (eds): *The IEBM Handbook of Organizational Behaviour*. International Thompson Business Press: London.

Burt, T (2002) Divorcees with a difference: Volvo. *Financial Times*, 4 March, 13.

Burton, F, Yamin, M and Young, S (eds) (1996) *Europe in Transition*. MacMillan: London.

Business Notebook (2003) Old expressions. *Guardian*, 2 July, 16.

Butler, R (1997) Decision making. In A Sorge and M Warner (eds): *The IEBM Handbook of Organizational Behaviour*. International Thompson Business Press: London.

Butler, VG (1985) *Organisation and Management*. Prentice Hall: London.

Buzzell, RD and Gale, BT (1987) *The PIMS Principles – Linking Strategy to Performance*. Free Press: New York, USA.

Byars, LL (1984) *Strategic Management: Planning and Implementation*. Harper & Row: London.

Bywater PLC (1997) *Executive Briefings: The Executive Role in Sponsoring Change – Making It Happen*. Bywater PLC: Reading.

Caldwell, R (2001) Champions, adapters, consultants and synergists: the change agents in HRM. *Human Resource Management Journal*, 11(3), 39–52.

Caldwell, R (2003) Models of change agency: a fourfold classification. *British Journal of Management*, 14(2), 131–42.

Callinicos, A (1989) *Against Postmodernism*. Polity: Cambridge.

Camp, RC (1989) *Benchmarking*. ASQC Quality Press: Milwaukee, USA.

Campbell, A and Warner, M (1988) Organization of new forms of manufacturing operations. In M Wild (ed): *International Handbook of Production and Operations Management*. Cassells: London.

Cant, M and Jeynes, L (1998) What does outsourcing bring you that innovation cannot? How outsourcing is seen – and currently marketed – as a universal panacea. *Total Quality Management*, 9(2/3), 193–202.

Carew, A (1987) *Labour Under the Marshall Plan: The Politics of Productivity and the Market*. Manchester University Press: Manchester.

Carlson, S (1951) *Executive Behaviour*. Strombergs: Stockholm.

Carnall, CA (1990) *Managing Change in Organizations*. Prentice Hall: London.

Carnall, CA (1995) *Managing Change in Organizations* (2nd edition). Prentice Hall: London.

Carnall, CA (2003) *Managing Change in Organizations* (4th edition). FT/Prentice Hall: Harlow.

Carr, C, Tomkins, C and Bayliss, B (1991) Strategic controllership – a case study approach. *Management Accounting Research*, 2, 89–107.

Carr, P and Donaldson, L (1993) Managing healthily: how an NHS region is managing change. *Personnel Management*, October, 48–51.

Carroll, DT (1983) A disappointing search for excellence. *Harvard Business Review*, November–December, 78–88.

Carroll, GR (ed) (1988) *Ecological Models of Organisations*. Ballinger: Cambridge, MA, USA.

Cartwright, D (1951) Achieving change in people: some applications of group dynamics theory. *Human Relations*, 6(4), 381–92.

Cartwright, D (ed) (1952) *Field Theory in Social Science*. Social Science Paperbacks: London.

Carvel, J (2002) Long working hours harming family life. *Guardian*, 25 September, 13.

Cassidy, J (2002) *Dot.con: the Greatest Story Ever Sold*. Allen Lane: London.

Caulkin, S (2003) The bosses we love to hate. *Observer*, 6 July, available at www.guardian.co.uk.

Caves, R (2001) *Creative Industries*. The Free Press: New York, USA.

Cellan-Jones, R (2003) *Dot.bomb: The Strange Death of Dot.com Britain*. Arum: London.

Chamberlin, EH (1933) *The Theory of Monopolistic Competition*. Harvard University Press: Cambridge, MA, USA.

Chandler, AD (1962) *Strategy and Structure: Chapters in the History of American Industrial Enterprise*. MIT: Cambridge, MA, USA.

Chang, T-L (1997) Cultivating global experience curve advantage on technology and marketing capabilities. *Journal of Marketing Practice: Applied Marketing Science*, 3(4), 230–50.

Chapman, L (1978) *Your Disobedient Servant Published*. Chatto & Windus: London.

Chapman, SD and Chassagne, S (1981) *European Textile Printers in the Eighteenth Century. A Study of Peel and Oberkampf*. Heinemann: London.

Chawla, S and Renesch, J (1995) *Learning Organizations: Developing Cultures for Tomorrow's Workplace*. Productivity Press: Portland, OR, USA.

Child, J (1972) Organizational structure, environment and performance: the role of strategic choice. *Sociology*, 6(1), 1–22.

Child, J (1984) *Organization*. Harper & Row: Cambridge.

Child, J and Ellis, T (1973) Predictors of variation in managerial roles. *Human Relations*, 26(2), 227–50.

Child, J and Smith, C (1987) The context and process of organisational transformation – Cadbury Limited in its sector. *Journal of Management Studies*, 24(6), 565–93.

Chin, R and Benne, KD (1976) General strategies for effecting changes in human systems. In WG Bennis, KD Benne, R Chin and KE Corey (eds): *The Planning of Change* (3rd edition). Holt, Rinehart and Winston: New York, USA.

Choi, TY, Dooley, KJ and Rungtusanatham, M (2001) Supply networks and complex adaptive systems: control versus emergence. *Journal of Operations Management*, 19(3), 351–66.

Christopher, M (1998) *Logistics and Supply Chain Management* (2nd edition). Pitman: London.

Cipolla, C (ed) (1973) *The Fontana Economic History of Europe, Vol. 4*. Fontana: London.

Clark, P (1972) *Action Research and Organisational Change*. Harper & Row: London.

Clark, RC (1979) *The Japanese Company*. New Haven, CT, USA.

Clarke, L (1994) *The Essence of Change*. Prentice Hall: London.

Clarke, M (1999) Management development: a new role in social change. *Management Decision*, 37(10), 767–77.

Clegg, CW (1984) The derivation of Job Design. *Journal of Occupational Behaviour*, 5, 131–46.

Clegg, CW and Symon, G (1991) Technology-led change: a case study of the implementation of CADCAM. *Journal of Occupational Psychology*, 64(4), 273–90.

Clegg, S (1990) *Modern Organisation: Organisation Studies in the Postmodern World*. Sage: London.

Coch, L and French, JRP, Jr (1948) Overcoming resistance to change. *Human Relations*, 1(4), 512–32.

Coghlan, D (1993) In defence of process consultation. In C Mabey and B Mayon-White (eds): *Managing Change* (2nd edition). The Open University/Paul Chapman Publishing: London.

Cohen, MD, March, JG and Olsen, JP (1972) A garbage can model of organizational choice. *Administrative Science Quarterly*, 17, 1–25.

Cole, RE (1979) *Work, Mobility and Participation: A Comparative Study of Japanese and American Industry*. University of California Press: Los Angeles, USA.

Collier, A (1994) *Critical Realism*. Verso: London.

Collins, D (1998) *Organizational Change*. Routledge: London.

Collins, J and Porras, J (1997) *Built to Last: Successful Habits of Visionary Companies*. Harper Business: New York, USA.

Collins, JC and Porras, JI (1991) Organizational vision and visionary organizations. *California Management Review*, Fall, 30–52.

Connelly, J (2000) A realistic theory of health sector management: the case for critical realism. *Journal of Management in Medicine*, 14(5/6), 262–71.

Conner, PE (1977) A critical enquiry into some assumptions and values characterizing OD. *Academy of Management Review*, 2(1), 635–44.

Constable, J and McCormick, R (1987) *The Making of British Managers*. British Institute of Management/Confederation of British Industry: London.

Cook, T (1998) New Labour, new NHS ... new internal market? *Management Accounting*, 76(3), March, 24–6.

Cooke, B (1999) Writing the left out of management theory: the historiography of the management of change. *Organization*, 6(1), 81–105.

Cool, K and Schendel, D (1988) Performance differences among strategic group members. *Strategic Management Journal*, 9(3), 207–23.

Coombs, R and Hull, R (1994) The best or the worst of both worlds: BPR, cost reduction, and the strategic management of IT. Paper presented to the OASIG Seminar on Organisation Change Through IT and BPR: Beyond the Hype, September, London.

Cooper, CL and Jackson, SE (eds) (1997) *Creating Tomorrow's Organizations*. Wiley: Chichester.

Cooper, J and Fazio, RH (1984) A new look at dissonance theory. In L Berkowitz (ed): *Advances in Experimental Social Psychology*, Vol. 17, 229–67. Academic Press: New York, USA.

Cooper, R and Burrell, G (1988) Modernism, postmodernism and organizational analysis: an introduction. *Organization Studies*, 9, 91–112.

Coopey, J and Burgoyne, J (2000) Politics and organisational learning. *Journal of Management Studies*, 37(6), 869–85.

Copley, FB (1923) *Frederick Winslow Taylor: Father of Scientific Management*, Vol. 2. Harper & Row: New York, USA.

Coram, R and Burnes, B (2001) Managing organizational change in the public sector: lessons from the privatisation of the property services agency. *International Journal of Public Sector Management*, 14(2), 205–20.

Coram, WR (1997) The privatisation of the Property Services Agency, Vols 1 & 2. Unpublished PhD Thesis. UMIST: Manchester.

Coulson-Thomas, C and Coe, T (1991) *The Flat Organization*. British Institute of Management: London.

Coupland, D (1995) *Microserfs*. Regan Books: New York, USA.

Courtney, H, Kirkland, J and Viguerie, P (1997) Strategy under uncertainty. *Harvard Business Review*, 75(6), 67–79.

Covin, JG (1991) Entrepreneurial versus conservative firms: a comparison of strategies and performance. *Journal of Management Studies*, 28, 439–62.

Cowe, R (1995) Compete carefully. *Guardian*, 25 March, 40.

Crainer, S (ed) (1995) *The Financial Times Handbook of Management*. FT Pitman: London.

Crainer, S (1998) *Key Management Ideas*. FT/Pitman: London.

Crawford, M, Rutter, D and Thelwall, S (2003) *User Involvement in Change Management: A Review of the Literature*. Department of Psychological Medicine, Imperial College: London.

Cressey, P (1996) Enriching production: perspectives on Volvo's Uddevalla plant as an alternative to lean production. *Industrial Relations Journal*, 27(1), 77–80.

Cringely, RX (1992) *Accidental Empires: How the Boys of Silicon Valley Make their Millions, Battle Foreign Competition, and Still Can't Get a Date*. Addison-Wesley: Reading, MA, USA.

Crosby, PB (1979) *Quality is Free*. McGraw-Hill: New York, USA.

Crossan, MM and Guatto, T (1996) Organizational learning research profile. *Journal of Organizational Change Management*, 9(1), 107–12.

Crouch, C and Streeck, W (eds) (1997) *Political Economy of Modern Capitalism*. Sage: London.

Crozier, M (1964) *The Bureaucratic Phenomenon*. Tavistock: London.

Cruise O'Brien, R and Voss, C (1992) *In Search of Quality*. Working Paper, London Business School: London.

Cummings, TG and Huse, EF (1989) *Organization Development and Change* (4th edition). West: St Paul, MN, USA.

Cummings, TG and Worley, CG (1997) *Organization Development and Change* (6th edition). South-Western College Publishing: Cincinnati, OH, USA.

Cummings, TG and Worley, CG (2001) *Organization Development and Change* (7th edition). South-Western College Publishing: Mason, OH, USA.

Cuthbert, N (1970) Readings from Henri Fayol, General and Industrial Management. In A Tillett, T Kempner and G Willis (eds): *Management Thinkers*. Pelican: Harmondsworth.

Cyert, RM and March, JG (1963) *A Behavioral Theory of the Firm*. Prentice Hall: Englewood Cliffs, NJ, USA.

Daft, RL (1998) *Organizational Theory and Design* (6th edition). Southwestern: Cincinnati, OH, USA.

Dakin, SR and Hamilton, RT (1990) How 'general' are your general managers? *Management Decision*, 28(2), 32–7.

Dale, BG (ed) (1999) *Managing Quality* (3rd edition). Blackwell: Oxford.

Dale, BG and Cooper, CL (1992) *TQM and Human Resources: An Executive Guide*. Blackwell: Oxford.

Dale, PN (1986) *The Myth of Japanese Uniqueness*. Croom Helm: London.

Darwin, J, Johnson, P and McAuley, J (2002) *Developing Strategies for Change*. FT/Prentice Hall: Harlow.

Dastmalchian, A (1984) Environmental dependencies and company structure in Britain. *Organization Studies*, 5(3), 222–41.

Davenport, TH (1993) *Process Innovation: Re-engineering Work Through IT*. Harvard Business School Press: Boston, MA, USA.

Davies, C (1995) *Gender and the Professional Predicament in Nursing*. Routledge: London.

Davis, E and Star, J (1993) The world's best performing companies. *Business Strategy Review*, 4(2), 1–16.

Davis, JA (1989) Industrialisation in Britain and Europe before 1850. In P Mathias and JA Davis (eds): *The First Industrial Revolutions*. Blackwell: Cambridge.

Davis, LE (1979) Job Design: historical overview. In LE Davis and JC Taylor (eds): *Design of Work*. Goodyear: Santa Monica, CA, USA.

Davis, LE and Canter, RR (1955) Job Design. *Journal of Industrial Engineering*, 6(1), 3.

Davis, LE, Canter, RR and Hoffman, J (1955) Current job design criteria. *Journal of Industrial Engineering*, 6(2), 5–11.

Davis, R (1928) *The Principles of Factory Organization and Management*. Harper & Row: New York, USA.

Davis, TRV (1985) Managing culture at the bottom. In R Kilmann, M Saxton, R Serpa and Associates (eds): *Gaining Control of the Corporate Culture*. Jossey-Bass: San Francisco, CA, USA.

Dawkins, W (1993) Costly burden of tradition. *Financial Times*, 1 December, 10.

Dawkins, W (1994) Loosening of the corporate web. *Financial Times*, 30 November, 15.

Dawson, P (1994) *Organizational Change: A Processual Approach*. Paul Chapman Publishing: London.

Dawson, P (2003) *Organizational Change: A Processual Approach*. Routledge: London.

Day, C, Elliott, J, Somekh, B and Winter, R (eds) (2002) *Theory and Practice in Action Research*. Symposium Books: Oxford.

Day, J, Reynolds, P and Lancaster, G (1998) A marketing strategy for public sector organisations compelled to operate in a compulsory competitive tendering environment. *International Journal of Public Sector Management*, 11(7), 583–95.

De Witte, K and van Muijen, JJ (1999) Organizational culture: critical questions for researchers and practitioners. *European Journal of Work and Organizational Psychology*, 8(4), 583–95.

Deal, T and Kennedy, A (1982) Culture: a new look through old lenses. *Journal of Applied Behavioural Science*, 19(4), 497–507.

Deming, WE (1982) *Quality, Productivity and Competitive Position*. MIT Press: Boston, MA, USA.

Dent, EB and Goldberg, SG (1999) Challenging resistance to change. *Journal of Applied Behavioral Science*, 35(1), 25–41.

Deresky, H (2000) *International Management: Managing Across Borders and Cultures* (3rd edition). Prentice Hall: Upper Saddle River, NY, USA.

Derrida, J (1978) *Writing and Difference*. Routledge and Kegan Paul: London.

Dess, GG and Davis, PS (1984) Porter's (1980) generic strategies as determinants of strategic group membership and original performance. *Academy of Management Journal*, 27(3), 467–88.

Dickens, L and Watkins, K (1999) Action research: rethinking Lewin. *Management Learning*, 30(2), 127–40.

Dixit, A (1980) The role of investment in entry deterrence. *Economic Journal*, 90, 95–106.

Dobson, P (1988) Changing culture. *Employment Gazette*, December, 647–50.

Docherty, P, Forslin, J, Shani, AB and King, M (2002) Emerging work systems: from intensive to sustainable. In P Docherty, J Forslin, AB Shani, AB and M King (eds): *Creating Sustainable work Systems: Emerging Perspectives and Practices*. Routledge: London.

Doherty, TL and Horne, T (2002) *Managing Public Services: Implementing Change – A Thoughtful Approach*. Routledge: London.

Dolvik, JE and Stokland, D (1992) Norway: the 'Norwegian Model' in transition. In A Ferner and R Hyman (eds): *Industrial Relations in the New Europe*. Blackwell: Oxford.

Domberger, S (1998) *The Contracting Organization*. Oxford University Press: Oxford.

Done, K (1994) Up to strength once again: Volvo. *Financial Times,* 2 December.

Donkin, R (2002) How to preserve the soul of management: the increasing sophistication of measurement techniques threatens to reduce executives to robots. *Financial Times*, 19 Sept, 12.

Donovan, P (1995) Saatchis in row over share deal. *Guardian*, 15 February, 22.

Drennan, D (1992) *Transforming Company Culture*. McGraw-Hill: London.

Drory, A and Romm, T (1988) Politics in the organization and its perception within the organization. *Organization Studies*, 9(2), 165–79.

Drucker, PF (1974) *Management: Tasks, Responsibilities, Practices*. Harper & Row: London.

Drucker, PF (1985) *Innovation and Entrepreneurship*. Pan: London.

Dudley, G (1999) British Steel and the government since privatisation: policy 'framing' and the transformation of policy networks. *Public Administration, 77(1)*, 51–71.

Dukakis, MS and Kanter, RM (1988) *Creating the Future*. Summit Books: New York, USA.

Duncan, WJ (1975) Organisations as political coalitions: a behavioral view of the goal function process. *Journal of Behavioral Economics*, 5, Summer, 25–44.

Dunham, AL (1955) *The Industrial Revolution in France*. Exposition Press: New York, USA.

Dunphy, DD and Griffiths, A (1998) *The Sustainable Corporation: Organisational Renewal in Australia*. Allen & Unwin: St Leonards, Australia.

Dunphy, DD and Stace, DA (1988) Transformational and coercive strategies for planned organizational change: beyond the OD model. *Organization Studies*, 9(3), 317–34.

Dunphy, DD and Stace, DA (1992) *Under New Management: Australian Organizations in Transition*. McGraw-Hill: Roseville, NSW, Australia.

Dunphy, DD and Stace, DA (1993) The strategic management of corporate change. *Human Relations*, 46(8), 905–18.

Dunphy, D, Griffiths, A and Benn, S (2003) *Organizational Change for Corporate Sustainability*. Routledge: London.

Easterby-Smith, M (1997) Disciplines of organizational learning: contributions and critiques. *Human Relations*, 50(9), 1085–113.

Easterby-Smith, M, Crossan, M and Nicolini, D (2000) Organizational learning: debates past, present and future. *Journal of Management Studies,* 37(6), 783–96.

Easton, G (2000) Case research as a method for industrial networks: a realist apologia. In S Ackroyd and S Fleetwood (eds): *Realist Perspectives on Management and Organisations*. Routledge: London.

Eccles, T (1993) The deceptive allure of empowerment. *Long Range Planning*, 26(6), 13–21.

Economist Intelligence Unit (1992) *Making Quality Work – Lessons from Europe's Leading Companies*. Economist Intelligence Unit: London.

Economist (1998) All fall down. *Economist,* 28 February.

Economist (2002) *Globalisation: Reasons, Effects and Challenges*. Economist Books: London.

Eden, C and Huxham, C (1996) Action research for the study of organizations. In SR Clegg, C Hardy and WR Nord (eds): *Handbook of Organization Studies*. Sage: London.

Edwardes, M (1983) *Back from the Brink*. Collins: London.

Egan, G (1994) Cultivate your culture. *Management Today*, April, 39–42.

Elden, M and Chisholm, RF (1993) Emerging varieties of action research: introduction to the special issue. *Human Relations*, 46(20), 121–42.

Eldridge, JET and Crombie, AD (1974) *A Sociology of Organizations*. George Allen and Unwin: London.

Elliot, K and Lawrence, P (1985) *Introducing Management*. Penguin: Harmondsworth.

Elliott, L (1997) The weightless revolution. *Guardian*, 10 November, 17.

Elliott, L (2003) The lost decade. *Guardian*, 9 July, 1–2.

Elliott, L and Brittain, V (1998) The rich and poor grow further apart. *Guardian*, 9 September, 18.

Elrod II, PD and Tippett, DD (2002) The 'death valley' of change. *Journal of Organizational Change Management,* 15(3), 273–91.

Erridge, A and Nondi, R (1994) Public procurement, competition and partnership. *European Journal of Purchasing and Supply Management*, 1(3), 169–79.

Etzioni, A (1975) *A Comparative Analysis of Complex Organizations*. Free Press: New York, USA.

European Commission (1998) *Work Programme*. The Directorate General for Energy, DG XVII / 148 / 98–EN: Brussels.

Evans, MG (1970) The effects of supervisory behaviour on the path–goal relationship. *Organizational Behavior and Human Performance*, 5, 277–98.

Evans, R, Traynor, I, Harding, L and Carroll, R (2003) Web of state corruption dates back 40 years. *Guardian*, 13 June, available at www.guardian.co.uk.

Ezzamel, M, Green, C, Lilley, S and Willmott, H (1994) *Change Management: Appendix 1 – A Review and Analysis of Recent Changes in UK Management Practices*. The Financial Services Research Centre, UMIST: Manchester.

Fahy, J (2000) The resource-based view of the firm: some stumbling-blocks on the road to understanding sustainable competitive advantage. *Journal of European Industrial Training*, 24(2–4), 94–104.

Farrell, D and Petersen, JC (1983) Patterns of political behaviour in organizations. *The Academy of Management Review*, 7, 403–12.

Fawn, J and Cox, B (1985) *Corporate Planning in Practice*. Strategic Planning Society: London.

Fayol, H (1949) *General and Industrial Management* (trans). Pitman: London.

Fazio, RH, Zanna, MP and Cooper, J (1977) Dissonance and self-perception: an integrative view of each theory's proper domain of application. *Journal of Experimental Social Psychology*, 13, 464–79.

Featherstone, M (1988a) In pursuit of postmodernism: an introduction. *Theory, Culture and Society*, 5, 195–215.

Featherstone, M (ed) (1988b) *Postmodernism*. Sage: Newbury Park, CA, USA.

Ferguson, CH (1988) From the people who brought you Voodoo Economics. *Harvard Business Review*, May–June, 55–62.

Ferlie, E, Ashburner, L, Fitzgerald, L and Pettigrew, A (1996) *The New Public Sector in Action*. Oxford University Press: Oxford.

Ferner, A and Hyman, R (eds) (1992) *Industrial Relations in the New Europe*. Blackwell: Oxford.

Festinger, L (1957) *The Theory of Cognitive Dissonance*. Stanford University Press: Stanford, CA, USA.

Fiedler, FE (1967) *A Theory of Leadership Effectiveness*. McGraw-Hill: New York, USA.

Fiedler, FE and Chemers, MM (1984) *Improving Leadership Effectiveness: The Leader Match Concept* (2nd edition). Wiley: New York, USA.

Filby, I and Willmott, H (1988) Ideologies and contradictions in a public relations department. *Organization Studies*, 9(3), 335–51.

Filley, AC, House, RJ and Kerr, S (1976) *Managerial Process and Organization Behavior*. Scott, Foresman and Company: Glenview, IL, USA.

Financial, The [of Greece] (2000) When would consumers get a better service: if service utilities were government- or privately-owned? *Financial, The* [of Greece], 6 October, 14–15.

Financial Times (2003) The madness in Marconi's fall: the FSA report obscures important lessons. *Financial Times*, 14 April, 20.

Finch, J and Treanor, J (2003) Shares down 24%. Average earnings up 3%. Boardroom pay up 23%. *Guardian*, 31 July, 1.

Finstad, N (1998) The rhetoric of organizational change. *Human Relations*, 51(6), 717–40.

Fiol, MC and Lyles, MA (1985) Organizational learning. *Academy of Management Review*, 10(4), 803–13.

Fitton, R and Wadsworth, A (1958) *The Strutts and the Arkwrights 1758–1830*. Manchester University Press: Manchester.

Fitzgerald, LA (2002a) Chaos: the lens that transcends. *Journal of Organizational Change Management*, 15(4), 339–58.

Fitzgerald, LA (2002b) Chaos speak: a glossary of chaordic terms and phrases. *Journal of Organizational Change Management*, 15(4), 412–23.

Fleisher, CS and Bensoussan, BE (2003) *Strategic and Competitive Analysis: Methods and Techniques for Analysing Business Competition*. Prentice Hall: Upper Saddle River, NJ, USA.

Fleishman, EA (1953) The description of supervisory behaviour. *Personnel Psychology*, 37, 1–6.

Fleishman, EA (1969) *Manual for the Leadership Opinion Questionnaire*. Science Research Associates: USA.

Flynn, J, Dawley, H, Templeman, J and Bernier, L (1995) Suddenly British carmaking is burning rubber. *Business Week*, 3 April, 21.

Foegen, JH (1999) Why not empowerment? *Business and Economics Review*, 45(3), April–June, 31.

Fohlen, C (1973) France 1700–1914. In C Cipolla (ed): *The Fontana Economic History of Europe*, Vol. 4. Fontana: London.

Ford, TM (1981) Strategic planning – myth or reality? A chief executive's view. *Long Range Planning*, 14, December, 9–11.

Fortune (1990) Global 500: the world's biggest industrial corporations. *Fortune*, 30 July.

Foucault, M (1977) *The Archaeology of Knowledge*. Tavistock: London.

Foucault, M (1983) The subject and power. In HL Dreyfus and P Rabinow (eds): *Michel Foucault: Beyond Structuralism and Hermeneutics* (2nd edition). University of Chicago Press: Chicago, USA.

Fox, JM (1975) Strategic planning: a case study. *Managerial Planning*, 23, May/June, 32–8.

Fox, M (1994) *The Reinvention of Work: A New Vision of Livelihood for Our Times*. Harper: San Francisco, USA.

Francks, P (1992) *Japanese Economic Development: Theory and Practice*. Routledge: London.

Franklin, B (1997) *Newszak and News Media*. Arnold: London.

Frederick, WC (1998) Creatures, corporations, communities, chaos, complexity: a naturological view of the corporate social role. *Business and Society*, 37(4), 358–76.

Freeman, C (1988) The factory of the future: the productivity paradox, Japanese just-in-time and information technology. *ESRC PICT Policy Research Paper 3*. ESRC: Swindon.

French, JRP, Jr and Raven, BH (1959) The bases of social power. In D Cartwright (ed): *Studies in Social Power*. Institute for Social Research: Ann Harbor, MI, USA.

French, WL and Bell, CH (1973) *Organization Development*. Prentice Hall: Englewood Cliffs, NJ, USA.

French, WL and Bell, CH (1984) *Organization Development* (4th edition). Prentice Hall: Englewood Cliffs, NJ, USA.

French, WL and Bell, CH (1995) *Organization Development* (5th edition). Prentice Hall: Englewood Cliffs, NJ, USA.

Friedman, G (1961) *The Anatomy of Work*. Heinemann: London.

Frith, M (2003) Brain drain: the men who won't let jobs deprive them of fatherhood. *The Independent*, 14 June, 7.

Froebel, F, Heinrichs, J and Kreye, O (1980) *The New Industrial Division of Labour: Structural Unemployment in Industrialized Countries and Industrialization in Developing Countries*. Cambridge University Press: Cambridge.

Frost, PJ and Hayes, DC (1979) An exploration in two cultures of a model of political behaviour in organizations. In RW Allen and LW Porter (eds): *Organizational Influence Processes*. Scott, Foresman and Co: Glenview, IL, USA.

Fruin, WM (1992) *The Japanese Enterprise System*. OUP: Oxford.

Fullerton, H and Price, C (1991) Culture change in the NHS. *Personnel Management*, March, 50–3.

Fulton, The Lord (1968) *The Civil Service: Report of the Committee Cmnd 3638*. HMSO: London.

Galagan, PA (1997) Strategic planning is back. *Training and Development*, 51, 32–38.

Galbraith, JR (2000) The role of formal structures and processes. In M Beer and N Nohria (eds): *Breaking the Code of Change*. Harvard Business School Press: Boston, MA, USA.

Gandz, J and Murray, VV (1980) The experience of workplace politics. *Academy of Management Journal*, 23, 237–51.

Gardner, J (1990) *On Leadership*. Free Press: New York, USA.

Garratt, B (1987) *The Learning Organization*. Fontana: London.

Garratt, B (1999) The learning organisation 15 Years on: some personal reflections. *The Learning Organization*, 6(5), 202–6.

Garvin, DA (1993) Building a learning organization. *Harvard Business Review*, July–August, 78–91.

Gastil, J (1994) A definition and an illustration of Democratic Leadership. *Human Relations*, 47, 953–75.

Gay, CL and Essinger, J (2000) *Inside Outsourcing*. Nicholas Brealey Publishing: London.

Gellerman, W, Frankel, MS and Ladenson, RF (1990) *Values and Ethics in Organizational and Human Systems Development: Responding to Dilemmas in Professional Life*. Jossey-Bass: San Francisco, CA, USA.

Gell-Mann, M (1994) *The Quark and the Jaguar*. Freeman: New York, USA.

Genus, A (1998) *The Management of Change: Perspective and Practice*. International Thompson: London.

Gephart, RP, Thatchenkery, TJ and Boye, DM (1996) Reconstructing organizations for future survival. In DM Boye, RP Gephart and TJ Thatchenkery (eds): *Postmodern Management and Organizational Theory*. Sage: Thousand Oaks, CA, USA.

Gergen, KJ (1992) Organization theory in the postmodern era. In M Reed and M Hughes (eds): *Rethinking Organization: New Directions in Organization Theory and Analysis*. Sage: London.

Gersick, CJG (1991) Revolutionary change theories: a multilevel exploration of the punctuated equilibrium paradigm. *Academy of Management Review*, 16(1), 10–36.

Ghemawat, P (1991) *Commitment: The Dynamics of Strategy*. Free Press: New York, USA.

Ghoshal, S and Bartlett, CA (2000) Rebuilding Behavioural Context: A Blueprint for Corporate Renewal. In M Beer and N Nohria (eds): *Breaking the Code of Change*. Harvard Business School Press: Boston, MA, USA.

Gibb, CA (1969) Leadership. In G Lindzey and E Aronson (eds): *Handbook of Social Psychology*, Vol. 4 (2nd edition). Addison-Wesley: Reading, MA, USA.

Gibbons, PT (1992) Impacts of organisational evolution on leadership roles and behaviors. *Human Relations*, 45(1), 1–18.

Gibson, JL, Ivancevich, JM and Donnelly, JH (1988) *Organizations: Behaviour–Structure–Processes*. Business Publications: Plano, TX, USA.

Gibson, O (2003a) Napster: hopes to relaunch before end of year. *Guardian*, 24 February, available at www.guardian.co.uk.

Gibson, O (2003b) Web piracy hits music sales. *Guardian*, 10 February, available at www.guardian.co.uk.

Gibson, O (2003c) EMI to sell music downloads. *Guardian,* 23 April, available at www.guardian.co.uk.

Giddens, A (1976) *The Constitution of Society*. Polity Press: Cambridge.

Giddens, A (2002) *Runaway World: How Globalisation is Reshaping Our Lives*. Profile: London.

Gilbert, RJ and Newbury, DMG (1982) Preemptive patenting and the persistence of monopoly. *American Economic Review*, 72, 514–26.

Gilbert, X and Strebel, P (1992) Developing competitive advantage. In H Mintzberg and JB Quinn (eds): *The Strategy Process: Concepts, Contexts and Cases*. Prentice Hall: London.

Gilbreth, FB and Gilbreth, LM (1914) *Applied Motion Study*. Sturgis and Walton: New York, USA.

Gilchrist, A (2000) The well-connected community: networking to the edge of chaos. *Community Development Journal*, 3(3), 264–75.

Gillespie, R (1991) *Manufacturing Knowledge: A History of the Hawthorne Experiments*. Cambridge University Press: Cambridge.

Gillett, C (1996) *The Sound of the City: The Rise of Rock & Roll* (3rd edition). Souvenir Press: London.

Gittings, J (1998) Weakest pay the price for recession as African poverty comes to Asia. *Guardian*, 17 October, 16.

Gleick, J (1988) *Chaos: The Making of a New Science*. Heinemann: London.

Globalisation Guide.org (2003) Is globalisation shifting power from nation states to undemocratic organisations? Available at www.globalisationguide.org.

Glueck, WF (1978) *Business Policy and Strategic Management*. McGraw-Hill: New York, USA.

Gold, KA (1982) Managing for success: a comparison of the private and public sectors. *Public Administration Review*, November–December, 568–75.

Gold, M (1992) Metatheory and field theory in social psychology: relevance or elegance? *Journal of Social Issues*, 48(2), 67–78.

Gold, M (ed) (1999): *The Complete Social Scientist: A Kurt Lewin Reader*. American Psychological Association: Washington, DC, USA.

Golding, D and Currie, D (2000) *Thinking About Management: A Reflective Practice Approach*. Routledge: London.

Golzen, G (1995) Jobbing guru. *Human Resources*, 16, January/February, 42–8.

Goodwin, B (1994) *How the Leopard Changed its Spots*. Weidenfeld and Nicholson: London.

Goold, M, Campbell, A and Alexander, M (1994) *Corporate-Level Strategy: Creating Value in the Multi-Business Company*. Wiley: Chichester.

Gordon, G (1985) The relationship of corporate culture to industry sector and corporate performance. In R Kilmann, M Saxton, R Serpa and Associates (eds): *Gaining Control of the Corporate Culture*. Jossey-Bass: San Francisco, CA, USA.

Gould, SJ (1989) Punctuated equilibrium in fact and theory. *Journal of Social Biological Structure*, 12, 117–36.

Gow, D (1999a) Vultures still circling Rover plant as BMW remains silent on investment. *Guardian*, 6 February, 11–12.

Gow, D (1999b) BMW to put £3bn into Rover car plants. *Guardian*, 24 June, 25.

Gow, D (1999c) Finance: EC plans global assault: Simpson pledges to double value within five years after Marconi defence sale. *Guardian*, 6 May. 25.

Gow, D and Traynor, I (1999) BMW split raises fears for Rover plant. *Guardian*, 2 February, 1.

Graen, GB and Cashman, JF (1975) A role making model of leadership in formal organizations: a developmental approach. In JG Hunt and LL Larson (eds): *Leadership Frontiers*. Kent State University Press: Kent, OH, USA.

Graetz, F, Rimmer, M, Lawrence, A and Smith, A (2002) *Managing Organisational Change*. Wiley: Milton, Queensland, Australia.

Graham, G, Burnes, B and Hardaker, G (2002) The peer-to-peer revolution: how the Internet is transforming the supply chain for music. *The International Journal of New Product Development & Innovation Management*, 4(2), June/July, 115–30.

Grant, A (1983) *Against the Clock*. Pluto: London.

Grant, GM (1991a) *Contemporary Strategy Analysis*. Blackwell: Oxford.

Grant, GM (1991b) The resource-based theory of competitive advantage: implications for strategy formulation. *California Management Review*, 33(3), 114–22.

Greenberg, P and Erios, L (2001) One year ago: MP3.com caves in to legal blow, *Ecommercetimes*, 1–3, 5 November, available at www.ecommercetimes.com.

Greenwald, J (1996) Reinventing Sears. *Time*, 23 December, 53–5.

Greiner, L (1972) Evolution and revolution as organizations grow. *Harvard Business Review*, July–August, 37–46.

Griffin, D (2001) *The Emergence of Leadership: Linking Self-Organisation and Ethics*. Routledge: London.

Griffin, D (2002) *The Emergence of Leadership: Linking Self-Organization and Ethics*. Routledge: London.

Grinyer, PH, Mayes, DG and McKiermon, P (1988) *Sharpbenders: The Secrets of Unleashing Corporate Potential*. Blackwell: Oxford.

Grove, G (1998) The automotive industry – the customer's perspective: a study of Rover group. In B Burnes and B Dale (eds) (1998): *Working in Partnership*. Gower: Aldershot.

Grundy, T (1993) *Managing Strategic Change*. Kogan Page: London.

Guest, RH (1957) Job enlargement – revolution in Job Design. *Personnel Administration*, 20, 9–16.

Gyllenhammar, PG (1977) *People at Work*. Addison-Wesley: Reading, MA, USA.

Habakkuk, HJ and Postan, M (eds) (1965) *The Cambridge Economic History of Europe*, Vol. VI. Cambridge University Press: Cambridge.

Hackman, JR and Lawler, EE (1971) Employee relations and job characteristics. *Journal of Applied Psychology*, 55, 259–86.

Hackman, JR and Oldham, GR (1980) *Work Redesign*. Addison-Wesley: Reading, MA, USA.

Haigh, C (2002) Using chaos theory: the implications for nursing. *Journal of Advanced Nursing*, 37(5), 462–9.

Hales, CP (1986) What do managers do?: a critical review of the evidence. *Journal of Management Studies*, 22(1), 88–115.

Hall, DT and Nougaim, KE (1968) An examination of Maslow's need hierarchy in an organizational setting. *Organizational Behaviour and Performance*, 3, February, 12–35.

Hall, R (1933) A framework linking intangible resources and capabilities to sustainable competitive advantage. *Strategic Management Journal*, 14, 607–18.

Hambrick, DC (1983) High profit strategies in mature capital goods industries: a contingency approach. *Academy of Management Journal*, 26, 687–707.

Hamel, G and Prahalad, CK (1989) Strategic intent. *Harvard Business Review*, May–June, 63–76.

Hamel, G and Prahalad, CK (1994) *Competing for the Future*. Harvard Business School Press: Boston, MA, USA.

Hammer, M and Champy, J (1993) *Re engineering the Corporation*. Nicolas Brealey: London.

Hammersley, B (2002) Working the web: P2P technology. *Guardian*, 7 March, available at www.guardian.co.uk.

Handfield, RB and Nichols, EL Jr (1999) *Introduction to Supply Chain Management*. Prentice Hall: Englewood Cliffs, NJ, USA.

Handy, C (1979) *Gods of Management*. Pan: London.

Handy, C (1984) *The Future of Work*. Blackwell: Oxford.

Handy, C (1986) *Understanding Organizations* (3rd edition). Penguin: Harmondsworth.

Handy, C (1989) *The Age of Unreason*. Arrow: London.

Handy, C (1993) *Understanding Organizations* (4th edition). Penguin: Harmondsworth.

Handy, C (1994) *The Empty Raincoat*. Hutchinson: London.

Handy, C (1997) *The Hungry Spirit*. Hutchinson: London.

Handy, C, Gow, I, Gordon, C, Randlesome, C and Moloney, M (1987) *The Making of a Manager*. NEDO: London.

Hannagan, T (2002) *Management: Concepts and Practices* (3rd edition). FT/Pearson: Harlow.

Hannam, R (1993) *Kaizen for Europe*. IFS: Kempston.

Hannan, MT and Freeman, J (1977) The population ecology of organizations. *American Journal of Sociology*, 82, 929–64.

Hannan, MT and Freeman, J (1988) *Organizational Ecology*. Harvard University Press: Cambridge, MA, USA.

Hanson, P (1993) Made in Britain – the true state of manufacturing industry. Paper presented at the Institution of Mechanical Engineers' Conference on Performance Measurement and Benchmarking, Birmingham, June.

Hardaker, G and Graham, G (2001) *Wired Marketing: Energising Business for e-Commerce*. Wiley: Chichester.

Hardaker, G and Graham, G (2001) *Wired Marketing: Energizing Business for e-Commerce*. Wiley: Chichester.

Hardy, C (1996) Understanding power: bringing about strategic change. *British Journal of Management*, 7(Special Issue) March, S3–S16.

Harré, R (1972) *The Philosophies of Science*. OUP: Oxford.

Harré, R and Madden, EH (1975) *Causal Powers*. Blackwell: Oxford.

Harré, R and Secord, PF (1972) *The Explanation of Social Behaviour*. Blackwell: Oxford.

Harrigan, RK (1980) *Strategy for Declining Businesses*. Lexington Books: Lexington, MA, USA.

Harris, PR (1985) *Management in Transition*. Jossey-Bass: San Francisco, CA, USA.

Harrison, M (2002) Lord Simpson speaks out for the first time since leaving Marconi. *Independent*, 28 November, 24.

Harrison, M (2003) Swipe card strike wipes £40m off BA. *Independent*, 1 August, 19.

Harrison, R (1970) Choosing the depth of an organisational intervention. *Journal of Applied Behavioural Science*, 6, 181–202.

Harrison, R (1972) How to describe your organization. *Harvard Business Review*, 50, September–October.

Harrison, R (2002) *Learning and Development* (3rd edition). CIPD: London.

Hartley, J, Bennington, J and Binns, P (1997) Researching the roles of internal-change agents in the management of organizational change. *British Journal of Managment*, 8(1), 61–73.

Harukiyo, H and Hook, GD (eds) (1998) *Japanese Business Management: Restructuring for Low Growth and Globalization*. Routledge: London.

Harung, HS, Heaton, DP, and Alexander, CN (1999) Evolution of organizations in the new millennium. *Leadership and Organization Development Journal*, 20(4), 198–207.

Harvey, D and Brown, DR (2001) *An Experiential Approach to Organization Development* (6th edition). Prentice Hall: Upper Saddle River, NJ, USA.

Harvey, F (2001) Microsoft's direct connection to the customer. *Financial Times*, 31 December, 7.

Hassard, J (1990) An alternative to paradigm incommensurability in organization theory. In J Hassard and D Pym (eds): *The Theory and Philosophy of Organizations*. Routledge: London.

Hassard, J (1993) *Sociology and Organization Theory: Positivism, Paradigms and Postmodernity*. Cambridge University Press: Cambridge.

Hassard, J and Parker, M (eds) (1993) *Postmodernism and Organizations*. Sage: London.

Hassard, J and Sharifi, S (1989) Corporate culture and strategic change. *Journal of General Management*, 15(2), 4–19.

Hatch, MJ (1997) *Organization Theory: Modern, Symbolic and Postmodern Perspectives*. Oxford University Press: Oxford.

Hatvany, N and Pucik, V (1981) An integrated management system: lessons from the Japanese experience. *Academy of Management Review*, 6, 469–80.

Hax, CA and Majluf, NS (1982) Competitive cost dynamics. *Interfaces*, 12, October, 50–61.

Hax, CA and Majluf, NS (1996) *The Strategy Concept and Process* (2nd edition). Prentice Hall: New Jersey, USA.

Hax, CA and Nicholson, SM (1983) The use of the growth share matrix in strategic planning. *Interfaces*, 13, February, 46–60.

Hayes, J (2002) *The Theory and Practice of Change Management*. Palgrave: Basingstoke.

Hayles, KN (2000) From chaos to complexity: moving through metaphor to practice. *Complexity and Chaos in Nursing*, 4, available at www.southernct.edu/scsu/chaos-nursing/chaos4.htm.

Hedberg, B (1981) How organizations learn and unlearn. In PC Nystrom and WH Starbuck (eds): *Handbook of Organizational Design*. Oxford University Press: London.

Hedberg, B, Nystrom, P and Starbuck, W (1976) Camping on seesaws: prescriptions for a self-designing organization. *Administrative Science Quarterly*, 17, 371–81.

Hedlund, G and Nonaka, I (1993) Models of knowledge management in the West and Japan. In P Lorange (ed): *Implementing Strategic Processes*. Blackwell: Oxford.

Heller, F (1970) Group feed-back analysis as a change agent. *Human Relations*, 23(4), 319–33.

Heller, R (2002) A legacy turned to tragedy. *The Observer*, 18 August, available at www.observer.co.uk.

Hendry, C (1979) Contingency theory in practice, I. *Personnel Review,* 8(4), 39–44.

Hendry, C (1980) Contingency theory in practice, II. *Personnel Review*, 9(1), 5–11.

Hendry, C (1996) Understanding and creating whole organizational change through learning theory. *Human Relations*, 48(5), 621–41.

Herzberg, F (1968) One more time: how do you motivate employees? *Harvard Business Review*, 46, 53–62.

Herzberg, F, Mausner, B and Snyderman, B (1959) *The Motivation to Work*. John Wiley: New York, USA.

Hickman, CF (1990) *Mind of a Manager, Soul of a Leader*. John Wiley: New York, NY, USA.

Hickson, DJ and Butler, RJ (1982) Power and decision-making in the organisational coalition. Research report presented to the Social Science Research Council.

Hickson, DJ, Pugh, DS and Pheysey, DC (1969) Operations technology and organisation structure: an empirical reappraisal. *Administrative Science Quarterly*, 14, 378–97.

Hines, P (1994) *Creating World Class Suppliers: Unlocking Mutual Competitive Advantage*. Pitman: London.

Hinkin, TR and Tracey, JB (1999) The relevance of charisma for transformational leadership in stable organizations. *Journal of Organizational Change Management*, 12(2), 105–19.

Hirschhorn, L (1988) *The Workplace Within*. MIT Press: Cambridge, MA, USA.

Hirschhorn, L (2000) Changing structure is not enough: the moral meaning of organizational design. In M Beer and N Nohria (eds): *Breaking the Code of Change*. Harvard Business School Press: Boston, MA, USA.

Hirst, C (2002) Marconi's £3bn debt lifeline. *Sunday Independent*, 7 April, 1.

Hlavacka, S, Bacharova, L, Rusnakova, V and Wagner, R (2001) Performance implications of Porter's generic strategies in Slovak hospitals. *Journal of Management in Hospitals*, 15(1), 44–66.

HMSO (1989) *Working for Patients*, Cmnd 555. HMSO: London.

HMSO (1991) *Competing for Quality,* Cmnd 1730. HMSO: London.

Ho, DYF (1976) On the concept of face. *American Journal of Sociology*, 81(4), 867–84.

Hobsbawm, EJ (1968) *Industry and Empire*. Pelican: Harmondsworth.

Hobsbawm, EJ (1979) *The Age of Revolution*. Abacus: London.

Hock, D (1999) *Birth of the Chaordic Age*. Berrett-Koehler: San Francisco, CA, USA.

Hofer, CH and Schendel, DE (1978) *Strategy Formulation: Analytical Concepts*. West: St Paul, MN, USA.

Hofstede, G (1980) *Culture's Consequences: International Differences in Work-Related Values*. Sage: London.

Hofstede, G (1990) The cultural relativity of organizational practices and theories. In DC Wilson and RH Rosenfeld (eds): *Managing Organizations: Text, Readings and Cases*. McGraw-Hill: London.

Hofstede, G (1993) Cultural constraints in management theories. *Academy of Management Executive*, 7(1), 81–94.

Holden, N and Burgess, M (1994) *Japanese-Led Companies*. McGraw-Hill: London.

Hoogerwerf, EC and Poorthuis, A-N (2002) The network multilogue: a chaos approach to organizational design. *Journal of Organizational Change Management*, 15(4), 382–90.

Horne, JH and Lupton, T (1965) The work activities of 'middle managers' – an exploratory study. *Journal of Management Studies*, 2(1), 14–33.

Horsley, W and Buckley, R (1990) *Nippon New Superpower; Japan Since 1945*. BBC Books: London.

Horton, S (1996) The Civil Service. In D Farnham and S Horton (eds): *Managing the New Public Services* (2nd edition). MacMillan: Basingstoke.

Hoskin, K (1990) Using history to understand theory: a re-consideration of the historical genesis of 'strategy'. Paper prepared for the EIASM Workshop on Strategy, Accounting and Control, Venice, Italy.

House, JS (1993) John R French, Jr: a Lewinian's Lewinian. *Journal of Social Issues*, 49(4), 221–6.

Howarth, C (1988) Report of the Joint Design of Technology, Organisation and People Growth Conference – Venice, 12–14, October. *Information Services News and Abstracts*, 95 November/December, Work Research Unit: London.

Huber, GP (1991) Organizational learning: the contributing processes and the literatures. *Organization Science*, February, 88–115.

Huczynski, AA (1993) *Management Gurus*. Routledge: London.

Huczynski, A and Buchanan, D (2001) *Organizational Behaviour* (4th edition). FT/Prentice Hall: Harlow.

Hughes, M (1995) Halifax and Leeds clear the courts. *Guardian,* 29 March, 15.

Hunter, JE (1989) *The Emergence of Modern Japan*. Longman: London.

Hurley, RF, Church, AH, Burke, WW and Van Eynde, DF (1992) Tension, change and values in OD. *OD Practitioner*, 29, 1–5.

Huse, EF (1980) *Organization Development and Change*. West: St Paul, MN, USA.

Hussey, D and Jenster, P (1999) *Competitive Intelligence: Turning Analysis into Success*. John Wiley: Chichester.

Hussey, DE (1978) Portfolio analysis: practical experience with the Directional Policy Matrix. *Long Range Planning*, 11, August, 2–8.

Hutton, W (1995) *The State We're In*. Cape: London.

Inagami, T (1988) *Japanese Workplace Industrial Relations*. Japan Institute of Labour: Tokyo.

Inagami, T (1995) *Enterprise Unions in a Mature Society*. Japan Institute of Labour: Tokyo.

Industrial Society (1997) *Culture Change. Managing Best Practice 35*. Industrial Society: London.

Institute of Management (1995) *Finding the Time – A Survey of Managers' Attitudes to Using and Managing Time*. Institute of Management: London.

Ishikawa, K (1985) *What is Total Quality Control? The Japanese Way*. Prentice Hall: Englewood Cliffs, NJ, USA.

Ishizuna, Y (1990) The transformation of Nissan – the reform of corporate culture. *Long Range Planning*, 23(3), 9–15.

Ivancevich, J (1970) An analysis of control, bases of control, and satisfaction in an organizational setting. *Academy of Management Journal*, December, 427–32.

Jacques, E (1952) *The Changing Culture of a Factory*. Dryden Press: New York, USA.

Jacques, E (1998) On leaving the Tavistock Institute. *Human Relations,* 51(3), 251–7.

Jenner, RA (1998) Dissipative enterprises, chaos, and the principles of lean organizations. *Omega: International Journal of Management Science*, 26(3), 397–407.

Johnson, G (1987) *Strategic Change and the Management Process*. Blackwell: Oxford.

Johnson, G (1993) Processes of managing strategic change. In C Mabey and B Mayon-White (eds): *Managing Change* (2nd edition). The Open University/Paul Chapman Publishing: London.

Johnson, G and Scholes, K (1993) *Exploring Corporate Strategy*. Prentice Hall: London.

Johnson, G and Scholes, K (eds) (2001) *Exploring Public Sector Strategy*. FT/Prentice Hall: Harlow.

Johnson, G and Scholes, K (2002) *Exploring Corporate Strategy* (6th edition). FT/Prentice Hall: Harlow.

Johnson, R and Ouchi, W (1974) Made in America (under Japanese management). *Harvard Business Review,* 52(5), 61–9.

Jones, EE (1990) *Interpersonal Perception*. Freeman: New York, USA.

Jones, GR, George, JM and Hill, CWL (2000) *Contemporary Management* (2nd edition). McGraw-Hill: Boston, MA, USA.

Jones, H (1989) Private property. *New Civil Engineer,* 29 June, 23.

Jones, RJB (1995) *Globalization and Interdependence in the International Political Economy: Reality and Rhetoric*. Pinter: London.

Jorberg, L (1973) The Nordic countries 1850–1914. In C Cipolla (ed): *The Fontana Economic History of Europe* Vol. 4. Fontana: London.

Joyce, P and Woods, A (2001) *Strategic Management: A Fresh Approach to Developing Skills, Knowledge and Creativity*. Kogan Page: London.

Juran, JM (1988) *Quality Control Handbook*. McGraw-Hill: New York, USA.

Kahn, H and Weiner, A (1978) *The Year 2000*. Macmillan: London.

Kamata, S (1982) *Japan in the Passing Lane*. Pantheon: New York, USA.

Kanter, RM (1977) *Men and Women of The Corporation*. Basic Books: New York, USA.

Kanter, RM (1979) Power failure in management circuits. *Harvard Business Review,* 57(4), 65–75.

Kanter, RM (1983) *The Change Masters*. Simon & Schuster: New York, USA.

Kanter, RM (1989) *When Giants Learn to Dance: Mastering the Challenges of Strategy, Management, and Careers in the 1990s*. Unwin: London.

Kanter, RM (1997) *World Class: Thriving Locally in the Global Economy*. Simon & Schuster: New York, USA.

Kanter, RM, Kao, J and Wiersema, F (eds) (1997) *Innovation: Breakthrough Thinking at 3M, DuPont, GE, Pfizer, and Rubbermaid*. HarperBusiness: New York, USA.

Kanter, RM, Stein, BA and Jick, TD (1992) *The Challenge of Organizational Change*. Free Press: New York, USA.

Kaplan, PJ (2002) *F'd Companies: Spectacular Dot-com Flameouts*. Simon & Schuster: New York, USA.

Karlsson, C (1996) Radically new production systems. *International Journal of Operations and Production Management*, 16(11), 8–19.

Karlsson, LE (1973) *Experiences in Employee Participation in Sweden: 1969–1972*. Mimeograph, Cornell University: New York, USA.

Kauffman, SA (1993) *Origins of Order: Self-Organisation and Selection in Evolution*. OUP: Oxford.

Kawakita, T (1997) Corporate strategy and human resource management. In M Sako and H Sato (eds): *Japanese Labour and Management in Transition*. Routledge: London.

Kay, J (1993) *Foundations of Corporate Success*. OUP: Oxford.

Kazunori, O (1998) New trends in Enterprise Unions and the Labour Movement. In H Harukiyo and GD Hook (eds): *Japanese Business Management: Restructuring for Low Growth and Globalization*. Routledge: London.

Kellaway, L (1998) Manage with mother. *Financial Times*, 2 March, 14.

Kellaway, L (2001) A boast too far: Tom Peters' 'confession' that he faked the data for his most famous management book shows how attitudes have changed in 20 years. *Financial Times*, 3 December, 16.

Kelly, JE (1982a) Economic and structural analysis of Job Design. In JE Kelly and CW Clegg (eds): *Autonomy and Control at the Workplace*. Croom Helm: London.

Kelly, JE (1982b) *Scientific Management, Job Redesign and Work Performance*. Academic Press: London.

Kemp, T (1979) *Industrialization in Nineteenth Century Europe*. Longman: London.

Kempner, T (1970) Frederick Taylor and scientific management. In A Tillett, T Kempner and G Wills (eds): *Management Thinkers*. Pelican: Harmondsworth.

Kennedy, C (1994) *Managing with the Gurus*. Century Business Books: London.

Kerr, C and Fisher, L (1957) Plant sociology: the elite and the Aborigines. In M Komarovsky (ed): *Common Frontiers of the Social Sciences*. Greenwood: Westport, CT, USA.

Kerr, S, Schriesheim, CA, Murphy, CJ and Stogdill, RM (1974) Towards a contingency theory of leadership based upon the consideration and initiating structure literature. *Organizational Behavior and Human Performance*, 12, 62–82.

Keshavan, K and Rakesh, KS (1979) Generating future scenarios – their use in strategic planning. *Long Range Planning*, 12, June, 57–61.

Keuning, D (1998) *Management: A Contemporary Approach*. Pitman: London.

Keys, JB and Miller, TR (1984) The Japanese management theory jungle. *Academy of Management Review*, 9, 342–53.

Kidd, P and Karwowski, W (eds) (1994) *Advances in Agile Manufacture*. IOS: Amsterdam.

Kiel, LD (1994) *Managing Chaos and Complexity in Government*. Jossey-Bass: San Francisco, CA, USA.

Kimberley, J and Miles, R (eds) (1980) *The Organizational Life Cycle*. Jossey Bass: San Francisco, CA, USA.

Kipnis, D, Schmidt, SM and Wilkinson, I (1980) Intraorganizational influence tactics: explorations in getting one's way. *Journal of Applied Psychology*, August, 440–52.

Kipnis, D, Schmidt, SM, Swaffin-Smith, C and Wilkinson, I (1984) Patterns of managerial influence: shotgun managers, tacticians, and bystanders. *Organizational Dynamics*, Winter, 58–67.

Kippenberger, T (1998a) Planned change: Kurt Lewin's legacy. *The Antidote*, 14, 10–12.

Kippenberger, T (1998b) Managed learning: elaborating on Lewin's model. *The Antidote*, 14, 13.

Kirton, MJ (1989) *Adaptors and Innovators: Styles of Creativity and Problem Solving*. Routledge: London.

Kjellberg, A (1992) Sweden: can the model survive. In A Ferner and R Hyman (eds): *Industrial Relations in the New Europe*. Blackwell: Oxford.

Klein, N (2001) *No Logo*. Flamingo: London.

Koch, R (1995) *The Financial Times Guide to Strategy*. FT Pitman: London.

Kodz, J, Davis, S, Lain, D, Sheppard, E, Rick, J, Strebler, M, Bates, P, Cummings, J, Meager, N, Anxon, D, Gineste, S and Trinczek, R (2003) *Working Long Hours in the UK: Excutive Summary*. Department of Trade and Industry: London, available at www.dtigor.uk/emar/longhours.htm.

Koji, O (1998) Small headquarters and the reorganisation of management. In H Harukiyo and GD Hook (eds): *Japanese Business Management: Restructuring for Low Growth and Globalization*. Routledge: London.

Kotler, P (1978) Harvesting strategies for weak products. *Business Horizons*, 21(4), August, 15–22.

Kotter, J (1990) *A Force for Change: How Leadership Differs from Management*. Free Press: New York, USA.

Kotter, JP (1982) *The General Manager*. Free Press: New York, USA.

Kotter, JP (1995) Leading change: why transformation efforts fail. *Harvard Business Review*, March–April.

Kotter, JP (1996) *Leading Change*. Harvard Business School Press: Boston, MA, USA.

Kotter, JP (1999) What effective general managers really do. *Harvard Business Review*, 77(2), 145–59.

Kotter, JP and Hesketh, JL (1992) *Corporate Culture and Performance*. Free Press: New York, USA.

Krell, TC (1981) The marketing of organization development: past, present and future. *Journal of Applied Behavioral Science*, 10(2), 485–502.

Kreps, DM and Wilson, R (1982) Reputation and imperfect information. *Journal of Economic Theory*, 27, 253–79.

Kriedt, P, Medick, H and Schlumbohm, J (1981) *Industrialization Before Industrialization*. Cambridge University Press: Cambridge.

Kuhn, TS (1962) *The Structure of Scientific Revolutions*. University of Chicago Press: Chicago, IL, USA.

Kumar, K (1995) *From Post-Industrial to Post-Modern: New Theories of the Contemporary World*. Blackwell: Oxford.

Laage-Hellman, J (1997) *Business Networks in Japan*. Routledge: London.

Lacey, R (1986) *Ford: The Men and the Machine*. Heinemann: London.

Laird, L (1998) Predators hover over Lonrho's African diamonds. *Guardian*, 14 November, 28.

Lamming, R (1993) *Beyond Partnership: Strategies for Innovation and Lean Supply*. Prentice Hall: Hemel Hempstead.

Lamming, R (1994) *A Review of the Relationships Between Vehicle Manufacturers and Suppliers*. DTI/SMMT: London.

Landes, DS (1969) *The Unbound Prometheus*. Cambridge University Press: Cambridge.

Landsberger, HA (1958) *Hawthorne Revisited: 'Management and the Worker'. Its Critics and Developments in Human Relations in Industry*. Cornell University Press: New York, USA.

Lanford, HW (1972) *Technological Forecasting Methodologies: A Synthesis*. American Management Association: New York, USA.

Larson, LL, Hunt, JG and Osborne, RN (1976) The great hi-hi leader behavior myth: a lesson from Occam's razor. *Academy of Management Journal*, 19, 628–41.

Laudon, K and Starbuck, WH (1997) Organization information and knowledge. In A Sorge and M Warner (eds): *The IEBM Handbook of Organizational Behaviour*. International Thompson Business Press: London.

Lawler, EE (1985) Challenging traditional research assumptions. In EE Lawler and Associates (eds): *Doing Research That is Useful for Theory and Practice*. Jossey-Bass: San Francisco, CA, USA.

Lawler, EE and Suttle, JL (1972) A causal correlation of the need hierarchy concept in an organizational setting. *Organization Behaviour and Human Performance*, 7, April, 265–87.

Lawler, EE, Mohrman, SA and Ledford, GE (1998) *Strategies for High Performance Organizations*. Jossey-Bass: San Francisco, CA, UK.

Lawrence, PR (1973) How to deal with resistance to change. In GW Dalton, PR Lawrence and E Grenier (eds): *Organizational Change and Development*. Dorsey: Homewood, IL, USA.

Lawrence, PR and Lorsch, JW (1967) *Organization and Environment*. Harvard Business School: Boston, MA, USA.

Lawson, H (1985) *Reflexivity, the Post Modern Predicament*. Hutchinson: London.

Learned, EP, Christensen, CR, Andrews, KR and Guth, WD (1965) *Business Policy: Texts and Cases*. Irwin: Homewood, IL, USA.

Lee, J (1978) Labour in German industrialization. In P Mathias and M Postan (eds): *Cambridge Economic History of Europe*, Vol. VII. Cambridge University Press: Cambridge.

Lee, M (1999) The lie of power: empowerment as impotence. *Human Relations*, 52(2), 225–62.

Lee, RG and Dale, BG (2003) Policy deployment. In BG Dale: *Managing Quality* (4th edition). Blackwell: Oxford.

Leemhuis, JP (1990) Using scenario development strategies at Shell. In B Taylor and J Harrison (eds): *The Manager's Casebook of Business Strategy*. Butterworth-Heinemann: Oxford.

Left, S (2001) Nike. *Guardian Unlimited*, 23 February, available at www.guardian.co.uk.

Leifer, R and Huber, GP (1977) Relations amongst perceived environmental uncertainty, organisation structure and boundary-spanning behaviour. *Administrative Science Quarterly*, 22, 235–47.

Lenin, VI (1918) The immediate tasks of the Soviet government. Reprinted in: *On the Development of Heavy Industry and Electrification*. Progress Publishers: Moscow, Russia.

Leontiades, M (1986) *Managing the Unmanageable*. Addison-Wesley: Reading, MA, USA.

Leslie, K, Lindsay, V, Mullings, H and Salkeld, N (1999) Why companies have much to learn from charities. *The Financial Times*, 9 February, 16.

Lessem, R (1998) *Management Development Through Cultural Diversity*. Routledge: London.

Levine, AL (1967) *Industrial Retardation in Britain 1880–1914*. Basic Books: New York, USA.

Lewin GW (ed) (1948a) *Resolving Social Conflict*. Harper & Row: London.

Lewin, GW (1948b) Preface. In GW Lewin (ed) (1948): *Resolving Social Conflict*. Harper & Row: London.

Lewin, K (1939) When facing danger. In GW Lewin (ed) (1948): *Resolving Social Conflict*. Harper & Row: London.

Lewin, K (1943/4) Problems of research in social psychology. In D Cartwright (ed) (1952): *Field Theory in Social Science*. Social Science Paperbacks: London.

Lewin, K (1943a) Psychological ecology. In D Cartwright (ed) (1952): *Field Theory in Social Science*. Social Science Paperbacks: London.

Lewin, K (1943b) The special case of Germany. In GW Lewin (ed) (1948): *Resolving Social Conflict*. Harper & Row: London.

Lewin, K (1946) Action research and minority problems. In GW Lewin and GW Allport (eds) (1948): *Resolving Social Conflict*. Harper & Row: London.

Lewin, K (1947a) Frontiers in group dynamics. In D Cartwright (ed) (1952): *Field Theory in Social Science*. Social Science Paperbacks: London.

Lewin, K (1947b) Group decisions and social change. In TM Newcomb and EL Hartley (eds): *Readings in Social Psychology*. Henry Holt: New York, USA.

Lewin, K (1999a) Group decisions and social change. In M Gold (ed): *The Complete Social Scientist: A Kurt Lewin Reader*. American Psychological Association: Washington, DC, USA.

Lewin, K (1999b) The dynamics of group action. In M Gold (ed): *The Complete Social Scientist: A Kurt Lewin Reader*. American Psychological Association: Washington, DC, USA.

Lewin, M (1992) The impact of Kurt Lewin's life on the place of social issues in his work. *Journal of Social Issues*, 48(2), 15–29.

Lewis, R (1994) From chaos to complexity: implications for organizations. *Executive Development*, 7(4), 16–17.

Lichtenstein, BM (1997) Grace, magic and miracles: a 'chaotic logic' of organizational transformation. *Journal of Organizational Change Management*, 10(5), 393–411.

Likert, R (1961) *New Patterns of Management*. McGraw-Hill: New York, USA.

Likert, R (1967) *The Human Organization: Its Management and Values*. McGraw-Hill: New York, USA.

Lincoln, JR and Kalleberg, AL (1985) Work organisation and workforce commitment: a study of plants and employees in the US and Japan. *American Sociological Review*, 50, 738–60.

Lindblom, CE (1959) The science of muddling through. *Public Administration Review*, 19, Spring, 79–88.

Lindblom, CE (1968) *The Policy-Making Process*. Prentice Hall: Englewood Cliffs, NJ, USA.

Lines, WL (2002) *Open Air Essays*. New Holland Publishers: Sydney, Australia.

Linneman, RE and Klein, HE (1979) The use of multiple scenarios by US industrial companies. *Long Range Planning*, 12, February, 83–90.

Linstead, S (1993) From postmodern anthropology to deconstructive ethnography. *Human Relations*, 46(1), 97–120.

Lippitt, G (1982) Management development as the key to organisational renewal. *Journal of Management Development*, 1(2).

Lippitt, R and White, R (1960) *Autocracy and Democracy: An Experimental Inquiry*. Harper & Row: New York, USA.

Lippitt, R, Watson, J and Westley, B (1958) *The Dynamics of Planned Change*. Harcourt, Brace and World: New York.

Litschert, R and Nicholson, E (1974) Corporate long range planning groups – some different approaches. *Long Range Planning*, 7, August, 62–6.

Little, R (1984) Conglomerates are doing better than you think. *Fortune*, 28 May, 60.

Littler, CR (1978) Understanding Taylorism. *British Journal of Sociology*, 29(2), 185–202.

Lloyd, AR, Dale, BG and Burnes, B (1994) A study of Nissan Motor Manufacturing (UK) Supplier Development Team Activities. *Proceedings of the Institute of Mechanical Engineers, 208, Part D: Journal of Automobile Engineering*, 63–8.

Locke, EW (1982) The ideas of Frederick W Taylor. *Academy of Management Review*, 7(1), 14–24.

Loden, M (1986) *Feminine Leadership, or How to Succeed in Business Without Being One of the Boys*. Time Books: New York, NY.

Long, P (1986) *Performance Appraisal Revisited*. IPM: London.

Lorenz, E (1979) *Predictability: Does the Flap of a Butterfly's Wing in Brazil Set off a Tornado in Texas?* Address at the American Association for the Advancement of Science, Washington, DC, USA.

Lorenz, E (1993) *The Essence of Chaos*. UCL Press: London.

Lorsch, JW (1970) Introduction to the structural design of organizations. In GW Dalton, PR Lawrence and JW Lorsch (eds): *Organization Structure and Design*. Irwin-Dorsey: London.

Lorsch, JW (1986) Managing culture: the invisible barrier to strategic change. *California Management Review, 28*(2), 95–109.

Lovell, R (1980) *Adult Learning*. Croom Helm: London.

Lu, DJ (1987) *Inside Corporate Japan*. Productivity Press: Cambridge, MA, USA.

Luthans, F (1989) Conversation with Edgar H Schein. *Organizational Dynamics*, 17, Spring, 70–5.

Luthans, F, McCaul, HS and Dodd, NG (1985) Organizational commitment: a comparison of American, Japanese and Korean employees. *Academy of Management Journal*, 28, 213–19.

Lynch, R (1997) *Corporate Strategy*. Pitman: London.

Lyon, D (2000) Post-modernity. In G Browning, A Halcli and F Webster (eds): *Understanding Contemporary Society*. Sage: London.

Lyotard, J-F (1984) *The Postmodern Condition*. Manchester University Press: Manchester.

Mabey, C and Mayon-White, B (1993) *Managing Change* (2nd edition). The Open University/Paul Chapman Publishing: London.

Macalister, T (1999) Fury over further 6000 job cuts in utilities. *Guardian*, 15 December, available at www.guardian.co.uk.

Macalister, T (2003) Swiss join oil bribery inquiry. *Guardian,* 7 May, available at www.guardian.co.uk.

Macbeth, DK (2002) Emergent strategy in managing cooperative supply chain change. International Journal of Operations and Producton Management, 22(7), 728–40.

Macdonald, M, Sprenger, E and Dubel, I (1999) *Gender and Organizational Change: Bridging the Gap between Policy and Practice*. Royal Tropical Institute: Amsterdam.

Machiavelli, N (1515) *The Prince*. Available at www.constitution.org/mac/prince06.htm.

MacIntosh, R and MacLean, D (1999) Conditioned emergence: a dissipative structures approach to transformation. *Strategic Management Journal*, 20(4), 297–316.

MacIntosh, R and MacLean, D (2001) Conditioned emergence: researching change and changing research. *International Journal of Operations and Production Management*, 21(10), 1343–57.

Maddock, S (1999) *Challenging Women*. Sage: London.

Magex (2000a) Liberating the digital economy – creating commercial success in the digital marketplace. Magex.com Whitepaper, 21 February, available at www.magex.com/downloads/W_Paper_1(1).pdf.

Magex (2000b) Online music piracy. Magex.com Whitepaper, 22 June, available at www.magex.com/news/library/list.

Maguire, K, Milner, M and Watt, N (2000) The Secret Deal That Left Rover a Museum Piece. *The Guardian*, 18 March, 4–5.

Mahoney, MJ (1974) *Cognition and Behavior Modification*. Ballinger: Cambridge, MA, USA.

Maitland, A (2001) Managers resort to old tools in a crisis. *Financial Times*, 18 July, 10.

Malaska, P, Malmivirta, M, Meristo, T and Hansen, SO (1984) Scenarios in Europe – who uses them and why? *Long Range Planning*, 17, October, 45–9.

Mallory, G (1997) March, James Gardner (1928–) and Cyert, Richard Michael (1921–). In A Sorge and M Warner (eds): *The IEBM Handbook of Organizational Behaviour*. International Thompson Business Press: London.

Mangham Working Party (1987) *The Mangham Working Party Report: A Survey of the In-house Activities of Ten Major Companies*. British Institute of Management/Confederation of British Industry: London.

Manicas, P (1980) The concept of social structure. *Journal of the Theory of Social Behaviour*, 10(2), 65–82.

Mansfield, R (1984) Formal and informal structures. In M Gruneberg and T Wall (eds): *Social Psychology and Organizational Behaviour*. Wiley: Chichester.

Mantoux, P (1964) *The Industrial Revolution in the Eighteenth Century*. Cape: London.

Marczewski, J (1963) The take-off hypothesis and French experience. In WW Rostow: *The Economics of Take-Off into Sustained Growth*. Macmillan: London.

Marglin, SA (1976) What do bosses do? In A Gorz (ed): *The Division of Labour: The Labour Process and Class Struggle in Modern Capitalism*. Harvester: Brighton.

Markus, L M, Manville, B and Agres, C E (2000) What makes virtual organisations work? Lessons from the open-source world. *Sloan Management Review*, Fall, 13–26.

Marrow, AJ (1957) *Making Management Human*. McGraw-Hill: New York, NY.

Marrow, AJ (1969) *The Practical Theorist: The Life and Work of Kurt Lewin*. Teachers College Press (1977 edition): New York, USA.

Marsh, N (1986) Management development and strategic management change. *Journal of Management Development*, 5(1).

Marsh, RM and Mannari, H (1976) *Modernization and the Japanese Factory.* Princeton University Press: Princeton, NJ, USA.

Marshak, RJ (1993) Lewin meets Confucius: a re-view of the OD model of change. *The Journal of Applied Behavioral Science,* 29(4), 393–415.

Martin, J (1992) *Cultures in Organizations: Three Perspectives.* Oxford University Press: Oxford.

Martin, J, Feldman, MS, Hatch, MJ and Sitkin, SB (1983) The uniqueness paradox in organizational stories. *Administrative Science Quarterly,* 28, 438–53.

Martin, R (2000) Breaking the code of change: observations and critique. In M Beer and N Nohria (eds): *Breaking the Code of Change.* Harvard Business School Press: Boston, MA, USA.

Masayoshi, I (1998) Globalisation's impact on the subcontracting system. In H Harukiyo and GD Hook (eds): *Japanese Business Management: Restructuring for Low Growth and Globalization.* Routledge: London.

Masayuki, M (1998) The end of the 'mass production system' and changes in work practices. In H Harukiyo and GD Hook (eds): *Japanese Business Management: Restructuring for Low Growth and Globalization.* Routledge: London.

Maslow, AH (1943) A theory of human motivation. *Psychology Review,* 50, 370–96.

Massie, JL (1965) Management theory. In JG March (ed): *Handbook of Organizations.* Rand McNally: Chicago, IL, USA.

Mathias, P (1969) *The First Industrial Nation.* Methuen: London.

Mathias, P and Davis, JA (eds) (1989) *The First Industrial Revolutions.* Blackwell: Cambridge.

Matthews, R (2002) Competition, archetypes and creative imagination. *Journal of Organizational Change Management,* 15(5), 461–76.

May, B and Singer, M (2001) Unchained melody. *The McKinsey Quarterly,* 1, available at www.Mckinseyquarterly.com.

Mayes, BT and Allen, RW (1977) Towards a definition of organizational politics. *Academy of Management Review,* October, 672–8.

Mayo, E (1933) *The Human Problems of Industrial Civilization.* Macmillan: New York, USA.

Mayon-White, B (1993) Problem-solving in small groups: team members as agents of change. In C Mabey and B Mayon-White (eds): *Managing Change* (2nd edition). The Open University/Paul Chapman Publishing: London.

McCalman, J and Paton, RA (1992) *Change Management: A Guide to Effective Implementation.* Paul Chapman Publishing: London.

McGill, I and Beaty, L (1995) *Action Learning.* Kogan Page: London.

McGregor, D (1960) *The Human Side of Enterprise.* McGraw-Hill: New York, USA.

McGregor, D (1967) *The Professional Manager.* McGraw-Hill: New York, USA.

McIvor, G (1995) Retuned Volvo rises from the ashes. *Guardian,* 24 June, 37.

McKenna, S (1988) 'Japanisation' and recent developments in Britain. *Employee Relations,* 10(4).

McKiernan, P (1992) *Strategies for Growth: Maturity, Recovery and Internationalization.* Routledge: London.

McKracken, JK (1986) Exploitation of FMS technology to achieve strategic objectives. Paper to the 5th International Conference on Flexible Manufacturing Systems, Stratford-upon-Avon.

McLaughlin, H and Thorpe, R (1993) Action Learning – a paradigm in emergence. *British Journal of Management*, 4(1), 19–27.

McLennan, R (1989) *Managing Organizational Change.* Prentice Hall: Englewood Cliffs, NJ, USA.

McMillan, J (1985) *The Japanese Industrial System.* De Gruyter: Berlin.

McNamee, BP (1985) *Tools and Techniques of Strategic Management.* Pergamon: Oxford.

McNiff, J (ed) (2000) *Action Research in Organisations.* Routledge: London.

McNulty, CAR (1977) Scenario development for corporate planning. *Futures*, 9(2), 128–38.

Meek, VL (1988) Organizational culture: origins and weaknesses. *Organization Studies*, 9(4), 453–73.

Meyer, MW and Zucker, LG (1989) *Permanently Failing Organizations.* Sage: Beverly Hills, CA, USA.

Meyerson, D and Martin, J (1987) Cultural change: an integration of three different views. *Journal of Management Studies*, 24(6), 623–47.

Michaelson, GA (2001) *Sun Tzu: The Art of War for Managers: 50 Strategic Rules.* Adams Media: Avon, MA, USA.

Miewald, RD (1970) The greatly exaggerated death of bureaucracy. *California Management Review*, Winter, 65–9.

Miles, RE and Snow, CC (1978) *Organisational Strategy, Structure and Process.* McGraw-Hill: New York, USA.

Milgrom, P and Roberts, J (1982) Predation, reputation and entry deterrence. *Journal of Economic Theory*, 27, 280–313.

Mill, J (1994) No pain, no gain. *Computing*, 3 February, 26–7.

Miller, D (1992) The generic strategy trap. *Journal of Business Strategy*, 13(1), 37–41.

Miller, D (1993) The architecture of simplicity. *Academy of Management Review*, 18(1), 116–38.

Miller, D and Friesen, PH (1984) *Organizations: A Quantum View.* Prentice Hall: Englewood Cliffs, NJ, USA.

Miller, E (1967) *Systems of Organisation.* Tavistock: London.

Miller, E (1993) *From Dependency to Autonomy – Studies in Organization and Change.* Free Association Books: London.

Milner, M (1998) Productivity as seen by hamsters. *Guardian*, 22 October, 27.

Milward, A and Saul, SB (1973) *The Economic Development of Continental Europe 1780–1870.* George Allen & Unwin: London.

Minett, S (1992) *Power, Politics and Participation in the Firm.* Ashgate: Brookfield, VT, USA.

Mink, OG (1992) Creating new organizational paradigms for change. *International Journal of Quality and Reliability Management*, 9(3), 21–35.

Mintzberg, H (1973) *The Nature of Managerial Work*. Harper & Row: New York, USA.

Mintzberg, H (1975) The manager's job: folklore and fact. *Harvard Business Review*, 53(4), 49–61.

Mintzberg, H (1976) Planning on the left side and managing on the right. *Harvard Business Review*, July/August, 49–58.

Mintzberg, H (1978) Patterns in strategy formation. *Management Science*, 24(9), 934–48.

Mintzberg, H (1979) *The Structure of Organizations*. Prentice Hall: Englewood Cliffs, NJ, USA.

Mintzberg, H (1983) *Power in and Around Organizations*. Prentice Hall: Englewood Cliffs, NJ, USA.

Mintzberg, H (1987) Crafting strategy. *Harvard Business Review*, 19(2), 66–75.

Mintzberg, H (1994) *The Rise and Fall of Strategic Planning*. Prentice Hall: London.

Mintzberg, H and Quinn, JB (1991) *The Strategy Process: Concepts, Contexts and Cases*. Prentice Hall: London.

Mintzberg, H, Ahlstrand, B and Lampel, J (1998a). *Strategy Safari*. Prentice Hall: Hemel Hempstead.

Mintzberg, H, Quinn, JB and Ghoshal, S (1998b) *The Strategy Process*. Prentice Hall: London.

Mirvis, P (1988) Organizational development: an evolutionary perspective. In W Pasmore and R Woodman (eds): *Research in Organizational Change and Development*, Vol. 2. JAI Press: Greenwich, CT, USA.

Mirvis, PH (1990) Organization development: Part 2 – a revolutionary perspective. *Research in Organizational Change and Development*, 4, 1–66.

Mitroff, II and Mason, RO (1981) *Challenging Strategic Planning Assumptions*. Wiley: New York, USA.

Moore, JI (1992) *Writers on Strategy and Strategic Management*. Penguin: Harmondsworth.

Morgan, G (1986) *Images of Organizations*. Sage: Beverly Hills, CA, USA.

Morgan, G (1988) *Riding the Waves of Change*. Jossey-Bass: San Francisco, CA, USA.

Morgan, G (1990) *Organisations in Society*. Macmillan: London.

Morgan, G (1997) *Images of Organization* (2nd edition). Sage: London.

Morieux, YUH and Sutherland, E (1988) The interaction between the use of information technology and organization change. *Behaviour and Information Technology*, 7(2), 205–13.

Morris, J and Imrie, R (1992) *Transforming Buyer–Supplier Relationships*. Macmillan: Basingstoke.

Mougayar, W (1998) *Opening Digital Markets: Battle Plans and Business Strategies for Internet Commerce*. McGraw-Hill: Maidenhead.

Mullins, L (1989) *Management and Organisational Behaviour.* Pitman: London.

Mullins, LJ (1993) *Management and Organisational Behaviour* (3rd edition). Pitman: London.

Mullins, L (2002) *Management and Organisational Behaviour* (6th edition). FT/Pearson: Harlow.

Mumford, A (1987) Myths and reality in developing directors. *Personnel Management,* 19(2), February, 29–33.

Mumford, E (1979) The design of work: new approaches and new needs. In JE Rijnsdorp (ed): *Case Studies in Automation Related to the Humanisation of Work.* Pergamon: Oxford.

Mumford, MD, Marks, MA, Connelly, MS, Zaccaro, SJ and Reiter-Palmon, R (2000). Development of leadership skills: experience and timing. *Leadership Quarterly,* 11, 87–114.

Murray, F (1989) The organizational politics of information technology: studies from the UK financial services industry. *Technology Analysis & Strategic Management,* 1(30), 285–97.

Myers, CS (1934) *An Account of the Work Carried out at the National Institute of Industrial Psychology during the Years 1921–34.* NIIP: London.

Nadler, DA (1988) Concepts for the management of organizational change. In ML Tushman and WL Moore (eds): *Readings in the Management of Innovation.* Ballinger: New York, USA.

Nadler, DA (1993) Concepts for the management of strategic change. In C Mabey and B Mayon-White (eds): *Managing Change* (2nd edition). The Open University/Paul Chapman Publishing: London.

Nadworthy, M (1957) Frederick Taylor and Frank Gilbreth: competition in scientific management. *Business History Review,* 31(1), 23–34.

Nahavandi, A (2000) *The Art and Science of Leadership* (2nd edition). Prentice Hall: Upper Saddle River, NJ, USA.

NAO (1995) *Interim Report: PSA Services, The Sale of PSA Projects. Report by the National Audit Office.* HMSO: London.

NAO (1996) *PSA Service: The Transfer of PSA Building Management to the Private Sector. Report of the National Audit Office.* HMSO: London.

Naoi, A and Schooler, C (1985) Occupational conditions and psychological functioning in Japan. *American Journal of Sociology,* 90, 729–52.

Naylor, TH (1979) *Simulation Models in Corporate Measuring.* Draeger: New York, USA.

Naylor, TH (1981) Strategic planning models. *Managerial Planning,* 30, July/August, 3–11.

NEDC (1991a) *The Experience of Nissan Suppliers: Lessons for the United Kingdom Engineering Industry.* NEDC: London.

NEDC (1991b) *Winning Together: Collaborative Sourcing in Practice.* NEDC: London.

Nelson, RR and Winter, SG (1982) *An Evolutionary Theory of Economic Change.* Harvard University Press: Cambridge, MA, USA.

New, C (1989) The challenge of transformation. In B Burnes and B Weekes (eds): *AMT: A Strategy for Success?* NEDO: London.

New, S and Burnes, B (1998) Developing effective customer–supplier relationships: more than one way to skin a cat. *Journal of Quality and Reliability Management,* 15(4), 377–88.

Newstrom, J (1985) Modern management: does it deliver? *Journal of Management Development,* 4(1).

Nonaka, I (1988) Creating organizational order out of chaos: self-renewal in Japanese firms. *Harvard Business Review,* November–December, 96–104.

Nonaka, I (1991) The knowledge-creating company. *Harvard Business Review,* November/December, 96–104.

Nord, W (1985) Can organizational culture be managed: a synthesis. In R Kilmann, M Saxton, R Serpa and Associates (eds): *Gaining Control of Corporate Culture.* Jossey-Bass: San Francisco, CA, USA.

Norrie, J (1993) *Winning By Continuous Improvement: Facilitators' Guide.* Norrie: Northampton.

Norse, D (1979) Scenario analysis in interfutures. *Futures,* 11(5), 412–22.

Nystrom, PC and Starbuck, WH (1984) To avoid crises, unlearn. *Organizational Dynamics,* 12(4), 53–65.

O'Brien, GE and Kabanoff, B (1981) The effects of leadership style and group structure upon small group productivity: a test of discrepancy theory of leader effectiveness. *Australian Journal of Psychology,* 33(2), 157–8.

Odaka, K (1975) *Towards Industrial Democracy: Management and Workers in Modern Japan.* Harvard University Press: Cambridge, MA, USA.

OECD (1996) *The OECD Economic Survey: the UK 1996.* OECD: Paris, France.

Ohmae, K (1986) *The Mind of the Strategist.* Penguin: Harmondsworth.

Ohmae, K (1990) Untitled article in *Special Report 1202, The Management Briefing, Economist,* London.

Ohmi, N (1997) The public sector and privatisation. In M Sako and H Sato (eds): *Japanese Labour and Management in Transition.* Routledge: London.

Olsen, BD (2002) Applied social and community interventions for crisis in times of national and international conflict. *Analyses of Social Issues and Public Policy* 2(1), 119–29.

O'Reilly, C (1989) Corporations, culture and commitment. *California Management Review,* 31(4), 9–24.

Osborne, D and Gaebler, T (1992) *Reinventing Government: How the Entrepreneurial Spirit is Transforming the Public Sector.* Addison-Wesley: Reading, MA, USA.

Oticon (1994) *Oticon's Fundamental Human Values – Vision and Reality.* Oticon: Copenhagen, Denmark.

Ouchi, W (1981) *Theory Z: How American Business Can Meet the Japanese Challenge*. Addison-Wesley: Reading, MA, USA.

Outhwaite, W (1987) *New Philosophies of Social Science: Realism, Hermeneutics and Critical Theory*. Macmillan: London.

Owen, G (2002) The man who built GEC into an industrial giant. *Financial Times*, 24 July, 23.

Pang, K and Oliver, N (1988) Personnel strategy in eleven Japanese manufacturing companies. *Personnel Review*, 17(3).

Parikh, M (1999) The music industry in the digital world: waves of changes. *Putting the 'e' in Entertainment: e-Music as a Case in Point, Industry Round Table*, June 17. The New York Information Technology Center, available at www.ite.poly.edu.

Parker, D (1998) Privatisation in the European Union: an overview. In D Parker (ed): *Privatisation in the European Union: Theory and Policy Perspectives*. Routledge: London.

Parker, D (2003) Performance, risk and strategy in privatised, regulated industries: the UK's experience. *International Journal of Public Sector Management*, 16(1), 75–100.

Parker, M (2000) *Thatcherism and the Fall of Coal: Politics and Economics of UK Coal*. Cambridge University Press: Cambridge.

Parsons, T (1947) Introduction. In M Weber (ed): *The Theory of Social and Economic Organization*. Free Press: Glencoe, IL, USA.

Partnership Sourcing Ltd (1991a) *Case Studies in Partnership Sourcing*. Partnership Sourcing Ltd: London.

Partnership Sourcing Ltd (1991b) *Partnership Sourcing*. Partnership Sourcing Ltd: London.

Partnoy, F (2003) When greed is fact and control is fiction. *Guardian*, 14 February, available at www.guardian.co.uk.

Pascale, RT (1993) The benefit of a clash of opinions. *Personnel Management*, October, 38–41.

Pascale, RT and Athos, AG (1982) *The Art of Japanese Management*. Penguin: Harmondsworth.

Patel, P and Younger, M (1978) A frame of reference for strategy development. *Long Range Planning*, 11, April, 6–12.

Paton, N (2003) Leadership skills hold Britain back. *Guardian: Jobs and Money*, 22 February, 23.

Paton, R, Clark, G, Jones, G, Lewis, J and Quintas, P (eds) (1996) *The New Management Reader*. Routledge/Open University: London.

Pavlov, IP (1927) *Conditioned Reflexes* (trans). Oxford University Press: London.

Peacock, A (1984) Privatisation in perspective. *Three Banks Review*, December, 3–25.

Pearson, AE (1987) Muscle-build the organization. *Harvard Business Review*, 65(4), 49–55.

Pearson, B (1977) How to manage turnarounds. *Management Today*, April, 75.

Pedler, M (1996) *Action Learning for Managers*. Lemos & Crane: London.

Pedler, M, Boydell, T and Burgoyne, JG (1989) Towards the learning company. *Management Education and Development*, 20(1), 1–8.

Pelling, H (1960) *American Labor*. Chicago University Press: Chicago, IL, USA.

Penrose, E (1959) *The Theory of Growth of the Firm*. Blackwell: Oxford.

Perez, C (1983) Structural change and the assimilation of new technologies in the economic and social systems. *Futures,* 15, 357–75.

Perrow, C (1967) A framework for the comparative analysis of organizations. *American Sociological Review*, 32, 194–208.

Perrow, C (1970) *Organizational Analysis: A Sociological View*. Tavistock: London.

Perrow, C (1983) The organizational context of human factors engineering. *Administrative Science Quarterly*, 28, 521–41.

Peters, T (1989) *Thriving on Chaos*. Pan: London.

Peters, T (1993) *Liberation Management*. Pan: London.

Peters, T (1995) *The Pursuit of WOW!* Macmillan: London.

Peters, T (1997a) *The Circle of Innovation: You Can't Shrink Your Way to Greatness*. Alfred A Knopf: New York, USA.

Peters, T (1997b) Foreword. In RM Kanter, J Kao and F Wiersema (eds): *Innovation: Breakthrough Thinking at 3M, DuPont, GE, Pfizer, and Rubbermaid*. HarperBusiness: New York, USA.

Peters, T and Waterman, RH (1982) *In Search of Excellence: Lessons from America's Best-Run Companies*. Harper & Row: London.

Pettigrew, AM (1973) *The Politics of Decision-Making*. Tavistock: London.

Pettigrew, AM (1979) On studying organizational culture. *Administrative Science Quarterly,* 24(4), 570–81.

Pettigrew, AM (1980) The politics of organisational change. In NB Anderson (ed): *The Human Side of Information Processing*. North Holland: Amsterdam, The Netherlands.

Pettigrew, AM (1985) *The Awakening Giant: Continuity and Change at ICI*. Blackwell: Oxford.

Pettigrew, AM (1987) Context and action in the transformation of the firm. *Journal of Management Sciences*, 24(6), 649–70.

Pettigrew, AM (1990a) Longitudinal field research on change: theory and practice. *Organizational Science*, 3(1), 267–92.

Pettigrew, AM (1990b) Studying strategic choice and strategic change. *Organizational Studies*, 11(1), 6–11.

Pettigrew, AM (1997) What is a processual analysis? *Scandinavian Journal of Management*, 13(40), 337–48.

Pettigrew, AM (2000) Linking change processes and outcomes: a commentary on Ghosal, Bartlett and Weick. In M Beer and N Nohria (eds): *Breaking the Code of Change*. Harvard Business School Press: Boston, MA, USA.

Pettigrew, AM and Whipp, R (1993) Understanding the environment. In C Mabey and B Mayon-White (eds): *Managing Change* (2nd edition). The Open University/Paul Chapman Publishing: London.

Pettigrew, AM, Ferlie, E and McKee, L (1992) *Shaping Strategic Change*. Sage: London.

Pettigrew, AM, Hendry, C and Sparrow, P (1989) *Training in Britain: Employers' Perspectives on Human Resources*. HMSO: London.

Pfeffer, J (1978) *Organizational Design*. AHM Publishing: Arlington Heights, IL, USA.

Pfeffer, J (1981) *Power in Organizations*. Pitman: Cambridge, MA, USA.

Pfeffer, J (1992) *Managing with Power: Politics and Influence in Organizations*. Harvard Business School Press: Boston, MA, USA.

Pfeffer, J (1996) *Competitive Advantage Through People: Unleashing the Power of the Work Force*. Harvard Business School Press: Boston, MA.

Phillips, A (2003) Childcare before money: as BA has discovered, working mothers will not give up their childcare arrangements without a fight. *Guardian*, 30 July, 17.

Pilling, D (2003) How could a corporate sector that dominated the world a decade ago have become so unproductive? *Financial Times*, 21 April, 15.

Piore, M and Sabel, C (1984) *The Second Industrial Divide*. Basic Books: New York, USA.

Plowden, The Lord. (1961) *Control of Public Expenditure*, Cmnd 1432. HMSO: London.

Pollard, S (1965) *The Genesis of Modern Management*. Pelican: Harmondsworth.

Pollard, S (1981) *Peaceful Conquest: The Industrialization of Europe, 1760–1970*. Oxford University Press: Oxford.

Pontusson, J (1990) The politics of new technology and job redesign: a comparison of Volvo and British Leyland. *Economic and Industrial Democracy*, 11, 311–36.

Porter, LW (1976) Organizations as political animals. *Presidential Address, Division of Industrial Organizational Psychology, 84th Annual Meeting of the American Psychological Association*, Washington, DC, USA.

Porter, LW, Allen, RW and Angle, IIL (1983) The politics of upward influence in organizations. In RW Allen and LW Porter (eds): *Organizational Influence Processes*. Scott, Foresman and Co: Glenview, IL, USA.

Porter, M (1980) *Competitive Strategy*. Free Press: New York, USA.

Porter, M (1985) *Competitive Advantage*. Free Press: New York, USA.

Porter, ME (2001) Strategy and the Internet. *Harvard Business Review*, March, 63–78.

Prahalad, CK and Hamel, G (1990) The core competence of the corporation. *Harvard Business Review*, May/June, 71–91.

Prigogine, I (1997) *The End of Certainty: Time, Chaos, and the New Laws of Nature*. Free Press: New York, NY.

Prigogine, I and Stengers, I (1984) *Order out of Chaos: Man's New Dialogue with Nature*. Bantam Books: New York, USA.

Probst, G and Buchel, B (1997) *Organizational Learning*. Prentice Hall: London.

Pruijt, HD (1997) *Job Design and Technology: Taylorism vs Anti-Taylorism*. Routledge: London.

PSA (1988) *PSA Annual Report 1987–88*. HMSO: London.

PSA (1989) *PSA to be Privatised*. PSA Press Release No. 96, 27 September. DoE: London.

Public Power Corporation (1999) *Human Resource Management*. The PPC Sector of Education: Athens, Greece.

Public Power Corporation (2001) *Offering Circular: 35,000,000 Shares in the Form of Shares and Global Depository Receipts*. Hellenic Republic: Athens, Greece.

Pugh, DS (1993) Understanding and managing organizational change. In C Mabey and B Mayon-White (eds): *Managing Change* (2nd edition). The Open University/Paul Chapman Publishing: London.

Pugh, DS (ed) (1984) *Organization Theory*. Penguin: Harmondsworth.

Pugh, DS and Hickson, DJ (1976) *Organizational Structure in its Context: The Aston Programme 1*. Saxon House: Farnborough.

Pugh, DS, Hickson, DJ, Hinings, CR and Turner, C (1969a) The context of organization structures. *Administrative Science Quarterly*, 14, 91–114.

Pugh, DS, Hickson, DJ and Hinings, CR (1969b) An empirical taxonomy of structures of work organisation. *Administrative Science Quarterly*, 14, 115–26.

Quinn, JB (1980a) Managing strategic change. *Sloan Management Review*, 21(4), 3–20.

Quinn, JB (1980b) *Strategies for Change: Logical Incrementalism*. Irwin: Homewood, IL, USA.

Quinn, JB (1982) Managing strategies incrementally. *Omega*, 10(6), 613–27.

Quinn, JB (1993) Managing strategic change. In C Mabey and B Mayon-White (eds): *Managing Change* (2nd edition). The Open University/Paul Chapman Publishing: London.

Quinn, RE (1996) *Deep Change: Discovering the Leader Within*. Jossey-Bass: San Francisco, CA, USA.

Quinn, RE and McGrath, MR (1985) The transformation of organizational cultures: a competing values perspective. In PJ Frost, LF Moore, MR Louis, CC Lundberg and J Martin (eds): *Organizational Culture*. Sage: Newbury Park, CA, USA.

Rafferty, K (1995) Tokyo and Mitsubishi banks to merge to create world's largest bank. *Guardian*, 25 March, 15.

Raven, BH (1965) Social influence and power. In ID Steiner and M Fishbein (eds): *Current Studies in Social Psychology*. Holt, Rinehart, Winston: New York, USA.

Raven, BH (1993) The bases of power – origins and recent developments. *Journal of Social Issues*, 49(4), 227–51.

Raven, BH (1999) Kurt Lewin address: influence, power, religion, and the mechanisms of social control. *Journal of Social Issues*, 55(1), 161–89.

Reed, M (1992) *The Sociology of Organizations*. Harvester Wheatsheaf: Hemel Hempstead.

Reed, M and Hughes, M (eds) (1992) *Rethinking Organization: New Directions in Organization Theory and Analysis*. Sage: London.

Reed, MI (2000) In praise of duality and dualism: rethinking agency and structure in organisational analysis. In S Ackroyd and S Fleetwood (eds): *Realist Perspectives on Management and Organisations*. Routledge: London.

Reich, R (1997) The menace of prosperity: widening inequality poses a threat to US and other societies. *Financial Times*, 3 March, 20.

Reich, S (1998) *What is Globalization? Four Possible Answers*. Working paper No 261. The Helen Kellogg Institute for International Studies, University of Notre Dame, IN, USA.

Rescher, N (1996) *Complexity: A Philosophical Overview*. Transaction Publishers: New York, USA.

Reynolds, CW (1987) Flocks, herds and schools: a distributed behaviour model. Proceedings of SIGGRAPH '87'. *Computer Graphics*, 21(4), 25–34.

Ricks, DA (1999) *Blunders in International Business*. Blackwell: Oxford.

Rigby, D (2001) *Management Tools 2001: An Executive's Guide*. Bain & Co: Boston, MA, USA.

Rigby, D and Gillies, C (2000) Making the most of management tools and techniques: a survey from Bain & Company. *Strategic Change*, 9, 269–74.

Ringland, G (1998) *Scenario Planning: Managing for the Future*. Wiley: Chichester.

Robbins, SP (1986) *Organizational Behavior: Concepts, Controversies, and Applications*. Prentice Hall: Englewood Cliffs, NJ, USA.

Robbins, SP (1987) *Organization Theory: Structure, Design, and Applications*. Prentice Hall: Englewood Cliffs, NJ, USA.

Robbins, SP (1997) *Managing Today!* Prentice Hall: Upper Saddle River, NJ, USA.

Roethlisberger, F and Dickson, WJ (1938) *Management and the Worker*. Wiley: New York, USA.

Rogers, R (1997) Handy man. *Training*, November, 19.

Roll, E (1930) An early experiment in industrial organisation: Boulton and Watt, 1775–1805. Reprinted in M Berg (ed) (1979): *Technology and Toil in Nineteenth Century Britain*. CSE Books: London.

Rollinson, D (2002) *Organisational Behaviour and Analysis* (2nd edition). FT/Prentice Hall: Harlow.

Romanelli, E and Tushman, ML (1994) Organizational transformation as punctuated equilibrium: an empirical test. *Academy of Management Journal*, 37(5), 1141–66.

Rose, M (1988) *Industrial Behaviour*. Penguin: Harmondsworth.

Rosenbrock, H (1982) *Unmanned Engineering*. Report 12 to the FMS Steering Committee. UMIST: Manchester.

Rosenzweig, PM (1994) When can management science research be generalized internationally? *Management Science*, 40(1), 28–39.

Rost, JC (1991) *Leadership for the Twenty-First Century*. Greenwood: Westport, CT, USA.

Rothwell, S (1994) Human resources management. *Manager Update*, 5(3), Spring, 22–35.

Rubin, I (1967) Increasing self-acceptance: a means of reducing prejudice. *Journal of Personality and Social Psychology*, 5, 233–8.

Rumelt, RP (1991) How much does industry matter? *Strategic Management Journal*, 12(3), 167–85.

Saigol, L (2003) Sex discrimination case could spell the end for City's secretive pay structure. *The Financial Times*, 4 April, 8.

Sakai, K (1992) The feudal world of Japanese manufacturing. In RM Kanter, BA Stein and TD Jick: *The Challenge of Organizational Change*. Free Press: New York.

Sako, M (1997) Introduction. In M Sako and H Sato (eds): *Japanese Labour and Management in Transition*. Routledge: London.

Sako, M and Sato, H (eds) (1997) *Japanese Labour and Management in Transition*. Routledge: London.

Salaman, G (1979) *Work Organisations*. Longman: London.

Salauroo, M and Burnes, B (1998) The impact of a market system on public sector organisations: a study of organisational change in the NHS. *The International Journal of Public Sector Management*, 11(6), 451–67.

Sathe, V (1983) Some action implications of corporate culture: a manager's guide to action. *Organizational Dynamics*, Autumn, 4–23.

Saul, JR (1997) *The Unconscious Civilization*. Penguin: London.

Saunders, M (1997) *Strategic Purchasing & Supply Chain Management* (2nd edition). Pitman: London.

Sayer, A (1989) Post-Fordism in question. *International Journal of Urban and Regional Research*, 13(4), 666–95.

Sayer, A (2000) *Realism and Social Science*. Sage: London.

Schein, EH (1969) *Process Consultation*. Addison-Wesley: Reading, MA, USA.

Schein, EH (1984) Coming to a new awareness of organizational culture. *Sloan Management Review*, 25(2), 3–16.

Schein, EH (1985) *Organizational Culture and Leadership: A Dynamic View*. Jossey-Bass: San Francisco, CA, USA.

Schein, EH (1988) *Organizational Psychology* (3rd edition). Prentice Hall: Englewood Cliffs, NJ, USA.

Schein, EH (1989) Organizational culture: what it is and how to change it. In P Evans, T Doz and A Laurent (eds): *Human Resource Management in International Firms*. Macmillan: London.

Schein, EH (1996) Kurt Lewin's change theory in the field and in the classroom: notes towards a model of management learning. *Systems Practice*, 9(1), 27–47.

Schein, VE and Mueller, R (1992) Sex role stereotyping and requisite management characteristics: a cross cultural look. *Journal of Organizational Behaviour*, 13, 439–47.

Schilit, WK and Locke, EA (1982) A study of upward influence in organizations. *Administrative Science Quarterly*, June, 304–16.

Schmalensee, R (1983) Advertising and entry deterrence: an exploratory model. *Journal of Political Economy*, 91(4), 636–53.

Schmuck, R and Miles, M (1971) *Organizational Development in Schools*. National Press: Palo Alto, CA, USA.

Schoeffler, S (1980) *Nine Basic Findings on Business Strategy*. The Strategic Planning Institute: Cambridge, MA, USA.

Schonberger, RJ (1982) *Japanese Manufacturing Techniques*. Free Press: New York, USA.

Schriesheim, CA and Murphy, CJ (1976) Relationships between leader behavior and subordinate satisfaction and performance: a test of some situational moderators. *Journal of Applied Psychology*, 61, 634–41.

Schumacher, EF (1973) *Small is Beautiful: A Study of Economics as if People Mattered*. Vintage Books: London.

Schuyt, TNM and Schuijt, JJM (1998) Rituals and rules: about magic in consultancy. *Journal of Organizational Change Management*, 11(5), 399–406.

Schwartz, H and Davis, S (1981) Matching corporate culture and business strategy. *Organizational Dynamics*, 10, 30–48.

Schwartz, P and Leyden, P (1997) The long boom: a history of the future, 1980–2020. *Wired*, July, 1–16, available at www.wired.com.

Scott, WR (1987) *Organizations: Rational, Natural and Open Systems*. Prentice Hall: Englewood Cliffs, NJ, USA.

Seike, A (1997) Ageing workers. In M Sako and H Sato (eds): *Japanese Labour and Management in Transition*. Routledge: London.

Selznick, P (1948) Foundations of the theory of organization. *American Sociological Review*, 13, 25–35.

Senge, PM (1990) *The Fifth Discipline: The Art and Practice of the Learning Organization*. Century Business: London.

Senge, PM (2000) The puzzles and paradoxes of how living companies create wealth: why single-valued objective functions are not quite enough. In M Beer and N Nohria (eds): *Breaking the Code of Change*. Harvard Business School Press: Boston, MA, USA.

Senior, B (1997) *Organisational Change*. Pitman: London.

Senior, B (2002) *Organisational Change* (2nd edition). Pitman: London.

Shapiro, C (1989) The theory of business strategy. *RAND Journal of Economics*, 20(1), 125–37.

Sheahan, J (1969) *An Introduction to the French Economy*. Merill: Columbus, OH, USA.

Sheldrake, J (1966) *Management Theory: From Taylorism to Japanization*. International Thompson Business Press: London.

Shelton, CK and Darling, JR (2001) The quantum skills model in management: a new paradigm to enhance effective leadership. *Leadership and Organization Development Journal*, 22(6), 264–73.

Sheridan, K (1993) *Governing the Japanese Economy*. Polity Press: Oxford.

Shiflett, SC (1973) The contingency model of leadership effectiveness: some implications of its statistical and methodological properties. *Behavioral Science,* 18(6), 429–40.

Shirai, T (1997) Foreword. In M Sako and H Sato (eds): *Japanese Labour and Management in Transition.* Routledge: London.

Short, JE and Venkatraman, N (1992) Beyond business process redesign: redefining Baxter's business network. *Sloan Management Review,* Fall, 7–21.

Shortell, S and Zajac, E (1990) Perceptual and archival measures of Miles and Snow's strategic types: a comprehensive assessment of reliability and validity. *Academy of Management Journal,* 33, 817–32.

Silverman, D (1970) *The Theory of Organizations.* Heinemann: London.

Silverman, D and Jones, J (1976) *Organizational Work.* Macmillan: London.

Silverman, S (2002) Weill wields his power at Citigroup: revamp represents ongoing structural changes. *The Financial Times,* 13 June, 30.

Simon, HA (1957) *Administrative Behaviour: A Study of Decision-making Processes in Administrative Organizations* (2nd edition). Macmillan: New York, USA.

Sirower, M (2003) When mergers can be a scandal. *Financial Times,* 14 August, 17.

Sissons, K (ed) (1989) *Personnel Management in Britain.* Blackwell: Oxford.

Sissons, K and Storey, J (1988) Developing effective managers: a review of the issues and an agenda for research. *Personnel Review,* 17(4), 3–8.

Sjöstrand, SV (1997) *The Two Faces of Management: The Janus Factor.* Thomson: London.

Skinner, BF (1974) *About Behaviourism.* Cape: London.

Sloan, AP (1986) *My Years with General Motors.* Penguin: Harmondsworth.

Smircich, L and Calás, M (1987) Organizational culture: a critical assessment. In F Jabin, L Putnam, K Roberts and L Porter (eds): *Handbook of Organizational Communication.* Sage: Newbury Park, CA, USA.

Smith, A (1776) *The Wealth of Nations,* Volume 1. Methuen (1950 edition): London.

Smith, JG (1985) *Business Strategy.* Blackwell: Oxford.

Smith, JH (1987) Elton Mayo and the hidden Hawthorne. *Work, Employment and Society,* 1(1), 107–20.

Smith, JH (1998) The enduring legacy of Elton Mayo. *Human Relations,* 51(3), 221–49.

Smith, M, Beck, J, Cooper, CL, Cox, C, Ottaway, D and Talbot, R (1982) *Introducing Organizational Behaviour.* Macmillan: London.

Smith, MK (2001) Kurt Lewin: groups, experiential learning and action research. *The Encyclopedia of Informal Education,* 1–15, available at www.infed.org/ thinkers/et-lewin.htm.

Smith, PB and Misumi, J (1989) Japanese management – a sun rising in the West. In CL Cooper and I Robertson (eds): *The International Review of Industrial and Organizational Psychology.* Wiley: London.

Smith, S and Tranfield, D (1987) The implementation and exploitation of advanced manufacturing technology – an outline methodology. *Change Management Research Unit, Research Paper No 2*, Sheffield Business School.

Smith, T (1994) Flexible production and capital/wage labour relation in manufacturing. *Capital and Class,* 53, Summer, 39–63.

Smithers, R (1995) Power chiefs pay themselves £72m in share options. *Guardian,* 13 February, 20.

Snow, C, Miles, R and Coleman, H (1993) Managing 21st century network organizations. In C Mabey and B Mayon-White (eds): *Managing Change* (2nd edition). The Open University/Paul Chapman Publishing: London.

Sorge, A (1997) Organization behaviour. In A Sorge and M Warner (eds): *The IEBM Handbook of Organizational Behaviour.* International Thompson Business Press: London.

Sosik, JJ and Megerian, LE (1999) Understanding leader emotional intelligence and performance: the role of self–other agreement in transformational leadership perceptions. *Group and Organization Management,* 24(3), 367–90.

Speller, S (2001) The Best Value initiative. In G Johnson and K Scholes (eds): *Exploring Public Sector Strategy.* FT/Prentice Hall: Harlow.

Spiller, K (2003) Realism replaces grand visions. *Financial Times,* 12 March, 2.

Stace, DA and Dunphy, DD (1994) *Beyond the Boundaries: Leading and Re-Creating the Successful Enterprise.* McGraw-Hill: Sydney, Australia.

Stace, D and Dunphy, D (2001) *Beyond the Boundaries: Leading and Re-Creating the Successful Enterprise* (2nd edition). McGraw-Hill: Sydney, Australia.

Stacey, R (1990) *Dynamic Strategic Management for the 1990s.* Kogan Page: London.

Stacey, R (1992) *Managing Chaos: Dynamic Business Strategies in an Unpredictable World.* Kogan Page: London.

Stacey, R (1993) *Strategic Management and Organisational Dynamics.* Pitman: London.

Stacey, RD (2003) *Strategic Management and Organisational Dynamics: The Challenge of Complexity.* FT/Prentice Hall: Harlow.

Stacey, RD, Griffin, D, and Shaw, P (2002) *Complexity and Management: Fad or Radical Challenge to Systems Thinking.* Routledge: London.

Stalk, G, Evans, P and Shulman, LE (1992) Competing on capabilities – the new rules of corporate strategy. *Harvard Business Review,* March–April, 57–69.

Stata, R (1989) Organization learning – the key to management innovation. *Sloan Management Review,* Spring, 63–74.

Statistics Bureau (2003) *Labour Force Survey – Monthly Results, June 2003.* Ministry of Public Management, Home Affairs, Posts and Telecommunications, available at www.stat.go.jp.

Steiner, GA (1969) *Top Management Planning.* Macmillan: London.

Stewart, H (2003) The day investors said enough is enough. *Guardian,* 20 May, available at www.guardian.co.uk.

Stewart, R (1976) *Contrasts in Management*. McGraw-Hill: London.

Stewart, R (1982) *Choices for the Manager: A Guide to Understanding Managerial Work*. Prentice Hall: Englewood Cliffs, NJ, USA.

Stickland, F (1998) *The Dynamics of Change: Insights into Organisational Transition from the Natural World*. Routledge: London.

Stolh, C and Cheney, G (2001) Participatory processes/paradoxical practices. *Management Communication Quarterly*, 14(3), 349–407.

Storey, J (1989) Management development: a literature review and implications for future research – Part 1: conceptualisations and practices. *Personnel Review*, 18(6), 3–19.

Storey, J (1990) Management development: a literature review and implications for future research – Part 2: profiles and context. *Personnel Review*, 19(1), 3–11.

Storey, J (1992) *Developments in the Management of Human Resources*. Blackwell: Oxford.

Stournaras, Y (1999) *The Converging Greek Economy: Developments, Policies and Prospects*. Ministry of National Economy: Athens.

Streeck, W (1987) The uncertainties of management and the management of uncertainties: employers, labour relations and industrial adjustments in the 1980s. *Work, Employment and Society*, 1(3), 281–308.

Stuart, R (1986) Social learning. *Management Decision*, 24(6), 32–5.

Student, J (1968) Supervisory influence and work-group performance. *Journal of Applied Psychology*, June, 188–94.

Styhre, A (2002) Non-linear change in organizations: organization change management informed by complexity theory. *Leadership and Organization Development Journal*, 23(6), 343–51.

Sugeno, K and Suwa, Y (1997) Labour law issues in a changing labour market: in search of a new support system. In M Sako and H Sato (eds): *Japanese Labour and Management in Transition*. Routledge: London.

Sullivan, J (1983) A critique of Theory Z. *Academy of Management Review*, 8, 132–42.

Sullivan, J and Nonaka, I (1986) The application of organizational learning theory to Japanese and American management. *Journal of International Business Studies*, Fall, 127–47.

Sullivan, TJ (1999) Leading people in a chaotic world. *Journal of Educational Administration*, 37(5), 408–23.

Sviokla, JJ (1998) Virtual value and the birth of virtual markets. In SP Bradley and RL Nolan (eds): *Sense and Respond: Capturing Value in the Network Era*. Harvard Business School Press: Boston, MA, USA.

Taguchi, G (1986) *Introduction to Quality Engineering*. Asian Production Organization: Dearborn, MI, USA.

Talbot, C (2001) UK public services and management (1979–2000): evolution or revolution? *International Journal of Public Sector Management*, 14(4), 281–303.

Talbot, R (1993) Creativity in the organizational context: implications for training. In SG Isaksen, MC Murdock, RL Firestien and DJ Treffinger (eds): *Nurturing and Developing Creativity*. Ablex: Norwood, NJ, USA.

Talbot, R (1997) Taking style on board. *Creativity and Innovation Management*, 6(3), 177–84.

Taylor, FW (1911a) *The Principles of Scientific Management*. Dover (1998 edition): New York, NY.

Taylor, FW (1911b) *Shop Management*. Harper (1947 edition): New York, USA.

Teather, D (2002) Trying to close a can of worms. *Guardian*, 11 October, available at www.guardian.co.uk.

Teather, D (2003) US labels to sue individuals for net music piracy. *Guardian*, 26 June, 13.

Teece, DJ, Pisano, G and Shuen, A (1997) Dynamic capabilities and strategic management. *Strategic Management Journal*, 18(7), 509–33.

Terry, PT (1976) The contingency theory and the development of organisations. *Paper presented to the British Sociological Association*.

Tetenbaum, TJ (1998) Shifting paradigms: from Newton to chaos. *Organizational Dynamics*, 26(4), 21–32.

Tett, G (1994) Partnerships in business grow. *Financial Times*, 28 June, 12.

Thickett, M (1970) Gilbreth and the measurement of work. In A Tillett, T Kempner and G Willis (eds): *Management Thinkers*. Pelican: Harmondsworth.

Thomas, AB (1993) *Controversies in Management*. Routledge: London.

Thomas, AB (2003) *Controversies in Management: Issues, Debates, Answers*. Routledge: London.

Thompkins, JM (1990) Politics – the illegitimate discipline. *Management Decision*, 28(4), 23–8.

Thompson, AA Jnr and Strickland, AJ (1983) *Strategy Formulation and Implementation*. Business Publications Inc: Illinois, USA.

Thompson, J (1967) *Organizations in Action*. McGraw-Hill: New York, USA.

Thompson, JW (1995) The renaissance of learning in business. In S Chawla and J Renesch (eds): *Learning Organizations: Developing Cultures for Tomorrow's Workplace*. Productivity Press: Portland, OR, USA.

Thompson, M (1996) Effective purchasing strategy: the untapped source of competitiveness. *Supply Chain Management*, 1(3), 6–8.

Thornberry, NE (1987) Training the engineer as project manager. *Training and Development Journal*, 41(10).

Tighe, C (2002) Less means more in engineering. *Financial Times*, 17 October, 15.

Tillett, A (1970) Industry and Management. In A Tillett, T Kempner and G Willis (eds): *Management Thinkers*. Pelican: Harmondsworth.

Tobach, E (1994) Personal is political is personal is political. *Journal of Social Issues*, 50(1), 221–44.

Toffler, A (1970) *Future Shock*. Random House: New York, USA.

Tomaney, J (1990) The reality of workplace flexibility. *Capital and Class,* 40, Spring, 29–60.

Total Quality Engineering Inc (2003) Hoshin Kanri, available at www.tqe.com/hoshinTR.html.

Trade (2003) 15 facts to remember about trade, wealth and the unequal world we live in. *Trade*. The Guardian/Action Aid: London.

Tran, M (2003) $1.4 bn Wall Street settlement finalised. *Guardian*, 28 April, available at www.guardian.co.uk.

Treanor, J and Finch, J (2003) Directors gains stir revolt by investors. *Guardian,* 31 July, 4.

Treanor, J and Wray, R (2003) Marconi chiefs defy FSA censure: no apology for shareholders in wake of City watchdog's warning on rules breach. *Guardian,* 12 April, available at www.guardian.co.uk.

Trice, HM and Beyer, JM (1984) Studying organizational cultures through rites and ceremonials. *Academy of Management Review,* 9, 653–69.

Trice, HM and Beyer, JM (1990) Using six organizational rites to change culture. In RH Kilmann, MJ Saxton, R Serpa and Associates (eds): *Gaining Control of the Corporate Culture*. Josey Bass: San Francisco, CA, USA.

Trist, EL, Higgin, GW, Murray, H and Pollock, AB (1963) *Organisational Choice.* Tavistock: London.

Trompenaars, F (1993) *Riding the Waves of Culture*. Nicholas Brealey: London.

Tsang, EWK (1997) Organizational learning and the learning organization: a dichotomy between descriptive and prescriptive research. *Human Relations,* 50(1), 73–89.

Tschacher, W and Brunner, EJ (1995) Empirical-studies of group-dynamics from the point-of-view of self-organization theory. *Zeitschrift fur Sozialpsychologie*, 26(2), 78–91.

Tsoukas, H (1992) Postmodernism, reflexive rationalism and organisation studies. *Organisation Studies*, 13(4), 643–9.

Tsoukas, H (2000) What is management? An outline of a metatheory. In S Ackroyd and S Fleetwood (eds): *Realist Perspectives on Management and Organisations*. Routledge: London.

Turnbull, P (1986) The Japanisation of production and industrial relations at Lucas Electrical. *Industrial Relations Journal*, 17(3), 193–206.

Turner, B (1971) *Exploring the Industrial Subculture*. Macmillan: London.

Turner, B (1986) Sociological aspects of organizational symbolism. *Organization Studies*, 7(2), 101–17.

Turner, D (2003) Unemployment falls to two-year low. *Financial Times*, 17 July, 3.

Turner, I (1990) Strategy and organisation. *Manager Update*, 1(3), 1–10.

Tushman, M and Virany, B (1986) Changing characteristics of executive teams in an emerging industry. *Journal of Business Venturing*, 37–49.

Tushman, ML and Romanelli, E (1985) Organizational evolution: a metamorphosis model of convergence and reorientation. In LL Cummings and BM Staw (eds): *Research in Organizational Behavior*, 7, 171–222. JAI Press: Greenwich, CT, USA.

Udy, SH Jnr (1959) 'Bureaucracy' and 'rationality' in Weber's organization theory. *American Sociological Review*, 24, December, 791–5.

Urabe, K (1986) Innovation and the Japanese management system. Keynote address, First International Symposium on Management, Japan Society for the Study of Business Administration, Kobe University, 11–49.

Ure, A (1835) *The Philosophy of Manufactures*. Frank Cass (1967 edition): London.

Ure, A (1836) *The Cotton Manufacture of Great Britain*, Vol. 1. Johnson (1970 edition): London.

Urwick, L (1949) Introduction. In H Fayol (ed): *General and Industrial Management* (trans). Pitman: London.

Uttal, B (1983) The corporate culture vultures. *Fortune*, 17 October, 66–72.

Van der Wiele, A (1998) *Beyond Fads*. Eburon: Delft, The Netherlands.

Van Maanen, J and Kunda, G (1989) Real feelings: emotional expression and organisational culture. In B Staw and L Cummings (eds): *Research in Organizational Behaviour*, 11, 43–103.

Vecchio, RP (1983) Assessing the validity of Fielder's contingency model of leadership effectiveness: a closer look at Strube and Garcia. *Psychological Bulletin*, 93, 404–8.

Vickers, J and Yarrow, G (1991) Economic perspectives on privatisation. *Journal of Economic Perspectives,* 5(2), 111–32.

Vinnecombe, S (1987) What exactly are the differences in male and female working styles? *Women in Management Review*, 3(1).

von Clausewitz, C, von Ghyczy, T, von Oetinger, C and Bassford, C (2001) *Clausewitz on Strategy: Inspiration and Insight from a Master Strategist*. Wiley: Chichester.

Voss, CA (1985) *Success and Failure in Advanced Manufacturing Technology*. Warwick University Working Paper.

Vroom, VH and Jago, AG (1988) *The New Leadership: Managing Participation in Organizations*. Prentice Hall: Englewood Cliffs, NJ, USA.

Vroom, VH and Yetton, PW (1973) *Leadership and Decision Making*. Pittsburg Press: Pittsburg, PA, USA.

Wack, P (1985) Scenarios: uncharted waters ahead. *Harvard Business Review*, September/October, 73–89.

Waclawski, J (2002) Large-scale organizational change and performance: an empirical examination. *Human Resource Development Quarterly*, 13(3), 289–305.

Wagner, JA (1994) Participation's effects on performance and satisfaction: a reconsideration of research evidence. *Academy of Management Review,* 19, 312–30.

Wakisata, A (1997) Women at work. In M Sako and H Sato (eds): *Japanese Labour and Management in Transition*. Routledge: London.

Waldersee, R and Sheather, S (1996) The effects of strategy type on strategy implementation actions. *Human Relations*, 49(1), 105–22.

Wall, TD, Burnes, B, Clegg, CW and Kemp, NJ (1984) New technology, old jobs. *Work and People*, 10(2), 15–21.

Wallace, J and Erickson, J (1992) *Hard Drive: Bill Gates and the Making of the Microsoft Empire*. Wiley: New York, USA.

Waller, DL (1999) *Operations Management: A Supply Chain Approach*. International Thompson: London.

Wang, CL and Ahmed, PK (2003) Organisational learning: a critical review. *The Learning Organization*, 10(1), 8–17.

Warner, M (1984) New technology, work organisation and industrial relations. *Omega*, 12(3), 203–10.

Warner, M (1997) The year of the very big deals. *Fortune,* 24, November, 3.

Warr, P (ed) (1987) *Psychology at Work*. Penguin: Harmondsworth.

Warwick, DP and Thompson, JT (1980) Still crazy after all these years. *Training and Development Journal,* 34(2), 16–22.

Wastell, DG, White, P and Kawalek, P (1994) A methodology for business process redesign: experience and issues. *Journal of Strategic Information Systems,* 3(1), 23–40.

Watson, G (1994) The flexible workforce and patterns of working hours in the UK. *Employment Gazette*, July, 239–47.

Watson, T (1982) Group ideologies and organisational change. *Journal of Management Studies*, 19(3), 259–77.

Watson, TJ (1986) *Management Organisation and Employment Strategy: New Directions in Theory and Practice*. Routledge and Kegan Paul: London.

Watson, TJ (1997) *Sociology, Work and Industry* (3rd edition). Routledge: London.

Watts, J (1998) Japanese 'bullied' out of work. *Guardian*, 29 August, 13.

Weber, M (1928) *General Economic History*. George Allen and Unwin: London.

Weber, M (1947) *The Theory of Social and Economic Organization* (trans). Free Press: Glencoe, IL, USA.

Weber, M (1948) *From Max Weber: Essays in Sociology* (translated, edited and with an introduction by HH Gerth and C Wright Mills). Routledge and Kegan Paul: London.

Weick, KE (1979) *The Social Psychology of Organizing*. Addison-Wesley: Reading, MA, USA.

Weick, KE (1987) Substitute for Corporate Strategy. In DJ Teece (ed) *The Competitive Challenge: Strategies for Industrial Innovation and Renewal*. Ballinger: Cambridge, MA, USA.

Weick, KE (1995) *Sensemaking in Organizations*. Sage: London.

Weick, KE (2000) Emergent change as a universal in organisations. In M Beer and N Nohria (eds): *Breaking the Code of Change*. Harvard Business School Press: Boston, MA, USA.

Wernerfelt, B (1995) The resource-based view of the firm: ten years after. *Strategic Management Journal*, 16, 171–4.

West, P (1994) The concept of the learning organization. *Journal of European Industrial Training*, 18(1), 15–21.

Wetlaufer, S (1999) Organizing for empowerment: an interview with AES's Roger Sante and Dennis Bakke. *Harvard Business Review,* January–February, 120–1.

Wheatley, MJ (1992a) *The Future of Middle Management.* British Institute of Management: London.

Wheatley, MJ (1992b) *Leadership and the New Science: Learning about Organization from an Orderly Universe.* Berrett-Koehler: San Francisco, CA, USA.

Wheelan, SA, Pepitone, EA and Abt, V (eds) (1990) *Advances in Field Theory.* Sage: Newbury Park: CA, USA.

Wheelen, TL and Hunger, DJ (1989) *Strategic Management and Business Policy.* Addison-Wesley: Reading, MA, USA.

Whitaker, A (1992) The transformation in work: post-Fordism revisited. In M Reed and M Hughes (eds): *Rethinking Organization: New Directions in Organization Theory and Analysis.* Sage: London.

White, M (1999) PM's deadline to end child poverty. *Guardian*, 19 March, 10.

White, S and Mitchell, T (1976) Organization development: a review of research content and research design. *Academy of Management Review*, 1(2), 57–73.

Whitehill, AM (1991) *Japanese Management: Tradition and Transition.* Routledge: London.

Whitley, R (1998) *Divergent Capitalisms.* Oxford University Press: London.

Whittington, R (1989) *Corporate Strategies in Recovery and Recession: Social Structure and Strategic Choice.* Unwin Hyman: London.

Whittington, R (1993) *What is Strategy and Does it Matter?* Routledge: London.

Whittington, R (1994) Sociological pluralism, institutions and managerial agency. In J Hassard and M Parker (eds): *Towards a New theory of Organisation.* Routledge: London.

Whyte, J and Witcher, B (1992) *The Adoption of Total Quality Management in Northern England.* Durham University Business School: Durham.

Whyte, WH (1960) *The Organization of Man.* Penguin: Harmondsworth.

Wickens, P (1987) *The Road To Nissan.* Macmillan: London.

Wickens, P (1995) *The Ascendent Organization: Combining Commitment and Control for Long Term Sustainable Business Success.* Macmillan: London.

Wilkinson, A (1991) *TQM and HRM.* Working Paper, Manchester School of Management, UMIST.

Wilkinson, HE and Orth, DC (1986) Soft skill training in management development. *Training and Development Journal*, 40(3).

Willbur, J (1987) Does mentoring breed success? *Training and Development Journal*, 41(11).

Willcocks, SG (1994) Organizational analysis: a health service commentary. *Leadership & Organization Development Journal*, 15(1), 29–32.

Williams, K, Cutler, T and Haslan, C (1987) The end of mass production? *Economy and Society,* 1(3), 404–39.

Williams, K, Haslam, C and Williams, J (1991) Management Accounting: the Western Problematic Against the Japanese Application. *9th Annual Conference of the Labour Process,* UMIST, Manchester.

Williamson, O (1991) Strategizing, economizing and economic organization. *Strategic Management Journal,* 12, 75–94.

Willmott, H (1995) Strength is ignorance; slavery is freedom: managing culture in modern organizations. *Journal of Management Studies,* 30(40), 511–12.

Willmott, R (2000) Structure, culture and agency: rejecting the current orthodoxy of organisational theory. In S Ackroyd and S Fleetwood (eds): *Realist Perspectives on Management and Organisations.* Routledge: London.

Wilson, DC (1992) *A Strategy of Change.* Routledge: London.

Wilson, JF (1995) *British Business History, 1720–1994.* Manchester University Press: Manchester.

Wisdom, J (ed) (2001) *Digital Futures: Living in a Dot-Com World.* Earthscan: London.

Witcher, B (1993) *The Adoption of Total Quality Management in Scotland.* Durham University Business School: Durham.

Witzel, M (2002) The sustainable business: continuous search for improvement. *Financial Times,* 19 August, 2002, 9.

Witzel, M (2003a) *Fifty Key Figures in Management.* Routledge: London.

Witzel, M (2003b) The master strategist: Michael Porter. *Financial Times,* 15 August, 11.

Witzel, M (2003c) The great iconoclast: Henry Mintzberg. *Financial Times,* 5 August, 11.

Womack, JP, Jones, DT and Roos, D (1990) *The Machine That Changed the World.* Rawson Associates: New York, USA.

Wood, S (1979) A reappraisal of the contingency approach to organization. *Journal of Management Studies,* 16, 334–54.

Wood, S (1991) Japanisation and/or Toyotaism? *Work, Employment and Society,* 5(4), 567–600.

Woodward, J (1965) *Industrial Organization: Theory and Practice.* Oxford University Press: London.

Woodward, J (1970) *Industrial Organization: Behaviour and Control.* Oxford University Press: London.

Wooten, KC and White, LP (1999) Linking OD's philosophy with justice theory: postmodern implications. *Journal of Organizational Change Management,* 12(1), 7–20.

Worrall, L and Cooper, CL (1997) *The Quality of Working Life: The 1997 Survey of Managers' Changing Experiences.* Institute of Management: London.

Worrall, L and Cooper, CL (1998) *The Quality of Working Life: The 1998 Survey of Managers' Changing Experiences.* Institute of Management: London.

Wren, D (1994) *The Evolution of Management Thought*. Wiley: Chichester.

www.dei.gr. The official website of PPC SA.

www.rae.gr. The official website of the Greek Regulatory Authority for Energy.

Young, H (1990) *The Iron Lady: A Biography of Margaret Thatcher*. Farrar Straus and Giroux: London.

Yukl, G (1994) *Leadership in Organizations* (3rd edition). Prentice Hall: Englewood Cliffs, NJ, USA.

Yukl, G (2002) *Leadership in Organizations* (5th edition). Prentice Hall: Upper Saddle River, NJ, USA.

Yutaka, N (1998) Japanese-style industrial relations in historical perspective. In H Harukiyo and GD Hook (eds): *Japanese Business Management: Restructuring for Low Growth and Globalization*. Routledge: London.

Zairi, M, Letza, S and Oakland, J (1994) Does TQM impact on bottom line results? *TQM Magazine*, 6(1), 38–43.

Zaleznik, A (1970) Power and politics in organisational life. *Harvard Business Review*, May–June, 47–60.

Zentner, RD (1982) Scenarios, past, present and future. *Long Range Planning*, 15, June, 12–20.

Zimmerman, BJ (1992) *Chaos and Self-Renewing Organizations: Designing Transformation Processes for Co-evolution*. Faculty of Administrative Studies, York University: Ontario, Canada.

Zinn, H (1980) *A People's History of the United States*. Longman: London.

Zwerman, WL (1970) *New Perspectives in Organization Theory*. Greenwood: Westport, CT, USA.

Glossary

Action Learning This approach to management development was devised in the 1940s in the UK by Reg Revans and involves small groups of managers tackling a set problem or case study. The aim is not only that managers learn how to approach problems together, but also that they learn about themselves and challenge the appropriateness of their own attitudes and behaviours.

Action Research This is an approach to change which, first, emphasises that change requires action, and is directed at achieving this; and second, it recognises that successful action is based on analysing the situation correctly, identifying all the possible alternative solutions and choosing the one most appropriate to the situation at hand. It is one of the four elements of Lewin's Planned approach to change (*see* **Planned change**).

Activity planning This involves constructing a schedule or 'road map' for a change programme, citing the main activities and events that must occur if the change is to be successful.

Adaptation–Innovation theory This maintains not only that people exhibit different degrees of creativity, but also that they express their **creativity** in different ways, along a spectrum which runs from adaptors to innovators. Those who tend towards the adaptor end of the spectrum prefer to work within the existing system to improve things. Innovators tend to ignore or challenge the system and to come up with radical proposals for change.

Analytical stream This phrase is used to describe writers on strategy and change who are more interested in understanding how organisations actually formulate **strategy** and manage change than prescribing how they should conduct these activities (*see* **Prescriptive stream**).

Artifacts At the highest level of cultural awareness are the artifacts and creations that are visible manifestations of the other levels of culture. These include observable behaviours of members, as well as the structures, systems, procedures, rules and physical aspects of the organisation (*see* **organisational culture**).

Aston Group The work of this Group constitutes one of the key building blocks of **Contingency Theory**. Working in the 1960s, they found that size was the most powerful predictor of specialisation, use of procedures and reliance on paperwork. In effect, what they found was that the larger the organisation, the more likely it was to adopt (and need) a **mechanistic** (bureaucratic) **structure**. The reverse was also found: the smaller the organisation, the more likely it was to adopt (and need) an **organic** (flexible) **structure**.

Audits and post-audits During and after a change initiative, an audit or a post-audit should be carried out (a) to establish that the objectives have really been met, and (b) to ascertain what lessons can be learned for future projects.

Authority In organisational terms, authority is the right to act, or command others to act, toward the attainment of organisational goals. The right to act is given legitimacy by the authority figure's position in the organisation. Therefore, the level of authority a person possesses is related to their job.

Autonomy This is the ability or requirement of individuals, groups and organisations to act independently and proactively, and without seeking the permission of higher authority, when pursuing organisational goals. Peters and Waterman link it to entrepreneurship and it is seen as an essential attribute of excellent organisations (*see* **Culture–Excellence approach**).

Backstaging This is concerned with the exercise of power skills during the change process. In particular, it involves influencing the recipients of change to accept it. Buchanan and Boddy (1992) see this as being an essential skill of a **change agent**.

Basic assumptions These are seen as one of the core components of **organisational culture**. They operate at the deepest level of cultural awareness and are unconscious, taken-for-granted assumptions about how organisational problems should be solved, as well as about the nature of human beings, human activity and human relationships.

Behaviourist psychology This maintains that all human behaviour is learned and that the individual is the passive recipient of external and objective data. One of the basic principles of the Behaviourists is that human actions are conditioned by their expected consequences. Behaviour that is rewarded tends to be repeated, and behaviour that is ignored tends not to be. Therefore, in order to change behaviour, it is necessary to change the conditions that cause it.

Benchmarking This is the term given to the process of comparing an organisation's performance, or the performance of part of an organisation, e.g. a product or service, against a range of internal and external comparators.

Bias for action This is one of Peters and Waterman's eight key attributes of excellent companies. Even though such companies may have an analytical approach to problems, they are predisposed towards taking rapid and appropriate action rather than getting bogged down in analysis (*see* **Culture–Excellence approach**).

Bold Strokes These are major strategic or economic initiatives, e.g. restructuring an organisation. They can have a clear and rapid impact on an organisation's performance, but they rarely lead to any long-term change in habits or culture. Bold Strokes are initiatives taken by a few senior managers, sometimes only one; they do not rely on the support of the rest of the organisation for their success (*see* **Long Marches; Culture–Excellence approach**).

Boston Consulting Group *see* **Growth-Share Matrix.**

Bottom-up change This is the opposite of top-down change. Instead of change being driven by a few senior managers from the top, this approach sees change as coming from bottom-up initiatives which emerge from local responses to issues, threats or opportunities in the environment. The size of such responses will vary but, because they are local responses, they can never be large-scale (*see* **Emergent change**).

BPR *See* **Business Process Re-Engineering.**

Bureaucracy This form of organisational structure is characterised by the **division of labour**, a clear hierarchical authority structure, formal and unbiased selection procedures, employment decisions based on merit, career tracks for employees, detailed rules and regulations, impersonal relationships, and a distinct separation of members' organisational and personal lives. It is one of the core elements of the **Classical approach to organisations** and corresponds with the **mechanistic structure** identified by **Contingency theorists** (*see* **Contingency Theory**).

Business ethics These are moral principles or beliefs about what is right or wrong. These beliefs guide managers and others in organisations in their dealings with other individuals, groups and organisations, and provide a basis for deciding whether behaviour is socially responsible.

Business Process Re-Engineering (BPR) This is an approach that aims to achieve a radical rethinking and redesign of organisational processes in order to significantly improve key performance measures, such as quality, cost and delivery.

Cash-cows These are companies whose rate of market growth is in decline but which still achieve significant cash surpluses. They became market leaders, during the early days when the market was rapidly growing, and have maintained that position as the growth tapered off. They are regarded as businesses with low growth but high market share (*see* **Growth-Share Matrix**).

Causal mechanisms According to the **realist** perspective, these are the (usually hidden) processes or pathways through which an outcome is caused to be brought about. An example of a causal mechanism is the process by which a rise in interest rates leads to a fall in house prices. In this case, the causal mechanism linking cause to effect involves decisions by each individual house purchaser about the mortgage repayments they can and cannot afford. It is the aggregate behaviour of these individuals that leads to the overall fall in house prices (*see* **realism**).

Causal powers These are the capabilities or potential for systems and mechanisms to act in a particular way, or to be capable of acting in a particular way (*see* **realism**).

Change agents These are the people responsible for directing, organising and facilitating change in organisations (*see* **backstaging**).

Chaordic This term was coined by Hock (1999) to describe organisations which are poised between **order** and **chaos** (*see* **edge of chaos; complexity theories**).

Chaos For **complexity theorists**, chaos describes a complex, unpredictable, and orderly disorder in which patterns of behaviour unfold in irregular but similar forms (*see* **edge of chaos; complexity theories**).

Chaos Theory This is one of the main **complexity theories**. It seeks to construct mathematical models of systems at the macro level (i.e. whole systems and populations). It portrays natural systems as both **non-linear** and **self-organising**.

Classical approach to organisations This approach to organisations is characterised by the horizontal and hierarchical **division of labour**, the minimisation of human skills and discretion, and the attempt to construe organisations as rational-scientific entities. It comprises the work of Frederick Taylor (*see* **Scientific Management**), Henri Fayol (*see* **principles of organisation**) and Max Weber (*see* **bureaucracy**).

Classical approach to strategy This is the oldest and most influential approach to **strategy**. It portrays strategy as a rational process, based on analysis and quantification, and aimed at achieving the maximum level of profit for an organisation.

Closed systems This is a view of organisations which sees them as being relatively unaffected by events outside their boundaries. It considers organisations to be closed, changeless entities. Once organisations have structured themselves in accordance with the correct precepts, then, regardless of external or even internal developments, no further changes are necessary or desirable (*see* **Open Systems school**).

Coercive power The use of threats, sanctions or force to gain compliance.

Cognitive dissonance This theory states that people try to be consistent in both their attitudes and behaviour. When they sense an inconsistency either between two or more attitudes or between their attitudes and behaviour, people experience dissonance; that is, they feel frustrated and uncomfortable with the situation, sometimes extremely so.

Competitive Forces model This is an approach to **strategy** which stresses the need to align the organisation with its **environment**, the key aspect of which is the industry or industries in which it competes. Proponents of this view believe that industry structure strongly influences the competitive rules of the game as well as the range of strategies open to the organisation. This model is most closely associated with the work of Michael Porter (1980, 1985).

Complexity theories These are concerned with how order is created in dynamic **non-linear**

systems. In particular, those applying this approach to organisations maintain that successful organisations need to operate at the 'edge of chaos' and can only maintain this position by the presence of appropriate **order-generating rules.**

Contextual approach to leadership This is an approach which argues that effective leadership is situation-dependent, i.e. a manager's performance will depend on his or her personal characteristics and the overall context within which they operate (*see* **transactional management** and **convergent state**, and **transformational leadership** and **divergent state**).

Contingency Theory This maintains that the structures and practices of an organisation, and therefore its performance, are dependent (i.e. contingent) on the circumstances it faces. The main contingencies – **situational variables** – identified by its proponents are environmental uncertainty and dependence, technology and organisation size (*see* **environment**).

Continuous change This model of change, also referred as to as the continuous transformation model, is based on the assertion that the **environment** in which organisations operate is changing, and will continue to change, rapidly, radically and unpredictably. Consequently, only by continuous transformation will organisations be able to keep aligned with their environment and thus survive.

Contracting-out *See* **outsourcing.**

Control The ability to impose a desired pattern of activity or behaviour on processes and people (*see* **authority** and **power**).

Convergent state This occurs when an organisation is operating under stable conditions, where there are established and accepted goals, and a predictable external and internal environment (*see* **transactional management**).

Creativity The ability to produce new, novel or original ideas and solutions.

Cross Impact method This is a **scenario-building** technique which asks a panel of

experts to assign subjective probabilities and time priorities to a list of potential future events and developments supplied by an organisation.

Culture *see* **organisational culture.**

Culture–Excellence approach Based on the work of Peters and Waterman, Kanter and Handy, this maintains that an organisation's performance (excellence) is determined by the possession of an appropriate, strong and clearly articulated culture. It is culture which ensures that the members of the organisation focus on those activities which lead to effective performance.

Delphi method This is a **scenario-building** technique which uses a panel of experts, who, independently of each other, are interrogated about a number of future issues within their area of expertise.

Design school The proponents of this approach to **strategy** emphasise the need to achieve a fit between the internal capabilities of an organisation and the external possibilities it faces. Flowing from this, they place primary emphasis on the appraisal of an organisation's external and internal situations.

Dissipative structures These are systems that exist in far-from-equilibrium conditions (i.e. are in a state of constant fluctuation) and which, therefore, use (dissipate) energy. The concept of dissipative structures is one of the core ideas in **complexity theories.** They are most closely associated with the work of the Nobel Prize-winning physicist, Ilya Prigogine (Prigogine and Stengers, 1984; Prigogine, 1997).

Divergent state This situation occurs when environmental changes challenge the efficiency and appropriateness of an organisation's established goals, structures and ways of working (*see* **contextual approach to leadership** and **transformational leadership**).

Diversity *see* **workforce diversity.**

Division of labour The hierarchical and horizontal separation of tasks and responsibilities into their component parts so that individuals are only responsible for a limited set of activities instead of the whole task.

Dogs These are businesses that have low market share and which operate in markets with low growth potential (*see* **Growth-Share Matrix**).

Double-loop learning This process involves challenging the appropriateness of an organisation's basic **norms, values**, policies and operating procedures (*see* **single-loop learning; triple-loop learning**).

Edge of chaos This is a state where systems are constantly poised between order and disorder (*see* **complexity theories**).

Emergent change This approach to change is based on the assumption that change is a continuous, open-ended and unpredictable process of aligning and re-aligning an organisation to its changing **environment**.

Empowerment The delegation of power and responsibility to subordinates.

Entrepreneurship The encouragement and pursuit of innovative ideas, products and services (*see* **Culture–Excellence approach**).

Environment Those forces external to an organisation, such as markets, customers, the economy, etc., which influence its decisions and internal operations.

Equifinality This concept, coined by Child (1972), states that different sorts of internal arrangements and structures can be perfectly compatible with identical contextual or environmental states. Put simply, this means that there is more than one way for organisations to structure themselves in order to achieve their goals.

Esteem needs These reflect a person's desire to be respected – esteemed – for their achievements (*see* **hierarchy of needs**).

Excellence *See* **Culture–Excellence approach**.

Extrinsic motivators These are material rewards, such as money and promotion, provided by others (*see* **intrinsic motivators** and **physiological needs**).

Felt-need This is an individual's inner realisation that change is necessary. If felt-need is low in a group or organisation, introducing change becomes problematic.

Field theory This is an approach to understanding group behaviour by trying to map out the totality and complexity of the field in which the behaviour takes place. It is one of the four elements of Lewin's **Planned approach to change** (*see* **Planned change**).

Firm-in-sector perspective This view of **strategy**, developed by Child and Smith (1987), maintains that the conditions operating in a sector shape and constrain the strategies which organisations in that sector can pursue.

Fordism This is named after Henry Ford's approach to car assembly. Fordism is seen as the application of **Scientific Management** to mass production industries through the utilisation of automation, e.g. the moving assembly line.

Game theory This approach to **strategy** can be traced back to the study of war. Game theory has two core assumptions: first, that competitors are rational and will try to win; second, that each competitor is in an interdependent relationship with the other competitors. So all competitors are affected by and will react to what other competitors do.

Generative structures *see* **causal mechanisms**.

Gestalt-Field psychology This sees an individual's behaviour as the product of their environment and reason. Behaviour arises from the way in which an individual uses reason to interpret external stimuli. Consequently, to change behaviour, an individual must be helped to change their understanding of themselves and the situation in question.

Globalisation There is a great deal of dispute as to what this term means. However, at its most basic, it refers to the worldwide integration of markets and cultures, the removal of legal and political barriers to trade, the 'death of distance' as a factor limiting material and cultural exchanges.

Group Dynamics This concept refers to the forces operating in groups. It is concerned with what gives rise to these forces, their consequence and how to modify them. Group Dynamics stresses that group behaviour, rather than that of individuals, should be the main focus of change. It is one of the four elements of

Lewin's **Planned approach to change** (*see* **Planned change**).

Group Dynamics school As a component of change theory, this school originated with the work of Kurt Lewin and has the longest history. Its emphasis is on bringing about organisational change through teams or work groups, rather than individuals.

Growth-Share Matrix This is a strategic planning tool developed by the Boston Consulting Group. Using pictorial analogies, it posits that businesses in an organisation's portfolio can be classified into **stars, cash-cows, dogs** and **problem children**.

Hawthorne Experiments These were carried out at Western Electric's Hawthorne Works in Chicago in the 1920s and 1930s. As a result of this work, two major propositions were put forward: that work is a collective, cooperative activity which is influenced by formal and informal aspects of an organisation; and that humans have a deep need for recognition, security and belonging, rather than being purely economic beings (*see* **Human Relations approach**).

Hierarchy of needs Developed by Maslow (1943), this sees human motivation as based on an ascending order of needs: **physiological needs; safety needs; social needs; esteem needs** and **self-actualisation needs.** Only when a lower order need has been met, does the next level of need begin to motivate an individual.

Hoshin Kanri Also known as policy deployment, this is a Japanese approach to communicating a company's policy, goals and objectives throughout its hierarchy in a structured and consistent fashion in order to ensure that its strategic priorities inform decision-making at all levels in the organisation.

Human Relations approach This was a reaction against the mechanistic view of organisations and the pessimistic view of human nature put forward in the **Classical approach to organisations.** It reintroduces the human element into organisational life by contending that people have emotional as well as economic needs, and that organisations are cooperative systems which comprise informal structures and **norms** as well as formal ones (*see* **hierarchy of needs** and **Hawthorne Experiments**).

Humanisation of work *see* **Job Design.**

Incremental model of change Advocates of this view see change as being a process whereby individual parts of an organisation deal incrementally and separately with one problem and one goal at a time.

Individual Perspective school This school of thought is concerned with understanding and promoting behaviour change in individuals. It is split into two camps: the **Behaviourists** and the **Gestalt-Field psychologists.**

Informal organisations *see* **Human Relations approach.**

Intrinsic motivators These are non-material rewards, such as praise, satisfaction and recognition which are internal to the individual (*see* **extrinsic motivators, esteem needs** and **social needs**).

Japanese approach Pascale and Athos (1982) argue that the effectiveness and uniqueness of the Japanese approach to **management** comes from their ability to combine 'soft' (personnel/industrial relations) elements and 'hard' (business/manufacturing) practices (*see* **7 S framework**).

Job Design Also called work humanisation, and arising from the work of the **Human Relations** approach, proponents of this view argue that the fragmentation of jobs promoted by the **Classical approach to organisations** creates boring, monotonous, meaningless and de-motivating jobs. To reverse this, and to make jobs interesting and intrinsically motivating, they should be designed to provide variety, task completeness and, above all, **autonomy.**

Kaizen This is a Japanese process of incremental, systematic, gradual, orderly and continuous improvement which utilises a range of techniques, tools and concepts, such as quality circles.

Knowledge power This is **power** based on the control of unique information that is necessary for decision-making.

Leadership The process of establishing goals and motivating others to pursue and achieve these goals.

Long Marches The Long March approach to change favours relatively small-scale and operationally-focused initiatives, which are slow to implement and whose full benefits are achieved in the long term rather than the short term. The Long March approach can impact on culture over time but it does require the involvement and commitment of most of the organisation (*see* **Bold Strokes**).

Long-range planning This is an approach to **strategy** based on plotting trends and planning the actions required to achieve the identified growth targets. It is heavily biased towards financial targets and budgetary controls.

Management The process of planning, organising and controlling resources and people in order to produce goods or provide services.

Management development This is concerned with the training and education of managers so as to equip them with the competences and skills necessary to carry out their duties effectively.

Mechanistic structure This forms one end of the structure continuum identified by **Contingency theorists**, the other end being **organic structure**. A Mechanistic structure equates to the bureaucratic-type structure advocated by the **Classical approach to organisations** (*see* **bureaucracy**).

Metaphor This is a linguistic device for describing or seeing one type of experience by suggestion that it is similar to something else, e.g. using the metaphor of a machine to describe a bureaucratic type of organisational structure.

Mission statement This states an organisation's major strategic purpose or reason for existing. It can indicate such factors as the organisation's products, markets and core competences. It is part of an organisation's **vision**.

Modernism This is a term used to describe the values, rationale and institutions that have dominated Western societies since the Age of Enlightenment in the eighteenth century. The essence of modernism is a strong belief in progress, economic and **scientific rationality**, a search for the fundamental rules and laws which govern both the natural world and human nature, and a commitment to a secular, rationalist and progressive individualism (*see* **postmodernism; realism**).

Moving This is the second step in Lewin's **Three-Step model** of change. It involves identifying and evaluating the various types of change on offer, and implementing the chosen one (*see* **unfreezing; refreezing**).

Non-linear systems This is a term used by **complexity theorists** to describe constantly-changing systems where the laws of cause and effect appear not to apply. **Order** in such systems is seen as manifesting itself in a largely unpredictable fashion, in which patterns of behaviour emerge in irregular but similar forms through a process of **self-organisation**, which is governed by a small number of simple **order-generating rules**.

Normative power This describes the allocation and manipulation of symbolic rewards, such as status symbols, as inducements to obey.

Norms These are one of the key components of culture. They represent unwritten rules of behaviour which guide how members of an organisation should behave in particular situations (*see* **organisational culture**).

OD (Organization Development) This is an approach to change developed in the USA. It is based on the work of Kurt Lewin and, originally at least, was concerned with improving the effectiveness of the human side of the organisation through participative change programmes.

'One best way' approach This is a term used to describe any theory or approach which claims to be universally superior to all others on offer, e.g. the **Classical approach to organisations**.

Open-ended change This is a term used especially by proponents of **Emergent change** to indicate that change is a continuous and unpredictable process which does not have a beginning, middle and end.

Open Systems school Proponents of this view see organisations as systems composed of a number of interconnected sub-systems, where any change to one part of the system will have an impact on other parts of the system, and, in turn, on its overall performance. Organisations are seen as open systems in that they are open to, and interact with, their external **environment** (*see* **closed systems**).

Order From a **complexity** perspective, order refers to the patterns of behaviour which emerge in irregular but similar forms in **non-linear systems** through a process of **self-organisation**.

Order-generating rules In complex systems, the emergence of **order** is seen as being based on the operation of simple **order-generating rules** which permit limited chaos whilst providing relative order (*see* **Complexity theories**).

Organic structure This forms one end of the structure continuum identified by **Contingency theorists**, the other end being **mechanistic structure**. An organic structure is seen as being flat, informal, flexible and highly adaptable, i.e. the reverse of a bureaucratic structure.

Organisation Development: *see* **OD**.

Organisational culture This is the name given to the collection of **basic assumptions, values, norms** and **artifacts** that are shared by and influence the behaviour of an organisation's members.

Organizational learning This term describes the process of collective, as averse to individual, learning in an organisation. Its aim is to improve the performance of the organisation by involving everyone in collecting, studying, learning from and acting on information.

Outsourcing This is the practice of seeking outside organisations to take over activities and services previously carried out within an organisation, e.g. catering, security and IT.

Paradigm This is a way of looking at and interpreting the world; a framework of basic assumptions, theories and models that are commonly and strongly accepted and shared within a particular field of activity at a particular point in time.

Participation This is the process of involving people in decision-making and change activities within organisations.

Person culture The individual and his or her wishes are the central focus of this form of culture. It is associated with a minimalistic structure, the purpose of which is to assist those individuals who choose to work together (*see* **organisational culture**).

Phases of change This is an elaboration of **Planned change** based on a four-phase model which describes change in terms of two major dimensions: change phases, which are distinct states through which an organisation moves as it undertakes **Planned change**; and change processes, which are the methods used to move an organisation from one state to another.

Physiological needs These relate to hunger, thirst, sleep, etc. (*see* **hierarchy of needs**).

PIMS (Profit Impact on Marketing Strategy) This is a quantitative strategic planning tool based upon the belief that there are three major factors which determine a business unit's performance: its **strategy**, its competitive position, and the market/industry characteristics of the field in which it competes.

Planned change This term was coined by Kurt Lewin in the 1940s to distinguish change that was consciously embarked upon and planned by an organisation, as averse to types of change that might come about by accident, by impulse or that might be forced on an organisation. Lewin's Planned approach to change consists of four interrelated elements: **Field theory, Group Dynamics, Action Research** and the **Three-Step model** of change.

Politics This describes the efforts of people in organisations to gain support for or against policies, rules, goals, or other decisions where the outcome will have some effect on them. Politics is seen as the exercise of **power**.

Population ecology This concept is borrowed from the physical sciences. It is a Darwinist-type approach that focuses on how organisations adapt and evolve in order to survive within the general population of organisations to which they belong.

Positioning school This approach to **strategy** is based on the argument that organisations which enjoy higher profits than their competitors do so because they have achieved advantageous and easily-defended positions in their markets.

Postmodernism This is a loosely-defined philosophical movement which, though originally based in the arts, has become increasingly influential in the social sciences over the last 20 years. It is a way of looking at the world that rejects the rationality of **modernism** and concentrates on the ways in which human beings attempt to shape reality and invent their world (*see* **realism**).

Power An individual's capacity to influence decisions, to exert their will and achieve outcomes consistent with their goals and priorities.

Power culture This is frequently found in small entrepreneurial organisations such as some property, trading and finance companies. It is associated with a web structure with one or more powerful figures at the centre, wielding **control** (*see* **organisational culture**).

Prescriptive stream This phrase is used to describe writers on **strategy** and change who are more interested in developing prescriptions for telling organisations what they should do rather than analysing what they actually do (*see* **Analytical stream**).

Principles of organisation: These are a set of rules governing the running of organisations developed by Fayol (1949). He claimed that they were universally applicable to all organisations. The principles of organisation form one of the core elements of the **Classical approach to organisations**.

Privatisation The process of transferring state assets from the public to the private sector.

Problem children Also known as **question marks**, these are units or businesses which have a high growth rate and low market share. They have high cash requirements to keep them on course, but their profitability is low because of their low market share. They are so named because, most of the time, the appropriate **strategy** to adopt is not clear (*see* **Growth-Share Matrix**).

Processual approach to change This approach sees change as a complex and dynamic process which cannot be solidified or treated as a series of linear events. In particular, it focuses on the need to analyse the **politics** of managing change.

Processual approach to strategy This perspective concentrates on the nature of organisational and market processes. It views organisations and their members as shifting coalitions of individuals and groups with different interests, imperfect knowledge and short attention spans.

Profit Impact on Marketing Strategy *see* **PIMS**.

Psychological contract This concept is based on the assertion that there is an unwritten set of expectations operating at all times between every member of an organisation and the various managers and others in that organisation.

Punctuated equilibrium model This view of change sees organisations as evolving through relatively long periods of stability (equilibrium periods) in their basic patterns of activity that are punctuated by relatively short bursts of fundamental change (revolutionary periods).

Question marks *see* **problem children**.

Rationality The use of scientific reasoning and logical arguments to arrive at decisions.

Realism This philosophical perspective asserts that social entities, such as markets, class relations, gender relations, ethnic groupings, social rules, etc., exist, are real and can be discovered. However, whilst it rejects the notion of multiple realities, it still acknowledges that social entities arise though a process of **social**

construction. This distinguishes it from both **modernism** and **postmodernism**.

Refreezing This is the third step in Lewin's **Three-Step model** of change. It seeks to stabilise new behaviours in order to ensure that they are relatively safe from regression (*see* **unfreezing; moving**).

Remunerative power This is the use or promise of material rewards as inducements in order to gain people's cooperation.

Resource-Based model This approach to **strategy** sees competitiveness as coming from the effective deployment of superior or unique resources, such as equipment, patents, brands and competences, which allow firms to have lower costs or better products than their competitors.

Ringi system This is a Japanese approach to decision-making which promotes extensive and open debate over decisions, in order to ensure that they fit in with the company's objectives rather than those of sectional interests.

Role A set of observable behaviours associated with, and expected of, an identifiable position or job in an organisation.

Role culture This type of **organisational culture** is appropriate to bureaucracies, and organisations with **mechanistic**, rigid structures and narrow jobs. Such cultures stress the importance of procedures and rules, hierarchical position and **authority**, security and predictability. In essence, role cultures create situations in which those in the organisation stick rigidly to their **role**.

Safety needs The desire for security and protection against danger (*see* **hierarchy of needs**).

Scenario-building This is an approach to strategy development that allows organisations to construct and test pictures of possible futures and to select the one which is most likely to meet their needs. It is based on the assumption that, if you cannot predict the future, then by considering a range of possible futures, an organisation's strategic horizons can be broadened, and managers can be receptive to new ideas (*see* **vision-building**).

Scientific Management This is an approach to work organisation developed by Frederick Taylor in the early twentieth century. He claimed that this approach to designing jobs and supervising workers is based on the scientific study of work. It emphasises the **division of labour**, the removal of workers' discretion and the right of management to make what changes it thinks are necessary for efficient working. It is one of the core elements of the **Classical approach to organisations**.

Scientific-Rational approach This is an alternative title used to describe the **Classical approach to organisations**.

Self-actualisation needs These constitute the need to achieve one's full potential. According to Maslow (1943), this will vary from person to person, and may differ over time as a person reaches a level of potential previously considered unattainable and so goes on to strive for new heights (*see* **hierarchy of needs**).

Self-organisation This is a term used by **complexity theorists** to describe how **order** emerges and is maintained in complex systems (*see* **order-generating rules**).

Semistructures This is a term used by **Complexity theorists** to describe structures which are sufficiently rigid so that change can be organised, but not so rigid that it cannot occur.

7 S framework This is a tool for analysing organisational performance and was developed by Tom Peters, Robert Waterman, Richard Pascale and Anthony Athos when they all worked at McKinsey in the late 1970s. The 7 Ss comprise four 'soft' Ss (staff, style, shared values, and skills) and three 'hard' Ss (**strategy, structure and systems**) (*see* **Japanese approach**).

Simple order-generating rules *see* **order-generating rules**.

Single-loop learning This is adaptive learning which involves detecting and rectifying errors or exceptions within the scope of the organisation's existing practices, policies and **norms** of behaviour (*see* **double-loop learning; triple-loop learning; organisational learning**).

Situational variables *see* **Contingency Theory.**

Size *see* **Contingency Theory.**

Social construction This is an approach concerned with the processes by which people construct, maintain and change social and organisational reality. It is a term used in both **postmodernism** and **realism**. For postmodernists, social construction is seen as creating a number of competing 'realities', none of which possess ultimate truth or reality. Realists, on the other hand, believe in just one socially-constructed reality which does exist.

Social needs The need to belong, to gain love and affection; to be in the company of others, especially friends (*see* **hierarchy of needs**).

Socio-Technical Systems theory This is a variant on **Job Design** which involves a shift of focus from the individual job to the organisation as a whole. It sees organisations as being composed of interdependent social and technical systems.

Stars These are business units, industries or products with high growth and high market share. Because of this, stars are assumed to use and generate large amounts of cash. However, they are also likely to be very profitable (*see* **Growth-Share Matrix**).

Strategic Conflict model This is an approach to strategy which harks back to the military metaphor, and portrays competition as war between rival firms. In particular, this model draws on the work of military strategists, and attempts to apply their military aphorisms to modern business organisations.

Strategic intent This is a term which was originally coined to describe the commitment of Japanese managers to create and pursue a **vision** of their desired future.

Strategic management Though often used as a generic term to describe the process by which managers identify and implement their organisation's **strategy**, it was originally applied only to quantitative, mathematical approaches to strategy.

Strategy This is a plan of action stating how an organisation will achieve its long-term objectives.

Sustainability This term was originally coined by environmental and ecological campaigners to describe the development of economic, social and industrial practices which would contribute to sustaining the natural environment. It has been extended to include the promotion of organisational practices that contribute to the health of the planet, the survival of humans and other species, the development of a just and humane society, and the creation of work that brings dignity and self-fulfilment (Dunphy *et al*, 2003).

SWOT analysis This is a strategic planning tool which assesses the Strengths, Weaknesses, Opportunities and Threats possessed and faced by an organisation.

Systems Theory *see* **closed systems** and **Open Systems school.**

Task culture This type of **organisational culture** is job- or project-orientated; the onus is on getting the job in hand (the task) done rather than prescribing how it should be done. Such types of culture are appropriate to organisations with **organic structures** where flexibility and teamworking are encouraged.

Taylorism *see* **Scientific Management.**

Technology *see* **Contingency Theory.**

Theory X This is a management theory expounded by Douglas McGregor (1960) which states that the average person dislikes work and will avoid it wherever possible, unless coerced to do so (*see* **Theory Y**).

Theory Y This is a management theory expounded by Douglas McGregor (1960) which states that most people can view work as being as natural as rest or play, they are willing to take responsibility, and are capable of exercising self-direction and self-control (*see* **Theory X**).

Three-Step model This model of change was developed by Kurt Lewin and sees change as going through three stages: **unfreezing, moving** and **refreezing**. It is one of the four elements of Lewin's **Planned approach to change** (*see* **Planned change**).

Total Quality Management (TQM) This was developed in Japan and is the systematic application of quality management principles to all aspects of an organisation's activities, including customers and suppliers, and their integration with key business processes.

Transformational leadership This approach portrays leaders as charismatic or visionary individuals who seek to overturn the status quo and bring about radical change. Such leaders use the force of their personality to motivate followers to identify with the leader's **vision** and to sacrifice their self-interest in favour of that of the group or organisation. Transformational leadership is seen as being appropriate to **divergent states** (*see* **contextual approach to leadership** and **transactional management**).

Transactional management This approach stems from the notion that the manager-subordinate relationship is based on a transaction between the two, whereby managers exchange rewards for subordinates' performance. Transactional managers focus on task completion, goal clarification and optimising the performance of the organisation through incremental changes within the confines of existing policy, structures and practices – basically, they seek to work within and maintain the status quo. This approach to management is seen as being appropriate in **Convergent states** (*see* **contextual approach to leadership;** **Transformational leadership**).

Triple-loop learning This involves questioning the rationale for the organisation and, in the light of this, radically transforming it (*see* **single-loop learning; double-loop learning; organisational learning**).

Uncertainty This relates to the degree of doubt, unpredictability and ambiguity that exists in any situation.

Unfreezing This is the first step in Lewin's **Three-Step model** of change. It seeks to destabilise (unfreeze) the complex field of driving and restraining forces which prevent human behaviour from changing (*see* **moving** and (**refreezing**).

Values These are one of the key components of culture. They relate to how things ought to be done in an organisation; they tell members what is important in the organisation (*see* **organisational culture**).

Vision This is a view of an organisation's desired future state. It generally has two components: a description of the organisation's core **values** and purpose; and a strong and bold picture of the organisation's future which identifies specific goals and actions (*see* **vision-building**).

Vision-building This is the process of creating a **vision**. It is an iterative process which involves the conception by a company's senior management team of an 'ideal' future state for their organisation; the identification of the organisation's **mission**, its rationale for existence; and a clear statement of desired outcomes and the desired conditions and competences needed to achieve these.

Workforce diversity This term refers to the dissimilarities – differences – among an organisation's workforce owing to age, gender, race, ethnicity, religion, sexual orientation, nationality, socio-economic background, capabilities/disabilities, etc. It draws attention to the need to take account of these differences when seeking to recruit, retain and motivate staff. In particular, it identifies the need to treat different groups differently if an organisation is to treat all its employees in an ethical and fair manner.

Index